From National Development to Global Community

Essays in Honor of Karl W. Deutsch

From National Development to Global Community

Essays in Honor of Karl W. Deutsch

Edited by
RICHARD L. MERRITT
Professor of Political Science and Research Professor in Communications, University of Illinois at Urbana-Champaign

and

BRUCE M. RUSSETT
Professor of Political Science, Yale University

London
GEORGE ALLEN & UNWIN
Boston   Sydney

First published in 1981

This book is copyright under the Berne Convention. All rights are reserved. Apart from any fair dealing for the purpose of private study, research, criticism or review, as permitted under the Copyright Act, 1956, no part of this publication may be reproduced, stored in a retrieval system, or transmitted, in any form or by any means, electronic, electrical, chemical, mechanical, optical, photocopying, recording or otherwise, without the prior permission of the copyright owner. Enquiries should be sent to the publishers at the undermentioned address:

GEORGE ALLEN & UNWIN LTD
40 Museum Street, London WC1A 1LU

© George Allen & Unwin (Publishers) Ltd, 1981

British Library Cataloguing in Publication Data

From national development to global community.
  1. Political science — Addresses, essays, lectures
I. Deutsch, Karl Wolfgang II. Merritt, Richard L III. Russett, Bruce M
320   JA66

ISBN 0-04-327060-3
ISBN 0-04-327061-1 Pbk

Set in 10/11pt Times by Preface Ltd., Salisbury
and Printed in Great Britain
by Mackays of Chatham.

Contents

EDITORS' INTRODUCTION: *page*
Karl W. Deutsch and the Scientific Analysis of World Politics   *Richard L. Merritt and Bruce M. Russett*   1

PART ONE   NATIONALISM AND SOCIAL MOBILIZATION

1. Modernization and Nation-Building: The Social Mobilization Model Reconsidered   *William J. Foltz*   25
2. Social Mobilization Theory and Arab Politics   *Michael C. Hudson*   46
3. Territories, Nations, Parties: Toward a Geoeconomic-Geopolitical Model for the Explanation of Variations within Western Europe   *Stein Rokkan*   70
4. Limits to Governmental Growth   *Charles Lewis Taylor*   96
5. Developmental Crises and Modernization: The Role of the State in the Redistribution Crisis in Developed Countries   *Frieder Naschold*   115

PART TWO   POLITICAL INTEGRATION AND UNIFICATION

6. Integration Theory and the Study of International Relations   *Donald J. Puchala*   145
7. The Political Sociology of Integration and Social Development: A Comparative Analysis of Emile Durkheim and Karl W. Deutsch   *Andrei S. Markovits and Warren W. Oliver III*   165
8. Public Opinion on International Affairs in Less Developed Countries   *Jorge I. Domínguez*   184
9. Political Disintegration in Postwar Berlin   *Richard L. Merritt*   206

PART THREE   INTEGRATION AND DEPENDENCE

10. Karl W. Deutsch and the New Paradigm in International Relations   *Arend Lijphart*   233

11	Domestic Structures and Political Strategies: Austria in an Interdependent World *Peter J. Katzenstein*	252
12	Dissociation and Autocentric Development: An Alternative Development Policy for the Third World *Dieter Senghaas*	279
13	A Formal Model of 'Dependencia Theory': Structure and Measurement *Raymond Duvall, Steven Jackson, Bruce M. Russett, Duncan Snidal, and David Sylvan*	312

PART FOUR POLITICAL CYBERNETICS AND WORLD ORDER

14	From Political Cybernetics to Global Modeling *Hayward R. Alker, Jr*	353
15	Can the Global System Learn to Control Conflict? *Manfred Kochen*	379
16	Periodicity, Inexorability, and Steersmanship in International War *J. David Singer and Thomas Cusack*	404
17	Critical Factors of North–South Relations Seen from a Long-Term Socioecological Perspective *Bruno Fritsch*	423

Karl W. Deutsch: A Bibliography	447
ABOUT THE CONTRIBUTORS	464
NAME INDEX	468
SUBJECT INDEX	476

Editors' Introduction:

Karl W. Deutsch and the Scientific Analysis of World Politics

RICHARD L. MERRITT and BRUCE M. RUSSETT

It is our pleasure to edit and introduce this collection of writings on the analysis of politics and international relations. One purpose of the volume is, of course, to honor our friend and former teacher, Karl Wolfgang Deutsch. Karl Deutsch is one of the outstanding personages in the social sciences during the post-Second World War era, someone who has had a powerful impact upon both the direction and the quality of work in the scientific community. With this volume, comprising chapters written by people who were, at one time or many, his students or his collaborators, we mark his retirement from full-time teaching at Harvard University and a new stage in his ever-developing scholarly career.

This book is nevertheless much more than just the celebration of that distinguished career. It is organized around a set of topics that constitutes not merely Karl Deutsch's major professional interest, but central concerns of anyone who considers the future of social and political organization on this planet. It considers the development of ethnic and national consciousness, as expressed in the modern nation-state – that now almost universal instrument of social control, source of reward and punishment, bringer of security and insecurity. It then turns to questions of how nation-states interact with one another in the larger global system, of how they may become 'integrated' with one another without necessarily becoming politically unified. It is concerned with wars and their causes, and with prospects for a future where, in a world system, poverty, war, and ecological collapse pose central – and interacting – threats to human society.

Karl Deutsch has written prolifically on all these topics, producing a corpus of work that addresses each topic individually and also examines how they impinge on one another. In these chapters we review and seek to expand upon some of his principal contributions to each. Scientific investigation, not encomium, is our goal. Thus Karl's work is viewed in terms of the larger intellectual context from which it sprang and to which it contributed. It is evaluated both in terms of that literature and by the wider standards of modern social science. It is 'appreciated' both for its strengths and for its human weaknesses. But, most important, it is set into the context of subsequent work on these topics.

This is, therefore, a book about politics and society, about what Karl Deutsch has told us and about what others have added and continue to add to Karl's contributions. Some of the chapters consider Karl's work in depth; others almost take it as a starting point to move directly to the task of new research and scientific cumulation. That each of the contributors has been heavily influenced by Karl Deutsch's intellect will be readily apparent. Our purpose, none the less, is to honor Karl not by praising him but by continuing the work which we have in part shared with him. We honor him with a book not about himself, but with contributions to help understand the problems with which he has wrestled.

Education and Career

Karl Wolfgang Deutsch was born in 1912 in Prague, Czechoslovakia. His father was an optician. His mother, active in various political causes both at home and internationally, eventually became one of Czechoslovakia's first woman parliamentarians. After graduating with high honors in 1931 at the German Staatsrealgymnasium in Prague, Deutsch went on to take his first degree in 1934 at the Deutsche Universität in Prague. His advanced studies at the same university were interrupted because of his outspoken leadership of anti-nazi groups. After a clash with the then pro-nazi majority of the faculty of the Deutsche Universität, he left for a period to study optics in England. His study of mathematics and optics helped prepare him for his later pioneering work in quantitative political science. On returning to Czechoslovakia he was granted admission to the Czech-national Charles University – a signal honor for a German-ethnic Czech – where he attained high honors in seven fields and received his doctorate in law (JUDr) in 1938. Shortly thereafter, Karl Deutsch and his new bride, Ruth, went to the United States for what was intended to be a brief stay. But with the capitulation of Britain and France to Hitler at Munich, and the nazi takeover of the Sudetenland, the Deutsches decided it would be unsafe to return.

In 1939 Karl Deutsch began a new life in the United States. The recipient of a student-funded scholarship for refugees from nazism, he entered Harvard University for further graduate training. During his first years in America he toured the country extensively, speaking on behalf of the Free Czechoslovak movement. America's entry into the war led Deutsch into the service of the United States government, where among other things he was a major contributor to the famous 'Blue Book' on Peron's efforts to extinguish democracy in Argentina. Later he participated as a member of the International Secretariat of the San Francisco Conference of 1945 that created the United Nations Organization.

The war over, Deutsch resumed his doctoral studies at Harvard University, while teaching at the Massachusetts Institute of Technology. Simultaneously, he began publishing articles that showed both his mature scholarship and, more significantly, perspicacity in his view of society and politics. His dissertation, 'Nationalism and social communication', was awarded Harvard's Sumner Prize in 1951. The

INTRODUCTION 3

following year Deutsch was promoted at MIT to the rank of professor of history and political science, and a year after that his dissertation appeared as a book, entitled *Nationalism and Social Communication*.[1]

Almost immediately Deutsch was in great demand in the scholarly community. In 1953-4 he was at the Center for Research on World Political Institutions at Princeton University, where he pulled together the findings of an interdisciplinary group, integrated them with his own thinking, and turned the result into a highly significant theoretic analysis of large-scale political integration, *Political Community and the North Atlantic Area*.[2] The year 1956-7 was spent as a fellow at the Center for Advanced Study in the Behavioral Sciences at Palo Alto, California. There he completed the basis for a book, *The Nerves of Government*,[3] that would constitute one of his most significant contributions. During the same period he held a visiting appointment at the University of Chicago (1954) and received his first Guggenheim Fellowship (1955).

In 1957 Karl Deutsch went to Yale University as visiting professor, and a year later accepted a permanent appointment as professor of political science. His first substantive accomplishment there was the completion of a book (with Lewis J. Edinger), *Germany Rejoins the Powers*,[4] which used data on public opinion, the background of elites, and economics to analyze the Federal Republic's postwar progress, and which, in our view, remains the most highly original study written to date on politics and society in West Germany. During his ten years at Yale he completed the intellectual framework and set up an organization – the Yale Political Data Program – to develop quantitative indicators for testing significant theories and propositions in social science; organized a multi-university research team, sometimes called the Yale Arms Control Project, to investigate the prospects for arms control, disarmament, and steps toward unification in the West European environment; and took on an increasingly important role in the development of international social science. A majority of the contributors to this volume first made Karl's acquaintance during those exciting Yale years. In 1960 he also held a visiting appointment at Heidelberg University, and in 1962 he was a visiting fellow at Nuffield College of Oxford University.

Deutsch moved to Harvard University in 1967, becoming Stanfield Professor of International Peace in 1971. Despite the fact that the demand for guest lectures on his part increased, and despite his dramatically expanding role in international social science, he continued his steady record of initiating and completing new projects. He has held guest professorships at the Goethe University in Frankfurt-am-Main, the University of Geneva, Heidelberg University, the University of Mannheim, the University of Paris, and the University of Zurich. He has lectured at major universities throughout the world, and served as consultant to various government agencies. And he has received such honors as a second Guggenheim Fellowship (1971) and appointment as resident scholar at the Aspen Institute of Humanistic Studies (1973, 1974).

That his standing is recognized by his colleagues is clear from the numerous offices to which they have elected him. Deutsch was president of the New England Political Science Association in 1964–5. He was elected president of the American Political Science Association in 1969–70, after having served as program chairman of its 1963 annual meeting. In 1973 he was elected president of the Peace Science Society (International). He has served the International Political Science Association as a member of the program committee (1970–6), co-ordinator of the triennial IPSA world congress (Montreal, 1973), vice-president, and finally as president for 1976–9. He has received six honorary degrees from American and European Universities.

Although this volume will of necessity emphasize Karl Deutsch's written contributions to knowledge, in fact his impact upon scholarship derives equally from the force and manner of his personal presentations. His commitment to teaching is manifested in both lectures and seminars. His undergraduate lectures, although quite often extemporaneous, almost always nevertheless combine profundity with wit. At Yale, we heard him deliver uncounted lectures to packed lecture halls, and each lecture, literally without exception, was greeted with an ovation. Yale undergraduates honored his contribution in 1965 when they awarded him the William Benton Prize of the Yale Political Union for having done most to stimulate and maintain political interest on campus: of the many honors he has received, this award alone is prominent in the Deutsch home. His graduate seminars have produced some of the more productive scholars currently in the fields of international and comparative politics. The combination of Karl's intellect and verve proved enormously stimulating, especially during a period when many graduate students were seeking a degree of analytical rigor and concern for quantitative evidence that was only beginning to be important in political science. Karl's teaching skills also are evident in two significant textbooks – *The Analysis of International Relations*[5] and *Politics and Government*[6] – that are not merely expositions of familiar material, but efforts to get students involved in the serious analysis of political phenomena.

Deutsch sees as an important part of his task as educator the presentation of guest lectures at universities and elsewhere in the United States and abroad. Within the bounds set by his continuing commitments, he is generous with his time and his thoughts. He seems happiest when he has engaged an individual or audience in an intellectual dialogue in which there is give and take, in which there are both challenges and stimulation, and which provides the opportunity for him, too, to learn something new. People invariably remark about the excitement he generates with these visits. He has always been noted for his ability to generate enormous numbers of ideas, in rapid-fire. His style typically has been virtually to free-associate, to take a piece of data or an idea and immediately throw it back with a requirement for more information, or with a new hypothesis, or even a full-blown theory. There is a certain risk in such a style – not every idea is well considered, or sound. But the sheer volume of intellectual sparks generates more fire in an hour than many scholars see in days.

Karl Deutsch's willingness to share his time and thoughts with students and colleagues around the world is a measure of the man. Knowledge is to be shared, not hoarded. Deutsch is firmly committed to the maximum sharing of scientific information as soon as possible after its generation. Neither should knowledge be used to enhance one's own status. The purpose of his lecturing is rather to increase the usefulness to others of our general pool of knowledge, to enlarge our understanding through interaction. All too often it is he who must perform the lion's share of the work in such interactions, and it is we, his audience, who benefit. But even then he is laying the basis for much more fruitful discussions in the future, for the enlargement of our pool of data and techniques as well as, more significantly, the understanding of politics and society.

Those of us who worked with Karl both as students and as young colleagues saw another facet of his style and his values. Karl was already in his mid-forties when he first began to teach graduate students on a regular basis. At this stage in life some scholars may begin to see their students more as competitors than as colleagues. Karl never did. His relationship with students has always been interactive, nurturent, generative. Partly this is simply a reflection of the way he keeps himself intellectually alive – giving and taking, with never a hint of feeling any personal threat. If a student had some technical ease that Karl lacked, so much the better; Karl would swap with a full measure of erudition and insight. Moreover, Karl has really cared, in a personal sense, about his students and former students. Much more than could be expected, he helped them get jobs, writing assignments, conference invitations, and other opportunities to show their intellectual wares. He wrote many articles and books with students and junior colleagues, sharing work and authorship equitably. The most unkind comment either of us can recall him making concerned a senior colleague who was, said Karl, 'the sort who never sends the elevator back down'.

Karl Deutsch has made important contributions to knowledge in many areas of the social sciences and humanities. In political science, for instance, there is hardly a field in the modern discipline in which one or another aspect of his work does not form a critical part. There are none the less several fields in which his work can be singled out as being truly pathbreaking, as having revolutionized scholarly thought and research: large-scale political community formation at the national and international levels; cybernetic approaches to politics and society; and the development and use of quantitative data to test and reformulate political theories. This volume has organized its chapters along these lines.

Nationalism and Social Mobilization

Karl Deutsch's youth was spent in a multinational state destined to endure a series of tragedies. Doubtless in response to his observation of the horrors brought to Europe by narrow-minded nationalism, before and during the Second World War, Karl early put his emotional and intellectual energies into scholarship focused upon nationalism and the formation of large-scale political communities. He decided to write his doctoral dissertation on nationalism – a brave decision, given both the flood of past writing on the topic and the strong emotions it engendered among even the most intellectual of scholars. His literature search alone encompassed over 2,000 titles – the intellectual and research thrust of each one of which he can discuss in detail today.[7]

The contribution of the dissertation, published in 1953 as *Nationalism and Social Communication*, was to recast the traditional literature into a more rigorous form, enriched by concepts from such social science disciplines as anthropology and social psychology as well as Deutsch's own insights, and, more innovatively, tested by the application of quantitative data from the real world. The book presented a new model of nationalism based upon the idea of a 'people' bound together by habits of, and facilities for, communication. New data creatively derived from four case studies of national growth and decay demonstrated the validity of the model and set the stage for further data-gathering efforts and tests of the basic model. The paradigm offered by Deutsch in these books and elsewhere[8] has dominated the scholarly study of nation-building and international integration.

The first main section of this book is devoted to the analysis and extension of work on nation-building by Deutsch and others. In his chapter 'Modernization and nation-building: the social mobilization model reconsidered', William J. Foltz considers Deutsch's early analysis and his subsequent efforts to apply relevant cross-national data to key propositions. Foltz recognizes – and was himself much stimulated by – the intellectual excitement of these developments, but then goes on to discuss how later research complicates Deutsch's relatively simple initial formulations. His wide-ranging review considers difficulties arising from using the nation-state as a unit of analysis and measurement, and from the earlier views of 'traditional societies' as consisting largely of people who were not politically mobilized. Instead, he indicates the pervasiveness of politics in such societies, and concludes with an appreciation of political actors not as passive, but as active, goal-seekers with changing purposes. This, too, resonates from Deutsch's work, and is a theme to which various contributors return later in the volume.

Michael Hudson, examining 'Social mobilization theory and Arab politics,' returns to Deutsch's analysis to find that his theory of social mobilization explains fairly well recent political transformations in the Arab world. Like Foltz, he points to ambiguities and limitations to the theory, and questions some of the sharp distinctions Deutsch makes between 'traditional' and 'modern'. Nevertheless, again like Foltz, he concludes that the theory is essentially sound, a fact that derives especially from the depth of historical knowledge that Deutsch brought to his theoretical formulations.

In the third contribution of this section, Stein Rokkan, 'Territories, nations, parties: toward a geoeconomic-geopolitical model for the explanation of variations within Western Europe', continues the analysis of nation-building by outlining a model which synthesizes work on the processes of mobilization with Rokkan's recent work on the geopolitical and geoeconomic history of Europe. It is an extraordinarily complex and comprehensive undertaking that begins with the early history of territorial organization, state-building, and resource combination, and outlines the different sequences of subsequent steps in different areas of Europe. It is a systematization in the best tradition of grand European macrohistory and sociology, a tradition from which Deutsch himself draws deeply and to which he contributes.

The remaining two chapters in this section deal with social mobilization in modern industrial states. Charles L. Taylor, 'Limits to governmental growth', notes that social mobilization implies the uprooting of people from their old ways, leading them to new expectations and demands for goods and services – demands which often are then made upon governments. Governments must enlarge their capabilities to meet these demands, and indeed then further mobilize the population in an effort to generate or co-opt support. As a result, the government's share of total national product continues to grow. Taylor considers this and other explanations for the growth in government share which he displays, as Deutsch often does, with simple but effective tabular and graphical presentations of data on many countries.

Whereas Taylor speaks of a positive reciprocal relationship between government growth and social mobilization, Frieder Naschold expresses concern in 'Developmental crises and modernization' that the apparent devolution to the state of important social functions has also been accompanied by decreasing rates of mobilization – that is, declines in political participation in liberal-capitalist societies and a failure to achieve substantial redistribution. Examining the German social security system over the past hundred years, he rejects conventional political mobilization theory, and then lays the framework for a competing paradigm, which combines theories of institutionalization of mobilization and demobilization by the state, long-range cycles of dynamic class crystallization and class conflict, and the role of a state in the world system.

Political Integration and Unification

Many of the theoretical perspectives that animated Karl Deutsch's analysis of nationalism and social mobilization apply equally to his work on large-scale political integration and unification. He used these perspectives effectively to focus the sometimes divergent research performed by members of the research group at Princeton University's Center for Research on World Political Institutions. Each individual member had worked on a case study of national integration or disintegration but, alas, the various pieces, each, to be sure, with considerable merit of its own, had not jelled into a coherent whole that was anything more than an accumulation of case studies. When Deutsch was asked to join the project it was with the specific hope that, by applying his historical knowledge of nationalism and his concepts derived from the study of communication in societies, he could integrate these insightful but disparate pieces.⁹ The result, published in 1957, was a major pioneering study, *Political Community and the North Atlantic Area*. In this view of political integration, the formation of large-scale community rests less upon such factors as a common language or common enemy than upon the complementarity of value systems and high levels of mutual responsiveness. As with the development of nationalism, two-way channels of communications between elites and mass, and among non-elites, are central to his conception of successful integration.

While nation-building and integration are closely linked in Deutsch's theorizing, the aspects identified with integration theory have become associated more with international relations than with nation-building *per se*. One manifestation of political integration may indeed be the creation of a new state by amalgamating two or more previously separate units. Even so, much of the most enduring of Deutsch's thought on integration deals with the creation of 'expectations of peaceful change', that is, 'security communities' among peoples who may or may not be unified under a single government.

This focus on community formation, rather than on amalgamation *per se*, is central to Deutsch's work and to that of the whole school of 'integration theorists' who worked with Deutsch or otherwise attempted to apply his insights. Donald J. Puchala in 'Integration theory and the study of international relations' considers this body of work, especially the efforts in the 1960s to comprehend and predict political integration in West Europe. Like the contributors to the earlier section, Puchala is by no means uncritical of some of Deutsch's formulations. Deutsch distinguished between integration (absence of expectations of war) and amalgamation (political unification). This distinction, and his attempted explanations of the phenomena, are at the heart of Deutsch's work. Nevertheless, he left several aspects of the analysis incomplete, such as specification of the dynamics of moving from integration to amalgamation, or of the process whereby attitudes become the basis for government action. Puchala also points out the severe problems that have arisen in devising measures for these concepts. Still, Puchala concludes with an appreciation of the great value and originality of Deutsch's contribution. While much work remains to be done, Deutsch's formulations lend themselves well to cumulative research.¹⁰

In 'The political sociology of integration and social development: a comparative analysis of Emile Durkheim and Karl W. Deutsch', Andrei S. Markovits and Warren W. Oliver III continue the analysis of Deutsch's work on integration by noting its striking parallels with that of Emile Durkheim. Both Deutsch and Durkheim have had great impact on modern social science, often dealing with similar problems and theories, yet apparently developing quite separate lines of inquiry. Both are characterized by strong efforts to create a discipline subject to the rigorous verification procedures of science. Both focus on solidarity and community in all aspects of human life, and how this shapes the political process. After a detailed analysis of how much Deutsch and Durkheim share in common, the authors conclude with an appreciation of the benefits that might be achieved by more self-conscious blending of the two traditions.

In contrast with these two chapters on intellectual history, the remaining two contributions in this section are primarily empirical. Jorge I. Domínguez, in 'Public opinion on international affairs in less developed countries', relates to theory on political integration data from survey research on attitudes toward international affairs in less developed countries. He concludes that mass publics in such countries pay relatively little attention to international affairs and, perhaps surprisingly, that the initial phases of modernization may shift the balance of interest between international and national affairs even more in the direction of the latter. Furthermore, the content of these attitudes is as likely to be hostile as co-operative. Mass support for international political integration thus appears slim and precarious in such countries.

Finally, Richard L. Merritt, 'Political disintegration in postwar Berlin', studies the effect of political division on feelings of community in Berlin. His chapter epitomizes many of the central features of Deutsch's work on integration: a special concern with Germany, and particularly an extensive and intensive empirical study of patterns of social communication. From this detailed analysis he provides one of the very few documentations we have of a process of disintegration, and concludes that, for Berliners across the boundary of East and West, community has been replaced by social as well as political estrangement.

Integration and Dependence in the Global System

Inherent in Karl Deutsch's discussions of integration at the national and supranational levels is his insight that unified government is neither a necessary nor a sufficient condition for peace in an area. Indeed, in some cases it may even be destructive of that end. On the one hand, premature steps toward unification, those taken before certain background conditions have been met, can lead to conflict and breakdown. Unification of unequal partners, on the other hand, can rigidify the inequality and give a cachet of legitimacy to the exploitation of the weak by the strong. These ideas are central to the more general study of international politics.

Arend Lijphart, in his chapter 'Karl W. Deutsch and the new paradigm in international relations', stresses Deutsch's analysis of the paradox of premature unification at the international level. For three centuries and more, Lijphart writes, leading statesmen and writers had seen anarchy as the dominant characteristic of that arena. Sovereign states, the sole protectors of their subjects, engaged in a never-ending war of all against all. Each feared for its own safety should any of its neighbors become stronger than itself; only world government could ensure tranquillity.

Such a view of the world led to differing strategies. Given the unlikelihood that states would offer up their cherished sovereignty to such a body, to 'realists' it seemed prudent for practical statesmen to worry less about its prospects in the future than to preserve their own states' autonomy in the here and now. Thus they elaborated schemes to balance power, to prevent competing states from establishing hegemony. 'Idealists', whether academicians writing on international political theory or leaders such as Woodrow Wilson bent on changing the world, rather looked for means to achieve global peace through world government. After the Second World War, attention focused on whether West Europe was marching toward economic and eventually political unification. Could a united Europe end the anarchy that had bred internecine warfare for more than a thousand years?

In the midst of this debate, Lijphart continues, Deutsch stepped in to question underlying premisses and suggest a new paradigm of international politics. He found that relations among states are in critical regards similar to interactions in other arenas of politics. To some specifiable degree, nation-states are isomorphic with states in a federal system, interest groups and parties competing for power, and still other actors at other levels of politics. International conflict is similarly one kind in larger classes of conflicts and behaviors. Close analysis of interaction at other levels of social organization can help us understand international politics. Such insights, together with Deutsch's own efforts to apply cross-systemic approaches to international phenomena, have served to bring the study of international relations back into its proper context of scientific analysis of politics.

Central to Deutsch's new paradigm is his view of anarchy, war, and amalgamation. Picking up an earlier strand of political thought from Hugo Grotius, Deutsch argued that no axiomatic relationship exists between anarchy and war. Indeed, historical evidence suggests that ineffective or premature efforts to mitigate anarchy may even cause war. Using the language of communications theory, Deutsch showed that amalgamation engenders transactions that increase loads on a governmental system. If the system does not have or is unable to develop capabilities commensurate with these added loads, the consequence may be mutual frustration and hostility. Accordingly, the search for world government can become self-defeating.

This concern, derived from his theoretic study of communications and his empirical examination of nationalism and political community in the North Atlantic area, informed the investigation undertaken in the mid-1960s by Deutsch and others of arms control and unification in West Europe. The project rested on systematic interviews with French and West German political and economic leaders, studies of public opinion, and quantitative analyses of the press in four countries. It sought most immediately to determine what trends existed, and then to project these trends into the short-range future.[11] In general, the study found an imbalance between what was commonly expected from a united Europe and the infrastructural support needed to create whatever institutions were necessary to satisfy these expectations. On the basis of this research Deutsch cautioned against further immediate steps toward unification of the Six.

Another form of imbalance, equally dangerous from Deutsch's point of view, consists of strong ties among unequal partners. A structure enforcing a rigorous division of labor between the masters and the enslaved may indeed enhance overall production in a society. The appearance of stability may none the less be deceptive. As Puchala and others have pointed out in this volume, Deutsch's own studies of nationalism and national integration have shown that an imbalanced scheme for organizing society, in which some pay an extraordinary price while others enjoy extraordinary benefits, is inherently unstable, and hides the development of patterns of social communication which can lead to unrest and even revolution. In the global system, too, members of some nation-states, especially those with poorly developed economic systems, fear that their involvement in the world economy and the political system produces an extremely disproportionate distribution of benefits both globally and within their own states. This leads them to question the legitimacy of the prevailing structures. At the same time, however, the costs of dissociating themselves from those structures would be immense. These conflicting demands pose one of the great dilemmas of our times.

This dilemma, spawned by economic and political interdependence in the non-communist world, has led to furious debate and some scientific analysis. Analyses directed against the industrialized states, which are perceived as those benefiting most in the long run from the status quo, have become commonplace. Similarly, we have seen strident exhortations to the less developed world to dissociate itself from the prevailing system, whatever the immediate cost might be. From Deutsch, we have heard an insistence on scientific analysis directed to questions such as how accurately do conflicting interpretations of this great dilemma reflect the real world? How can we devise means to ascertain the direction and speed of current developments? His contribution, then, in addition to cool analysis of the assumptions and logic of theories about 'dependencia' and 'structural imperialism',[12] has been to force us to search for objective, reproducible, and, when possible, quantitative data which can test derivative propositions and, eventually, the theories themselves.

Peter J. Katzenstein, in his chapter 'Domestic structures and political strategies: Austria in an interdependent world', points to the possibility of maintaining political autonomy while analyzing the patterns of dependence of small, developed states. After seven years of nazi rule and a decade of occupation by the victors of the Second World War, a poor and politically contentious Austria regained its sovereignty in 1955, but it was deeply penetrated by the world market. Simple dependence on foreign trade was not the worst of it, but structural imbalances existed as well. Lagging industrialization had meant that Austria emphasized 'traditional' industries for exports and 'modern' industries for imports. Lacking the potential for investment to create its own automotive industry, for example, the country opted to import automobiles from Italy. Current interest in setting up an indigenous automotive industry faces a similar economic stumbling block, plus the fact that Austria has much farther to go to catch up than was the case two decades ago. And, in the meantime, the country has had to strengthen its traditional industries to pay for the imported Fiats.

What has saved Austria from complete economic dependence, in contrast to other countries with similar problems, is in Katzenstein's view the stability of its domestic structures which, for historical and political reasons, are more autonomous from the international arena than are those of developing countries. The keystone is the principle of social compensation, aimed at providing employment for the working class, a low inflationary rate for the business community, and both political stability and economic prosperity for the general public. The Austrians preferred stable domestic political structures to a destabilizing, rapid internationalization of their economy. Unable to dissociate themselves from that economy, Austrians in effect bargained among themselves to achieve the greatest possible measure of autonomy in the international arena.

Dieter Senghaas, writing about 'Dissociation and autocentric development: an alternative development policy for the Third World', deals with a substantially different aspect of the dilemma of development and autonomy. Without stable domestic structures, and with an economy dominated by foreign governments and businessmen, the typical less developed country faces a severe challenge in choosing and implementing its own values and political goals. Elites frequently continue the state's dependence on the prevailing international economy in exchange for the wherewithal to pursue a policy of rapid but distorted economic expansion. Accepting such a bargain, however, merely exacerbates the imbalance between the industrial and the developing countries, and permits the former to control the latter more easily.

As a first step toward autocentric development, Senghaas urges countries of the Third World to dissociate themselves from the prevailing international economy. They must initiate protective policies to encourage development of their productive forces; trade selectively with the industrialized countries, always with the aim of building up viable domestic structures; and, instead of continuing to produce raw materials which are processed in the metropolitan countries, concentrate on creating their own industries. Secondly, they should restructure themselves to meet priorities in their own economy. This may retard the rate of economic growth, at least at the outset, since they will have to invent or reinvent or adapt appropriate technologies, pay attention to the basic needs of consumers, and simultaneously develop a broadly effective infrastructure. All this entails both economic and political costs. But the alternative, satisfying immediate needs by continued reliance on metropolitan countries, inevitably leads to penetration and control from abroad. The third prong of Senghaas's strategy calls for the developing countries to create among themselves new infrastructures of co-operation at the subregional, regional, and continental levels. Although such steps may actually limit autocentric development, they also prevent dependence and may ultimately allow countries in the Third World to create a multicentric international economy.

Raymond Duvall and his associates, in their chapter 'A formal model of "dependencia" theory: structure and measurement', outline a plan for research to test some of the assumptions and hypotheses of theories like that offered by Senghaas. Their goal here is to make a rigorous theoretical specification of central 'dependence' propositions, to suggest empirical referents for key concepts in such theories, and to suggest sources of relevant data. This requires as a first step reviewing the literature on poor countries' political, economic, and social penetration by rich countries, including the alleged effects of economic distortions, internal economic disintegration and inequalities, the increase of social conflict, and the interaction of that conflict with coercive authoritarian rule. They formalize a theory of 'dependencia' in terms of three sets of variables affecting social processes. The concern (a) economic and political ties between states at the center and those at the periphery, (b) the creation of export enclaves and various aspects of internal economic distortion, and (c) violent conflict and government coercion to suppress that conflict. The measurement of some variables is fairly straightforward, but others, such as economic and cultural penetration, or economic dis-integration, rest on complex concepts and measurement. Some variables interact, allowing for different national contexts and different modes of involvement in the capitalist world economy. The authors have now compiled the large-scale data required to test such hypotheses; the project thus moves from speculation and argument about important political phenomena to formal statements evaluated in the light of empirical evidence. It also adopts a research style typical of Deutsch: Russett, a former student of Deutsch, works with a team of younger scholars, including three of his students who form a 'third generation' in descent from Karl.

The emphasis in this section of the volume on dysfunctional integration – whether it be due to an imbalance of loads and capabilities in a formally amalgamated government or inequities in the distribution of burdens and rewards in a wide range of formal and informal arrangements – should not be interpreted as a sign that Deutsch himself is pessimistic about prospects for broadening the area of common decision-making and peace. On the contrary, Deutsch argues that formal unification is not required to create a security-community among states and other actors with a common interest in preventing armed conflict with each other. More creative paths to this end are conceivable and have in fact been implemented. Secondly, even if the intent is to create common governmental institutions, a concern with dysfunctional integration aims at isolating problems which must be solved if unification is to be successful. Imbalances between the system's loads and capabilities and among the partners in terms of burdens and expected rewards should be ameliorated.

Political Cybernetics and World Order

Studies in the previous sections bear implications for the scientific study of politics far beyond questions of nationalism, national development, and integration at the supranational level. They point to Karl Deutsch's fundamental interest in communication and control, his emphasis on the use of quantitative data to test important political theories, and his pioneering efforts with respect to both. The final section of this volume includes chapters on these interrelated concerns.

Political Cybernetics

The field of cybernetics was first developed by Norbert Wiener of the Massachusetts Institute of Technology. It was Karl Deutsch, however, who saw and spelled out its importance for the study of politics and society. Cybernetics, derived from the Greek word for steering, focuses on communication and control in systems. A cybernetic approach, by trying to specify and put into operational terms the variables that permit such steering, opens the way for the measurement of these variables and a more precise assessment of their interaction within such systems as a national decision-making unit. The central elements are the flow of communication through a system and the ways in which it can be controlled – topics vital to the formation of national and supranational communities, of course. Cybernetics forces us to examine such aspects as the conditions under which certain types of information are accepted into or screened out of the system, the critical role of consciousness, and the process of making decisions in a way that permits us to substitute probability statements for assertions based on intuition or often conflicting personal experiences.

Deutsch spelled out the political implications of cybernetics in a series of impressive articles which formed the basis for *The Nerves of Government* which in turn, since its publication in 1963, has attained near-classic standing among social scientists. His own subsequent research examined such aspects of political communication as the ratio between internal and external communications and transactions of a country as an indicator of the degree of its self-preoccupation or self-closure over time, governments' share of facilities for controlling the flow of information and the effect of this variable on governmental performance, the ways in which decision-making systems deal with communications overload, and, most recently, the forms and consequences of decentralization in governmental decision-making.

In his chapter 'From political cybernetics to global modeling', Hayward R. Alker, Jr looks into the longer-range impact of some of Deutsch's work in this field. Generally speaking, Alker says, the introduction into scientific discourse in the 1940s and early 1950s of cybernetic systems theory was as important in changing thought as the Newtonian revolution. Going beyond 'simple rejection of mechanistic, lawful explanation and related equilibrium analysis', it used 'richer, often teleological metaphors suggested by medicine, physiology, and modern computers' and paid attention to the causal nature of feedback systems. The virtue of Deutsch's early cybernetic work, Alker continues, was its focus on central political problems (although, he laments, such insights were by and large not made operational).

Even more exciting was what Alker terms second- and third-generation cybernetics. An emerging theory of automata facilitated progress in linguistic understanding, itself necessary for operationalizing central concepts. Political scientists paid more attention to the shift from maximization to optimal control, to the need for counterfactual analyses of decision-making bodies. Developments in heuristics, creativity, and artificial intelligence were in turn important for theories of automata and optimal control. Remaining problems include structural analysis and the study of notions about pathological performance such as corruption and irrationality in a wide range of systems. The 'new cybernetics' of the third generation deals with autopoietic (self + producing) cellular systems and genetically programmed processes. Alker concludes with some reinterpretations and extensions of automata theory as relevant to world order theorizing.

Some uses of cybernetic insights have already been seen in earlier chapters of this volume. Studies of the conscious formation of political communities by Foltz, Merritt, and others, the consequences of governmental growth by Taylor, and self-reliance by Senghaas are indicative. So, too, is the emphasis in many of these chapters on what J. David Singer calls 'steersmanship'. Manfred Kochen picks up this theme of consciousness and steering in his chapter entitled, provocatively, 'Can the global system learn to control conflict?' He recognizes that some kinds of conflict, such as creative tension, serve a useful function in societies. But any system, if it is to survive, must be able to keep its conflicts within bounds.

For the global system as such to remain in control of its conflicts, in Kochen's view, requires 'a search for conditions under which self-regulating mechanisms in the total system maintain stable equilibria or smooth (non-catastrophic), non-equilibrium changes'. Balance-of-power systems, it therefore turns out, are too easily destabilized in their search for equilibrium. What is required is *adaptive learning*. This occurs if a system 'forms and uses a consensual representation of the world to recognize and control or master an increasing variety' of challenges. Changes in the values assigned to a fixed set of hypotheses (or in the procedures used for generating them), the hypotheses themselves, or the conceptual repertoire (and its structure) from which hypotheses are formed are all means to that end.

Easy to say, Kochen recognizes, but difficult to follow. The problem is that 'we are uncertain and inconsistent about what we will consider desirable or valuable in the future'. This means coping with complexity, coming up with creative imagery of situations we have not yet experienced. It also means detecting and correcting errors of perception, cognition, and conation, as well as improving our ability to use and communicate information. Conflict can be controlled 'if each party behaves so that the long-term consequences are preferred by all parties, each according to its own basic values, even if it means forgoing short-term consequences that are preferable to each party'.

Political Theory and Quantitative Data

What cybernetic thinking applied to politics makes absolutely clear is the need for data – impersonal, replicable, quantitative – that can test significant propositions derived from major theories. And, indeed, in Deutsch's own works he assembled a considerable amount of data on population movements, language assimilation, and the flow of such international transactions as trade and mail. In a seminal article of 1960, 'Toward an inventory of basic trends and patterns in comparative and international politics',[13] Deutsch generalized this research experience and assessment of needs to suggest how large-scale data banks could aid in the development and testing of theory on such topics as political development and the probabilities of war and peace.

Deutsch's ideas on the development of cross-national data banks contained four elements. First, it was necessary to use data which, however insufficient they might be, could be obtained fairly readily to show that the entire notion had intellectual merit and theoretic promise. Secondly, efforts would have to be undertaken, always within a theoretic frame of reference that informed the researcher's criteria of relevance and reliability, to gather systematically sets of better data. Thirdly, since it seemed clear that no single scholar, regardless of that scholar's discipline or nationality, could accomplish alone the task of assembling adequate data relevant to political theories, data programs should comprise multidisciplinary and, he hoped, multinational research teams. If this was not always possible, then it was imperative to create a multidisciplinary and cross-national network of conferences and other means of communication to exchange scientific information, evaluate each other's efforts, and search out new directions for future research and analysis. Fourthly, new techniques must be developed to analyze the data in a theoretically meaningful way.

Deutsch has viewed these tasks as simultaneous and mutually reinforcing, requiring prodigious organizational and intellectual work. It is not exaggerating to say that Karl Deutsch was in the forefront of all these developments. As suggested above, his early work was exemplary in showing that data could be generated to test important propositions; and, by the time his article in 1960 on the need for data banks had appeared, as well as another one, 'Social mobilization and political development',[14] published the next year, the point had been sufficiently well established to proceed to a more ambitious undertaking.

With the intellectual collaboration of Harold D. Lasswell and the practical support of two younger political scientists, Richard L. Merritt and Bruce M. Russett,[15] Karl Deutsch secured the pilot funds necessary to set up the Yale Political Data Program. Under Russett's direction, the YPDP aimed at developing quantitative indicators which could help test significant propositions and theories in social science. Its first major publication, *World Handbook of Political and Social Indicators*, by Russett and Alker, Deutsch, and Lasswell, contributed to reorienting social scientists to the use of such data;[16] and a plethora of scholarly articles by Deutsch, Russett, and others used the data to make very specific contributions to the development of empirically based theory.[17]

Eight years later, in 1972, the greatly revised and expanded second edition of the *World Handbook*, by Charles L. Taylor and Michael C. Hudson, appeared;[18] and a third edition is currently being prepared by Taylor and David Jodice at the International Institute for Comparative Social Research of the Science Center Berlin. Karl's insistence on the speedy publication of these volumes, and on the widespread dissemination of the machine-readable data sets, epitomizes his commitment to the sharing of scientific information. His early example helped to make this norm as generally accepted as it now is in political science.

Deutsch's influence and the importance of quantitative data made themselves felt in other ways as well. For one thing, Deutsch, together with Stein Rokkan and others, helped to create a series of conferences to discuss questions of quantitative data, data banks, and social science theory. Many of these resulted in substantial volumes that contributed to what some have called the data movement.[19] Then, too, this work has stimulated other collections of political and social indicators developed by scholars across the world.[20] In short, the increasing use of aggregate data and the increasing sophistication of modes of mathematical analysis have revolutionized the study of politics, especially in the subfields of comparative and international politics.

Toward Global Modeling

Data are of critical importance if we are to understand how world politics has developed and where it is likely to head in the future. J. David Singer and Thomas Cusack, discussing 'Periodicity, inexorability, and steersmanship in international war', proceed *inter alia* from Deutsch's argument that enhanced knowledge of ourselves, the instruments we use, and our environment – but also awareness of the limits of our autonomy – improves our capacity to determine our own fate. Understanding the causes of war may help us to recognize the signs of its imminent onset and prevent its occurrence. But what if wars are the result of stochastic processes over which we have little or no control? Much traditional writing, for instance, has claimed that wars occur in cycles. If this is true, then there may be little more we can offer than to predict and prepare ourselves for the inevitable turning of the martial wheel.

Is there a cyclical pattern in the occurrence of war? The 'correlates of war' project scrutinized every international conflagration from the Congress of Vienna in 1815 until 1965 in terms of three variables: the intervals between their outbreak, their outcomes, and their costs. Statistical analysis reveals no evidence that the passage of time alone makes war more probable for any major power. Defeat similarly makes little difference, although victory in the most recent war tends to increase the nation-state's likelihood of getting involved in a new one. The cost of the previous war, indicated by the number of fatalities and the war's duration, was not significantly related to the chances of a new war. Taking outcomes and costs together made little difference if the country's previous war had ended in victory; if that last war had been lost, however, then its greater length was associated with a shorter interval before the country warred again, and its greater cost in fatalities was associated with a longer interval. The longer the interval between wars, the greater were the costs of the ensuing war. These data strongly suggest that war is not a simple cyclical phenomenon for the international system, though nation-states may make choices based in part on their previous experience in war.

This returns us to the concept of steersmanship: nation-states can act in ways to enhance or diminish the chances of war. Steersmanship is even more possible when we have data and models for projecting nation-states' behavior into the future. Only in recent years have scholars developed data-based econometric and sociometric models sufficiently sophisticated to permit reasonably accurate forecasting and hypothetical adjustments of variables to stimulate contingent futures. The possibility of creating comprehensive models for world politics none the less seemed remote to most scholars.

The possibility of global modeling doubtless intrigued Karl Deutsch not only because of the challenge it posed but also because it brings together all his interests and skills: a concern with preventing the outbreak of violence, the need of nation-states for strategic roadmaps to help them steer their way in the global system, and a focus on generating hypotheses about human behavior, testable at least in principle by data from the real world, which can be used to model social processes. Early efforts at global modeling, of substantial intrinsic interest to be sure, he found disappointing because of their questionable assumptions and lack of attention to key social and especially political variables.[21]

The next logical step, then, was to create the organizational framework to make global modeling more useful for political decision-makers. The opportunity came in 1976 when Karl Deutsch was asked to help found and co-direct the International Institute for Comparative Social Research of the Science Center Berlin. There he has created a research team on global modeling, led by Stuart Bremer and aided by such consultants as Bruno Fritsch, Manfred Kochen, and J. David Singer. The target is to produce by the early 1980s a functioning, computerized model of global society based not only on an integrated set of mathematical equations but also on hard data about political and social processes.

Bruno Fritsch's contribution to this volume, 'Critical factors of North–South relations seen from a long-term socioecological perspective', represents some of the thought going into the global model being developed at the Science Center Berlin. Starting from the fact of interdependence in today's world, Fritsch asks how we can meet the material needs of people without falling short in meeting their non-material needs. A continuation of present trends spells trouble, he says. Expected population growth alone will produce by the year 2020 a world population of 8 billion people, 5 billion of them in the less developed countries. Continued inequalities in the distribution of resources notwithstanding, there are likely to be more highly gifted people in these latter countries than in the developed North as well as ever more desperados disinclined to accept this inequality. The renewal of resources which are being used requires energy, itself a resource in short supply.

These and similar trends emphasize the importance of the developed countries' problem-solving capabilities. Fritsch outlines three indicators of change in a nation-state's capabilities: its reinforcement potential, indicated by the proportion of worldwide defense expenditures accounted for by the country in question and its degree of self-sufficiency in supplies of energy; a structuring capacity index (which interacts with the reinforcement potential), comprising the ratio of 'social communication and information potential' and 'material energy turnover'; and dependence on foreign trade. The North's problem-solving capabilities, Fritsch concludes, must be turned to the tasks of increasing significantly its own energy supply and achieving an overall economic growth rate consistent with both a social and thermodynamic equilibrium. If it cannot do this, then the political climate for support of the less developed countries will deteriorate.

Advances in global modeling make clear the fact that the stress on data and the use of increasingly sophisticated modes of mathematical analysis have revolutionized the study of politics. Karl Deutsch was and is at the forefront of this movement. His own research broke new paths, and his teaching has inspired others to push out even farther the frontiers of knowledge. His organizational efforts at the international level have contributed significantly to a worldwide network of scholars and data-based research programs which can provide a firm basis for still further developments. His new program in West Berlin promises new breakthroughs in the specific field of global modeling and, more generally, demonstrates once again his continuing commitment to the development and use of knowledge for the betterment of humankind.

Notes: Editors' Introduction

1 Karl W. Deutsch, *Nationalism and Social Communication: An Inquiry into the Foundations of Nationality* (Cambridge, Mass.: Technology Press of the Massachusetts Institute of Technology, and New York: Wiley, 1953; 2d edn, Cambridge, Mass.: MIT Press, 1966).
2 Karl W. Deutsch, Sidney A. Burrell, Robert A. Kann, Maurice Lee, Jr, Martin Lichterman, Raymond E. Lindgren, Francis L. Loewenheim, and Richard W. Van Wagenen, *Political Community and the North Atlantic Area: International Organization in the Light of Historical Experience* (Princeton, NJ: Princeton University Press, 1957).
3 Karl W. Deutsch, *The Nerves of Government: Models of Political Communication and Control* (New York: The Free Press, 1963; 2d edn, 1966).
4 Karl W. Deutsch and Lewis J. Edinger, *Germany Rejoins the Powers: Mass Opinion, Interest Groups, and Elites in Contemporary German Foreign Policy* (Stanford, Calif.: Stanford University Press, 1959).
5 Karl W. Deutsch, *The Analysis of International Relations* (Englewood Cliffs, NJ: Prentice-Hall, 1968; 2d edn, 1978).
6 Karl W. Deutsch, *Politics and Government: How People Decide Their Fate* (Boston, Mass.: Houghton Mifflin, 1970; 3d edn, 1980).

7 This background work appears separately in Karl W. Deutsch, *An Interdisciplinary Bibliography on Nationalism, 1935–1953* (Cambridge, Mass.: Technology Press of MIT, 1956). An updated and greatly expanded version is Karl W. Deutsch and Richard L. Merritt, *Nationalism and National Development: An Interdisciplinary Bibliography* (Cambridge, Mass.: MIT Press, 1970).
8 See, for example, Karl W. Deutsch and William J. Foltz (eds), *Nation-Building* (New York: Atherton Press, 1963); Karl W. Deutsch, *Nationalism and Its Alternatives* (New York: Knopf, 1969); Karl W. Deutsch, *Nationenbildung-Nationalstaat-Integration*, ed. A. Ashkenasi and P. Schulze (Düsseldorf: Bertelsmann Universitätsverlag, 1972); and numerous articles.
9 Deutsch spelled out his own ideas in *Political Community at the International Level* (Garden City, NY: Doubleday, 1954).
10 Karl Deutsch's basic ideas on nationalism and integration have stimulated numerous monographs exploring their implications, and often leading to independent contributions. To name but a few of these: Bruce M. Russett, *Community and Contention: Britain and America in the Twentieth Century* (Cambridge, Mass.: MIT Press, 1963); William J. Foltz, *From French West Africa to the Mali Federation* (New Haven, Conn., and London: Yale University Press, 1965); Arend Lijphart, *The Trauma of Decolonization: The Dutch and West New Guinea* (New Haven, Conn., and London: Yale University Press, 1966); Richard L. Merritt, *Symbols of American Community, 1735–1775* (New Haven, Conn., and London: Yale University Press, 1966); Michael C. Hudson, *The Precarious Republic: Political Modernization in Lebanon* (New York: Random House, 1968); Hugh Stephens, *The Political Transformation of Tanganyika, 1920–67* (New York: Praeger, 1968); Gebhard Ludwig Schweigler, *National Consciousness in Divided Germany* (Beverly Hills, Calif., and London: Sage, 1975); and Peter J. Katzenstein, *Disjoined Partners: Austria and Germany since 1815* (Berkeley and Los Angeles: University of California Press, 1976).
11 A summary of the findings is in Karl W. Deutsch, 'Integration and arms control in the European political environment: a summary report', *The American Political Science Review*, vol. 60, no. 2 (June 1966), pp. 354–65. The main publications of the project are Karl W. Deutsch, Lewis J. Edinger, Roy C. Macridis, and Richard L. Merritt, *France, Germany and the Western Alliance: A Study of Elite Attitudes on European Integration and World Politics* (New York: Scribner, 1967); Karl W. Deutsch, *Arms Control and the Atlantic Alliance: Europe Faces Coming Policy Decisions* (New York: Wiley, 1967); Bruce M. Russett and Carolyn C. Cooper, *Arms Control in Europe: Proposals and Political Constraints* (Denver, Colo.: University of Denver, Social Science Foundation and Graduate School of International Studies, Monograph Series in World Affairs No. 2, 1967); Richard L. Merritt and Donald J. Puchala (eds), *Western European Perspectives on International Affairs: Public Opinion Studies and Evaluations* (New York: Praeger, 1968); and J. Zvi Namenwirth and Thomas L. Brewer, 'Elite editorial comment on the European and Atlantic communities in four countries', in *The General Inquirer: A Computer Approach to Content Analysis*, ed. Philip J. Stone, Dexter C. Dunphy, Marshall S. Smith, and Daniel M. Ogilvie with associates (Cambridge, Mass., and London: MIT Press, 1966), pp. 401–27.
12 See Karl W. Deutsch, 'Imperialism and neocolonialism', in Peace Science Society (International), *Papers: The Fifth Cambridge Conference, November 1973*, ed. Walter Isard and T. M. Fogarty, 23 (1974), pp. 1–26.
13 Karl W. Deutsch, 'Toward an inventory of basic trends and patterns in comparative and international politics', *The American Political Science Review*, 54, no. 1 (March 1960), pp. 34–57.
14 Karl W. Deutsch, 'Social mobilization and political development', *American Political Science Review*, vol. 55, no. 3 (September 1961), pp. 493–514.
15 For its underpinnings, see Karl W. Deutsch, Harold D. Lasswell, Richard L. Merritt, and Bruce M. Russett, 'The Yale Political Data Program', in *Comparing Nations: The Use of Quantitative Data in Cross-National Research*, ed. Richard L. Merritt and Stein Rokkan (New Haven, Conn., and London: Yale University Press, 1966), pp. 81–94.
16 Bruce M. Russett, Hayward R. Alker, Jr, Karl W. Deutsch, and Harold D. Lasswell, *World Handbook of Political and Social Indicators* (New Haven, Conn., and London: Yale University Press, 1964).

17 See David H. Jodice, Charles Lewis Taylor and Karl W. Deutsch, *Cumulation in Social Science Data Archiving: A Study of the Impact of the Two World Handbooks of Political and Social Indicators* (Konigstein/Ts.: Anton Hain, 1980). An earlier review is Bruce M. Russett, 'The *World Handbook* as a tool in current research', in *Aggregate Data Analysis: Political and Social Indicators in Cross-National Research*, ed. Charles Lewis Taylor (Paris: Mouton, 1968), pp. 143–63.
18 Charles Lewis Taylor and Michael C. Hudson, *World Handbook of Political and Social Indicators*, 2d edn (New Haven, Conn., and London: Yale University Press, 1972).
19 See, for example, Merritt and Rokkan (eds), *Comparing Nations*, op. cit.; Stein Rokkan (ed.), *Data Archives for the Social Sciences* (Paris and The Hague: Mouton, 1966); Mattei Dogan and Stein Rokkan (eds), *Quantitative Ecological Analysis in the Social Sciences* (Cambridge, Mass., and London: MIT Press, 1969); Hayward R. Alker, Jr, Karl W. Deutsch, and Antoine H. Stoetzel (eds), *Mathematical Approaches to Politics* (San Francisco, Calif.: Jossey-Bass, 1973); and Karl W. Deutsch and Rudolf Wildenmann (eds), *Mathematical Political Analysis: From Methods to Substance*, vol. 5 of *Sozialwissenschaftliches Jahrbuch für Politik*, ed. Rudolf Wildenmann (München and Wien: Günter Olzog Verlag, 1976).
20 Among these are Ellen Propper Mickiewicz (ed.), *Handbook of Soviet Social Science Data* (New York: The Free Press, 1973); J. David Singer and Melvin Small, *The Wages of War, 1816–1965: A Statistical Handbook* (New York: Wiley, 1972); and J. David Singer (ed.), *The Correlates of War, I: Research Origins and Rationale* (New York: The Free Press, 1978).
21 See Karl W. Deutsch, 'Toward Drift Models and Steering Models', in *Problems of World Modeling: Political and Social Implications*, ed. Karl W. Deutsch, Bruno Fritsch, Hélio Jaguaribe, and Andrei S. Markovits (Cambridge, Mass.: Ballinger, 1977), pp. 5–10.

Part One

Nationalism and Social Mobilization

1

Modernization and Nation-Building: The Social Mobilization Model Reconsidered

WILLIAM J. FOLTZ

Karl Deutsch's 'Social mobilization and political development' was first presented in draft version at a 1959 meeting of the Social Science Research Council's Committee on Comparative Politics and was published in the September 1961 issue of the *American Political Science Review*.[1] This was a time of ferment and excitement in American social science, particularly in political science where the so-called 'behavioral revolution', having seized the center of the study of American politics, was busy establishing far-flung beachheads in the study of non-Western areas. Behavioralism had turned the discipline from political history, legal philosophy, and institutional description toward attempts at the greater methodological rigor thought to be associated with the natural sciences. It put the emphasis on quantification and systematic generalization, and equally on establishing intellectual links with allied social sciences, particularly psychology and sociology, which had earlier undergone similar transformations.[2] 'Social mobilization' reflected that intellectual excitement and contributed to it. It occupied a central position in the analysis of modernization and of political development, especially the development of effective structures of the nation-state, a process to which Deutsch soon gave the name of 'nation-building'.[3] In reconsidering the social mobilization model, one perforce raises questions about this larger constellation of mid-twentieth-century social science thought.

As the 1961 article explains, 'Social mobilization is a name given to an overall process of change, which happens to substantial parts of the population in countries which are moving from traditional to modern ways of life. It ... brackets together a number of more specific processes of change ... It implies that these processes tend to go together in certain historical situations and stages of economic development ... It is not identical, therefore, with this process of modernization as a whole, but it deals with ... a recurrent cluster among its consequences'.[4] Social mobilization is thus a phenomenon of the social and economic realms, produced by the historic process of modernization. It in turn connects these realms with the realm of the political, because 'these changes tend to influence and sometimes to transform political behavior'. Within the social and economic realms, social mobilization is not just a 'consequence' of modernization, as it may appear when viewed in a short timespan; over the long run it also can be a 'significant cause' of modernization 'in the well-known pattern of feedback or circular causation'.[5]

The particular importance of social mobilization is that it introduces human action and reaction into a broad historical process; in effect, it brings the vast changes adumbrated by Durkheim, Tönnies, Marx, and Weber down to the level of discernible actions which can be studied and measured. The consequences of modernization are seen as quantitative and eventually qualitative changes in attitudes, needs, and actions of real persons; these changes in turn permit, and perhaps compel, other changes in the social and economic realms. As people change they also affect the political realm directly, by generating demands for government to satisfy, and indirectly, by producing new social structures which both generate demands and create new resources on which national governments can draw. The social mobilization of substantial parts of the population, then, can both push and permit national government to expand and modernize their operations. Social mobilization thus becomes a motor of political development.

For the people who undergo it, social mobilization is a two-stage process. In the first stage they 'break away' from their old loyalties and patterns of behavior. If this is all that happens, they are left as 'uprooted, impoverished and disoriented masses'.[6] In the second stage they are 'inducted' into 'some relatively stable new patterns of group membership, organization, and commitment'.[7] The level and rate of change in each stage is susceptible to measurement using readily available (and, it is presumed, highly intercorrelated) national-level statistical indicators. Measurement of the first stage gives an indication of the burdens likely to be placed on government; measurement of the second stage indicates something of the capabilities of government for bearing these burdens. Comparison of changes in the two measures thus can tell us something of the likelihood that the state might remain stable and pursue a successful path of political development or that it might collapse under its new burdens. It is no small tribute to Deutsch's article that well before Huntington raised the spectre of 'political decay'[8] or Kasfir demonstrated the necessity and willingness of some Third World governments artificially to restrict political participation,[9] Deutsch was attempting to *measure* the likelihood that particular governments would find themselves in such parlous straits.

Deutsch's social mobilization model has stimulated and provided intellectual support for social and political research in many different fields. Most immediately, it spurred the systematic hunt for collection and analysis of aggregate data, notably in the two editions of the *World Handbook of Political and Social Indicators*.[10] Major studies of political mobilization[11] and of historic and contemporary processes of state and national consolidation[12] are deeply marked by their debt to Deutsch's formulation. Contemporary cross- and intranational studies on political participation command our particular attention because they descend from the aggregate level of analysis to look at the behavior of smaller groups and of individuals. They provide more precise tests of the model by asking the questions: who actually does participate in politics? To what degree and in what ways have they been socially mobilized as compared with those who do not participate? Predictably, succeeding research, especially that requiring the analysis of historically specific and micro-level data, has entailed complications for Deutsch's simple original formulation of the relationship between social mobilization and political development.

Domínguez[13] looks at Latin America during the period of revolution against Spanish rule in the early nineteenth century to see how much popular participation in these mass events can be explained by social mobilization. He finds, rather reluctantly one feels, that 'the social mobilization hypothesis is *not* a general, adequate explanation of political participation during the wars of independence period. The levels of social mobilization in the four colonies were far below the thresholds of significance which must be approached if the hypothesis is to be relevant'.[14] Whether or not the population of a colony rose in arms was independent of its ranking on a scale of social mobilization; where the people rose, 'political mobilization depended on leaders and organizations acting upon a fairly inept, non-civic mass'.[15] While Domínguez then goes on to show that the low degree of social mobilization retains its utility in that it predicts the failure of the wars of independence to be followed by 'sustained civic participation', it is clear to him that 'one must look to other hypotheses and independent variables' to explain the revolutions themselves.

Looking at considerably less dramatic and less remote situations through a survey of individual political behavior in five nations, Nie, Powell, and Prewitt show that economic change does indeed affect political participation, but that it does so in two different and complex ways.[16] It increases the size of the middle class whose members are more likely to have access to political information, to pay attention to politics, and to feel politically efficacious than is the case with economically and socially deprived persons. It is these intervening personal attributes that explain political participation among individuals of higher socioeconomic status. In addition, economic growth facilitates the expansion of an 'organizational infrastructure' which 'may represent an alternative channel for political participation for socially disadvantaged groups'.[17] Nowhere do they show, however, that economic development is *necessary* for the construction of organizations capable of involving low SES people in political activities. For them it is at least an open possibility that, as Domínguez subsequently showed in his four cases, major political action can take place in the absence of any significant level of aggregate social mobilization.

In a particularly well-argued attack, Cameron[18] looks at a wide range of nineteenth- and twentieth-century cases in the United States, Europe, and China and finds the social mobilization model deficient in three respects. First, social mobilization by itself fails to explain how persons are actually 'inducted' into the new patterns of political commitment that Deutsch foresees coming about as the result of social and economic change. Using quite different types of data from those used by Nie, Powell, and Prewitt, Cameron extends their emphasis on organizations as mediators between the individual and political actions to demonstrate that specifically political organizations must be seen as active participants in the induction process. In politically active situations organizers may penetrate local society 'from within', using 'traditional social organizations as the vehicles of party organization'.[19] Secondly, he argues that 'mobilization may be conceived as a change process relatively free of the various "end state biases" associated with modernization'.[20] Thus, as many of Deutsch's followers have ignored, 'national development' is in no way implicit in the changes summarized by social mobilization. Cameron stresses that in many settings a historically significant form of mobilization has been that of the periphery organizing itself – even in the absence of ethnic or linguistic splits – in reaction against the activities of the national center. Finally, Cameron rejects the general pattern of argument which views political mobilization as 'socially determined and the dependent variable in a process of social change'. Rather, he argues, 'The critical independent variable which gives rise to mobilization efforts involves not the patterns of social cleavage and social change *per se* but, rather, the context of public policy . . . it is in the structures, processes, and outputs of national policy that one must look for an explanation of why mobilization first occurs'.[21] More specifically than either Domínguez or Nie, Powell and Prewitt, but entirely consistent with their arguments, Cameron finds political development impossible to explain on the basis of independent variables drawn exclusively from the social and economic realms.

While Cameron emphasizes the national context of politics, Connor,[22] in a broadside attack on the linkage between social mobilization and nation-building, argues that the most important political reality often lies at levels below that of the central government. He finds political mobilization increasingly taking place in both old and new 'nations' on the basis of ethnic and other primordial divisions at a substate level. Furthermore, he argues that much of the existing literature suffers from an 'unwarranted exaggeration of the influence of materialism upon human affairs'.[23] Thus, rising levels of per capita GNP, even rising ratios of a subgroup's income to that of the rest of the population, in no way need betoken either an increase in that group's functional integration into the larger polity or an increase in its loyalty to the central government. Again, factors other than aggregate social and economic data must be taken into account.

Duvall and Welfling,[24] in the most technically sophisticated of the studies reviewed here, look at social mobilization in relation to four political variables: party system institutionalization; turmoil; internal war; and elite conflict. Of these, they find social mobilization to be 'the least useful variable in explaining changes in the other variables'.[25] Like Cameron explicitly, and the others cited above implicitly, Duvall and

Welfling stress 'the importance of political linkage mechanisms for processes of development and stability' and conversely, that 'conflict, as an interactive process, is a function of linkages between actors as well as attributes of actors'.[26] If neither the development and extension of political organization, nor the development of political conflict, can be shown to have a 'direct basis in social mobilization',[27] in a careful study using aggregate data from twenty-eight countries, some rethinking of the social mobilization model is required.

The weaknesses of the social mobilization model, I believe, are not so much specific to the model itself, either in its 1961 formulation or in the many studies it spawned, but stem from more fundamental weaknesses implicit in the broader paradigms of nation-building and modernization. These can legitimately be called paradigms in that they are not so much models or theories as sets of basic assumptions that have conditioned the questions scholars have asked, the data they have collected, and therefore the sorts of theories they have constructed.[28] The problem with each originates in the misapplication of nineteenth-century macrosociological theorizing. This is not the place to do a full critique of these paradigms or to analyze the reasons for their persistence, but it is possible here to develop two central points which have the virtue of suggesting ways out of the present theoretical muddle.

The Unit of Analysis Problem

The nation-building literature, of course, deals with the problem of how nations (or more precisely nation-states) come about, whether they are viewed as conscious constructions or as organically evolving entities.[29] The unit of analysis, therefore, is the internationally recognized national state. Political development and modernization come to be defined in national terms. Thus, for Organski, 'Political development can be defined as *increasing governmental efficiency in utilizing the human and material resources of the nation for national goals* ... Today political development requires national unification ...'.[30] And for Huntington, 'Political modernization involves assertion of the external sovereignty of the nation-state against transnational influences and of the internal sovereignty of the national government against local and regional powers. It means national integration and the centralization or accumulation of power in recognized national lawmaking institutions'.[31] These are, of course, gratuitous assumptions about what 'developed' or 'modern' means or ought to mean, assumptions not at all shared by writers of a decade previous concerned with, for example, European integration, nor by those of the succeeding decade for whom 'small' had become 'beautiful'. Gratuitous they may be, but the assumptions reflect the profession's intellectual acquiescence in the present structure of the international system of national sovereignty.

For those doing quantitative studies, the acceptance of the nation as the basic unit of analysis is reinforced by the simple fact that most readily available data come pre-packaged at the national level (and by national statistical bureaus). This, it should be noted, is particularly the case for data on exchanges which cross national boundaries; very few of these data indicate the subnational region or group from which or to which the exchanges flow. Even when data are available on social or other cleavages at a lower unit level, these are almost inevitably presented in relation to the national unit which retains its power as the framework within which these divisions are to be examined.[32] The first of the Social Science Research Council's Studies in Political Development illustrated the problem. The substantive chapters all had headings denoting broad geographical regions; in each case the analysis dealt exclusively with the development prospects of individual nation-states.[33]

At a deeper analytic level, the tendency to use the nation-state as the unit of analysis is reinforced by the macrosociological models from which most modernization research derives. From Durkheim on, the unit of analysis has been the 'society', but one does not have to read far in the works of contemporary macrosociologists to see that 'society' becomes transformed into nation-state, either in actual practice or as a normative construct toward which a given entity is supposedly evolving. Thus Edward Shils begins the section of a recent work entitled 'Society' with a highly formal presentation of the eponymous concept as being characterized by a 'relationship with a central zone' which is 'a phenomenon of the realm of values and beliefs' and 'also a phenomenon of the realm of action'.[34] Eight pages later, however, we are brought down from such realms with the statement: 'The size of nominally revolutionary parties in France and Italy is a measure of the extent to which French and Italian societies have not been modernized'. Quite aside from whether the statement is true, it clearly assumes that French and Italian societies consist of those people over whom the French and Italian states claim dominion. Or some pages later, the 'effort of East Bengal to free itself from Pakistan' is presented as an instance 'of the organized efforts of one part of a society to become independent of some dominant or central part of that society, and to become a society which is significantly separate from other societies'.[35] Formal definitions aside, the meaning of such a statement becomes clear only if the word 'state' is substituted for 'society'. The reader is invited to try a similar re-reading of other macrosociological theorists.

Other sociologically inclined scholars, of course, have more clearly distinguished between, and have built more careful analyses on, the distinctions between society and the state and the practical difficulties of relating the two. Too often, however, they have done so at the expense of mapping the possibly great range of different societies within a state boundary. Thus Apter's *Gold Coast in Transition* and *The Political Kingdom in Uganda*[36] confine detailed social analysis to one significant ethnic group which comes to stand for all in those multi-ethnic societies. Likewise Pye's and Landé's analyses of why the Burmese and Philippine states malfunction deal only with the psychosocial character of the dominant population groups, neglecting what are significant and politically relevant minority groups.[37]

One now popular approach to dealing with subnational differentiation distinguishes analytically between center and periphery. One must be aware, however, that the definition of the center is an arbitrary analytic decision. While there is no *a priori* reason why the center should not turn out to be the internationally recognized central government of the nation-state (or alternatively of those individuals and social categories associated most closely with that government), if the concept is to be of any analytic help it must be defined and measured in relation to the actual behavior and attitudes of actual people. It must be theoretically possible for a state to have more than one center, or for it to have one which does not coincide well with the official and internationally recognized state structure. It is easiest to talk of center and periphery in a historic developmental context (cf. Rokkan in this volume) because the analyst has the advantage of knowing how the story came out, which group or region triumphed over its competitors to establish itself as the center of the political or social order. When the concepts of center and periphery are used in contemporaneous research, they must be treated as problematic. The first task of the analyst is to find out what *is* the center – or how many 'centers' may be competing with one another.

The nation-state as a unit of analysis has been attacked from both above and below. From above, the flood of writings of the various 'dependency theory' and structural imperialism schools have sought, and sometimes succeeded, in showing that the effective 'center' may not lie anywhere within a poor state's national boundaries, that economic, social, and political change depend on decisions and forces located outside. The general approach is familiar enough not to require elaboration here, and its impact on studies of development (or more often lack of development) has been profound.[38] Among its strengths have been its insistence on treating national boundaries as problematic and on perceiving that state structures, or more precisely the persons occupying roles in those structures, may act in terms of stimuli and goals having little to do with social or other facts originating within those boundaries. If the nation-building approach has erred in reifying national boundaries and state structures, the structural imperialism and dependency approaches, at least in the hands of lesser practitioners, have tended to err in treating them as epiphenomenal, or at best as objects of external control. To repeat, the reality of such structures and boundaries must be a matter of empirical investigation, not a matter of definition.

The attack from below has been less extensive, but no less intense. As in Connor's critique cited earlier, this approach has looked at subnational social units as the prime political reality and analyzed 'national' politics as little more than a fight for hegemony of the winning over the losing groups. The pitfall with this approach – into which Connor tumbles – is the tendency simply to reify the subnational ethnic or other group identities, to treat them as absolutes such as the literature being criticized treats the nation-state. Such groups and their boundaries as well must be treated as problematic, fluctuating and redefining themselves in response to processes like social mobilization and to decisions at the political center, whether that center is a national one (as in Cameron's article) or one outside the country.[39]

The Traditional Society Problem

The modernization paradigm has in recent years been subject to a wide range of attacks, the most devastating of which have undermined the logical and empirical bases for the functionalist and evolutionist mechanisms used to explain progress, and indeed, so often to make it seem inevitable.[40] These particular attacks, however, do not touch those parts of the modernization paradigm involved in the social mobilization model. Here we shall concentrate on modernization's starting point, the view of traditional society whose broad outlines have remained unchanged since they were laid down by the armchair theorists of the nineteenth century. Shils provides a contemporary statement of this view in discussing the 'positive content' of traditional beliefs:

> Beliefs which assert the moral rightness or superiority of institutions or a society of the past and which assert that what is done now or in the future should be modelled on the past ... are traditional beliefs ... These have often been described by sociologists and anthropologists; they are the beliefs of the Gemeinschaft, of the folk or peasant societies. They are beliefs in the virtue of authority, of respect for age and the rightful allocation of the highest authority to the aged. They are beliefs in the value of the lineage and the kinship group and in the primacy of obligations set by membership in these groups. Traditional beliefs are deferential. They express an attitude of piety ... Traditional beliefs enjoin ceremonial-ritual performances. They are particularistic in the sense that they recommend the primacy of obligations and attachments to bounded collectivities, above all the primordial collectivities of lineage, tribe, locality, ethnicity ... Closely connected with this is the frequent disposition in traditional belief to perceive a sharp disjunction between one's own collectivity and others and therefore to accept the appropriateness of war as a normal relationship between societies.
>
> Traditional beliefs of the substantive sort have no place for rational scientific theory or the results of scientific research ... This short list of the substantive properties of traditional beliefs could be extended ...[41]

Even without extending the list and risking belaboring what to most is the obvious, Shils has given the basic elements of the traditional social science view of the 'traditional': subordination of the present to the past; deference to authority and age; primordial community sentiment; absence of – even hostility toward – systematic or scientific curiosity and innovation.

Since it is now hardly contestable that the so-called 'traditional' societies exhibit a wide variety of forms, with widely varying norms and structures, permitting an equally wide variety of patterns of action (one need only compare the two societies featured in the Apter studies cited above), one must be impressed with the ability of this consensus vision of the traditional to persist. Certainly important in any explanation is the fact that the originators of the paradigm were for the most part not fieldworkers themselves but historically oriented sociologists whose primary task was the explanation of the changes Europe was undergoing in the nineteenth and early twentieth centuries. Even as their minds strove to bridge physical and historical distance, they were nevertheless men of their time and place, and that place was a superior one. Their vision, reinforced by more popular understandings current in their cultural milieu, provided the intellectual paradigm out of which their twentieth-century successors worked. Their view of 'traditional society' shaped the questions fieldworkers asked, and the way they heard and interpreted the answers. Research reports forced elaborations on the paradigm and deepened its structure, but provided no central challenge to its dominion. Indeed, as more recently the volume of observations has increased by astronomical proportions, the information overload has forced increased reliance on the paradigm to introduce order into the welter of data.[42]

Implicit in this view of traditional society is a view of traditional man, perhaps romanticized as the Happy Savage, perhaps savagely dismissed as, in Marx's image, a 'sack of potatoes', but always steady, uncomprehending, politically apathetic, a usually passive but sporadically violent obstacle to new ideas and to progress in all its forms. This image is the point of departure of Deutsch's social mobilization process, the first stage of which merely 'uproots' the villager from the protective soil of his traditional community and threatens to leave him and his colleagues 'impoverished and disoriented', unless the 'political elite' of the central government has 'increased the scope' of the central government to bring him safely the rest of the way into the modern world. Such a point of departure can no longer stand up to the scrutiny of contemporary research which for the first time in its study of 'traditional' societies has succeeded in getting past those societies' official myths by collecting and analyzing the detailed data which alone permit one to follow the actions, interpret the beliefs, and understand the motivations of ordinary individuals.

Much of this research has been conducted by historians who have learned to use new materials. In Europe the *Annales* school of historiography through painstaking analysis of ecclesiastical and court records, of deeds, wills, and population registers, has produced a new picture of the medieval 'little tradition' in action that ill accords with the homogeneous, solidaristic stereotype of the *Gemeinschaft*.[43] In tropical Africa the systematic collection of Arabic script documents and the development of reliable techniques for preserving, collating, and comparing oral histories have built a new portrait of human action and of societal complexity and change quite different from the purposeless and 'unrewarding gyrations of barbarous tribes' dimly perceived by

Oxford's Regius Professor of History as the sum total of pre-colonial experience.[44]

Economic historians and economic anthropologists have found that careful attention to the actual life situation of producers permits the application of modern techniques of formal economic analysis to their materials. From such studies emerges a new portrait of the peasant producer as a rational actor, responding to real incentives and opportunities much as do modern entrepreneurs. Peasant 'conservatism', reliance on past practice for guidance, familial solidarity, and the like are more adequately understood as reactions to highly uncertain conditions than to any immutable cultural traits. When conditions change, so do appropriate aspects of peasant behavior. Thus, North and Thomas have catalogued European peasant responses to technological innovation and market incentives over a broad range of European history.[45] Bundy, Schneider, and Hill have shown that African farmers from very different sections of the continent and at different historical moments act according to the principles of *homo oeconomicus*.[46] Cancian and Alatas have recorded similar findings for Central American and South-East Asian farming communities.[47] Lest it be thought that what we have here is a group of Western intellectuals leaning over backward to be kind to the Third World producer, Green and Hymer have compared results produced by African peasant farmers against those of European experts and found:

> In terms of both economic rationality and calculation and of relevant technical and institutional knowledge and adaptability, the Gold Coast cocoa farmers, despite very real limitation, had significantly better records than the Gold Coast Department of Agriculture throughout the period 1890–1940.[48]

Counter to what the *Gemeinschaft* metaphor might suggest, one of the cocoa farmers' main limitations was their emphasis on individual rather than social benefits! Hopkins concludes his major reinterpretation of West African economic history with words that speak for the spirit of all these studies:

> The pre-colonial economy was complex, efficient and adaptable ... long before the impact of the Western world was felt ... It was not the will to achieve that was lacking, but the means of achieving which were limited. The expansion of the domestic market was retarded not by institutional rigidities determined by anti-capitalist values, but by identifiable economic obstacles ....[49]

If the traditional portrait of traditional man must be altered to make room for *homo oeconomicus*, so must it also make room for *homo politicus*. As anthropologists and others have shifted their focus from elucidating timeless societal norms to observing how individuals actually behave in relation to those norms, they have come to discover, like modern *Bourgeois Gentilhommes*, that they have been observing politics all along![50] The image of pervasive political apathy holds only if one defines out of the realm of the political the vast majority of authoritative decisions that actually affect the lives of the persons being studied. It is true that much of the relevant politics is local, and furthermore it may be expressed in indirect ways not readily accessible to the curious outsider. For that, it is no less intense, no less consequential, and no less political.

If the central government does not figure prominently in such politics it is often because the central government has little to offer, indeed frequently it is perceived as a source of danger to the rational ordering of local affairs.[51] The track record of dealings with rural peoples of most central governments in history – and perhaps a majority even today – belies the facile assumption that the peasants, if only they knew what was good for them, should want to be involved. Recent painstaking research among rural peoples in West and East Africa and in Central America challenges the assumption that non-participation in national level politics is based on ignorance of doings at the center.[52] It reveals a much higher level of political awareness than less careful observers had picked up, and indeed, a higher appreciation of the salience of politics in specific areas of life than is readily apparent in, say, much of the American electorate.

Similar micro-level research in Africa substantiates a further point: in contradiction to earlier assumptions, peasant political activity does not take primarily a ritual or consummatory form, but is highly instrumental and pragmatic in orientation. In summarizing his own and others' work, Barrows finds 'fundamental agreement on the relative unimportance of such oft-used categories as tribalism, rural–urban rifts, traditional–modern cleavages, and ideology. Instead stress is put on the instrumental behavior of ambitious leaders and followers and the groups – such as factions – that emerge as agents of political competition ... Utility serves as a more powerful [analytic] device than identity'.[53] These same studies (Barrows's most elegantly) strongly emphasize the complex linkages that can exist between center and seemingly isolated periphery. Far from these linkages being a one-way affair, as much of the nation-building literature assumes, what one sees increasingly is that when it clearly serves their purposes, 'those on the periphery are already attempting to penetrate the center'.[54]

All of these studies point toward the difficult task of developing reliable research methods adequate to understand and interpret small-scale societies very different from our own. Political and other social scientists can learn much from the work of two sets of colleagues. The first are the cross-cultural cognitive psychologists, the recent rapid development of whose field is reflected in the pages of the new *Journal of Cross-Cultural Psychology*. Moving far beyond the *Mentalité Primitive* of Lévy-Bruhl, their painstaking and methodologically self-critical experimental work has laid bare the daunting dimensions of the task of translation from one cultural idiom to another of the basic and common abilities and limitations of mankind.[55] Particularly notable is the implicit critique of most common interview and survey methods, and the revelation of the distorting effect that the implied relationship of power inequality between a Western investigator and a rural Third World subject has on the responses of the latter. The second are the Third World scholars themselves, especially the anthropologists who have begun doing systematic critiques of the methods and hidden assumptions of the classic Western works analyzing their own societies.[56] Their criticisms are not the sort that are met by the mere employment of local scholars and interviewers in a project whose principal outlines are set by outsiders. They should also be distinguished from the many meretricious railings against research done by anyone who does not share the personal and ideological background of the critic. Though the central point of a few of these critics is sometimes difficult to disentangle from an excess of angry rhetoric, their writings have provided particularly effective criticisms of the indicators Western scholars have chosen to mark processes of individual change and have consistently shown how overarching political relationships have distorted the analysis of data.[57]

The task announced by the social mobilization model – that of relating the experiences of the individual undergoing change to the political structures around him – remains to be accomplished. But we now at least know a little more about how to understand the individual, and also a little more about how to analyze the relevant political structures. Our explorations have shown us an image of man who is more than a passive plaything of social forces; he is consciously and actively contending with alternatives and able to integrate different patterns of activity and of allegiance into his personal repertoire. The two-stage model of mobilization, in which a person is first 'uprooted' and only then 'inducted' into new social patterns, falsifies the continuity of human experience and denies the demonstrated ability of ordinary persons throughout history creatively to interpret and order their own existences, by combining old and new patterns of thought and action.

Much of human activity is political. Political participation in non-Western, non-industrial societies differs in outward form and perhaps in scale from that in our own; it is not, however, different in kind. When men or societies seem to remain essentially unchanged, it is incumbent on the analyst to examine carefully the alternatives actually open to them, and the likely costs and risks that would be borne by persons acting differently. When change does take place, it, too, must be explained in terms of human choice in relation to perceived opportunities and constraints and in terms of the resultant interactions of more and less powerful groups of persons, whose individual identities and fields of operation span various levels of social inclusiveness.

Social mobilization and nation-building attempt to deal with changes in political scale, and with the creation of new and more inclusive structures of power and authority. Appropriate theory must be able to describe and explain actions at these higher levels using analytic elements which are common to all levels; the analysis must be able to move continuously up and down the scale of inclusiveness without betraying the reality of interaction at each level, and without subordinating the complexity of interaction to some preconceived sense of overall process or of final state. In examining political and other social structures, we might best start from an assumption of the indeterminancy of social life, in which structures of regularity are always and in all societies in competition with processes of change.[58] The nation-state no more defines a goal toward which human actions ineluctably tend than the local community represents a set of structures which must be abandoned or crushed in the process.

Toward Theoretical Reconstruction

There is no better foundation for a task of theoretical reconstruction than the early, challenging writings of Karl Deutsch. As all who have studied under him are aware, in the many-storeyed house of Deutsch's thought are many mansions, not all of them connected by lighted passageways and doors that open readily to the curious. The ground floor consists of Deutsch's first book, *Nationalism and Social Communication*, and his many early articles later reworked into *The Nerves of Government*.[59] These works point to unexplored passageways that lead out of social mobilization's theoretical dead end.

In this early work Deutsch creatively applies insights and models derived from information theory and the then new science of cybernetics to the understanding of political processes. It emphasizes processes of feedback, growth, adaptation, change, goal-seeking, and intercommunication of 'autonomous and semi-autonomous groups' to replace earlier models based on 'mechanism and the equilibrium concept'.[60] The earliest and simplest cybernetic models were homeostatic, that is, they described systems which used information brought back from their environment via feedback loops in order to regulate and maintain their internal structure or to correct for deviations from a pre-selected goal. While such models represent an advance over earlier mechanistic and equilibrium models (as a heat-seeking missile represents an 'advance' over a time-fused anti-aircraft shell) they are still far too simple, as Deutsch recognized, to represent the complexity of actual political processes characterized by creative rearrangement of internal structures, growth, and the selection of new goals. The discussion of these 'higher order processes' takes up much of *The Nerves of Government*. What Deutsch sketches out in these pages are the basic elements for an open systems model of action going well beyond the 'black box' models of political systems that have led others only to involuted and sterile descriptions of political life.[61] Walter Buckley has developed Deutsch's starting point into a general model of social interaction based on what he calls 'complex adaptive systems'. Characteristic of such systems is their property of being 'open internally as well as externally in that the interchanges among their components may result in significant changes in the nature of the components themselves with important consequences for the system as a whole'.[62]

By following Deutsch's and Buckley's leads and focusing on the internal openness of social systems, we are led to direct our attention to the conflicting ongoing pressures toward both change and continuity of structure. Rather than being immutable, '"structure" is only a relative stability of underlying, ongoing micro-processes'.[63] We cannot understand either the persistence or the change in overall structures without understanding the micro-processes, just as those processes cannot be understood without reference to the larger structures which constrain and incite their actions. The researcher must always be prepared to move continuously up and down in level of analysis, taking with him to each level the same principles of inquiry. Only in the lowest form of system functioning can purpose and form be treated as constant. A heat-seeking missile has its *telos* built in; any human social system, by contrast, contains the ability to reprogram its goals, and indeed to change its form. Except in the most trivial sense, development (economic, social, or political) cannot be linked with a particular form (such as the nation-state), nor can such a form be considered immanent in any historical or evolutionary process. If nation-states exist, they do so because of specific conjunctures between internal micro-processes and external environmental constraints, all of which are subject to change, and subject to study.

The study of any process of systemic change requires constant reference to that system's environment; indeed, the very 'dichotomy of sets of related objects into system and environment depends essentially on the point of view at hand'.[64] The decision to group one particular set of structures and to call them a political system must be taken as a conscious analytic choice, and one subject to revision if evidence indicates that more explanatory power is to be derived from different rules for grouping phenomena. An important first step is the mapping of 'uneven cluster distributions' of institutions, communications links, population, and other structures which Deutsch undertakes in Chapter 2 of *Nationalism and Social Communication*. Some of these clusters will coincide with political boundaries (national or subnational) others will spill over them and demonstrate actual or latent opportunities for disrupting bounded political structures. At the very least, mapping of these clusters 'could help us to start out with a more detailed and realistic picture of the very uneven world in which politics must function'.[65] Such a mapping should provide the analyst with a picture of the ecology of various systems and of system discontinuities, or boundaries, on the basis of which he can make his subsequent analytic choices. An essential part of any such mapping should be a study of the extent and clustering patterns of political and other politically relevant organizations. In periods of rapid social and political change, perhaps nothing would be so helpful to the analyst as a good organizational census. Since, as Nie *et al.* and Cameron have shown, in the absence of a large middle class political participation is likely to be largely a function of organization, an organizational survey and the study of relationships between organizations are likely to yield much more relevant information than, say, a survey of political attitudes and opinions. Detailed studies of countries undergoing rapid social change regularly show a proliferation of voluntary organizations catering for the needs and aspirations of those who have left their former communities.

Those organizations which are not overtly political nevertheless provide infrastructures and principles of association between individuals which augment their collective power and which are capable of direct political mobilization.

Who studies systems studies boundaries. If boundaries are effective, they have two politically relevant characteristics. First, they increase the collective power of those within them by providing the potential for organization and preventing the diffusion of effort and energy. As a function of that presumed advantage, however, boundaries also constrain the freedom of those within. Even in the most extreme theoretical case, a system which succeeds in promoting the absolute freedom of its members must deny them the identity of those who are not members. A study which begins with mapping the ecology of human organizations should proceed to study the characteristics of their boundaries. A first question is, are they defined and maintained primarily by internal or by external action? Although some situational co-operation between members and non-members is usually required to maintain a systemic boundary, one can readily distinguish between the case of a social group like the American Amish who cling to their customs and reinforce the boundary between them and their surrounding farmers by highly visible symbols, and the case of urban South African blacks who are forced to accept an identity like 'Xhosa' or 'Zulu' by a structurally superior level of organization and are deprived in most respects of the legal identity of 'South African' or even 'African', which most would prefer. In situations of rapid change the consequences of such boundaries are likely to be quite different.

One may further want to study the way boundaries are maintained from within. For this, organizations may be placed along a continuum measuring degrees of internal power differentiation. At one extreme boundaries are maintained by total elite domination which attempts to lock in the mass of ordinary persons by manipulation of symbols and, ultimately, by force. Feudal manors and slave-labor plantations are close to pure examples. At the middle of the continuum are voluntaristic groups with circulating or situational leadership chosen on the basis of ability to facilitate group tasks. At the other extreme are found the pathological cases of boundary maintenance through participation in a 'group mind' characterized by what Erich Fromm described as an 'escape from freedom'.[66] These cases are familiar to those working with experimental groups[67] and find their closest real-world analogues in groups devoted to the service of a distant (and perhaps non-existent) charismatic leader who plays only a symbolic role as a focus of adoration for the group.[68] Each of these positions on the continuum implies different relationships with the environment, with the extremes most dependent on supportive environmental conditions. Such a continuum cuts across any traditional/modern distinction; examples can be found as readily in industrial as in non-industrual settings.

Boundaries are intimately involved with power differentials. Within a social field, existing 'power differences enable *relational control*, i.e. influence over the existing matrix of action possibilities, action outcomes, and orientations within which social interaction occurs'.[69] Such control permits further accumulation of power and both provides the resources for and encourages the construction of boundaries to constrain emigration from the social system and 'compel subordinate or disadvantaged groups to accept their inferior positions'.[70] Nowhere is this power element more apparent than in the competition over the choice of national boundaries during the break-up of colonial empires or other large-scale political systems, or as part of the process of amalgamating smaller units into a single state. The delineation of state sovereignties will be influenced by environmental factors such as economic and communications discontinuities, but it will be determined by the competition of different power interests, each seeking the boundary configuration which will maximize its ability to exert further relational control. That intensely political competition must be a central focus of any study of the process by which national states are formed. So too must be the study, at a lower level of analysis, of power differentials resulting from the elaboration of structures within the state's boundary.

Social system boundaries are never absolute barriers to exchange with the environment. Every system establishes formal or informal rules for boundary-crossing and gate-keeper roles for those who regulate exchanges. These roles are major power positions capable of generating further resources for extended relational control within the system. Such roles are likely to be particularly important in subordinate systems dependent on external patronage or on a large volume of exchanges with the environment, whether or not 'traditional' or 'modern' structures are involved. An officially recognized tribal chief in a French or British colony was placed in a position to play such a role, as may be the president of the new state which came into being after that colony's political independence. The primary similarity in role is structural; only in a trivial sense may it be cultural.

Boundaries constrain action by raising the cost of passing across them. The cost may be paid literally and directly in terms of tariffs, export licenses, bribes, and residence permits. Less directly they may be paid in terms of the opportunity cost of forgoing activities within a social system or established channel of communications. Such costs are potentially quantifiable, and it should not be beyond the resources of determined researchers to derive appropriate indicators for them.[71] We can attain much greater analytic power if we think of the process of change to which social mobilization addresses itself as one involving conscious individuals who calculate these costs at least in approximate terms. As studies like those of the economic anthropologists and historians referred to earlier indicate, such an assumption does not violate reality.

Individuals and their activities are the basic elements of our ecology of interacting systems. Rather than passive reactors to historical forces, they are, in Allport's term, *pro-active*.[72] Or as Deutsch might put it, they too are goal-seeking, self-governing systems which 'must therefore remake [their] own memories and inner structures as [they] act.[73] Social mobilization, thus, has to do with men choosing to learn different things, including new ways of learning. Men integrate these new things into their lives as they serve their changing purposes. The most important thing about what they learn is that it is new and different, and appropriate to new and different purposes and settings, not that it is more 'developed' or 'advanced'. The study of this learning process is best approached as one of cross-cultural analysis, requiring an understanding of something of both cultures and of the possibilities of combining major features of both.[74] What particularly must be clarified is what items of behavior are both characteristic and essential to each cultural setting, and what is the range of feasible variation in behavior. Concentration on norms and ideology rather than behavior can hopelessly mislead analysis. The entrance of individuals into new and larger organizational settings will link them with other individuals in new ways: it will impose new constraints on their action, but also open new opportunities and perhaps new and greater powers. We should not underestimate their ability to act, to understand, and to transform their situations.

What has been presented here is far, yet, from a comprehensive model. Rather, it is an intellectual framework and set of principles permitting the systematic elaboration of models which reflect the realities of social change and the creation of new political structures better than those commonly in use. Chief among these realities are the indeterminate nature of social and political structures and the active participation of individuals and groups in creating and changing them in the pursuit of their own goals. Such a framework directs our attention to new sorts of empirical information and suggests that many of our prevailing techniques for collecting data are inadequate or badly biased. The increasing participation of Third World scholars in the leadership of research enterprises promises to accelerate our assimilation of more adequate intellectual formulations as well as to improve our ability to collect accurate information in the field. Nevertheless, we have far to go in learning how to construct adequate models of the actual behavior of our fellow men, and of ourselves.

The Nerves of Government concludes with invoking a powerfully simple goal for our labors as political scientists, 'that men should be more able to act in politics with their eyes open'.[75] If we are to join with Karl Deutsch in working toward that end, we should not start out by building models in which men can only react to change with their eyes shut.

Notes: Chapter 1

1 Karl W. Deutsch, 'Social mobilization and political development', *American Political Science Review*, vol. 55, no. 3 (September 1961), pp. 493–514.
2 Robert A. Dahl, 'The behavioral approach in political science: epitaph for a monument to a successful protest', *American Political Science Review*, vol. 55, no. 4 (December 1961), pp. 763–79.
3 Karl W. Deutsch and William J. Foltz (eds), *Nation-Building* (New York: Atherton Press, 1963).
4 Deutsch, 'Social mobilization', p. 493.
5 loc. cit.

6 ibid., p. 498
7 ibid., p. 494.
8 Samuel P. Huntington, 'Political order and political decay', *World Politics*, vol. 16, no. 3 (1965), pp. 386–430.
9 Nelson Kasfir, *The Shrinking Political Arena* (Berkeley and Los Angeles: University of California Press, 1976).
10 First edition by Bruce Russett and Hayward R. Alker, Jr, Karl W. Deutsch, Harold D. Lasswell (New Haven, Conn.: Yale University Press, 1964); 2d edn ed. Charles Lewis Taylor and Michael C. Hudson (New Haven, Conn.: Yale University Press, 1972).
11 For example, J. P. Nettl, *Political Mobilization: A Sociological Analysis of Methods and Concepts* (London: Faber, 1967).
12 For example, S. N. Eisenstadt and Stein Rokkan (eds), *Building States and Nations*, 2 vols (Beverly Hills, Calif.: Sage, 1973–4).
13 Jorge I. Domínguez, 'Political participation and the social mobilization hypothesis: Chile, Mexico, Venezuela, and Cuba, 1800–1825', *Journal of Interdisciplinary History*, vol. 5, no. 2 (Autumn 1974), pp. 237–66.
14 ibid., p. 265.
15 ibid., p. 266.
16 Norman H. Nie, G. Bingham Powell, Jr, and Kenneth Prewitt, 'Social structure and political participation: developmental relationships', *American Political Science Review*, vol. 62, no. 2 (June 1969), pp. 361–78; and vol. 62, no. 3 (September 1969), pp. 808–32.
17 ibid., p. 819.
18 David R. Cameron, 'Toward a theory of political mobilization', *Journal of Politics*, vol. 36, no. 1 (February 1974), pp. 138–71.
19 ibid., p. 153.
20 ibid., p. 144.
21 ibid., p. 169.
22 Walker Connor, 'Nation-building or nation-destroying', *World Politics*, vol. 24, no. 3 (April 1972), pp. 319–55.
23 ibid., pp. 342–3.
24 Raymond Duvall and Mary Welfling, 'Social mobilization, political institutionalization, and conflict in black Africa: a simple dynamic model', *Journal of Conflict Resolution*, vol. 17, no. 4 (December 1973), pp. 673–702.
25 ibid., p. 691.
26 ibid., p. 700.
27 ibid., p. 701.
28 Thomas S. Kuhn, *The Structure of Scientific Revolutions*, 2nd edn (Chicago: University of Chicago Press, 1970), esp. pp. 176–91.
29 Karl W. Deutsch, 'Nation-building and national development: some issues for political research', in *Nation-Building*, ed. Deutsch and Foltz, p. 3.
30 A. F. K. Organski, *The Stages of Political Development* (New York: Knopf, 1965), p. 7. Italics in the original.
31 Samuel P. Huntington, *Political Order in Changing Societies* (New Haven, Conn.: Yale University Press, 1968), p. 34.
32 See Donald G. Morrison, Robert C. Mitchell, John N. Paden, and Hugh M. Stevenson, *Black Africa: A Comparative Handbook* (New York: The Free Press, 1972), for a vigorous, but not quite successful, attempt to escape from this pre-packaging.
33 Gabriel, A. Almond and James S. Coleman (eds), *The Politics of the Developing Areas* (Princeton: Princeton University Press, 1960).
34 Edward Shils, *Center and Periphery: Essays in Macrosociology* (Chicago: University of Chicago Press, 1975), p. 3.
35 ibid., p. 54.
36 David E. Apter, *The Gold Coast in Transition* (Princeton, NJ: Princeton University Press, 1955); and *The Political Kingdom in Uganda* (Princeton, NJ: Princeton University Press, 1961).
37 Lucian W. Pye, *Politics, Personality and Nation-Building* (New Haven, Conn.: Yale University Press, 1962); and Carl H. Landé, *Leaders, Factions, and Parties: The Structure of Philippine Politics* (New Haven, Conn.: Yale University, Southeast Asia Studies, Monograph No. 6, 1965).

38 Johan Galtung, 'A structural theory of imperialism', *Journal of Peace Research*, vol. 8, no. 2 (1971), pp. 81–117; André Gunder Frank, *Capitalism and Underdevelopment in Latin America* (New York: Monthly Review Press, 1969); and Samir Amin, *L'Afrique de l'Ouest Bloquée* (Paris: Editions de Minuit, 1971) are representative works. See also the chapters by Duvall *et al.* and Senghaas in this volume for sophisticated assessments of these approaches.
39 On the dependence of ethnic identity on situation, see Fredrik Barth (ed.), *Ethnic Groups and Boundaries* (Boston, Mass.: Little, Brown, 1969); Abner Cohen (ed.), *Urban Ethnicity* (London: Tavistock Publications, 1974); and William J. Foltz, 'Ethnicity, status, and conflict', in *Ethnicity and Nation-Building*, ed. Wendell Bell and Walter E. Freeman (Beverly Hills, Calif.: Sage, 1974), pp. 103–16.
40 C. S. Whitaker, Jr, 'A dysrhythmic process of political change', *World Politics*, vol. 19, no. 2 (January 1967), pp. 190–217; A. James Gregor, 'Political science and the uses of functional analysis', *American Political Science Review*, vol. 62, no. 2 (June 1968), pp. 425–39; and Anthony D. Smith, *The Concept of Social Change* (London: Routledge & Kegan Paul, 1973).
41 Edward Shils, *Center and Periphery*, p. 197.
42 For an informed view of one aspect of this process, see Philip D. Curtin, *The Image of Africa* (Madison, Wis.: University of Wisconsin Press, 1964), esp. pp. 479–80.
43 Emmanuel Le Roy Ladurie, *Montaillou, Village Occitan de 1294 à 1324* (Paris: Gallimard, 1975), pp. 415–18.
44 H. R. Trevor-Roper, *The Rise of Christian Europe* (London: Thames & Hudson, 1965), p. 9. For a comprehensive example of the new African historiography, see Philip D. Curtin, Steven Feierman, Leonard M. Thompson, and Jan Vansina, *African History* (Boston, Mass.: Little, Brown, 1978).
45 Douglas North and Robert Paul Thomas, *The Rise of the Western World: A New Economic History* (Cambridge: Cambridge University Press, 1973).
46 Colin Bundy, 'The emergence and decline of a South African peasantry', *African Affairs*, vol. 71, no. 285 (October 1972), pp. 369–88; Harold K. Schneider, 'A model of African indigenous economy and society', *Comparative Studies in Society and History*, vol. 7, no. 1 (October 1972), pp. 37–55; Polly Hill, *The Migrant Cocoa Farmers of Southern Ghana: A Study in Rural Capitalism* (Cambridge: Cambridge University Press, 1963). Also B. Marie Perinbam, 'Homo Africanus: antiquus or oeconomicus', *Comparative Studies in Society and History*, vol. 19, no. 2 (April 1977), pp. 156–78.
47 Frank Cancian, *Change and Uncertainty in a Peasant Economy: The Maya Corn Farmers of Zinacantan* (Stanford, Calif.: Stanford University Press, 1972); and S. H. Alatas, *The Myth of the Lazy Native* (London: Cass, 1976).
48 Reginald H. Green and Stephen H. Hymer, 'Cocoa in the Gold Coast: a study in the relations between African farmers and agricultural experts', *Journal of Economic History*, vol. 26, no. 3 (September 1966), p. 319.
49 A. G. Hopkins, *An Economic History of West Africa* (New York: Columbia University Press, 1973), p. 293.
50 F. G. Bailey, *Stratagems and Spoils* (Oxford: Blackwell, 1969); and Fredrik Barth, *Political Leadership Among Swat Pathans*, London School of Economics Monographs on Social Anthropology, No. 19 (London: Athlone Press, 1959). For an analogous discovery in the field of legal anthropology, see Richard L. Abel, 'Customary laws of wrongs in Kenya: an essay in research method', *American Journal of Comparative Law*, vol. 17, no. 4 (1969), pp. 573–626.
51 F. G. Bailey, 'The peasant view of the bad life', *Advancement of Science*, vol. 23, no. 114 (December 1966), pp. 399–409.
52 Fred M. Hayward, 'A reassessment of the conventional wisdom about the informed public: national political information in Ghana', and Joel D. Barkan, 'Comment: further reassessment of the "conventional wisdom": political knowledge and voting behavior in rural Kenya', in *American Political Science Review*, vol. 70, no. 2 (June 1976), pp. 433–51, 452–5. See also John A. Booth and Mitchell A. Seligson, 'Peasants as activists: a revaluation of political participation in the countryside', *Comparative Political Studies*, vol. 12, no. 1 (April 1979), pp. 29–59.
53 Walter L. Barrows, *Grassroots Politics in an African State: Integration and Development in Sierra Leone* (New York: Africana Publishing Co., 1976) p. 246. The

works referred to are Nicholas S. Hopkins, *Popular Government in an African Town: Kita, Mali* (Chicago: University of Chicago Press, 1972); Maxwell Owusu, *Uses and Abuses of Political Power: A Case Study of Continuity and Change in the Politics of Ghana* (Chicago: University of Chicago Press, 1970); and Joan Vincent, *African Elite: The Big Men of a Small Town* (New York: Columbia University Press, 1971).
54 Barkan, 'Comment: "conventional wisdom" ', p. 455.
55 Lucien Lévy-Bruhl, *La Mentalité Primitive* (Paris: F. Alcan, 1922). Among the important résumés of modern work, see John W. Berry and Pierre R. Dasen, *Culture and Cognition: Readings in Cross-Cultural Psychology* (London: Methuen, 1974); Michael Cole and Sylvia Scribner, *Culture and Thought* (New York: Wiley, 1974); and H. A. Witkin and J. W. Berry, 'Psychological differentiation in cross-cultural perspective', *Journal of Cross-Cultural Psychology*, vol. 6, no. 1 (March 1975), pp. 4–87.
56 Talal Asad (ed.), *Anthropology and The Colonial Encounter* (New York: Humanities Press, 1973); Archie Mafeje, 'The fallacy of dual economics', *East Africa Journal*, vol. 7, no. 9 (1972), pp. 30–4; T. V. Sathyamurthy, 'Social anthropology in the political study of new nation states', *Current Anthropology*, vol. 14, no. 5 (December 1973), pp. 557–79; Maxwell Owusu, *Uses and Abuses of Political Power: A Case Study of Continuity and Change in the Politics of Ghana* (Chicago, Ill.: University of Chicago Press, 1970).
57 Bernard Magubane, 'A critical look at indices used in the study of social change in colonial Africa', *Current Anthropology*, vol. 12, nos 4 and 5 (October–December 1971), pp. 419–45. Among the many studies that would fail to meet the intellectual and methodological tests of these newer critics, perhaps none would fail more spectacularly than the massive six-nation interview project on individual modernization, Alex Inkeles and David Smith, *Becoming Modern* (Cambridge, Mass.: Harvard University Press, 1974). Conceived originally in 1962, the project stood, by the time of its final publication, as a monument to the inadequacy of modernization theory and to the deleterious effect on individual level research of macrosociological assumptions.
58 Sally Falk Moore, 'Epilogue: uncertainties in situations, indeterminacies in culture', in *Symbol and Politics in Communal Ideology*, ed. S. F. Moore and Barbara G. Myerhoff (Ithaca, NY: Cornell University Press, 1975), pp. 210–40.
59 Karl W. Deutsch, *Nationalism and Social Communication: An Inquiry into the Foundations of Nationality* (Cambridge, Mass.: Technology Press; and New York: Wiley, 1953); and Karl W. Deutsch, *The Nerves of Government: Models of Political Communication and Control* (New York: The Free Press, 1963).
60 Deutsch, *The Nerves of Government*, p. 79.
61 For example, David Easton, *A Systems Analysis of Political Life* (New York: Wiley, 1965).
62 Walter Buckley, 'Society as a complex adaptive system', in *Modern Systems Research for the Behavioral Scientist*, ed. Walter Buckley (Chicago: Aldine, 1968), p. 490.
63 ibid., p. 497.
64 A. D. Hall and R. E. Fagen, 'Definition of systems', in *Modern Systems Research*, ed. Buckley, p. 84.
65 Deutsch, *Nationalism and Social Communication*, p. 45.
66 Erich Fromm, *Escape From Freedom* (New York: Rinehart, 1941).
67 Wilfred R. Bion, *Experiences in Groups* (London: Tavistock, 1959); A. K. Rice, *Learning for Leadership: Interpersonal and Intergroup Relations* (London: Tavistock, 1965).
68 Margaret J. Rioch, '"All we like sheep . . ." (Isaiah 53:6): followers and leaders', *Psychiatry*, vol. 34, no. 3 (August 1971), pp. 258–73.
69 Tom Baumgartner, Walter Buckley, Tom R. Burns, and Peter Schuster, 'Meta-power and the structuring of social hierarchies', in *Power and Control: Social Structures and Their Transformation*, ed. Tom R. Burns and Walter Buckley (Beverly Hills, Calif.: Sage, 1976), p. 218.
70 ibid., p. 219.
71 Albert O. Hirschman, *Exit, Voice, and Loyalty* (Cambridge, Mass.: Harvard University Press, 1970).

72 Gordon W. Allport, 'The open system in personality theory', *Journal of Abnormal and Social Psychology*, vol. 61, no. 3 (November 1960), pp. 301–10.
73 Deutsch, *The Nerves of Government*, p. 221.
74 One of the few books to study in detail the actual process of individual change is Leonard W. Doob, *Becoming More Civilized* (New Haven, Conn.: Yale University Press, 1960). With no significant exceptions, the twenty-seven hypotheses about the changes undergone in modernization could be recast to reflect the crossing of any cultural boundary.
75 Deutsch, *The Nerves of Government*, p. 255.

2
Social Mobilization Theory and Arab Politics

MICHAEL C. HUDSON

The upsurge of theoretical creativity in comparative politics reached a high point with the publication of Karl Deutsch's landmark article 'Social mobilization and political development' in 1961.[1] In it he put forth a model of social and political change that crystallized the best of what had come before (for example, in the work of Lerner, Rustow, and Almond)[2] and foreshadowed some important advances yet to come (notably, Huntington).[3] The 'overall process of change' from traditional to modern ways would influence and 'sometimes transform' political behavior. The politically relevant strata would be enlarged and political pressures would increase. The quality of politics would change as new needs for housing, social security, public health care, and the like became politically salient demands. Government and administration would expand, and the scope of governmental services would increase. Elites would be broadened and modernized in their functions, recruitment, and communications. Yet communications between elites and masses might not grow apace. The newly politicized masses would demand significant political participation and express their frustration at the lack of it through demonstrations, riots, and strikes. But institutionalized participation, such as voting, would also increase in polities where such institutions existed. Rapid social mobilization presaged a shift of public attention from the parochial and the cosmopolitan toward the territorial state and also a tendency toward economic autarchy and a decline of foreign trade in the economy. Deutsch concluded his argument with two significant propositions. First, rapid social mobilization would tend to consolidate states that already shared basic cultural and social characteristics while it would inhibit the integration of states whose populations did not share such common characteristics. Secondly, political systems whose governments failed to develop the capabilities to deal with the new loads imposed by social mobilization could look forward to instability, disorder, and possible destruction.

Modernization Theory Under Attack

Nearly two decades have passed since Deutsch presented us with this modernization paradigm. In the meantime the modernization 'approach' in comparative politics has come under attack, much of it justified. Today many scholars feel that modernization theory as a whole has proven a failure: to some it seems naively optimistic, to others bourgeois rationalization. Third World polities do not appear to have 'developed' according to its forecasts: expected transformations have not occurred, 'new men' have not arisen, 'new middle classes' have not emerged, liberal democracies have not evolved, modernizing military regimes have not lived up to expectations, and even the dour projections of the critics of 'liberal' modernization theory – in their prediction of praetorian chaos as the new norm – have failed to encompass present realities.

In light of this disenchantment, and in as much as Deutsch's work is very much a part of the modernization-development 'persuasion' in comparative politics, one must ask whether it too is vulnerable to these criticisms. At the general theoretical level, Deutsch's model has had its critics, as William Foltz has demonstrated in the previous chapter. I too share some of their reservations, as I will indicate below. But I would like to argue that his contribution, unlike much of the writing on political modernization, actually has worn well and has not lost its relevance or validity when re-evaluated in light of Third World political experience in the past two decades. The reason, I believe, is that Deutsch infused his analysis with a knowledge and sense of history that few other of the more behaviorally oriented students of political modernization possessed. We find, therefore, greater complexity and sophistication in Deutsch's formulation than in much of the literature. To be sure, such subtlety has rendered Deutsch much harder to apply than one would expect from one so known for his advocacy of the quantitative approach; but the merit of analytic insight, in my view, far outweighs the cost in operational simplicity.

What I propose to do here in order to support my argument is to assess the Deutschian approach applied to a very important area of the Third World – the Arab Middle East. The Arab world represents not only a case of frenetic and uneven modernization, with a variety of political consequences, but also a most interesting 'laboratory' for the study of political integration. So it is in its way ideal as a testing ground for Deutsch's central theoretical concerns. Such a test, I believe, leads to three basic conclusions. First, Deutsch was basically right in his delineation of the multiple, complex, and sometimes contradictory consequences of rapid and uneven social mobilization; he provides the analytic lens for perceiving the Arabs' political malaise. Secondly, his analysis of social mobilization and political integration, when the political unit of analysis is specified, illuminates the Arab experience and helps explain what I would call the integration puzzle in Arab politics. Thirdly, I do not believe that competing analytic perspectives, such as the Marxist or the conservative ethnicity approach, have provided more satisfactory explanations of Arab politics than his.

This is not to say, however, that the Deutschian approach is without its own flaws. To an analyst of Arab politics, several difficulties are evident. Most serious is an inadequate treatment of the shift from tradition to modernity. But there are others too. We cannot assume that the sovereign state is the only appropriate unit for analysis. Certain indicators are arbitrarily assigned certain kinds of political significance that they may not in fact represent. The predictive power of the social mobilization approach is uncertain, indeed almost Delphic in its possible interpretations. Specifically political intervening variables, such as ideology and leadership, are ignored in the explanation of political outcomes. Social structure is incompletely developed as a variable in the formula; thus while we may rightly reject reified notions of classes as political actors, we still lack the kind of map of social structures (especially the interaction of traditional formations and specific economic conditions) that might allow us to plot the impact of social mobilization more precisely. Finally, we are troubled by Deutsch's conspicuous (and surprising) inattention to the impact of external political and economic forces – forces which cannot be ignored for an understanding of Arab political behavior. I shall comment on these and other difficulties as we juxtapose specific Deutschian hypotheses against the Arab political situation in the following pages.

The Arab World

The Arab world consists of over 140 million people in twenty-two political units stretching from Morocco to Kuwait.[4] Its inhabitants are overwhelmingly Arabic-speaking and orthodox Muslim. The Arab societies clearly belong among those whom Deutsch would classify as undergoing rapid social mobilization. Since the formation of the modern Arab state system, beginning at the end of the First World War and culminating in the achievement of independence after the Second World War, the Arabs have been 'exposed to modernity' in a most substantial way.[5] The mass media, notably through the transistor radio, have penetrated the most remote villages. Literacy and the availability of public education have greatly expanded. Population growth and urban migration have undoubtedly altered the values and worldviews of hundreds of thousands of Arabs. The struggle for independence brought political movements of various kinds into the experience of ordinary people.

At the same time, those processes that signify the growth of governmental capability have also developed, but generally at a lesser pace. Income and per capita income, except for the small oil-exporting countries, has increased modestly; industrialization has been relatively slow; measurable assimilation of linguistic or cultural minorities has been, so far as one can determine, quite limited at best; and administrative performance, while it has expanded considerably since the 1960s in most countries, still appears to lag behind the needs and demands of an awakening, changing society. Thus the Arab world fits comfortably into Deutsch's category of societies in the 'middle stages' of development – that is, considerably beyond the exclusively traditional and very poor but still far from the levels of modernization associated with the industrialized states.

Of such societies Deutsch asserts that 'a cumulative strain on political stability may be expected'. Certainly, political instability has not been lacking in the modern Arab polities. Indeed, some of the most modernized countries have undergone some of the most significant upheavals – Syria, Iraq, Egypt, Lebanon, Jordan. Only the super-rich traditional states of Arabia and the Gulf have not experienced some form of anomic popular participation – riots, demonstrations, and the like. Even those states that have not experienced extensive instability could not have avoided it without pervasive internal security organization.

Deutsch's Model Applied

It is one thing to observe, *grosso modo*, that the Arab countries (*a*) fall into the 'high instability potential' category of the social mobilization spectrum, and (*b*) are, for the most part, quite unstable. It is something else to conclude that their social mobilization configuration is the primary cause of their instability. To evaluate this conclusion, we must inspect the several hypotheses that comprise the social mobilization-political development model and juxtapose them against Arab social and political behavior. One of the model's strengths is its complexity. It proposes a rich set of causal links between the social and the political spheres that are both intrinsically plausible and applicable to the Arab case.

The key idea is that those interrelated social trends called social mobilization expand the politically relevant strata of the population. Media exposure and physical mobility 'advertise' new ideas and values to people whose political horizons hitherto may have been limited. These people are presented with objective conditions, opportunities, and especially problems that may galvanize them for political activity. Modernization also threatens important elements and at the same time creates avenues of political recruitment. The 'modernization' of Algeria by French settlers who created a plantation economy created such tensions between the dominant and subservient societies that a successful mass uprising of 'traditional' people was possible.[6] A threat by 'modernizers' to the traditional Lebanese fishing industry at Saida was one of the chief precipitants of the 1975–6 civil war.[7] The growth of organized, politicized trade unionism at Aden port set in motion the uprising against British rule.[8] Probably the most striking example is the case of the Palestine refugees whose camps constituted a virtual hothouse of social mobilization – a most effective incubator for a political movement.[9]

Deutsch is also right to assert that these new elements bring pressures for political change of one sort or another. Expansion of the political arena gives opposition politicians the leverage to exert demands for power-sharing and policy change. The rise of the Wafd Party in Egypt during and after the First World War is a case in point. Politicized junior officers in the modernizing post-independence Arab armies frequently spearheaded demands for political change; and in a number of countries, including Egypt, Iraq, Syria, Sudan, and Libya, they successfully seized power.

The most dramatic expression of the pressure of the newly mobilized on established governments was that of the 'Nasser constituency' throughout the Arab world. Gamal Abdel Nasser discovered that he could project vast influence via Egypt's 'Voice of the Arabs' radio station once he had established himself as a hero in the cause of Arabism. When the masses in the teeming Arab megalopoli from Casablanca to Baghdad heard Nasser's voice, regimes and elites trembled. Had Nasser or other Arab nationalist forces been able to transform this broad but diffuse support into institutionalized action, the monarchies of Jordan, Saudi Arabia, Morocco, and Libya might not have survived as long as they did.

From these newly salient strata came, as Deutsch predicted, a rise in political tensions. One need only to inspect the political instability event tables and computer-drawn plots in the *World Handbook of Political and Social Indicators* (second edition) to observe the agitation in the Arabian polities during the post-independence period following the Second World War.[10] With the exception of the still-dependent, highly traditional and wealthy oil principalities, the Arab states experienced both governmental instability and popular anomic turbulence. In general, this agitation was an expression of demands for what Deutsch calls 'the transformation of political practices and institutions'. Calls for major political reform, democracy, socialism, Arab unity, and anti-Western imperialism were incessantly voiced by the new elements, civil and military, seeking to share or seize power in the 1950s and 1960s.

At the same time, there were growing demands for social and administrative development. As urban migration swelled, Arab regimes sought to cope with what Deutsch foresaw as a change in the 'range of human needs' and the 'quality of politics'. Nascent labor organizations and new political movements, some of them illegal, put pressure on the governments for better public administration, civil service reform, health and welfare programs. When one recalls that the 'natural' scope of government activities was limited essentially to 'night-watchman' and taxation functions in most Arab countries up until the 1940s, the shift in attitudes and expectations is considerable. In an Arab world nearly half-urbanized into vast cities, regimes were hard-pressed to respond to the changing social environment. A case in point is the Iraqi monarchy in the middle 1950s which established the Iraq Development Board. The Board drew up important long-term plans for developing water resources and hydroelectric power. But as a source of regime legitimacy its impact was negligible, especially on the hundreds migrating into the Greater Baghdad area. In fact, the regime's concentration on such projects and its neglect of the growing urban social problems was a major cause of the 1958 revolution.

Deutsch hypothesizes that social mobilization not only changes the issues in the political arena but also encourages bigger government. To address the new issues and the unrest that may accompany them, governments establish new bureaucracies and enlist new technologies; in short, they acquire new capabilities. Certainly, the Arab states have followed this pattern. We observe an almost universal increase in the government final consumption expenditure share of gross domestic product between 1960 and 1972; and several countries (e.g. Libya, Syria, Iraq, Saudi Arabia, and the United Arab Emirates) more than doubled their government budgets within a period of five to six years in the early 1960s.[11] Between 1959 and 1964 at least nine Arab states enacted new or expanded social security laws (Algeria, Iraq, Jordan, Lebanon, Libya, Morocco, Saudi Arabia, Syria, and Egypt).[12] Perhaps even more important than the creation of agencies to cope with new needs was the development of control organizations – internal security agencies, domestic intelligence networks, and military establishments. The growing control capabilities of Arab regimes cut across ideological and structural cleavages: it is a trend as observable in Saudi Arabia, Morocco, and Jordan as it is in Iraq, South Yemen, or Algeria.

Another political consequence of social mobilization involves a general transformation of political elites. Traditional elites are pushed aside because they are inadequate to deal with the new demands and functions required of the state, and they are replaced by parties and movements led by modernized, dissatisfied, 'marginal' men and women. Why are these elites now 'inadequate'? Not (as Deutsch perhaps implies) because their mind-sets cannot grasp new realities, but rather because new elites are developing new centers of power in an expanding politicized sector. These new elites can mobilize the new urban masses or the new military establishment. In Arab states governed by movement-parties (usually military-dominated) we have seen reform-minded officers or other professionals displacing 'incompetent' feudal-bourgeois politicians and kings. These states include Algeria, Libya, Egypt, the Sudan, Syria, Iraq, and the two Yemens. The case of Syria is instructive. Here nationalist politicians who had bungled Syria's participation in the 1948–9 Arab–Israeli War and who were seen as intolerably corrupt in domestic affairs were overthrown by disgruntled officers from the newly independent Syrian army. After over a decade of instability Syria finally came under the control of the Ba'th Party. A country at a much earlier stage of social development – North Yemen – presents another example. The medieval imamate in San'a struggled to deal with new realities but failed and was overthrown by nationalist officers. As in Syria, however, the new 'modern' men did not appear to be markedly more competent than the 'traditionals', but they had access to the new power resources generated by social mobilization.

Elites will have trouble keeping in touch with the newly politically relevant social strata; this 'communications intake' problem may cause them to underestimate the nature and intensity of issues (and opposition), at least until demonstrations, riots and rebellion break out. In the Arab world there are some notable cases of elite unawareness. The French–Algerian elite was totally surprised by the outbreak of the Algerian liberation movement in 1954. The *coup d'état* in Egypt in 1952 revealed that the elite had lost any effective support base; much the same thing happened in Libya in 1969. The troubles in Tunisia toward the end of Habib Bourguiba's rule would seem to indicate that the Supreme Combattant and his Destourian Socialist Party – widely regarded as a textbook example of good elite–mass linkages – are ignorant of current Tunisian realities. One can speculate in a similar vein as to whether some other seemingly secure Arab elites are in fact also suffering from a 'communications intake' problem.

Deutsch sees participation among the newly mobilized taking the form of proliferating political and ostensibly non-political organizations and, in polities with electoral systems, increased voting participation. Tocqueville made a similar observation about the nineteenth-century United States, but whether what we see in the twentieth-century Arab world is functionally the same thing is more problematical. It is safe to assume that there has been an organizational proliferation. But it is not clear whether these organizations function as 'marshalling grounds for entry' of the socially mobilized into Arab political life, and if they do, whether the net effect is in the direction of political development or instead the maintenance of political tradition. One reason for doubt is that the political coloration of many of these 'non-political' organizations is traditional rather than modern. For example, the *diwaniyyas* of the Arabian peninsula, despite their seemingly modern function, lend structural support to the traditional political system.[13] In fact, they may serve to 're-traditionalize' the modernized young men beginning their careers in government or business. Moore has noted in a study of professional syndicates in Egypt that 'these most modern and prestigious professionals (doctors and engineers) practice the most traditional political styles'.[14] Our difficulty in applying this particular hypothesis to the Arab world arises out of the model's principal weakness – its failure to account adequately for the persistence of tradition. We shall comment further on it below.

A second reason for doubt about organizational proliferation is that in most Arab countries organizations that are other than clearly (and traditionally) social or professional are, if not proscribed, only established by the regime itself or the ruling party. Arab regimes (leftist or rightist) are all in favor of marshalling mobilized strata into political life as long as they maintain control and supervision. This being the case, some organizational proliferation may amount to little more than spurious institutionalization. The creation of such organizations may do little to develop a general (as opposed to partisan) consensus and may not confer much legitimacy on the political system as a whole. Probably the most famous case of spurious institutionalization was the Arab Socialist Union in Egypt – a mass organization designed to harness all civic-minded Egyptians to co-operate in the development of the country. The ASU in fact performed useful functions on the local level, but it was widely and rightly regarded by politically aware Egyptians as a government-inspired device for pre-empting and controlling serious opposition to the regime. It became the target of so many cynical jokes that when President Sadat decided to abandon it for a new but scarcely more liberal three-party system it was hardly missed. Whether the officially sanctioned trade union federations, professional societies, women's and student organizations in several other Arab one-party states are also effective participatory structures cannot be taken for granted. Much the same might be said about the electoral process, where pro-government votes of 99 per cent are the rule and where voting participation is either compulsory or, where it is not, the actual turnout may be a closely kept secret. In my view, Deutsch's social mobilization hypotheses, when taken together, constitute a persuasive explanation for the political instability and autocracy so evident in the Arab world. Expansion of the politically relevant population has taken place everywhere. Social change has given opportunities for opposition movements to develop. Coups and mass turbulence, as Deutsch would predict, have in fact occurred and continue to do so. The range of political and administrative obligations has increased and with it the ideological spectrum. Governments in the Arab world have indeed become bigger. Established elites have been forced out of power by new aspirants who, in turn, have trouble maintaining their incumbency. Despite better communications technologies, Arab elites still appear distant from and ignorant of opinions and movements among the governed. Politically relevant organizations have proliferated, though not necessarily performing 'positive' modernizing functions; and we cannot assume that all of this growth represents the 'institutionalization' so crucial to political development modernization theorists. So, while we may demur from the linear development notions implicit even to some extent in Deutsch's approach, we conclude that the Arab world largely conforms to his social mobilization hypotheses.

Fragmentation v. Integration: Loads v. Capabilities

In addition to the propositions we have discussed, the social mobilization model proposes two more overarching, interrelated hypotheses that, to my mind, possess exceptional originality and insight, and lift Deutsch's theory to a level well above conventional modernization and political development theory. One is his notion that social mobilization facilitates the integration of states whose societies already share certain basic common values and traits, while it may accelerate the disintegration of states whose societies are not so endowed. The other is the idea that political 'development' is a function of the ratio of loads to capabilities. These are propositions of critical importance for understanding problems of Arab political development. But they need to be applied not just at one level but at three: supranational, national, and subnational. Deutsch, while obviously aware of levels of identity questions (the subject, indeed, of his *Nationalism and Social Communications*),[15] is focusing in his social mobilization article essentially on the integration of the political community within given state boundaries. But the Arab world cannot be properly analyzed only as a disparate collection of states because there is also an Arab political community embracing the entire area.[16] *Al-umma al-arabiyya* ('the Arab nation') is too frequently used in the Arab political lexicon to be dismissed as a fictitious or rhetorical term, and it is too widely used, by leaders and politicians of different ideologies and locales, to be considered as a narrowly partisan concept. In fact, the Ba'th Party, the principal pan-Arab organization, refers to the whole Arab world as the nation, and what we called the national (or state) level as the sector. There is also, however, a subnational dimension to the Arab identity problem: the existence of ethnic and religious minority communities within given states or across adjacent states. These communities include the Kurds of Iraq, Syria, Iran, and Turkey; the Shi'ites (heterodox Muslims), various sects of whom are found in Iraq, Syria, North Yemen, and Lebanon; the non-Muslim blacks of the southern Sudan; the Coptic Christians of Egypt; the Maronite and Ammenian Christians of Lebanon, the Orthodox Christians of Lebanon, Syria, Jordan, and Palestine–Israel; and the Berber communities of Algeria and Morocco.

Because in the Arab world we have three significant foci of identity, not just one, we must examine Deutsch's two grand hypotheses at each level.

The Arab Nation as the Unit of Analysis

Let us begin by considering the Arab world as a single nation. We may assume that the 130 million people of this entity, in Deutsch's words, 'already share the same language, culture, and major social institutions'.[17] Only a tiny minority (probably less than 2 per cent) are not Arabic-speaking, probably less than 5 per cent are non-Muslims, and the various Shi'ite Muslim sects must comprise less than 10 million people. A problem arises with 'shared major social institutions'. In anthropological terms the Arabs share a patrilineal, patrilocal, patriarchal, and extended family structure and a great many customs and values – diet, ritual, music, history, and the like. But they also share a certain parochialism and conflict in their social relations; it has been remarked that 'the Arabs are one nation and a thousand tribes'. Nevertheless, there is indeed a wealth of common elements in the social substructure of Arab political culture. Given the rapid social mobilization that has been occurring throughout the region, do we then observe a trend toward what Deutsch calls political consolidation? If by consolidation is meant what Foltz calls 'nation-building' or Huntington 'political institutionalization' then the answer is negative. All unification efforts until now have failed: the United Arab Republic of Egypt and Syria, 1959–61, the Federation of Arab Republics of Egypt, Syria, and Libya in the early 1970s, the various efforts at unity between the two Yemens, the aborted plans for Fertile Crescent unity, and the stalled efforts at Maghreb unity. Indeed, the existence of serious inter-Arab hostilities (such as, in the late 1970s, Morocco v. Algeria, Egypt v. Libya, Iraq v. Syria, Saudi Arabia v. South Yemen) suggests that basic cultural similarities are too far removed from the political environment to serve as useful predictors of integration.

'We can understand more fully these failures by referring to Deutsch's second grand hypothesis: political development (or the lack of it) depends upon the balance of 'loads' and 'capabilities'. Some aspects of social mobilization (such as economic growth, scientific and technological development, and the spread of education) can help government, the political leadership, interests, and organizations to cope effectively with the new demands (loads). Considering the Arab world as a single unit, it is clear that the demands being made upon it are extremely burdensome. The Arab nation is called upon to solve the Palestinian-Israeli problem on terms acceptable to the Arabs. It is also called upon to redistribute wealth within the Arab world, now so geographically skewed, and to break down the obstacles (which some, of course, consider to be protective shields) to fuller economic integration.[18] But the greatest immediate 'load' on the Arab nation is political: conflict over who shall run it and how.

If the loads on this hypothetical political unit are enormous, its capabilities are virtually nil. This is because this area now is only a hypothetical unit and lacks even nominal all-Arab institutions. As we have seen, the efforts to create broader-scope institutions and the attendant political and administrative capabilities have thus far been unsuccessful. The experience of the United Arab Republic is most instructive in this respect. The combined leadership of the UAR, under Nasser, proved unable to generate the requisite institutionalized support from the Syrian 'region', nor could it provide the policy-making and administrative performance necessary to cope with growing discontent in Syria. Another area of potential all-Arab capabilities is the efforts of the principal pan-Arab parties – the Ba'th, the Arab Nationalists' Movement, and the Nasserite groups – to create political structures and capabilities on the all-Arab level. But it is unmistakably clear that they have been unable to do so effectively and have indeed lost ground to existing states with their narrow and competing interests.

Decisive as these data may appear, however, they do not necessarily deny that cultural homogeneity plus social mobilization may lead to political consolidation in the Arab nation. There is other evidence for consolidation beneath the surface of these seemingly disintegrative facts. Since this is a unit that lacks the elementary attributes of sovereignty and central government, one must expect the process of consolidation to take longer than it would in a state. Furthermore, the analysis of integration of disparate political communities involves additional loads: among them, the intra-regional identification, habits, and vested interests that cluster around existing sovereignties.[19] Even though all efforts at political unity so far have failed, its member states have shown consistent solidarity on most regionwide issues, especially Palestine. The League of Arab States has become a significant armature for functional integration; and numerous regionwide elite and professional associations have been created. Under Nasser, Egypt projected itself as the active core area of the Arab world, and, more importantly, implanted the idea of Arab solidarity firmly in the political arena. Moreover, with the dramatic increase of oil revenues, the volume of elite transactions increased markedly. The expansion of airline routes between Arab capitals is just one dramatic illustration of the new closeness of once geographically and psychologically distant cities. An Arab communications satellite and other linkage technologies will accelerate this trend. The proliferation of a dense network of functional linkages between the growing – and similar – megalopoli from Kuwait to Casablanca suggests that the Arab world may be on the same historical track that united France and other European countries, which Stein Rokkan discusses below in this volume.

Even the seemingly negative instability may be a sign of 'national' vitality. Much of this turmoil has arisen from demands from the newly mobilized urban and rural lower classes. These were the classes that gave such enthusiastic, if diffuse, support to Nasser's pan-Arabism and which continue to serve as the constituency for today's Palestinian and progressive Arab nationalist organizations. Much of the turmoil of the eastern Arab world – for example, Lebanon, Syria, Jordan, Iraq, Bahrain, and the Yemens – can be traced to conflicts of identity priorities between these Arab states and the Arab nation. Finally, it is not just the failure of unity efforts that deserves attention; the persistence of such efforts indicates that the mobilization-integration hypothesis may yet be valid over the long run. Therefore, despite the numerous examples of intra-region conflict, we should not exclude the possibility that the Arab world may yet become what Deutsch would call a pluralistic security community. The Arab world may yet enter the process (as Deutsch's social mobilization and regional integration theory would predict) of increased social, economic, and eventual political consolidation. But to do so – again according to Deutsch – it will also have to develop region-wide institutions to enhance the capabilities of an all-Arab political system.

The Arab States as Units of Analysis

The question of integration at the all-Arab level is obviously affected by processes of consolidation occurring at the state level within the Arab world. These processes may well have enhanced the possibility of regional integration understood as the policy co-ordination of independent or autonomous units, as has apparently been the case in Western Europe. But they have also retarded regional integration when it is understood as the process of political fusion of separate states into a larger unified entity. Conversely, Arabism has constituted a legitimacy resource for particular regimes at various times, but it has also complicated political life throughout the states of the region, especially those of the pan-Arab heartland (Syria, Iraq, Egypt, Lebanon, Jordan, and Palestine). A state or regime that violates the all-Arab consensus may find its own internal cohesion weakened. A correct application of Deutsch's social mobilization and integration ideas therefore requires that we examine the states as well as the 'nation'.

When we shift the unit of analysis from the Arab nation to the Arab states, we find that what is true for the Arab world as a whole – namely, that its people 'already share the same language, culture, and major social institutions' – is also true for almost all of the Arab states; and so social mobilization is also promoting (among other things) the already substantial consolidation of these polities. Many analysts believe that the Arab states have become stronger and more cohesive, particularly in the last decade.[20] Ever since the failure of the merger of Egypt and Syria in the ill-fated United Arab Republic (1958–61) there has been no successful challenge to the existing sovereignties: no states have disappeared,[21] although Lebanon has approached political oblivion. There is more political stability in the 1970s than there was in the 1950s and early 1960s. Some observers feel that identification with specific states (if not loyalty or respect for a given regime) has grown; people have become accustomed, at least, to the political reality of Syria, Kuwait, or Libya whereas a quarter- or a half-century earlier these entities were considered artificial. The growth of governmental capabilities in recent years has been significant: today there are far fewer areas outside the control of a central government than there were at the end of the Second World War, and the information and propaganda media of governments have doubtless instilled ordinary people with an awareness of their state citizenship they they did not have earlier.

In as much as the Arab states are already homogeneous (i.e. the 'assimilated' population is a high proportion of the total population)[22] one would expect, following Deutsch,[23] the 'consolidation' of such states to increase under conditions of rapid social mobilization. This is all very well as long as two important factors, both of which are at least implicit in Deutsch's overall position, are considered. One may be indicated by a not-so-simple question: 'assimilation to what ?' Writing in 1961, shortly before the break-up of the UAR, Deutsch states that 'social mobilization may thus assist to some extent in the consolidation of the United Arab Republic ... '[24] To be sure, we see a huge majority population in each country assimilated to Arabism – to an identity and a community transcending the boundaries of either Egypt or Syria. What we may not see (yet what is surely implicit in the theory) is that people are also mobilized on behalf of Arabism in their particular state. Many of these people are not just mobilized on the level of sentiment but also on the level of interest, particularly since the structures and presence of each state governmental apparatus have also developed. It follows that a merger between two such states may not quickly eradicate the parochial state orientations that constitute continuing hidden cleavages in the new union.

The second factor is the numerous and essentially disruptive effects of social mobilization referred to earlier in this paper. Even a state with a largely 'assimilated' population may be beset with serious problems arising out of the concern of the mobilized populations over issues other than national identity – issues such as authority, social justice, and foreign policy. Such issues certainly bedeviled Syrian politics before and during the merger with Egypt and undoubtedly had much to do with the collapse of the unity effort. It must be added that social mobilization also activates the small non-assimilated communities within the state, and these 'mobilized but differentiated' groups may exacerbate separatist currents within the state.

Social mobilization's contribution to consolidation in the Arab world is not mainly by enhancing already existing assimilation; rather it is through its stimulation of the growth of government capabilities. The consolidation we observe in the various Arab states today is due less to a general consensus-building and development of civic attitudes focused on the state itself than to the growth of state bureaucracies, symbol manipulation capabilities, and above all control technologies. The strong man of Iraq, Saddam Hussein, has remarked that it is no longer possible to make a *coup d'état* simply by taking over the broadcasting station. The route from social mobilization to political consolidation does not run so much via the growth of common values and consensus but rather through the preponderance of capabilities over loads. If Arab governments are stronger than they used to be, it is not just that their populations are more harmonious and supportive of the system. More important is the fact that it is very largely the system that can exert increasingly pervasive influence (both positive and negative) over individuals and society.

Obviously one cannot for long maintain the 'other things equal' condition in trying to evaluate the multifarious political effects of social mobilization. But if we could insist on that condition for a moment, would we see even a rough verification of the fragmentation-integration hypothesis at the state level? While there is overall ethnic, linguistic, religious, and cultural homogeneity in the Arab world, some states are less homogeneous on these grounds than others. Are the states with the less homogeneous societies also less stable as we would expect? If we were to dichotomize the Arab states into 'more homogeneous' and 'less homogeneous' categories, we could probably elicit general agreement that the Arabian peninsula desert states fall into the former category. These include Kuwait, Saudi Arabia, Qatar, the United Arab Emirates. We would also include Egypt, Libya, Tunisia, and the People's Democratic Republic of Yemen (South Yemen). The relatively heterogeneous countries would include the Yemen Arab Republic (North Yemen) (Zaydis and Shafi'is), the Sudan (Muslims and non-Muslims), Bahrain (Sunnis and Shi'ites), Lebanon (pervasive ethnoreligious fragmentation), Oman (coastal and interior doctrinal differences), Morocco and Algeria (Arabs and Berbers), Syria (Alawites and Orthodox Muslims), Iraq (Kurds and Muslims; Sunni and Shi'a Muslims), and Jordan (east Jordanians and Palestinians).

Categorizing in terms of political stability is not as easy, but for our rough, nominal-scale dichotomization, let us call 'stable' those countries that have not experienced generalized civil strife (as opposed to sporadic rioting and strikes), that have not experienced any irregular changes of regime (accompanied by violence or the direct threat of violence), and that have not experienced more than three serious (potentially successful 'near-miss') abortive coups during the twenty-five year period 1953–78, or in the case of newly independent states during their post-independence history. Using these criteria, we may classify Kuwait,

Table 2.1 *The Arab Polities Classified According to Stability and Political Culture Homogeneity*

	Homogeneous	Heterogeneous
Stable	Kuwait Saudi Arabia Qatar United Arab Emirates Tunisia Egypt	Bahrain
Unstable	South Yemen Libya	Algeria North Yemen Sudan Lebanon Oman Morocco Syria Jordan Iraq

Saudi Arabia, Qatar, the United Arab Emirates, Egypt, Tunisia, and Bahrain as 'stable'; while Algeria, North Yemen, South Yemen, Sudan, Lebanon, Libya, Oman, Morocco, Syria, Jordan, and Iraq are 'unstable'.

Table 2.1 suggests that Deutsch's hypothesis associating homogeneity with stability and heterogeneity with instability is valid for the Arab world. Only Libya and South Yemen among the homogeneous political cultures (and, one must admit, the strong tribal cleavages in South Yemen almost qualify it for the heterogeneous category) are considered unstable; while Bahrain is the only heterogeneous polity to be considered stable (and this only with some misgivings, in light of its considerable labor and political dissidence, compared to the other Gulf states). But these are the exceptions; basically we find the Arab states grouped in two clusters: homogeneous-stable and heterogeneous-unstable.

Substate and Trans-state Political Communities

The differential political effects of social mobilization are nowhere better illustrated than in the development of communal consciousness among the several ethnic and religious minorities of the Arab world. Albert Hourani has rightly indicated the centrality of such quasi-political identifications in the historical development of nationalism in the Ottoman Empire – the last of the great pre-national, religiously legitimized political systems.[25] The Christian and Jewish minorities of Turkey and the Arab east – notably the Armenians, Maronites, Copts, and Greek Orthodox – displayed an intense desire for education and Western cultural contact, a desire which the American and European missionaries, Protestant and Catholic, of the nineteenth century helped fulfil. Communal consciousness was also inevitably strengthened by the fact of minority status itself, which in Islam was one of 'protected' separateness – but not quite equality. The *millet* system of the Ottoman Empire provided for substantial local communal autonomy under the aegis of religious authorities. Non-orthodox Muslim communities (like the Kurds and Berbers) were not given *millet* status, but they still preserved an important degree of communal autonomy and self-consciousness. While these groups have not had the Western linkage of the Christian minorities, they nevertheless have been touched by social mobilization as the state extends its apparatus throughout the society and as the economy develops, sometimes with enormous speed, as in the oil-rich Kurdish areas of Iraq.

If states with relatively homogeneous populations, according to Deutsch's hypothesis, consolidate themselves because of social mobilization, then is it not logical that these proto-national communities, assuming they dominate a particular territory, should also consolidate their communal nationalism and institutions? Indeed, such seems to have been the case with the Armenians in the late nineteenth and early twentieth centuries in Turkey, the Arabs themselves (when they were a distinct minority in the Ottoman Empire), the Kurds, the Maronites, and the non-Muslim, non-Arab peoples of the southern Sudan. In all cases ethnoreligious communalism turned into assertive nationalism. Interestingly, there has been relatively less assertiveness of this sort among communities more widely diffused throughout the society at large and less tightly interlinked within themselves: the Christian Orthodox Arabs of the Fertile Crescent, the Copts of Egypt, and the Berbers of North Africa are cases in point. In short, Deutsch's argument seems applicable at the sub- or transnational level as well: areas dominated by groups with basic common characteristics may enhance their solidarity and extend their national aspirations under conditions of rapid social mobilization, especially if they also possess the potential structural capabilities, as in several cases embodied in the *millet* organization, to handle their new political tasks.

But in dealing with subnational communities within a given state system it is important to avoid confusion and pay careful attention to Deutsch's sophisticated formulations. If Kurds, for example, comprise only 10 per cent of the Iraqi population, social mobilization theory hastily applied might suggest that Kurds will steadily be assimilated into the Iraqi political system. Such an inference would not be warranted, however, because it ignores an important boundary factor: the Kurds comprise 90 per cent of the population of Kurdistan, the non-state territory that lies athwart parts of Iran, Turkey, Syria, and the Soviet Union, as well as northern Iraq. We might therefore expect an increase in Kurdish national solidarity throughout Kurdistan. But the 'loads' imposed by the hostility of established governments (Iraq, Turkey, and Iran) appear to outweigh the limited organizational capabilities the Kurds can muster, so we cannot mechanically infer that a Kurdish nation is likely to become a reality. Such inferences also ignore Deutsch's emphasis on the importance of *rates* of assimilation and *rates* of mobilization.[26] If the rate of assimilation of Kurds into an essentially

Arab political culture exceeds the rate of mobilization of Kurds into politically active roles, then we may expect a diminution of Kurdish separatism, whereas if the mobilization rate exceeds the assimilation rate then we may expect continuing tension and conflict. Thus far, it appears that the latter situation has existed, and it remains an open question whether the integration policies of Baghdad following its victory over the Kurdish rebels in 1975 will alter these rates.

The Case of Lebanon and Other Examples

Lebanon presents the most dramatic example of an Arab country rent asunder by socially mobilized ethnoreligious fragmentation. It is a tragic confirmation of Deutsch's mobilization-integration and loads-capabilities hypotheses. Here also we find the intermingling of supranational, state-national, and subnational identities – at best in uneasy tension, at worst in violent conflict. With a half-dozen religious communities and numerous regional cleavages defined by quasi-feudal fiefdoms, Lebanon is almost a caricature of divided society. At the same time, it has been undergoing explosive and uneven social mobilization since the middle 1940s. That there has been a powerful centrifugal tendency germinating in Lebanese political culture, as Deutsch's hypothesis predicts, has been all too well demonstrated by the virtual collapse of the state in civil war. A quarter-century of social mobilization gradually awakened new political strata and new elites, or would-be elites, in the subordinate non-Maronite half of the population. This sector, religiously mixed (although dominated by Sunnite and Shi'ite Muslims and Druze), was the breeding ground for radical reformist, socialist, and secular ideologies and pan-Arab or pan-Syrian nationalism that challenged the Lebanese identity. Thus, instead of social mobilization helping build consensus, it (a) generated new non-traditional 'loads' upon the system and (b) strengthened subnational ethnolinguistic identification at the expense of a common Lebanese civic consciousness to which both Christians and non-Christians could feel an attachment. As for the growth of capabilities, mobilization could have strengthened governmental and political institutions. The economy was burgeoning; the government possessed surplus revenue; a skilled manpower pool and strong educational resources existed to buttress the political system. Unfortunately, these positive factors were overwhelmed by the preponderant negative effects of mobilization; indeed, the structural solution itself to the problem of Lebanon's fragmented political culture only exacerbated the new loads. The device of proportional representation by sect, in the principal political offices, the parliament, the entire state bureaucracy (military as well as civil), inhibited the development of efficient or effective administration.[27] Sectarianism thwarted the development of political parties and movements that could appeal to all fragments of Lebanese political culture.[28] According to a rough, aggregate comparison of the loads/capabilities equation in Lebanon with other countries at similar levels of modernization, Lebanon is politically underdeveloped.[29] Lebanon's 'neighbors' on several rank-ordered indicators of social mobilization were 'ahead' of Lebanon on several indicators of 'political development' (including voting percentages, government expenditures, and executive instability). Its 'political neighbors' ranked well below Lebanon on the social mobilization indicators. By 1968, the unstable regional situation – characterized by Israel's new conquests and the rise of the Palestinian movement – was precipitating a new kind of tension in the Lebanese system, and in defensive reaction the principal right-wing Maronite organizations began to prepare themselves for what they saw as the inevitable future conflict. When it came in 1975–6 it was a war not mainly between religious communities (for there were substantial Christian and even Maronite elements on the so-called Muslim side). Basically, it was a sociopolitical struggle that took on a sectarian character. On one side were the newly mobilized and politically relevant elements, mostly urban, Muslim, middle and lower class, many of whom were secular and supranational in their ideology. On the other was the incumbent, Maronite-dominated establishment, which became increasingly subnational and parochial in its ideology. The old, elite-level alliance of wealthy Muslim *za'ims* (bosses) with the Maronites crumbled, and the Muslim traditionalists found themselves the captives of their erstwhile 'flocks' and ranged reluctantly against their former elite partners.

One of the mysteries of the social mobilization hypothesis is the location of thresholds. Where is the threshold of basic culture integration beyond which social mobilization is a consolidating factor, and the threshold of the loads/capabilities ratio beyond which the political system can effectively cope with socioeconomic growing pains? Available quantitative indicators alone do not seem adequate for making precise calculations of these thresholds, Deutsch's ingenious efforts notwithstanding. But perhaps one can hazard an intuitive calculation, using the extreme Lebanese case as a benchmark, about the break-even point for other political systems in the Arab world, in which a basically similar political culture is a constant. To explore this question fully is beyond the scope of this chapter, but one or two comparative examples may at least illuminate it. In Lebanon high fragmentation coupled with unusual impediments to institution-building led to chaos. Similarly in North Yemen, another mountainous country, a bipolar sectarian cleavage coupled with complex tribal rivalries has caused almost chronic instability. Notwithstanding these cleavages, one could argue that Yemenis still possess a stronger national identity than do Lebanese: but the Yemenis lack even the most rudimentary institutions of government, and their efforts to build them are constantly impeded by both persisting cleavages within the traditional sector and pressure from the small but growing mobilized sector.

Iraq, on the other hand, is almost as ethnoreligiously diverse as Lebanon. To be sure, Iraq has also had a history of political instability; but there is now reason to suppose that Iraq is on a path toward consensus and consolidation rather than endless chaos. In 1978 the ruling Ba'th Party celebrated ten years of uninterrupted rule – a real milestone in modern Iraqi history. By developing a disciplined party organization, the Ba'thists had succeeded in imposing an effective control system over this unruly political culture and had converted enough of the political fallout of social mobilization into capabilities to cope with the also-increasing loads on the system.

At the other end of the spectrum, Tunisia, a country very much like Lebanon in many ways, is one of the most culturally homogeneous in the Arab world. A textbook case of 'political development', Tunisia under Bourguiba and his Destourian Socialist Party had displayed a relatively tranquil political scene. Without the additional loads of cultural fragmentation, Bourguiba was able to generate the capabilities to run the country smoothly through his own charisma and the penetrative apparatus of his party. But the recent turbulence in Tunisia, as Bourguiba nears the end of his rule, should deter us from accepting what might be called the 'happily-ever-after' fallacy – the idea that nothing but harmony and order lie beyond the thresholds. At the same time it should provide us with a clue to the puzzle of mobilization and political development. If Tunisia is headed for a major political crisis in spite of favorable environmental conditions and a good record of effective government, the explanation would seem to lie in a failure of institutional capabilities.

Capabilities are not just a function of social trends: they depend as well upon unrelated political factors. In addition to material potentialities, the political system, to become truly 'capable', needs legitimacy; and legitimacy requires more than pervasive control mechanisms or administrative effectiveness. It requires leadership, an effective ideology or set of common principles, and – especially in a situation of rapid social mobilization – it requires effective participation. Lebanon, unfortunately, lacked not only control and administrative effectiveness, but also leadership, a set of common principles, and effective participation for the newly relevant strata. In North Yemen, despite its extremely underdeveloped levels compared to Lebanon, the situation is very much the same. But in Iraq, by contrast, despite an unfavorable environment, a political party has succeeded (for the time at least) in harnessing the considerable wealth and manpower resources of that country. It has generated an effective, if often ruthless, control apparatus and its administration, despite inefficiencies, does appear to deliver the kind of services needed by a socially mobilized Iraqi population more effectively than its predecessor regime. In short, it has invested the stability (and to some extent perhaps the legitimacy) secured through its initial authoritarian capabilities into new and different capabilities for economic and social development. It would be premature to suppose that Iraqis now accord to their political system the legitimacy enjoyed by governments in the more settled industrialized societies, but it seems clear that the leadership is at least respected and the ideology of the ruling party widely supported. As for the Tunisian case, the lesson is obvious enough: even a homogeneous political environment requires political legitimacy, and legitimacy depends upon responsive leadership, administrative competence and popular participation. The main problem in linking social mobilization to political modernization in each of the countries discussed here – and one that is present throughout the Arab polities – is whether the modalities for effective political participation can be found before their absence becomes a critical problem.

Conclusion: A Critique of the Model

I have attempted to assess the plausibility of Deutsch's social mobilization hypotheses in the Arab world with special attention to the propositions relating cultural integration/fragmentation and the loads/capabilities ratio to 'political development'. On the whole, I find the Deutschian approach fruitful. Yet in the process of carrying out the assessment I also find certain problems and inadequacies.

But before turning to my own critique, let me briefly note two critical alternatives to the model that, in my view, are off the mark. One is the assertion that the Deutschian approach, like that of conventional political development theory in general, neglects the salience of ethnicity.[30] In light of what we have already said, this is an absurd charge. It is hardly accurate to accuse Deutsch of underestimating ethnicity. It may be that the assimilation of ethnic groups is a much slower process than the other aspects of social mobilization, but the model on balance is quite successful in accounting for ethnic assertiveness and fragmentation as well as integration; and, as I have tried to show, there is no need to apply it only to existing states. The second, more serious alternative is offered by Marxists and other economic determinists. From their perspective Deutsch's approach, representative of 'bourgeois' social science, profoundly misinterprets the realities of development in the Third World. The optimistic version of this school sees the inevitability of radical transformation arising out of the gradual creation of subjective class-consciousness congruent with objective class interests. But the social mobilization hypotheses depict a much more complex world, making revolution only one of the many possible outcomes of the social change that all agree is taking place. In the pessimistic and more sophisticated form of neo-Marxist theory, the underdeveloped societies are seen as fundamentally dependent upon the needs and interests of the 'central' economy of the industrialized societies. The notion of a gradual 'awakening' of traditional sectors into modernity is rejected in favor of an image whereby the engines of world finance and production, through their client elites in the Third World, systematically suppress the efforts of exploited classes to obtain political power and economic independence.[31] These matters are taken up at greater length in the chapters by Duvall *et al.* and Senghaas in this volume. From this perspective the social mobilization theory is naive and romantic in its essentially liberal assumptions. But as we have seen, Deutsch's vision of social and political change, while it does not exclude liberal solutions, certainly does not insist on them. It is, rather, prudently 'pluralistic' in the type of political consequences it foresees.

While it does neglect external linkages, a weakness we shall mention below, it avoids the doctrinaire assertion of dependency, the reification of class, and the exaggeration of economic interests as the fundamental motivating force in Third World politics.

The greatest misconception in the social mobilization model is the expectation that people pass rather suddenly from an essentially passive traditional orientation into an active one that prepares them to function in complex, modern social settings. The theory also appears to imply, in places, that social mobilization homogenizes people, makes them more capable of working together, sharing goals, employing rational, pragmatic means to achieve them. Implicit as well is the notion of stages of development: people can be predicted not only to move from 'tradition' to 'modernity' but also — although here the argument becomes murkier — to move toward more modern forms of political behavior. Neither recent theory nor practical experience in the Arab world supports this simplistic image. Indeed, one of the most significant aspects of modern Arab politics is the ability of people at all levels (including the 'traditional' rural poor) to comprehend and function with purpose in the political process. South Yemen highlanders were not too 'traditional' to make a Marxist revolution; but at the same time the resurgence of popular religion and 'traditional' cynicism toward governments and parties causes considerable despair for the modernizers in both 'progressive' and 'conservative' regimes. There is considerable rethinking of the hypothesized mobilizing effects of urbanization, and not just in the Middle East, as Foltz indicates in his chapter above.[32] While we may be able to isolate the socially mobilized sectors in terms of aggregate data indicators, we do not find similarly distinct 'new' political sectors. Much has been spoken about the 'new middle class' or the 'new men' in the Arab world, but they seem to have the same old political habits as their aristocratic predecessors.

Perhaps it is for this reason that we cannot easily discern stages of Arab political development and cannot trace an onward-and-upward curve toward 'modern' political order. In so far as Deutsch's formulation envisages the possibility of developing nations passing beyond the troubled adolescence of political development into a new era of modern leadership, sufficient capabilities, and general consensus, it may be guilty of the 'happily-ever-after fallacy' referred to earlier, which assumes a take-off into political harmony, as if societies governed by strong central governments were immune to serious political disorders.[33]

If the core concept is so flawed, how can anything of value be found in the rest of the theory? Fortunately, Deutsch the political scientist comes to the rescue of Deutsch the social theorist, and he provides us with a sophisticated range of political possibilities none of which depends on the notion of social mobilization as a transformationist phenomenon. Social mobilization does indeed expand the politically relevant population, but it does not necessarily modernize or homogenize it; indeed, the real value of Deutsch's work, for example in *Nationalism and Social Communication*, is in showing the various ways and conditions under which it divides and complicates political life. We have tried to illustrate the fruitfulness of these formulations with our examples from Arab politics.

More serious are the ambiguities and omissions. We have already suggested some of the problems that must be faced in a region, such as the Arab world, where the state is not the only locus of political identity: social mobilization theory must also be applied at the supranational and subnational levels; and it can be if due recognition is given to the different institutional configuration at each level. In the operational expression of the concept there is some ambiguity in the interpretation of politically positive and negative indicators: why, for example, should increase in voting participation be treated as a load rather than a capability factor, and why should change from rural to urban residence be treated as a capability rather than a load factor? Why, indeed, should population growth be treated as a load factor in underpopulated areas such as the Arab world (Egypt excepted)? Is there not also a problem about timespans? Linguistic or cultural assimilation, in the Arab experience at least, is a glacial phenomenon, measured in generations or longer, not years or decades. An individual, we are led to think, may undergo his (or her) mobilization experience out of a traditional lifestyle and into a modern one at some point or during some stage of fifty years of adulthood. Yet has anyone ever discovered an individual who could clearly be shown to have gone through this experience? Or is this dramatic shift in outlook, habits, and political beliefs observable only between generations?

We find the social mobilization approach useful for explaining the incoherence in Arab politics, but we do not find it particularly helpful in a predictive sense. This may be because of ambiguities in the social mobilization concept itself, as we have suggested, and it may also be due in part to the fact that the dependent variable, 'political development' (as in the title of the article) or 'the politics of development' (p. 497) is not clearly specified. As it stands, social mobilization can explain or predict almost any kind of political behavior, from riots to voting participation to revolutions and welfare policy outcomes. But it may also be due to the omission of certain other key variables. We have already alluded to the absence of political factors as possible or necessary intervening variables between social mobilization and political outcomes; and in the light of Deutsch's subsequent imaginative work on the cybernetic character of political systems, and his emphasis on the 'steering' functions of government, it is a little surprising not to find more emphasis on the political system then is provided in a rather routine reference to feedback. In the Arab world it is hard to analyze politics without some reference to ideology, leadership policy, and other overtly political structures, and how they are affected by social mobilization. One also senses an omission of social structure as an important intervening variable. The differential impact of social mobilization (and its component parts) on the urban labor force, the peasantry, the professional bureaucracies, and the political elite still needs theoretical elaboration, unless these important structures are to be left entirely to Marxist analysts.

Finally, the social mobilization formulation, like most comparative politics theory, hardly recognizes external factors. One does not need to go as far as the dependency theorists in asserting the subordination of politics in the Third World countries to the economic and strategic interests of the industrialized societies, but the modern history of Arab politics is certainly difficult to interpret without considering the impact of Western governments on local political processes. I am not referring merely to the examples of covert intervention by outside powers through attempted coups and the like, but more broadly to the influence which the outside world, the West in particular, brings to bear in the economic and cultural as well as political spheres. We have noted the significance of the growing inter-Arab network of social communications; but one should also look at an airline route map of the area to comprehend the far greater density of elite traffic between the main Arab centers and the industrialized world. It would be naive to suppose that the 'political development' of Saudi Arabia and Egypt, among other states, is not being strongly influenced by the United States, although not as directly as Great Britain in an earlier age created and maintained political elites in the territories it dominated. Lebanon, referred to earlier, is also a dramatic case of a political system whose fate has been heavily determined by outside political forces – Arab, Israeli, and Western.

Karl Deutsch's hypotheses on social mobilization and political development, when applied to the Arab world, lack perhaps the scope and power of 'grand theory', and we have found real difficulties with the social mobilization concept itself. But as an explanatory guide to the convulsions, the trend toward autocracy, and the dilemma of participation in Arab politics, these 'middle-range' ideas, in my view, have proven eminently sound.

Notes: Chapter 2

1 Karl W. Deutsch, 'Social mobilization and political development', *American Political Science Review*, vol. 55, no. 3 (September 1961), pp. 493–514.
2 Daniel Lerner, *The Passing of Traditional Society: Modernizing the Middle East* (Glencoe, Ill.: The Free Press, 1958); Dankwart A. Rustow, *Politics and Westernization in the Near East* (Princeton, NJ: Princeton University, Center of International Studies, 1956); and Gabriel Almond and James S. Coleman (eds), *The Politics of the Developing Areas* (Princeton, NJ: Princeton University Press, 1960).
3 Samuel P. Huntington, *Political Order in Changing Societies* (New Haven, Conn.: Yale University Press, 1968).
4 They include Morocco, Algeria, Tunisia, Libya, Egypt, Sudan, Jordan, Syria, Lebanon, Iraq, Kuwait, Bahrain, Saudi Arabia, Qatar, the United Arab Emirates, Oman, the People's Democratic Republic of Yemen (South Yemen), and the Yemen Arab Republic (North Yemen). The League of Arab States also includes Mauritania, Somalia, and Djibouti (which are not overwhelmingly Arab), and the Palestine Liberation Organization (which is not a state).
5 For a description and analysis, see Michael C. Hudson, *Arab Politics: The Search for Legitimacy* (New Haven, Conn.: Yale University Press, 1977), ch. 5.

6 On Algeria, see Pierre Boudieu, *The Algerians* (Boston, Mass.: Beacon Press, 1969), esp. pp. 145–6.
7 See, for example, Paul D. Starr, 'Lebanese fishermen and the dilemma of modernization', in *Those Who Live from the Sea*, ed. M. Estelle Smith (St Paul, Minn.: American Ethnological Society and West Publishing Co., 1977).
8 See Fred Halliday, *Arabia Without Sultans* (New York: Vintage Press, 1974), chs 6 and 7, esp. pp. 192–201.
9 For an excellent treatment of the political effects of refugee camp life see the following articles by Rosemary Sayigh in the *Journal of Palestine Studies*: 'The Palestinian identity among camp residents', vol. 6, no. 3 (Spring 1977), pp. 3–22; 'Sources of Palestinian nationalism: a study of a Palestinian camp in Lebanon', vol. 6, no. 4 (Summer 1977), pp. 17–40; and 'The struggle for survival: the economic conditions of Palestinian refugees in Lebanon', vol. 7, no. 2 (Winter 1978), pp. 101–19.
10 Charles L. Taylor and Michael C. Hudson, *World Handbook of Political and Social Indicators*, 2d edn (New Haven, Conn.: Yale University Press, 1972), section 3.
11 Hudson, *Arab Politics*, pp. 155–6.
12 US Department of Health, Education, and Welfare, Social Security Administration, *Social Security Programs Throughout the World – 1969* (Washington, DC: US Government Printing Office, 1969).
13 The *diwaniyya*, according to two Kuwait University political scientists, is a traditional group where Kuwaitis meet to express their thoughts about political and other matters. It is something like a men's private club; an informal, yet structured periodic gathering of men who sit together in a loose circle, drink tea and coffee, and talk. Tawfic E. Farah and Faisal Al-Salem, 'Size, affluence, and efficacy: regime effectiveness in Kuwait', paper delivered at the 1978 annual meeting of the Midwest Political Science Association, mimeo., p. 13.
14 Clement Henry Moore, 'Professional syndicates in contemporary Egypt: the "containment" of the new middle class', paper delivered at the 1973 annual meeting of the Middle East Studies Association, mimeo., p. 27.
15 Karl W. Deutsch, *Nationalism and Social Communication: An Inquiry into the Foundations of Nationality* (Cambridge, Mass.: Technology Press; and New York: Wiley, 1953).
16 On the origins of Arab nationalism, George Antonius's *The Arab Awakening* (London: Hamish Hamilton, 1938, 1961) remains indispensable despite its flaws. See also the collection of Arab nationalistic writings in Sylvia Haim (ed.), *Arab Nationalism: An Anthology* (Berkeley, Calif.: University of California Press, 1964); and Kemal Karpat, *Political and Social Thought in the Contemporary Middle East*, Pt I (New York: Praeger, 1963). A noteworthy recent comment is offered by the distinguished Palestinian political scientist Walid Khalidi: 'The Arab states' system is first and foremost a "Pan" system. It postulates the existence of a single Arab Nation behind the facade of a multiplicity of sovereign states. In pan-Arab ideology, this Nation is actual, not potential. It is a present reality, not a distant goal. The manifest failure even to approximate unity does not negate the empirical reality of the Arab Nation.' Quoted in 'Thinking the unthinkable: a sovereign Palestinian State', *Foreign Affairs*, vol. 56, no. 4 (July 1978), pp. 695–713, at p. 695.
17 Deutsch, 'Social mobilization and political development', p. 501.
18 On the problem of Arab economic integration, see Abdelhamid Brahimi, *Dimensions et Perspectives du Monde Arabe* (Paris: Economica, 1977).
19 Deutsch, of course, has made major contributions to the study of regional integration in Deutsch *et al.*, *Political Community and the North Atlantic Area* (Princeton, NJ: Princeton University Press, 1957), esp. chs 2 and 3.
20 On pan-Arabism as a transitional ideology, giving way to stable state nationalisms, see Richard H. Pfaff, 'The function of Arab nationalism', *Comparative Politics*, vol. 2, no. 2 (January 1970), pp. 147–68.
21 Even the seven city-states that now comprise the United Arab Emirates cannot be said to have lost any more autonomy than they had under the former British domination.
22 Deutsch, *Nationalism and Social Communication*, pp. 97–104.
23 *idem*, 'Social mobilization', p. 501.
24 ibid.

25 Albert Hourani, 'Race, religion, and nation-state in the Middle East', in *A Vision of History*, ed. Albert Hourani (Beirut: Khayat's, 1961), pp. 71–105.
26 Deutsch, *Nationalism and Social Communication*, ch. 6, esp. pp. 99–104.
27 See, for example, Ralph Crow, 'Religious sectarianism in the Lebanese political system', *Journal of Politics*, vol. 24, no. 3 (1962), pp. 489–520.
28 The best comparative study of Lebanese parties is Michael W. Suleiman, *Political Parties in Lebanon* (Ithaca, NY: Cornell University Press, 1967), esp. chs 2 and 3.
29 Michael C. Hudson, 'A case of political underdevelopment', *Journal of Politics*, vol. 30, no. 4 (November 1967), pp. 821–37; on Lebanon in general see Michael C. Hudson, *The Precarious Republic: Political Modernization in Lebanon* (New York: Random House, 1968).
30 Walker Connor, in 'Nation building or nation destroying?' *World Politics*, vol. 24, no. 3 (April 1972), pp. 319–55, makes such a charge. For an argument about the renaissance of ethnicity in the Middle East, see Iliya Harik, 'The ethnic revolution and political integration in the Middle East', *International Journal of Middle East Studies*, vol. 3, no. 3 (July 1972), pp. 303–23.
31 An intriguing Marxist interpretation of Arab politics, stressing its dependency on world capitalism, is Samir Amin, *La Nation Arabe* (Paris: Les Editions de Minuit, 1976).
32 See, for example, Janet Abu-Lughod, 'Varieties of urban experience: contrast, coexistence, and coalescence in Cairo', in *Middle Eastern Cities*, ed. Ira Lapidus (Berkeley, Calif.: University of California Press, 1969), pp. 159–87.
33 I am not suggesting that Deutsch is a mechanistic social determinist; indeed, his later work (e.g. *The Nerves of Government*, New York: Free Press, 1963, esp. chs 13 and 14) emphasizes the need for political systems continually to learn if they are to survive and prosper. But 'Social mobilization and political development (p. 505) calls for 'deliberate political and economic intervention into the social mobilization process ... in favor of more rapid and more balanced growth; a somewhat more even distribution of income; ... the more productive investment of available resources; and a sustained growth in the political and administrative capabilities of government ...' Otherwise, Third World states face instability or 'absorption into the communist bloc'. The implication is that 'political development' will result from enhanced growth and capabilities. Yet the question remains whether Third World nations are likely to develop such a preponderance of capabilities and, if they do, whether the resulting kind of political and social life would merit the term 'political development'.

3

Territories, Nations, Parties: Toward a Geoeconomic-Geopolitical Model for the Explanation of Variations within Western Europe

STEIN ROKKAN

Karl Deutsch taught my generation of social scientists to develop models and to test them against the data of history. My own early research on steps in the extension of political rights[1] and on the mobilization of peripheries[2] was heavily influenced by Deutsch's ideas. My later work on dimensions of state formation and nation-building[3] was directly inspired by Deutsch's pathbreaking study *Nationalism and Social Communication*: he taught me to look out for the decisive characteristics of the center-building networks and to study the functions of the printed media and of educational institutions in the fashioning of territory-wide identities. In this tribute to Karl Deutsch's intellectual leadership, I propose to try my hand at a first rough synthesis of these two sets of studies: I want to trace the outlines of a possible unifying model by linking elements from my early work on processes of mobilization with elements in my current search for a pattern in the geopolitical-geoeconomic history of Western Europe.

Background

I first developed the rudiments of a 'model of Western Europe' in an effort to offer a parsimonious set of explanations of the well-documented contrasts in party alignments across Western Europe.[4] This was essentially a stepwise taxonomy: I posited a sequence of 'critical junctures' from the Reformation to the Russian Revolution and I generated on this basis a typology of alliance options and consequent party systems. In this first effort each political system was treated in isolation from the others: there were no elements of geopolitics or geoeconomics in the model. I took a first step in this direction in a subsequent comparison of the marked variations in sequences of suffrages extension since the Great French Revolution:[5] in this I was forced to consider not only the timing of movements of territorial unification or secession but also the geopolitical weight of metropolitan *v.* peripheral centers. This first analysis of contiguities and interdependencies in the larger system of territories led on to a study of the underlying structure of differentiation within Western Europe: I summarized this graphically in a simplifying 'Conceptual map of Europe'.[6] The primary purpose of this exercise was to develop a typology of the distinctive preconditions for the development of mass politics in each territory but I never found time to link up this work on the timing and the characteristics of the territory-building processes with my earlier analyses of sequences of suffrage extensions and steps in the formation of party systems. My further work on the 'conceptual map' has concentrated on the analysis of the center-building process and of the successes or failures of territorial integration[7] but much work still remains to be done at the interface between this effort of geopolitical macrohistory and my earlier comparisons of rhythms of mass mobilizations between 1848 and 1920. In this tribute to Karl Deutsch I shall try to bring together in one outline model elements from these two sets of studies. I shall start out from my systematization of 'preconditions' and move on to an analysis of the key components of the processes of interaction triggered by the twin revolutions of the nineteenth century: the political, triggered by the French, and the industrial, launched by the English.

The model is still very much a sketch. It has still to be worked out in detail component by component, but it has already proven of some use as an engine for the generation of hypotheses for testing through comparisons by pairs of countries. Much work remains to be done before the model can offer systematized accounting schemes for the variations at each step in the long historical process: from the early decisions on the survival or dismantling of representative institutions, through the sequences of democratization and mass organization, to the great strains produced within each system by the rise of nationalist-fascist movements and their efforts to overthrow the gradually built-up institutions of competitive electoral democracy. These are tasks of great complexity: progress can only be made step by step. Nothing decisive is likely to be developed within the perspective of one single scholar: progress is much more likely to be made through the confrontation of a variety of paradigms and through attempts to combine elements from several part-theories in parsimonious schemata.

The Model

The model spans the entire history of state formation, nation-building, and mass politics in Western Europe: it represents an attempt to identify the crucial variables in the long and complex process that led up to the current constellations of territories, economies, and political alignment systems. The essential message of the model is simple enough: you cannot explain the marked variations in the structuring of mass politics in Western Europe without going far back in history, without analyzing the differences in the initial conditions and the early processes of territorial organization, of state building, of resource combination.

In practice this means going back to the fall of the Western Roman

Empire and the long sequence of efforts to establish a viable successor empire to the north of the Alps. To understand the later development we have to identify the decisive differences across this Western European territory in the conditions of center formation and territorial expansion. These constellations of conditions in their turn set the stage for the further sequences of change: the fragmentations of the German–Roman Empire, the build-up of strong dynastic states at the edges of that loosely structured system, the violent upsurge of Atlantic capitalism, and the establishment of Western empires across the oceans.

Dimensions and Stages

The primary elements of the model are set out in Figure 3.1. The elements are grouped by period and by type. The grouping by period reflects the basic analytical design: there is a set of precondition variables, a set of intervening process variables, and there is finally a set of explicanda. The precondition and the intervening variables are again grouped by type into essentially economic variables, territorial variables and cultural variables. There is a corresponding typology at the level of the explicanda: there a distinction is made between variables characterizing the extent of rights of participation and variables describing the alternatives set for mass politics, whether at the total-system level or at the level of parties.

The model does not cover the whole of Europe: to keep it within manageable bounds it concentrates on the Europe of the Celtic, the Latin, and the Germanic peoples. There is some fuzziness on the Eastern marches: most of the accounting schemes include Finland because of the heavy dominance of the Swedes until 1809 but exclude Estonia, Hungary, and the Slavic states re-established or reorganized after 1918.

The model starts out from a simple classification of sources of variation in the early Middle Ages: it identifies as an important economic variable the type of agrarian structure predominant in each area; it identifies as a territorial variable *par excellence* the degree of exposure to the efforts of empire-building under Charlemagne and his successors, and it suggests as an equally important cultural variable the ethnic-linguistic composition of the population of the given territory.

The model proceeds to a corresponding specification of variables for the first major periods of structural change: the establishment of a strong network of cities running from the Mediterranean to the North Sea during the High Middle Ages and the consolidation of strong nation-states during the troubled decades of economic expansion and internecine religious conflict from 1492 to 1648.

The model does not specify the same broad range of variables for the period of consolidation from the Treaty of Westphalia to the French Revolution: for this stage of development the model retains only one source of variation, the strength of representative institutions during the reign of absolutism.

This complex set of 'precondition variables' offers a springboard for the analysis of a set of 'intervening process variables' in the model: these are the variables posited as essential in any systematic account of the generation of cleavage fronts during the century and a half after the French Revolution. This was again a period of great political turmoil: the French Revolution set the stage for a wide variety of efforts of centralization, territorial consolidation, national self-assertion, and the Industrial Revolution brought about even greater contrasts between the economically advanced core territories and the stagnant provinces and peripheries. The interaction of these parallel revolutions generated complex variations in cleavage structures and these in their turn produced marked differences in the style and the structure of the emerging politics of mass mobilization across Western Europe.

This complex set of intervening process variables finally offers a springboard for the analysis of the 'explicanda', the variations in political response structures. Here again the model specifies two stages and three sectors of variation. At the first stage, questions are asked about the structuring of political alternatives: what sorts of options were set for the emerging mass citizenries and how stable, how vulnerable did these structures turn out to be? At the final stage questions are asked about the decisive dimensions of mass alignments in each territorial system: what is the weight of ethnic-religious-cultural commitments, what difference can be found between ascending and stagnant classes and strata, between the old and the new middle class, between the peasantry and the industrial working class?

The resulting system of variables is set out in Figure 3.1. Each of the variables is indicated in simple keyword style: full explication would take us far beyond the confines of this first statement.

The model reduces the great complexity of territorial histories to a series of concatenated constellations of variables over time. The variables can be used to characterize units at different levels of complexity. To use the term so dear to the *Annales* school, you can read the scheme *en aval*, downstream, as well as *en amont*, upstream. Reading the scheme *en aval*, you can use the variables as direct attributes of historical regions, *pays*, *Landschaften*, or you can characterize the regions contextually on the basis of the values for the larger units they become part of. An example: Alsace as a region can be characterized directly as located within the central city belt (var. I:T) but also contextually as integrated into the absolutist French system during the seventeenth to eighteenth centuries (var. III:T). By contrast, reading the scheme *en amont*, you start off with the territorial units established after, say, 1945, and characterize these either directly or through aggregations for their constituent units. To use France again as our example: post-1945 France may be characterized directly as administratively unitary and centralized (an extrapolation from var. II:T) but not as ethnically/linguistically homogeneous because of the incorporation of such culturally diverse territories as Brittany, Flanders, Lorraine, Alsace, Savoie and Nice, Occitania, Roussillon, and the Basque region. In most of the accounting schemes presented here we

74 FROM NATIONAL DEVELOPMENT TO GLOBAL COMMUNITY

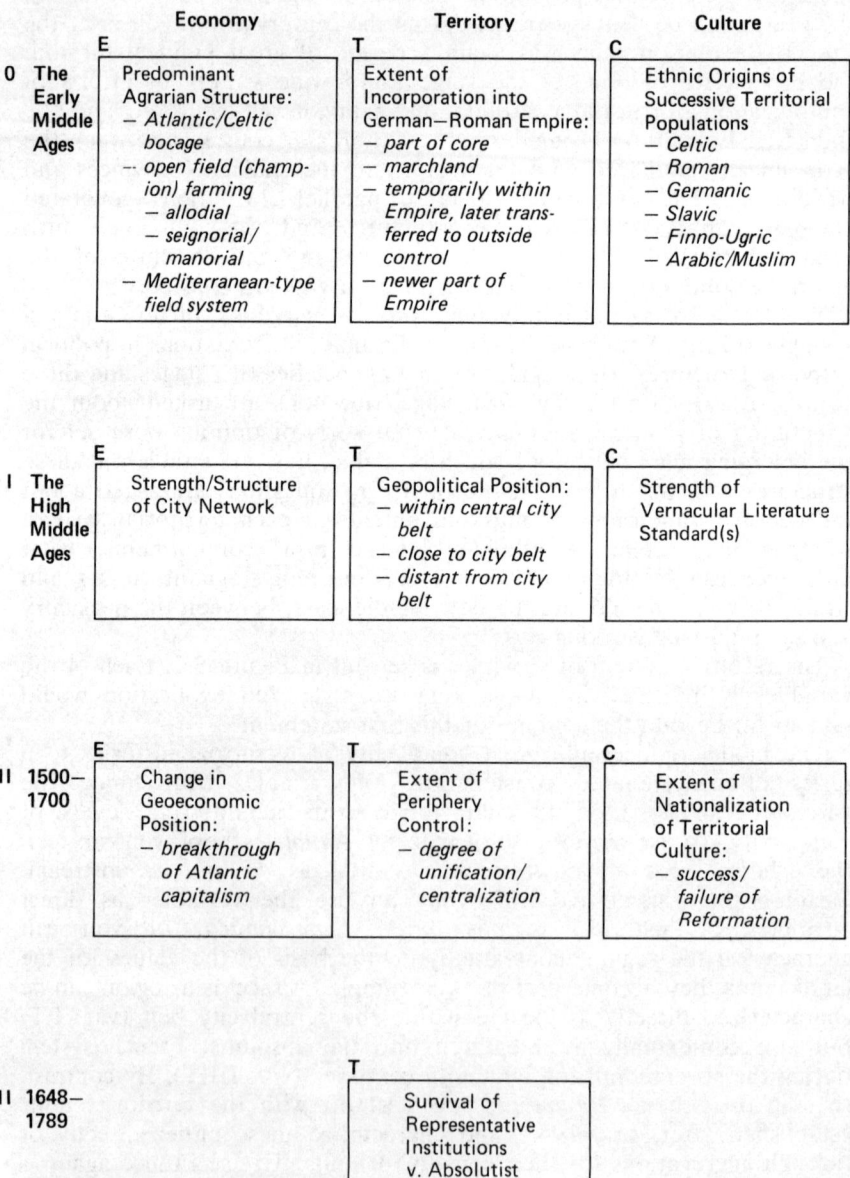

Figure 3.1 *The primary elements of the model.*

TOWARD AN EXPLANATION OF VARIATIONS IN W. EUROPE

INTERVENING PROCESS VARIABLES:
INTERACTION OF
NATIONAL WITH INDUSTRIAL REVOLUTION
1789–1920s

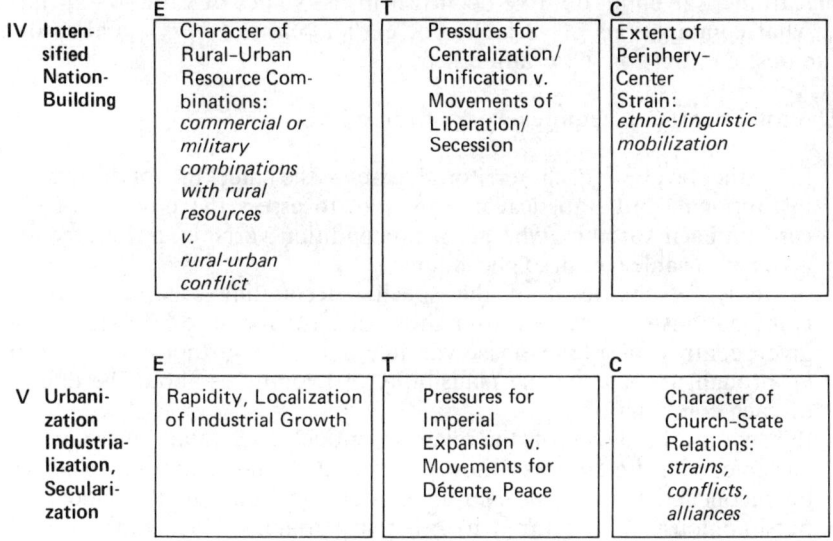

	E	T	C
IV Intensified Nation-Building	Character of Rural-Urban Resource Combinations: *commercial or military combinations with rural resources v. rural-urban conflict*	Pressures for Centralization/ Unification v. Movements of Liberation/ Secession	Extent of Periphery-Center Strain: *ethnic-linguistic mobilization*
V Urbanization Industrialization, Secularization	Rapidity, Localization of Industrial Growth	Pressures for Imperial Expansion v. Movements for Détente, Peace	Character of Church-State Relations: *strains, conflicts, alliances*

EXPLICANDA:
VARIATIONS IN POLITICAL RESPONSE STRUCTURES
1848–1950s

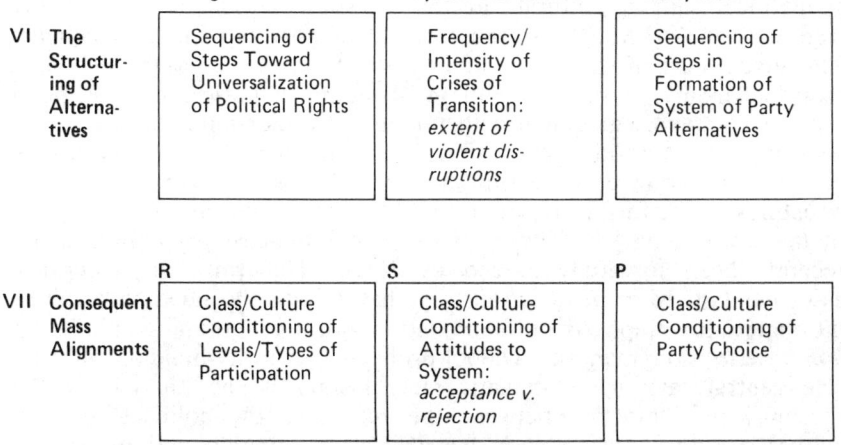

	Rights: extension	System alternatives	Party alternatives
VI The Structuring of Alternatives	Sequencing of Steps Toward Universalization of Political Rights	Frequency/ Intensity of Crises of Transition: *extent of violent disruptions*	Sequencing of Steps in Formation of System of Party Alternatives
	R	S	P
VII Consequent Mass Alignments	Class/Culture Conditioning of Levels/Types of Participation	Class/Culture Conditioning of Attitudes to System: *acceptance v. rejection*	Class/Culture Conditioning of Party Choice

shall follow this *en amont* procedure but we shall on several occasions have to break up our post-1945 units in order to bring out analytically important distinctions.

Reading the scheme *en amont* we proceed by way of retrospective diachronics: given an observed contrast in the values of variables at time t_i, what combinations of variables for earlier phases t_{i-1}, t_{i-2}, and so on, can best account for these differences.

The total operation requires work at three levels:

- first, the level of each territorial case – the checking of historical, institutional, and statistical information, to assess the position of the case on each variable, whether a precondition variable, an interactive process variable, or an explicandum.
- secondly, at the level of the specific accounting scheme – which combinations of variables offer the best basis for an explanation of a given contrast in a later-phase variable and what further evidence can be brought to bear on the plausibility of hypotheses about the effects of each combination?
- thirdly, at the level of the over-all model and total inventory of variables and dimensions – how can the different accounting schemes be reconciled within the over-all model and how can the model be parsimoniously restructured to bring in variables which have proved important elements in particular accounting schemes?

This is not the place to go into all the complexities of this effort at systematization. What needs to be emphasized is the multidimensionality of the model: at each stage it gives equal weight to economic-technological, political-territorial, and cultural-ethnic-religious dimensions. There is no economic determinism in the model, nor a geopolitical, nor a cultural: in this sense it seeks to combine the traditions of Karl Marx with those of Max Weber and Emile Durkheim. The model recognizes the great importance of the breakthrough to a world economy in the fifteenth to sixteenth centuries: on this point there is complete agreement with Immanuel Wallerstein. But the model also stresses the political and cultural preconditions of this breakthrough and the importance of territorial organizations and cultural identity structures in the further processes of change triggered by the emergence of the world economy. The need for a multidimensional approach has recently been forcefully argued by Jürgen Habermas in his critical assessment of Marxian macrohistory: he stresses the need to combine the materialist emphasis on *homo faber* with a cybernetic emphasis on *homo pictor*, on man the symbol-producing, identity-building animal.[8] The central task for systematic macrohistory is the analysis of the dynamics of interaction between the economic, the political, and the cultural systems: each system has its specific rhythm and its specific boundaries but the fate of a particular territory and its institutions is determined through processes of interaction among the systems, across their boundaries.

The model seeks to balance contextual totality against systematic parsimony. No single explanatory or intervening variable can be linked up with a dependent variable in isolation from the context, whether across systems or across stages. And no variable can justify its position in the scheme simply because it helps to describe the conditions in one particular system at one particular stage: to qualify for inclusion in the analysis a variable must specify a necessary or a sufficient condition for a patent difference in later-stage outcomes between at least two distinct systems. So far only part of the model has been subjected to detailed testing against such criteria. The bulk of the efforts thus far have concentrated on the link-ups between 'cleavage generation' variables (rows IV and V in Figure 3.1) and variables for the 'structuring of political alternatives' (row VI), particularly the steps in the extension of suffrage rights and the genealogies of party systems. An attempt has also been made at a systematization of the links between the precondition variables and the intervening process variables: these links have been expressed in a 'topological typology' of territories, in what has been called a 'conceptual map of Europe'. But very little has been done to link up variables across the entire range of stages in the model: this statement in fact represents a first serious effort in this direction.[9]

To make it possible to assess the potentialities of the model we shall first review quickly some of the simpler accounting schemes generated through the concatenations of several variables over time and then proceed to a discussion of analysis tasks at a higher level of complexity.

A 'Conceptual Map' of Europe

Three of the precondition variables combine to produce a 'conceptual map of Europe'. This is a schematized system of co-ordinates generated through the combination of one territorial, one economic, and one cultural variable in the model:

> I:T   Geopolitical position
> I:E   Strength/structure of city network
> II:C   Outcome of Reformation.

Variables I:T and I:E combine to produce a five-step west–east typology.[10] Variable II:C divides the Europe once dominated by the Roman Church into three slices from south to north. This gives the two-dimensional map set out in Figure 3.2.

This effort of schematization represents an attempt to come to grips with the 'great paradox of European development': the fact that the strongest and the most durable systems emerged at the periphery of the old empire; the heartlands, the Italian and German territories, remained fragmented and dispersed until the nineteenth century.

To quote from an early presentation of the 'map':

To reach some understanding of this paradox we have to reason in several steps:

(1) The heartland of the old Western Empire was studded with

THE 'STATE-ECONOMY' DIMENSION: WEST-EAST AXIS

Territorial centers City networks	Weak Weak *Seaward peripheries*	Strong Strong *Seaward empire nations*		Weak Strong *City-state Europe*		Strong Weak *Landward empire-nations*		Strong Weak *Landward buffers*
Conditions of Consolidation	Distant from city belt	Close to city belt	Integrated into larger system	Consociational formation	Fragmented until 19th century	Close to city belt	Distant from city belt	
Protestant State Church	Iceland ⟶ Scotland Wales	Norway ⟵ Denmark England			Hanse Germany	Sweden Prussia	Finland	
Mixed territories				Netherlands Switzerland	Rhineland Bohemia			Baltic territories
National Catholic Church	Ireland Brittany	France	'Lotharingia' Burgundy Arclatum			Bavaria	Poland ⟶	
Counter-Reformation		Spain Portugal	Belgium ⟵ Catalonia		Italy	Austria	Hungary ⟶	

THE 'STATE-CULTURE' DIMENSION: SOUTH-NORTH AXIS

* Arrows indicate change in geopolitical position. Territories underlined were sovereign powers 1648–1789

Figure 3.2 *A 'conceptual map' of sixteenth- to eighteenth-century Western Europe.*

cities in a broad trade route belt stretching from the Mediterranean to the east as well as west of the Alps northward to the Rhine and the Danube.
(2) This 'city belt' was at the same time the stronghold of the Roman Catholic Church; this territory had a high density of cathedrals, monasteries, and ecclesiastical principalities.
(3) The very density of established centers within this territory made it difficult to single out any one as superior to all others; there was no geography-given core area for the development of a strong territorial system.
(4) The resurrection of the Holy Roman Empire under the leadership of the four German tribes did not help to unify the territory; the emperors were prey to shifting electoral alliances; many of them were mere figureheads and the best and the strongest of them expended their energies in quarrels with the pope and with the Italian cities.
(5) By contrast, it proved much easier to develop effective core areas at the edges of the city-studded territories of the old empire; in these regions, centers could be built up under less competition and could achieve command of the resources in peripheral areas too far from the cities in the central trade belt.
(6) The earliest successes in such efforts of system-building at the edges of the old empire came in the west and in the north, in France, in England, in Scandinavia, later also in Spain; in all these cases the dynasties in the core areas were able to command resources from peripheral territories largely beyond the reach of the cities of the central trade belt.
(7) The second wave of successful center-building took place on the landward side: first the Habsburgs, with their core area in Austria; then the eastern march of the German Empire; next the Swedes; and finally, and decisively, the Prussians.
(8) The fragmented middle belt of cities and petty states was the scene of endless onslaughts, counter-moves and efforts of reorganization during the long centuries from Charlemagne to Bismarck: first, the French monarchs gradually took over the old Lotharingian-Burgundian buffer zone from Provence to Flanders and incorporated such typical trade cities as Avignon, Aix, and Lyons; secondly, the key cities to the north of the Alps managed to establish a defense league against all comers and gradually built up the Swiss confederation; similar leagues were established along the Rhine and across the Baltic and the North Sea but never managed to establish themselves as sovereign territorial formations; thirdly, the Habsburgs made a number of encroachments both on the west and on the east of the belt and for some time controlled the crucial territories at the mouth of the Rhine triggering the next successful effort of consociational confederation, the United Netherlands; finally, in the wake of the French Revolution, Napoleon moved across the

80 *FROM NATIONAL DEVELOPMENT TO GLOBAL COMMUNITY*

middle belt both north and south of the Alps and set in motion a series of efforts of unification which ended with the successes of the Prussians and the Piedmontese in 1870.[11]

A remarkably similar classification of the territories of Western Europe has been proposed by the French geographers Juillard and Nonn.[12] They distinguish between three main types of urban network and consequently three types of regional structure: the first

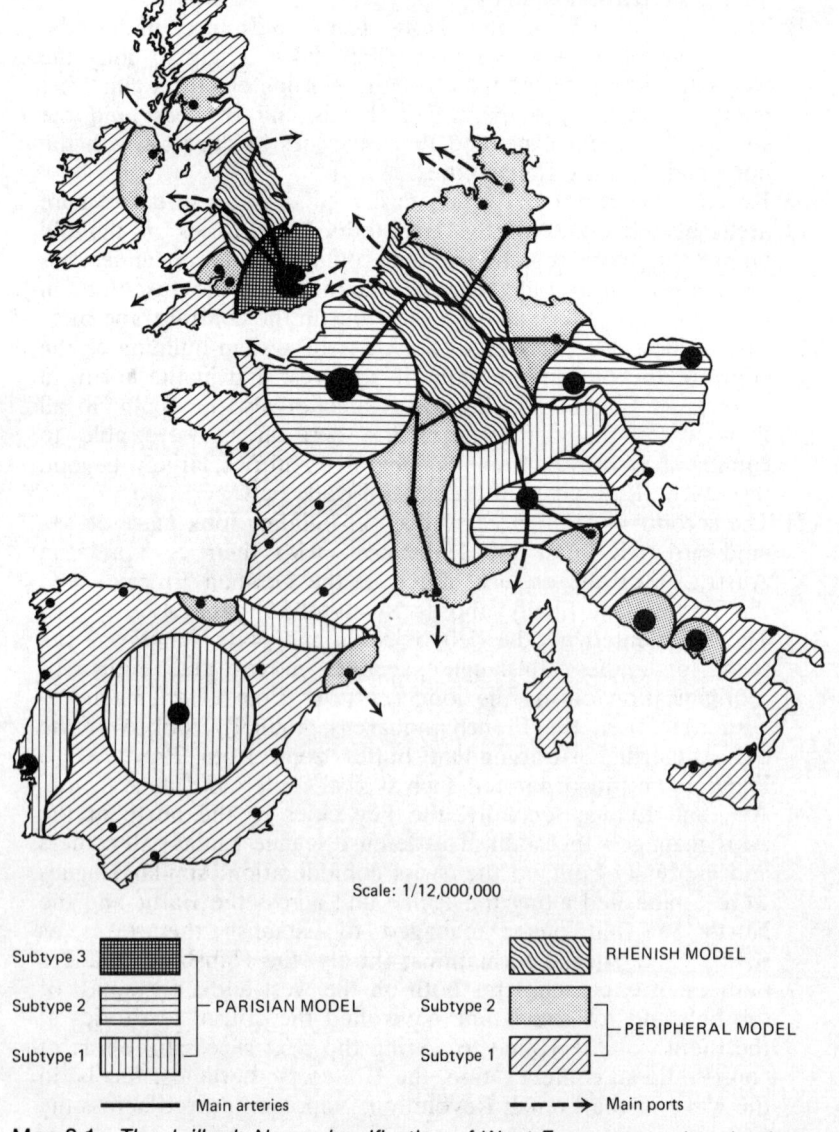

Map 3.1 *The Juillard–Nonn classification of West European center structures*

they call the *modèle rhénan*, the second the *modèle parisien* (three subtypes), and the third they call the *modèle périphérique* (two subtypes). The distribution of these territorial models is given in Map 3.1. The *modèle rhénan* corresponds to our city belt: Juillard and Nonn place this along the Rhine and in the English midlands. The *modèle parisien* corresponds to the seaward or the landward center formations in our conceptual map: Paris, London and Madrid, Munich and Vienna. There is a difference in the classification of Italy, however. Juillard and Nonn consider this a polycephalic constellation of three Parisian models: Milan, Rome, and Naples. This, of course, is a matter of cut-off points in the definition of network structures: what is important is that Italy contains at least three major centers within the same territory. The *modèle périphérique* finally covers the rest of Western Europe: these territories are either regions dominated by externally oriented centers (Dublin–Belfast, Glasgow–Edinburgh, Hamburg–Bremen, Bilbao–Catalonia) or simply backward regions with only weak centers.

The Juillard–Nonn scheme is essentially based on twentieth-century statistics for the central cities and their regions: for this very reason it is remarkable how close a fit we find with our own historical classification of territories.

Whichever the precise delimitations of each cell in the map, this 'typological-topological' scheme has proved useful in our efforts to sort out the preconditions for a broader range of variations across Western Europe at later stages of political development.

Applications to Concrete Tasks of Explanations: Examples

Let us first review the simplest schemes of explanation within this over-all model and then proceed to the discussion of the possibilities of combining this essentially geopolitical scheme with the geoeconomic dimensions pinpointed by Wallerstein.

Variations in Sequences of Suffrage Extension

The simplest scheme is probably the one proposed for the explanation of variations in the sequences of steps toward universal suffrage (see Figure 3.3).[13]

One message stands out clearly: a long history of continuous center-building favors a slow, step-by-step sequence of suffrage extensions. Systems passing abruptly from absolutism to representative rule also tended to pass quickly to maximal suffrage, at least for men: Denmark, Prussia, France. Threats of territorial secession also tended to trigger rapid increase in suffrage: Switzerland after the Sonderbundkreig, Norway in the 1890s, Finland in 1906. By contrast, the countries marked by strong Counter-Reformation traditions generally tended to go through longer series of steps towards full manhood suffrage: Austria, Spain, Belgium, Italy. Rapid democratization was clearly a strategy of national unification against entrenched particularisms, whether social, linguistic, or religious. Where the nation-building alliances had had early successes (England, Sweden) there was little

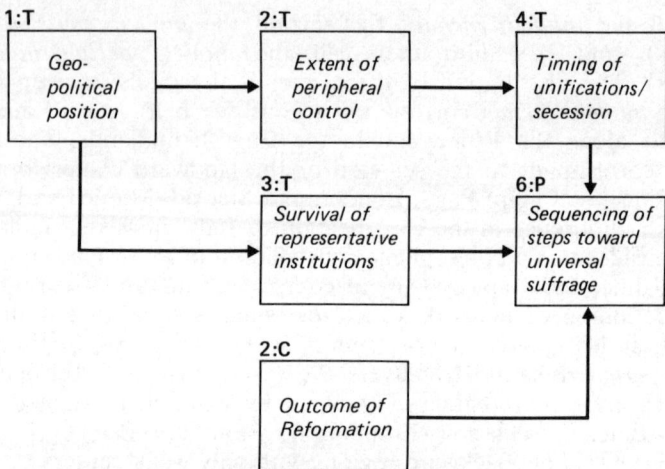

Figure 3.3 *An accounting scheme for variations in the processes leading to universal suffrage.*

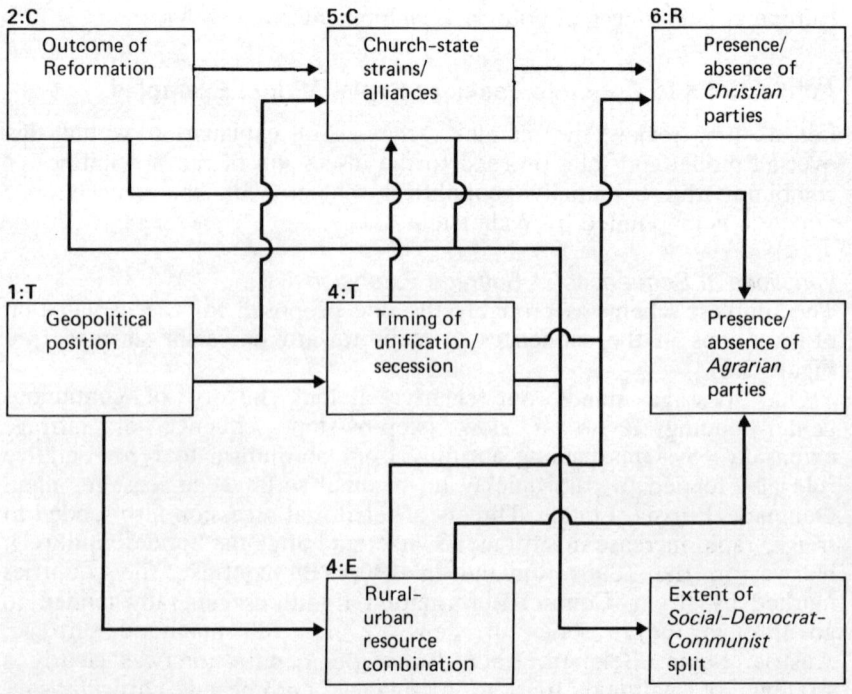

Figure 3.4 *An accounting scheme for variations in the structure of party systems under full suffrage.*

The values of the six variables in this scheme were linked up in these combinations:

Stage I Geopolitical position	Stage II Periphery control	Outcome of Reformation	Stage III Representative institutions	Stage IV Unification/secession	Stage V Sequencing of steps
Distant from central city belt	Extensive	Protestant domination	Minor interruptions only	Early unification	*Slow:* Great Britain Sweden
"	Extensive	"	"	Late secession	*Sudden:* Finland
"	Middling	"	Absolutist rule	Earlier secession	*Slower:* Norway
"	"	"	"	Late secession	*Slower:* Iceland
Close up to or in city belt	Minor	"	Representative rule	Early unification	*Slow:* Netherlands
"	"	"	"	Same, but *threat of secession*	*Sudden:* Switzerland
"	Middling	"	Absolutist rule	Early unification	*Sudden:* Denmark
"	Extensive	"	"	Late unification	*Sudden:* Prussia
"	"	National Catholicism	"	Early unification	*Sudden:* France
(any values)		Counter-Reformation dominant	"	(any value)	*Slow:* Austria Belgium Italy Spain

need to use this strategy. Where the Catholic Church was particularly well entrenched, it proved able to slow down the process of democratization and mass mobilization, at least for some time.

Variations in Party Systems

The explanation of variations in the content of mass politics calls for a very different structure of linkage: the focus changes from territoriality to functionality, from external to internal generation of cleavage fronts.

The simplest scheme for the explanation of variations in party systems would have to link up at least five conditioning variables with the most distinctive components of the structures of electoral alternatives.[14] See Figure 3.4.

The full combinatorics of this scheme are too complex to warrant presentation in this context. A few simple tables will help to bring out the gist of the scheme.

Let us first review the combinations of variables generating differences in the conditions for the emergence of distinctively Christian party fronts in the competitive pressures for mass mobilization. Conditions for the success of this type of political entrepreneurship differ markedly between the Protestant north and the Catholic south of Western Europe. See Table 3.1.

The table tells us that the conditions for the emergence of distinctive Christian parties are most favorable in the territories of the city belt, whether religiously mixed or predominantly Catholic. Such parties are least likely to occur in the peripheral territories last to achieve full independence: Iceland, Ireland, Finland. The table also brings out a difference among the long-established Catholic empire-nations at the edges of the city belt: no distinctive Christian parties in the countries where the church–state conflict was intense and protracted (France, Spain), strong Christian parties wherever there were closer links between church and state.

A very similar scheme can be established for the identification of the conditions for the emergence of distinctive agrarian parties (see Table 3.2). Three of the five key dimensions turn out to discriminate significantly in a parallel scheme proposed for the explanation of variations in the severity of splits within the working-class party fronts in Western Europe (see Table 3.3). The message is simple: in Protestant Europe the latest nation-states to be unified or to secede were most vulnerable to severe splits within the working class; in Catholic Europe the same was the case in the territories which had experienced the sharpest conflict over church–state relations. In both cases there was a clear-cut syndrome: difficulties of elite integration in an early phase of nation-building made for strains within the working-class leadership and set the stage for deeper communist–social democrat splits than elsewhere in Europe.

The Use of the Model in the Explanation of Fascist Victories

Having given these examples of the basic style of reasoning in this topological-typological effort of systematization we shall now proceed to

Table 3.1 The 'conceptual map' of variations in the mass politicization of church–sect–state conflicts

II: C: Outcome of Reformation	I: T: GEOPOLITICAL POSITION				
	Seaward peripheries	Seaward empire-nations	City belt	Landward empire-nations	Landward peripheries
– Protestant domination, few Catholics IV: T: Timing of unification/ secession – early		Denmark: Broad liberal front: recently minor Christian party		Sweden: Liberals split over prohibition: minor Christian party	
– late	Iceland: Broad agrarian front. *No* Christian party	Norway: Broad liberal front: split in 1920s. *Significant* Christian party			Finland: Christian movement aggregated within *nationalist* front
– Significant Catholic minority	Ulster: Significant Catholic party	Rest of UK: Christian movements aggregated within *liberal* front	Netherlands: Significant Calvinist and Catholic parties. Rhineland, Germany, Switzerland Important Catholic parties	Prussia: Broad conservative front. *No* Christian party	
– Catholic domination V: C: Church–state relations – Alliance 19th century	Ireland: Church interests aggr. within *Nationalist* fronts			Belgium: Strong Catholic party	Austria: Strong Catholic party
– Conflict		France, Spain: Church interests defended within *right* fronts	German Reich, Italy: Strong Catholic parties		

Table 3.2 The 'conceptual map' of variations in the mass politicization of rural–urban conflicts

	Seaward peripheries	Seaward empire-nations	City belt	Landward empire-nations	Landward peripheries
II: C Outcome of Reformation – Protestant			All Nordic countries: Strong agrarian parties Netherlands: minor peasant party Switzerland: agrarian party (PAB)		IV: E Rural–urban alliances – none
– Protestant	UK: rural interests defended within conservative front			Prussia: same as for UK	– rural–commercial (UK) or rural–military (Prussia)
– Catholic	Ireland: Minor farmers' party		All other Catholic countries: Rural interests defended within Catholic or conservative fronts		

broaden the range of the 'explanatory potential' of the model by adding further dimensions.

The initial accounting scheme generated by the model focused on variations that had largely manifested themselves in each country by the end of the First World War: variables VI:R and VI:P in Figure 3.1.

Very different variables seemed to be required in accounting for the contrasting developments within Europe during the late 1920s and the 1930s: in identifying the conditions that made for victories or defeat for the nationalist-fascist monolithic party fronts that emerged during this period (variable VI:S).

Scholars have diverged in their definitions and their interpretations of fascism ever since the March on Rome. The divergencies increased dramatically after Hitler's *Machtergreifung* in 1933 and the Dolfuss coup in 1934. What did these ideologies, these movements, these strategies have in common? Was there a core concept of fascism and how could this essence be identified in the welter of complex interactions in each concrete development?

However difficult this search for conceptual communalities, there was, by the time of the final confrontation during the Second World War, not

Table 3.3 A 'Conceptual map' of the cases of deep Communist–Socialist split

	Seaward peripheries	Seaward empire-nations	City belt	Landward empire-nations	Landward peripheries
IV: T: Timing of unification/ secession – Early Protestant					
– Late	Iceland: deep split	Norway: split early 1920s	Reich-Prussia: deep split during Weimar Republic		Finland: deep split
V: C: Church state relations – Alliance Catholic					
– Conflict		France, Spain deep splits	Reich-Prussia: deep split during Weimar Republic Italy: deep split		

much doubt about the actual alignment of cases: five of the countries of Western Europe had succumbed to movements of this general type and been turned into plebiscitarian one-party dictatorships.

However divergent their national trajectories, these five countries, Italy, Germany, Austria, Spain, and Portugal, had succumbed to similar fates:

- they had all experienced a number of competitive elections under broadening suffrage criteria and had passed through a shorter or longer period of rapid mobilization of new strata of the territorial population under mass parties and parallel movements and agencies;
- they had all run into a series of constitutional crises in the management of these waves of competitive mobilization, and had finally succumbed to a movement determined to put an end to such pluralistic tolerance and to introduce monolithic control of mass politics;
- these monolithic movements had all reached their positions of dominance through extensive use of extra-legal violence against political opponents and had maintained their power through ruthless mobilization against internal no less than external enemies.

Other countries in Western Europe had been through similar phases of development: extensions of the suffrage, phases of competitive mass mobilization, sequences of crises in the management of the strains generated by such competitive pressures. But they had not succumbed to monolithic control under one mass movement. Some of the countries came near to the breaking point: England during the Irish crisis just before the First World War, Finland during the first couple of decades after independence, France in 1934. But of the seventeen countries within what we would today call Western Europe only five fell prey to a monolithic movement dedicated to the overthrow of the pluralist system of multi-party competition.

We exclude from this reckoning the whole of Eastern Europe. In none of these countries do we find anything approaching the step-by-step sequence that led up to the fascist victories in the five Western cases. What we find are at best brief and erratic periods of competitive politics preceding the onset of military–authoritarian rule and, after the Second World War, the victory of monolithic parties exerting strict control of all sources of pluralism. The one exception is Czechoslovakia. Here we find an impressive series of regularly organized competitive elections after independence, but no endogenously generated victory of monolithic forces: national socialism was imposed from outside, through military occupation.

There were obviously movements of fascist–national socialist inspiration all across Eastern as well as Western Europe and they are certainly all worth detailed scrutiny. Our concern in this analysis, however, is not with the proliferation of movements or ideologies of this type, but with the conditions for their success within systems of competitive politics: with the characteristics of the national coalition structure which made it possible for such movements to seize central power and to establish effective monolithic control. This leaves us with five Western cases: Germany and Italy, Austria, Spain, and Portugal.

To avoid misunderstanding: we do not claim that the regimes established in each of the theses five cases were 'fascist'. There were indeed important differences in the structure and the contents of the victorious ideologies and these were clearly reflected in the institutions built up and the practices followed by the victors. Our analysis concentrates on the one feature these five cases have in common: the sequence leading from a series of competitive elections under multiparty systems to the victory of a monolithic alliance and the abolition of rights of pluralist opposition. This is the sequence we find in our five cases[15] and not in the other twelve. How can we account for these differences in the outcomes of the mobilization processes between these five and the others? How can we identify the prerequisites for success and the conditions leading to failure in the struggle to maintain competitive pluralism under full-suffrage mobilization?

Let us go back to the conceptual maps set out in full detail in Figure 3.2. One conclusion is clear: our five cases fall into several distinctive cells of the map; they do not form one single cluster. They do share one basic set of characteristics, however: they are either located inside the central belt of cities from the Mediterranean across the Alps to the North Sea and the Baltic or their territories were historically closely linked to this belt, whether on the seaward side as in the cases of Spain and Portugal, or on the landward, as in the case of Prussia-Austria. But these characterizations suffer from a considerable margin of imprecision: there were other territories within as well as close to the city belt and these did not succumb to monolithic movements of the fascist type. To identify a distinctive configuration for the five, to develop an adequate accounting scheme, we have to incorporate further variables.

Three variables appear crucial in the further specification of conditions for violent breakdowns in the process of mass democratization.

The first of these was not explicitly spelled out in the original model: it is implicit, however, in the ordering of the basic variable I:T: 'geopolitical position'. We shall call this component the 'strength of the imperial heritage'. The early history of Europe can be telescoped into three successive failures of internally generated empire-building: the fall of Rome; the fragmentation and ultimate disintegration of the empire of Charlemagne and its German successors; the failure of the Habsburgs to achieve control of Europe from their strongholds in the two corner territories, Austria and the Iberian peninsula. These successive failures left bitter memories of past glory in four territories: in a fragmented Italy, in the vast German congeries of petty princedoms and free cities, in Austria, and in Spain and Portugal.

What made these failures of empire an even greater source of pent-up aggression was the subsequent peripheralization within the emerging geoeconomics of capitalism. This is our variable II:E: the central variable in Immanuel Wallerstein's pathbreaking reinterpretation of European history since 1492. The opening up of new territories across the oceans and the rapid expansion of trade set the stage for a gigantic struggle between south and north in Europe: the Habsburgs tried desperately to establish a new great empire across the dorsal spine of Europe but to no avail. The Middle Ages had left too strong a heritage of multi-centered diversity: the city-studded belt from Northern Italy to the North Sea, the empire-nations on the seaward and later the landward edges. The decisive battle was fought out between the Habsburgs and France: this ended with bankruptcy and the stalemate Treaty of Cateau-Cambrésis in 1559. In the next round, the hegemony moved to the north-west: Atlantic capitalism established its core territories in the Netherlands and in England and the old strongholds of imperial power in Europe were reduced to what Wallerstein calls 'semi-peripheries'. The final *dénouement* came with the Treaty of Westphalia and the subsequent division of the Habsburg territories: Austria and Spain were left each in their corner and could no longer hope to achieve mastery in Europe. Portugal, for sixty-two years a territory under Spain, retained her overseas empire but her influence in European affairs was severely reduced. In the central belt, Germany and Italy were left fragmented and stagnant: both territories strongly marked by imperial traditions, both of them culturally unified through remarkably vigorous standard languages, both of them characterized by dispersed networks of cities and princedoms dominated by patriciates embittered by centuries of stagnation.

The fates of Austria, Spain, and Portugal were largely sealed during this stage of geoeconomic restructuring from 1500 to 1789. The trajectories of Germany and Italy were decisively changed in the wake of the French Revolution and the short-lived spurt of empire-building that ended at Waterloo. The Napoleonic Wars set the stage for a massive upsurge of nationalism in the two territories and the subsequent spread of the Industrial Revolution increased the pressures for joint action against the hegemonic core of world capitalism. The massive movements of territorial unification were triggered through the interaction of the two revolutions: the national and the industrial. In fact the one revolution fed on the other. The dynamic sectors of the bourgeoisie saw great opportunities in the new industrial technologies but they could only defend themselves against competition from the advanced economies through alliances with unified territorial powers. In addition, the traditionalist elements of the bourgeoisie, the artisans and the family-sized merchant firms, tended to rally to the nationalist fronts simply in the hope that unification would protect them against the worst ravages of rapid industrialization. The representatives of the bourgeois corporations proved unable to solve these problems of national unity against foreign economic pressures at the Frankfurter Parliament in 1848. The next step was an alliance with a stronger territorial power to the east: this was Bismarck's great achievement. He extended the alliance already established in Prussia between the territorial administration and the landowners to a broader alliance with large chunks of the bourgeoisie of western and southern Germany: this alliance built up the power of the Reich and made it a real threat to the dominant capitalist powers England, France, and later the United States. A parallel development took place in Italy. The heartland of the Roman Empire was again unified but there was an important difference in the direction of integration: in Germany, the decisive movement of integration originated in the rural east, in the militarized periphery; in Italy the final decisions were taken in the urban north and the movement spread southward into a stagnant periphery.

Our five cases clearly differ on a number of important variables but they still share three decisive characteristics:

- first, the imperial heritage;
- secondly, the geoeconomic peripheralization brought about by the two great waves of capitalist advance, first the restructuring of trade flows in the sixteenth century, secondly the lags in the spread of industrial technology in the nineteenth;
- thirdly, the successive attempts to re-establish their position in the international system through deliberate military-industrial alliances.

The first of these characteristics can be generated through a combination of two successive territorial variables: I:T and II:T in Figure 3.1.

The second characteristic represents a value of variable II:E 'change in geoeconomic positions' but this is again linked to the much later variable V:E 'rapidity, localization of industrial growth'.

And the third characteristic finally represents one of the possible resource combinations listed under variable IV:E in Figure 3.1.

However similar on these three variables, the five cases clearly differ in their territory-building histories: early center-building but arrested national integration in Austria and in Spain, early nation-building but frustrated empire-building in the case of Portugal, late center-building within culturally highly homogeneous territories in Germany and in Italy.

Let us now go back to the 'conceptual map' to pin down the additional sources of differentiation: see Figure 3.5. The recast map brings out the crucial contrasts in territorial fates: the north-western geoeconomic core against the peripheralized territories to the south and

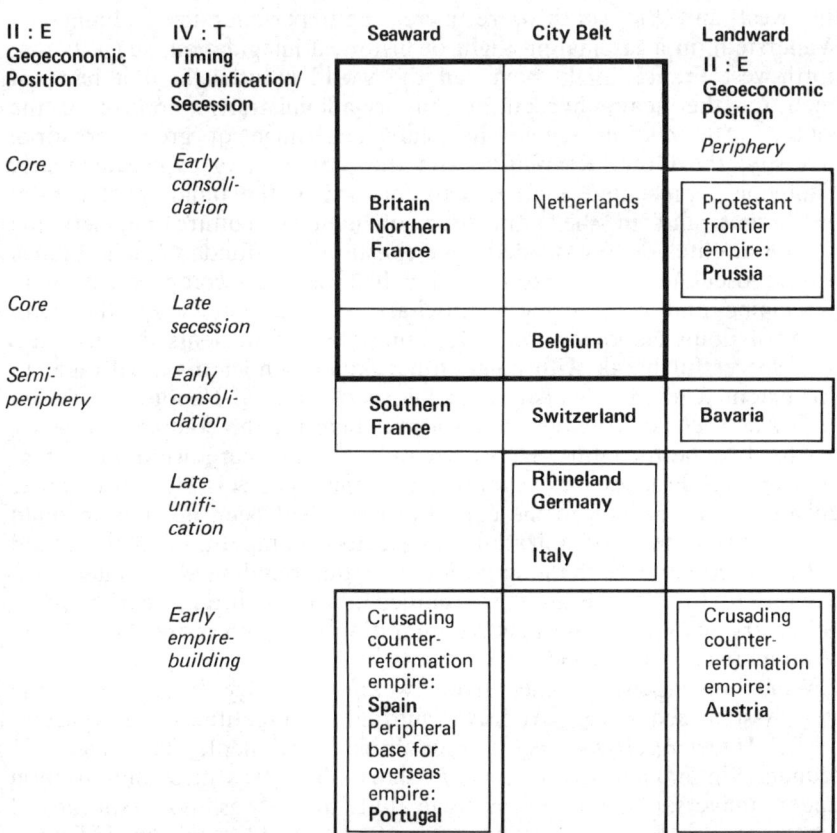

Figure 3.5 Geoeconomics, geopolitics, and territorial consolidation: a recasting of the 'conceptual map' for Western Europe.
Note: territories enclosed in double frames made up the five key cases of violent breakdown of competitive mass politics; those in heavy frame were the capitalist core from the seventeenth century on.

to the east; the early histories of consolidation in the four corners and, remarkably, at two transition areas in the city belt, the Netherlands and Switzerland; the much later consolidation or secession of the units within the rest of the city belt.

Perhaps the most intriguing of all the comparisons suggested by these juxtapositions is the one between France and our five cases of fascist victory. France was built up through continuous accretion of territories in all directions from the initial core. This congeries of differently structured units was kept together against heavy odds: the constant threats of 'exit' at the borders[16] could only be contained through the build-up of a highly centralized military-bureaucratic machinery but even this heavy machinery could not move towards full unification of institutional structures during the *ancien régime*. What proved even more important was the extreme unevenness of economic developments: the north-west was part of the early core of capitalist expansion while the west and the south were increasingly peripheralized. Immanuel Wallerstein, in a fascinating flight of historical imagination, suggests that north-west France might have led the world industrially if it had not been for the heavy burden of military-administrative control of the south.[17] The *ancient régime* had left a heritage of great territorial diversity: the Great Revolution and the paroxysm of expansion under Napoleon represented a great leap forward in the building of central institutions and in the unification of national culture but left the territorial elites deeply divided over constitutional fundamentals. France was to oscillate for a century and a half between complex corporate bargaining and centralizing plebiscitarianism. In one sense the *coup d'état* of Louis Napoleon on 2 December 1851 represents the first case of a successful break with competitive politics under mass suffrage: to this extent Karl Marx's analysis of the social basis of Napoleon's victory in *Der achtzehnte Brumaire* offers a paradigm for the comparative study of the twentieth-century fascist victories.[18] But there were important differences: France had experienced one or two elections under universal suffrage before the coup but there had been no time to build up nationwide mass organizations for electoral competition. What turned out to be crucial was the long period of nation-building at the mass level from 1875 to 1914: France was unified not only through conscription, obligatory schooling, and massive migration but even more through the development of nationwide party fronts.[19]

What distinguished the five twentieth-century cases was the step-by-step sequence: extensive suffrage, competitive mass parties, crisis, *Machtergreifung* by a monolithic movement. The 1848–51 sequence in France was simply too short: there was mass mobilization under universal manhood suffrage but there was no tradition of organized electoral competition, no party system to break up. If France had succumbed to fascism in 1934 the parallel with Germany and Italy would have been only too obvious: a long period of multiparty elections under the Third Republic and then the violent overthrow of party competition by a monolithic movement. But France did not succumb to internal disruption: the process of nation-building, at the mass as well as the elite levels, had gone far enough to prevent an effective coalition with the radical right.

The analysis of the French case is important in several perspectives. In my own 'typological-topological' scheme France represents a nodal area: halfway between the inland city belt and the advancing ocean-based empires to the west, halfway between the nation-building Protestantism of the north and the cross-territorial Church of Rome to the south. In Wallerstein's 'map' of Europe, the north of France maintained a position within the core of the emerging world economy, while the south was part of the peripheralized Mediterranean area. This position at the 'cross-roads' helps to account for the two Napoleons and for the long series of constitutional crises in the era of mass politics: it also helps to account for the extraordinary viability of the Third Republic and the resistance against the attempts at fascist takeover.[20]

Concluding Note

Generalizing beyond Wallerstein's initial design, we might conclude, at least for the period up to 1939, that the chances for the survival of competitive multiparty politics was greatest within the capitalist core of the world economy, that the likelihood of fascist-type victories was greatest in the semi-peripheralized territories of earlier city-studded empires – and that the probability of communist-type victories was greatest in the much more markedly peripheral areas of earlier empires of the 'agrarian bureaucracy' type, empires with poorly developed commercial-industrial bourgeoisies. This formulation comes very close to Barrington Moore's in his great work *The Social Origins of Dictatorship and Democracy*: again an attempt to identify in the early configurations of state-building alliances the preconditions for the defeat or victory of totalitarian mass movements at a much later stage in the history of each system. The structure of Wallerstein's analysis differs fundamentally from Moore's but it still leads to a very similar classification of long-term trajectories.

This reinforces us in our belief that progress can be made toward some higher level of systematization – if not strict formalization – of the basic dimensions of macrohistory. We are the first to concede the inadequacies of the current efforts of systematization, yet we venture to believe that this step-by-step process of confrontation, recasting, and retesting of models will eventually help us forward toward the construction of a unified theory of sociocultural, economic, and political change, at least for the territories of Europe once under the domination of the Roman Empire or the Church of Rome. What is important is that these efforts of schematization and of systematization be taken seriously by work-a-day historians and data-handling social scientists: that efforts be made to broaden the empirical bases for the testing and the questioning of the implications of the models, not only within particular territories but across them. If our discussions of alternative schemes of interpretation will also have consequences at this level of concrete historical analysis we shall not have worked in vain.

Notes: Chapter 3

1 'The comparative study of political participation', first published in *Essays on the Behavioral Study of Politics*, ed. Austin Ranney (Urbana, Ill.: University of Illinois Press, 1962); later reprinted as ch. 1 of Stein Rokkan, *Citizens, Elections, Parties* (Oslo: Universitetsforlaget, 1970).
2 'The mobilization of the periphery', originally published in *Approaches to the Study of Political Participation*, ed. Stein Rokkan (Bergen: Chr. Michelsen Institute, 1962); later reprinted as ch. 6 of *Citizens*.
3 'Dimensions of state formation and nation-building', in *The Formation of National States in Western Europe*, ed. Charles Tilly (Princeton, NJ: Princeton University Press, 1975), pp. 562–600; and S. N. Eisenstadt and Stein Rokkan (eds), *Building States and Nations*, 2 vols (Beverly Hills, Calif.: Sage, 1973–4).
4 S. M. Lipset and Stein Rokkan, 'Introduction', in *Party Systems and Voter Alignments*, ed. S. M. Lipset and Stein Rokkan (New York: The Free Press, 1967); further developed in Stein Rokkan, *Citizens*, ch. 3.
5 A first formulation was presented in 'The structuring of mass politics in the smaller European democracies', *Comparative Studies in Society and History*, vol. 10, no. 2 (1968), pp. 173–210; this was later incorporated in ch. 3 of Rokkan, *Citizens, Elections, Parties*.
6 A first version was published in Vol. I of *Building States and Nations*, ed. Eisenstadt and Rokkan. Later versions are found in 'Dimensions of state formation and nation-building'; and in 'Entries, voices, exits', *Social Science Information*, vol. 13, no. 1 (1974), pp. 39–53.
7 Stein Rokkan et al., *Centre-Periphery Structures in Western Europe. A Data Workbook* (in preparation).
8 *Zur Rekonstruktion des historischen Materialismus* (Frankfurt/Main: Suhrkamp Verlag, 1976).
9 A first, cryptic formulation was presented in 'Entries, voices, exits'. This was expanded a bit further in two notes prepared for meetings of the Association Française de Science Politique in June 1974 and in December 1976: 'Macro-histoire et analyse comparative des processus de développement politique' and 'Une famille de modèles pour l'histoire comparée de l'Europe Occidentale'. A parallel version of the scheme has been worked out in Bernt Hagtvet and Stein Rokkan, 'The conditions of fascist victory', in *Who Were the Fascists?*, ed. B. Hagtvet, S. U. Larsen, and J. P. Myklebust (Oslo: Universitetsforlaget, 1980).
10 This West–East gradient represents a central dimension in two much-discussed works of macrohistorical analysis: Immanuel Wallerstein, *The Modern World-System* (New York: Academic Press, 1974), chs 2 and 6; Perry Anderson, *Passages from Antiquity to Feudalism* (London: NLB, 1974), pp. 1–3 and 213–64; and *Lineages of the Absolutist State* (London: NLB, 1974), pp. 195–235 and 430–1. The West–East array in the 'conceptual map' combines two different dimensions, however, and establishes a typology of conditions for political-economic development: a city-studded belt with only minimal *Flächenstaat* elements in the middle, in the West a set of seaward empires-turned-nation-states with extensive peripheries as well as strong commercial cities, in the east similar expanses of periphery waiting to be mastered but much weaker city networks. Jürgen Habermas, commenting on an earlier version of my 'conceptual map', has brought out with great clarity the double significance of the city belt for the territorial fates of Germany and Italy: the cities played a crucial role in the initial development of capitalism but could not compete with the *Flächenstaaten*, the territorial nation-states, at the stage of the generalization (*Durchsetzung*) of capitalist modes of production (see his *Zur Rekonstruktion des historischen Materialismus*, p. 258). This contrast between city belt and territorial nation-state clearly needs further differentiation in the light of Wallerstein's analysis. The contrast between the two first core territories of the new Atlantic–Indian Ocean geoeconomy, Portugal and the United Provinces, can clearly be analyzed within the combinatories of the conceptual map: both were able to exploit their position at the edge of the Atlantic but the Dutch core territory was closer to the North Sea–Rhine–Italy trade routes and could benefit from the multiplier effects across this dense network of well-established

cities. The Netherlands was in its turn handicapped in the contest with other core territories with larger peripheries: England and later the United States.
11 Stein Rokkan, 'Cities, States . . .', p. 81.
12 E. Juillard and H. Nonn, *Espaces et régions en Europe occidentale* (Paris: Editions de GNRS, 1976).
13 For a detailed discussion of the sources of variation, see Stein Rokkan, *Citizens, Elections, Parties*, pp. 79–87.
14 For a detailed discussion, see ibid., pp. 96–138.
15 We are well aware that there are important differences between the five countries in the character of the sequences leading up to the victory of the monolithic alliances. Portugal is clearly a marginal case in this classification. Stanley Payne has established the following comparative table of sequences for Italy, Spain, and Portugal:

Phase	Italy	Spain	Portugal
Elitist doctrinaire liberalism	1860–1876	1843–1881	1833–1857
Two-party *trasformista* liberalism	1876–1898	1881–1899	1857–1906
Pre-mass politics reformism	1899–1915	1899–1923	1910–1917
Authoritarian interlude	1915–1918	1923–1931	1917–1918
Compulsive mass politics	1919–1922	1931–1936	1919–1926

But Payne comments that the last category 'does not fully fit Portugal, which *never really knew a phase of genuine mass politics*' (my italics); see 'Spanish fascism in comparative perspective', pp. 142–69 in *Reappraisals of Fascism*, ed. Henry A. Turner, Jr (New York: Watts, 1975). We still feel justified in including Portugal with the other four: even though the level of mass mobilization was low, there was a sequence leading from competitive electoral politics to the victory of a monolithic movement.
16 For a further development of this theme see S. E. Finer, 'State-building, state boundaries and border control', *Social Science Information*, vol. 13, nos 4 and 5 (1974), pp. 79–126.
17 Wallerstein, *Modern World-System*, p. 296. The north–south, east–west gradients within France have fascinated scholars at least since the revolution. The early collection of thematic maps by Adolphe d'Angeville, *Essai sur la statistique da la population française* (Paris, 1836), reprinted with an introduction by E. LeRoy Ladurie (Paris: Mouton, 1969), called attention to the important dividing line from St Malo to Geneva: the economically advanced regions to the north of this line, the backward regions to the south and west. François Furet and Jacques Ozouf have recently added another perspective on these regional contrasts: they have analyzed in great detail data on the spread of literacy since the sixteenth century and have concluded that the most marked contrast opposes the north–east and the west (a triangle running roughly from the Spanish border on the Atlantic, northward to Brittany and eastward toward Valence on the Rhône), see *Lire et écrire: L'alphabétisation des français de Calvin à Jules Perry* (Paris: Editions de Minuit, 1977), esp. vol. 1, concluding chapter.
18 For an example of the use of Marx's *Brumaire* analysis in current theorizing about fascism, see Axel Kuhn, *Das faschistische Herrschaftssystem und die moderne Gesellschaft* (Hamburg: Hoffmann & Campe, 1973), ch. III A.2, 'Das Vorbild: Die Bonapartismus-theorie von Karl Marx', pp. 102–13.
19 For a fresh reinterpretation of this late phase of nation-building see Eugen Weber, *Peasants into Frenchmen* (Stanford, Calif.: Stanford University Press, 1976).
20 For a detailed analysis of the French–German differences in levels of economic organization and their consequences for the vulnerability to fascist takeover, see Charles S. Maier, *Recasting Bourgeois Europe* (Princeton, NJ: Princeton University Press, 1975), especially ch. 8: 'The Radical Socialist constituency avoided fascism in the 1930s for the same reason that it had endured economic confusion in the 1920s: *the continuing viability of economically archaic modes*. French democracy was to remain buffered by the society's *proverbial reluctance to organize*' (p. 511, my italics).

4
Limits to Governmental Growth

CHARLES LEWIS TAYLOR

Governmental expenditures in most countries have grown rapidly in recent years.[1] Modern governments are expected to provide a much wider range of services than were traditional ones and the costs of these services, relative to those offered privately, have risen.[2] Opposition is occasionally registered by such movements as the Poujardists in France, the followers of Glistrup in Denmark, and the supporters of Proposition 13 in California; but pressures toward further expansion have generally been stronger. Governments continue to grow both in absolute terms and in relation to the total size of the economy.

One does not have to be very conservative, economically or politically, to recognize that this kind of growth cannot go on for ever. Whatever the ideological program of the decision-makers, there is a practical limit to the proportion of total economic resources that can be absorbed by the government. Not even the most ideologically committed socialist regime has been willing to eliminate the private sector; the administrative costs would be far too high.[3] Identifying this practical limit, however, is likely to prove difficult. The mixture of market forces and political allocation depends at least in part on the total economic resources available.[4] It also depends upon policy preferences of elite and population. The point beyond which government cannot go without dire consequences differs from country to country and by circumstances within country.

Charting the size and growth of governments, nevertheless, may allow us to answer some questions related to the limits of expansion. Is the rate of growth in government revenue speeding up or slowing down? Are there clues as to whether or not revenues are outgrowing available resources? Are the trends the same in all countries or do various countries follow differing patterns? In other words, is the rate of growth slowing down in some countries but speeding up in others? Can these countries be distinguished in terms of their levels and rates of economic growth, their political orientation, or their degrees of social mobilization? What in fact is the situation with regard to government growth cross-nationally?

One explanation for governmental growth is provided by Karl Deutsch's theory of social mobilization. As noted already by Foltz, the uprooting of people from their old ways and their induction into new ways bring increasing expectations of goods and services, many of which can be supplied by government. People turn to the national government with new demands and new supports which both allow it and push it to expand and to mobilize. Indeed, according to Deutsch, governments which do not change face major problems. In his article on the measurement of political development,[5] he insisted that as social mobilization increases, a government must enlarge its capabilities to find resources for the budget, to limit inflation, to maintain full employment, to redistribute land, to slow down population growth, to strengthen the armed forces, to promote education, to accelerate economic development, and to carry through other domestic policies and reforms.

Expansion of these capabilities in turn requires increased mobilization of the population. A government cannot operate effectively without the intelligent and skillful co-operation of its people. Social mobilization then is both a cause of and is caused by modernization of which governmental expansion is an integral part. Whether as cause or as product, however, social mobilization is a source of additional political and economic demands.

Deutsch argues that the balance between demands made upon a government and the level of that government's capabilities is of critical importance for stable social change. It is not surprising, therefore, that governments have attempted to expand in order to meet the demands levied upon them in increasing degree during the last twenty-five years or more. Elites have not gotten all the stability, nor masses all the services they wanted, but both social mobilization and government capabilities have certainly increased.[6] And growth in the proportion of economic resources used by governments has kept pace.

Much of this postwar social and political change has occurred during a period of relatively rapid growth in the world economy. New resources were sufficient to support both higher governmental expenditures and enlarged private income simultaneously. Although the former was growing as a proportion of the total, the total itself was also growing rapidly enough to allow the aggregate level of the latter to increase. Even so, balance between demands and capabilities has not always been maintained even under these favorable conditions. To what extent will such a balance be possible if economic growth rates turn downward or if the growth rate of gross domestic product is unable to keep up with the growth rate of government expenditure? Will the socially mobilized people expect too much and be willing to pay too little when additional public benefits can be provided only by reducing real private income? Will the taxpayers' revolt become a standard part of the political scene and, at the same time, will citizens continue to demand services which governments are no longer able to provide?

We can only speculate on answers to these questions. At some point in each country, some kind of limit will be imposed on the proportion of gross national product which the government can take as revenue. If rapid or even moderate social mobilization continues after that point and has the effects that Deutsch has suggested, imbalance between demands and capabilities is likely.[7] Is it possible to identify signs of imbalance among economic resources, social mobilization, and government growth in some countries? In what types of countries is the imbalance most likely to take place?

More complete answers to questions on the limits to government growth require more direct measurements of demands being placed upon governments – not only by people but also by the changing environment. They require more direct measurements of the abilities of governments to respond to these challenges and of the probable reactions of people to likely government responses. Also needed are estimates of the degree to which governments are overloaded in terms of diminished authority and increased value conflict,[8] the extent to which government bureaucrats themselves cause the growth of government,[9] and the amount of communications breakdown brought on by the growing size and internal complexities of government.[10] Analysis of interactions between pressures upon governments and the ability to respond to these pressures are currently among the interests of Karl Deutsch. He and his colleagues at the Wissenschaftszentrum in Berlin intend to develop a world model that can be used to investigate a number of problems of this kind.[11] A model of this complexity will take several years to complete, of course. In the meantime, we can take at least a tentative look at the problem.

One of Karl Deutsch's major contributions to social science has been his emphasis upon understanding macrosocial processes through the analysis of cross-national data. Broad historical processes, he argued, could be fruitfully investigated with comparative aggregate data across countries and over time. This approach has always been viewed as a supplement, not a replacement, for other methods and other kinds of data. It can make its own particular contribution but will not take the place of comparative case studies of the kind undertaken, for example, by Rokkan elsewhere in this volume. A variety of approaches should be pursued simultaneously.

A criticism levelled at the cross-national approach by Foltz (and others) is that it focuses upon the nation-state to the neglect of both subnational and transnational political actions and social movements. This is true. Nevertheless, there are many political phenomena for which the national state is *ipso facto* the appropriate unit of analysis. Clearly one of these is the national government budget. For problems such as this, the Deutsch approach to cross-national data collection and analysis remains a valid means of studying social and political change.

The Indicators

Total current revenue as a percentage of general government is employed as an index of government size. In general, data refer to the central authority, to all other government levels, and to public enterprises.[12] Revenue rather than expenditure was selected as a measure because consistent data are more readily available for it. Since the two follow a similar pattern both across countries and over time, either is a reasonably good indicator of the other.[13] Revenue, therefore, is used to indicate general limits to total public expenditure.

Government budgets rather than government personnel or government services and other activities are used in the analysis not because finances are more important or more meaningful but because data for them are more readily available. Comparative indicators of services delivered would provide an excellent means for charting the size and growth of governments. They could deflate for the presumed growth of inefficiency as government becomes larger and would be a more direct indicator of the capabilities of government than total revenue. The measurement of services remains a controversial matter, however, even within the context of particular countries for which it has been tried. Certainly comparable data for a number of countries do not yet exist.[14] Even the somewhat more easily quantifiable indicator, government personnel, has yet to be collected in a comparable cross-national manner. No series of data on government employees (other than armed forces) has been undertaken either by an international agency or by a private scholar, so far as I know.

The situation is different for budget data. We do not have everything we would like, but a great deal of progress has been made. Based upon the National Accounts System of the United National Statistical Office, most countries are now reporting increasingly comparable data to the international statistical offices. These offices in turn are applying more and more sophisticated methods in order to detect error and to enhance comparability. Adjustments are made to remove inconsistencies and discrepancies and occasionally data are estimated on the basis of information possessed by the staffs of the statistical offices. One such compilation of comparable governmental budget data is that put together by the Economic and Social Data Division of the World Bank. A shortened version of this compilation has been published as *World Tables 1976* and a more complete dataset is available on magnetic tape. This collection provides the revenue data and gross domestic product used in this chapter.

Current government revenue represents the economic resources more or less at the direct command of the government. Less directly, a government also has at its disposal at least some share of the total economic resources of a society. These total resources are measured by the gross domestic product, the total final output of a country's economy. GDP at constant market prices is the basis for the index numbers reported in this analysis.

Several measures are available for social mobilization. Most of these, as noted in numerous studies, are highly related to one another and any one may substitute for the others. The indicator chosen for this paper is school enrollment at the secondary level, as collected by Unesco. Secondary education puts the citizen into position both to make intelligent demands upon the government and to support or challenge that government in its undertakings. This measure, however, is believed to stand for the whole of social mobilization as defined by Deutsch.

The Size of Governments

The proportion of gross domestic product going to government differs significantly from country to country. According to Table 4.1, revenue as a percentage of GDP in 1973 ranged from a high of 51·7 per cent in Sweden to a low of 1·6 per cent in Mali. Virtually all of the developed, industrialized countries are in the top quartile of the rank order. Only Switzerland, the Mediterranean countries, Japan, and South Africa fall lower. Several oil-producing countries are also near the top. The relatively sudden appearance of this wealth and the ease of taxing it probably account at least in part for this fact. Third World countries fill up most of the lower three-quarters of the ranks and the poorest of them are concentrated in the fourth quartile. Although Africa is the poorest region of the world, it shares the bottom quarter of the ranks with countries from all the Third World regions.

It would be very interesting to know where the communist countries should be placed in this distribution. Unfortunately, the reporting systems of the centrally planned economies do not correspond for the most part with the United Nations System of National Accounts used by the World Bank. The discrepancies between systems are too large for easy adjustments that would make the data comparable. For that reason, the World Bank excludes these countries from its dataset. Earlier Pryor,[15] however, adjusted budgetary expenditures and other data for seven market economies and seven centrally planned economies to common definitions. He found government expenditures as a percentage of GNP in 1962 to range from 18 to 30 per cent for the market economies and from 17 to 33 per cent for the centralized economies. From this evidence of the early 1960s we can suspect that size of government in the centrally planned economies is not very different from that in the market economies of roughly equivalent economic development. Nevertheless, we do not know currently. Available data simply do not allow direct comparisons.

Among non-communist countries, the relationship between size of government and degree of official socialist rhetoric is not especially high. To be sure the proponents of Western-style socialism, for example, Sweden and Denmark, are at the very top of the list, and for industrialized countries taken alone there seems to be some rough association between the proportion of domestic product taken as government revenue and ideological positions held by recent leaders. The United States, Switzerland, Japan, and South Africa, all bastions of private enterprise, are much lower than most of the other developed countries.

This association is less apparent for the less developed areas. Chile and Brazil, not notable socialist countries, rank a great deal higher than Ethiopia and Benin although other very leftist countries, for example, Somalia, are at the higher level. This may be due in some measure to the fact that leftist language is fashionable in much of Asia, Africa, and Latin America, but the countries are not rich enough to afford large governments. Radical politics alone is not sufficient to cause a large

Table 4.1 *Size of government and national production (1973)*

	Government revenue as % of GDP	GNP per capita in US$
Mean for all countries	22·4	1,369
Median	20·1	475
Standard deviation	10·4	1,881
1 Sweden	51·7	6,360
2 Netherlands	49·0	4,670
3 Libya	48·4[b]	3,590
4 Norway	47·9	5,190
5 Denmark	45·0	5,870
6 West Germany	40·8	5,690
7 Oman	39·1	1,130
8 Luxembourg	39·0[c]	5,460
9 Finland	39·9	4,120
10 Saudi Arabia	38·9	2,070
11 Israel	38·7[c]	3,080
12 United Kingdom	38·0	3,270
13 France	37·6	4,810
14 Nigeria	37·2	230
15 Belgium	36·6	4,990
16 Canada	35·7	4,480
17 Algeria[a]	35·3	660
18 Lesotho[a]	34·9	110
19 Austria	33·5	3,900
20 Italy	33·0	2,520
21 New Zealand	33·0	3,980
22 Ireland	32·6	2,150
23 United States	32·3	6,230
24 Sudan	31·6[b]	200
25 Uruguay	31·4	1,070
26 Iraq	30·6	880
27 Chile	30·0	740
28 Malta	29·6	1,220[d]
29 Australia	28·4	4,650
30 Brazil	28·1	790
31 Egypt[a]	27·8	250
32 Somalia[a]	27·5[c]	90
33 Equador	27·3	400
34 Barbados[a]	26·4	1,090
35 Tunisia	26·0	550
36 Guyana[a]	25·9	440
37 Switzerland	25·6	7,060
38 Jamaica	25·3	1,050
39 Turkey	25·0[b]	650
40 Greece	24·8	1,980
41 Zaïre[a]	24·6[c]	130
42 Malaysia	24·0	590
43 Panama	23·6	940
44 Botswana	23·3	250
45 Portugal	22·7	1,440
46 Spain	22·5	2,170
47 Congo	22·4	400
48 Mauritius	22·3	500
49 Sri Lanka	22·2	120
50 Fiji[a]	22·0	750
51 Gabon[a]	21·9	1,650
52 Japan	21·6	3,800

Table 4.1 *continued*

		Government revenue as % of GDP	GNP per capita in US$
53	Ivory Coast	21·2	420
54	Rhodesia	21·1[b]	450
55	Venezuela	20·8	1,730
56	Central African Empire[a]	20·4[c]	200
57	Zambia	20·3[c]	450
58	South Africa	20·2	1,060
59	Gambia[a]	20·1	140
60	Kuwait	20·1	9,380
61	Singapore[a]	20·0	1,940
62	Cyprus	19·4	1,480
63	Taiwan[a]	19·3	750
64	Morocco	19·1	360
65	Costa Rica	18·9	740
66	Guinea[a]	18·6	100
67	Peru	18·5	650
68	Iran[a]	18·4	1,020
69	Malagasy	18·4	170
70	Kenya[a]	18·2	180
71	Swaziland	18·1	320
72	Nicaragua	17·6	550
73	Cameroon	17·3	230
74	Jordan[a]	17·3	380
75	Tanzania[a]	17·2	150
76	Mauritania[a]	17·1	220
77	Papua New Guinea	17·1[b]	440
78	Liberia[a]	16·9	360
79	Hong Kong[a]	16·3	1,490
80	Sierra Leone	16·3	170
81	India	16·2	130
82	Trinidad and Tobago	15·9	1,490
83	South Korea	15·8	410
84	Benin[a]	15·7	110
85	Dominican Republic	15·5	560
86	Colombia	14·8	440
87	Indonesia[a]	14·8	150
88	Pakistan	14·8	120
89	Chad[a]	14·4	90
90	Thailand	14·1	280
91	Burma	13·9	90
92	Togo[a]	13·9	220
93	Lebanon[a]	13·8	940
94	Bolivia	13·6	250
95	Malawi[a]	13·4	120
96	Senegal[a]	13·3	290
97	Syria	13·3	440
98	Philippines	12·7	290
99	Uganda[a]	12·6[c]	230
100	El Salvador[a]	12·5	360
101	Honduras	12·1	310
102	Ghana[a]	11·7	390
103	Upper Volta[a]	11·7	80
104	Niger[a]	11·4	100
105	Burundi[a]	11·3	80
106	Ethiopia[a]	11·1	90
107	Paraguay	10·1	440

Table 4.1 continued

	Government revenue as % of GDP	GNP per capita in US$
108 Argentina	9·3	1,310
109 Guatemala	9·1	510
110 Mexico[a]	8·5	980
111 Cambodia[a]	8·4[c]	70
112 Rwanda[a]	8·3[c]	80
113 Afghanistan[a]	7·2[c]	100
114 Laos[a]	5·6	60
115 Nepal[a]	5·5	90
116 Mali	1·6	70

Notes:
a Central government only.
b 1971.
c 1972.
d 1974.
Sources: International Bank for Reconstruction and Development, *World Tables 1976* (Baltimore, Md: Johns Hopkins University Press, 1976) and International Bank for Reconstruction and Development, *World Bank Atlas: Population, Per Capita Product and Growth Rates* (Washington, DC, 1976).

proportion of GDP to go for government purposes. In the Third World, the largest governments are in the oil-producing countries and these include traditional states such as Saudi Arabia and Oman as well as radical ones such as Libya and Nigeria.

Gross national products per capita for 1973 are listed in the second column of Table 4.1. These data allow a visual analysis of the relation between the distribution of wealth and the distribution of revenue. Clearly there is a strong but by no means perfect correlation between the two. Indeed, using the equation

$$Y = \alpha + \beta_1 \cdot \ln X + \beta_2 \cdot \ln X^2 + \varepsilon$$

it is possible to explain 48 per cent of the variance in Y (government revenue as a percentage of GDP) by X (GNP per capita).[16] In their study of structural change in economic development, Chenery and Syrquin[17] regressed government revenue on GNP per capita and on population allowing for non-linearity and controlling for time. They were able to use 1,111 observations for eighty-nine countries in a World Bank data file not generally available to the public.

For a hypothetical country of 10 million people, they used their equation to predict government revenue at various levels of GNP per capita in the development range. These predictions were as follows:

	Sample mean under	$100	12·5%
		$100	15·3%
		$200	18·1%
		$300	20·2%

	$400	21·9%
	$500	23·4%
	$800	26·8%
	$1,000	28·7%
Sample mean over	$1,000	30·7%

These predictions reflect the slight upward tendency of the regression curve allowed for in the equations above. The higher the GNP per capita, the more effect an increase has on government revenue.

Deviations from the relationship remain interesting, however. Some of the more obvious of these are identified by label in Figure 4.1. Deviants on the lower side of the regression line include some but not all of the better-known 'conservative' states of the world. On the upper side are several of the well-known 'radical' states, but many of the governments with socialist rhetoric have not moved their countries very far from

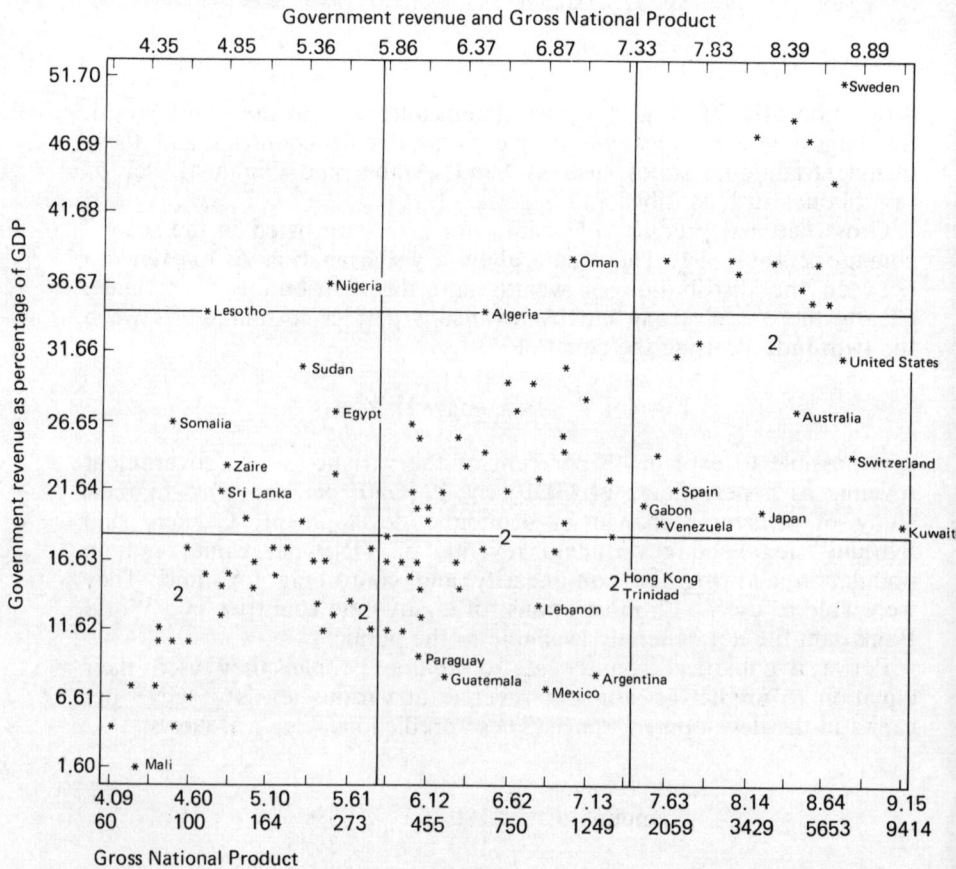

Figure 4.1 *Government revenue and gross national product.*

where they would be expected given their GNP per capita. Obviously, we need far better comparative public policy indicators than we now have in order to improve the cross-national prediction of government expenditure.

The Growth of Governments

Governments have been growing rapidly during the last few years. According to the World Bank[18] government revenue in the developing countries stood at 15·6 per cent of GDP in 1960, but this figure had risen to 19·9 per cent by 1973.[19] In the industrial countries during the same period, this percentage rose from 28·8 to 33·5. The same kind of growth pattern holds for further divisions of income.

	1960	1973
high-income	17·2%	20·0%
middle-income	12·5%	18·8%
low-income	11·7%	14·8%
oil-producing	17·3%	26·6%

In both rich and poor countries, therefore, government revenue not only has been growing but has been growing more rapidly than GDP. Alternatively stated, an increasing share of total production has come under direct government control.

Chenery and Syrquin found, as reported earlier, a slight upward tendency of the regression curve for government revenue predicted by GNP and population. On the basis of both cross-sectional and time-serial data, they suggested an exogenous upward shift of about 1 per cent per decade. In other words, the growth rates reported by the World Bank are due to the basic regression effect of income size on government revenue and to some additional factor. This finding is quite consistent with the social mobilization explanation of governmental growth. Social mobilization accompanies economic development and brings with it increasing demands for services. The pressures created by newly mobilized people outrun the increase in productive capacity. This used to be called the revolution of rising expectations.

For the average country then governmental growth seems to be speeding up and appears to be outgrowing resources. That is, government revenue is approaching some practical limit although we cannot say how closely. These average figures assume, however, the existence of universal causal factors that produce worldwide regularity in the processes of change. Group factors may also be important in determining rates of growth in many countries. For this reason, I have divided the countries for which adequate time series are available into groups according to the patterns of change which they follow. First, GDP and government revenue – each stated in national currencies at constant prices – were converted into index numbers (1960 = 100). Then these numbers were plotted separately for each country and the plots were compared. Several distinct patterns became evident in these

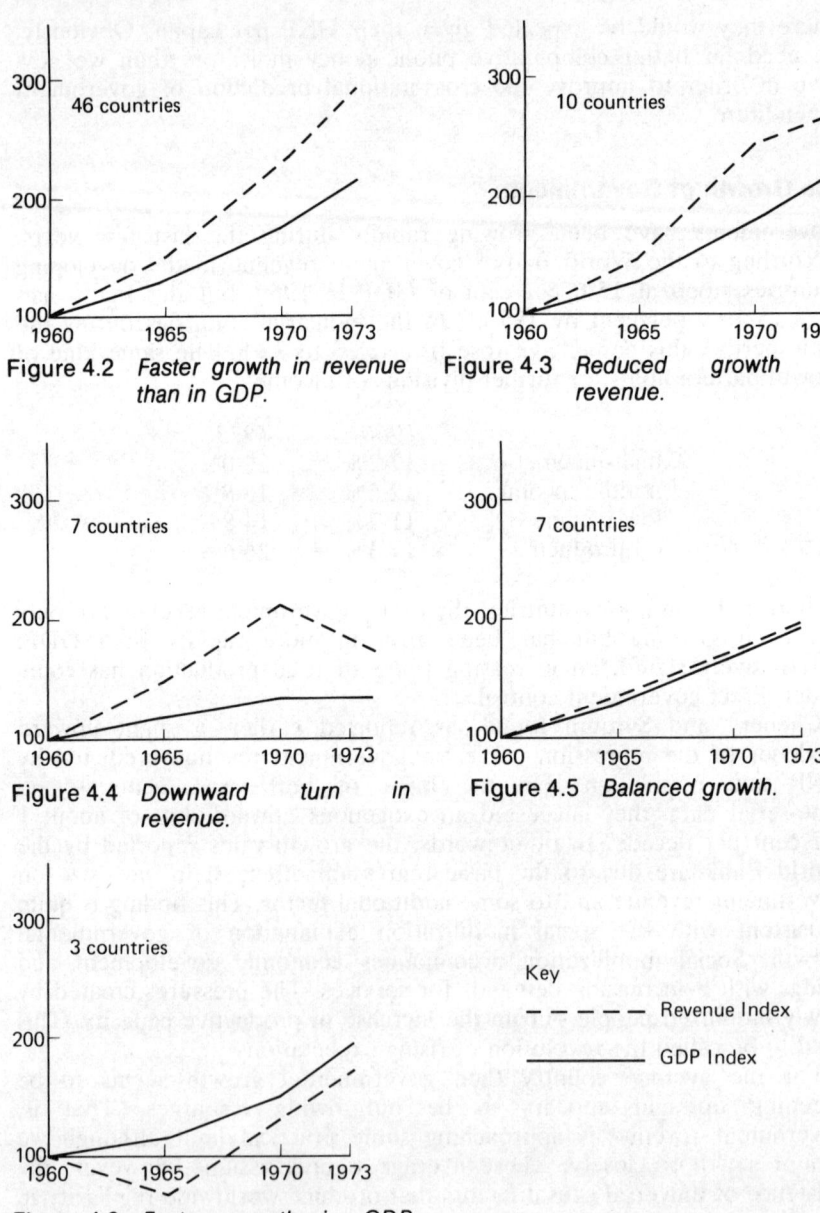

Figure 4.2 Faster growth in revenue than in GDP.

Figure 4.3 Reduced growth in revenue.

Figure 4.4 Downward turn in revenue.

Figure 4.5 Balanced growth.

Figure 4.6 Faster growth in GDP than in revenue.

Key
- - - - - Revenue Index
———— GDP Index

comparisons. For the countries fitting each of these, index numbers were averaged to obtain the mean time series experience of the group. These mean index numbers are shown in Figures 4.2–4.6.

The pattern followed by the greatest number of countries is one of more rapid growth in government revenue than in GDP. This is to be expected, of course, given the average percentage growths reported above. Almost two-thirds of all countries for which data are available fit this pattern represented in Figure 4.2. In five countries the growth rate in real revenue between 1960 and 1965 was lower than the rate for real GDP (indicated by negative number in Table 4.2) and in one the rates

Table 4.2 *More rapid growth in revenue than GDP 1960–1973 (1960 = 100)*

	Revenue index 1973	GDP index 1973	Revenue index minus GDP index		
			1965	1970	1973
Nigeria	720	209	13	62	511
Mauritania	617	227	135	247	390
Saudi Arabia	701	465	59	67	236
Gabon	463	285	69	135	178
Panama	400	265	11	59	135
Nepal	252	133	16	105	119
Denmark	297	181	18	84	116
Central African Empire	235	121	61	61	114
Brazil	349	245	−18	28	104
Israel	395	292	3	63	103
Malta	278	180	27	55	98
Sweden	254	161	25	63	93
Togo	320	228	7	75	92
Netherlands	282	192	13	50	90
Congo	278	189	30	59	89
Jamaica	277	193	20	50	84
Hong Kong	384	306	13	67	78
Ireland	234	161	14	53	73
Canada	270	198	10	56	72
Norway	252	182	12	36	70
Nicaragua	293	225	21	15	68
India	222	155	43	46	67
Equador	266	200	13	49	66
Fiji	268	202	34	53	66
Morocco	231	167	5	62	64
Belgium	249	187	15	44	62
Spain	311	251	−5	54	60
Benin	200	142	6	47	58
Philippines	261	203	−6	15	58
Costa Rica	270	213	13	42	57
Japan	421	368	6	33	53
Guyana	187	139	−1	40	48
Iraq	279	231	1	28	48
Peru	247	200	26	44	47
South Africa	247	200	12	32	47
Finland	237	193	8	24	44
Ivory Coast	293	252	19	23	41
Gambia	229	191	11	38	38
Mexico	273	235	10	19	38
Liberia	202	168	8	28	34
Lebanon	242	209	21	23	33
Australia	215	183	9	30	32
West Germany	207	179	0	8	28
United States	197	172	−1	12	25
Italy	216	192	8	17	24
France	229	208	13	19	21

were equal. Otherwise, in all countries and for all periods government revenue advanced more rapidly than GDP. In none of these countries during any of the three periods (1960–5, 1965–70, 1970–3) did either revenue or GDP actually decline.

Information specific to each country is listed in Table 4.2. The revenue index numbers for 1973 give revenue of that year stated as a percentage of revenue in 1960; the GDP index does the same for domestic product. (Both are based on constant prices.) Nigeria's revenue for 1973, for example, was 720 per cent of what it was in 1960 and its GDP was 209 per cent. The difference between these two appears in the final column and is the basis on which the rank order of the table is determined. Similar figures for 1965 and 1970 are also reported. These differences measure the increased burden of government on the society's economic resources relative to the burden in 1960. They indicate not the increasing share of total production taken by the government but that share adjusted for the real growth in the economy. If government were growing only as rapidly as GDP, the difference between growth rates would be zero and the increased burden on resources would also be nil. The more rapidly government grows, relative to GDP, the heavier the increased burden is. When government grows more slowly than GDP, the burden is lightened (and the difference is represented as a negative number).

The second most frequently followed pattern is a variant on the first. It is pictured in Figure 4.3. Both GDP and government revenue grow throughout the period and, for the first ten years, the latter advances more rapidly than the former. After 1970, however, the rate of growth in real government revenue slackens and becomes smaller than the rate of growth in real GDP. The differences between revenue index numbers and GDP index numbers for 1973 listed in Table 4.3 are only somewhat smaller than the bulk of those for 1973 in Table 4.2 but they are smaller than their counterparts for 1970 in Table 4.3. In these ten countries some effort was made to bridge the gap between the growth rates. The burden of government on resources was somewhat less in

Table 4.3 *Reduced growth in revenue in 1973 (1960 = 100)*

	Revenue index 1973	GDP index 1973	Revenue index minus GDP index		
			1965	1970	1973
Barbados	304	192	24	115	112
Guinea	230	161	46	79	69
South Korea	382	317	−14	108	65
Portugal	281	224	20	68	57
Greece	323	271	20	66	52
Colombia	246	202	0	62	44
United Kingdom	189	145	14	51	44
Thailand	278	257	13	30	21
Bolivia	211	193	23	47	18
Austria	207	190	16	29	17

Table 4.4 Downward turn in revenue in 1973 (1960 = 100)

	Revenue index 1973	GDP index 1973	Revenue index minus GDP index		
			1965	1970	1973
Chad	168	94	52	120	74
Niger	242	108	56	41	34
Uruguay	148	114	5	34	34
Chile	188	159	10	52	29
Malagasy	141	129	26	37	12
Paraguay	183	186	-12	40	-3
Zambia	150	156	48	117	-6

1973 than in 1970. As was the case with the countries of the first pattern, revenue generally outgrew GDP throughout the period (with the exception of only two countries between 1960 and 1965). In no country also did real GDP or real revenue decline during one of the three subperiods.

The situation was different in another seven countries that followed the pattern plotted in Figure 4.4. In four of the seven (listed in Table 4.4) real GDP actually declined between 1970 and 1973 and in all seven real government revenue fell. For the first ten years the pattern is similar to the previous two except that growth in GDP is more sluggish. Revenue outgrew GDP in most subperiods for most countries. As with the second pattern, the burden of government on resources was less in 1973 than in 1970, but this was due to an actual decline in the revenues themselves. Even so, in no country did real revenues decline below 140 per cent for their 1960 level.

Growth of revenue and GDP were closely balanced in another seven countries. This is demonstrated in Figure 4.5 and the countries are listed in Table 4.5. Both real GDP and real government revenue grew steadily during the period. In most of the countries, GDP tended to increase somewhat more rapidly in the earlier part of the period and revenue in the later part. Nevertheless, the differences between the two indexes remained very low. The burden of government on total resources was about the same in 1973 as in 1960.

Table 4.5 GDP and revenue growth in balance 1960–1973 (1960 = 100)

	Revenue index 1973	GDP index 1973	Revenue index minus GDP index		
			1965	1970	1973
Cyprus	248	226	-9	8	22
New Zealand	184	169	-5	2	15
Trinidad and Tobago	154	164	-10	10	9
El Salvador	207	199	-6	-18	8
Honduras	182	180	-5	12	2
Venezuela	202	201	5	-7	1
Guatemala	183	208	10	0	-25

Table 4.6 GDP growth greater than revenue growth 1960–1973 (1960 = 100)

	Revenue index 1973	GDP index 1973	Revenue index minus GDP index		
			1965	1970	1973
Indonesia	217	186	−76	−27	31
Argentina	136	171	−34	−15	−35
Dominican Republic	177	222	−41	−25	−45

In only two countries, Argentina and the Dominican Republic, was the growth of GDP consistently more rapid than the growth of government revenue. In a third, Indonesia, this was true for the decade from 1960 to 1970, although revenue grew much more rapidly after 1970. These three were made to form the pattern in Figure 4.6. In all three countries, GDP grew steadily and so did government revenue after an initial dip in 1965 (see Table 4.6). The government burden on economic resources tended for the most part to decline in these three countries, primarily because of the drop in 1965.

These patterns only begin to identify similar cases in the sense that Rokkan finds Portugal, Italy, Germany, and Austria to be similar. We cannot take a single country or a small group of countries from a pattern and call it or them representative of the whole group. To identify 'similar cases' in this stricter sense, we need similarity on several variables simultaneously. Thus far we have determined membership in the patterns only on the basis of a single variable: the growth of government burden on the total production of the economy. The causes of this increased burden and the circumstances under which it takes place can vary greatly within patterns. Certainly the countries listed in Tables 4.2 to 4.6 do not appear to be divided on the basis of political orientation of their regimes. Both radical and conservative countries show up in virtually all patterns. Nor did countries within a pattern necessarily begin their growth from a single position in 1960. The first

Table 4.7 Mean levels and growth rates for government revenue and GDP by pattern of growth

	Revenue index 1973	GDP index 1973	Revenue as % GDP 1973	GDP per capita 1973
Faster growth in revenue than in GDP	375	207	26·5	1,968 ($)
Reduced growth in revenue	265	215	22·2	1,316
Balanced growth	194	192	17·4	1,408
Downward turn in revenue	174	135	19·4	437
Faster growth in GDP than in revenue	177	193	13·2	673

pattern, particularly, holds for countries at a variety of levels of economic development.

Nevertheless, relationships do exist between the patterns, on the one hand, and GDP and government revenue, on the other. The patterns can be put into rank as in Table 4.7 if we assume that they represent the following ordering:

(a) the consistently growing government burden on the economy;
(b) the recent effort to control the growing burden, by reducing growth in revenue;
(c) the avoiding of growth in the burden;
(d) the recent reduction of real revenue to control the burden;
(e) a significant reduction in the burden during the earlier years.

When ranked in this way the patterns are clearly related to levels and growth rates of GDP and government revenue.

The relationship with growth rates is not surprising. The burden scores, on which the patterns are based, can be completely explained as a function of the two sets of index numbers. The same cannot be done for the patterns because the latter measure not simply the size of burden but also the growth or decline of it over time. The mean index numbers are given in Table 4.7 to demonstrate that the more persistently the burden of government increases, the higher are the growth rates – of GDP as well as of government revenue. This might partly be explained by the fact that growing GDP provides a surplus that allows government revenue to grow even more rapidly; increasing public expenditures do not come out of private pockets. Unfortunately for this hypothesis, however, burdens are correlated with GDP growth at 0·25 but with revenue growth at 0·86. Burdens grow wherever it is that government revenue grows.[20]

They also tend to grow where government revenue is already large. Countries whose growth rates in government revenue consistently outpaced their growth rates in GDP have, on the average, the highest percentages of GDP devoted to government. Countries with slower growth rates in government revenue than in GDP have the lowest average percentages. This relationship may partially reflect differing conceptions of the role of the state, but it is also undoubtedly a reflection of the underlying relationship between wealth and government growth. The countries with consistently faster growth in revenue than in GDP are the wealthier countries; those with a downward turn in revenue are the poorest; and those with faster growth in GDP than in revenue are only slightly more wealthy. This is closely related to a finding in the cross-sectional analysis. There it was shown that wealthy countries devote larger shares of their wealth to government revenue than do poor countries. Here it can be seen that they do so at an increasing rate over time, whereas the percentage growth of government in poorer countries remains lower.

Is it possible to link social mobilization to these findings? According to Deutsch and consistent with a large amount of empirical evidence, social mobilization takes place within the context of modernization and wealth-getting. Measures of the process such as the secondary school enrollment ratio are closely related to GNP per capita and other measures of development; therefore, it should also be related to the rate of growth in government revenue and to the growing burden of government on the economy. As Deutsch has said, all of these things go together and it is very difficult to separate the effects of each from the others. Any regression containing several of them will inevitably contain some multicollinearity.

Nevertheless, the results may be interesting. In a forward stepwise procedure, I regressed burdens as defined above upon GNP per capita, government revenue as a percentage of GDP, the growth rate in secondary school enrollment as a ratio of the proper age-group between 1960 and 1970, and the ratio itself as of the beginning of the period. The first and second variables to enter the regression were revenue as a percentage of GDP and the school enrollment ratio for 1960.[21] Each alone could explain only 6 or 7 per cent of the variance in burdens. Together they explained 26 per cent. When controlling for level of government revenue already attained, social mobilization could provide additional explanation. But the explanation was not in the direction predicted! The slope for school enrollment ratio was a negative one. That is, at any given size of government, the effect of higher school enrollment would be to lower the gap between revenue growth and GDP growth. Perhaps it can be argued that the level of school enrollment measures past growth in demands upon the government; the earlier increases of social mobilization may have already had their effect upon government revenue. According to this argument, what should be related to increased burdens is the growth rate in school enrollment ratio. Unfortunately, however, this variable was the last to be entered in the stepwise regression and then added only 2 percentage points to the variance explained. (Taken alone, it accounts for only 3 per cent.) In short, there is little direct evidence in these data to prove that social mobilization, as opposed to other phenomena associated with modernization, is the cause of growth in government expenditures.

Conclusion

Explanations for the increase in government share of economic output have been numerous. Deutsch's social mobilization theory is an important one. Another argues that growing income leaves more resources for government consumption after other needs have been met. Still a third emphasizes the tolerable level of taxation which may be increased from time to time during major social upheavals. A fourth makes the case for incrementalism in budgeting. The first two theories appear appropriate to the data between 1960 and 1973 and either, or both in combination, can provide a credible explanation for the growth of government revenue during that period. We would need longer time series to consider the third explanation and more detailed data for the fourth. It has not been possible here to make comparative assessments of these theories since this would require a much more extensive study.

Nevertheless, some questions about governmental growth have been answered. For the period under study, the rate of government growth was speeding up in most countries. Government revenue was growing not only absolutely but also relative to GDP. In forty-six of the seventy-three countries for which time-serial data were available, the discrepancy between government growth and GDP growth continued throughout the period. This still leaves one-third of the countries in which revenue growth has slowed down or has only kept pace with or been surpassed by GDP growth. These countries tend to be the poorer ones in which government revenue is not already high, although countries whose growth curves still show an upward sweep include many poor countries as well as the rich ones.

Obviously government growth cannot go on for ever. The increasing cost of public services and the growing demand for them must inevitably run into the opposition of taxpayers' revolts. Seven of the seventy-three countries decreased their rate of government growth between 1970 and 1973, and another seven actually reduced their revenues. This may be an indication of the limits to government growth. And if the theory of social mobilization is correct, a great many countries may require imaginative leaders to avoid serious troubles in the years ahead.

Notes: Chapter 4

1 Total government expenditure in the United States increased from $3·2 billion in 1902 to $135·5 billion in 1970 (stated in 1929 constant dollars) or from 6·8 per cent of GNP to 34·1 per cent. See Thomas E. Borcherding, 'One hundred years of public spending, 1870–1970', *Budgets and Bureaucrats: The Sources of Government Growth*, ed. Thomas E. Borcherding (Durham, NC: Duke University Press, 1977), pp. 19–44. Similar expansion took place in the British and German economies. See Richard A. Musgrave, *Fiscal Systems* (New Haven, Conn.: Yale University Press, 1969). Data for more recent years for a larger number of countries are reported in Tables 4.2 to 4.6 above.

2 W. J. Baumol, 'Macroeconomics of unbalanced growth: the anatomy of the urban crisis', *American Economic Review*, vol. 57, no. 3 (June 1967), pp. 415–26. Baumol's model implies very low or zero growth in productivity in the public sector relative to the private sector. Many other economists have concluded the same.

3 Kampuchea appears to have tried hard, if recent news reports are reliable. But directing all payments and purchases through government is a very inconvenient way of managing an economy.

4 Hollis Chenery and Moises Syrquin, *Patterns of Development: 1950–1970* (New York: Oxford University Press, 1975).

5 Karl W. Deutsch, 'Toward an inventory of basic trends and patterns in comparative and international politics', *American Political Science Review*, vol. 54, no. 1 (March 1960), pp. 34–57.

6 Relevant data are found in Bruce M. Russett *et al.*, *World Handbook of Political and Social Indicators* (New Haven, Conn.: Yale University Press, 1964); and in Charles Lewis Taylor and Michael C. Hudson, *World Handbook of Political and Social Indicators*, 2d edn (New Haven, Conn.: Yale University Press, 1972).

7 What is missing in the social mobilization theory, as well as in the whole modernization paradigm, is a prediction of what occurs at the end of the process. Various recent hypotheses have been suggested but we have no generally agreed upon model of what happens when people are mobilized within the concept of a 'fully modernized' society. See Daniel Bell, *The Coming of Post-Industrial Society* (New York: Basic Books, 1973); and Ronald Inglehart, *The Silent Revolution* (Princeton, NJ: Princeton University Press, 1977).

8 Brian Crozier, Samuel Huntington, and Jōji Watanuki, *Crisis of Democracy* (New York: New York University Press, 1975); and Richard Rose, *New Trends in British Politics* (London: Sage, 1977).
9 James M. Buchanan, 'Why does government grow?,' *Budgets and Bureaucrats*, ed. Borcherding, pp. 3–18.
10 Karl W. Deutsch, *The Nerves of Government: Models of Political and Communications and Control* (New York: The Free Press, 1963).
11 Much of this work has yet to be published. See, for example, Stuart A. Bremer, 'Technological advance and limits to growth' (Berlin: Wissenschaftszentrum, International Institute for Comparative Social Research, 1978, mimeo.).
12 For some countries, it has been necessary to use data for the central government only. These are identified in Table 4.1. Total current revenue includes direct taxes on households and corporations, all indirect taxes, receipts from government enterprises, rents and royalties, fees, fines, private donations, compulsory social security payments, and so on. Grants and borrowing from abroad, however, are excluded.
13 Chenery and Syrquin, *Patterns of Development*, p. 26.
14 Henry Teune and Adam Przeworski, *The Logic of Comparative Social Inquiry* (New York: Wiley Interscience, 1970).
15 Frederic L. Pryor, *Public Expenditures in Communist and Capitalist Nations* (Homewood, Ill.: Irwin, 1968).
16 Results of this regression include the following:

$R = 0.69$
$R^2 = 0.48$ s.e. $= 7.56$
$b_1 = 4.46$ s.e. $= 5.23$
$b_2 = 0.75$ s.e. $= 0.40$

17 Chenery and Syrquin, *Patterns of Development*.
18 World Bank, *World Tables 1976* (Baltimore, Md: Johns Hopkins University Press, 1976).
19 The publicly available World Bank data type contains only central government accounts. For general government, we must rely upon *World Tables 1976* in which 1973 is the most recent year reported for government revenue; ibid.
20 Government revenue growth and GDP growth are correlated at 0·69.
21 Results at each of the four steps were as follows:

Step 1

$R = 0.27$
$R^2 = 0.07$ s.e. $= 78.02$
$b_1 = 2.09$ s.e. $= 0.90$

Step 2

$R = 0.51$
$R^2 = 0.26$ s.e. $= 70.19$
$b_1 = 3.88$ s.e. $= 0.91$
$b_2 = -2.01$ s.e. $= 0.48$

Step 3

$R = 0.55$
$R^2 = 0.30$ s.e. $= 68.91$
$b_1 = 5.59$ s.e. $= 1.27$
$b_2 = -1.47$ s.e. $= 0.56$
$b_3 = -0.02$ s.e. $= 0.01$

Step 4

$R = 0.56$
$R^2 = 0.32$ s.e. $= 68.36$
$b_1 = 5.81$ s.e. $= 1.27$
$b_2 = -2.29$ s.e. $= 0.79$
$b_3 = -0.01$ s.e. $= 0.01$
$b_4 = -0.34$ s.e. $= 0.23$

Where b_1 = revenue as a percentage of GDP
b_2 = education enrollment ratio
b_3 = GNP per capita
b_4 = growth in educational enrollment ratio.

5

Developmental Crises and Modernization: The Role of the State in the Redistribution Crisis in Developed Countries

FRIEDER NASCHOLD

The creation of the modern world is generally recognized as one of the few great watersheds in the history of mankind.[1] As early as the nineteenth century, the idea of social modernization as a single, global process shaped the perspectives of the emerging European bourgeoisie. It enjoyed a renascence after the Second World War with both the expanding economic, political, and ideological hegemony of the United States and the parallel decolonization struggle in the Third World. Countervailing these were pressures from the Soviet bloc. Agreement on this constellation of interest and power notwithstanding, the logic and substance of the process of modernization are evaluated quite differently. Conservative, liberal, and social systems of values and interests produce a variety of interpretations and draw different conclusions with respect to domestic and international strategies for development.

Such perspectives are none the less merely vague images and ideal concepts[2] which generally rest upon experiences carried over indirectly from our daily lives. Because of its great theoretic and strategic importance, a systematic and theoretic conceptualization of modernization processes stands 'at the center of most contemporary social science theory'.[3]

Alternative Theories: Some Assumptions

Renewed interest in nineteenth-century theories of value along with the structural-functional approach to systems – especially that of Talcott Parsons – contributed, above all in the United States, to early formulations of a theory of modernization. Its concepts, categories, and assumptions gradually spread to the liberal, free-enterprise, industrialized countries of Western Europe as well. Since the 1950s there has been sharp scholarly debate on individual substantive and methodological aspects of modernization theory: circumscriptive definitions of traditional and modern societies; stages, trends, and typologies of the developmental process; and varying assessments of both the key historical turning points and the most significant social forces and events.[4] The debate, to be sure, did not lead to a single, comprehensive theory of modernization. In large part this was because of not inconsiderable substantive heterogeneity and the varying methodological approaches used. That an explanatory sketch (such as that by Hempel) emerged out of all this along with a set of categories, definitions, and propositions was due in no small measure to the extensive work by Karl W. Deutsch.[5] Despite the many different ways it has been explained, this sketch may be viewed as a 'theory design', the paradigm of a theory of modernization that tries to measure up to the claim of being a discipline in its own right.[6]

In accordance with this theory design, the theory of modernization deals 'with an epochal, long-range, not infrequently violent transformation that began in Western Europe but soon involved the entire world'. The transformation was at once 'a systematic process, entailing general problems', and 'a historical process producing vastly different solutions'.[7] More narrowly, and at the same time more abstractly defined, modernization means the 'increasing capacity to control the problems facing particular societies (or individuals)'.[8]

The individual concepts and plethora of significant empirical hypotheses characterizing modernization theory need not be discussed here. In this regard it is essential only to note the controversy that has further refined the comprehensive theory design. The two most important strands in this controversy stem from revisionists and radical revisionists. Whereas the former aim at a further development of the modernization theory within its paradigm, the latter pursue a research strategy of 'modernization: requiescat in pace'[9] and the development of an alternative theory design in the form of a historically oriented, political and economic (not economistic) theory of transformation.

The present state of the scholarly controversy on the theory of modernization may be summarized as follows.[10] On the one hand, there is an elaborate concept of social modernization that is relatively homogeneous in its basic assumptions but otherwise extremely differentiated and dynamic. On the other hand, those representing the original modernization theory and revisionists alike have spawned a 'proliferation of versions of a theory' within the framework of the basic assumptions. This circumstance may be viewed as a 'common sign of paradigmatic crisis'.[11] To counter this, incisive and intensive efforts are being made to revise radically the theory of modernization by replacing it with an alternative theory design. These different theory designs engender problems of strategic and practical as well as theoretic relevance. Given this situation, a comparative examination of the controversial theory designs is more urgent at this time than further isolated studies reflecting one or another of the paradigms.[12]

The discussion that follows essays such a theoretic and empirical examination of several controversial theory designs. It also hopes to avoid the trap of mere ideological criticism that slashes in both directions but is ultimately fruitless. This task can, however, only be accomplished – if it can be accomplished at all! – by looking briefly at a few selected examples. Such an examination requires, moreover, a multitude of delimitations and specifications that in turn depend on criteria of theoretic and practical political relevance. The theoretic sphere of political development together with its various subconcepts is especially controversial in a theoretic sense and especially relevant in a political sense. Most relevant are the concepts of political mobilization and governmental capacity for control as well as hypotheses correlating economic, social, and political developmental processes.

Specifying the objective problem-area requires focusing on an important developmental issue within the framework of modernization theory: in the present case, the choice has fallen upon a modernization conflict involving the welfare state, more specifically, the development of national health care in developed ('modernized') countries. This conflict has been conceptualized as the 'transformation crisis of political modernization'.[13] Methodological delimitation requires that the empirical data come from two closely connected areas: in this instance a comparative examination of the general development of the welfare state in Germany, England, and the United States and, more specifically, the longitudinal analysis of individual cases from almost a century of national health care in Germany (Legislative Health Insurance) which in this chapter will be discussed only for the sake of cross-sectional international comparison.[14]

Meta-methodologically, the examination is patterned on recent developments in critical rationalism to which modernization theory is especially indebted. According to Lakatos, a confrontation among several theories must adhere to a number of strict rules: one theory is better than another if and only if, in addition to the same empirical content, it has 'corroborated excess empirical content over its predecessors'.[15] Specifically, our examination follows several criteria for differentiation. For one, it follows the criterion formulated most precisely by Durkheim: a definition of the problem that is empirically based and anchored in reality as a necessary basis for conceptualization, as opposed to ideal notions as the basis for 'ideological analysis'.[16] Another is Abraham Kaplan's criterion of the extent to which a set of categories and concepts can tell us more than some other scheme of categorization.[17] Finally, there is the criterion emphasized most strongly by Kuhn: the extent to which evidence at once extra- or counterparadigmatic and empirical is capable of disrupting the core of a paradigm.[18] Such a strategy for examining theories can have one of several results. It may lead to the retention of the theory design; there may be a progressive or degenerative shift in the statement of the issue within the theory design; or the theory design may be dropped and an alternative one developed. At this point, according to Lakatos, two further criteria must be observed. First, no single observation of a lower order may by itself falsify a hypothesis. Secondly, 'there is no falsification before the emergence of a better theory'.[19]

The issue under discussion here may, therefore, be specified and circumscribed as follows. (1) We accept as given the empirically based and objectively accepted description of the 100-year development of the welfare state, more specifically, of the Legislative Health Insurance (LHI) in a 'modernized' country like Germany along with a limited international comparison, especially with England and the United States. (2) Also accepted as given are the prevailing theory of modernization and competing theory designs. (3) The question to be resolved is: using the alternative interpretation offered by a competing theory design, which theory design can provide (*a*) a more adequate empirical statement of the issue as an objective starting point for scientific conceptualization and theory creation (external validity), and (*b*) greater conceptual and empirical content (internal validity) in accordance with the above-mentioned theoretic criteria?

These goals can only be sought in a summary and crude fashion, and with only limited attention paid to their plausibility. They cannot lead to a definite conclusion.

The Redistribution Crisis and the Development of the Welfare State

An empirical description of the real-world situation as the necessary basis for a scientific conceptualization, and an analysis of the genesis and development of the modern welfare state as a problem-solving strategy in the face of the redistribution crisis, reveal substantial similarities as well as dissimilarities among various political theories of development comprising the general theory of modernization.[20] The basic assumptions and definitions, theoretic concepts, and analytic categories as well as the empirical and normative evaluations are relatively similar. As supporting evidence we might point to the theoretic variations in the stages of social development and the creation of the welfare state as presented by authors like Rostow, Organski, and Black on the one hand and, on the other, the quantitative causal model of Karl W. Deutsch. The creation and expansion of a welfare state and a national health care program are conceptualized as subsequent to, and the result of, the political development of fundamentally different elements of modernization: the similarity of economic, social, and political civil rights, combined with an intensification of the political processes of mobilization and participation; and the secular increase in a state's steering capacity resting on and as a result of economic and social developments following the onset of industrialization.

According to one theory of political modernization, modernization leads to a universal developmental syndrome consisting of three essential characteristics: structural differentiation, expansion of the political capacity for control, and equality among citizens. The inherent tensions, especially between the principle of equality on the one hand, and those of differentiation and the state's capacity for control, on the other hand, are a threat to the three universal functions of the political system – its legitimation and its procedural functions and especially its productivity function (resource mobilization and distribution). All these interrelated frictions give rise to social developmental crises. In the historical situation under discussion here these manifest themselves as a political modernization crisis of redistribution, together with crises of penetration, political participation, and integration. The political processes together with economic and social tendencies toward modernization pass through historical and crisis management mechanisms peculiar to each individual state. The final result of the process may be any one of a variety of patterns and levels of solution to the issues of welfare state development and a national health care system.

The discussion that follows, and that will serve as the basis of a new theory, concentrates on selected aspects of the external validity of the empirically drawn situation and proceeds along three lines: (1) a description of the factual characteristics of the development of the welfare state and a national health care system; (2) empirical and strategic estimation of the level and quality of political problem-solving (goal attainment) in the redistribution crisis; and (3) the affective adjustment of genetic political intentions and resulting changes in system functions.

Welfare State and National Health Care: Central Issues

In describing and conceptualizing the substantive issue – the genesis of the redistribution crisis and development of the welfare state – three essential and significant problems come immediately to mind: first, the large number of imprecise and vague definitions of the real issue; secondly, the high level of abstraction in these definitions, and thirdly, the relatively homogeneous economic and geopolitical realm of experience, that is, the fact that empirical evidence for scientific conceptualizations is drawn from the core states of Western Europe and the United States, all of whose liberal economies are based on private ownership.

The vagueness and abstractness of the description of the real issue are essentially and methodologically speaking a result of combining generalizations that are empirically weak with abstractions that are ideal types. A central problem resulting from this strategy of conceptualization is a highly substantive and formal randomness in defining the issue. This manifests itself, for one thing, in the fact that the internal variance in modernized states – for instance, in the solutions to national health problems – is at times much greater than the external variance between certain developing and modernized states.[21] Above all, the very abstractness of the definitions leads to such a far-reaching separation of the real problem that is inherent to the development of the welfare state (defined as the redistribution crisis) from the fundamental issues, interests, and power structures of the sociopolitical forces, that the definitions begin to resemble almost purely analytical artifacts or empty tautologies. At the same time, there is an undeniable meta-methodological contradiction between the high level of generalization in the categories and the narrow range of experience defined spatially, temporally, economically, and politically. The same contradiction exists between the demand for bias-free analysis and implicit normativism. In this way 'ideal notions are turned into substitutes for reality' (Durkheim) as the basis for such scientific conceptualizations.

An analogous and theoretic proof of these hypotheses can be found in a more empirically detailed manner by looking at the development of national health care as an aspect of state welfare policies aimed at solving the redistribution crisis, in this case the development of the Legislative Health Insurance.[22] The genesis in 1883 of this program – a product in part of confusing economic and political as well as ideological strategies of co-operation among classes, parties, and political elites – is frequently viewed as an epochal event for the beginning of the modern welfare state. Although it also provided a number of other services, its major function was to make cash payments for salaries lost due to illness. Five major changes have taken place since its inception:

- the expansion of the number of persons insured from 10 per cent of the working population in 1890 to over 90 per cent today, or in other words almost the maximum limit of insurable persons;
- an increase in the range of services offered, determined by criteria of need;
- an ever-increasing political and ideological separation between the LHI and the working-class movement;
- the expansion of individual measures aimed at the early detection of disease, as well as similar efforts on the part of the state and corresponding agencies;
- the development of a planning and information system for the more efficient control of this area of policy which, as indicated by its fiscal and informational volume, is constantly growing in size and importance.

Such changes notwithstanding, the basic principles underlying the LHI remain to this day.

At first glance the genesis, functions, and structures of the LHI seem to correspond to the assumptions and concepts of political modernization theory with respect to strategies for solving the universal redistribution crisis and the developmental problems of equality. Empirical and theoretical studies, however, have pointed out a number of significant gaps relevant to the criticism mentioned above as well as other basic problems. Here, too, a fundamental aspect of conceptualization lies in describing the central concept of health insurance as an aspect of state policy on welfare and relating this analytic concept to the real-world issue.

One need only look at such controversial phrases as 'health insurance' and 'preventive medicine' to see that different, and at times contradictory or even opposing, social forms and social ideas (Heimann) are concealed behind the notion of a universal problem of social and political development – surmounting the physical and psychological consequences of industrialization – and that these are combined into a single, homogeneously defined, abstract concept. Significant empirical and theoretic research none the less provides extra- and counterparadigmatic evidence.[23] Such research, both prior to and during the LHI's developmental period as well as during some of its later years, shows that more or less opposing social configurations – economic and political societal configurations and ideological social concepts as well as strategies of social and political stabilization *v*. transformation – are in constant conflict with one another. One of the societal configurations was composed of the dominant political and economic alliance among diverse hegemonic capitalist groups, extensive portions of the traditional middle class, and the ruling political elite. The social concepts of its members included a narrowly defined, negative view of illness; a compensatory and curative notion of the benefits system; a separation of the LHI from measures to protect the worker; controls on the benefits system by the state and the industrialists together with the simultaneous destruction of any existing or developing autonomy among the workers; fragmentation of the organizational structure of the LHI; and encouragement of the traditional middle class (especially doctors) to serve as a buffer against the working-class movement.

In contrast to this, a broad spectrum of leadership groups within the working-class movement created a societal configuration with almost diametrically opposed societal ideas. These included a broadly defined, positive view of health with full recognition given to the societal causes of most health problems and their unequal social distribution; a strategy focusing on the prevention of illness; the integration of the LHI and measures to protect workers; a unified and public health service with extensive provisions for self-government on the part of workers; transformation of members of the traditional and new middle class into public servants; and, along the same lines, the transformation of pharmacies and doctors' practices from private into public enterprises.

The counterparadigmatic evidence revealed in this extremely condensed description of the real-world issues surrounding the LHI unequivocally contradicts the explanatory sketch offered by the political modernization theory. It confirms, in both a concrete and an empirical way, that the theory can hardly be expected to explain in an adequate fashion an empirically based issue. This strategy for dealing with a real-world problem, which is the basis for most research on modernization, will be counterposed in a selective and summary fashion with the outlines of a research strategy for an alternative theory.[24] Such a theory requires that empirically drawn issues be empirically described according to the concrete economic, political, and ideological interests of the existing social classes and strata and taking into account society's balance of power and material productivity in both the national and international context.

These issues in turn form the empirically drawn starting point for conceptualized and theoretic strategies of research. Based on the foregoing example of the development of the welfare state and the national health plan, this means that the core structure of the welfare state is not at all a single, relatively homogeneous, and definable unit of analysis with equally homogeneous and clear-cut definitions of the problem and other characteristics. It consists rather of a relatively large number of extremely heterogeneous configurations that are temporally, factually, and socially and politically variable, at times even antagonistic. Accordingly, an aggregation of these occasionally contradictory configurations can only lead to exaggerated generalizations, poor abstraction of definitions, and consequently to merely analytic artifacts which elude the true dimensions of the issue.[25] This evaluation does not in the least suggest a further development of the theory along the lines of a simple comparative or longitudinal differentiation of the welfare state concept. Instead, the description and conceptualization of an alternative theory should show that the development and characteristics of the welfare state, as represented by the German case, rested on several divisible and partially contrary economic, political, and ideological power constellations, interests, and strategies – based on differing and distinguishable, even contrasting, classes and strata as well as alliances among them. Only by ignoring strict scientific standards can these socially contradictory societal configurations be artificially abstracted into an artifact called redistribution crisis and development of the welfare state; to summarize them would require distortion of the real issues.[26]

Strategies for Resolving the Redistribution Crisis

The welfare state program, which is described in the political theory of modernization and development as relatively homogenous, has two goals for resolving the redistribution crisis:[27] first, a state-guaranteed minimum in terms of income, nutrition, health, housing, and education as a civic right and not an act of charity; and secondly, a redistribution of income among the various classes and social strata. Another assumption is also basic to this perspective: in the course of the modernization process, the redistribution crisis is clearly not resolved in either a unilinear or a secularly circumscribed fashion. Rather, modernized societies in the twentieth century reach a solution at once appropriate in level and quality to their peculiar national traditions and, what is more, responsive to new demands arising within their own historical contexts.[28]

A series of case studies on the development of the welfare state appears to confirm these universal assumptions.[29] In modernized countries, according to these studies, the state welfare policy goals – including a high level of achievement and satisfactory quality – give way to the continuing necessity for gradual reform. What has frequently happened, especially among 'new' political economists, is that analysts make a normative strategic judgement about the optimum functional level of the welfare state and conclude that that level has been overshot and that solving the redistribution crisis will create considerable problems in the areas of economic, financial, and employment policy.

A detailed examination of such empirical hypotheses and normative evaluations of the welfare state's level of goal attainment, however, produces empirical evidence contradicting the basic assumptions of the theory of political development. It is, of course, undeniable that the strategy of using the welfare state to solve the redistribution crisis has become increasingly popular throughout the world since the Second

World War. Equally undeniable, however, are the results of empirical studies showing that no modernized nation anywhere in the world has come close to meeting the goals sought by state welfare policies.[30]

(1) It has not been possible to attain for every citizen a standard of living above the level of mere subsistence.
(2) Grants of money, goods, and services in the welfare state continue to be better described as acts of charity on the part of the society or social bureaucracy than as social and political rights guaranteed to every citizen.
(3) The desired redistribution of income has not been achieved. In fact, it would be more appropriate to speak of an inverse relationship between material grants and the social stratum of their recipients. In contrast to the announced political goals, only minimal redistribution took place at the lower social strata. Even more significantly, however, the structures used by most welfare programs for financing, organizing, and selecting recipients are apt to have a regressive or at least neutral effect on income distribution. If we also include in the private sector what Titmuss calls 'occupational welfare benefits', which are clearly and consciously set up in a regressive manner, the contrary hypothesis is empirically more supportable: the total complex of social welfare, in its public as well as private aspects, is more likely to benefit the higher social strata than the truly needy. Indeed, at times the former benefit at the expense of the latter. As Martin Rein has put it so aptly: 'So pervasive has been our failure to cope with poverty and dependency that this tendency can be called the iron law of social welfare.'[31]
(4) In the course of modernization, a series of new, qualitative welfare requirements emerged, and in recent decades further demands were defined as issues which, in their quantitative and qualitative ramifications, correspond to the shift from 'pauperism to poverty' of which Rein speaks. These changes cover a wide range of problems. They include humanizing the workplace through modernization strategies in the private and public economic sectors, reducing the growing disparities in the deteriorating living and working conditions of certain geographic areas, and basic questions about industrial democracy and the reduction of relative deprivation.[32] None of these 'qualitative' developmental crises, however, could readily be defined in a political sense, let alone be studied as an aspect of a more highly developed state policy.
(5) According to the political theory of modernization, traditional societies can also experience a 'modernization reversal' and 'political decay' (Huntington). But, as a rule, in modernized industrial states with liberal economies based on private ownership, the expectation is that the political and socioeconomic level of development will stabilize following the resolution of developmental crises; further development, it is assumed, is likely to be secular in nature. Demodernization of modern systems 'is regarded as hard to imagine in the twentieth century'.[33] The empirical data mentioned above on

the long-term development of the welfare state in the twentieth century also argue significantly against this theory.

Looking superficially at the LHI's development and its prevailing system of goals, it would seem that, given gradual expansion and accommodation, the LHI went far toward solving the redistribution crisis by combating illness among the general public. It would also seem that its quantitative growth, which is indeed remarkable, would substantiate this conclusion: expansion of health insurance to an almost comprehensive insurance system, enormous increases in expenditures and services, changes in the structure of services rendered by emphasizing practical services and by the limited introduction of early intervention measures, and the LHI's thorough professionalization, especially among its doctors.[34]

This primarily quantitative expansion of the LHI cannot be underestimated as an empirical example. It must none the less be contrasted with two other empirically verifiable developments.[35] These are widespread stagnation and the relative regression – in several areas – of the quantitative structural development. Characteristic of the first is the continuing dominance and limitation of the LHI's curative-compensatory organization alongside its only barely expanded definition of goals in terms of negative illness. In addition, there are the structures of the welfare system which foster fragmented organization and specific selectivity.

Symptomatic of the second is a historically relative but also absolute regression in the level and quality of problem-solving. There is a great deal of evidence to support this view, including: the absolute increase in numerous chronic diseases and decreasing life expectancy among a large proportion of the population (with the lower classes and strata suffering most); a clear-cut shift in the power structure of the LHI as indicated by the weakening of self-administrative positions, sharply strengthened state controls, and the enhanced, juridically fixed predominant role increasingly exercised by industry during the last seventy years; the almost total loss of direct control by the working class over the LHI's facilities, techniques, and goals of production, both through increased 'professional dominance' (Friedson) by traditional groups within the middle class, such as doctors with their mixed status of self-employment and representation in public and legally recognized corporate bodies, as well as through the sharply increasing economic and political weight of the medical-industrial complex as the predominant supply structure opposed by a fragmented demand structure; the widespread disappearance of public facilities such as, in particular, outpatient facilities for participants in state insurance programs and the crisis in public health which, if anything, has intensified in recent years; the increasing tendency toward reprivatization of the profitable portions of the welfare system through a financial arrangement based on collective solidarity among the insured and the introduction and tendentious expansion of the number of insured persons who bear a portion of their own medical costs.

Thus the history of the German LHI projects an image in which the quantitative and the structural or qualitative dimensions have undergone fractionated and uneven modernization. The quantitative development of the LHI, though not the shift in diseases, seems to provide empirically verifiable support for the traditional theory of modernization. (The fact that this conclusion can be only partially proven will become apparent when we get to the functional analysis of the LHI.) With respect to the relationship between the core structure of the LHI and the problems of eradicating disease – problems such as chronically degenerative and socially oriented diseases, primary prevention, and treatment and control of those affected which have actually always been with us but which arè now much more intense – there is none the less fairly unequivocal counterparadigmatic and empirical evidence supporting the theory presented here. This assertion is based on the relative stagnation and partial regression of the core structures of the system and the stagnating, at times even worsening, morbidity and mortality rate for the general public. It is precisely this relative stagnation and partial regression of the system's core structures together with its efficiency and effectiveness that strengthen the counterparadigmatic evidence. This evidence indicates that a reversal of the modernization process is possible even in a modernized society of the twentieth century with a liberal economy based on private ownership.

Explaining the Failure to Resolve the Redistribution Crisis
Empirical data on the negligible and at times even negative ability of public welfare policies in modernized systems to attain their goals for dealing with redistribution crises may be explained in three ways: contingency factors, restrictions inherent in the system and its structure, and substantial changes during the course of the modernization process in the functions – or even a reversal of functions – described in the original social and political goals.

All available literature categorically refutes the first interpretation. In contrast to other policy areas, political developments in the area of welfare state activities are noteworthy for having achieved a number of far-reaching breakthroughs in overcoming the redistribution crisis. Moreover, nowhere in the political history of the welfare state's emergence in the West, especially in Germany, the United States, and Great Britain, can one find a significant accumulation of contingency factors that would hamper development.[36]

In the case of the other two interpretations, the empirical evaluation typically – again conforming to the political theory of modernization – assumes that the historical and systematic growth of the redistribution crisis and the development of the welfare state grew out of problems associated with increasing industrialization (linked primarily with the developmental theme of equality and the state's capacity to control) along with the new safety and health problems emerging from them. The results of long-term developments in the welfare state, however, cannot be measured, or can only be measured to a very limited degree, by comparisons with goals set in such a genetic fashion. For, given all the differences in the way nations have developed, the effects of the welfare state cannot adequately be explained by its goals but only, if at all, on other grounds: preservation of the family, humanitarian values, anti-recession instruments, and especially the education of the masses as a means of restructuring the qualification system.[37]

It is certainly true that the 'social side of sociopolitical regulations' (Heimann) in the welfare state should not be overlooked or dismissed as 'capitalist ideology' (Offe). As a significant counterpoint stands the secular development of 'pauperism to poverty' (Rein). 'But it is for precisely this reason that one must not forget the fundamental importance of social policies for productivity policy.'[38] The reference to the structurally 'characteristic bipolarity' of state welfare policies provides an opportunity for a comprehensive (though cursory) and empirical description that is closer to the true picture of the actual and most significant functions of the welfare state system; it can also show the system's dynamics and relative strengths in relation to the redistribution crisis in modernized societies. First, due to its increasing involvement in the societal web of interest groups and power blocs, the historically ascribed 'characteristic bipolarity'[39] of the welfare state contributed to a gradual differentiation of the social and political goals by adding and overlapping various economic, political, and ideological functions with the state. Secondly, the quantitative as well as the qualitative expansion of the welfare state was not so much the result of endogenous sociopolitical developments within the system itself. Rather, it was to a large extent the result of the penetration of the welfare state through redirected and redefined conflicts among the most widely differing areas of the society and the dynamics that developed out of them:[40] economic functionalization through preparatory efforts in isolated branches of the economy as well as through cyclical and growth demands in the total economy;[41] a political functionalization through attempts to pacify and reduce solidarity among workers, to exert social control over deviant behavior, and to subsidize traditional and newer middle-class groups as carriers of the welfare state measures;[42] an ideological functionalization in which the welfare state displayed a new and relatively low-cost method for reaching a consensus while avoiding fundamental changes in the existing social structure with its inequalities and dependencies.[43] Thirdly, on the one hand, this conglomerate of welfare state functions was – in its differentiation and hierarchy of priorities – variable and partially substitutable.[44] On the other hand, there were systemic and longstanding restrictions against further expansion of its socially and politically oriented goals – in the cost and productivity pressure exerted by the private-ownership economy; in the fiscal problems of the liberal taxation state; and in the bureaucratized, juridicized, and professional structures.[45] Fourthly, within the framework of welfare state developments resulting from the prevailing and contradictory power relationships in society, the original sociopolitical goals are to a large extent only a byproduct of its primary economic and political functions.

Thus the developments experienced to date suggest not merely a shifting of functions but rather a reversal in its functional priorities.

A closer look at the actual functioning of the LHI confirms the empirical results outlined above.[46] As is true of welfare state policy in general, the LHI has manifested a 'characteristic bipolarity' since its inception and its system is subject to similar dynamics. Since the scope of the LHI in society, however, is ruled to a far greater extent by strong societal forces – in comparison to, let us say, the numerous fringe groups involved in public assistance – the developmental dynamics are characterized by increased social conflict. From the very outset, the ruling elite tried hard to use the LHI as a means to further its own argument in the prevailing societal dialogues by: destroying the voluntary and self-administered welfare programs for workers; having the state gradually take over the administration of the LHI; internally blocking that administration through the factual supremacy of business and industry; fractionating the working-class movement on the question of individualizing socially related illnesses; and trying to undo both the individual and collective rights of the working-class and union movements.

The LHI, meanwhile, turned increasingly into an agency concerned with realizing the profit motives of industrial interests and the status concerns of the middle class. In contrast, from almost the beginnings of the LHI, the working-class movement had used available strategies to protect its own reproduction interests and to build up its political strength as an opposition power. Thus the development of the real functions of the LHI is to a significant degree the story of conflict among opposing power blocs over what should be the real functional priorities.

In this section the comparison among competing theories of social development has concentrated on political theories of modernization and development and how they describe the actual and substantive structure of the welfare state, specifically the health care system, and conceptualize this problem through appropriate explanatory sketches and assumptions. Were this central issue not dealt with, then our theories would rest upon 'ideas ... as products of everyday experience', whose main purpose is to 'harmonize our behavior with our environment'. The result would be that, 'instead of a scientific discipline concerned with realities, we produce nothing more than ideological analyses'.[47] The successful solution to this problem determines all further scientific undertakings such as the development of definitions, categories, and concepts, of empirically verifiable hypotheses and theories. To summarize, the foregoing analysis has shown that:

(1) The political theory of development correctly identifies numerous aspects of real-world and substantive problems, at least as they appear in isolated and empirical form. In the process, however, the dynamics of the system are overlooked. This circumstance frequently leads to incorrect judgements about the empirical

evidence. (See, for instance, the expansion of the welfare state, which is less easily explained in terms of endogenous social policy than as a result of the overlapping of other functions that have been detoured from other social conflicts.)

(2) In the case of several such aspects, the investigation revealed counterfactual and counterparadigmatic empirical evidence (such as the long-term 'demodernization' and the 'political decay' of twentieth-century states with liberal, private-ownership economies).

(3) Given the central notion of the political theory of modernization and development under discussion here – the concept of a redistribution crisis – it has been possible to show by examining the basic assumptions, goal attainment level, and actual functional development of the welfare state that the description of the real-world and substantive issue is highly inadequate. The conceptualization of the welfare state and the health care system proved to be largely an artifact that runs counter to the actual issues in the countries under consideration.

(4) If it is true that the conceptualizing strategy of the theory design's core idea distorts reality, then it would be difficult to avoid basic 'ideological analyses' growing out of a structurally rooted and implicit normativism. The most significant reasons for this are twofold: the limited scope of historical and socioeconomic political experience on which the conceptualizing strategies rest, together with a selective perception regarding specific classes and strata. This means that middle-range studies related to this theory design can hardly prevent the gaps described in the explanatory sketch and the basic assumptions mentioned earlier from being wholly reproduced in subsequent analytic categories and concepts that seek to spell them out or in their empirically defined hypothesis and theories.

Alternative Theories: Concepts, Realities, and Comparisons

The second part of our comparison of alternative theories will examine the internal validity of the analytic concepts and the empirical hypotheses as they relate to the assumptions analyzed earlier. Here the basic empirical issue derives from the prerequisites and forms of the political, economic, and ideological arguments surrounding the welfare state as a strategy for resolving the redistribution crisis. As an illustration of this crisis we shall continue with our example of the LHI. Such a task does not require a thorough analysis of the political theory of development since that theory is part of the more general modernization theory and is subject to a similar fundamental criticism.[48] It will, however, be necessary to examine briefly the basic elements of the historically oriented political and economic theory, since this theory is not yet widely known in its non-economistic form.

For this reason the following analysis concentrates on the conceptual and empirical examination of two central and functionally equivalent concepts found in both theories: the role of political mobilization or class conflicts together with the significance of intervention by the state in the development of the German LHI. Empirical data will be brought to bear on the analytic and empirical qualities of five conceptual configurations: (1) the structure, function, and processes of political mobilization and class conflict; (2) the role of the state in this particular developmental process; (3) the issue of linkages within the political system; (4) linkages between the political system and especially economic development; and (5) the possible impact of the international system on these endogenous political developments. In this case, too, the total analysis can be illustrative only, not definitive, and must concentrate on evaluative contrasts among a few, carefully selected core notions of the actual developmental process and particularly significant aspects of the theory.

Some Analytic Concepts

According to the political theory of development, processes of political mobilization – as expressions of a secular trend toward the expansion of participation in a wide variety of political structures – are a 'central component of the political process and a central means for the analysis of political problems and social change'.[49] As 'the most important and central functions of many political groups', processes of political mobilization are rooted either in structural and historical cleavages and specific conflicts of interest, or in political conflicts that are relatively endogenous.[50]

Historically speaking, these processes of political mobilization are the 'latest and most recent form of social mobilization', resulting from both the liberal political revolution and the Industrial Revolution. During these periods questions about the distribution of resources, economic gains, and production became central societal issues. Differentiated roles for landowners and the bourgeoisie, for ownership classes and the lessees and workers, grew out of these cleavages and conflicts. The two central societal functions of political mobilization – the articulation of interests and the legitimation of the state's authority – also produced the two most significant societal forms: solidarity within specific interest groups and political conflicts among relatively opportunistic alliances for the purpose of distributing society's surplus and creating general rules for distribution (pluralistic process and distribution policies); and creating instruments for political mobilization to support and legitimate the state's authority (system-oriented policies).

History shows that processes of mobilization become increasingly institutionalized. Those movements that are not institutionalized, those which maintain their diffuseness, solidarity, and ideology, assume marginal importance; those politics that are controlled by the state enjoy a disproportionately greater weight than the politics of pluralistic interest representation.[51] According to the prevailing political theory of development, processes of political mobilization usually proceed according to specific developmental sequences. In contrast to this, and on the basis of the Chinese experience, recent studies have tried to take into account such factors as strategy and tactics, organization and the ideology of political actors, and counter-mobilization and demobilization.[52]

Besides the political processes of mobilization, the key element of political development is thought to be the national and secularized state.[53] The state, viewed externally as sovereign and internally as relatively autonomous with regard to economic and social processes, is considered to be a central, powerful, and relatively neutral center of control for accomplishing social goals. Typically, historical development leads to an increase in the state's capacity to control, a differentiation and rationalization of state structures, and the dominance of the state's internal politics as opposed to other types of politics.

Within the political system there is thus typically a movement toward disengagement and independence on the part of the state's control mechanism *vis-à-vis* the pluralistic policies pertaining to the masses. Mutual interdependence takes place during those historically rare occasions of political realignment.[54] At one time the relationship between the political, economic, and social subsystems of a society was regarded as relatively strongly deterministic. In the revisionist views, however, the economic and social systems provide conditions for both limiting and encouraging state control and are in turn controlled by it.[55] With respect to the international system, to be sure, there are increasing numbers of interdependencies. The key element in the political theory of development is nevertheless the sovereign national state with its own relatively high endogenous weight. External penetrations of the international system are viewed as either somewhat peripheral or difficult to explain.[56]

In political-economic theory, conflict among social classes is viewed as the motor of social development (primacy of the class struggle in contrast to an economistic view). Following the formation of commercial, industrial, and financial capital, a social structure was developed whose sociopolitical conflicts and configurations were determined by the economic division of labor, political elite structure, and ideological value system.

This social structure is a link between classes engaged in agrarian production and those involved in capitalist production, as well as among the numerous strata and factions in both. The relationship between classes does not change simply according to the changing trends in the predominant means of production. Rather, there also exists considerable historical variation in the crystallization of classes, the relationship of the dominance and hierarchy among classes, and the possibilities for alliances among them. The extent to which opportunistic alliances may be formed, however, is determined by the major economic, political, and ideological contradictions among them.[57]

According to this view the dynamics and direction of political development emanate from the economic, political, and ideological contradictions among the various classes. Sociopolitical development is not regarded as a long-term, linear process of maturation or as catastrophic collapse, but rather as a long, drawn-out war entailing various configurations of the class struggle. During this war – in which economic, political, and ideological factors all play their own important role – the various factions and alliances of at least the two main classes pursue goals that are ultimately antagonistic, do not follow a balanced developmental process, and therefore cannot result in a final compromise. Fluctuations in the class struggle are differentiated according to offensive and defensive stages, according to phases of varying imbalance and strategic reversals each of which signifies a variation in the relational organization among classes. The specific fluctuations depend on objective factors in the power relationship among the classes and their economic, political, and ideological strategies and tactics at a given moment.

The primacy of its class aspects notwithstanding, this struggle is none the less also directed at the state. The state in contradistinction to its instrumental or institutional-functional conceptualizations is interpreted as the materialized massing and grouping process that takes place among the classes. Its origins are traced back to a union of the absolutist state with the interests of the bourgeoisie. This union sought to elevate specific functions into a centralized body for control and intervention. The special purposes of such a state consisted of holding together the splinter groups of the bourgeoisie as well as fragmenting, pacifying, and subjugating the working class. The structural foundation of the state rests on the alliance between monopolistic and non-monopolistic groups within the bourgeoisie. From time to time this alliance produces a hegemonic power bloc based on coalitions between traditional and newer middle classes which in turn vary according to the strength of individual classes at any given moment in history.

It is in the bourgeois state that the bloc in power discovers its political representation which is exercised by competing political factions. In the course of history such political representation has varied from configurations based on total identity and correspondence to those with a crisis-like tendency toward dissolving the state's ties to its roots in social class. In all this the state does not appear as a unified, well-organized body but rather reflects in its manifold apparatuses the structural contradictions and subordinations of hegemonic and hierarchically organized groups.[58] Consequently, specific functions of the state are characterized by a structural selectivity: certain social problems are never defined as political by the state and are not seen as within its purview; similarly, its instruments of intervention are limited structurally in a historical, real, and social sense. The state's political autonomy and neutrality, therefore, depend upon the relationship among the classes which is basic to its existence. It is also for this reason that the state's capacity to control cannot expand, since with every fluctuation in the long drawn-out war of the class struggle the strength, direction, and quality of state control are altered, as are the forms, functions, and structures of the state's exercise of power.[59] Given this theoretic perspective, the linkage problem in a political system may be regarded as the momentary and specific manifestation of the relationship that evolves from political representation. This will alternate – depending on class relationships and contacts among the political elites – between correspondence/identification and an extensive capacity to control from the perspective of hegemonic groups and bloc formations, that is, political crisis.

The search for linkages among the economic, social, and political aspects of the system, however, contradicts the basic precepts of this theory. For according to its developmental and accumulation model of society it is not possible to isolate a deterministic economy as it relates to politics; one cannot find the opposite situation either. Rather, the primacy of the class struggle determines economic tendencies in the long drawn-out war, such as the development of profit rates as well as technical tendencies, such as the development of productivity forces. This does not mean, however, that the state is center stage for the class struggle. Rather, separate economic apparatuses exist outside the state in the form of individual capital goods that can develop their own economic, political, and ideological mobilization processes.

Of fundamental significance to the processes of political mobilization, and especially for the role of the state, is its position within the universal system, the world economy.[60] From this perspective it is fundamentally incorrect to use the nation-state as a unit of analysis. Depending on the historical configurations within the world's economy at a given moment, a certain and limited number of core states emerge as nation-states. These, however, are balanced by numerous peripheral and semi-peripheral areas with weak or non-existent state functions and structures. Thus the extent to which nation-states (and political mobilization as defined by the theory of modernization) develop depends in large measure on the world economic system at any given moment.

Phases in the Development of the LHI

Against the foregoing background of alternative explanations and their respective concepts, definitions, categories, hypotheses, and theories, we turn now to the history of the German LHI from the perspective of the process of political development and its determinants. This history will of necessity be sketchy and descriptive. Even so, it will be possible to use specific, illustrative aspects of this development in testing the strengths and weaknesses of the individual theories.

The history of the German LHI may be divided roughly into eight phases.[61]

(1) The precursors of the LHI, which took the form of self-help organizations within the working-class movement as well as state and communal assistance to the poor.
(2) The beginnings of state-imposed insurance and the destruction of the self-help organizations through an alliance of landownership and heavy industry with feudal-conservative political elites opposed to the efforts of a politically active working-class movement.
(3) The struggle for power between 1890 and 1914 between both social entities and the creation of the LHI within the unstable political structure that rested on an alliance between the two.

(4) In the period from 1918 to 1920, a partial strategic reversal in conjunction with external intervention.
(5) The unstable political balance during the Weimar era, reliant upon bourgeois domination and accompanied by the search on the part of both social entities for appropriate structures, functions, and progress for the LHI.
(6) The polarization of social groupings into explicitly antagonistic alliances (1930–3) and the strategic reversal that occurred during the 'counter-revolution' of fascism (1933–45).
(7) External intervention on the part of the conquering powers (in both parts of Germany) with the goal of restoring a liberal, private-ownership economy together with an internal system that is politically, economically, and ideologically unstable.
(8) The strategic shift in 1948–9 and the 'balance of imbalances' which began in 1951 with the re-establishment along traditional lines of the LHI.

This chaotic history points up widely divergent characteristics of political development: several different offensive and defensive phases or a differentiated balance among economic, political, and ideological forces; four strategic shifts of varying scope in the course of long, drawn-out political altercations; and two phases of explicit penetration and intervention on the part of the international system into the national development of the LHI.

Comparisons between Two Theories

On the basis of some carefully chosen configurations of political development from these phases, the two theories will now be compared with respect to how well their central concepts and categories as well as their empirical hypotheses and theories can be used for explanatory purposes. The comparison will be limited to the five concepts discussed earlier and can, of course, only be illustrative, not systematic.[62]

Political conflict, mobilization, and social class. Given the tumultuous history of the German LHI, there is much to be said for the argument that both the analytic sweep of the concepts as well as a series of empirical findings are better explained by the notion of class conflict than that of political mobilization. It is relatively easy to explain the political development of the LHI as a long, drawn-out war involving social entities that are to some extent antagonistic and using strategic goals that are to some extent contradictory; it is rather more difficult to explain it as the mobilization of interests, especially those of the working class, as a part of the secular expansion of rights of participation aimed at the ultimate goal of common problem-solving. It is equally difficult to find any sort of inexorable process in the LHI's history. Instead, this history is a product of various fluctuations in the class struggle consisting of various phases – sometimes on the offensive, sometimes defensive, sometimes balanced and sometimes not, with occasional strategic shifts. Finally, but no less significantly, it becomes apparent that the LHI's political development was not merely a *political* mobilization, but really an all-inclusive conflict involving economics, politics, and ideology.

It is especially noteworthy, we might add, that those concepts included by the political theory of development in dealing with political mobilization systematically exclude significant aspects of the social and political conflict. Political mobilization cannot be understood merely as the activation of social collectives such as the working class and the traditional or new middle class.

Political mobilization is primarily also class crystallization of commercial, industrial, and financial capital, that is, of the power bloc and its hegemonic faction. This was especially apparent in the period from 1930 to 1933 and again between 1948 and 1951.[63] The forms of mobilization among these dominant factions were simply of a different type. They include political intervention in the political elite, active forms of struggle in the economic sphere (such as policies on investments, productivity, pricing, the job market, and employment); they also include mobilization through inactivity. An analogous systematic exclusion characterizes the mobilization of the working class. At least in the early decades of the LHI, mobilization of the working class cannot be described simple as the articulation of interests in conjunction with legitimation of the existing order. Rather, it is the strategic attempt to establish a transformational counterweight, the aim of which is the reformation of the entire social fabric.[64] Last but not least, political mobilization may be regarded only in part as an aspect of a secular expansion of citizen participation. For the history of the LHI itself confirms – most clearly in the destruction of the unions (Mason) and the creation of the Fuehrer principle during the Third Reich – the long-term reversal in levels of participation by insured workers within autonomous bodies and in organizational elections (including numbers of voters as well as numbers of elections held). This early history illustrates quite clearly the strategically successful attempt to push back and destroy through a variety of mechanisms the workers' right to negotiate on matters of national health insurance, and in any case, to 'permit subordinate forms of participation'.[65]

Role of the state in development. According to the theory of political development, the state is the central and relatively autonomous controlling agency of a society. The state regulates by mediating as a neutral force among interests, and its capacity for control in modern societies increases secularly. The history of the LHI provides an overwhelming amount of conceptual and empirical data to counter this view. The very manner in which the state set up the LHI proves the structural selectivity and ambivalence of its class-oriented control mechanism.[66] All aspects of the LHI's implementation, internal make-up, organization, financing, and power structure corresponded to the interests of the class originally addressed. Any deviations were the result of political compromises at the expense of the working class or compromises among contradictory capital interests.

It is equally incorrect to describe the state as a relatively autonomous control mechanism for a society. The history of the LHI confirms the enormous variability in the history of the state's capacity for control. This widely differentiated ability to control includes the strong authoritarian state under Bismarck, the 'emergence state' under fascism, the unstable compromise of the Weimar era, the total immobilism and disorientation of the political elite between 1930 and 1933, and the practically non-existent state after 1945. Structural selectivity and variability on the part of the state's controlling capacity also determine the type and extent of relative autonomy enjoyed by the state. Independent of the influence exerted by the international system, it is only possible to speak of the state's autonomy when either a balance of power among the classes has been achieved or when, vice versa, one class clearly dominates over all the others. It is only by means of such configurations that the elites achieve room in which to maneuver – but always and only within the framework of the existing class balance and the state's structural selectivity.

Linkages within the political system and between the political and economic systems. A pervasive conceptual dilemma of both theories lies in the manner and intensity of relating the economic and political systems to each other. The history of the LHI shows that the revisionist political theory of development is correct when it rejects an unequivocal determinism in political development based on economic laws and makes them subject to a significant number of autonomous state responses. The political-economic theory of development is better able, both conceptually and empirically, to deal with this relational issue. First, it is precisely the long-term as well as the short-term development that confirms the state's dependence upon economic growth and fluctuations. Furthermore, the state's manner of responding to economic developments is not haphazard or accidental. It is rather determined to a substantial degree by the class relationships on which the state itself rests. National responses ('reforms') to the economic crisis of 1930–3 or the one that has persisted since 1974 confirm this counter-thesis. Even the political theory of development, according to which economic processes either encourage or discourage national control of social policies, does not provide an adequate explanation. For the structures of the private economy determine in large measure the direction and intensity of the activity of the state's structures and functions, and hence the extent of their ability to maneuver.[67] The history of the LHI does not provide, in any case, examples of anti-capitalist social policy within the framework of the existing social order.

Impact of the international system. In the case of the revisionist version of the political theory of development, either the influence of the international system is historically contingent or else the causal relationships cannot be clearly proved. For the political-economic theory, too, internal political processes of mobilization and national functions are dependent in large measure on the position of the state in the world economic system. The history of the German LHI provides fairly substantial proof for this latter conception. Reference has already been made to the fact that at different times, especially in 1918 and 1945, state functions and structures varied in their capacity to control due to Germany's varying situation in the world system. Especially after 1946 the core nations in the capitalist world were keenly interested in restoring West Germany to a central position – albeit an extremely dependent one. At the same time, the outside interventions were aimed at the contents of core-state restoration in West Germany. This post-1946 restoration was to correspond to the liberal parliamentary and private-ownership structures of the core nations. This was also the aim of Allied involvement in the LHI, whose fundamental structures and functions were not to be altered. The penetration of the core economic states into the process of political development is thus an integral and systematic part of the history of the German LHI.[68]

These few illustrative examples from the LHI's history – and research on the American and English development of health care services produces similar results – are sufficient to suggest the basic weaknesses of the political theory of development and its component elements, political mobilization and the theory of the state: (1) as a fundamental analysis this conceptualization is unable or only partially able to deal with significant and central issues of the LHI's development; (2) its concepts and categories, as a rule, can incorporate only limited portions of the total reality and even then frequently juxtapose them in a mutually contradictory way; and (3) in the case of several important hypotheses there is a significant amount of counterparadigmatic and empirical evidence to oppose them.

Conclusions and Prospects for a Comparison of Competing Theories

Our review of the revisionist version of the political theory of modernization as exemplified by the theoretic constructs of the redistribution crisis, political mobilization, and development of the state has shown: (1) the model is not sufficient to explain adequately the real issue nor to translate it into an adequate, scientifically conceptualized strategy; (2) there are serious gaps in the basic analytic concepts and categories; and (3) there is much counterparadigmatic evidence regarding numerous empirical hypotheses. In contrast, empirical evidence suggests that the competing political-economic theory possesses far greater explanatory power. According to Lakatos, however, a theory is falsified only when a better theory is presented which fulfills three criteria: it must have greater empirical and conceptual content than the first; it must include those aspects of the original theory that were not disproved; and the excess content must at least in part have been verified.[69]

In the case of the LHI, the alternative political-economic theory seems to fulfill the first criterion. With respect to the second, the discussion raised plausible arguments showing that, for instance, the concept 'behavior-steering norms' – a central point in the theory of modernization – has not been dealt with sufficiently.[70] And, with respect to the third criterion, the only thing that is certain is that here, too, there are gaps and much that is unclear about a great many of the basic assumptions of this 'explanatory sketch', its central analytic concepts, and empirical hypotheses. Certainly, they are in need of further study.[71]

In view of this situation it seems fruitless either to stick with a dogmatic confrontation and rule out the alternative theory at every turn, or to avoid the entire question and seek refuge in research that is oriented to history or 'middle-range' hypotheses. What does seem fruitful from a research point of view, however, are two possible strategies. One calls for an attempt at progressive issue reorientation of the theory of modernization through further revision of its explanatory sketch, basic concepts, and hypotheses. Secondly, and more important, there should be an intensive examination of the gaps in the political-economic theory. Even though the steps described above for the second research strategy promise greater success, the first variant should not be entirely dismissed. As a further research strategy we might rather relate empirically and theoretically oriented investigations to the significant and functionally equivalent core structures of both theories. This might further the process of evaluation and at the same time clarify substantive political issues. Such a research endeavor ought not, however, either to fall prey to the error of demanding too much theoretic rigor or to set up the prevailing competitive theory as a straw man only to knock it down.

To avoid the twofold experiential predicament for scientific conceptualization, it is essential that the theory of modernization assimilate the historical experience of societal developments such as the liberal-European and Chinese-Asian 'revolutions' into its scientific conceptualization, categories, and hypothesis formation. For both these social developments present transformations of basic societal structures and not merely 'modernization' within predetermined and pre-ordained societal structures. Such an expanded perspective also reveals once again the fundamental relationship of scientific insight and societal interest, and as a research strategy might even produce results of practical relevance.

Notes: Chapter 5

1 As a source for many other authors, see Immanuel Wallerstein, *The Modern World-System* (New York, San Francisco, London: Academic Press, 1974), pp. 3ff.
2 Emile Durkheim, *The Rules of Sociological Method* (New York: The Free Press, 1938), pp. 14ff.
3 Wallerstein, *Modern World-System*, p. 3.
4 For two examples, see Dean C. Tipps, 'Modernization theory and the comparative study of societies: a critical perspective', *Comparative Studies in Society and History*, vol. 15, no. 2 (1973), pp. 199–226; and Peter Flora, *Modernisierungsforschung: zur empirischen Analyse der gesellschaftlichen Entwicklung* (Opladen: Westdeutscher Verlag, 1974).
5 William J. Foltz, 'Modernization and nation-building: the social mobilization model reconsidered', in this volume.
6 On the theoretic discussion under consideration here, see Wolfgang Fach, 'Autonome Wissenschaft', *Zeitschrift für Soziologie*, vol. 3, no. 1 (February 1974), pp. 31–43.
7 Wolfgang Zapf, 'Die Soziologische Theorie der Modernisierung', unpublished manuscript (1974), p. 1.

8 Nelson Kasfir, *The Shrinking Political Arena: Participation and Ethnicity in African Politics, with a Case Study of Uganda* (Berkeley, Los Angeles, London: University of California Press, 1976), p. 55; for a general overview of the literature on this point, see Foltz, 'Modernization and nation-building'; Flora, *Modernisierungforschung*, pp. 18–93; Hans-Ulrich Wehler, *Modernisierungstheorie und Geschichte* (Göttingen: Van den Hoeck & Ruprecht, 1975); Chong-Do Hah and Jeanne Schneider, 'A critique of current studies on political development and modernization', *Social Research*, vol. 35, no. 1 (1968), pp. 130–58; Robert A. Packenham, 'Approaches to the study of political development', *World Politics*, vol. 17, no. 1 (October 1964), pp. 108–20.

9 Wallerstein, 'Modernization: requiescat in pace', in *The Uses of Controversy in Sociology*, ed. Lewis A. Coser and Otto N. Larsen (New York, London: The Free Press, 1976), pp. 131ff.

10 For an example of the revisionist view, see Reinhard Bendix, 'Tradition and modernity reconsidered', *Comparative Studies in Society and History*, vol. 9, no. 3 (1967), pp. 292–346.

11 Thomas Kuhn, *The Structure of Scientific Revolutions* (Chicago: University of Chicago Press, 1962), pp. 69–72.

12 It is interesting to note that while, as a rule, Americans are concerned with the internal paradigmatic aspects of theoretic and empirical research, Western Europeans make a greater attempt to compare and contrast the various theoretic frameworks at a theoretic and empirical level; on this point, for the Federal Republic, see Gerhardt Brandt, 'Industrialisierung, Modernisierung, gesellschaftliche Entwicklung', *Zeitschrift für Soziologie*, vol. 1, no. 1 (January 1972), pp. 5–14; Friedrich Eberle, 'Bemerkungen zum Stand der Diskussion um die Modernisierungstheorie', in *Jahrbuch der Arbeiterbewegung*, ed. Claudio Pozzoli (Frankfurt: Fischer Verlag, 1976), vol. 4, pp. 242–58; Wehler, *Modernisierungstheorie und Geschichte*, pp. 51–7.

13 Theoretic justification for such a focus may be found in the conceptualization of the Committee on Comparative Politics of the Social Science Research Council and in the social mobilization model developed by Karl W. Deutsch; political support may be found in the ongoing discussion concerning the crisis in the welfare state and the creation and development of a national health system in modernized societies.

14 For the methodological approach used, see Seymour Martin Lipset, Martin A. Trow, and James S. Coleman, *Union Democracy* (Garden City, NY: Doubleday, 1962), pp. 471ff.

15 Imre Lakatos 'Falsification and the methodology of scientific research programmes', in *Criticism and the Growth of Knowledge*, ed. Imre Lakatos and Alan Musgrave (Cambridge: Cambridge University Press, 1970).

16 Durkheim, *The Rules of Sociological Method*.

17 Abraham Kaplan, *The Conduct of Inquiry: Methodology for Behavioral Science* (San Francisco: Chandler, 1964).

18 Kuhn, *The Structure of Scientific Revolutions*.

19 Lakatos, 'Methodology of scientific research programmes', pp. 116–19.

20 For a brief overview, see Flora, *Modernisierungsforschung*, pp. 44–52, 56–64, 79–83.

21 Empirical support and bibliographic references for this may be found in Frieder Naschold *et al.*, *Systemanalyse des Gesundheitswesen in Österreich*, 2 vols, 2nd edn (Vienna: Montan-Verlag, 1978).

22 Basic explanations of how the German Legislative Health Insurance system developed, together with further bibliographic references, may be found especially in Florian Tennstedt, 'Sozialgeschichte der Sozialversicherung', in *Handbuch der Sozialmedizin*, ed. Maria Blohmke *et al.* (Stuttgart: Enke-Verlag, 1976), pp. 385–492; Naschold *et al.*, *Systemanalyse des Gesundheitswesen in Österreich*; Marianne Rodenstein, 'Arbeiterselbsthilfe, Arbeiterselbstverwaltung und staatliche Krankenversicherungspolitik in Deutschland', unpublished manuscript (1978); Alfons Labisch, 'Ursprünge sozialdemokratischer Gesundheitspolitik', *Die Neue Gesellschaft*, vol. 4 (1977), pp. 304–08; Harald Bogs and Christian von Ferber, *Soziale Selbstverwaltung*, vol. 1: *Aufgaben und Funktion der Selbstverwaltung in der Sozialversicherung* (Bonn: Verlag der Ortskrankenkassen, 1977); Florian Tennstedt, *Soziale Selbstverwaltung*, vol. 2: *Geschichte der Selbstverwaltung in der Krankenversicherung* (Bonn: Verlag der Ortskrankenkassen, 1977); Erich Standfest *et*

al., *Sozialpolitik und Selbstverwaltung: zur Demokratisierung des Sozialstaats* (Cologne: Bund-Verlag, 1977).

23 In this connection, see especially Labisch, 'Ursprünge sozial-demokratischer Gesundheitspolitik'; Tennstedt, 'Sozialgeschichte der Sozialversicherung' and *Soziale Selbstverwaltung*; Naschold (ed.), *Systemanalyse des Gesundheitswesen in Österreich*; Rodenstein, 'Arbeiterselbsthilfe, Arbeiterselbstverwaltung und staatliche Krankenversicherungspolitik'; and Standfest *et al.*, *Sozialpolitik und Selbstverwaltung*; see also note 36.

24 Some insights into this perspective are provided by the theoretic research of Durkheim, *Rules of Sociological Method*; Kuhn, *Structure of Scientific Revolutions*; Lakatos, 'Methodology of scientific research programmes'; and Kaplan, *Conduct of Inquiry*. Not to be overlooked are the more historically oriented, non-economistic variations of political-economic theories such as Wallerstein, *Modern World-System*; Nicos Ar. Poulantzas, *Faschismus und Diktatur* (Munich: Trikont Verlag, 1973); Nicos Ar. Poulantzas, *Klassen im Kapitalismus, heute* (Berlin: Verlag für das Studium der Arbeiterbewegung, 1975); Timothy W. Mason, *Sozialpolitik im Dritten Reich* (Opladen: Westdeutscher Verlag, 1977).

25 This situation is very clearly described by Eduard Heimann, a leading social political theoretician in the SPD during the Weimar Republic; in his *Soziale Theorie des Kapitalismus: Theorie der Sozialpolitik* (Tübingen: Mohr, 1929), p. 234, Heimann speaks of the conflict between the two societal structures and the social ideas embodied in them.

26 An analogous argument based on the two basic concepts of the argument may be found in Foltz, 'Modernization and nation-building'. See the analyses made by Erik Boettcher, 'Sozialpolitik und Sozialreform', in *Sozialpolitik und Sozialreform*, ed. Erik Boettcher (Tübingen: Mohr [Paul Siebek], 1957), pp. 3–42; A. Bönisch, 'Probleme der bürgerlichen sozialdemokratischen Theorie vom Wohlfahrtsstaat', *Wirtschaftswissenschaft*, vol. 13, no. 3 (1965), pp. 417–33. On the situation in the United States, see especially Martin Rein, *Social Policy* (New York: Random House, 1970), pp. 50ff. As counter-examples of a simple, concrete differentiation of the artifically constructed welfare state, see Gaston V. Rimlinger, *Welfare Policy and Industrialization in Europe, America and Russia* (New York: Wiley, 1971); as well as Hugh Heclo, 'Towards a new welfare state?', unpublished manuscript (1978).

27 For further references see Harold L. Wilensky, 'The problems and prospects of the welfare state', in *Industrial Society and Social Welfare: The Impact of Industrialization on the Supply and Organization of Social Welfare Services in the United States*, ed. Harold L. Wilensky and Charles N. Lebeaux (New York: The Free Press, 1965), p. xii. Similar conclusions are reached by Richard Titmuss, *Income Distribution and Social Change* (London: Allen & Unwin, 1962); Gunnar Myrdal, *Asian Drama* (New York: Pantheon, 1968); Maurice Bruce, *The Rise of the Welfare State: English Social Policy, 1601–1971* (London: Weidenfeld & Nicolson, 1973); and Boettcher, 'Sozialpolitik und Sozialreform'.

28 Passing references to the general issue are made by Flora, *Modernisierungsforschung*. Among the large quantity of literature on the subject, see especially Heclo, 'Towards a new welfare state?', which contains the most recent bibliographic references; Bruce, *Rise of the Welfare State*; Rimlinger, *Welfare Policy and Industrialization*; Standfest *et al.*, *Sozialpolitik und Selbstverwaltung*, pp. 135–72. As examples of the strategic and normative evaluations mentioned here, see Samuel Brittan, 'The economic contradictions of democracy', *British Journal of Political Science*, vol. 5, no. 2 (April 1975), pp. 129–59; Morris Janowitz, *Social Control of the Welfare State* (New York: Elsevier, 1976); James M. Buchanan and Richard E. Wagner, *Democracy in Deficit: The Political Legacy of Lord Keynes* (New York: Academic Press, 1976).

29 See Rimlinger, *Welfare Policy and Industrialization*; Bruce, *Rise of the Welfare State*; as well as Harold L. Wilensky, *The Welfare State and Equality* (Berkeley, Calif.: University of California Press, 1975).

30 A different conclusion may be reached only if welfare state politics is reduced (as it is by Wilensky) to a kind of fringe politics, or extended social welfare; this is not an atypical historical configuration. A summary of many of the international studies dealing with the discussion that follows may be found in Tim Guldimann, *Die Grenzen*

des Wohlfahrtsstaates (Munich: Beck, 1976); Adrian Sinfield, 'Transmitted deprivation and the social division of welfare', unpublished manuscript, 1976; Wilensky, 'Problems and prospects of the welfare state', p. xii; see also Margaret S. Gordon, *The Economics of Welfare Policies* (New York; Columbia University Press, 1963); Titmuss, *Income Distribution and Social Change*; Rein, *Social Policy*, pp. 21ff.; Wilensky, *Welfare State and Equality*.

31 Rein, *Social Policy*, p. 94.
32 As representative examples of this perspective, see Horst Kern, 'Qualität und Humanität des Arbeitslebens', in *Krise und Reform in der Industriegesellschaft*, ed. IG-Metall (Frankfurt: Europäische Verlagsanstalt, 1976); Frieder Naschold, *Alternative Raumpolitik* (Krosberg: Athenäum-Verlag, 1978); W. G. Runciman, *Relative Deprivation and Social Justice: A Study of Attitudes to Social Equality in Twentieth-Century England* (London: Routledge & Kegan Paul, 1966), chs 2–5; Rein, *Social Policy*, pp. 89ff.
33 For a discussion of both points, see Kasfir, *Shrinking Political Arena*, pp. 22ff.
34 Suffice it to say that the effectiveness and efficiency of medical and technical progress in the area of public health is increasingly disputed in recent literature; see A. L. Cochrane, *Effectiveness and Efficiency* (Nuffield: Nuffield Provincial Hospitals Trust, 1971).
35 For supporting arguments, see Standfest *et al.*, *Sozialpolitik und Selbstverwaltung*; Rodenstein, 'Arbeiterselbsthilfe, Arbeiterselbstverwaltung und staatliche Krankenversicherungspolitik'; Naschold *et al.*, *Systemanalyse des Gesundheitswesen in Österreich*; see also note 36.
36 On this point, see Bruce, *Rise of the Welfare State*; Wilensky and Lebeaux, *Industrial Society and Social Welfare*; Rimlinger, *Welfare Policy and Industrialization*; Boettcher, 'Sozialpolitik und Sozialreform'; Rein, *Social Policy*; Gordon, *Economics of Welfare Policies*; Titmuss, *Income Distribution and Social Change*; Heclo, 'New welfare state?'
37 On this point see especially Wilensky, 'Problems and prospects of the welfare state', pp. xviff.
38 Heimann, *Soziale Theorie des Kapitalismus*, p. 137.
39 Wilensky, 'Problems and prospects of the welfare state', p. xxv; Rimlinger, *Welfare Policy and Industrialization*, pp. 1ff., 333ff.
40 Rein, *Social Policy*, pp. 305ff.
41 Wilensky, 'Problems and prospects of the welfare state', pp. xviff; Rein, *Social Policy*, pp. 3ff.
42 Frances F. Piven and Richard A. Cloward, *Regulating the Poor: The Functions of Public Welfare* (London: Tavistock, 1972); Rimlinger, *Welfare Policy and Industrialization*, pp. 8ff., 335ff.
43 Claus Offe, 'Demokratische Legitimation der Planung', in *Strukturprobleme des kapitalistischen Staates: Aufsätze zur politischen Soziologie*, ed. Claus Offe (Frankfurt: Suhrkamp Verlag, 1972).
44 Rein, *Social Policy*; Piven and Cloward, *Regulating the Poor*.
45 Heclo, 'New welfare state?', pp. 16ff., Rein, *Social Policy*, pp. 103–219.
46 In addition to the above-mentioned German research, see especially Robert Alford, *Health Care Politics: Ideological and Interest Group Barriers to Reform* (Chicago: University of Chicago Press, 1975); and Vincente Navarro, *Class Struggle, the State and Medicine* (Oxford, Robertson, 1978).
47 Durkheim, *Rules of Sociological Method*, pp. 14ff.
48 Reference has already been made to several works which join in this fundamental criticism of the political theory of development, among them. Tipps, 'Modernization theory and the comparative study of societies'; Wallerstein, *Modern World-System*; Foltz, 'Modernization and nation-building'; two other studies should also be mentioned: Marion J. Levy, Jr, *Modernization and the Structure of Societies: A Setting for International Affairs* (Princeton, NJ: Princeton University Press, 1966), pp. 10ff.; and Lucian W. Pye, 'The concept of political development', *The Annals of the American Academy of Political and Social Science*, no. 358 (March 1965), pp. 1–13.
49 John Peter Nettl, *Political Mobilization: A Sociological Analysis of Methods and Concepts* (New York: Basic Books, 1967), pp. 25, 110, 125.
50 This is one of the points of difference between the economic and social determinism of the classic political theory of development and the newer revisionist variations. For

more on this, see especially Stein Rokkan, *Citizens, Elections, Parties* (Oslo: Universitetsforlaget and New York: McKay, 1970); and David R. Cameron, 'Toward a theory of political mobilization', *Journal of Politics*, vol. 36, no. 1 (February 1974), pp. 138-71.
51 This historical development – or scientific conceptualization – forms a basis for recent discussions on 'new corporatism'. For an overview of this discussion, see the special issue on 'Corporatism and policy-making in contemporary Western Europe', ed. Philippe C. Schmitter, *Comparative Political Studies*, vol. 10, no. 1 (April 1977), pp. 3-152.
52 So far this discussion has relied on the major points made by Nettl, *Political Mobilization*, and Rokkan, *Citizens, Elections, Parties*. On the newer developments, see especially Franz Schurmann, *Ideology and Organization in Communist China* (Berkeley, Calif.: University of California Press, 1968); Cameron, 'Toward a theory of political mobilization'; as well as Norman Nie, G. P. Powell, and Kenneth Prewitt, 'Social structure and political development: developmental relationships', *American Political Science Review*, vol. 62, no. 2 (June 1969), pp. 361-78, and vol. 62, no. 3 (September 1969), pp. 808-32.
53 Among the overwhelming amount of literature on the subject see Nettl, *Political Mobilization*; Samuel P. Huntington, *Political Order in Changing Societies* (New Haven, Conn.: Yale University Press, 1968); Kasfir, *Shrinking Political Arena*; Cameron, 'Toward a theory of political mobilization'; Rokkan, *Citizens, Elections, Parties*; and Bendix, 'Tradition and modernity reconsidered'.
54 See the specific references in such works as Kasfir, *Shrinking Political Arena*, and Nettl, *Political Mobilization*.
55 See especially Cameron, 'Toward a theory of political mobilization', and Rokkan, *Citizens, Elections, Parties*.
56 See Bendix, 'Tradition and modernity reconsidered'. On the latter point, see especially Kasfir, *Shrinking Political Arena*, p. 270, n.2.
57 The thematic summary of political and economic theory of class structure as it relates to the political mobilization process is based on examples taken from the analysis by Poulantzas, *Faschismus und Diktatur* and *Klassen im Kapitalismus, heute* (see note 34); and Mason, *Sozialpolitik im Dritten Reich*.
58 On this and the following points, see Naschold, *Alternative Raumpolitik*.
59 This might serve as the basis for further analyses in the area of political formations on the one hand, and on the other the specific manifestations of political representation among class relationships in a government of interest groups, the administration, party competition, or of 'liberal corporatism'. On this point, see Gerhard Lehmbruch, 'Liberal Corporatism and Party Government', *Comparative Political Studies*, vol. 10, no. 1 (April 1977), pp. 91-126.
60 In addition to Wallerstein, *Modern World-System*, see especially Dieter Senghaas, *Weltwirtschaftsordnung und Entwicklungspolitik* (Frankfurt: Suhrkamp Verlag, 1977); as well as Gernot Müller, Charles Sabel, Frank Stille, and Winfried Vogt, 'Ökonomische Krisentendenzen im gegenwärtigen Kapitalismus', unpublished manuscript (1976).
61 See notes 35 and 36.
62 On similar methodological limitations, see Flora, *Modernisierungsforschung*, p. 18.
63 For further empirical evidence and bibliographic references, see, for instance, Mason, *Sozialpolitik im Dritten Reich*.
64 In the place of numerous references, see Heimann, *Soziale Theorie des Kapitalismus*.
65 Rodenstein, 'Arbeiterselbsthilfe, Arbeiterselbstverwaltung und staatliche Krankenversicherungspolitik'; Tennstedt, 'Sozialgeschichte der Sozialversicherung' and *Soziale Selbstverwaltung*; Mason, *Sozialpolitik im Dritten Reich*, pp. 99-123; Lelio Basso, *Gesellschaftsformation und Staatsform* (Frankfurt: Suhrkamp Verlag, 1975), pp. 99ff.
66 On this see descriptive contents of this chapter, pp. 120ff.; see also Basso, *Gesellschaftsformation und Staatsform*, pp. 136ff.
67 In addition to Poulantzas, *Faschismus und Diktatur* and *Klassen im Kapitalismus, heute*, see Müller et al., 'Ökonomische Krisentendenzen im gegenwärtigen Kapitalismus'; Wilensky, 'Problems and prospects of the welfare state'.
68 On this restoration period, see Eberhard Schmidt, *Die verhinderte Neuordnung*

1945–1952: zur Auseinandersetzung um die Demokratisierung der Bundesrepublik Deutschland (Frankfurt: Europäische Verlagsanstalt, 1970); as well as Tennstedt, 'Sozialgeschichte der Sozialversicherung' and *Soziale Selbstverwaltung*.
69 Lakatos, 'Methodology of scientific research programmes', p. 116.
70 Brandt, 'Industrialisierung, Modernisierung, gesellschaftliche Entwicklung', pp. 9ff.
71 Eberle, 'Bemerkungen zum Stand der Diskussion um die Modernisierungstheorie', pp. 242ff.; Wehler, *Modernisierungstheorie und Geschichte*, pp. 51ff.; and especially Rudolf Bahro, *Die Alternative* (Frankfurt: Europäische Verlagsanstalt, 1977).

Part Two

Political Integration and Unification

6
Integration Theory and the Study of International Relations

DONALD J. PUCHALA

It is highly appropriate that a volume compiled in celebration of Karl W. Deutsch's scholarship should contain a major section devoted to problems of international integration. Karl Deutsch pioneered in integration studies. This chapter attempts to place his work in perspective and to underline his influence and contributions. However, it is neither an uncritical testimonial to a retiring master nor a reminiscence about past controversies among integration theorists. A good deal will be said about the last twenty years' efforts to formulate and validate a theory of international integration. But the purpose of the exercise is to examine relationships between the subfield of integration studies and the broader discipline of international relations. The point to be emphasized is that the apparent failures of the integration theorists, as for example in their inabilities to predict accurately outcomes in Western Europe, are rather unimportant in comparison to their successes in adding entire new dimensions to the study of international relations.

Integration Theory: A Footnote to Intellectual History

When the intellectual history of twentieth-century social science is written, there is likely to be at least one chapter on 'the study of international integration'. Somewhere in that chapter there may be a rather long, but not especially prominent, footnote that will explain how a series of events in Western Europe after the Second World War prompted two generations of scholars to proliferate abstract explanations of what was happening.[1] It will further tell how the European experience and forthcoming explanations inspired some of these scholars to ask whether what was happening on the Old Continent was also happening elsewhere.[2] The early consensus among these scholars was to label the phenomenon under consideration 'international integration', (although, as it turned out, there was little consensus about what this label meant). Under the influence of the prevailing social 'scientism' of the 1950s and 1960s, newly generated abstractions about international integration were clustered and elevated to the status of 'integration theories'.[3] There then ensued a prolonged debate among scholars concerning the power and accuracy of the various theories, and schools of analysis consequently emerged – federalists, functionalists, neofunctionalists, and transactionalists – all mutually critical and highly self-critical as well; and each claiming exclusive insight almost as in the parable of the 'blind men and the elephant'.[4]

As this debate among theorists gathered momentum, and indeed as it was beginning to yield some rather imaginative efforts to 'integrate' integration theory,[5] whatever had been happening in Western Europe apparently stopped happening. It stopped happening elsewhere as well, and to the intellectual embarrassment of scholars involved, 'integration theory' offered no satisfactory explanation for these turns of events.[6] At this juncture some suggested that the so-called integration theories were probably not theories at all but simply *post hoc* generalizations about current events. Others suggested that the integration theories had been moralizations and utopian prescriptions only. Still others offered that they were accurate generalizations, but that since they were addressed to explaining time-bound, non-recurrent events, they were prone to obsolescence as theories.[7]

Integration theory as it developed from the middle 1950s to the early 1970s was directed primarily toward explaining political unification among states. Karl Deutsch and some of his students defined integration more broadly, as will be explained below. But most other theorists tended to agree that political unification was the object of their inquiries. While the exact meaning of 'political unification' differed from theoretical school to theoretical school, most imagined the end-product to be an entity similar to the modern nation-state, or multinational federation. This being the case, the main questions of integration theory were: within what environment, under what conditions, and by what processes does a new transnational political unit peacefully emerge from two or more initially separate and different ones? These questions are quite legitimate, and the answers would have been (and perhaps will be) interesting, but they were not provided by the integration theorists of the 1950s and 1960s. They could not be provided largely because inappropriate cases were selected for empirical analysis and theoretical generalization. The Western European Common Market, the different Latin American and African customs unions, and various other regional ventures over the last twenty years have not turned out to be cases of political unification, so that using them to generate a theory about political unification proved impossible.

Students of international integration recognized this, of course, and they agreed that to the extent that they were working inductively from contemporary cases, they were not studying political unification. But they then fell into intellectual disarray trying to define exactly what they were studying. Their controversy came to be called the 'dependent variable' problem in integration theory, and in Ernst Haas's interpretation it was an 'anguishing' one.[8] If no end-product of the processes afoot in Europe and elsewhere could be defined, how could it be possible to explain transformation toward or away from it? Empirically, how could one devise a metric to measure progress toward an unspecified, perhaps unknowable end? Whether anguishing or not, this 'dependent variable' problem was sufficiently serious to bring productive efforts at formulating a theory of political unification to a halt in the early 1970s when the college of integration theorists disbanded. Since that time the study of the politics of common markets and regional associations has continued, but most analysts are currently more concerned with practical policy issues in regional co-operation than with theoretical generalizations about unification.[9]

Integration Studies and the Origins of the Challenge to Political Realism

The efforts of twenty years of formal theorizing about international integration are here relegated to the status of a 'footnote' to intellectual history because in a broader and more meaningful context these were neither the most enduring nor the most important accomplishments of the integration theorists of the 1950s and 1960s. To understand why this is so, one must distinguish between *integration theory* (or theories) as represented by the generalizations of federalists, functionalists, neo-functionalists, and transactionalists about international political unification, and *integration studies* as represented by the concerns, questions, observations, and findings of all of those scholars, including the integration theorists, who undertook to discover in the broadest sense 'what was happening' within customs unions, common markets, and other regional associations. Clearly, not all who studied regional co-operation were prompted to do so out of interest in political unification, and many of those who began by seeking insights into unification found in their case-study materials wealths of new and interesting information about cognate occurrences in subject areas currently called international administration, transnational and transgovernmental relations, international political economy, international bargaining, linkage politics, interdependence, Third World political and economic development, and more. Each of these diversions into cognate areas produced a literature and several led to new bodies of theory. Together they came to constitute integration studies. Whereas the common interest among those working at integration 'theory' was, as noted, to explain political unification, the common interest among those in integration studies came to center more comprehensively in explaining collaborative behavior at the international level.

The broadening of the concerns of the integrationists was almost bound to follow as they probed the empirical reality of postwar international relations, especially those realms in customs unions and common markets where productive collaboration was actually taking place. Moreover, their findings were almost bound to be significant (and indeed controversial) because they were turning up patterns of international behavior, outcomes, and events of importance that according to conventional wisdom in international relations were either *not supposed to happen or that were not supposed to be very consequential if and when they did happen*. That is, from the very beginning of their investigations in the early 1950s, students of international integration were making observations and reporting discoveries that directly contradicted the prevailing political realist or 'power politics' paradigm of the discipline of international relations.[10] With emphases on conflict and coercion, states as unitary actors, and state security as an end, this paradigm conditioned the philosophic assumptions of scholars and their research priorities in studying international relations from the early 1940s onward. By the 1950s, with the eclipse of early idealism about the United Nations, political realism also became the prevailing paradigm for the study of international organization, thus leaving integration studies as a distinct, rather isolated, philosophically unorthodox subculture within international relations. As Table 6.1 shows, there was no place in political realist thinking for the kinds of findings that the integrationists were making. For one thing, in the 1950s and early 1960s the integrationists were virtually alone in holding that international collaboration for welfare ends was an important aspect of contemporary international relations. They were also alone in arguing that in terms of quantity and intensity, such collaboration was something new under the post-Second World War sun.

Of course the new findings of the integrationists were no more representative of the total subject-matter of international relations than were the more traditional ones of the realists. But they were valid findings arrived at by focusing upon cases of collaborative behavior. For example:

- widespread and consequential collaboration does occur in international relations;
- supranationality is both practicable and practiced in international relations;
- international pursuits of welfare ends tend often to be highly, or more highly, politicized than international pursuits of security ends;
- transnationally organized non-governmental organizations are consequentional actors in international relations;
- transgovernmentally linked bureaucrats and officials co-ordinate foreign policies and foreign policy-making;
- interdependence constrains states' autonomy and it complicates determinations of relative power;
- to the extent to which they serve welfare ends, the domestic and foreign policies of modern states, both industrialized and less developed, are integrally and inextricably linked.

In as much as these new findings were valid, they opened the way and lent academic legitimacy to the study of international co-operation at a time when the world seemed engulfed in all-pervading, protracted conflict, and when our discipline seemed fixed in the notion that conflict was the beginning and the end of the subject-matter of international relations. Although it was not clearly articulated until the 1970s, integration studies in the 1950s and 1960s embodied the philosophic elements of an alternative disciplinary paradigm that contrasted sharply with the Welftanschauung of political realism. In the light of this, it is

Assumptions of political realism as applied to international relations	Findings of integration studies in the 1950s and 1960s	Impacts on the discipline of international relations
(1) States and nation-states are the only consequential actors in international relations, and therefore the study of international relations should be focused upon the motives and behavior of states and nation-states or their representatives. Other actors exist but they are consequential only as agents or instruments of states.	(1) States and nation-states are not the only consequential actors in international relations. Indeed, some outcomes in international relations can be understood only in terms of the motives and behavior of international public organizations and bureaucracies, formal and *ad hoc* coalitions of officials transnationally grouped, transnationally organized non-governmental associations, multinational business enterprises, international social classes, and other actors traditionally deemed inconsequential.	(1) Orthodoxy was brought into question, and theoretical and empirical inquiries were initiated that led eventually to theories of transnational relations.
(2) International relations result from foreign policies directed toward enhancing national security, defined in terms of military might, and territorial and ideological domain. Other goals are pursued by international actors, but these are 'low politics' and hence command little priority in foreign policy and are of little consequence to international relations.	(2) International relations result from foreign policies directed toward enhancing national welfare defined in terms of per capita income, employment, and general well-being. The importance which governments attach to such goals and the domestic penalties and rewards surrounding their attainment or sacrifice render their pursuit 'high politics'.	(2) Orthodoxy was brought into question and theoretical analyses were initiated that led to the emergence and prominence of international political economy as a central disciplinary concern.
(3) International relations are fundamentally conflict processes played out in zero-sum matrices, i.e. all significant outcomes take the form of aggrandizement for one actor or coalition at the expense of other actors or coalitions. Conflict is the international mode.	(3) International relations are fundamentally collaborative processes played out in positive sum matrices, i.e. all significant outcomes take the form of realizing and distributing rewards among collaborating actors or coalitions. Co-operation is the international mode.	(3) Orthodoxy was brought into question and theoretical and empirical inquiries were initiated that led to the emergence and prominence of bargaining theory as applied to international relations.
(4) Influence in international relations follows from the application of power defined as military or economic capability, actual or potential. Coercion is the modal means to influence.	(4) Influence in international relations follows from the manipulation of bonds of interdependence that connect actors. Persuasion is the modal means to influence.	(4) Orthodoxy was brought into question and theoretical and empirical inquiries were initiated that led ultimately to theories of interdependence.

small wonder that integrationist writings were greeted with incredulity by more realist-oriented colleagues, whose frequent criticisms were either that politics within common markets were basically competitions for national power, like all international politics, or that they were not really politics at all but technocratic dealings of little international political consequence.[11] Interestingly, and ironically, at the time that the findings of integration studies were raising serious questions about the assumptions of political realism, the integrationists were so engaged in intellectual conflict with one another that they largely ignored what their work was doing to their discipline.[12]

Enlightened by twenty years of hindsight, and cognizant of recent developments in the study of international relations, one can say with some confidence that the impact of the study of international integration was the confrontation with disciplinary orthodoxy that it fomented in the 1950s and 1960s. This is its contribution to the history of social science. Without taking credit from any of those who have pioneered new theoretical domains in the 1970s, it should be underlined that integration studies were precursors to transnational and transgovernmental relations, to interdependence studies, and to the revitalization of the study of international organization presently so apparent.[13] In this sense, integration studies remain relevant, alive, well, and quite vibrant in the 1970s because the integrationists' earlier curiosities about international collaboration via transnational processes within settings of interdependence have become central concerns of international relations and new avenues for theoretical growth.[14]

Karl Deutsch and the Philosophical Foundations of Integration Studies

It is unfortunate that for many years Karl Deutsch the methodologist was confused by critics with Karl Deutsch the theorist. The controversies about quantitative analysis sparked by Deutsch's publications too often diverted attention from their theoretical content and philosophical underpinnings. The term 'philosophical' is used here deliberately to distinguish between the motivations and assumptions underlying Deutsch's work on international integration and the models and propositions that can be more properly called his integration theory. His *theory*, like the integration theories of others, is an attempt to explain international political unification; his *philosophy*, by contrast, is a set of assumptions about peace in international relations. These carry through all of his work on integration, and beyond, and summarize to the convictions that continuing peace and peaceful change are attainable in international relations, and their foundations are in the attitudes and identifications of peoples.

Karl Deutsch's work on international integration was motivated by his belief that peace could be attained if its conditions were understood and nurtured.[15] These conditions were in evidence as certain phenomena occurred in international relations, most notably during peaceful changes in the size of political units or the jurisdictions of governments, and in particular neighboring governments' abilities to resolve their mutual conflicts peacefully for prolonged periods of time. The assignment that Karl Deutsch chose to execute was to examine such phenomena and to determine their causes.

In this regard, the prompting to the project that produced *Political Community and the North Atlantic Area* was Deutsch's belief that violent conflict could be eliminated from international relations (though probably not via conventional practices such as balances of power, collective security, or military deterrence). Underlying this belief was his observation that there have always been pairs and clusters of countries whose relations have been characterized by peaceful conflict resolution and whose leaders and peoples conceived of no contingencies in their mutual relations that could bring resorts to violence. Such experiences in lasting peace were extraordinary in international relations, but this is precisely why they warranted study. Knowing their origins and the bases of their continuity is important to understanding international peace, perhaps even to attaining it more broadly and frequently.

Relatedly, while the mode of change in the international system has always been through conflict and war, these have not effected the totality of change. History records instances of states entering or leaving the international system, or getting larger or smaller in territory and population without conflict or war. There are instances as well of peoples shifting their social-political identities and loyalties to either prompt or accommodate peaceful changes in international political structure. Again, such instances of peaceful change are extraordinary. But this is what attracted Deutsch's attention. Accepting that peaceful change was possible, and believing it to be desirable in the light of the alternatives, he determined to understand better the conditions under which it occurred and the practices that facilitated it.

Karl Deutsch has never really conceived of international relations strictly as interactions among states. Rather, his writings have constantly pictured a world of peoples, communities, or identitive groupings, characterized by 'within and without', 'we and they' perceptions and relationships.[16] How peoples perceive each other, feel about each other, and especially the degree to which they respect and trust each other, all condition the substance of their political relationships and the styles of their diplomatic dealings. Most important, degrees of mutual identification among peoples will influence probabilities of peaceful conflict resolution among their governments. From this it follows that to understand international relations, and especially those conducted non-violently, it is essential to understand how peoples perceive and feel about one another, from whence stem such perceptions and sentiments, how and why they change, and especially how and why they sometimes change in ways that increase or diminish degrees of mutual identification. As noted below, Deutsch's most important contributions to the study of international integration are in his findings concerning sentimental relations among peoples. Indeed, it is his preoccupation with such relationships that distinguishes his work in integration theory from that of other major theorists.

Karl Deutsch was not alone among theorists of international relations in the 1950s holding to convictions about the attainability of lasting peace. But he was certainly in a minority. Followers of David Mitrany embraced such assumptions, as did the world federalists and the few figures in the field of international organization whose inspirations had been fired at San Francisco and still remained aglow.[17] Yet, it must be underlined that Deutsch's early works on integration, *Nationalism and Social Communication* (1953), *Political Community at the International Level* (1954), and *Political Community and the North Atlantic Area* (co-authored, 1957) were injected into a scholarly community widely committed to political realism, and into a world dominated by East–West cold warfare where current events lent credibility to realist propositions (and incredibility to alternative ones!).[18] In this setting much of what Deutsch assumed and wrote was unorthodox. His presentations in numbers and graphs symbolizing a science of the study of peace were even more unorthodox. These were the most frequent targets of critics' commentaries,[19] and the philosophical questions that Deutsch's work raised were not debated to the extent that their importance warranted. Only the hindsight of twenty years reveals that Deutsch's deviance from the philosophical orthodoxy of the discipline of international relations in the 1950s contributed not only to the launching of integration studies but to the beginning of the revision of disciplinary paradigms. It took many years after Deutsch's early work (and that of the other integration theorists) to bring the study of international collaboration to prominence as a disciplinary concern. Yet, as a result of this early work, international collaboration definitely became a legitimate disciplinary concern, and Deutsch's students pursued it with enthusiasm.[20]

Karl Deutsch and Integration Theory

Deutsch's most direct statements concerning international integration are set forth in *Political Community and the North Atlantic Area*, which he wrote in collaboration with colleagues at Princeton University between 1952 and 1956. In this work, Deutsch offers an inventory of concepts pertinent to the analysis of peaceful relations among countries and peaceful change in international relations. *Integration*, Deutsch specifies, is to be distinguished from *amalgamation*, in that the former has to do with the formation of communities, and the latter with the establishment of organizations, associations, or political institutions. Communities are groups of people who share attributes in common, who display mutual responsiveness, confidence, and esteem and who self-consciously self-identify. A minimum condition of community is a shared expectation among members that their conflicts will be peacefully resolved.[21] This minimum community is called a *security community*.[22]

International communities, may be either *amalgamated* or *pluralistic*. If amalgamated, the community would look very much like a federation or nation-state, with institutions of central government regulating the internal and external relations of an integrated population. (A fully amalgamated community would in fact be indistinguishable from a federation or nation-state.) By contrast, the pluralistic international community is a population integrated into at least a security community, but politically fragmented into two or more separate sovereign states. Typical of the various kinds of international communities would be the thirteen American states in 1781 as an example of a newly amalgamated international community, Americans and Canadians at present as an example of a pluralistic international community, and the Benelux Union as an example of an intermediate entity between a pluralistic and an amalgamated community.

It should be underlined that for Deutsch, both integration and amalgamation are quantitative concepts. Both are to be measured with regard to degree or intensity and both range along continua that extend from incipience to fulfillment. Notably, this gives rise to an almost infinite variety of entities defined by the combination of their degrees of integration and amalgamation. Many of these exist empirically. What is fascinating here is that the behavioral properties of the various entities created by combination of integration and amalgamation tend to differ markedly with regard to both their internal and external relations. Compare, for example, differences in internal and external relations among the states of Scotland, the United Kingdom, the British Empire, and the British Commonwealth of Nations, each of which can be located at a different integration-amalgamation intersect. What is theoretically challenging is to determine precisely the behavioral properties of the various bi-variately defined entities, and to explain whether and exactly why variations in behavior relate to varying degrees of integration and amalgamation in combination.

Deutsch took up this theoretical challenge by nominally distinguishing between amalgamated and pluralistic communities (and implicitly between amalgamated and pluralistic non-communities). But the more refined theorizing suggested by the quantitative conceptualization of amalgamation and integration never reached fruition in either Deutsch's work or that of his students, because the metrics that would permit accurate assessment of degrees of amalgamation and integration could not be devised. Operationalization proved insuperable.[23] 'Integration', for example, is in one sense an attitudinal phenomenon having to do in the broadest way with people's degrees of feelings of 'we-ness'. In another sense, integration is a process of attitudinal change that creates or culminates in such feelings of 'we-ness'. In neither sense is 'integration' readily observable or measurable, except perhaps in the very limited number of very recent cases where mass opinion data are available, accurate, and appropriate.[24] But even in such cases indices of integration are rather unsatisfactory, because it is unclear what a satisfactory index would be. What kind of questions should a pollster ask to tap meaningfully into people's mutual identifications? Moreover, in order to generalize about degrees of integration and kinds of related behavior, a much larger inventory of cases would be required than is represented by contemporary stores of public opinion studies. But to find the largest number of cases, research must turn to history, and how is one to measure attitude and attitudinal change within and between populations long dead and gone? It would, of course, be possible to assess the attitudes of some elements of historical populations, namely, some elites and literary figures via their recorded oratory and writings. However, to use such a data base in a theoretically appropriate fashion would require revising and complicating descriptions of international communities by noting stratifications within their populations and weighing the relative significance of the attitudes of political elites, literary groups, and so on. Falling back upon flows of communications, which have been recorded historically, to index attitude and attitudinal change within and between populations is questionable, because questions remain about the connections between communications and attitudes. Even if one is satisfied with the answers offered, there are perplexities about whether changes in communications flow precede and cause attitudinal change or follow and reflect it. Some of these issues are taken up below.

Amalgamation similarly defies precise quantification, partly because it has no precise definition. Deutsch defines it as 'the formal merger of two or more independent units into a larger unit, with some type of common government after amalgamation'.[25] But what does 'formal merger' mean in an operational sense, and how does one know it when one sees it? Most historical cases, and all of the contemporary ones, intuitively suggest that 'formal merger' tends to take place in piecemeal fashion, one institution or one institutionalized task at a time. But, empirically, it remains extremely difficult to determine whether there is more of it or less of it in evidence[26] in particular cases at particular times. These became crucial concerns for the analysis of Western European unification during the 1960s, and a considerable effort was invested in index construction, with the result that 'amalgamation' became 'institutionalization', which then became a multivariate concept embodying degrees of authority, scope of authority, and resources available to authorities. Measures of institutionalization were then questioned as indices of amalgamation because they ignored 'political system' attributes on the input side.[27] Amalgamation then became the 'coming into being of a political system' as this was variously defined by leading theorists in comparative politics.[28] Indicators and metrics were sought for degrees of political socialization, interest articulation, demand and support, and the like. By this time 'amalgamation' operationally defined had become a matrix of attributes. But their indicators tended to vary in different directions at different rates in different contexts and hence to render confusing (and fruitless) any attempts to devise composite measures of amalgamation. Of course, too, as soon as one moved from contemporary cases to historical ones, measurement problems were exacerbated by data problems.

None of this is to suggest that the methodological problems generated in attempts to operationalize and measure integration and amalgamation should detract from the heuristic value of the concepts. Nor should difficulties in trying to devise systematic indicators for historical cases preclude rigorous measurements on contemporary and future ones. By beginning to make and bank appropriate data now, the potential for sophisticated measurement and theoretical generalization in the future is accordingly enhanced. For Deutsch, of course, encouraging such data banking has been a cause pursued with considerable zeal.[29]

It also must be borne in mind that even rather primitive measurement, at the level of nominal typology or even simple dichotomy, often opens the way to productive research and theorizing. As alluded to above, in terms of Deutsch's concepts, we can develop an interesting fourfold typology by distinguishing between integrated and non-integrated international communities, and between amalgamated and non-amalgamated ones. Operationalization here is readily accomplished by defining security communities (i.e. minimally integrated transnational populations) as peoples who have managed peacefully to resolve their conflicts over relatively prolonged periods of time (say, fifty years or longer). Amalgamated entities are identified by the existence of central governing institutions, and pluralistic ones are groups of interacting, yet separate and different sovereign states. From this classification, we get four entities: (1) state systems (non-integrated and non-amalgamated), (2) empires (non-integrated but amalgamated), (3) pluralistic security communities (integrated but non-amalgamated), and (4) amalgamated security communities (integrated and amalgamated). The first two have been the foci of traditional research and theorizing in international relations for many years; number 4 was the particular object of integration theorizing, and number 3 is the threshold for a number of the recent departures in international relations theory discussed earlier.

The Process of Political Unification

Examining the amalgamated security community and the forces that produce and maintain it is tantamount to examining international political unification. To the extent that Deutsch's writings concern this entity, they are in the tradition of 'integration theory' and thus closely related to the efforts of the neo-functionalists and federalists. Except for the historical case studies included in *Political Community and the North Atlantic Area*, and other volumes from the Princeton project,[30] the principal empirical focus for the investigation of the amalgamated security community was the Western Europe of the Six. Here the work of Deutsch, his students and colleagues was directed toward ascertaining the existence of a security community among the peoples of the Six, ascertaining the degree of political amalgamation in evidence, and projecting both integration and amalgamation into the future in order to draw conclusions about European unification. Deutsch's most ambitious efforts at analyzing developments in Western Europe appear in his book with Merritt, Macridis, and Edinger, *France, Germany and the Western Alliance*.[31]

Aside from their substantive importance as attempts to understand better the course of European unification, these exercises were also a test of a developmental model of political unification devised by Deutsch and initially contained in his work on nationalism.[32] In this model, international political unification, or the coming into being of amalgamated security communities, is a phenomenon similar to the coming into being of nation-states. Therefore, what one would observe at the international level as political unification occurs is comparable to what one would observe at the national level when nation-states are born. First, functional linkages develop between separate communities. Such ties in trade, migration, mutual services, or military collaboration prompted by necessity or profit generate flows of transactions between communities and enmesh people in transcommunity communications networks. Under appropriate conditions of high volume, expanding substance, and continuing reward, over extended periods of time, intercommunity interactions generate social-psychological processes that lead to the assimilation of peoples, and hence to their integration into larger communities.[33] Such assimilatory processes are essentially learning experiences of the stimulus–response variety.[34] Once such community formation has taken place, the desires of members and the efforts of the elites may be directed toward institutionalizing, preserving, and protecting the community's integrity and distinctiveness and regulating internal social relations. Such desires, acted upon, lead to political amalgamation through the establishment of institutions of government. In overview, then, the model posits that political unification – national or international – consists in moving first from communi*ties* to community, and then from community to state. This follows from initial functional linkage, increased transaction, social assimilation, community formation, and ultimately political amalgamation. Integration therefore precedes amalgamation; sentimental change precedes institutional change; social change precedes political change. At the core of this formulation rests the assumption highlighted earlier that peaceful change in international relations has its origins in the perceptions and identifications of people.

As an *integration theory*, in the sense that the term is being used in this chapter, Deutsch's formulation is valuable in as much as it focuses attention on international community formation during unification. This sentimental dimension is largely ignored in other integration theories,[35] with the result that the end-product of unification processes is there left unspecified. In neo-functionalist formulations, for example, it is not clear whether the envisaged end-product is a nation-state-like entity (although nowhere is it indicated that the end-product is something else). If it is indeed a nation-state-like entity that the neo-functionalists envisage, then their formulations fall short of explaining the social assimilatory aspects of the unification process. On the other hand, if the end-product is not a nation-state-like entity and hence one in which social assimilation has not occurred, then its nature must be better described. Deutsch's formulations allow for a number of possible end-products, as noted, but to the extent that international political unification is under investigation, the end-product looks like a nation-state, and attaining this implies that both integration and amalgamation have occurred, most likely in sequence.

For all its elegance and intuitive promise, Deutsch's developmental model of the unification process has some rather serious shortcomings. For one thing, the conditions under which people in newly integrated communities will or will not initiate drives for political amalgamation are never specified. Therefore, one cannot predict future amalgamation from evidence of present integration, except possibly in terms of probability statements that tend to be so imprecise as to approximate 'refined guessing'. The relationship between integration and amalgamation is certainly not causal. Otherwise the pluralistic community could never exist. But there is a contingency linkage between the two which is never exactly specified in either Deutsch's work or that of his students. What is minimally needed is a list of conditions necessary and sufficient for moving from integration to amalgamation, or at least some stipulation of the decision rules involved. Deutsch's list of conditions for the maintenance of the amalgamated security community does not suffice in this regard because all it suggests is that people are more likely to accept amalgamation as community among them intensifies.[36] This still begs the question: what motivates people to *opt for* political unification, and how is this motivation influenced by levels of integration? Or, more elaborately, *who opts* for amalgamation, *when*, and *why*? In short, the motivational dynamics are missing from Deutsch's process model, and this opens a serious gap.[37]

Political dynamics are similarly missing from Deutsch's model and this too seriously affects its explanatory and predictive power. The underemphasis on political dynamics – that is, decision-making, organizational behavior, coalition behavior, and so on – in the Deutsch model is essentially a level-of-analysis problem. His formulation makes statements about people's attitudes and sentiments, individually and in the aggregate, and it also makes statements about governments' policies (i.e. to amalgamate or not). Therefore, as far as the theory informs us, we can believe that changes in people's attitudes and sentiments may prompt changes in governments' policies. This is reasonable, but not very helpful. What remains undisclosed is how, when, and why changes at the social-psychological level are converted into changes at the governmental level. Whose change of mind affects whose change of behavior, how, when, and why? In effect, there are no social or political structures or processes in Deutsch's integration models – no groups or classes (except elites and masses, and even these are seldom differentiated analytically) no decision-makers, no decisions, very little voluntaristic behavior, and no politics. These omissions generated considerable confusion among the neo-functionalists in the 1950s and 1960s (since they were preoccupied with the political-structural and procedural matters that Deutsch very seldom mentioned).[38] Their dismay was well founded because without social-political inners the Deutsch model forces unguided inferential leaps of considerable magnitude. Notably, some of the conceptual ingredients that would add structure and process to Deutsch's integration theory appear in some of his later work on cybernetics and national policy-making.[39] But these have yet to be added specifically to the integration models. Adding them would, of course, better establish the relationship between integration and amalgamation by more precisely specifying how the former gets converted into the latter.

Not only have time and testing raised questions about the relationships between integration and amalgamation in Deutsch's formulations, but they have also exposed problems in the assumed relationship between communication and integration. Recent Western European experience suggests, for example, that international communications may flow in great volume, between and among virtually all strata of population over prolonged periods of time, with perceived rewards to communicators, and yet register minimal effects on people's identifications, symbolic references, and the like. Communication, in short, does not seem to be creating an international community among Western Europeans, at least beyond minimal definition. In fact, with the emergence of separatisms and provincialisms in recent years, to say nothing of reinvigorated nationalisms, it would appear that sentimental developments in Europe contradict conclusions suggested by the theoretical linkage between transaction and assimilation. However, the linkage itself is not at issue here since there is sufficient evidence in historical cases of national and international community formation to establish its validity. What is needed, rather, is a statement of elaborations and qualifications that would stipulate the conditions under which the communication–integration linkage is strongest, moderated, weakest, and non-existent. With such conditions specified – and validated – yet another unguided inferential leap would be removed from the integration model, and it would become that much more useful analytically.

These criticisms of Deutsch's model of political unification suggest that it is incomplete, not inaccurate. Its strengths lie precisely in the fact that its explanatory and predictive power can be improved through further research into clearly definable problems. That is, it lends itself nicely to cumulative research and theorizing. Much could be accomplished, for example, by filling the gap between integration and amalgamation with the neofunctionalists' findings on the politics of integration, the conditions for 'spillover' and 'spillback', and the influence of national and international bureaucracies.[40] If political structure and dynamics were added in this manner, the power of the model would be greatly enhanced. Similarly, the gap between integration and amalgamation could be further filled by modelling the motivational dynamics of the unification process from the findings of the literatures of ideology and integration, liberal and Marxist political economy, domestic politics and integration, and the management of interdependence.[41] Generally speaking, if environmental conditions permit, movement toward unification occurs when motivational overdetermination prevails. That is, the phenomenon takes place when many people want it to happen for a broad and convergent variety of reasons. Integration theory could be improved to the extent that motivational overdetermination could be built into it. As for the relationship between communication and integration, a great deal of work remains to be done on attitudinal change between and within societies before this linkage is clarified. Until the work is done, inferring assimilation from communication will remain questionable and the social-psychological dynamics of community formation will remain theoretically murky.

The Pluralistic Security Community and International Relations in the 1970s

While Deutsch's considerations of the amalgamated security community led him into integration theory, his identification of the pluralistic security community pointed in the direction of much broader concerns. The term 'pluralistic security community' is rather cumbersome and therefore has not been widely used in the literature of international relations. But the entity it identifies has been the object of a great deal of investigation. This became especially the case in the late 1960s when after a decade or more of 'movement toward political unification' Western European states and peoples comprised neither a politically amalgamated international community nor a traditional unintegrated international state system. In fact, what Western Europe had come to resemble most closely was a pluralistic security community – a cluster of non-warring peoples and an arena of peaceful conflict resolution among governments, but not a political unit and certainly not a supranational state. What is even more interesting is that by the 1960s it was not only the Western Europeans who comprised a pluralistic security community, but the Europeans and the North Americans, the North Americans and the Japanese, the Japanese and the Europeans, in fact more or less the entire 'trilateral' world.

In recent years the bulk of research in the field of integration studies, as well as in the more focused subdisciplines that have evolved from integration studies, has concerned the nature and problems of the pluralistic security community. These are called problems of 'managing interdependence' or 'North–North' problems or 'OECD' problems or the like, but they have to do fundamentally with understanding relations among peoples who have ceased to expect or prepare for war among themselves, but who are nevertheless so closely bound politically and economically that their relationships generate constant friction which must be diplomatically handled in the common interest. This being the case, current research is focused upon how peaceful problem-solving is accomplished in the pluralistic setting and especially in the absence of regulatory institutions or mediating authorities. How are foreign policies co-ordinated in the absence of central co-ordinators? How are 'prisoners' dilemma' situations avoided in the setting of decentralized adjustment? Policy-prescriptive inquiries into these questions are directed toward setting guidelines to improve the workings of the pluralistic communities toward the end of making them more durable.

Deutsch's concerns with the pluralistic security community are more fundamental. When, where, and why do such entities form? How durable are they, and what affects this durability? Under what conditions do they deteriorate? Empirically, how are we to observe the emergence of such communities, what indexes their durability, and what signals their deterioration? Except for Russett's fascinating study of the Anglo-American security community in the twentieth century,[42] very little research has been directed toward answering these questions in the theoretical terms that Deutsch posed them. And yet they are crucial to understanding the foundations of the international relations of the contemporary Western World!

Unfortunately, Deutsch offers very little theoretical guidance concerning problems of the pluralistic security community. Beyond defining it, and listing characteristics of intracommunity relations, he says little about origins, developmental processes, or causal relationships. We can assume that the process of international community formation (i.e. integration) resembles the assimilatory process in nationalism, as discussed above. Communications and transactions have an assimilatory impact upon peoples, and attitudinal change is the product of a learning process of some kind. But, even if these assumptions are valid, the formulation remains limited in its analytic utility by concerns raised earlier. What also needs to be discovered is whether the learning that prompts attitudinal change during community formation follows from explicit *teaching*. That is, are symbols characterizing other peoples purposefully disseminated through populations in order to prompt changes in international perception? If so, who disseminates these, how, and why? Findings in the literature of nation-building have tended increasingly to emphasize voluntaristic aspects of the spread of nationalism.[43] That is, elites consciously and deliberately diffuse national symbols for a variety of reasons including political expediency. Are there similar voluntaristic aspects to international community formation? Who decides that 'these are not issues that we are ever going to go to war over', and that 'these are not people we are ever likely to fight with'? What considerations go into such decisions? What processes normalize and universalize such expectations? How precisely do such expectations, once normalized, affect diplomatic relations?

Analyzing Deutsch's thinking on the pluralistic security community underlines that we presently have no theory of international pluralism. The lesson in this is not that Deutsch has left his work unfinished, but rather that no one has carried forward what he began many years ago. This lesson ought to be a sobering one for those of us who have scurried to become 'policy relevant' in our work in recent years, and who, in so doing, have abandoned the more basic theoretical inquiries that Deutsch and his contemporaries launched and inspired one social science generation ago. Unless we understand better the fundamental nature and dynamics of the relationships our policy recommendations seek to preserve or change, we cannot confidently ask that these be taken very seriously.[44]

The Obsolescence of Integration Theory?

When Ernst Haas recently reviewed the history and shortcomings of neo-functionalist integration theory, somewhat as I have done here with Karl Deutsch's work, he concluded that with some effort the theories could be repaired, and improved. But he questioned the worth of making the effort, given the unlikelihood of significant international political unification during the remainder of our century.[45] In effect, why sharpen tools that may never again be used?

As one who has also experienced the 'joy and anguish' of theorizing about international integration, I sympathize with my colleague's position. Yet I cannot share it. If all integration theory is to be concerned with is international political unification or amalgamated security communities, there might be some question about the worth in sharpening conceptual tools. But, at least as far as Karl Deutsch's formulations are concerned, they are as applicable to national and subnational developments as they are to international ones, and they bring attention to a variety of outcomes aside from political unification *per se*. While we are likely to see little international political unification in coming years, we might very well expect new efforts at national unification, and international relations within pluralistic communities will continue to capture our interest.

Furthermore, Deutsch's concepts remain as useful for analyzing cases of disintegration and fragmentation as they are for examining cases of integration and amalgamation. Indeed, we are already witnessing manifestations of the breakdown of polity or community in places such as Canada, the United Kingdom, Belgium, perhaps in the European Communities, and most assuredly in Northern Ireland. Better understanding of these cases, and other inevitable ones, must remain high on our research agendas because reverberations from national dissolutions are bound to be internationally significant. There is therefore a good deal to be said for working out the problems in integration theory, especially since we have labored to isolate them, and improving our conceptual capabilities to understand national and international developments that will predictably continue to occur.

Finally, whatever the future of integration theory, integration studies and their progeny in transnational relations and interdependence studies will remain prominent in international relations into the foreseeable future. So too will the 'post-realist' paradigm that integration studies thrust upon our discipline. Whether peaceful problem-solving and peaceful change will ever become prevailing features of international relations is uncertain. But they have apparently become more frequent in our part of the twentieth century. If understanding these better could have anything to do with further increasing their frequency, then there is much to be said for heightening our understanding. Karl Deutsch and his colleagues set out to heighten this understanding almost three decades ago. Many of us remain committed to the task.

Notes: Chapter 6

1 See, for example, Ernst B. Haas, *The Uniting of Europe: Political Social, and Economic Forces, 1950–1957* (Stanford, Calif.: Stanford University Press, 1958); Ernst B. Haas, 'International integration: the European and the universal process', *International Organization* vol. 15, no. 3 (Summer 1961), pp. 366–92; and Leon N. Lindberg and Stuart A. Scheingold, *Europe's Would-Be Polity: Patterns of Change in the European Community* (Englewood Cliffs, NJ: Prentice-Hall, 1970).

2 Ernst B. Haas and Philippe C. Schmitter, 'Economics and differential patterns of political integration: projections about unity in Latin America', *International Organization*, vol. 18, no. 4 (Autumn 1964), pp. 705–37; Philippe C. Schmitter, 'Central American integration: spill-over, spill-around or encapsulation?' *Journal of Common Market Studies*, vol. 9, no. 1 (September 1970), pp. 1–48; Joseph S. Nye, Jr, 'Central American regional integration', in *International Regionalism: Readings*, ed. Joseph S. Nye, Jr (Boston, Mass.: Little, Brown, 1968), pp. 377–429; Joseph S. Nye, Jr, 'East African economic integration', in *International Political Communities: An Anthology* (Garden City, NY: Doubleday/Anchor Books, 1966), pp. 405–36; and Andrzej Korbonski, 'Theory and practice of regional integration: the case of comecon', *International Organization*, vol. 24, no. 4 (Autumn 1970), pp. 942–77.

3 For a comparative sampling of these 'theories', see Leon N. Lindberg and Stuart A. Scheingold (eds), *Regional Integration: Theory and Research* (Cambridge, Mass.: Harvard University Press, 1971); Charles Pentland, *International Theory and European Integration* (New York: The Free Press, 1973); Roger D. Hansen, 'Regional integration: reflections on a decade of theoretical efforts', *World Politics*, vol. 21, no. 2 (January 1969), pp. 242–71; Ronn D. Kaiser, 'Toward the Copernican phase of regional integration theory', *Journal of Common Market Studies*, vol. 10, no. 2 (March 1972), pp. 207–32; *Pour l'Etude de l'Intégration Européenne* (Montréal, Que.: Université de Montréal, Centre d'Études et de Documentation Européennes, 1977), pp. 3–91; and Marie-Èlisabeth de Bussy, Hélène Delorme, and Françoise de la Serre, 'Approches théoriques de l'integration européenne', *Revue Française de Science Politique*, vol. 20, no. 3 (June 1971), pp. 615–53.

4 Donald J. Puchala, 'Of blind men, elephants and international integration', *Journal of Common Market Studies*, vol. 10, no. 3 (March 1972), pp. 267–84.

5 See, for example, Pentland, *International Theory and European Integration*; and Lindberg and Scheingold (eds), *Regional Integration*.

6 Ernst B. Haas, 'The Uniting of Europe and the uniting of Latin America', *Journal of Common Market Studies*, vol. 5, no. 4 (June 1967), pp. 315–43.

7 Ernst B. Haas, 'Turbulent fields and the theory of regional integration', *International Organization*, vol. 30, no. 2 (Spring 1976), pp. 173–212; and also Ernst B. Haas, *The Obsolescence of Regional Integration Theory* (Berkeley, Calif. University of California, Institute of International Studies, 1975).

8 Ernst B. Haas, 'The study of regional integration: reflections on the joy and anguish of prethcorizing', *International Organization*, vol. 24, no. 4 (Autumn 1970), pp. 607–46; for a broader view of the 'dependent variable problem', see Bruce M. Russett, 'Transactions, community and international political integration', in his *Power and Community in World Politics* (San Francisco: Freeman, 1974), pp. 325–45.

9 See, for example, Helen Wallace, William Wallace, and Carole Webb (eds), *Policy-Making in the European Communities* (London and New York: Wiley, 1977). See also Donald J. Puchala, 'New trends in the study of European integration', in *Pour l'Étude de l'Intégration Européenne*, pp. 67–77.

10 Robert O. Keohane and Joseph S. Nye, Jr, 'Interdependence and integration', in *Handbook of Political Science*, ed. Fred I. Greenstein and Nelson W. Polsby (Reading, Mass.: Addison-Wesley, 1975), Vol. 8, pp. 363–414; Robert O. Keohane and Joseph S. Nye, Jr, *Power and Interdependence: World Politics in Transition* (Boston, Mass.: Little, Brown, 1977), pp. 3–62; and Donald J. Puchala and Stuart I. Fagan, 'International politics in the 1970s: the search for a perspective', *International Organization*, vol. 28, no. 2 (Spring 1974), pp. 247–66.

11 Stanley Hoffmann, 'Obstinate or obsolete? The fate of the nation-state and the case of Western Europe', in *International Regionalism*, ed. Nye, pp. 177–231; Stanley Hoffmann, 'Europe's identity crisis: between past and America', *Daedalus*, vol. 93, no. 4 (Fall 1964), pp. 1244–97; Raymond Aron, *Peace and War: A Theory of International Relations*, trans. Richard Howard and Annette Baker Fox (Garden City, NY: Doubleday, 1966), pp. 21–176, 643–66; Hans J. Morgenthau, *Politics Among Nations: The Struggle for Power and Peace*, 4th edn (New York: Knopf, 1967), pp. 511–16.

12 Ernst B. Haas, 'The challenge of regionalism', in *Contemporary Theory in International Relations*, ed. Stanley Hoffman (Englewood Cliffs, NJ: Prentice-Hall, 1960), pp. 223–40; Karl W. Deutsch, 'Towards Western European Integration: An Interim Assessment', *Journal of International Affairs*, vol. 16, no. 1 (1962), pp. 89–101; Karl W. Deutsch, Lewis J. Edinger, Roy C. Macridis, and Richard L. Merritt, *France, Germany and the Western Alliance: A Study of Elite Attitudes on European Integration and World Politics* (New York: Scribner's, 1967); Ronald A. Inglehart, 'An end to European integration?', *American Political Science Review*, vol. 61, no. 1 (March 1967), pp. 91–105; and William E. Fisher, 'An analysis of the Deutsch sociocausal paradigm of political integration', *International Organization*, vol. 23, no. 2 (Spring 1969), pp. 254–90.

13 Keohane and Nye, 'Interdependence and integration'.

14 See Joseph S. Nye, Jr, and Robert O. Keohane (eds), *Transnational Relations and World Politics* (Cambridge, Mass.: Harvard University Press, 1972); and Keohane and Nye, *Power and Interdependence*.

15 Karl W. Deutsch, *Political Community at the International Level* (Garden City, NY: Doubleday, 1954), pp. 3-38; and Karl W. Deutsch, Sidney A. Burrell, Robert A. Kann, Maurice Lee, Jr, Martin Lichterman, Raymond E. Lindgren, Francis L. Loewenheim, and Richard W. Van Wagenen, *Political Community and the North Atlantic Area: International Organization in the Light of Historical Experience* (Princeton, NJ: Princeton University Press, 1957), pp. 3-70.
16 Karl W. Deutsch, *The Analysis of International Relations*, 2nd edn (Englewood Cliffs, NJ: Prentice-Hall, 1978).
17 David A. Mitrany, *A Working Peace System* (Chicago: Quadrangle Books, 1966); Haas, *The Uniting of Europe*; Ernst B. Haas, *Beyond the Nation-State: Functionalism and International Organization* (Stanford, Calif.: Stanford University Press, 1964); Crane Brinton, *From Many, One: The Process of Political Integration* (Cambridge, Mass.: Harvard University Press, 1948); Leland M. Goodrich, *The United Nations* (New York: Crowell, 1959); Inis L. Claude, Jr, *Swords Into Plowshares: The Problems and Progress of International Organization*, 3rd rev. edn (New York: Random House, 1964).
18 Karl W. Deutsch, *Nationalism and Social Communication: An Inquiry into the Foundations of Nationality* (Cambridge, Mass.: MIT Press; and New York: Wiley, 1953).
19 See Fisher, 'An analysis of the Deutsch sociocausal paradigm'.
20 See, for example, Bruce M. Russett, *Community and Contention: Britain and America in the Twentieth Century* (Cambridge, Mass.: MIT Press, 1963); Donald J. Puchala, *European Integration: Progress and Prospects* (New Haven, Conn.: Yale University, Political Science Research Library, 1965); Hayward R. Alker, Jr, and Bruce M. Russett, *World Politics in the General Assembly* (New Haven, Conn., and London: Yale University Press, 1965); Richard L. Merritt, *Symbols of American Community, 1735-1775* (New Haven, Conn., and London: Yale University Press, 1966); Peter J. Katzenstein, *Disjoined Partners: Austria and Germany since 1815* (Berkeley and Los Angeles: University of California Press, 1976).
21 Deutsch et al., *Political Community and the North Atlantic Area*, pp. 5-7.
22 The concept 'security community' was introduced by Richard W. Van Wagenen in his *Research in the International Organization Field: Some Notes on a Possible Focus* (Princeton, NJ: Princeton University, Center for Research on World Political Institutions, 1952).
23 For attempts at such operationalization, see Donald J. Puchala, 'Patterns in West European integration', *Journal of Common Market Studies*, vol. 9 no. 2 (December 1970), pp. 117-42; Donald J. Puchala, 'Integration and disintegration in Franco-German relations, 1954-1965', *International Organization*, vol. 24, no. 2 (Spring 1970); pp. 183-208; Donald J. Puchala, 'International transactions and regional integration', *International Organization*, vol. 24, no. 4 (Autumn 1970), pp. 732-63; and Leon N. Lindberg, 'Political integration as a multidimensional phenomenon requiring multivariate measurement', *International Organization*, vol. 24, no. 4 (Autumn 1970), pp. 649-731.
24 Deutsch et al., *France, Germany and the Western Alliance*; Ronald A. Inglehart, 'Ongoing changes in West European political cultures', *Integration*, vol. 1, no. 4 (1970), pp. 250-73; Ronald A. Inglehart, 'Public opinion and regional integration', *International Organization*, vol. 24, no. 4 (Autumn 1970), pp. 764-95; Ronald A. Inglehart, 'Cognitive mobilization and European identity', *Comparative Politics*, vol. 3, no. 1 (October 1970), pp. 45-70; Donald J. Puchala, 'The Common Market and political federation in Western European public opinion', *International Studies Quarterly*, vol. 14, no. 1 (March 1970), pp. 32-59; Donald J. Puchala, 'National distinctiveness and transnationality in West European public opinion', *Integration*, vol. 1, no. 4 (1970), pp. 273-87.
25 Deutsch et al., *Political Community and the North Atlantic Area*, p. 6.
26 Lindberg and Scheingold (eds), *Regional Integration*; Puchala, 'Patterns in West European integration'; Karl W. Deutsch, 'Integration and arms control in the European political environment: a summary report', *American Political Science Review*, vol. 60, no. 2 (June 1966), pp. 354-65.
27 James A. Caporaso, *The Structure and Function of European Integration* (Pacific Palisades, Calif.: Goodyear, 1974).
28 See, for example, Gabriel A. Almond's 'Introduction: a functional approach to

comparative politics', in *The Politics of the Developing Areas*, ed. Gabriel A. Almond and James S. Coleman (Princeton, NJ: Princeton University Press, 1960), pp. 3–64; and David Easton, *A Systems Analysis of Political Life* (New York: Wiley, 1965).

29 Karl W. Deutsch, 'Toward an inventory of basic trends and patterns in comparative and international politics', *American Political Science Review*, vol. 54, no. 1 (March 1960), pp. 34–57; and Karl W. Deutsch, Harold D. Lasswell, Richard L. Merritt, and Bruce M. Russett, 'The Yale Political Data Program', in *Comparing Nations: The Use of Quantitative Data in Cross-National Research*, ed. Richard L. Merritt and Stein Rokkan (New Haven, Conn., and London: Yale University Press, 1966), pp. 81–94.

30 Robert A. Kann, *The Habsburg Empire: A Study in Integration and Disintegration* (New York: Praeger, 1957); and Raymond E. Lindgren, *Norway-Sweden: Union, Disunion, and Scandinavian Integration* (Princeton, NJ: Princeton University Press, 1959).

31 Deutsch et al., *Political Community and the North Atlantic Area*; see also Karl W. Deutsch, *Nationalism and Its Alternatives* (New York: Knopf, 1969).

32 Deutsch, *Nationalism and Social Communication*; and Puchala, 'International transactions and regional integration'.

33 Puchala, 'International transactions and regional integration'.

34 Donald J. Puchala, 'The pattern of contemporary regional integration', *International Studies Quarterly*, vol. 12, no. 1 (March 1968), pp. 38–64.

35 The work of Amitai Etzioni is an exception; see his *Political Unification: A Comparative Study of Leaders and Forces* (New York: Holt, Rinehart & Winston, 1965).

36 Deutsch et al., *Political Community and the North Atlantic Area*, pp. 46–58.

37 Katzenstein, in his *Disjoined Partners*, takes important steps toward filling this gap.

38 Haas, 'The challenge of regionalism'; and Joseph S. Nye, Jr, *Peace in Parts: Integration and Conflict in Regional Organization* (Boston, Mass.: Little, Brown, 1971), chs 1 and 2.

39 Karl W. Deutsch, *The Nerves of Government: Models of Political Communication and Control* (New York: The Free Press, 1963); and Deutsch, *The Analysis of International Relations*, 2nd edn, chs 8–10.

40 Nye, *Peace in Parts*; Lindberg and Scheingold (eds), *Regional Integration*; David L. Coombes, *Politics and Bureaucracy in the European Community: A Portrait of the Commission of the EEC* (London: Allen & Unwin, 1970); Glenda G. Rosenthal, *The Men Behind the Decisions: Cases in European Policy-Making* (Lexington, Mass.: D. C. Heath, Lexington Books, 1975); Helen Wallace, *National Governments and the European Communities*, PEP European Series No. 21 (London: Chatham House, 1973); Donald J. Puchala, 'Domestic politics and regional harmonization in the European Communities', *World Politics*, vol. 27, no. 4 (July 1975), pp. 496–520; Peter Busch and Donald J. Puchala, 'Interests, influence and integration: political structure in the European Communities', *Comparative Political Studies*, vol. 9, no. 3 (October 1976), pp. 235–54.

41 Joseph S. Nye, Jr, *Pan-Africanism and East African Integration* (Cambridge, Mass.: Harvard University Press, 1965); Richard N. Cooper, *The Economics of Interdependence: Economic Policy in the Atlantic Community* (New York: McGraw-Hill, 1968); Johan Galtung, *The European Community: A Superpower in the Making* (Oslo: Universitetsforlaget; and London: Allen & Unwin, 1973); and Keohane and Nye, *Power and Interdependence*.

42 Russett, *Community and Contention*.

43 See, for example, Thomas L. Hodgkin, *Nationalism in Colonial Africa* (New York: New York University Press, 1957); and Karl W. Deutsch and William J. Foltz, *Nation-Building* (New York: Atherton Press, 1963).

44 Consider, for example, various recommendations for 'bridge-building' between East and West that are founded on assumptions concerning the impacts of transactions and communications on political-diplomatic outcomes. In this regard, see Zbigniew K. Brzezinski, *Alternative to Partition: For a Broader Conception of America's Role in Europe* (New York: McGraw-Hill, 1965).

45 Haas, 'Turbulent fields and the theory of regional integration', p. 174.

7
The Political Sociology of Integration and Social Development: a Comparative Analysis of Emile Durkheim and Karl W. Deutsch

ANDREI S. MARKOVITS and WARREN W. OLIVER III

Introduction

Emile Durkheim and Karl W. Deutsch have affected greatly the disciplines of sociology and political science. Coming from two entirely different and distinct intellectual traditions (the lack of a manifest Durkheimian influence upon Deutsch is underlined by the near-total absence of references to Durkheim in Deutsch's work),[1] they none the less exhibit striking parallels between their social and political theories. The similarities may seem surprising;[2] but the independent yet parallel nature of their writings adds to their joint credibility. In this chapter we shall bring out and analyze the similarities and differences in their ideas on politics and society.

Even the harshest critic would not deny the impact of Durkheim and Deutsch upon the social sciences. Their looming presence manifests itself from introductory undergraduate-level courses in sociology and political science to advanced research articles published in the most prestigious journals of their respective fields.[3] Moreover, each thinker's powerful ideas and persuasive intellect created a school of thought wherein eminent scholars in their own right furthered and expanded the original formulations of their teacher. The Durkheimian school found its most tangible expression in the pages of the journal *Année Sociologique*, which gave a forum to some of the most important French social scientists. Although there has been no equivalent Deutschian journal to serve as a major locus for academic debate on Deutschian topics of concern, mainly among Deutsch's epigones, it would be fair to compare the *Année* school's role and influence in French sociology to that of the 'Yale school' of international politics in the United States.[4]

Emile Durkheim: A Brief Overview

Durkheim, with Marx and Weber, provides the foundations of modern sociology. Yet unlike the latter two, Durkheim has made little impact upon the discipline of political science. This is largely because, for

Durkheim, the 'social' is such an all-inclusive concept that it swallows up the 'political'. Precisely because of the broadness of 'social', however, his writings contain much material relevant to political science. For example, Durkheim's lifelong concern with the various types of social order and the changing basis of social cohesion in modern society produce a major contribution to the theory of social development, and therefore to the theory of political development as well. Consequently, we must briefly outline his work as a whole.

Durkheim always emphasized the salience of the social. He strongly reacted against the very popular English utilitarian school of the time, which argued that individuals act in order to maximize their personal utility, and equally against the French psychological school, which reduced all social action to psychological phenomena. Durkheim came to grips with the dimensions of the social *qua* social. In all of his work, Durkheim attempted to analyze and comprehend the integrative forces in society.

One central – although not the only or even always the most important – integrative element is the *conscience collective*, which includes in its meaning aspects of both of its English cognates, 'collective conscience' and 'collective consciousness'. The *conscience collective* emerges from the individuals making up society. 'The totality of beliefs and sentiments common to average citizens of the same society forms a determinate system which has its own life; one may call it the *collective* or *common conscience*'.[5]

By looking at such important human bonds as religion and law, Durkheim attempts to demonstrate their respective *social* origins, functions, and consequences. In a work that shaped the sociological study of religion, *The Elementary Forms of Religious Life*, Durkheim argues that all aspects of primitive religion, its meticulous rituals, institutionalized rites, totems, and taboos have one origin and one purpose: to maintain social cohesion. He carries this approach of looking for *social* causes to a logical extreme in *Suicide* (which is also the first truly modern comparative and quantitative case study in sociology). In this book he explores the social origins of suicide, which would on the surface seem to be the ultimate expression of the individual psyche.

Durkheim's theory of social development is largely contained in his first major work, *The Division of Labor in Society*. Social development is essentially the progress of the division of labor – the latter concept being used in a wider sense than the strictly economic meaning, including what is today called structural differentiation and functional specialization.

The division of labor constantly changes the bases of social solidarity and the components of the *conscience collective*. He terms the two ideal types of solidarity 'mechanical' (pre-modern) and 'organic' (modern), and sees the latter as becoming ever more important. 'Mechanical' denotes a single, self-contained, isolated unit without any inter- or intrasystematic communication. 'Organic', on the other hand, is analogized from the human body, a highly complex, diversified whole that is always more than the sum of its parts, each of which in turn fulfills a crucial function.[6]

Durkheim does not see the division of labor as wholly beneficial. The changing nature of social solidarity can lead to unresolved tensions and a pervasive sense of normlessness or *anomie*. At the same time, however, he places high hopes onto two types of institution which could counter anomie: education and secondary associations (particularly occupational associations). The latter are especially important, for they could be intermediate structures between the isolation of the individual and the anonymity of the society as a whole. Both types of institution could inculcate the individual with a collective morality enhancing his social behavior and mitigating excessive individualism.

Karl W. Deutsch: A Brief Overview

Karl W. Deutsch's work is a scientific attempt to explain social cohesion, integration, and community formation. Society, again a whole which is more than the sum of its parts, is used as an empirical starting point as well as a normative framework for analysis.

Deutsch, like Durkheim, has been preoccupied with a fundamental analysis of modernization and systemic development, both as a process and as a condition. His concept of social mobilization, 'a name given to an overall process of change, which happens to substantial parts of the population ... moving from traditional to modern ways of life',[7] provides an innovative framework for the study of the coexisting phenomena of social integration and change. It accounts for the clashes between the old and the new and describes the resulting synthetic integration.

If the underlying theme of Deutsch's work is integration, then the expression of that theme is in the form of communication and cybernetics. Although integration is not consistently and authoritatively defined, it is clear that Deutsch has in mind the continued existence of a community held together by the totality of a Durkheimian *conscience collective*. Significantly, for both Deutsch and Durkheim, the integrative elements of community formation and maintenance occur *between* as well as *within* societies, thereby negating any analytic differences between the 'domestic' and 'international' dimensions of integration.[8] Thus in a perceptive article Deutsch writes of integration: 'When we speak of integrating ... a human community, we are using integration to mean making a whole out of the previously separate components'.[9] Further on in the same place, integration is defined as involving 'building up [of] self-correcting and self-maintaining systems that serve people'.[10] This passage emphasizes the cybernetic nature of integration. In *The Nerves of Government*, Deutsch's theoretical masterpiece, the integration of a society is its 'ability to receive and transmit information on wide ranges of different topics with relatively little delay or loss of relevant detail',[11] which reflects the author's interest in communication. In yet another instance, Deutsch defines integration as the 'attainment, within a territory, of a "sense of community" and of institutions and practices strong enough and widespread enough to assure, for a "long" time, dependable expectation of "peaceful change" among its population'.[12] Here integration assumes a supranational level and extends to a community of nations.

The theme of integration and its cybernetic form pertain to the most diverse aspects of scientific inquiry and everyday occurrences. For example, in the realm of economics Deutsch has used the concept of integration in an imaginative fashion. By devising such innovative and useful diachronic and synchronic measures as the fluctuation of international trade flows, relative acceptance ratios, and foreign trade figures as percentages of a country's total trade, Deutsch succeeds in a sophisticated empirical substantiation of his theoretical proposition. The gathering of geographical and linguistic data for the same purpose underlines this point. Thus, mountain passes, trade routes, and natural waterways, for example, determine the development of social integration as much as the formation and crystallization of new written languages, evolution of dialects, and the codification of grammar. His original research concerning various aspects of communication data, such as mail flows, railroad grids, and telephone connections, has helped make clear many patterns of community formation. Lastly, political structures such as power constellations, administrative patterns, authority relations, and party systems have received new and original interpretations – quantitative and qualitative – with the help of Deutsch's theory of integration, innovatively elucidated by the frameworks of cybernetics and communication.

Durkheim's attempts to make sociology a discipline subject to the rigorous verification procedures of science, without, however, losing its moral imperatives and normative obligations, are paralleled by Deutsch's endeavors in political science. These efforts are manifested in Deutsch's pioneering quantifications of hitherto vague concepts which were neither testable nor verifiable by accepted scientific criteria. Furthermore, Deutsch's preoccupation with the 'scientification' of social science can be ascertained in his choice of language, metaphors, and analogies, many of which – as in the case of Durkheim – refer to the structures and functions of the human anatomy (nerves, muscles, cells, brains, memory) and to components of the 'hard' sciences including thermodynamics, electricity, and communication.

Deutsch's theory of integration and its multifaceted empirical applications culminate in various studies concerning the most unique and powerful integrative force of modern social life: nationalism. No other social bond has continued to dominate world politics to the extent that nationalism has. Deutsch's systematic investigation of the nation-building process reveals nationalism's diachronic and synchronic variety with respect to form and content. Thus, nationalism can have ethnic, political, linguistic, or other bases. Depending on the particular historical and geopolitical context and its major social carriers, nationalism can be a progressive, even revolutionary movement, or conversely can represent a retarding, even reactionary force. Conscious nationalism, usually first initiated and articulated by elites, remains politically impotent until it becomes an integral part of the mobilized population's value system.

Nationalism and its manifestations are subject to continuous change; the only constant remains its promise of *conscience collective* and social solidarity, which has yet to be challenged by any other structural formation.

However, Deutsch's keen awareness of the adverse dimensions of nationalism represents one of *the* major driving forces behind his scholarly inquiries.[13] Underlying his work one finds a genuine apprehension of uncontrolled nationalism and its potentially dangerous consequence. It is in this context that Deutsch's analysis of integration reaches frequently beyond the confines of the nation-state. It would not be unreasonable to argue that Deutsch's great contributions to the study of international relations – the subject area that more than anything else established his scholarly fame – are logical extensions of his prime concern with political integration and social solidarity. Believing in the ultimate virtues of mankind, Deutsch repeatedly states that integration on the supranational level increasingly will become a necessity for the survival of mankind. Moreover, as it was with the formation of the nation-state, supranational units may be able to provide more benefits for less cost to their citizens and may possess better capacities to learn and listen than the individually competing, frequently hostile parts. Thus, as Deutsch's research concerning supranational alliance structures shows, the process of integration beyond the nation-state has become a reality in some parts of the world. However, as Puchala demonstrates in his paper in this volume, the empirical extent of this integration has often been exaggerated.[14] In the final analysis, the true test of moral existence lies in mankind's capacity and willingness to make social action integrative and communal – a fundamental theme in the works of both Emile Durkheim and Karl W. Deutsch.

Emile Durkheim and Karl W. Deutsch: Some Comparative Analyses

In attempting to find some answers to the central question of their work, namely, 'What are the bonds that unite men?', Durkheim and Deutsch established certain normative parameters concerning man and his environment, some of which will be considered briefly. It may be an oversimplification – especially considering the voluminous writings of both thinkers – yet no false characterization to call Durkheim and Deutsch 'optimists'. Their strong belief in the enlightening powers of science, so thoroughly reflected in every aspect of their work; their emphatic scholarly engagement on the side of egalitarianism, merit and objective criteria; their concomitant open disdain for most forms of elitism and exclusivism; and their unmitigated hostility toward all manifestations of racism – convey a positive and human outlook, as well as hope, for mankind.

It is interesting to note that both thinkers were close to the values of social democracy in their private and public lives, though they both refrained from using their academic stature to espouse their political preferences in the lecture hall. The latter point is understandable given their preoccupation with academic rigor and scholarly objectivity. Durkheim, of course, lectured extensively on socialism.[15] Following

Saint-Simon, Durkheim extols socialism as the epitome of scientific rationalism and heralds its advent as the ideal type of progress, industrial development, and all-round modernization. Of further interest is the fact that communism – not communism, of course, in its post-1917 Leninist sense – to Durkheim is *not* a perfection of socialism, but rather its complete antithesis. Communism, Durkheim argues, is a backward, anti-modern, and retarding force that is predicated on a primitive form of social solidarity and human existence. Durkheim's association with progressive causes was also manifested in his strong public engagement on the side of Captain Dreyfus and his close friendship with his fellow graduate from the Ecole Normale Supérieure, Jean Jaures, one of the leading French socialist thinkers and politicians.

Deutsch's 'non-academic' values are steeped in the humanitarianism of Austro-Marxism, in which members of his family played a leading role. His writings and especially his lectures reflect a deep concern for egalitarianism, human rights, and the plight of the poor and disadvantaged. This concern pertains to intra-country analyses as well as to the global distribution of wealth and power.

Thus both Durkheim and Deutsch argue for the *moral* necessity as well as *realpolitikal* advantages of democracy as opposed to any other political form of government. Democracy's essence does not lie in the size of the political community, the number of its inhabitants, or the power of the government; rather, the criteria of open information and unimpeded feedback between the state and society, and the constant enhancement and guarantee of choice for the individual, determine its existence and success. The question of open two-way communication between the state and society is a central one in terms of democracy and its requirements, both for Deutsch and Durkheim. As Durkheim puts its:

> The true characteristics [of democracy] are twofold: (1) a greater range of the government consciousness, and (2) closer communications between this consciousness and the mass of individual consciousness ... This is what gives democracy a moral superiority. Because it is a system based on reflection, it allows the citizen to accept the laws of the country with more intelligence and thus less passively. Because there is a constant flow of communication between themselves and the State, the State is for individuals no longer like an exterior force that imparts a wholly mechanical impetus to them. Owing to constant exchanges between them and the State, its life becomes linked with theirs, just as their life does with that of the State.[16]

Deutsch and Durkheim recognize the important structural ramifications of the reciprocity in communication between state and society; namely, an elevation of social consciousness, hence individual freedom; and a curtailment – largely through the creation of secondary organizations – of the possible abuse of power on the part of the state. Giddens substantiates this view in arguing the following on Durkheim's concept of democracy:

A democracy, therefore, has two primary characteristics: the existence of close, and two-way, communication between government and governed; and the increasing extension of the contacts and ties of the state with other sectors of the society ... A democratic society therefore, according to Durkheim, is a society which is 'conscious of itself'.[17]

Both authors reject any dictatorship or any form of authoritarianism from above, no matter for what end or purpose. Both emphasize that every system's overall efficacy depends primarily on its legitimacy or *moral* authority. Coercive sanctions form only a distant deterrence, which in turn can never work without the presence of moral consensus. To paraphrase a thought from one of Deutsch's lectures, no state, no matter how coercive and totalitarian, can afford to 'bug' every room in a society. There simply would not be sufficient time and manpower available to listen to all the information, sift through the necessary evidence and pursue the 'culprits'. Thus, a society without common moral tenets and legitimate non-coercive channels of communication is bound to stagnate and eventually disintegrate from information overload due to lack of legitimation rather than technological deficiencies. The constraints of time and human capacities necessitate the existence in every society of what could be best labeled the 'non-contractual elements of contract'. People do not keep promises, abide by rules, and follow other patterns of peaceful and co-operative interaction because the enforcers of the law require them to do so; rather, they do so because of the legitimacy of certain 'unwritten rules', that is, because of the existence of the *conscience collective*.

This normative parameter assumes a benign interpretation of human mentality. Neither Durkheim nor Deutsch, however, has a Rousseauian or Promethean view of man. Although man is certainly not evil, power-hungry, and devious (as in the *homo-homini-lupus* view commonly held by conservative social theorists), his goodness is not biologically, instinctively, and/or psychologically inherent to his being. Rather, goodness, like everything else, is acquired through the social process. Institutional discipline teaches, transmits, and channels social attitudes and behavior. By limiting and disciplining the human being's individualistic desires, institutions simultaneously enhance his – and the community's – social existence. The fact that by their very limitation organizations widen human potential could be viewed as a dialectic of institutional constraint.

Moderation, constraint, and limitations with respect to most extremes are central to Durkheim's and Deutsch's normative and theoretical frameworks. Characterizing the tone of Durkheim's scholarship and his potential temperament in words that are equally applicable to Deutsch, Giddens writes:

Both in political temper and in sociological conviction, Durkheim was an opponent of revolutionary thought. Evolution, not revolution, provided the framework for his conception of social change: he frequently emphasized that significant change only takes place through the cumulation of long term processes of social development.[18]

Moderation pertains to all social phenomena. Thus Durkheim argues that even such antisocial, disruptive, morally reprehensible, and unpleasant occurrences as crime, suicide, and 'melancholy' (a state of mind we would call 'depression') are not only normal for individual and collective life – provided they exist in moderation – but are necessary for it. Hence their absence or eradication – apart from being impossible – would also be undesirable, indeed pathological.[19]

Deutsch's cybernetic model is the very essence of moderation and compromise. Any unmodified strains – positive or negative – on the system would lead most probably to increasing oscillations, periods of turmoil, and eventual breakdown. To take the four key components of the feedback model as examples, an exacerbated strain with respect to the system's capacities in three of the four could cause stagnation and/or disintegration: too high a *'load* in terms of information', too great a *'lag* in the response of the system', even too substantial a *'gain* in each corrective step taken by the system' has detrimental consequences for the whole.[20] Only the *lead*, that is, advanced knowledge available to a system, represents a factor the abundance of which may be unconditionally beneficial to the maintenance of an equilibrium.

Constraint and mediation also represent a common denominator with respect to the two authors' frameworks of the political. Durkheim's framework includes two elements. One is the fairly conventional idea that politics involves relations of authority between those who command and those who obey. The other, more unusual and complicated, involves notions of communication and a special state consciousness.

Not all associations with relations of authority are political, however. Authority exists within the family and the clan, but these do not thereby become political associations. A 'political society' results from the association of individual clans, castes, or guilds, which are not themselves political associations. 'We should then define the political society as one formed by the coming together of a rather large number of secondary social groups, subject to the same one authority which is not itself subject to any other superior authority duly constituted.'[21]

The most important form of political society in the modern world is a central, legitimate, and accessible structure known as the government or state, that is, 'the particular group of officials entrusted with representing this sovereign authority'.[22] The state is not above – or apart from – society in the sense that it encompasses an ideal embodiment of society. The state's presence is far from pervasive. Instead, the state is a highly neutral – almost asocial – corporation of rational administrators who embody, co-ordinate, and direct the rational realization of the public interest. One of the state's major tasks is to foster society's integration and maintenance.

In order for the state to mediate as a neutral arbiter, 'the state detaches itself from society ... The state thus does not express the collective representations arising from society as a whole; it rejects them deliberately in order to assure itself of perfect rational judgment. Hence the state acquires a strong independence which is precisely based on its own rationality'.[23] Despite the sharp distinction between the *conscience* of the state (*conscience gouvernemental*) and that of society, the former nevertheless is the prime agent of social solidarity. Its unique position in society's communication framework is mainly responsible for this phenomenon.

In no other area of Durkheim's and Deutsch's writings is the context of their common concern expressed in more similar form than with respect to the state and its functions. Durkheim's language describing the state and its activities abounds with analogies with the human anatomy and organism; the cybernetic framework employed to analyze the state's relationship with society is quite Deutschian.[24] Thus, the state's task for Durkheim is to operate like a 'brain' with the 'principal function to think'.[25] Durkheim differentiates between the state proper, which he likens to 'the central nervous system', and its administrative bodies, which are similar to 'the muscular system'.[26] In his actual usage, however, Durkheim sometimes expands the state to include the administrative staffs as well as the political decision-makers. The state, for Durkheim, functions above all as an efficient communication mechanism transmitting information both within society and between society and the environment. It therefore fulfills essential prerequisites of moral authority: guidance, control, and integration.

Durkheim's theory of the functions of the state grows out of his concept of the political. The state channels and centralizes currents of *conscience* and interests within society, but it does more than this alone. The state is also the 'organizing centre of the secondary groups themselves'.[27] Durkheim nowhere reduces the state to society (or vice versa). There are all sorts of collective representations arising from the various secondary groups within society, while the state produces its own characteristic collective representations. The state's representations are 'distinguished from the other collective representations by their higher degree of consciousness and reflection'.[28]

The ideal form of the state is a democracy, but the latter term is given an unusual twist. Democracy for Durkheim cannot be defined in the Aristotelian manner according to the number of rulers and their personal normative orientations *vis-à-vis* the ruled. In any but the smallest society some men govern and others are governed; the relative number of the former is not really very important. A democracy for Durkheim is a society in which 'communications between the state and other parts of society are many, and both regular and organized'.[29] Furthermore, the realm of consciously directed public activity is comparatively large. Justice, education, and the economy are brought into the conscious sphere of policy discussion and state action.

The democratic state may be compared with its feudal or absolutist predecessor. The most important difference is the far wider range of communication between state and society. Earlier forms of the state had little contact with society; the state was 'a kind of mysterious being to whom the ordinary man dared not lift his eyes and whom he even, more often than not, represented to himself as a religious symbol. The representatives of the state bore the stamp of a sacred character and, as such, were set apart from the commonality'.[30] Also the early state involved itself in little conscious direction of society. In this sense, Durkheim says, absolutism is a misnomer. The Bourbons were, of course, absolute in relation to any particular subject, but they were much less powerful in relation to secondary groups *qua* groups. Furthermore, in 'a society such as the monarchy of the seventeenth century, the number of things on which government deliberations have any bearing is very small'.[31]

Thus the development of the modern state is marked by an increase in communication and government activity. In addition, the state fulfills other functions. It permits the development of individual freedoms. In the Middle Ages, the individual was subordinated to a secondary grouping, whether guild or manor or family. The modern state, on the other hand, liberates the individual from the 'tyranny' of particular social groups. At one point, Durkheim even goes so far as to say that the 'stronger the state, the more the individual is respected'.[32]

Related to its promotion of the 'cult of the individual', the state takes over the role of 'calling the individual to a moral way of life ... It is, above all, the organ of moral discipline'.[33] The state accomplishes this function in a number of ways, the administration of justice, regulation of the economy, and establishment of educational institutions being among the more prominent.

Despite the liberating power of the modern state, it too can become oppressive. Individualism takes firmest root when a balance exists between the state and secondary groups. 'It is out of this conflict of social forces that individual liberties are born.'[34] The vitality of *both* state and secondary associations ensures both maximum individual liberty and maximum solidarity.

A related issue is the necessity of insulating the state from society, or more precisely from the mass popular electorate. There are two connected reasons for this requirement. In the first place, a certain separation of state and society is necessary for the minimization of anomie (and consequent maintenance of solidarity). In the second place, it is impossible for the state to fulfill its role as a planning and directing agency if it is subject to constant buffeting from the ebb and flow of unorganized and shifting currents among the population. In order to prevent the enervation of the directing power of the state by too close a contact with popular opinion, Durkheim proposes using professional associations as the basic electoral unit. This measure would both strengthen secondary associations and insulate the state from the mass electorate. The state must strike a balance between being independent and being in close communication with society.

Discounting some marginal corporatist overtones, it is quite clear why Durkheim, together with his famous compatriot Alexis de Tocqueville, can be regarded as one of modern pluralism's intellectual forefathers. Seeing an acute threat to the individual's freedom and well-being, hence moral and social existence, from the exigencies of modern life, Durkheim sought remedies in a structural balance between a *Gesellschaft*-type organization, like the state, and a new *Gemeinschaft*-type association, such as the secondary occupational group. (Durkheim observed correctly that primary ties such as kinship, extended family, religion, and geographic origin could not provide a sufficiently strong and enduring community for the individual in modern society.) Durkheim believed the stand-off between the state and secondary associations to be of great significance to the individual and to the community as a whole. An uncontrolled, powerful state may easily create what would later be called 'totalitarianism', whereas unaccountable groups could just as easily subjugate the individual.[35]

Durkheim is, of course, primarily concerned with sociology. His political theory is largely implicit in the bulk of his writings. Deutsch, on the other hand, is specifically interested in constructing political theory. The core of Deutsch's political theory is the cybernetic model of government (the state) and politics. Government for Deutsch has two basic elements. In the first place, it is conceived as a system of communication. Secondly, its function is to act as the conscious steering mechanism of society.

Viewing the state as a system of communication leads one to focus on elements neglected by other political theories. Also, Deutsch elaborates the concept of social communication further than does Durkheim, and thus requires a more detailed analysis.

Any system of communication relies upon the processing of information.[36] A government requires a 'flow of information' to those whom it rules and who are expected to obey. The government in its turn depends upon information from and about the ruled, ranging from the hard data of economic indicators and demographic variables to the more impressionistic soundings of the 'public mood'. Mistakes or garbled information can lead to serious errors in government decision-making; the breakdown of the channels of information can lead to stagnation and drift on the part of the state and apathy or rebellion on the part of the ruled. The opposite problem, but with similar harmful effects, is that of 'communications overload', where channels of information are swamped with messages.

The other aspect of government is its function as the agency of coordination and direction for the society as a whole.

> Governments may seek goals in domestic or foreign policies. In order to approach these goals they must guide their behavior by a stream of information concerning their own position in relation to these goals; their remaining distance from them; and the actual, as distinct from the intended, results of their own most recent step or attempt to approach them.[37]

The state as steering mechanism is liable to a number of dysfunctions which remain unexplained by Durkheim's theories of the state and social interaction. The steering capacity of the government may decline due to the stereotyping or ossification of institutions, with the dominance of government 'machinery over [government] performance'.[38] Even if established routines are not elevated from means to ends, such routines eventually will prove insufficient to deal with some new problem. Unless the state retains the ability to adapt and create new routines, it will suffer a loss of steering capacity from its inability to meet new challenges. If a state loses its steering capacity, it then drifts under 'external influences, or by coasting on momentum, or by some combination of these two'.[39]

Although there are fundamental similarities between the political theories of Deutsch and Durkheim, there are none the less differences of emphasis and nuance. Deutsch provides a more detailed analysis of social communication and connects it to political development or decay more systematically than does Durkheim. On the other hand, Durkheim provides a better analysis of the historical situations that permit a government to fulfill its role as a steering agency and of those that tend to subvert the government's independence or steering capacity, leading to drift. Durkheim is also more explicitly concerned with the relationship between society (particularly secondary associations) and the state than is Deutsch. This difference is probably a result of Deutsch's emphasis on political theory. It cannot be denied that Deutsch's analysis of the state apparatus itself is more detailed than Durkheim's. In general, Deutsch gains considerable analytic clarity from his narrower focus.

Both Deutsch and Durkheim have a fairly unusual conception of politics. In Deutsch's wording (which is compatible with Durkheim's view) the 'essence of politics [is the] dependable coordination of human effort and expectations for the attainment of the goals of the society'.[40] This conception of the political neglects many of the commonly accepted features of politics in much other social theory. Such phenomena as class struggle and the class nature of the state, the tensions between rulers and their staffs, or the dynamic of acceptance and rejection of claims to legitimacy are neglected or glossed over, as is Lasswell's question of 'who gets what, when, and how?' Perhaps the greatest lacuna of all is the begging of the question of how the 'goals of society' are themselves defined. They are assumed to be the rational outcome of a regulated process directed by a common public morality.

Emanating from their inclination toward rationalism and their all-pervasive preoccupation with morality, Durkheim and especially Deutsch tend to equate the two implicitly. Thus everything rational seems to be good, and vice versa. Conversely, irrational acts are seen as ethically wrong; irrationalism, thus, is equated with immorality, or at least with amorality.

The notion of rationality as a virtue and irrationality as pathological has been a dominant normative trend in the realm of American academic social science. The Anglo-Saxon empiricist tradition contributed to the evolution of this framework of inquiry, as did positivism and (especially in sociology via Talcott Parsons) Durkheim's normative and methodological legacy. The temporary triumph – and final fall – of fascism and national socialism in Europe corroborated the dangers – and eventual futility – of irrationality; they also provided excellent empirical examples for the inherently evil and powerful manifestations of unleashed and channeled irrationality.

Given his background and geographical origin, it seems hardly surprising that Deutsch adopted this liberal tenet prevalent in American academia. His inclination to equate irrationality with iniquity seems to derive from understandable reactions to recent events in world history. To Deutsch, as to Durkheim, all social action necessitates moral parameters. 'Is' and 'ought' are inseparable in real life, hence they should be as well to the social scientist, since the latter's task is not to create an artifact of the world, but rather to help clarify it. And it would seem that in the world rational action is good, whereas irrational action is bad.

By implicitly postulating this dichotomy, Deutsch and (to a lesser degree) Durkheim run the risk of being victimized by two equally undesirable occurrences: an ahistorical description of social change; and a tendency to allow their own normative preferences to intrude upon the interpretation of the action observed.[41] Concerning the former, both Deutsch and Durkheim neglect the turmoil and bloodshed of historical change. Societies are held together by common morality, *conscience collective*, social solidarity and consensus. But how do all these forces arise? And more important, who initiates them at whose cost? Why do communities break up and what are the benefits as well as costs to the formation of new social units? Why and how do values change?

Unlike Marx's analysis of the class struggle or Weber's sociology of domination, Deutsch's cybernetic approach to system formation and Durkheim's social progress propelled by the division of labor describe integration and modernization as a rational – almost abstract – process with little opposition. Commenting on this point in Deutsch's work, Pfaltzgraff writes:

> In his writings on integration, Deutsch has evolved a theoretical framework based on a consensual approach. Integration occurs as peoples ... find areas of commonality of interest and expectations of joint reward. Force is consigned to a minimal role. While core areas themselves are identified, we find little place in Deutsch's writings for the coercive capabilities which are often employed in the integrative process. To understand the unification of Germany without the 'blood and iron' of Bismarck; the unification of the United States without the conquest of the South in the Civil War; the building of modern Russia without the force employed by the Tsars and their successors; or ... the preservation of the Congo [Zaïre] by the defeat of secessionist movements is once again to ignore an important set of variables.[42]

Here we reject the notion of the Deutschian framework being unable to account for social change. Deutsch's steering and feedback mechanisms – both profoundly Durkheimian in the sense that they presuppose the existence of a common morality as a corrective between state and society, within the state as well as within society – are precisely the dimensions by which the Deutschian model goes beyond structural functionalism. Thus as Deutsch himself argues, his model does not have to stop at the issue of self-preservation, but indeed can account for systemic self-transformation.

Despite this important qualification, neither author emphasizes sufficiently the coercive side of integration. Moreover, there are no attempts to explain the crucial differences in the degrees of coercion exercised by the integrating agent. These coercive actions can range from brutal physical force to cunning and diplomatic manipulation; from an open display of power to the more subtle nuances of influence and authority. Durkheim's and Deutsch's preoccupation with rationality (and optimism) does not allow them to pay attention to the brutal sides of history and the costs exacted by every integration process.

By attempting to be all-inclusive and universally applicable, Deutsch's cybernetic model runs the risk of emphasizing form at the expense of content in explaining integration. This tendency is a problem with respect to all levels of the analysis. In *The Nerves of Government*, for example, Deutsch elucidates systemic goal changes using Sweden as an example.[43] He states the fundamental changes in the goals of the Swedish system, from a militarist state of the seventeenth century to the welfare state of the twentieth. He clarifies the salience of goal-setting for the survival of every system; he equally demonstrates the tremendous choice – and discrepancy – between goals. Yet the most pressing issue remains unresolved: why and how did Sweden change its goals so drastically in the course of three centuries? What were the objective conditions and subjective factors that induced – necessitated – this evolution? Above all, especially in our contemporary world, why was Sweden successful at this goal change; and can it be imitated?

The risk with the Deutschian model, as indeed with most models, is that its sophisticated analytical framework can distort reality, leading to two unintended consequences: the obfuscation of concepts and the reification of means. Notions such as system 'lag' and 'gain', 'feedback' and 'steering', just to name a few, must be anchored in concrete historical contexts lest they become reified. The same pertains to Durkheim's concepts of 'society' and 'social'. Both are frequently used as *deus-ex-machina*-type explanations, which, however, lack the necessary weight to be convincing. Thus, for instance, in analyzing the social bases of religion, Durkheim introduces the important concepts of 'sacred' and 'profane'. Both are prevalent in every society, each is a *sine qua non* for social order. Yet, by making society the cause, carrier, and outcome of both 'sacred' and 'profane', Durkheim diminishes its explanatory value and that of his own argument. It remains unclear, ultimately, why certain things become sacred and others remain profane. Is it a question of scarcity, force, authority, or charisma? When and how does the establishment of the sacred gain – and lose – legitimacy? What are the struggles involved in the creation of a new 'sacred' item?

Moreover, the two theorists' attempts to construct models which can at least formulate – if not answer – relevant questions pertaining to all social systems frequently necessitate too high a level of abstraction, which either entails a hiatus between the theoretical framework and its empirical substantiations, or indeed excludes the latter altogether. For instance, Deutsch's notion of 'system strain' may prove valuable for historical sociology though little work has yet been done along this line. But as presently constituted, 'system strain' is too vague a concept for useful historical application. It will require a more subtle differentiation and substantial concretization if it is to be of significant analytic and empirical value. Furthermore, the concept of democracy, as we mentioned above, implicit and central to the premises of both Durkheim and Deutsch, never receives full concretization in terms of its historical development, political content, and day-to-day functioning. Giddens is quite correct in describing Durkheim's failure to account for the structure of democracy: 'Democracy, for Durkheim, thus becomes a matter of the interplay of sentiments and ideas between government and mass; his discussion of democratic government contains no developed examination of the functioning of political parties, or of parliament, or of the franchise, and indeed these considerations are regarded as of purely minor significance'.[44] Although certainly less the case with Deutsch, there is no question that most concrete political and historical examples are not presented in his major theoretical contribution, *The Nerves of Government*, but rather in the more textbook-type publications such as *Politics and Government, The Analysis of International Relations, Nationalism and Its Alternatives*, and his excellent chapter on West Germany in *Modern Political Systems: Europe*, edited by Macridis and Ward.

Finally, both authors neglect the resilience – even resurgence – of pre-modern social formations in modern times. A unilinear and unidirectional modernization process assumes a 'critical mass' of modernity that serves as a 'point of no return' with respect to most aspects of traditional life. Thus, for example, Durkheim devotes almost no attention to the substantial remnants of 'mechanical solidarity' in modern society, just as Deutsch assumes that in the process of social mobilization all forms of urbanization imply a break with traditional life, such as the extended family and other social manifestations of pre-mobilized, rural existence. Thus it is ironic that in advanced industrial countries many political and social developments of the last decade have been precisely manifestations of a resurgence of dormant traditions in quest of community and integration on a more immediate scale, a process for which the Durkheimian and Deutschian frameworks should provide some of the most adequate explanations in the social sciences due to their preoccupation with the morality of social integration.

Conclusion

Few theories in the social sciences provide a more comprehensive explanation of integration and cohesion in the process of social development than Deutsch's and Durkheim's. The centrality of solidarity and community in all aspects of human life represents their fundamental concern. The common morality of social action shapes individual existence and the direction of the political process. It is this phenomenon that Durkheim and Deutsch have attempted to study with the help of innovative methodological propositions and applications.

A synthesis of the two frameworks of inquiry would go well beyond the welcome dismantling of artificially erected – and intellectually stultifying – barriers between the related academic fields of political science and sociology. Both disciplines would benefit from such a conceptual union. Sociologists might recognize that many of their thoughts could be applied to the political interaction of nations and states, and political scientists might pay more attention to the social dimensions of government. Sociologists could learn from Deutsch's innovative research on national and supranational integration, just as political scientists could improve their hitherto rudimentary knowledge of the political importance and ramifications of such phenomena as anomie, religion, and *conscience collective*.

These cross-disciplinary, integrative steps seem of increasing significance to some of the potentially most important research endeavors of the near future. Following up the internal logic of their theory, Deutsch and some of his colleagues have embarked on an analysis of integration and community formation on a global level.[45] Critical of certain 'world modeling' attempts that place undue emphasis on material constraints in postulating an inevitable global inequality, Deutsch and his colleagues have recognized – both empirically and normatively – the importance of social and moral phenomena for future regional integrative developments and global community formation. These issues, being profoundly Durkheimian in nature, may necessitate a fundamental understanding of some of Durkheim's concepts in order at least to help formulate the right questions if, regrettably, perhaps unable to provide any definitive answers.

Notes: Chapter 7

We would like to thank Jerome Karabel and David Swartz for comments on an earlier draft of this chapter. Due to strict space limitations, certain portions of the original study, including an extensive bibliography of the works of Karl W. Deutsch and Emile Durkheim, have been omitted. For an unabridged version, please contact the authors.

1 Indeed, the lack of an overt Durkheimian influence upon Deutsch is reflected by the presence of perhaps only one reference to Durkheim in Deutsch's work, and that on an inconsequential point. See Karl W. Deutsch, *The Nerves of Government: Models of Political Communication and Control* (New York: The Free Press, 1963), p. 250.
2 Only Steven Lukes appears to have remarked upon this similarity. See Steven Lukes, *Emile Durkheim — His Life and Work: A Historical and Critical Study* (Harmondsworth, Mddx: Penguin, 1975), p. 269.
3 Thus Durkheim is among the five most important sociologists 'regardless of the audience in question', according to a thorough study by Mark Jay Oromaner, 'The audience as a determinant of the most important sociologists', *American Sociologist*, vol. 4, no. 4 (November 1969), pp. 332–5; the study includes citations in

introductory sociology textbooks, appearance on graduate reading lists, and citations in articles published in the *American Sociological Review*. Deutsch, on the other hand, is far and away the most frequently cited author in international relations publications, appearing in three prestigious journals of political science during the period 1958–73 (Richard B. Finnegan and John J. Giles, 'A citation analysis of patterns of influence in international relations research', *International Studies Notes*, vol. 2, no. 4, Winter 1975, pp. 11–21). A table, 'Citation to scholars: 1958–1973', based upon a thorough analysis of the *American Political Science Review, World Politics*, and *The Journal of Politics*, shows that Deutsch leads all other scholars with 131 citations; the second person, has 83. 'The table reveals a great deal of attention to Karl Deutsch well beyond the citations of his major works. Deutsch is cited over a wider range of books, monographs, articles, etc. than any other scholar. It is fair to say that Deutsch not only is most influential in terms of citations but his influence is broader than for any other scholar' (ibid., pp. 15–16). Furthermore, many of Deutsch's books and articles, as tabulations of 'leading works' indicate, are central to the field of international politics. 'Most striking are the number of works directed at international integration in the later period [1966–73], indicating the pervasive influence of Karl W. Deutsch. Not only is *Political Community* in the first rank, but works in the 5th, 6th, 8th, and 9th ranks are in this conceptual orientation' (ibid., p. 14). These findings are corroborated by another study conducted by Bruce M. Russett ('Methodological and theoretical schools in international relations,' in *A Design for International Relations Research: Scope, Theory, Methods, and Relevance*, ed. Norman D. Palmer, American Academy of Political and Social Science Monograph No. 10, Philadelphia, Pa, October 1970, pp. 87–105.) Russett's analysis, even more than that of Finnegan and Giles, demonstrates Deutsch's dominant influence in political science as a whole since his study includes other subfields of the discipline, in addition to that of international relations narrowly defined (see esp. pp. 100–1).

4 For the significant influence of some of Deutsch's students and collaborators on the discipline of international relations, see Finnegan and Giles, 'Citation analysis'. More specifically, it is important to note that a disproportionately large number of them have been increasing their positions of influence in the top fifteen ranks 'rapidly' since 1966 (see especially p. 17). Russett's study ('Methodological and theoretical schools') not only shows the distinct existence of a 'Yale Factor' (p. 97) in American political science, but also provides ample data as to the importance and influence of its individual members. (See especially Table I.1 entitled 'Yale – International Integration' on p. 94.)

5 Emile Durkheim, *The Division of Labor in Society* (New York: The Free Press, 1964), p. 79; emphasis in original.

6 The terms 'mechanical' and 'organic' are derived from the 'hard' sciences, notably biology, reflecting Durkheim's desire to have sociology accepted as a legitimate science by the academic establishment. This conscious effort on the part of Durkheim, in addition to his choice of terminology referring to the anatomy of the human body, finds striking parallels in the work of Karl W. Deutsch in relation to the discipline of political science.

7 Karl W. Deutsch, 'Social mobilization and political development', *American Political Science Review*, vol. 55, no. 3 (September 1961), pp. 493–514, esp. p. 493.

8 For Durkheim's view of a continuity between domestic and international politics see Emile Durkheim and Marcel Mauss, 'Note on the notion of civilization', intr. and tr. Benjamin Nelson, *Social Research*, vol. 38, no. 4 (1971), pp. 808–13. It is appropriate to point out in this context that there are no epistemological or analytic differences between our discussions of Deutsch's concept of integration and those elaborated in this volume by Arend Lijphart and Donald Puchala, respectively. Whereas our colleagues chose to illustrate the Deutschian framework in the context of 'international relations', we emphasized its 'sociological' aspects. Thus, rather than being contradictory, both approaches complement each other in a manifestation of the widely valid and useful applications of Deutsch's integration theory. For an explicit corroboration of this view, see Arend Lijphart, 'Karl W. Deutsch and the new paradigm in international relations', in this volume, esp. pp. 246–7.

9 Karl W. Deutsch, 'Integration and autonomy: some concepts and ideas', *Ekistics*, vol. 30, no. 179 (October 1970), pp. 327–31.

10 loc. cit.
11 Deutsch, *The Nerves of Government*, p. 150.
12 Karl W. Deutsch, Sidney A. Burrell, Robert A. Kann, Maurice Lee, Jr, Martin Lichterman, Raymond E. Lindgren, Francis L. Loewenheim, and Richard W. Van Wagenen, *Political Community and the North Atlantic Area: International Organization in the Light of Historical Experience* (Princeton, NJ: Princeton University Press, 1957), p. 5.
13 We are grateful to Bruce M. Russett for alerting us to the centrality of this point.
14 For a detailed analysis of the concept of international integration, see Donald J. Puchala, 'Integration theory and the study of international relations', in this volume. Puchala contrasts the considerable intrinsic value of Deutsch's theory of integration with a pessimistic appraisal of the chances for any substantial international integration in the coming decades.
15 His lecture notes were posthumously edited and published by his nephew and student Marcel Mauss under the title *Le Socialisme*. As the English title, *Socialism and Saint-Simon*, ed. Alvin W. Gouldner, tr. Charlotte Sattler (Yellow Springs, Ohio: Antioch Press, 1958), indicates, Durkheim combined the study of socialism with an analysis of the work of the French utopian socialist Henri Saint-Simon.
16 Emile Durkheim, *Professional Ethics and Civic Morals* (London: Routledge & Kegan Paul, 1957), pp. 88, 91.
17 Anthony Giddens, 'Durkheim's political sociology', *Sociological Review*, vol. 19, no. 4 (November 1971), pp. 477–519, esp. pp. 500–1.
18 ibid., pp. 504–5.
19 Emile Durkheim, *Suicide* (New York: The Free Press, 1966), pp. 367–70; idem, *The Rules of Sociological Method* (New York: The Free Press, 1964), pp. 70–3.
20 Deutsch, *The Nerves of Government*, pp. 187–8; emphasis in original.
21 Durkheim, *Professional Ethics*, p. 45.
22 ibid., p. 47.
23 Pierre Birnbaum, 'La conception durkheimienne de l'État: l'apolitisme des fonctionnaires', *Revue Française de Sociologie*, vol. 17, no. 2 (April–June 1976), pp. 247–58, esp. p. 248.
24 It is interesting to note the intellectual comparisons and parallels that this particular context evoked in two eminent Durkheim scholars. Whereas Pierre Birnbaum (ibid., p. 251) connects Durkheim's 'cybernetic analogies' with David Easton's systems analysis ('It is stunning to observe how much the ambiguities which one can discern in David Easton's model are already present in Durkheim's'), Steven Lukes (*Emile Durkheim*, p. 269, n. 75) sees parallels between Durkheim's and Deutsch's views of the state: 'There is a very close but seemingly unwitting parallel between [Durkheim's] view of government (and, indeed, Durkheim's account of democracy), on the one hand, and the very similar ideas of Karl Deutsch and his followers, on the other: cf., for instance, K. Deutsch, *The Nerves of Government* . . .'.
25 Durkheim, *Professional Ethics*, p. 51.
26 loc. cit.
27 ibid., p. 49
28 ibid., p. 50.
29 ibid., p. 85.
30 ibid., pp. 81–2.
31 ibid., p. 83.
32 ibid., p. 57.
33 ibid., pp. 69–72.
34 ibid., p. 62.
35 On these points see especially the preface to the second edition of *The Division of Labor in Society*, entitled 'Some notes on occupational groups'; also, Durkheim, *Suicide*, pp. 374–92. To Deutsch, the existence of secondary groups, their relative autonomy from the state and each other, and their integrative mechanisms with respect to the individual are all important prerequisites for a successful pluralist society. For an excellent discussion on this topic, see Karl W. Deutsch, *Political Community at the International Level: Problems of Definition and Measurement* (1954; reprint edn, Hamden, Conn.: Archon Books, 1970), pp. 49–51.
36 Deutsch, *The Nerves of Government*, p. 145.

37 ibid., p. 185.
38 ibid., p. 225.
39 ibid., p. 128.
40 ibid., p. 124.
41 Ironically, both shortcomings would probably meet with the two thinkers' disapproval, judging from the theoretical and methodological premisses of their work.
42 Robert L. Pfaltzgraff, Jr, 'Karl Deutsch and the Study of Political Science', *Political Science Reviewer*, vol. 2 (Fall 1972), pp. 90–111, esp. pp. 105–6.
43 Deutsch, *The Nerves of Government*, p. 199.
44 Giddens, 'Durkheim's political sociology', p. 150.
45 For a collection of essays on this topic, including numerous contributions from Deutsch and his colleagues, see Karl W. Deutsch, Bruno Fritsch, Hélio Jaguaribe, and Andrei S. Markovits (eds), *Problems of World Modeling: Political and Social Implications* (Cambridge, Mass.: Ballinger, 1977). Deutsch's 'other' major academic preoccupation of recent years has been the establishment of peace research as an international, cross-disciplinary field of study. It is clear that issues of world modeling and global peace are normatively and empirically inextricable and, as Arend Lijphart suggests in his article in this volume, directly derivative of the Deutschian paradigm. See Arend Lijphart, 'Karl W. Deutsch and the new paradigm in international relations', p. 233.

8
Public Opinion on International Affairs in Less Developed Countries

JORGE I. DOMINGUEZ

The peoples of less developed countries have a special stake in the relationship between national development and the global community.[1] The task of national development, though of worldwide concern, is particularly pressing in less developed countries. Their pasts as well as their prospects are shaped by the impact of the global community on them. Colonialism, warfare, private foreign investment and multinational enterprises, international organizations, foreign trade and aid all mold the international circumstances and the internal processes of most of these still very vulnerable countries. Many of them were long integrated with European powers against their will as parts of colonial empires. Many more have long entered and are inserted in the international economy in ways which remain unsatisfactory to some of their elites; even for those untroubled by the difficulties of interdependence, the experience of varying kinds of dependence has posed problems for both national development and foreign policies. Their political attitudes, then, look toward the outside world as well as toward their own communities. And yet mass public attitudes toward international affairs in less developed countries and their relationship to modernization have been studied relatively little.

These facts about their collective histories suggest a high and lively concern with international affairs, and yet the scholarly literature presents contradictory hypotheses about the nature of public opinion on international affairs in these countries; this chapter seeks to sort these out. Four questions about their mass publics will be addressed. How attentive are they to international issues? How differentiated internally are they? To what do they pay attention? How responsive are they to changes in international politics?

Parts of Karl Deutsch's work, as will be seen, bear directly on these questions. His research on social mobilization addresses the first two of these questions, and still provides the best answers to them. His research (with Richard Merritt) on the fourth question continues to identify the principal elements of the answer, but has proved to be too conservative in assessing patterns of responsiveness to events.

Public attitudes help to shape the political environment for government policy. Very low public concern with international affairs would make it easier for a government to conduct its foreign policy autonomously from internal social forces, while allowing wide foreign policy variation over time as incumbents change, making sustained international political integration less likely. A higher public concern with international affairs might constrain short-run government action more; its impact on international political integration depends on the content and direction of public attitudes.

The first part of this chapter asks the prior question about the sheer volume of public concern with international affairs; the second part looks at content and direction. Both touch on a people's propensity toward international political integration with other countries and with international organizations. The chapter draws eclectically from various sources with three restrictions. Countries from different international subsystems are represented. No data were used unless the opinions of at least several dozen people were being reported. And elite data are used only if there is also some reference to at least mass urban public opinion in that country. Because of space constraints, this chapter will consider neither the impact of the foreign policy opinions of these mass publics on the making of foreign policy in their countries, nor the detailed distribution of opinion on particular substantive questions. Though these are critical questions, the chapter is focused on issues which precede these considerations.

Some Theoretical Issues: The Volume of International Attentiveness

The scholarly literature bearing on public attitudes toward international affairs in less developed countries shows two principal cleavages: the impact of modernization on these attitudes, and their direction. This section will consider the first of these. One school of thought argues that the least modernized countries are likely to have a parochial culture largely inattentive to issues other than those of immediate local concern, such as food and shelter. Modernization, in the view of these scholars, increases attention beyond parochial concerns. Within this school of thought, two different hypotheses emerge. Karl Deutsch has argued that an 'aspect of the process of social mobilization is the shift of emphasis away from the parochialism and internationalism of many traditional cultures to a preoccupation with the supralocal but far less than worldwide unit of the territorial, and eventually national, state'. There may be 'a more rapid rise of attention devoted to national topics than of that given to world affairs, on the one hand, and to purely local matters, on the other'.[2] Thus one hypothesis is that modernization increases public attention toward national issues more rapidly than toward international or local-parochial issues. Daniel Lerner's view has been, however, that modernization increases an individual's news range, illustrating 'his interest in matters beyond his immediate personal and local concerns'.[3] Thus public attentiveness to all supralocal issues, including international issues, increases secularly with modernization.

Other scholars argue that the least modernized countries may be among the most internationally concerned. Lucian Pye has suggested that the 'national leadership must appeal to an undifferentiated public'. Because interest groups are not explicitly organized and all participants are not continuously represented in politics, politicians must appeal for public support at a high level of generality and diffuseness, stressing emotional issues to mobilize the entire population. Precisely because the public is undifferentiated, 'leaders are encouraged to adopt more clearly defined positions on international issues than on domestic issues'.[4] Robert Good has argued that foreign policy for many of these countries flows out of mostly domestic considerations: anti-colonialism holds together domestic factions, it helps to establish the identity of these countries in their conflicts with major powers. Foreign policy serves to keep the in-group in power, and reduces foreign influence in internal politics.[5] George Liska has also argued that 'relatively uninhibited foreign relations encompassing conflicts and alliances may be the primary necessity in political development'.[6] Thus an international enemy can be identified and domestic support gathered. In sum, then, public opinion in less modernized countries may be more attentive to international issues than public opinion in somewhat more modernized countries, and more attentive to international than to internal issues.

Some scholars, in addition, have noted the general proposition, as James Rosenau put it, that 'the most predominant mood of the mass public is, of course, indifference and passivity'.[7] The attentive public is approximately one-tenth of the total. However, even Rosenau has noted that specific events and processes of change may increase the size of this attentive public.[8]

A closely related issue addressed by these scholars is the extent of internal differentiation of the mass public in its foreign policy views. For those who emphasize the common conditions of tradition, prior to modernization, there may be few significant differences in the amount, as well as in the direction and content, of international attention according to social class, ethnicity, place of residence, or related factors, because the weight of pre-modernity is overwhelming. For those who emphasize that modernization has begun in most countries, and that it makes a difference in international attentiveness, there may, on the contrary, be major variations in amount, direction, and content of international attentiveness according to these categories; these variations may derive from modernization or from a combination of traditional and modernizing experiences. With regard to the United States, a number of studies clearly show that age, sex, income, education, and place of residence do affect international attitudes. Some 'attention groups' may also appear within mass publics in response to issues that directly affect their common interests, even though they are normally uninterested. These often acquire structure through ethnic or religious organizations independent of level of modernity.[9]

Toward a Synthesis

Public opinion in the least modernized countries is likely to be more attentive to international than to national issues in comparison with the balance of attention of public opinion in middle modernized countries. Relatively new states may have not yet created a national consensus. In post-colonial situations much information still comes from the former colonial power, shaping attention toward diffuse international events and affairs. The chief effect, then, of the first phase of modernization is to increase relative attention toward national issues more rapidly than toward international issues as countries shift from low to middle levels of modernity. If parochial and international concerns coexisted in the least modernized countries, national issues predominate in the middle modernized countries. Modernization, however, does increase attention to all supralocal issues, but at different rates.

As levels of modernization increase further attentiveness toward international issues catches up, both in absolute volume and in relative terms so that modern countries' mass publics are the most attentive to all kinds of issues. Within countries, the most modernized are also the most likely to be internationally attentive even though they, too, pay even more attention to national concerns. Elites run the affairs of their societies, so that national affairs are largely their own affairs; their attitudes toward international issues are likely to be nationalistic, because the task of developing their country will be seen to have internal as well as international implications.

The Evidence

Hadley Cantril and his associates have gathered data from several large national samples in the late 1950s and early 1960s. The Cuban sample included the urban population only; however, the samples for Brazil, the Dominican Republic, India, Nigeria, Panama, and the Philippines were weighted according to census data to obtain an urban–rural distribution approximately equal to the national population. Subjects were asked cross-nationally comparable open-ended questions, about their hopes and fears for their nation; answers were subsequently coded into several major categories. Table 8.1 reports the average references – $\frac{1}{2}$(hopes + fears) – to the international situation, including war and peace, the average references about the independent status of their nation, and two measures of modernization for the approximate time samples were taken.

The most modern countries have above average concern with the international situation. The least modernized countries (Egypt, Nigeria, and India) have middle levels of concern. Middle modernized countries have low to middle levels of concern. Concern for one's nation's independent status seems to be independent of the level of modernization.

International context makes surprisingly little difference. The Indian survey was taken in the late summer, 1962. Border incidents with China had already begun, the level of international conflict between India and China was heating up, and war would break out in October. The Cuban survey was taken in April and May 1960. Conflict with the United States had been heating up since the previous fall; the Soviet Union and

Table 8.1 Percentage of average references about hopes and fears for one's nation on international subjects and rank orders for adult literacy and GNP per capita (1957 US$)

	International situation	Independent status	Adult literacy	Per capita GNP
Israel	71	27	3	3
United States	58	8	2	1
West Germany	56	15	1	2
Yugoslavia	55	6	5	7
Egypt	32	41	10	10
Philippines	28	13	6	9
Panama	15	5	7	5
India	14	9	11	12
Nigeria	12	16	12	11
Brazil	12	4	9	6
Cuba	9	12	4	4
Dominican Republic	6	5	8	8
Average	35	15	—	—

Source: Hadley Cantril, *The Pattern of Human Concerns* (New Brunswick, NJ: Rutgers University Press, 1965), pp. 176, 178; methodology discussed in Appendix B; and Bruce Russett et al., *World Handbook of Political and Social Indicators* (New Haven, Conn.: Yale University Press, 1964), pp. 155-7, 222-4.

other communist countries were quickly becoming Cuba's allies; the conflict with the United States would lead to Cuba's nationalization of US property and the suspension of Cuba's sugar quota to the United States within weeks of the survey. The Dominican survey was taken in April 1962. The last months of the Trujillo government had been deeply filled with international conflict, including sanctions by the Organization of American States, supported by the United States. In the fall of 1961 the US navy intervened, probably decisively, to shape the short-term future of the country. Thus the experiences of at least three of the countries in the bottom half of the scale were profoundly shaped by international politics. But their less modernized populations were much less attentive to international affairs than the more modernized populations of other countries at comparable levels of international engagement.

Table 8.2 shows the ratio of average internal economic and political concerns to whichever of the two columns in Table 8.1 is higher for each country. A score of 1·0 would indicate that such a country was equally concerned about internal and international issues; a score higher than 1·0 would indicate that such a country was more concerned about internal issues; a score below 1·0 would indicate that the country was more concerned about international issues.

The four countries at the top of Table 8.1's scale on the international situation are at the bottom of both scales in Table 8.2. They are all more concerned about international than internal political or economic issues (except for West Germany's equal concern about economics). The middle and least modernized countries rank toward the top end of both scales in Table 8.2. They are overwhelmingly concerned about internal

Table 8.2 Ratio of average internal to highest average international concerns

	Internal economic/ international	Internal political/ international
Dominican Republic	12·6	12·7
Cuba	4·2	3·3
Nigeria	3·9	3·8
Brazil	3·8	1·7
Panama	3·6	2·1
India	3·3	1·1
Philippines	1·2	1·3
Egypt	1·1	0·6
West Germany	1·0	0·7
Yugoslavia	0·9	0·6
Israel	0·9	0·4
United States	0·6	0·3
Average	1·5	1·1

Source: Computed from Table 8.1, and from Cantril, *The Pattern of Human Concerns*, pp. 174–5.

issues, especially economic issues. The least modernized countries (Egypt more than Nigeria) seem, nevertheless, to be more concerned about international affairs than some of the middle modernized countries, four of which rank among the top five in both scales of Table 8.2, thus indicating their high concern for internal issues. But Yugoslavia and the Philippines, on the other hand, though middle modernized, seem to have average or above-average concern with international affairs.

An international research team engaged in the study of values in politics across countries in September–December 1966, also asked similar questions of local political leaders in India, Poland, Yugoslavia, and the United States. Whenever subjects were asked about the hopes and wishes for the future of each country, social and economic development objectives predominated. Concern with international co-operation or world peace ranged from a high of 60 per cent in the United States to a low of 3 per cent in India, with Poland and Yugoslavia scoring 15 and 14 per cent respectively.[10] Even though India had just fought a war in 1965, and before that it had fought wars against China and Pakistan, while Poland and Yugoslavia had not been engaged similarly since the Second World War, the level of international attentiveness was far lower in India, and that is consistent with the view that modernization increases international attentiveness.

Cross-nationally comparable questions were also asked on behalf of the US Information Agency in Buenos Aires, Rio de Janeiro, Mexico City, and Caracas in 1964. Asked about the most important problem facing the country, international topics were not cited by more than 2 per cent in any of these cities. Asked about their interest in international affairs, only between one-sixth and one-quarter said that they were very interested, while majorities in all four cities proclaimed their lack or very low level of interest. Only 7 per cent of the respondents, on average, named a person outside of their own country when they were asked which political leader in Latin America they admired the most.[11]

Other evidence also suggests that specific contextual variables may be relatively insignificant. A 1974 national sample (N = 2,191) of Venezuelan opinion showed that four-fifths could name petroleum as the country's most important industry but only 4 per cent considered the petroleum 'question' to be one of the country's most important problems – even though the Venezuelan government was then engaged in serious negotiations over the expropriation of the petroleum industry and its actions in OPEC are of worldwide importance. As a national priority for the Venezuelan mass public, oil was in eleventh place.[12] Similarly, a survey of 1,000 literate adults in Calcutta, Madras, Bombay, and Delhi in the first two months of 1966 found that Indian disagreements with Pakistan and China were cited by only 3 and 1 per cent of respondents as the major problems facing the country, even though India had just been through the Tashkent negotiations to settle affairs after the 1965 war with Pakistan.[13]

International context – understood as a pattern of national experience over a long period of time – may, however, serve to distinguish among countries at a comparable level of modernization, such as Argentina and Chile. Even though international affairs have been very salient in the Argentine experience, especially for Peronists, and even though Argentina's high modernity might lead one to expect high concern with international affairs, Argentines are overwhelmingly preoccupied with their own national affairs to the exclusion of everything else. A March 1966 survey in greater Buenos Aires asked about the most important international problem: 12 per cent said there was none and 22 per cent said they did not know. The comparable statistics for internal problems were 2 and 8 per cent. When asked four questions about the recent intervention in the Dominican Republic by the Organization of American States, 'don't know'[14] responses ranged from 35 to 45 per cent. For questions on Vietnam, the range was 33 to 40 per cent. Kirkpatrick's survey of fall 1965 asked: 'What are the principal problems Argentina faces these days?' Less than 4 per cent of all Argentines, including less than 4 per cent of the 'core Peronists', mentioned anything related to international affairs.[15]

The international Gallup poll asked three general questions about the then forthcoming year, 1966, in eight countries. The average 'don't know' responses were 19.6, 44.5, and 41.6 per cent. Argentina scored last on the first (27 per cent), and next to last on the others (54, 47 per cent). Chile, however, scored first on all three: 6, 5, and 7 per cent. The other countries are all modern, industrial ones.[16] The Argentine puzzle thus extends to cross-national comparison.

There is also considerable within-country variation in attentiveness to national and international issues. For example, surveys of five Brazilian cities in November 1962 and of the rural north-east in March 1963 show that at worst 10 per cent of the respondents in Porto Alegre, São Paulo, Rio de Janeiro, and Belo Horizonte had never heard of Fidel Castro; ignorance in the north-eastern city of Recife reached about one-quarter but, in the rural areas, ignorance ranged between one-third and over three-quarters of the respondents.[17]

Five villages in Egypt's Menoufia province, north of Cairo (more modernized than the national average), were surveyed in August–September 1956. Only 8·2 per cent of the leisure-time discussion topics reported by females, and 26·4 per cent of the topics reported by males, concerned supralocal subjects. While 80 per cent of the males and 50 per cent of the females knew that Nasser was President of Egypt, only one out of ninety-nine females could identify the position of any foreign leader, and 27·7 per cent of the men could identify Churchill's past position (the highest score). On the other hand, a survey of forty-nine Egyptian professionals in 1951 showed that twenty-five respondents considered relations with the United Kingdom to be their country's main problem.[18] Their response linked their internal national and international concerns to yield a strongly nationalistic view of international affairs, somewhat at the expense of concern for 'pure' national issues.

Modernization in Brazil and Egypt increases attention and knowledge about both national and international issues though concern about the former increases faster than concern about the latter in the middle modernized Brazil. The Egyptian elite had a diffuse, strongly nationalistic international interest. This supports the view that in least modernized Egypt there is a coexistence of international and local-parochial concerns somewhat at the expense of more purely national concerns.

In general, as Karl Deutsch would have expected from his research on social mobilization, modernization appears to increase international attentiveness (though at a slower rate than national attentiveness). For each of the seven less modernized countries in Tables 8.1 and 8.2 for which there are data on education, two international hopes and two international fears are considered, computing their relationship to education. Thus we have twenty-eight observed relationships. In eighteen of these the most educated were most likely to express hopes or fears about international issues; and the least educated were least likely to do so. In only three of the twenty-eight were the most educated least likely to be internationally concerned and in only three were the least educated most likely to be internationally concerned.[19]

Inkeles has also shown that factory experience makes an independent contribution to knowledge about international affairs. The ability to identify correctly an international leader improved significantly if one compares low-educated, newly recruited factory workers (who had been employed in a factory from one to three months) with factory workers with at least four years' experience. This cognitive ability increased from 26 to 67 per cent in Argentina, 47 to 85 per cent in Chile, 1 to 31 per cent in India, 80 to 81 per cent in Israel, 11 to 17 per cent in Nigeria, and 2 to 26 per cent in East Pakistan.[20]

The argument has been aptly summarized by José Silva Michelena referring to his large, stratified random sample of Venezuelans: 'Those groups which had a larger proportion of people evaluating foreign influences, no matter the particular judgments, tended to have a larger proportion of upper-status persons who have experienced a great deal of change, whose normative orientation is congenial with development, and whose psychological state is autonomous'.[21]

Further Theoretical Issues: Direction and Responsiveness of International Attention

Deutsch and Merritt have studied the degree of public responsiveness to changes in international events. They noted the 'resistance of human thinking and imagining to sudden environmental pressures'. Images and attitudes change very slowly; for major changes to occur, they suggest that there must be the 'combination and mutual reinforcement of cumulative events with spectacular events and substantial government efforts as well as the absence of sizable cross-pressures'.[22] A good deal of empirical evidence, on such diverse countries as Japan and Canada, suggests that international attitudes, indeed, change slowly, but they do change.[23] Because so many less developed countries are former colonies, their public attention might still be fixed on the affairs of the former colonial powers, responding too slowly to changes in their own international environment. Alternatively, some would suggest that low attentiveness and low modernity of these mass publics would make for voluble or fickle public opinion.

There has been no more consensus among international relations scholars on the direction of international attention in these countries. Thus George Liska, writing about the 'non-aligned countries', noted that 'their chief concern centers on the relationships between the industrial nations of the "North" and the underdeveloped, ex-colonial countries of the "South"'.[24] There has been an explosion of literature in the 1970s pointing to the dominance of 'North–South' concerns.[25] Robert Good also stressed the direction of attention toward major and/or former colonial powers. Morton Kaplan's and Peter Fliess's discussions of loose bipolar politics define the situation of 'non-bloc actors' in the peripheries of the international system as a function of international bloc politics at its center.[26] Marxist scholars are no different on this point. Harry Magdoff defines international politics as the 'competitive struggle among the industrial nations for dominant positions with respect to the world market and raw material resources.[27] And the literature of dependency, by definition, focuses on the relationship between the weak and the strong, to the virtual exclusion of relations among less developed countries themselves.[28]

An alternative perspective has noted greater variety in the scope and domain of international relations. There are significant differences from one international subsystem to another in the identity of relevant actors, substantive interests, patterns of conflict, and power balances. Because the international system, at some of its levels, exhibits polycentric trends, relatively weak states can be rather more active and successful in international politics than was the case in the past.[29] The key hypothesis flowing from this literature is that subsystemic international politics may explain best the distribution of attention toward international issues.

Attention flows toward actors and issues in the international subsystems where less developed countries find themselves, rather than toward the central issues and actors of the international system.

These hypotheses have alternative implications for world order outcomes. If attention flows toward central actors and issues, world order outcomes may require a high awareness of, and support for, the United Nations and related organizations. But if attention is toward international subsystems, international political regional integration or common markets may result if the content of the attention emphasizes co-operation instead of rivalry.

Toward a Synthesis

Although considerable public attention flows toward the central issues of the international system, in part as a legacy of the colonial past, more attention flows toward actors and issues of the international subsystems in which these countries find themselves. This direction of foreign policy attention, moreover, holds regardless of the amount of attention toward international affairs, and regardless of the level of modernization. Attentive as well as inattentive publics focus on international subsystem actors and issues when they focus on international affairs at all.

There is also public responsiveness toward changing objective conditions in international affairs. Intervening international events shape attitudes toward international affairs. Independence itself was a major event shifting some attention from the metropolis to the new international subsystem. There is also public responsibility, because views tend not to change in the absence of objective international changes, nor do they persist in their presence. Views are, therefore, related to experience. They are neither fickle, nor stubborn, nor capricious. The mass public seems no less responsive and responsible than the attentive public.

Direction, content, and responsiveness, as well as attentiveness, are substantially shaped by internal differentiation within countries, but the specific differentiating variable differs from country to country. While modernization and social class are often major predictors, other variables – such as religion in India – are also key factors that may increase or nullify the importance of modernization as internal cleavages relevant for international attitudes.

International context, of only modest importance in explanations of attentiveness, is decisive for understanding responsiveness, direction, and content of international attention. There is a strong and increasing international subsystemic focus, away from the center of the international system. For these reasons, direction and content of international attention, and less so responsiveness, are likely to be independent of level of modernization.

The Evidence

Clues about the focus of mass publics on international subsystems emerge from a pair of comparatively modernized countries – Argentina and Chile. Of the seventy-three Argentines who were concerned about

Table 8.3 Chilean attitudes toward Argentina (N = 1,640) in 1957

Years of education	Most sympathy	Least sympathy
0–1 primary	49	18
2–3 primary	40	20
4–6 primary	38	22
1–3 secondary	27	31
4–6 secondary	19	33
1–4 university	10	39
5+ university	3	41

Source: Alain Girard and Raúl Samuel, 'Situation et perspectives du Chile en 1957 : une enquête d'opinion à Santiago', Sondages, vol. 19, no. 4 (1957), p. 41.

international affairs in a large survey in the mid-1960s, approximately 70 per cent cited problems with Chile as their chief international worry. The more diffuse, international-center-oriented issues were unimportant.[30]

Chileans are not, in fact, all that attentive to international affairs either. Not more than 3 per cent of the 1,640 respondents to a 1957 survey considered international affairs among Chile's most important problems. When asked about foreign affairs, however, Chileans agreed more easily on the distant and less pressing issues of the international center. They were far more divided over issues in their own 'local' international subsystem; the direction of their international attention thus seemed to focus more on this subsystem than on the international center. Chileans were sharply divided in opinions about Argentina: 30 per cent had the most sympathy for Argentina while 27 per cent had the least sympathy from a list of countries. On no other question on international affairs was the cleavage so sharp.[31] Argentina was near and real, and Chileans internalized their views about it in the domestic politics of their country. Chile's social stratification affected deeply views of Argentina. There was a sharp, inverse relationship between education and positive views toward Argentina whose then recently overthrown president, Juan Perón, had championed the Argentine lower class while seeking influence in Chile. In sum, both Argentina and Chile were more attuned to each other than to the distant international center.

Many African countries have had populations that are considered alien, including citizens from the former colonial power as well as the 'Asians' in East Africa. Attitudes toward these so-called aliens are often strongly shaped by international experiences. Table 8.4 presents the average country scores of the ratings given by each tribe to each alien minority on a Bogardus social distance scale[32] where 5 is the worst possible score; 727 Ghanaians and 564 Kenyans in secondary school or university were surveyed in 1966. Students were willing to trade – but not be friends – with some of these minorities (score 3). The Ghanaians wanted to have nothing to do with the Syrians, nor the Kenyans with most Indians. The Somalis, who were the only ones that could be feared for international reasons, because Somalia wanted to incorporate ethnic Somalis in Kenya in a 'greater Somalia', got the worst score even though

Table 8.4 *Country scores on a Bogardus social distance scale in 1966*

Peoples scored	Scoring host countries	
	Ghana	Kenya
British	2·91	3·34
Nigerians	3·10	—
Indians (Hindus)	3·26[a]	3·23
Indians (Sikhs)	—	4·10
Indians (Goans)	—	4·14
Syrians	3·47	—
Somalis	—	4·18

Note:
a All Indians.
Source: Computed from Roberta A. Mapp, 'Cross-national dimensions of ethnocentrism', paper presented at the annual meeting of the American Sociological Association, Denver, 1971, tables 2, 4.

their economic weight in Kenya was slight. Despite the larger numbers and wealth of the Indians in Kenya, the Somalis were still disliked more.

Attitudes toward the British in Ghana and Kenya were surprisingly benign, though bad memories of colonialism had faded more quickly in Ghana (which had become independent more easily and sooner than Kenya). Ghanaians got along better with the distant British than they did with their Nigerian neighbors, perhaps because that very nearness made them more suspicious. In sum, then, hostility to alien minorities is increased in both Ghana and Kenya by the intervention of a 'local' international subsystem variable, above and beyond the effect of these minorities on the country's social stratification.

A similar pattern is evident in a national survey of Nigerians conducted in September–November 1962 (N = 1,200). Asked to rank their opinions of several countries on a ten-point ladder, the lowest-ranking country was Ghana, topped by the more distant United States, Soviet Union, United Arab Republic, and even the former colonial power, the United Kingdom. The latter scored 58 per cent higher than Ghana.[33]

Attitudes toward the United Nations and Regional Integration

The United Nations appears to have rather different importance among various groups of less developed countries. Asked on behalf of the US Information Agency in 1964 whether they happened to know if 'our country is a member of the UN or not', three clusters of countries appeared: industrialized modern countries, less developed countries in Africa and Asia that recently achieved independence, and less developed countries in Latin America that had long been independent. Respondents in Caracas, Buenos Aires, Mexico City, and Rio de Janeiro were most likely to be uninformed or misinformed. Respondents in the capital cities of ten African, Near and Far Eastern countries and in urban India, were most likely to be correctly informed. The United

Nations had played an active role recently in Africa, especially in the Congo, but also in the supervision of decolonization in the former Trust Territories (Tanganyika, Cameroons, Togo); the foreign policies of many of these countries then paid special attention to membership in the UN as a symbol of their very independence. Thus while the median level of accurate information in Latin America was 67–8 per cent, it was 92 per cent in Africa and Asia. The national samples in European countries and Japan, while not strictly comparable to the Latin American capital city samples, still performed better, too.[34]

Asked on behalf of the USIA in 1965 about how much they had heard or read about the United Nations, four clusters appeared. Urban Africans in Nigeria, Senegal and Kenya had a 92 per cent median level of awareness. At the other end, urban Latin Americans in Caracas, Santiago, Mexico City, Buenos Aires, and Rio de Janeiro had only a 48 per cent median level of awareness. National samples taken in Europe and Japan all showed a level of awareness above the best-informed Latin Americans (in Caracas) but below the median urban African level. Asian respondents overlapped with both the European and Latin American countries.[35] These surveys, in sum, suggest the continuing high importance of the UN for African urban publics, aware of recent UN activity on their behalf, and the UN's low salience for Latin American urban publics, neither modernized enough to follow the UN for its own sake, nor having the UN close enough to home to make a difference.

An alternative view might be that the Latin Americans are relatively uninterested in the United Nations because they are more interested in regional integration. When pollsters for the USIA asked people in Buenos Aires, Caracas, Mexico City, Rio de Janeiro, and Santiago in the wake of the actions of the Organization of American States in the Dominican Republic in 1965 – which included sending troops from several member countries to join those the United States had already sent – whether they had heard of the OAS, the five-city average of the uninformed was 52 per cent. Although Brazilian troops had been sent to the Dominican Republic as the largest single Latin American component of the OAS force, less than a third of Rio de Janeiro respondents had heard about the OAS.[36]

Latin American urban mass publics do not even think of each other as best friends. Asked in 1964 about what country in the world is their best friend, other Latin American countries were mentioned only by 2 per cent in Rio, 1 per cent in Mexico City, 12 per cent in Caracas, and 15 per cent in Buenos Aires. In Buenos Aires, Rio, and Mexico, the mention of other Latin American countries trailed behind the United States, Western Europe, and 'no country'; in Caracas, Western Europe was rarely mentioned, but mention of Latin American countries remained third.[37] In 1961 a national sample of Brazilians (N = 2,168) were asked to rank their opinions of several countries on a ten-point ladder. The United States topped the list, while Argentina and Mexico only ranked between 5·5 and 5·7. Argentina ranked seventh – even below the Soviet Union and China – in a longer, simultaneously conducted survey of 100 Brazilian legislators.[38]

College students surveyed in Colombia, Mexico, and Paraguay in the mid-1960s gave apparently strong supranational responses. Asked about their countries' participation in the Latin American Free Trade Association (LAFTA), they were overwhelmingly favorable. Opposition was expressed by only 5·90 per cent of the Paraguayans, 3·78 per cent of the Mexicans, and 5·74 per cent of the Colombians. Sample sizes were 441, 794, and 1,551 respectively.

The views of students who reported a strongly favorable attitude toward LAFTA on two nationalistic statements are presented in Table 8.5. Between one-half and two-thirds of the college students who strongly favor LAFTA agree somewhat or strongly that their fellow nationals can do anything better than a foreigner, and between one-quarter and one-third of them agree that the health of a fellow national is of greater value than the life of a foreigner. In general, however, attitudes toward LAFTA among these college students are relatively independent statistically of their nationalistic feelings. Favorable statements about LAFTA probably did not curtail nationalistic feelings, rather they seemed a generalized, low-cost foreign policy preference with few other implications.

Studies of college students in eleven countries, using similar questionnaires, indicate that Egyptian, Turkish, Mexican, and non-English South African college students are far more nationalistic than college students in modern industrial countries. They are much more likely to prefer a world of unmodified nation-states, and much more likely to give nation-oriented responses to questions about their personal hopes for the future, what they will teach their children, or what they would be proud of.[39]

Two opinion surveys about federation, of approximately 1,800 and 1,400 respondents, were taken in 1963 and 1965 in the three countries of East Africa. The 1963 survey was allegedly a national sample; the 1965 survey covered the capital cities only: Nairobi (Kenya), Dar es Salaam (Tanzania), and Kampala (Uganda); there are some questions about the reliability of the 1963 survey. The differences between the two surveys should be considered a difference in the sampled populations.

Table 8.5 *Nationalistic attitudes of college students who strongly favored the Latin American Free Trade Association*

	[Fellow nationals] do anything better than a foreigner		The health of a [fellow national] is of greater value than the life of a foreigner	
	% agree	N	% agree	N
Colombia	68·8	662	27·1	657
Mexico	57·3	307	31·4	309
Paraguay	67·4	150	25·7	148

Source: Computed from surveys conducted under the auspices of the Comparative National Development Study, directed by Professor Seymour Martin Lipset, at that time of the Institute of International Studies of the University of California at Berkeley, and presently at Stanford University.

There is a combination of localism and supranationalism in East African mass public opinion that is characteristic of so many least modernized countries. For example, approximately four-fifths of the Kenyans, two-thirds of the Tanzanians, and half of the Ugandans supported the federation in both surveys. On the other hand, respondents preferred that the federation leader be drawn from their own country rather than from any other, and that the federation capital be located in their own country rather than elsewhere (except for Tanzanians in 1963 who preferred Nairobi). Between a sixth and a fifth of the 1963 national samples wanted major tribes to represent them at federation activities. Notwithstanding persistently high localism, the prevalence of supranational opinions in the mass public has not been encountered in the same way in other countries. Only the contextual, historical circumstances which long bound the three countries to each other in the now defunct East African community can explain them. Thus the modernization approach is not a complete substitute for contextual analysis, but a complement.[40]

Moreover, urban public attention was more focused on issues in the East African subsystem than on more diffuse issues, such as the Commonwealth, in East Africa's capital cities in 1965. The proportions of East Africans who held no opinion on the federation were 1 per cent for Kenya, 5 per cent for Tanzania, and 10 per cent for Uganda. The proportions who held no views about continued membership in the Commonwealth were 15, 17, and 18 per cent respectively.[41]

Responsiveness to International Events

Ghanaian likes and dislikes about foreign peoples remained rather stable over a decade, in the relative absence of international events to change their views. Jahoda's study of national stereotypes in Ghana, conducted between 1952 and 1956 – over a decade before Mapp's study – showed that Syrians were ranked at the bottom of ten nationality groups, while Indians were ranked fifth. The eight other nationalities referred to European peoples.[42]

Two other African cases, on the other hand, suggest that views can be changed by international events. In 1960, a random probability sample of 500 students from francophone Africa studying in France was taken. The fifty-one sampled students from Guinea differed from the others. One-third of the Guineans ranked at the top of the political interest scale, whereas at most one-quarter of the students from any other African country ranked so high. Only 8 per cent of Guineans (next to last) reported associating with French students. Only the Guineans reported by a majority (56 per cent) that they felt distant from the French way of life.[43] The then lively international conflict between France and Guinea probably shaped these views. Thus the difference between Guineans and other francophone African students in France can be attributed to intervening international factors.

A study of national stereotypes held by 100 western Nigerian university students, 'conducted soon after the end of the civil war in Nigeria' but at a date otherwise unspecified, suggests that international attitudes are shaped more by events in a country's own subsystem than in the international center. These randomly selected students were given a list of sixty-three adjectives, of which ten were to be applied to ten different nationalities. Egyptians, Israelis, Americans, Russians, British, Germans, Italians, and Indians were highly praised, but the French and the Chinese were condemned.[44] Neither the Cold War nor the Middle East conflict was paramount when these judgements were made. These attitudes were probably shaped by the positions taken by these countries during the Nigerian Civil War.

A detailed look at the Indian subcontinent may illustrate the issues. In Orissa, India, 200 randomly selected college freshmen and service-holders were asked in late 1957 to select traits about various peoples from a list of sixty adjectives. The Chinese were the only people (Indians included) for whom no 'bad' traits were selected. They tied for second (behind the Indians) for the largest number of 'good' traits.[45] At Patna University in the late 1950s, 200 randomly selected students were asked to select five traits out of eighty, indicating whether they were favorable or unfavorable. The Chinese were assigned no undesirable traits. All but one trait (which was neutral) were judged desirable.[46] The Indian Institute of Public Opinion (IIPO) surveyed a cross-section of members of the Lok Sabha (lower house of parliament) in the spring of 1958. Asked whether they were confident of 'even better relations over the next five years' with China, 82 per cent agreed. No parliamentarian in 1958 feared Chinese aggression.[47]

Then the Sino-Indian conflict broke out in 1959, gradually worsening until war erupted in October 1962. Two hundred Patna University students had been tested for ethnic stereotypes in February 1959, and then again after the conflict heated up in December 1959. There was no change at all in the stereotypes held about three peoples, and only trivial and statistically insignificant changes in stereotypes held about another five peoples. The only statistically significant, dramatic changes occurred in stereotypes held about the Chinese. The students at the beginning of the year thought the Chinese were friendly, progressive, honest, nationalistic, brave, cultured, and active; at the end of the year the same students thought that the Chinese were aggressive, cheats, selfish, war-mongers, cruel, shrewd, and stupid.[48] A Bogardus social distance scale, administered to 900 students, also at Patna University, prior to the war, but after the conflict had heated up, showed that Chinese ranked at the bottom of eleven peoples; 43·2 per cent would not even allow the Chinese to come to visit India.[49] One-quarter of the Indian parliamentarians surveyed in the summer of 1962 expected Chinese aggression. And 82 per cent did not think it likely that relations with China would improve in the years ahead. On a ten-point ladder, where 10 was the best score, the Indian mass urban public assigned China a 2·6 rating in the summer of 1962 and an 0·9 rating in November 1962.[50]

Table 8.6 shows three different patterns of Indian public opinion responsiveness to international affairs. Mass urban opinion of the Soviet Union has been highly positive. Opinion of the United States had been

Table 8.6 *Indian mass urban public attitudes about three foreign countries*[a]

	1966	1967	1968	1969	1970	1971	April 1972	August 1972
United States	183	123	132	176	157	71	−81	−23
Soviet Union	207	154	152	145	109	138	195	219
United Arab Republic	—	71	87	58	42	−6	−24	−39

Note:
a N = 1,000; weighted averages reported.
Source: Indian Institute of Public Opinion, 'International images after the Simla summit', *Monthly Public Opinion Surveys*, vol. 17, no. 11 (August 1972), pp. II, IV, VI.

highly positive until the third Indo-Pakistani war, when the United States 'tilted' toward Pakistan. Opinions of the United Arab Republic had been modestly positive, though steadily declining since 1968, turning negative at the time of the third Indo-Pakistani war; but the IIPO's more general finding is that Indian interest in and knowledge about its erstwhile friend of Nehru's day had been fading, as concern about issues of the international center declined, and concern about issues of India's south Asian international subsystem increased.

This shift of concern away from issues of the international center toward issues in India's own international subsystem can also be documented through other data. In 1958 Indian parliamentarians reported three internationally relevant hopes about their country, in an open-ended question. Thus 15 per cent each hoped that India would attain a position of world power, and that it would provide ideological and moral leadership; 1 per cent wanted it to be militarily strong. The respective hopes in 1962 were 0, 1, and 10 per cent. In 1958 no parliamentarian expressed fears concerning Pakistan and Kashmir, or Chinese aggression. In 1962 the scores were 11 and 25 per cent respectively. In the summer of 1962, 25 per cent of the sampled Indian mass urban public feared Chinese aggression; in November 1962, after the Sino-Indian War, 46 per cent feared it. The concern about Chinese aggression led to small declines in fear of Pakistan and in diffuse attitudes such as 'enhancing Indian national status'.[51]

There has been, however, very little change in public attitudes on Indo-Pakistani relations. No Indian parliamentarians in 1958 cited Pakistan as a fear for India in an open-ended question. But when asked directly about India's most important foreign policy problem, 35 per cent cited Kashmir, and 25 per cent cited other aspects of relations with Pakistan. Their concern about both Pakistan and China had increased in 1962. In 1958, 52 per cent of them thought that relations with Pakistan were not likely to improve, rising to 67 per cent in 1962.[52] The Indian urban public's views about Pakistanis have remained consistently unfavorable. In the late 1950s Patna University's 200 students assigned only 10 per cent favorable comments to Pakistanis; all other comments were unfavorable. Pakistanis ranked next to last (the Chinese) on a Bogardus social distance scale administered at Patna in 1962; 21·6 per cent would exclude them from India altogether.[53] After the third

Indo-Pakistani war, the Pakistanis outranked the Chinese as the most despised of fifteen peoples in a survey of 137 randomly selected college-educated North Indians, who were asked to choose five traits from an eighty-eight-item list.[54]

However, Indian Muslims dissent from this negative consensus about Pakistan. The IIPO surveyed the Indian urban public after the Simla summit meeting, called to settle the issues from the third Indo-Pakistani war. Asked whether India should have agreed to vacate Pakistani territories occupied during the war even without a final settlement of the Kashmir question, only 25 per cent of respondents agreed. Respondents do not differ by level of education. But they do by religion: whereas 22 per cent of the Hindus agree, 52 per cent of the Muslims do so. Asked whether they agreed that Pakistan would never again go to war with India, only 25 per cent of the respondents agreed. Here there are some slight differences by education, where the more educated are more pessimistic. But the sharp difference again appears only between religious groups: whereas 24 per cent of the Hindus agree, 69 per cent of the Muslims agree.[55]

Pakistanis reciprocate. A 1957 survey conducted among ninety-seven students at Dacca University showed that 76 per cent of the traits assigned to Indians were 'bad'. A replication of the experiment among 214 Karachi University students in 1963 showed that exactly the same percentage assigned 'bad' traits to the Indians. In February 1964, before the second Indo-Pakistani war, 217 students of Karachi University were given a Bogardus social distance scale; 17 per cent would exclude Indians from Pakistan – the next-to-last score (Russians).[56] And, not surprisingly, a study conducted among 200 undergraduate female students at Hyderabad during the second war, in September, 1965, showed that Indians were assigned 100 per cent unfavorable traits.[57]

Conclusions

Mass publics in less developed countries pay relatively little attention to international affairs, less so than mass publics in more modern countries. More interestingly, the impact of the first phases of modernization may be to shift the balance of attention away from international and toward national affairs; thus attention to international affairs may be a characteristic of modernity, but not so much of the process of modernization, as Deutsch would have expected from research on social mobilization. When mass publics in less developed countries do pay attention to international affairs, they are more likely to be concerned with their neighbors and with subsystemic issues than with actors and issues at the center of the international system, regardless of levels of attention or of modernization. The content of subsystemic attention is just as likely to be hostile as it is to be co-operative. Mass publics in less developed countries have also been strikingly responsive to changing international events. Far more change has occurred than one might expect from the writings of Deutsch and Merritt, and certainly far more than is ordinarily the case in stereotype studies.[58]

The consequences of these findings for world order and political integration are not reassuring. The low level of international attentiveness leaves a great deal of discretion for often transient public officials. Although awareness of the United Nations is quite high among the urban publics of Africa and Asia, it seems to be much less so in Latin America. Mass attitudinal support for integration, or even awareness of existing international regional organizations, is modest at best in Latin America. Latin American mass publics do not even think of other Latin American countries as their best friends, and may think of them as their principal rivals. The one area where support for integration was rather stronger – East Africa – has witnessed the federation's demise.

The orientation of public attention – when it exists – to regional subsystemic concerns might, at first sight, seem to favor political integration.[1] And yet, in the Indian subcontinent as in South America's southern cone, the content of the attention has emphasized rivalry or even war, rather than integration. Responsiveness to international events has also been highly asymmetrical. Changes in the direction of more cordial relations seem to have been glacial; changes in the direction of deeper hostility appear to have been quicker, and at times dramatic, as between India and China, or France and Guinea, or Nigeria and its enemies in the Biafran War. Trends toward conflict might have been developing far more swiftly than trends toward co-operation in these subsystems.

Notes: Chapter 8

1 Research support for my work has been provided by the Center for International Affairs at Harvard University.
2 Karl W. Deutsch, 'Social mobilization and political development', *American Political Science Review*, vol. 55, no. 3 (September 1961), p. 500.
3 Daniel Lerner, *The Passing of Traditional Society: Modernizing the Middle East* (New York: The Free Press, 1958), pp. 43–75, 98.
4 Lucian W. Pye, 'The nature of transitional politics', *Political Development and Social Change*, ed. Jason L. Finkle and Richard W. Gable, 2d edn (New York: Wiley, 1971), pp. 546–7.
5 Robert Good, 'State-building as a determinant of foreign policy in the new states', *Neutralism and Nonalignment*, ed. Lawrence W. Martin (New York: Praeger, 1962).
6 George Liska, 'Tripartism: dilemmas and strategies', in *Neutralism and Nonalignment*, p. 47.
7 James N. Rosenau, *Public Opinion and Foreign Policy* (New York: Random House, 1961), pp. 35–41.
8 James N. Rosenau, *The Attentive Public and Foreign Policy: A Theory of Growth and Some New Evidence* (Princeton, NJ: Princeton University, Center for International Studies, Research Monograph No. 31, 1968), p. 48.
9 Gabriel A. Almond, *The American People and Foreign Policy* (New York: Praeger, 1960), pp. 183–91; and Rosenau, *Public Opinion*, p. 37.
10 International Studies of Values in Politics, *Values and the Active Community* (New York: The Free Press, 1971), pp. 71, 321–7, 362.
11 US Information Agency, Research and Reference Service, 'Public attitudes in Latin America: some reassuring perspectives', R-148-64 (October 1964, mimeo.), pp. 2, 13–14. I am grateful to Dr Leo P. Crespi for making these and other declassified USIA surveys available to me.

12 US Information Agency, Research Service, 'Venezuelan opinion on nationalization of oil and attitudes toward foreign investment', N-1-75 (September 8, 1975, mimeo.), pp. 1–2.
13 *Polls*, Vol. 2, no. 4 (Summer 1967), p. 62.
14 'Don't know' responses on cross-national surveys present problems of interpretation. For methodological discussion, see Andrzej Sicinski, '"Don't know" answers in cross national surveys', *Public Opinion Quarterly*, vol. 34, no. 1 (Spring 1970), pp. 126–9; Clyde H. Coombs and Lolagene Coombs, '"Don't know": item ambiguity or respondent uncertainty', *Public Opinion Quarterly*, vol. 40, no. 4 (Winter 1976–7), pp. 497–514; and Jean M. Converse, 'Predicting no opinion in the polls', *Public Opinion Quarterly*, vol. 40, no. 4 (Winter 1976–7), pp. 515–30.
15 Encuestas Gallup de la Argentina in *Polls*, Vol. 2, no. 3 (Spring 1967), pp. 22, 24; and Jeane Kirkpatrick, *Leader and Follower in Mass Society: A Study of Peronist Argentina* (Cambridge, Mass.: MIT Press, 1971), pp. 187–91.
16 Gallup International in *Polls*, vol. 1, no. 4 (Summer 1966), p. 90.
17 Jonathan Lane, 'Isolation and public opinion in rural north east Brazil', *Public Opinion Quarterly*, vol. 33, no. 1 (Spring 1969), pp. 58–9, 61.
18 Gordon Hirabayashi and M. Fathalla El Khatib, 'Communications and political awareness in the villages of Egypt', *Public Opinion Quarterly*, vol. 22, no. 3 (Fall 1958), pp. 257–9; and Patricia Kendall, 'The ambivalent character of nationalism among Egyptian professionals', *Public Opinion Quarterly*, vol. 20, no. 1 (Spring 1956), p. 278.
19 Computed from Tables 8.1 and 8.2, and from Hadley Cantril, *The Pattern of Human Concerns* (New Brunswick, NJ: Rutgers University Press, 1965), pp. 397–9, 401, 404–6.
20 Alex Inkeles, 'Making men modern: on the causes and consequences of individual change in six developing countries', *American Journal of Sociology*, vol. 75, no. 2 (September 1969), p. 215; for a fuller statement, see Alex Inkeles and David H. Smith, *Becoming Modern: Individual Change in Six Developing Countries* (Cambridge, Mass.: Harvard University Press, 1974).
21 José A. Silva Michelena, *The Illusion of Democracy in Dependent Nations* (Cambridge, Mass.: MIT Press, 1971), p.198.
22 Karl W. Deutsch and Richard L. Merritt, 'Effects of events on national and international images', in *International Behavior: A Social-Psychological Analysis*, ed. Herbert C. Kelman (New York: Holt, Rinehard & Winston, 1965), p. 182–3.
23 Douglas H. Mendel, Jr, 'Japanese views of the American alliance in the seventies', *Public Opinion Quarterly*, vol. 35, no. 4 (Winter 1971–2), pp. 521–38; Kazuto Kojima, 'Public opinion trends in Japan', *Public Opinion Quarterly*, vol. 41, no. 2 (Summer 1977), pp. 206–16; J. Alex Murray and Lawrence LeDuc, 'Public opinion and foreign policy options in Canada', *Public Opinion Quarterly*, vol. 40, no. 4 (Winter 1976–7), pp. 488–96.
24 Liska, 'Tripartism', p. 211.
25 For a discussion of a portion of this burgeoning literature, see Jorge I. Domínguez, 'Consensus and divergence: the state of the literature on inter-American relations in the 1970s', *Latin American Research Review*, vol. 13, no. 1 (1978), pp. 87–126.
26 Good, 'State-building'; Morton A. Kaplan, *System and Process in International Politics* (New York: Wiley, 1957), ch. 2; and Peter J. Fliess, *International Relations in the Bipolar World* (New York: Random House, 1968), ch. 6.
27 Harry Magdoff, *The Age of Imperialism* (New York: Monthly Review Press, 1969), p. 15.
28 See, for example, Johan Galtung, 'A structural theory of imperialism', *Journal of Peace Research*, vol. 8, no. 2 (1971), pp. 81–117. For a discussion of variations within dependency perspectives, see Domínguez, 'Consensus and divergence'.
29 Oran Young, 'Political discontinuities in the international system', *World Politics*, vol. 20, no. 3 (April 1968), pp. 369–92; George Modelski, *The Communist International System* (Princeton, NJ: Princeton University, Center for International Studies, Research Monograph No. 9, 1960); Stanley Hoffmann, *Gulliver's Troubles, or the Setting of American Foreign Policy* (New York: McGraw-Hill, 1968), ch. 2, and 'Discord in community: the North Atlantic area as a partial international system', *International Organization*, vol. 18, no. 3 (Summer 1963), pp. 321–49; Jorge I.

Domínguez, 'Mice that do not roar: some aspects of international politics in the world's peripheries', *International Organization*, vol. 25, no. 2 (Spring 1971), pp. 175–208, and citations listed there.
30 Computed from Kirkpatrick, *Leader and Follower*, p. 190.
31 Alain Girard and Raúl Samuel, 'Situation et perspectives du Chili en 1957: une enquête d'opinion à Santiago', *Sondages*, vol. 19, no. 4 (1957), pp. 30, 40, 43.
32 Emory S. Bogardus, 'Measuring social distance', *Journal of Applied Sociology*, vol. 9, no. 4 (March–April 1925), pp. 299–308.
33 Lloyd A. Free, *The Attitudes, Hopes and Fears of Nigerians* (Princeton, NJ: Institute for International Social Research, 1964), p. 9.
34 US Information Agency, Research and Reference, 'A note on worldwide attitudes toward the UN', R-195-64 (December 1964, mimeo.), p. 1.
35 US Information Agency, Research and Reference Service, 'Some Worldwide opinions on UN issues', R-207-65 (December 1965, mimeo.), p. 1.
36 US Information Agency, Research and Reference Service, 'Latin American attitudes toward the US in the wake of the Dominican crisis', R-179-65 (December 1965, mimeo.), p. 5.
37 US Information Agency, Research and Reference Service, 'Some Latin American attitudes on current issues', R-113-64 (11 August 1964, mimeo.), p. 2.
38 Lloyd A. Free, *Some International Implications of the Political Psychology of Brazilians* (Princeton, NJ: Institute for International Social Research, 1961), p. 1.
39 James M. Gillespie and Gordon W. Allport, *Youth's Outlook on the Future* (Garden City, NJ: Doubleday, 1955), pp. 16, 22–4, 55; and Herbert Hyman, Arif Payaslioglu, and Frederick Frey, 'The values of Turkish college youth', *Public Opinion Quarterly*, vol. 22, no. 3 (Fall 1958), pp. 277–80, 282–4.
40 Marco Surveys Ltd, 'Public opinion', *Poll No. 12* (December 1963), p. 8; *idem*, 'Who wants an East African Federation?', *Poll No. 13* (August 1965), pp. 1, 2, 4, 9–10; and Joseph S. Nye, Jr, *Pan-Africanism and East African Integration* (Cambridge, Mass.: Harvard University Press, 1965). The answers of those who failed to say that they would be disappointed if federation did not come about were subtracted from those who said they believed federation was desirable in the first set of numbers. Leaders and cities from the same country were grouped in the reporting of subsequent numbers.
41 Marco Surveys Ltd, 'Who wants an East African Federation?', pp. 1, 22.
42 Gustav Jahoda, 'Nationality preferences and national stereotypes in Ghana before independence', *Journal of Social Psychology*, vol. 50, no. 2 (November 1959), pp. 165–74; Roberta Mapp, 'Cross-national dimensions of ethnocentrism', paper presented at the annual meeting of the American Sociological Association, Denver, Colo, 1971, tables 2 and 4.
43 Institut Français d'Opinion Publique, 'Les etudiants d'outre-mer en France', *Sondages*, vol. 23, no. 3 (1961), pp. 13, 57, 66, 71.
44 James O. Ogunlade, 'National stereotypes of university students in western Nigeria', *Journal of Social Psychology*, vol. 85, no. 2 (December 1971), pp. 309–10.
45 R. Rath and J. P. Das, 'Study in stereotypes of college freshmen and service holders in Orissa, India, towards themselves and four other foreign nationalities', *Journal of Social Psychology*, vol. 47, no. 2 (May 1958), pp. 373–85, esp. pp. 373–5, 378.
46 A. K. P. Sinha and O. P. Upadhyaya, 'Stereotypes of male and female university students in India toward different ethnic groups', *Journal of Social Psychology*, vol. 51, no. 1 (February 1960), pp. 93–102, esp. pp. 99–100.
47 Albert H. Cantril, *The Indian Perception of the Sino-Indian Border Clash* (Princeton, NJ: Institute for International Social Research, 1963), pp. 31, 34–5.
48 A. K. P. Sinha and O. P. Upadhyaya, 'Change and persistence in the stereotypes of university students toward different ethnic groups during the Sino-Indian border dispute', *Journal of Social Psychology*, vol. 52, no. 1 (August 1960), pp. 31–9.
49 A. K. P. Sinha and O. P. Upadhyaya, 'Eleven ethnic groups on a social distance scale', *Journal of Social Psychology*, vol. 57, no. 1 (June 1962), pp. 49–54, esp. pp. 49–50.
50 Cantril, *The Indian Perception*, pp. 18, 31, 34–5.
51 ibid., pp. 12–13, 30–1.
52 ibid., pp. 31, 34–5; and Lloyd A. Free, *Six Allies and a Neutral: A Study of the*

International Outlooks of Political Leaders in the United States, Britain, France, West Germany, Italy, Japan and India (Glencoe, Ill.: The Free Press, 1959), pp. 16-17.
53 Sinha and Upadhyaya, 'Stereotypes of male and female university students', pp. 99-100; *idem*, 'Eleven ethnic groups', p. 50.
54 Santokh S. Anant, 'Ethnic stereotypes of educated North Indians', *Journal of Social Psychology*, vol. 85, no. 1 (October 1971), pp. 137-8.
55 Indian Institute of Public Opinion, 'After the Simla summit: the hopeful outlook', *Monthly Public Opinion Surveys*, vol. 17, no. 10 (July 1972), pp. ii, iv, vi.
56 S. M. Hafeez Zaidi and Mesbahuddin Ahmed, 'National stereotypes of university students in East Pakistan', *Journal of Social Psychology*, vol. 47, no. 2 (May 1958), pp. 387-95; S. M. Hafeez Zaidi 'National stereotypes of university students in Karachi', *Journal of Social Psychology*, vol. 63, no. 1 (June 1964), pp. 73-85, esp. pp. 73-4; and S. M. Hafeez Zaidi, 'A study of social distance as perceived by students of Karachi University', *Journal of Social Psychology*, vol. 71, no. 2 (April 1967), pp. 197-207, esp. pp. 197, 199, 206.
57 Abdul Haque, 'Stereotypes of college students in Hyderabad (Pakistan) toward the ingroup and the outgroup during the Indo-Pakistan War', *Journal of Social Psychology*, vol. 74, no. 2 (April 1968), pp. 285-6.
58 Nelson R. Cauthen, Ira E. Robinson, and Herbert H. Krauss, 'Stereotypes: a review of the literature, 1926-1968', *Journal of Social Psychology*, vol. 84, no. 1 (June 1971), pp. 103-25, esp. p. 120.

9

Political Disintegration in Postwar Berlin

RICHARD L. MERRITT

At the core of the community is interdependency. Interdependency, in brief, is a relationship at once mutually beneficial for those party to it and binding in the sense that the parties would all perceive a real loss were it to be dissolved. There is thus a commitment on the part of members of the group to the maintenance of that interdependency. Its nature varies greatly from group to group, just as does the degree of commitment to it. A fully integrated community will enjoy an economic division of labor, political and other institutions responsible for making decisions for the territory populated by the group, common facilities for and habits of communication, and sets of procedures for determining what is important, resolving conflicts, socializing children into the community, and a host of other day-to-day tasks. Other groups may have more limited purposes, institutions, and processes.

When interdependencies within a social group break down, we speak of *disintegration*.[1] As is true of interdependency, the degree of disintegration is a relative matter. Moreover, both may have 'spillover' effects: steps toward or away from a high level of integration may be self-reinforcing and soon assume their own dynamic. The key to the disintegrative process is the collapse of people's commitment to the community's values, a decline in their willingness to make sacrifices in the expectation that the rewards of community life will significantly outweigh the costs.

Processes of disintegration in large-scale political communities have only rarely been the subject of systematic analysis. The most important such analysis found Karl W. Deutsch and his colleagues examining background conditions conducive to disintegration in four case studies: the break-up of the American Union in the mid-nineteenth century, the separation of Ireland from the United Kingdom in 1921, Norway's secession from Sweden in 1905, and the final dissolution in 1918 of the Habsburg Empire.[2] They found most particularly that excessive burdens, such as overly heavy military commitments or political mobilization at the periphery, together with increased ethnic or linguistic differentiation, tended to destroy 'amalgamated security communities', as did the reduced 'capabilities of their governments and political elites for adequate and timely action or response' which might derive from economic decline or stagnation, low upward social mobility and a closed political elite, especially an elite unable to adjust to a loss of dominance due to changed conditions, or else excessive delays in demanded and expected social, economic, or political reforms. Thus, for instance, the growing rigidity of Austro-German and Magyar political leaders, who felt threatened by the increasing social mobilization of other ethnic groups within the Habsburg Empire and by their demands for political equality, contributed greatly to the ultimate disintegration of that empire.

The case examined in this chapter, postwar Berlin, approaches disintegration from a rather different point of departure. Here we are not speaking of more or less distinct subgroups which, although retaining a greater or lesser degree of autonomy, are united in paying allegiance to main political values and institutions. The city's situation since 1945 is one in which a single political community without significant cultural, ethnic, religious, linguistic, or other differentiation was arbitrarily divided into two competing political systems with sharply different political institutions, processes, and values. The key questions are thus not identical with those addressed by Deutsch and his colleagues: whether or not a shared political system can bridge cultural or other 'non-political' differences, and the extent to which such differences add to the burdens and reduce the capabilities of the political system. The central issue is instead whether or not living in two separate but contiguous political systems will pull apart people who, before their political division, were pretty much like each other, viewed themselves as members of a single political community, and engaged in as much interaction as is normal in any metropolis.

A goal of both points of departure is to ascertain the relationship between formal political ties and processes of social communication. And, of course, the same issue informs numerous studies of political integration. We are familiar with cases in which ethnic or other differences contribute to varying perspectives that in turn erode the basis for political community. But what about circumstances in which political decisions divide an integrated people? Do the ties of social communication cease just as abruptly? Thus data on postwar Berlin address the more general question of the *process* of political integration – a process widely discussed in the social science literature and other chapters in this volume.

Political Division and Human Integration

Greater Berlin, one of the world's largest cities spatially and boasting almost $4\frac{1}{2}$ million inhabitants in 1943, suffered three successive waves of disruption during the next half-decade. The first came when aerial bombardments and, in April 1945, intensive streetfighting reduced great parts of the city to piles of rubble, forced evacuations of over a third of its population, and crippled Berlin's communication and transportation facilities and such municipal services as the electrical and water works.

This disruption, however, had a random effect on the eastern and western halves of the city, which were basically similar in their physical and socioeconomic structure. The effects of the second disruptive wave were distributed less equitably. In the two months between the city's fall on 2 May 1945, and the arrival of Western occupation troops on 1 July, Soviet occupation authorities extensively dismantled its industrial capacity – especially that in the sectors designated for American, British, and French control – for shipment to the Soviet Union as reparations.

The main dimensions of the third disruptive wave, the political division of Berlin itself, are well known.[3] The breakdown of Four-Power co-operation in Germany led ultimately to the currency reforms in 1948, the subsequent blockade of the city, and the creation of separate governments not only for the Western zones of occupation (Federal Republic of Germany, or FRG) and the Soviet zone (German Democratic Republic, or GDR) but also, by fall 1948, for East and West Berlin. What ensued were quite conscious efforts to split the city's formerly unified infrastructure of municipal services, traffic routes, and public transportation and communication facilities. This took time, of course. For the most part, however, the task of infrastructural division was completed by 1952. Today, very few elements of pre-1948 Berlin's infrastructure, among them parts of the sewage system and quadripartite control over air traffic, remain as living examples of an earlier, undivided past.

But what about the Berliners? How did they respond to the division of their city? Two aspects of behavior are particularly relevant here. One is their attitudes toward the political events and their consequences. Although this issue will not be discussed in this chapter, it may be worthwhile noting that on both sides of the border mass opinion, originally hostile to the new status quo, gradually grew accustomed to it whereas elite and official opinion was and continues to be sharply divided.[4] The idea of the original wartime agreements defining Greater Berlin within its boundaries of 1920 as a single political unit continues to dominate in the West – that is, West Berlin, the Federal Republic, and their Western allies – whereas the Eastern position is that subsequent events nullified the Four-Power agreements, turned the eastern sector of Berlin into the capital city of the German Democratic Republic, but left the western sectors, located on GDR territory, as an anomaly still occupied by the victors of the Second World War. Few in the West, however, and certainly not the American, British, and French commanders who retain sovereign control over West Berlin, are prepared to take any concrete action to support their legal claims that the entire city remains under Four-Power rule. Elaborate interpretations of its underlying meanings notwithstanding, the quadripartite agreement of September 1971 had the effect of giving the status quo of divided Berlin a seal of acceptance (albeit not, at least in Western eyes, approval).

The second relevant aspect of the Berliners' behavior comprises possible changes in their habits. Even after the division of 1948–9, the border between East and West Berlin remained open, at least in principle. Citizens of one side merely had to board a subway or elevated railway to get to the other side, or else simply walk across at any of the eighty-six border stations which connected the two sides of the city. But, of course, what was possible in principle was limited in fact. Just enough arrests or other unpleasantries occurred to remind most citizens that crossing the border entailed some risk. This risk, however small, remained fairly constant from the end of the blockade in 1949 to the construction twelve years later of a wall that virtually ended all Berliners' travel to the other side of their city during the next dozen years.

Ideally, what we would like to know is how the Berliners actually changed their daily lives in response to political division. Did they continue to visit friends who lived on the other side of the demarcation line? If they lived in one half of the city but worked in the other, did they give up their job or their residence – both of which were scarce indeed in postwar Berlin – or did they try to continue as they had in the past? Did they go to the same movie houses, lakes, and shopping centers as before? What was the nature of the contacts they had with people from the other side of the city? The most clear-cut answers to such questions, as Donald J. Puchala has stressed elsewhere in this volume, would rest on information gathered at the level of the individual – information that does not exist or, if it does, has not been made public.

It is nevertheless possible to obtain a picture of how such transaction patterns changed by examining indicators of behavior at the aggregate level. For instance, given the fact that a third of Greater Berlin's population lived in the East, we would normally expect that an opera house located near the center of the city will draw a third of its visitors from East Berlin. If the actual percentage is less than a third, then it would seem reasonable to assume that the political division had had some impact on the composition of the opera house's audience. Even if we conclude that we do not know what quota of visitors would 'normally' come from the East – since, perhaps, a taste for opera is strong only among certain social classes, and it turns out that most of the opera-lovers lived in one rather than the other half of the city – trends over time in the pattern of visits may indicate shifts in the flow of transactions between East and West Berlin. This example points also to the need to search for a multiplicity of indicators of any complex concept. One indicator pointing in a particular direction may not convince us that it adequately indicates what it is said to indicate. A set of independent indicators of slightly different aspects of the concept under investigation gives us, if the preponderance of them points in the same direction, more confidence in the general reliability of the indicators themselves and the validity of their findings.[5]

Indicators of personal interactions are important on several counts. Most relevant for present purposes is the fact that they indicate changing levels of community involvement on the part of the community's members. Absence makes the heart grow fonder, it is often said of lovers. Even so, few would encourage separated lovers to eschew communicating with each other via letters and telephone calls during periods when they are apart. Were the latter to occur, then the counter saying of folk wisdom, 'out of sight, out of mind', might be more apt as a prediction of the lovers' future. The extent to which these saws are applicable to social groups is a question that empirical indicators can begin to answer.

In this regard two prominent hypotheses emerge. The first says that the political division of Berlin did not significantly affect the dispositions of Berliners toward each other and toward their formerly unified political community. To this day officials in West Berlin and the Federal Republic publicly espouse such a position with respect to both Berlin and Germany as a whole. Former Chancellor Willy Brandt doubtless spoke for the majority of his compatriots in the West when he said that the *de facto* existence of two German states does not alter the fact that there is but a single German nation. This proposition, if true, bears a significant implication for personal interactions in divided Berlin. Even taking into account some absolute decline in the level of transactions due to individuals' wariness about entering the other half of the city, the relative level of such transactions should have remained fairly constant over the course of the dozen years from 1949 to 1961, that is, until the construction of the Berlin wall.

The alternative hypothesis derives from Ernst Renan's assertion of more than a hundred years ago that nationalism is a plebiscite of daily living. Over time, the individual living in a particular political system builds up a pattern of expectations, demands, and identifications relevant to that system but only tangentially so *vis-à-vis* other such systems. Emigrants set up new patterns in their new environment. The longer they are away from the homeland, the more the emigrants find it necessary to substitute memories of how things were in the homeland for present knowledge of how they are. Thus a common experience of emigrants returning in later years to their homeland is a sense of estrangement made only sharper by the recognition of remembered but transformed elements of the past. This line of thought, if accurate, would lead us to hypothesize that transactions between East and West Berliners dropped off during the 1950s even though the possibility of personal contacts remained open. Their new lives after 1949 would simply have made the other side of the city seem less relevant for them.

Should the latter proposition reflect more accurately than the former the actual developments in divided Berlin, then yet another question arises: what is the shape of the curve of declining transactions? One possibility is that a sharp drop-off occurred immediately after the political division of the city. Unfortunately, data are not available to test this notion. Before 1948, there seemed to be no reason for municipal officials to pay attention to the kinds of contacts that people in one borough had with those in another. An exception is in the field of public and private transportation, where periodic counts of traffic flows are made to permit an adjustment of services or the construction of new streets. Even these counts do not exist for the period immediately before and after, let us say, November 1948 when a new municipal administration was installed in East Berlin, or March 1949 when East Berlin's currency lost its validity in West Berlin.

Another possibility is that the level of transactions conformed to patterns of public sentiments. Throughout the 1950s there was a steady demand in both the East and the West for the reunification of Germany and Berlin. This can be seen in both the public statements of politicians and in public opinion polls (or, in the case of East Germans, for whom no data based on systematic interviews are available, polls of those visiting exhibits in West Berlin).[6] Only until the middle 1950s, however, did the West German public, including West Berliners, express great hopes that such a reunification would in fact be brought about. Afterwards it was also fairly clear to observers that neither the FRG in the west nor the GDR in the east was prepared to accept the sacrifices and risks entailed in such a step.[7] If transactions between East and West Berliners reflected their expectations about the future, then we might anticipate that a curve characterizing these transactions will remain fairly high for some years after the city's political division and only then begin to sink.

Other possible shapes of this curve also exist. One would indicate a steady decline of transactions, possibly growing logarithmically as time passed. Another might be an inverted S-shaped or logistics curve. In the latter case, we might hypothesize that transactions remained high for a brief time after division, declined sharply as Berliners on both sides of the city stopped crossing the boundary for casual purposes, and then flattened out and remained fairly constant at a level reflecting hardcore transactions, such as family contacts. Still another might show rising transactions following an initial decline. Such a curve would correspond to the West German government's expectations when, in the middle 1950s, it instituted a number of measures aimed at encouraging east–west contacts in Berlin. Finally, various curves might simply show random fluctuations in the pattern of transactions between East and West Berliners from 1949 to 1961.

Indicators of Interactions between East and West Berliners

The search for data on interactions from 1949 to 1961 between East and West Berliners could lead in several directions. Here we shall concentrate upon both official statistics and those produced by public and quasi-public agencies in the course of their normal operations but never published. In the absence of information gathered from sample surveys on the frequency, type, and quality of individuals' contacts, we must proceed on the basis of available data, such as traffic flows, visits by Easterners to events in West Berlin, correspondence, membership in organizations, and subscriptions by Easterners for West Berlin newspapers. After examining these indicators individually, it will then be possible to assess their overall meaning for the development after 1949 of political community in Berlin.

Passengers Carried by Public Transportation

An initial indicator shows less trends in interpersonal contacts than a structural change over time. Figures 9.1 and 9.2 depict the density of traffic in public transportation for two years, 1937 and 1958. Prewar traffic – and here the same holds true for automobiles and trucks as well as public carriers – was heavy in the inner city and radiated toward the suburbs. Moreover, an east–west axis is clearly visible. The densest traffic was in the borough of Mitte (or Center), which was in fact the governmental, cultural, and financial center of the city. The division of the city in 1945 into four sectors of occupation turned this borough over to Soviet control.

The traffic pattern in 1958, more than a dozen years after the end of the war and a decade after the city's government was split, shows two things. First, the overall level of traffic was sharply reduced compared to that which obtained in 1937. This fact reflects both the continuing economic hardships facing Berliners and, more significantly, the loss of the functions that pre-1945 Berlin had served for Germany as a whole. Secondly, in the place of a single traffic pattern centered in the heart of prewar Berlin, there were now two quite distinct patterns. That in West Berlin radiated from the Zoo Quarter, the main streets of which (Kurfürstendamm, Tauentzien Street, and Hardenberg Street) had become the most heavily traveled arteries in the new core. The core area of East Berlin had already begun to shift to Alexander Square, a trend that continues to the present day.

From 1937 to 1958, then, a city unified in its traffic system had split in two. The prewar links between what are now East and West Berlin, once the strongest in the entire system, were in 1958 to become virtually non-existent. Bus and streetcar lines had in fact been severed at the border. Only in the case of the more permanently situated subway and elevated railway lines was there a modicum of continuity. The Berlin wall, built in August 1961, was to reduce these tenuous links even further. East Berlin instituted controls and structural changes in the subway and elevated stations that made it impossible for its citizens to enter West Berlin via public transportation, and prevented those from the West from stopping at any station but that in Friedrich Street, where its border police provided visas (for all save, until 1972, West Berliners). Meanwhile, West Berlin instituted new bus services and began an extensive subway construction program that would enable Westerners, should they so wish, to avoid going through East Berlin at all. Weak links in 1958 had thus become sharp discontinuities three years later.[8]

Eastern Visitors to West Berlin Events

The openness of the east–west border in Berlin meant that residents of either side could (again, in principle) attend cultural, sports, and other events on the other side. Indeed, officials of both did their best to make their offerings attractive to those on the other side. Phrases characterizing West Berlin as the 'display window of democracy' and East Berlin as the site where 'socialist accomplishments' might be

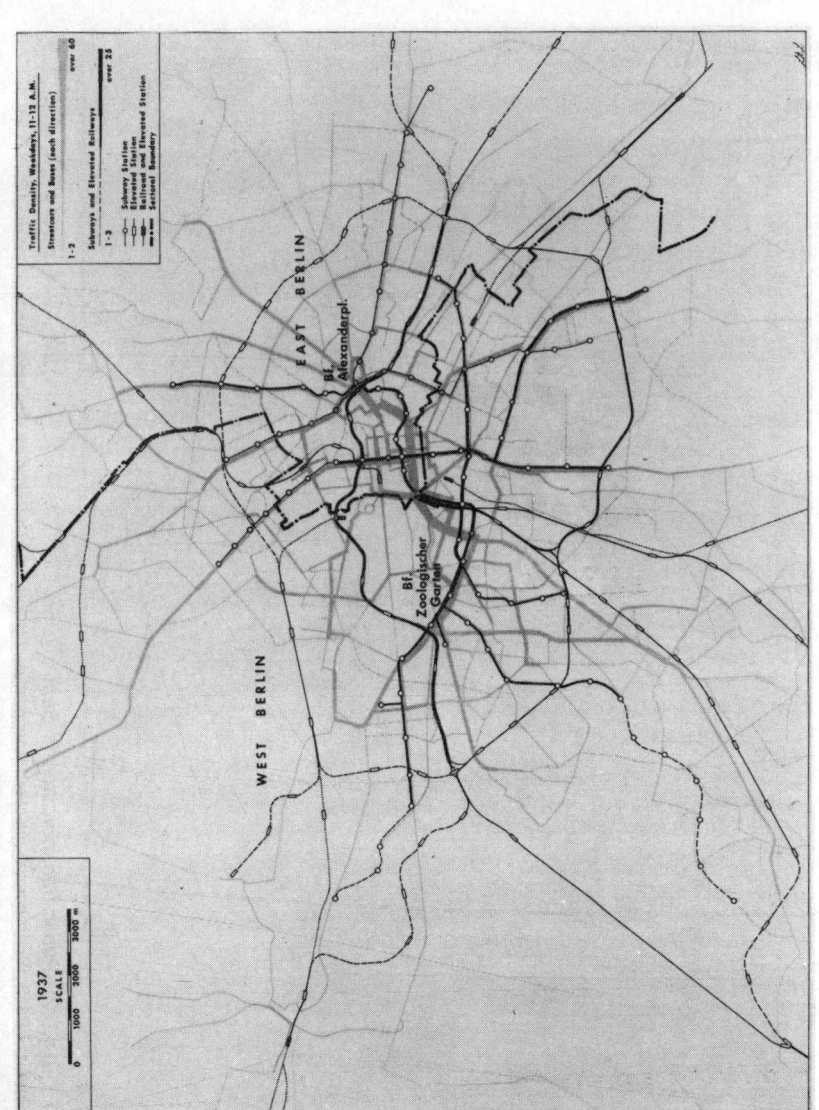

Figure 9.1 Public transportation in Berlin, 1937.
Source: After K. Schroeder, Deutscher Planungsatlas: Atlas von Berlin (Hanover, Jänecke, 1962).

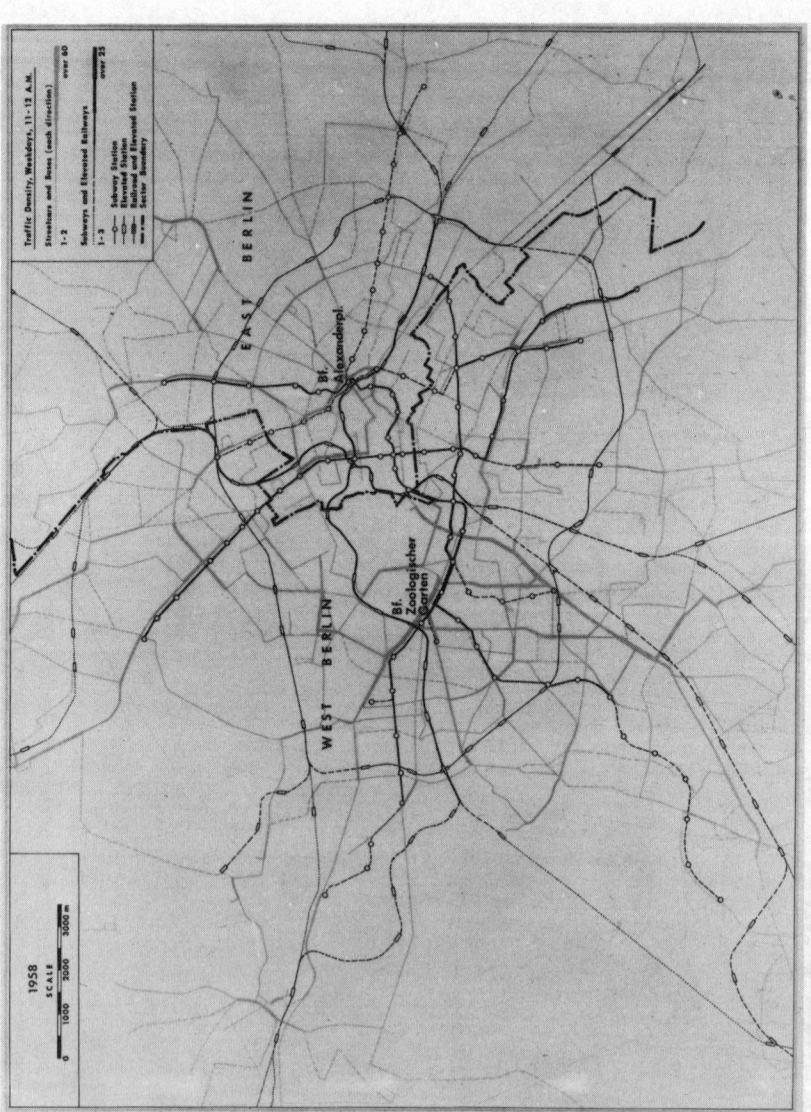

Figure 9.2 Public transportation in Berlin, 1958.
Source: After K. Schroeder, Deutscher Planungsatlas: Atlas von Berlin (Hanover, Jänecke, 1962).

admired were part of a broader propaganda effort that played such an important role during the height of the Cold War. The question of interest here is whether Berliners actually used the opportunity available to them – a question that can be answered with assurance only in the case of East Berliners attending events in West Berlin.

Most of West Berlin's cultural institutions – public and private theaters, the Municipal Opera, cinemas, the zoo, art galleries, the Exhibition Center, and still others – provided a financial break for Easterners wanting to attend their events. Why was this? There can be no denying that such a step in part enabled them to fill their unused capacities and in part accorded with the political program of the West Berlin and West German governments, but providing less expensive tickets was also a simple humanitarian gesture toward fellow Germans who, usually through no fault of their own, happened to be living in financially strapped East Berlin. Fortunately for later scholars, these ticket sales were carefully recorded.

Although the procedures for selling discounted tickets varied over the dozen years from 1949 to 1961, they were sufficiently similar to yield consistent data. The municipal theaters – the Municipal Opera, Schiller Theater, and Schloßpark Theater – may serve as a representative example.[9] Beginning with the 1949–50 season they sold tickets to Easterners in Eastmarks for double their Westmark price. But, since the value of the Eastmark fluctuated at West Berlin exchanges, occasionally dropping to a rate of six or even seven to one Westmark, it was necessary to adopt a new system. After September 1952 Easterners received a 50 per cent reduction in the price of tickets, but had to pay for them in Westmarks. Federal support beginning in mid-1957 for the All-Berlin Cultural Program enabled these theaters to use a one-to-one exchange rate for Eastern residents, even though the current rate was four Eastmarks to one Westmark. Thus the All-Berlin Cultural Program afforded the East Berliner willing to undertake the subway trip into West Berlin the opportunity to attend performances without paying a surcharge.

As Figure 9.3 shows, however, none of these steps stopped the declining tendency of Easterners to attend performances in West Berlin's municipal theaters. If we suppose that, in the absence of political and economic barriers, a third of the visitors to these theaters would have come from East Berlin alone, it is significant that, by 1957, less than 12 per cent came from East Berlin *and* the surrounding territories in the German Democratic Republic. The institution of the All-Berlin Cultural Plan retarded but did not reverse the declining trend. Moreover, if we assume that the linear trend for the period as a whole had continued and that the wall had not been built, then by 1968 there would have been *no* visitors from the East to West Berlin's municipal theaters.[10]

Roughly the same was true of Eastern visitors to four major events held almost every year at West Berlin's Exhibition Center. These included an Agricultural Fair held every January, a Sports Show in the spring, the Industrial Fair during the fall, and the Christmas Mart in

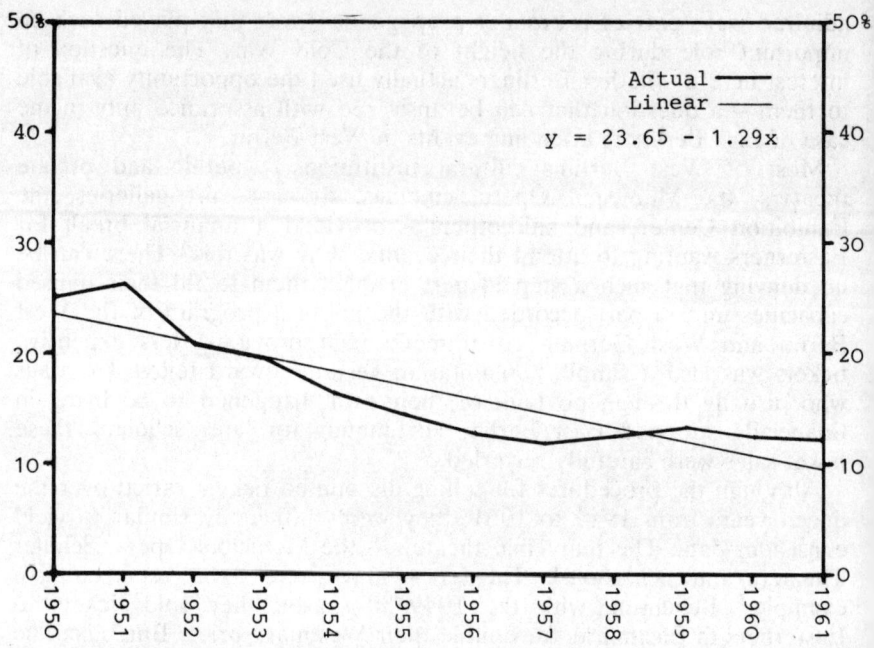

Figure 9.3 *Eastern visitors to West Berlin municipal theaters (as percentage of total ticket sales).*

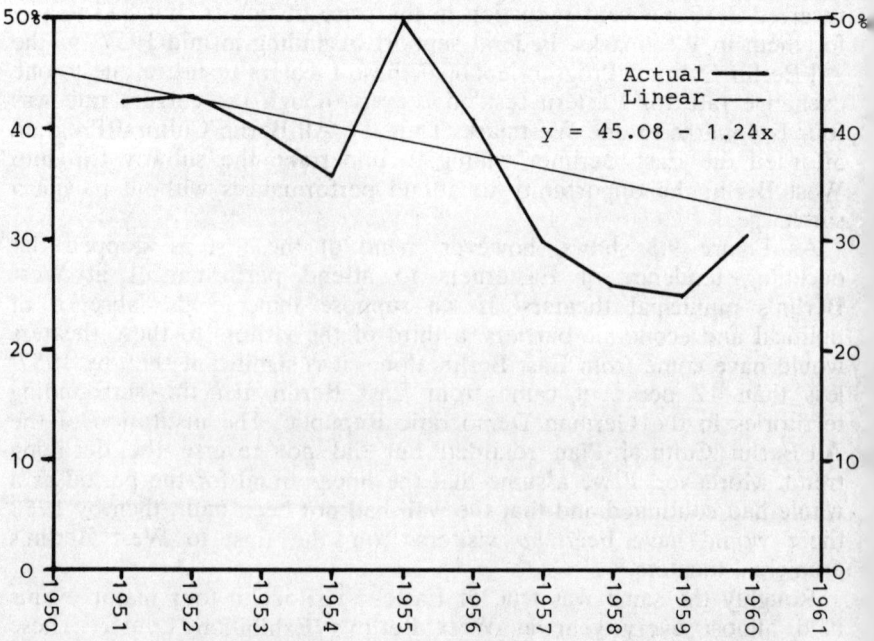

Figure 9.4 *Eastern visitors to four major West Berlin events (as percentage of total ticket sales).*

December. As Figure 9.4 shows, however, the average level of Eastern attendance at these exhibitions was higher than that at the municipal theaters. Reasons for this doubtless varied from person to person. For some, going to the exhibition was a daytime activity; this meant that they would be returning on the subway or elevated railway during the daylight hours or very early evening, that is, at a time when they would be less conspicuous to border patrols than were they returning to East Berlin in the late night hours. For others, living in a time when the GDR was still trying to survive with outmoded and poorly maintained agricultural and industrial equipment, seeing the latest technologies that the West had to offer was a treat. The chance to meet relatives or sample higher-quality food may have tempted still others. But, whatever the cause, the effect was that these exhibitions were enormously popular with Easterners and often attracted as many as half a million East Berliners and other citizens of the GDR.

Even so, the overall trend was one of declining shares of visitors from the East. The high point came in 1955, when Easterners comprised 45 per cent of those attending the 'Green Week' or Agricultural Fair and 58 per cent of visitors to the Industrial Exhibition.[11] By 1957, however, the average for the four exhibitions had fallen below a third of all ticket sales, and there it remained through 1960. The last full exhibition year before the wall went up saw an upswing in the Eastern attendance rates at all four major events.

The West Berlin Exhibition Center has two other attractions that continue to draw thousands of visitors every year. One is the Funkturm or Radio Tower. Upon the payment of a small fee a person can climb the stairs or take an elevator to a restaurant located 183 feet above the ground level, or take the elevator to the top of the 500-foot structure – the highest point in all Berlin until the completion in the early 1970s of East Berlin's 1,025-foot television tower. In many ways the Funkturm rivals the Brandenburg Gate as the best-known symbol of Berlin. Its uppermost platform, from which the visitor enjoys a panoramic view of the city as well as its surrounding Brandenburg March, remains one of West Berlin's most popular tourist attractions. Near the base of the Funkturm is yet another: the Summer Garden. Especially in the early postwar years, when Berliners had to use every bit of available land for raising vegetables and the city had no funds to reforest the parks, the formal Summer Garden, with its roses, fountains, and reflecting pool as well as an outdoor cafe, was a favorite spot for people to relax. Even today, a warm Sunday afternoon finds the Garden's paths and the cafe's tables filled with Berliners enjoying nature and sunning themselves.

In the early years at least, East Berliners were no exceptions. Indeed, from 1950 to 1952, the proportion of Eastern visitors was greater than the share of East Berliners in Berlin's total population (Figures 9.5 and 9.6). With time, however, ever fewer Easterners were inclined to take the time and trouble required to visit either the Funkturm or the Summer Garden – although, again, there was a slight upward trend in the curve after the introduction of the All-Berlin Cultural Program made entrance prices cheaper for Easterners. Had the overall trends

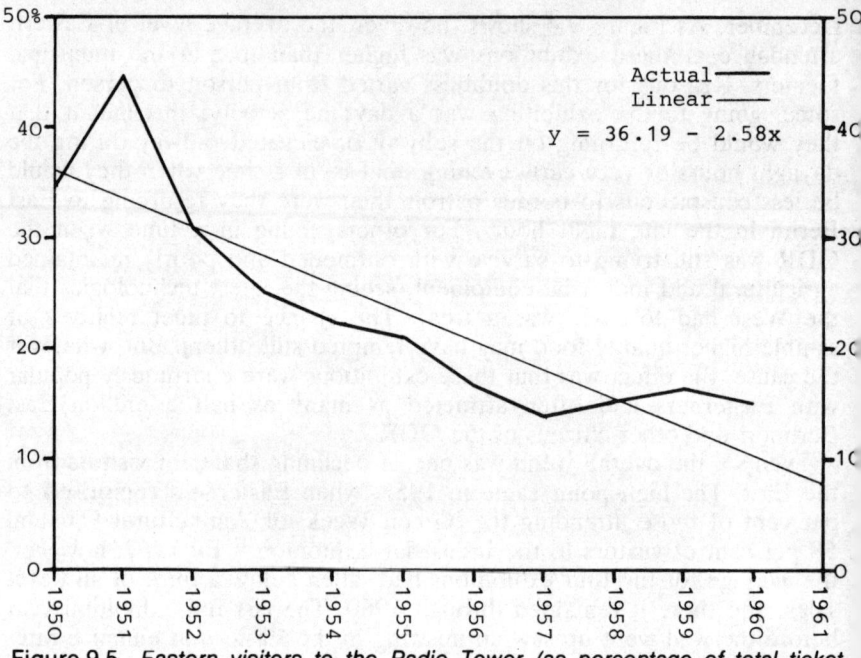

Figure 9.5 *Eastern visitors to the Radio Tower (as percentage of total ticket sales).*

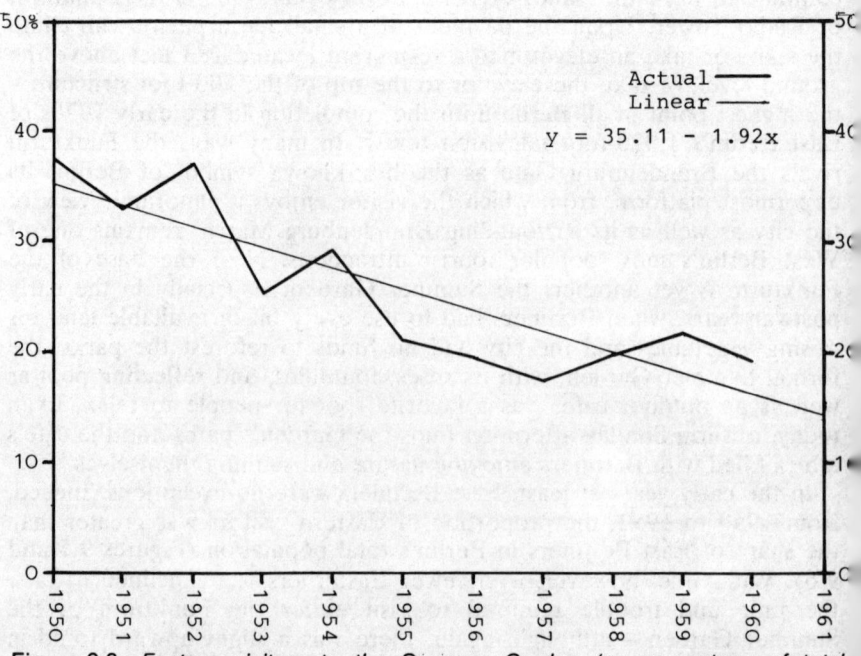

Figure 9.6 *Eastern visitors to the Summer Garden (as percentage of total ticket sales).*

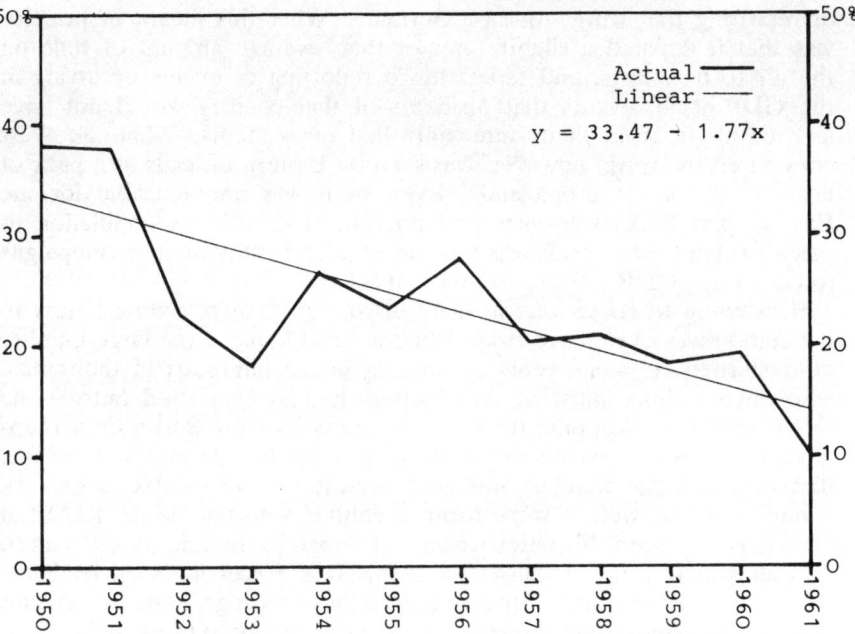

Figure 9.7 *Eastern letters to radio station RIAS (as percentage of total letters).*

continued, there would have been no more visitors from the East by 1964 to the Funkturm and 1969 to the Summer Garden.

The four sets of data shown in Figure 9.3 through 9.6 are consistent in depicting a declining tendency among Easterners to make use of whatever opportunities they had to maintain old contacts or develop new ones in West Berlin. Measures undertaken by the West German government to ease the financial burden of attending such events in the West had only a slight and temporary effect. In the absence of relevant data, it is of course difficult to be sure that the trends characterizing public behavior also held for private behavior, such as visits to the homes of friends or relatives in the West. Yet, such an extrapolation is reasonable. Limited information suggests that visits to public places were frequently undertaken jointly with people from the West. It is unlikely although possible that Easterners substituted for their visits to public events, with or without Westerners, a growing number of private visits.

Indirect East—West Contacts

Personal visits were not the only means by which people in West and East Berlin remained in contact. Another was by mail. Figure 9.7 shows the relative share of the mail received by the West Berlin radio station RIAS (Radio in the American Sector) that came from listeners in East Berlin and the GDR. Now, RIAS was not a common or garden-variety radio station. Throughout the 1950s it was owned and operated by the United States government, and saw as one of its chief missions the task of reporting the 'truth' to East Germans. What this meant in practice was that it devoted a slightly greater than average amount of time on the air to newscasts, and especially to reporting of events occurring in the GDR itself, events that residents of that country would not have learned about from their state-controlled news media. What the West considered the truth, however, was seen by Eastern officials as a pack of lies and disruptive propaganda. Even so it was impracticable for the East to jam RIAS transmissions and futile to forbid its population to listen to them. The result was a series of occasionally intense campaigns to encourage GDR citizens to tune out RIAS.

If listening to RIAS was strongly discouraged, then writing letters to the station was even more risky. What is remarkable is the large number of Easterners, in some years numbering in the hundreds of thousands, who did so. Since most of these letters had to be posted outside the GDR, either by dropping them in a mailbox in West Berlin or perhaps having friends or relatives in the West forward the letters, the mere fact that such a large number was sent indicates a formidable degree of commitment (as well as some form of contact with the West). RIAS, of course, encouraged this letter-writing, although cautioning its listeners to be judicious in sending the letters themselves. Receiving such feedback was vital to its continued effectiveness. To encourage it RIAS officials occasionally announced contests, with prizes (to be picked up in West Berlin!) awarded to the best letters on a particular topic.

Figure 9.7 none the less reveals a declining readiness on the part of Easterners either to take the risk of writing a letter to RIAS or to find some means to post it. That the percentage dipped sharply in 1953 – a year of intensified controls in the GDR that ultimately led to a number of small-scale revolts in June – suggests that low levels of letter-writing were definitely correlated with the degree of surveillance over citizens exerted by the GDR government. But, whatever the cause, during the part of 1961 before the wall was built only one in ten letters received by RIAS came from GDR citizens.

A slightly different picture emerges when we look at the relative share of letters and packages which West Berliners sent to and received from East Berlin and the GDR (Figure 9.8). After a sharp decline from 1952 to 1954, the curve dropped only very slowly through 1960. We might attribute the earlier phase either to rapidly increasing business activity in West Berlin, which would have produced a heavier flow of commercial mail to shrink the Eastern portion of the city's overall mail flow, or else to a growing fear by West Berliners and Easterners alike during these tense years that their postal exchanges were subject to political controls that could have nasty consequences, and it would also be possible to cite the relative smoothness of these exchanges from 1954 to 1960 as evidence that a degree of enduring stability had been reached.

Neither circumstance, however, even if true, could ignore the fact that the curve was declining (as was the absolute amount of Eastern mail). This was the case for three of the four categories of mail included in the curve; letters to the East as a proportion of all letters sent by West Berliners; letters from the East as a proportion of all letters received by

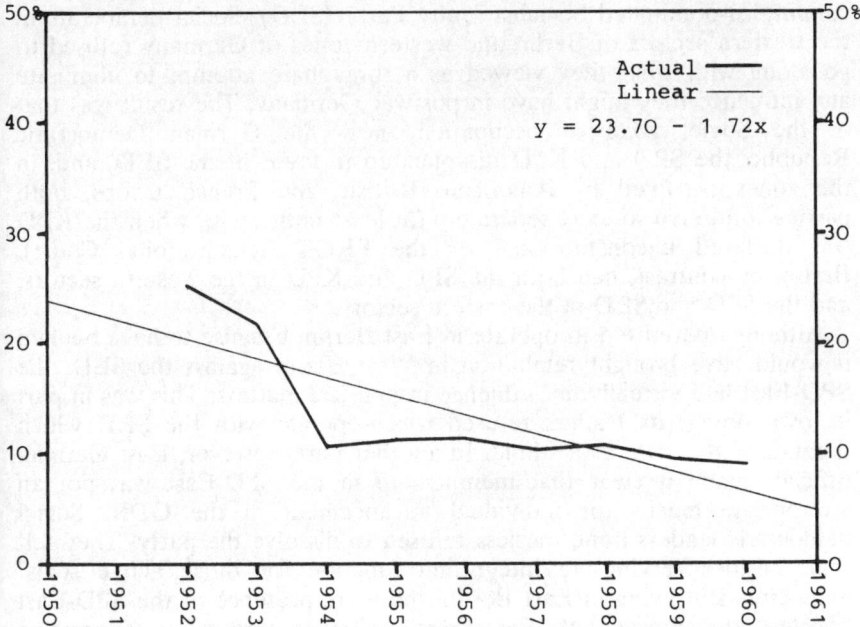

Figure 9.8 Letters and packages sent between West Berlin and the East (as percentage of West Berlin's total letters and packages).

West Berliners; and packages from the East as a proportion of all packages received by West Berliners. Only the category of packages sent to the East as a proportion of all packages sent by West Berliners rose, from an average of 5·5 per cent in 1952–5 to an average of 6·3 per cent during the next five years. The upward swing, which began at the same time as the All-Berlin Cultural Program instituted tax rebates for West Berliners sending packages to the East, reached a high point of 6·9 per cent in 1958 but quickly dropped off to 6·2 and 6·0 per cent, respectively, during the next two years.

The patterns of decline in postal contacts are too persistent to ignore. Whether we look at letters written by Easterners to RIAS or at various kinds of mail flows between West Berlin and the East, we find a decreasing proclivity to communicate by mail across West Berlin's borders. Even incentives, such as contests for letter-writers from the East and tax rebates for Westerners sending packages to friends and relatives in the East, had only a shortlived effect. Not long after such plans were implemented the curves of postal contacts between West Berlin and the East began to drop off again.

Partisan Activity

For international legal reasons, a small Social Democratic Party (SPD) continued to exist in East Berlin for a decade and a half after the 'official' SPD in both East Berlin and the rest of Soviet-occupied Germany had merged with the Communist Party (KPD) to form the communist-dominated Socialist Unity Party (SED). Social democrats in the western sectors of Berlin and western zones of Germany refused to go along with what they viewed as a threadbare attempt to eliminate any influence they might have in postwar Germany. The result was that in the Soviet zone of occupation, now the German Democratic Republic, the SPD and KPD disappeared in favor of the SED, and, in the zones occupied by American, British, and French troops, both parties continued to exist separately (at least until 1956, when the KPD was declared unconstitutional by the FRG's Constitutional Court). Berlin, by contrast, had both the SPD and KPD in the western sectors, and the SPD and SED in the eastern sectors.

Although permitted to operate in East Berlin, because to have banned it would have brought retaliation in West Berlin against the SED, the SPD-East had virtually no influence in political matters. This was in part its own doing: its leaders refused to co-operate with the SED which dominated the state as a whole. In another part, however, East German officials made it clear that membership in the SPD-East was not an appropriate means for individual advancement in the GDR. Social democratic leaders none the less refused to dissolve the party. They felt that, besides serving an integrating function for those active social democrats still living in East Berlin, the mere presence of the SPD-East boosted the morale of Easterners suffering under an oppressive regime.[12]

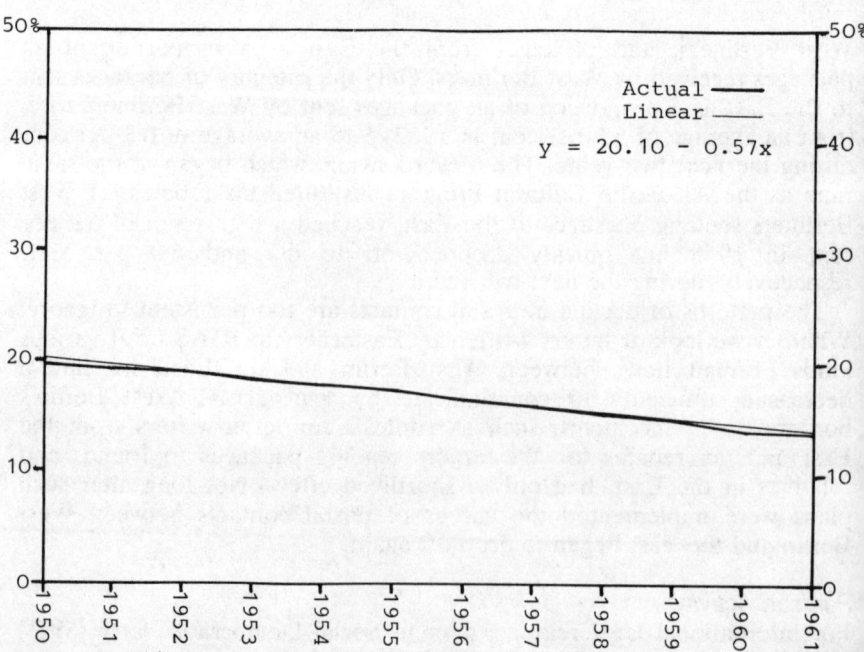

Figure 9.9 *East Berlin members of Social Democratic Party (as percentage of total SPD membership in Berlin).*

The costs of continued membership in the SPD-East on the part of East Berliners were thus substantial. It took a firm commitment to social democratic principles for someone to be willing to pay these costs. Forty per cent of its members dropped out during the twelve months after 31 March 1946, three weeks before the SED was formally promulgated, and only slightly over half of the rest continued their membership through the end of 1950. From then on, until the construction of the wall in August 1961, there was a steady decrease in the number of SPD-East members. The total number declined from 8,330 in December 1950 to 5,327 in June 1961; and, as Figure 9.9 shows, their share of SPD membership in all Berlin dropped during the same period from 20 to 14 per cent. A multiple regression model used to extend the membership trend past August 1961 projected that it would have dropped off to zero by the end of 1968. Shortly after the wall was built, however, the overall SPD leadership decided to dissolve its East Berlin branch rather than to run the risk that the SPD-East, now isolated from its sister organization in West Berlin, would succumb to political pressure exerted by the GDR government.

Eastern Subscribers to West Berlin Newspapers

During the winter months of the blockade, a few weeks after a new government was set up in East Berlin, Soviet-zone authorities banned the sale in their occupation zone and sector of Berlin of newspapers printed in the West. The open border, of course, permitted East Berliners interested in what these newspapers had to say to purchase them in the western sectors. After March 1949 West Berlin newspaper dealers refused to accept payment in Eastmarks on a one-to-one basis, since the coins they were amassing had little value in the West. The publishers themselves, however, arranged for Easterners to subscribe at reduced rates, with the proviso that the newspapers be picked up at some specified place in the West.[13]

Among Easterners willing to accept these terms, the most popular newspaper was the daily *Telegraf*. It may have been its strong social democratic orientation, which did not appeal much to West Berlin's newspaper readers as a whole, that made the newspaper most attractive to the 1,500 or so Easterners who subscribed to it.[14] Informal interviews revealed that it may have been members of the SPD-East who were most inclined to read the *Telegraf* in the first place. Even so, Eastern readership declined during the 1950s. At a time when the total sales of the *Telegraf* were slowly declining, the percentage going to Eastern subscribers dropped from 6·5 to 3·6 per cent (Figure 9.10). Yet the rate of decline was relatively low – about a quarter of a percentage point per year. At that rate the newspaper might have retained Eastern readers until the early 1970s.

Overall Trend of Declining Contacts

A comparative examination of the streams of evidence depicted in Figures 9.3 through 9.10 reveals striking convergence. Each curve declined during the decade of the 1950s. To be sure, they started out at

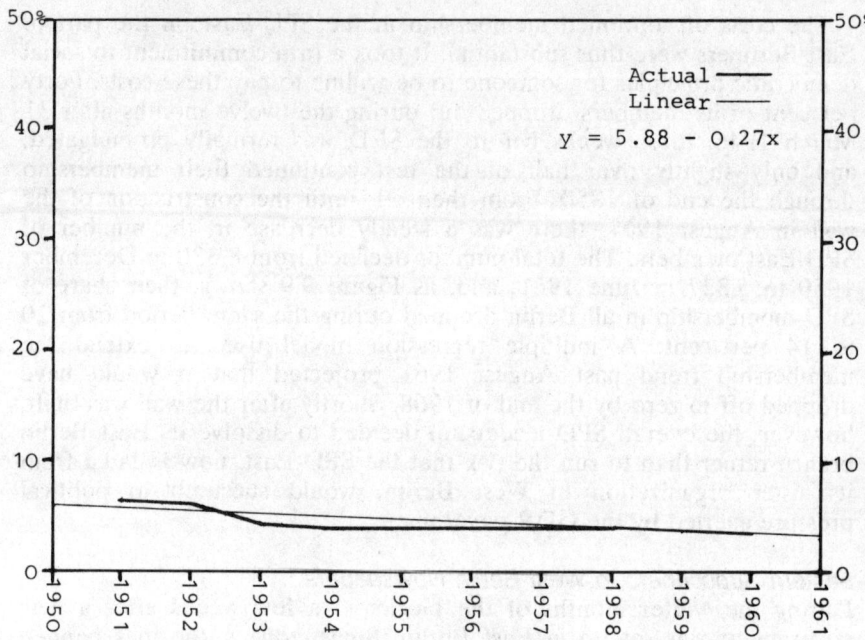

Figure 9.10 *Sales of newspaper* Telegraf *to Eastern subscribers (as percentage of total* Telegraf *sales).*

various levels and declined at varying rates – with the steepest linear curve dropping 2·6 percentage points per year and the least steep about a quarter of a percentage point per year – but the overall trend of declining contacts between East and West in Berlin is unmistakable. Moreover, in those cases in which there were clear-cut efforts by the West German government to revive flagging levels of contacts, the actual impact was brief before the curves began to decline again.

The composite curve in Figure 9.11 shows these trends clearly. For each set of data used in Figures 9.3 through 9.10, the average 'interaction rate' for 1952–60 was computed. Using this average rate as 100, the index figures for each year were then calculated. Figure 9.11, then, shows the average of these yearly index figures. For example, the average interaction rate for 1950, based on the available data, was 159, that is, 59 per cent greater than the average for the decade. By 1961, as Figure 9.11 also indicates, the average interaction rate was 70, or about 30 per cent below the average for the decade as a whole. The best-fitting straight line declines almost eight percentage points per year. A second-order curve, the broken line in Figure 9.11, fits the data still better (although both are significant at the $p < 0.001$ level). It suggests that the rate of declining contacts was greatest at the outset of the 1950s, and then, by about 1958, flattened out considerably.

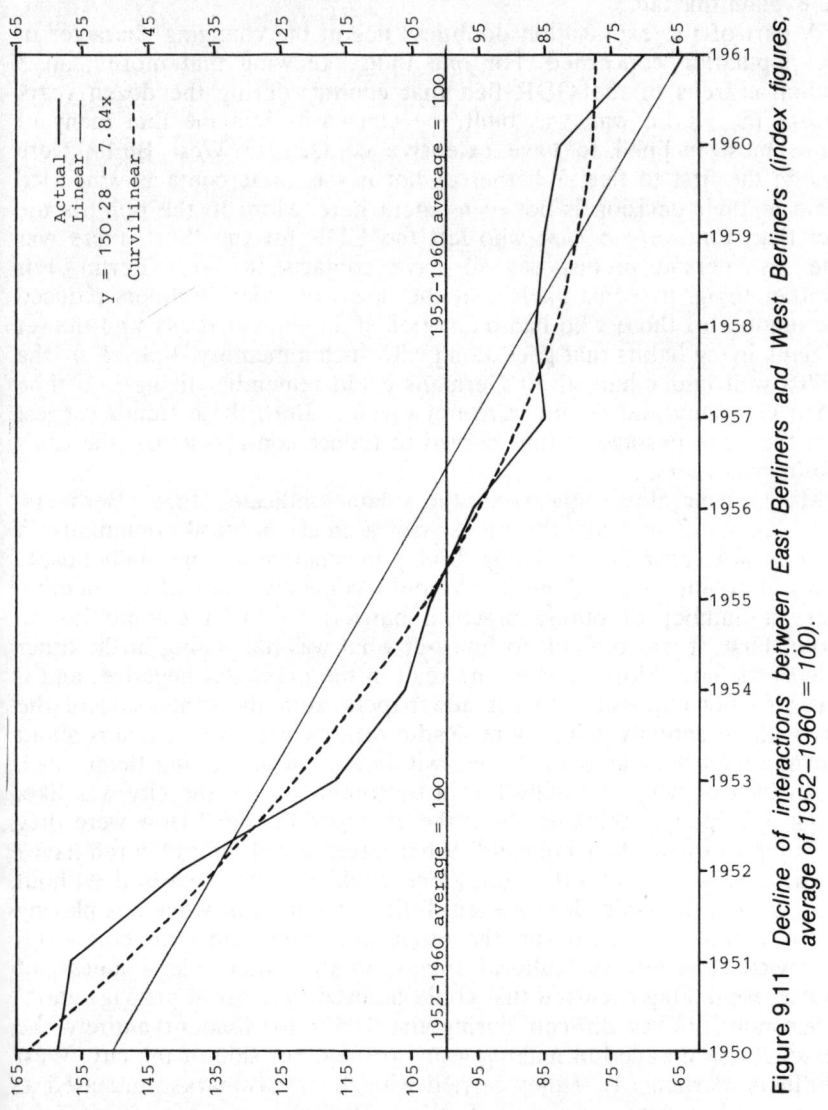

Figure 9.11 *Decline of interactions between East Berliners and West Berliners (index figures, average of 1952–1960 = 100).*

Political Disintegration in Postwar Berlin

The evidence reviewed in this chapter indicates that personal interaction between East and West in the divided Berlin of the 1950s declined – despite West German governmental efforts to encourage it.[15] How can we explain this fact?

A part of the explanation doubtless lies in the changing character of the population concerned. For one thing, knowing that more than 3 million citizens of the GDR fled that country during the dozen years before the Berlin wall was built, we can easily imagine that many of those most inclined to have extensive contacts in West Berlin were among the first to flee. Whether or not it was these contacts which led them to their decision is not of moment here. More to the point is the fact that, for every person who left the GDR for the West, there was one less person predisposed to have contacts in West Berlin. For another thing, it seems likely that the death of older Berliners reduced the number of those who had memories of an undivided city and the set of daily living habits that goes along with such a memory. Indeed, by the 1970s well under half of all Germans could remember living in a time when Germany and Berlin were not divided. Both these trends suggest that the mere passage of time served to reduce contacts across the city's arbitrary borders.

More generally, however, the data indicate that Berliners' expectations of and identifications with a single political community in the city were probably declining. Living in separate and mutually hostile political systems was taking its toll on a common sense of community. Here a number of purely practical barriers to social communication arose. First, it was difficult to find out what was happening in the other side of the city. Most of what one read in the press was negative; and it was virtually impossible to get newspapers from the other side of the city without actually going there. Radio reports might tell listeners about the more spectacular occurrences, without, however, giving them much of an idea of what the daily life in the other part of the city was like. What were people thinking about the events of the day? How were they planning to spend their holidays? What interests did their children have? These and a host of other questions could not be answered without visiting the other side. It was even difficult to find out what was playing at the theater or cinema on the other side. The media on both sides eschewed reporting on cultural events on the other side – unless, of course, something occurred that could be used as political propaganda.

Secondly, it was difficult during the 1950s to discount entirely the personal risk entailed in making visits to the other side of the city. West Berliners, particularly if they carried with them Eastmarks purchased at black market rates in one of West Berlin's many (and officially supported) exchange bureaux, always had before them examples of other West Berliners who had been detained and even imprisoned in East Berlin. East Berliners knew that visits to the West were officially discouraged. Those known to have too many contacts with the West might well find that they or their children were disadvantaged at the workplace or in school. In short, even though nothing was *likely* to happen – and, given the number of border-crossings each day, the percentage of incidents was minuscule – the thought that something *could* happen was ever present. Such a thought doubtless discouraged many casual visits across the border.

A third barrier to social communication across the border comprised the imperatives of Berliners' daily lives. That is, West Berliners had to deal every day and in virtually every way with the political system of the West – its public schools, marketing procedures, banking, tax laws, telephone system, consumer products, newspapers, and everything else in their immediate social environment. The same was true for East Berliners. The practical relevance to them of the other side of the city was slight. Moreover, the probability that anything they did would have an impact in the other part of the city was slighter. In such circumstances the findings of social psychologists that levels of relevance are correlated with levels of both knowledge and interest would lead us to expect Berliners to become increasingly indifferent about what was happening 'over there'. Renan's 'plebiscite of daily living' was day by day turning Berliners into either East Berliners or West Berliners.

All these factors contributed to the decline of interactions. What is equally important is the shape of the curve showing this decline. That is, interpersonal contacts did not drop off immediately after the political division. They endured, despite the element of risk involved, for at least a dozen years, and would doubtless have continued had not the GDR built a wall to break off almost all contacts between East and West Berliners. (What happened after 1972, when limited contacts again became possible, is a different story; in brief, the limited reversal of visits that began is consistent with the data presented in this paper.) Political institutions can be broken apart almost overnight, and such aspects of a community's infrastructure as traffic networks, municipal services, and even residential patterns can be changed with both considerable effort and some time. But separating a people tied together by habits and expectations of extensive social communication over a wide range of subject-matters takes a much longer time; it can, however, be done.

It would be equally inaccurate to say that the interpersonal contacts were unaffected by the political division. The hope expressed by the West and encouraged by such measures as the All-Berlin Cultural Program remained just that, a hope. By and large, the level of interaction at the beginning of the 1960s was less than half of that which obtained a decade earlier. Political community in the sense of shared expectations, demands, and identifications had not been sustained for Berlin as a whole.

The overall trend of declining interactions suggests that Berliners were learning to be different. In this sense it is the converse of the curve identified in other studies as the pattern by which a sense of community is learned.[16] Each aspect of behavior examined here in the aggregate moved steadily, albeit with fluctuations, in that direction. Governmental efforts to retard learning produced only a slight and temporary amount of regression, indicated by an upward swing in the curve. Nor is there any reason to think that the curve would have reversed itself had not the events of August 1961 taken place. By that time Berliners were well on their way toward complete separation.

The possibility of reversibility raises an interesting question: what would happen if Berlin were to be reunified today? Would not the old patterns of interactions, and with them the expectations, demands, and identifications associated with political community, simply re-emerge? In other words, have three decades of separation *really* made East and West Berliners distinct from each other?

In seeking to answer this question, it is tempting to think in terms of historical examples. Poles did not give up their sense of nationality despite a century and a quarter of division under alien rule; and similar nationality struggles were recurrent in the Balkans. Such examples, however, which would lead us to expect a sense of German nationality and Berlin community to persist for many decades to come,[17] may be misleading. The classic cases of reunited nationalities occurred at times and places in which there was a relatively low degree of organized complexity. Polish peasants in what were then the German, Russian, and Austro-Hungarian empires were fairly similar, more tied to the land and their peasant communities than to elaborate sets of imperial social communication systems. It is by no means clear that the Poland which re-emerged in 1918 was the result of spontaneous pressure from the masses, as opposed to an unusual set of international circumstances, effective organization by a small number of leaders, and the willingness of the masses to cast votes in plebiscites. How likely is it that a new international crisis would make the rest of the world accept a reunified Germany and Berlin? Moreover, although another element in the Polish case, a unifying thrust by determined leaders, may eventually exist in the German situation, what they will face is not a mass of peasants untied to any large-scale and complex system of government and communication, but rather populations with strong sets of interdependencies which are mutually exclusive.

The latter is a more likely scenario for a Berlin reunified at some future time. If the city is politically amalgamated on the basis of new international agreements, it will be fairly easy to rebuild a unified municipal government, and with time it will be possible to construct the links to tie together divided water and sewage systems, telephone networks, streets and subway lines, and the like. Still more difficult to reconstruct will be the sentimental ties of community. Reunification in the year, say, 2000 will come more than half a century after the city's political division and almost forty years after the appearance of the wall. By then there will be very few Berliners alive who will have a vivid memory of what it was like before 1945, and fewer still who will have any active contacts on the other side of the city. Changing residential, traffic, and other patterns by which people organize their daily lives will by then have produced two cities in a physical sense. East Berliners will be tied intimately to the social, economic, political, and other systems in the German Democratic Republic; West Berliners to quite different systems in the Federal Republic. Rebuilding a common set of expectations, demands, and identifications among Berliners will doubtless be a very slow process, quite possibly slower than that which had forced them apart in the first place.

What seems less likely in the present circumstances is that a nationalistic movement firmly grounded at the grass-roots level will emerge to force the German governments or those of the victorious Allies of the Second World War to reunify the country (or, still less likely, Berlin alone). The precondition for such a movement would be the kind of social communication networks which the GDR government still seems determined to prevent. Free mobility within Berlin and Germany will probably remain an impossible dream until there are no more economic incentives for citizens of one Germany to flee to the other, pacts have been reached for returning to their country of origin those who have left for political reasons (a possibility that most West German leaders would firmly reject now), and, more generally, neither country poses a threat to the other. It is unlikely that, in the absence of free mobility, an effective social communication network will emerge in the two Germanies.

The prospects, at least for the foreseeable future, are for the division of Berlin to continue. As each year passes, the underlying basis of political community in Berlin as a whole erodes a bit more. East Berliners become more closely tied to a network of systems that tries as much as possible to ignore the existence of West Berlin, while West Berliners form stronger links to a network of systems in which non-governmental processes in East Berlin are of little moment. In the place of community, estrangement is growing.

Notes: Chapter 9

1 Disintegration is thus different from both *decay*, which implies a loss in the unit's capabilities, abilities to frame goals commensurate with its capabilities, and combinatorial resourcefulness or ability to develop strategies to use available resources in a reasonably efficient manner to obtain realistic goals, and mere *disaggregation*, the division of the unit into its component parts. For further elaboration, see Richard L. Merritt, 'Decay in social systems', in *Systems in Society*, ed. Milton D. Rubin (Washington, DC: Society for General Systems Research, 1973), pp. 71–103; and the chapter in this volume by Donald J. Puchala.
2 Karl W. Deutsch, Sidney A. Burrell, Robert A. Kann, Maurice Lee, Jr, Martin Lichterman, Raymond E. Lindgren, Francis L. Loewenheim, and Richard W. Van Wagenen, *Political Community and the North Atlantic Area: International Organization in the Light of Historical Experience* (Princeton, NJ: Princeton University Press, 1957), pp. 59–65. For details on two of the cases, see Raymond E. Lindgren, *Norway–Sweden: Union, Disunion, and Scandinavian Integration* (Princeton, NJ: Princeton University Press, 1959); and Robert A. Kann, *The Habsburg Empire: A Study in Integration and Disintegration* (New York: Praeger, 1957). Donald J. Puchala, in his chapter in this volume, discusses Deutsch's approach to political integration at the international level, without, however, discussing the relevance of the approach at other levels of analysis. The contribution by Andrei S. Markovits and Warren W. Oliver III points to the general aspects of Deutsch's approach; and that of Arend Lijphart is even more explicit in stressing the impact elsewhere of Deutsch's 'new paradigm'.

3 See W. Phillips Davison, *The Berlin Blockade: A Study in Cold War Politics* (Princeton, NJ: Princeton University Press, 1958); and G. Keiderling and Percy Stulz, *Berlin 1945–1968: Zur Geschichte der Hauptstadt der DDR und der selbständigen politischen Einheit Westberlin* (East Berlin: Dietz Verlag, 1970).
4 For an example, see Richard L. Merritt, 'Political division and municipal services in postwar Berlin', in *Public Policy*, ed. John D. Montgomery and Albert O. Hirschman (Cambridge, Mass.: Harvard University Press, 1968), Vol. 17, pp. 165–98.
5 For data and some interpretations on the larger question of Germany as a whole, see Gebhard Schweigler, *National Consciousness in Divided Germany* (Beverly Hills, Calif., and London: Sage, 1972).
6 See Anna J. Merritt and Richard L. Merritt (eds), *Public Opinion in Semisovereign Germany: The HICOG Surveys* (Urbana, Ill.: University of Illinois Press, 1980).
7 See, for example, Ferenc A. Váli, *The Quest for a United Germany* (Baltimore, Md: Johns Hopkins University Press, 1967).
8 For a more thorough discussion of this topic, see Richard L. Merritt, 'Infrastructural changes in Berlin', *Annals of the Association of American Geographers*, vol. 63, no. 1 (March 1973), pp. 58–70.
9 For further data and analysis, see Richard L. Merritt, 'Politics, theater, and the East–West struggle: the theater as a cultural bridge in West Berlin, 1948–61', *Political Science Quarterly*, vol. 80, no. 2 (June 1965), pp. 186–215.
10 Western political leaders underscored the significance of the West Berlin stage as a cultural bridge between East and West by claiming it to be a place where East Berliners could see theater unfettered by political or ideological chains. A statistical analysis of attendance patterns, however, reveals that, at the Schiller Theater at least, East Berliners did not flock to plays that were banned in the GDR, but rather attended performances of plays popular among Western visitors as well.
11 From 1955 to 1957 no admission was charged to the Christmas Mart and hence no figures on Eastern visitors are available. To estimate these figures, I used straight-line extrapolations based on paid admissions to the other three events for each year.
12 For details, see Richard L. Merritt and Ronald A. Francisco, 'The SPD of East Berlin, 1945–1961', *Comparative Politics*, vol. 5, no. 1 (October 1972), pp. 1–28.
13 It was also possible for Easterners to read Western newspapers at libraries in the West. See Harold Hurwitz, *Der Heimliche Leser* (Cologne and Berlin: Kiepenheuer & Witsch Verlag GmbH, 1966).
14 For the six years for which comparable data exist for *Der Tagesspiegel* (average percentage of sales going to Easterners for 1955–60 = 1·3, as opposed to 3·9 per cent for *Telegraf*), there was a similar declining trend. A Pearsonian correlation showed $r = +0·885$. Although data for the more popular *Morgenpost* are not available, it is worth noting that its first appearance was in the same year (1953) in which the sharpest drop in Eastern *Telegraf* readers occurred.
15 Critics of the FRG's politics would argue that its stubborn refusal to work out a *modus vivendi* with the GDR actually hampered the policies the FRG professed to be pursuing. Leaving aside the claims of East German officials, it could be argued that the West's desire to end any reliance by West Berlin upon services provided by the East (such as electricity) contributed to the city's division; and that such disruptive tactics as supporting the system of exchange rates that disadvantaged those holding Eastmarks kept even more East Berliners from visiting the West.
16 See, for example, Richard L. Merritt, *Symbols of American Community, 1735–1775* (New Haven, Conn., and London: Yale University Press, 1966); and Donald J. Puchala, 'The pattern of contemporary regional integration', *International Studies Quarterly*, vol. 12, no. 1 (March 1968), pp. 38–64.
17 For some debate on this point, see Schweigler, *National Consciousness in Divided Germany*; and the several volumes produced by a project led by Peter Christian Ludz, the final volume of which is *Materialien zum Bericht zur Lage der Nation 1974* (Bonn: Bundesministerium für innerdeutsche Beziehungen, 1974).

Part Three

Integration and Dependence

10

Karl W. Deutsch and the New Paradigm in International Relations

AREND LIJPHART

The theoretical revolution in the scholarly study of international relations that began in the 1950s was characterized by major reorientations with regard to both methodological and theoretical perspectives. In this, as I have argued elsewhere, Karl W. Deutsch was one of the leading 'revolutionaries'.[1] Deutsch's role as a methodological innovator in international relations and, more generally, in political science has, of course, been widely recognized. For instance, Robert L. Pfaltzgraff finds that Deutsch gave momentum to the following behavioral trends in political science: 'a quest for concepts of sufficient precision and applicability to provide the basis for the development of theory; the creation of operational (quantifiable) indicators for the testing of hypotheses about political behaviour; and the adaptation and utilization of concepts, methodologies and insights from other disciplines'.[2]

Less recognition has been given, however, to Deutsch's intellectual leadership in the major *theoretical* reorientation in the discipline of international relations that has taken place during the past three decades. My discussion of the new theoretical paradigm in this essay will follow up and elaborate on two themes that are stressed in Donald J. Puchala's introduction to the previous section on political integration and unification: the challenge by studies of integration to the realist school in international relations and the innovative character of the concept of 'pluralistic security community' in Deutsch's theory of integration. I shall argue that the challenge extended to the entire traditional paradigm, of which realism was the most important post-second World War manifestation, and that Deutsch's conception of integration provided the crucial philosophical impetus both for the assault on the traditional paradigm and for the construction of a comprehensive new paradigm. In my discussion the concept of integration plays a prominent role, but it is worth emphasizing that my concern will be exclusively with 'integration' in its unconventionally broad Deutschian sense and with its significance not for the field of international integration studies but for the discipline of international relations as a whole.

It is particularly appropriate to begin the section on 'Integration and Dependence' with a discussion of the shift from the traditional to the new paradigm. In contrast with the traditional view of international relations as taking place within an anarchical framework and the related conception of the sovereign state as the only unified, uniform, and unique actor on the international scene, the new paradigm sees the world as less orderly in one respect but more orderly in another. It is a less orderly world in the sense that it is more complex: there are all kinds of actors in addition to, fundamentally different from, and operative both outside and inside the sovereign states; and there are social, economic, and cultural variables that should be considered in addition to the purely political forces. On the other hand, the new paradigm adheres to a view of a more orderly world, which can be traced back to Hugo Grotius's conception of a world society: international relations as a system with strong elements of order and even hierarchy – and definitely not anarchical. The new paradigm is clearly reflected in the chapters that follow in this section. They deal with a multiplicity of international, transnational, and domestic actors and factors within a systematically ordered world.

The main subject of this chapter will be the new international relations paradigm of the 1960s and 1970s of which Grotius was a precursor and to which Deutsch was a seminal contributor, and its consequences for international relations theory. I shall also try to answer the objections against my view that the new theoretical paradigm shaped by Deutsch and the methodological-behavioral paradigm that came to fruition in political science generally are closely related, and against my proposition that Deutsch played the commanding role in the attack on the traditional paradigm of 'international anarchy'.

The Traditional Paradigm: International Anarchy

Classical international relations theory revolved around the notions of state sovereignty and its logical corollary, international anarchy: the idea that sovereign states, recognizing no higher authority, are in an international state of nature with the resulting security dilemma forcing them to live in a condition of mutual competition and conflict.[3] In Martin Wight's terminology, this is the 'Machiavellian paradigm' of international relations.[4] However, the first theorist who explicitly described the relations among states in terms of the anarchic state of nature was Thomas Hobbes. In a frequently cited passage from the *Leviathan*, he argues that 'in all times kings and persons of sovereign authority, because of their independence, are in continual jealousies and in the state and posture of gladiators ... which is a posture of war'.[5] The most extensive discussion by a classical theorist of the basic notion underlying the traditional paradigm may be found in Jean-Jacques Rousseau's *The State of War*. He paid particularly close attention to the characteristics of the security dilemma: the state 'feels weak so long as there are others stronger than itself. Its safety and preservation demand that it makes itself stronger than its neighbors. It cannot increase, foster, or exercise its strength except at their expense'.[6]

The twin notions of sovereignty and international anarchy provided the basis for three interrelated theories: world government, collective security, and balance of power. The theory of world government follows logically from the premiss that international relations are in the state of nature. If anarchy is the root of international conflict, the logical way to escape this undesirable condition is to conclude a social contract among the states which abolishes the separate sovereignties and establishes a single sovereign world government. Because most classical writers regarded world government as either unattainable or, on the basis of other ethical criteria, undesirable, this theory remained embryonic, but the idea that ultimately world government is the only solution was a powerful, albeit implicit, assumption in virtually all theoretical treatments of international relations.

Balance-of-power theory is the most important and influential of the traditional theories; it attracted the greatest number of thinkers in the field of international relations prior to the twentieth century, and it has achieved the highest degree of theoretical development by the efforts of both these classical theorists and the post-Second World War realists. Briefly, this theory attempts to explain why and how the state of nature does not necessarily mean a state of war. It is the *laissez-faire* theory of international relations which holds that, although anarchy entails the absence of sovereign rule, it does not entail the absence of a large measure of international order. The struggle for power into which states are forced by the security dilemma tends to lead to an overall equilibrium among them instead of inevitable conflict.

The third theory based on the traditional paradigm, collective security, also concerns itself with the problem of order and peace in the anarchic international system. It rejects the notion of an automatic 'invisible hand' leading to equilibrium, and argues that states should reach a formal agreement to take collective action against any aggressor. Thus, aggression is either deterred or punished by overwhelming power. Collective security theory can be regarded as a partial acceptance of the social contract, in which international anarchy is not abolished but only reduced and in which the separate state sovereignties are left intact. This theory was a key element in the thinking of the interwar idealist scholars.

Inis L. Claude has shown conclusively that the three theories are closely related to each other. He treats them as 'successive points along a continuum' that ranges from a minimum to a maximum of central power and authority.[7] This continuum applies to the normative objectives of the theories; the paradigmatic point of departure of all three is the idea of anarchy among sovereign states.

The few pre-1950 theories of international relations that appear to constitute exceptions to the hegemony of the traditional Machiavellian or Hobbesian paradigm belong to what Kenneth N. Waltz calls the first and second 'images' in the study of international relations, which see human nature and the internal organization of the state rather than the anarchical character of the international system (Waltz's third image) as the basic sources of international conflict and war, and to what Wight labels the 'Grotian paradigm'. On closer inspection, however, many of the seemingly extraparadigmatic theories turn out either not to deviate far from the prevailing traditional paradigm or to be only marginal to the main body of theoretical thinking in international relations. One important set of exceptions consists of the Marxist and other economic theories of imperialism. They are generally second-image (the national state level of analysis) and to some extent first-image (the individual level) theories, and fall outside the level of analysis of the international system – the level of Waltz's third image and of the traditional paradigm of international anarchy.[8]

The most significant deviation from the traditional paradigm was the view, long submerged, of Grotius and his followers that the world should be seen as a society of states with a common framework of moral and legal norms. They maintained that the normative consensus of international society was sufficiently strong and pervasive to render the image of the state of nature, at least in the Hobbesian sense of international anarchy, inapplicable.[9] The Grotian conception of world society remained a minority viewpoint among the classical theorists, but from the late 1950s on it has been reasserted with increasing frequency.

Pluralistic Security Community v. International Anarchy

Although certain aspects of the traditional paradigm had been questioned before during the twentieth century – particularly by Charles E. Merriam and his colleagues of the Chicago school in the 1930s – the crucial and most explicit challenge to it was mounted by the comparative study, published in 1957, of integration in the North Atlantic area by a team of investigators led by Deutsch.[10] Their analysis, which marked the revival of the Grotian paradigm of world society, contains three fundamental attacks on the traditional notion of international anarchy: (1) it disputes the axiomatic character of the relationship between anarchy and war; (2) it disproves the hypothesis that such an empirical relationship exists; and (3) it argues that the imposition of a common government may well decrease rather than increase the chances of peace.

First, the point of departure of Deutsch and his collaborators is a clear distinction between amalgamation and integration. An amalgamated community has 'one supreme decision-making center'; its opposite, a non-amalgamated or pluralistic community, lacks such a single center of authority. In the terminology of the traditional paradigm, the contrast is between an anarchic community and a community ruled by one sovereign government. The term integration is defined unconventionally: an integrated community, also called a security community, is 'one in which there is real assurance that the members of that community will not fight each other physically, but will settle their dispute in some other way'.[11] In traditional terms, integration means a situation of lasting peace, and the opposite, non-integration, is a condition of actual or potential war. The cross-classification of the two dichotomous dimensions of amalgamation and integration produces Deutsch's well-known 2 × 2 conceptual scheme, of which Figure 10.1 is an adapted version. In the figure, the traditional equivalents of Deutschian terminology are presented first, and the original Deutschian terms are given in parentheses.

According to the axiomatic assumption of the traditional paradigm, the basic cause of war is anarchy and hence the normal state of affairs is that of either domestic peace or international war, actual or potential: cells II and III of Figure 10.1. This axiom is reduced to a mere hypothesis by the serious examination of the possibilities raised in cells I and IV: a firm and lasting international peace and actual or potential civil war. In contrast with the traditional paradigm, Deutsch and his colleagues assume that 'integration and amalgamation overlap, but not completely', and 'there can be amalgamation without integration [i.e. civil strife], and ... integration without amalgamation [i.e. international peace]'.[12]

Secondly, the hypothesis derived from the traditional paradigm is disconfirmed by the comparative analysis of ten North Atlantic cases by Deutsch and his colleagues. To their own surprise, they found 'pluralistic security communities ... to be somewhat easier to attain and easier to preserve than their amalgamated counterparts'. In traditional terminology, this means that anarchy is a better road to peace than

	Anarchy (non-amalgamation)	Sovereign government (amalgamation)
Lasting peace (*integration*)	I International peace (*pluralistic security-community*)	II Domestic peace (*amalgamated security-community*)
Actual or potential war (*non-integration*)	III International war (*not amalgamated, not security-community*)	IV Civil war (*amalgamated but not security community*)

Figure 10.1 *Patterns of amalgamation and integration*

sovereign rule. Twelve background conditions were found to be either essential or helpful for integration. Of these conditions, nine were definitely and three possibly essential for an amalgamated security community. In contrast, 'only two or possibly three' of the twelve conditions 'were found to be very important for a pluralistic security community as well'. The other factors were helpful but not necessary conditions.[13]

Thirdly, as far as methods of integration are concerned, Deutsch and his collaborators discovered that non-amalgamation offered considerable advantages compared with amalgamation: 'we found pluralistic security communities to be a more promising approach to the elimination of war over large areas than we had thought at the outset of our inquiry'. Moreover, amalgamation can be a clearly negative factor. Efforts to achieve over-all amalgamation and the establishment of a 'monopoly of violence' tended to be 'more of a burden than a help' to the attainment of lasting peace.[14] In his international relations textbook, Deutsch warns that 'neither a common government nor common laws and institutions can ensure ... internal peace and security to a country on the verge of civil war.... Indeed, the very effort to maintain the amalgamated community or political union by force may bring on exactly that large-scale warfare which a security community was intended to prevent'.[15]

The danger of amalgamated non-security communities may be related to what I think is one of the most important and fundamental elements of Deutsch's thinking: the concept of the 'transaction–integration balance', expounded in his 1954 theoretical monograph on political community. The growth of transactions among groups of people does not automatically lead to greater integration. Instead, 'it is the volume of transactions, political, cultural, or economic, which throws a *burden* upon the institutions for peaceful adjustment or change among the participating populations'. As the volume of mutual transactions increases, the opportunities for violent conflict also increase. Hence, a crucial concern in the quest for peace is 'the race between the growing rate of transactions among populations in particular areas and the growth of integrative institutions and practices among them'.[16] Sovereign governments may have integrative capabilities, but they are also the source of political and other transactions that may be disintegrative. In this sense, amalgamation itself can hamper integration – and sovereign control can be a danger to peace.

The Significance of the New Paradigm

The rejection of the traditional paradigm of international anarchy and the assertion of the new paradigm of world politics have had both practical and theoretical consequences. In this chapter I shall focus on the theoretical significance of the new paradigm, but its implication for the all-important practical question of world peace should be stated first.

As indicated above, the logic of the traditional paradigm points to the establishment of a sovereign world government as the ultimate solution.

The new paradigm, however, leads to the prescriptive conclusion that, in Deutsch's words, 'peace *can* be had in our time', not by instituting world government but by moving toward 'a pluralistic world of limited international law, limited, but growing, international co-operation, and regional pluralistic security communities'.[17] Elsewhere, he argues specifically against world government: 'the world is not ready for political amalgamation by the merger of national governments or by the creation of powerful international administrative agencies. At best, we can hope that pluralistic security communities among nations may develop'.[18] And in order to leave no doubt about the fundamental distinction between the policy consequences of the rival paradigms, he calls for the development of 'new methods, not for having nation-states replaced by world organizations but, rather, for having them co-operate more effectively with these organizations, which is a very different thing indeed'.[19]

The theoretical significance of the new paradigm is that it has liberated the study of international relations from five limiting assumptions implied by the traditional paradigm. In an illuminating article, R. Harrison Wagner points out that the image of an anarchic world naturally leads to (1) an exclusive attention to sovereign states as the *only* important actors in international politics, and (2) the view that these states are *unified* entities. He calls the first assumption the 'state-centric model' and the second the 'state-as-actor model'.[20] In order to avoid terminological confusion, it would be preferable to name the second model the state-as-unified-actor or the state-as-unitary-actor model. Both models are closely related to what Arnold Wolfers calls the 'billiard-ball' model of international politics: 'the stage is *pre-empted* by a set of states, each *in full control* of all territory, men, and resources within its boundaries. Every state represents a closed, impermeable, and sovereign unit, completely separated from all other states'.[21]

Three further restrictive assumptions are logically implied by the traditional paradigm. (3) The view of the state as sovereign means that it is a *unique* entity and that there is a fundamental distinction between the state and other political actors and between international and domestic politics.[22] (4) Because the crucial characteristic of states is their sovereignty, they are regarded as basically *uniform*, and differentiating traits tend to be ignored; the only important exception is that they differ in terms of power – a variable of central importance in balance-of-power and collective security theories. If we can envisage a billiard table with balls of different sizes, this fourth assumption is also represented quite well by Wolfers's billiard-ball model. (5) Finally, as indicated earlier, the traditional paradigm corresponds with Waltz's third image of international conflict, and the analysis is therefore limited to the *international system level*. This restriction overlaps with some of the other assumptions, particularly the second and third ones concerning the unified and unique character of the state.

The rejection by the new theoretical paradigm of the uniqueness of the sovereign state and of the fundamental difference between international and domestic politics has had two important consequences.

First, adherents of the new paradigm no longer view the field of international relations as qualitatively different from the other fields of political science. This means that analogies from domestic politics can profitably be used at the international level of analysis; Deutsch's theory of integration, which grew out of his first major research project on nationalism and national integration, is a prime example of this.[23] Secondly, the new paradigm induces receptivity to the idea that international relations is one of the social sciences and can make use of their knowledge and methods. One of the scholarly observers of the discipline who has called attention to this important point is Chadwick F. Alger. He points out that the 'removal of the intellectual shackles imposed by the image of uniqueness has freed international relations scholars to borrow from the full storehouse of social science knowledge'.[24]

Similarly, the rejection of the state-centric or state-as-the-only-actor assumption has paved the way for the study of 'transnational' relations, which are defined by Joseph S. Nye and Robert O. Keohane as 'contacts, coalitions, and interactions across state boundaries that are not controlled by the central foreign policy organs of governments'; their definition of a 'significant actor' goes far beyond the national state actor: 'any somewhat autonomous individual or organization that controls substantial resources and participates in political relationships with other actors across state lines'.[25] The repudiation of the state-as-unified-actor approach has led to the examination of the internal processes of the foreign policy-making of governments and the formulation of such alternative models as Graham Allison's 'organizational process' and 'bureaucratic politics' models.[26] The rejection of the state-as-unified-actor assumption together with that of the state-as-uniform-actor has opened up the possibilities of investigating the domestic sources of foreign policy as well as the comparative analysis of foreign policy-making in which both national characteristics and subnational factors are taken into consideration, as exemplified by James N. Rosenau's innovative 'pre-theory of foreign policy,' in which he tries to explain the relative influence on external state behavior of internal variables like the individual idiosyncracies of decision-makers, the constraints of their roles, the governmental structure, and so on, in different types of states.[27] These changes have obviously also entailed the abandonment of the exclusive attention to the level of the international system and a much greater emphasis on the national, subnational, and individual levels of analysis.

The New Paradigm and the Behavioral Revolution

It is my contention that the new theoretical paradigm is closely linked with the new methodological approaches and perspectives established by the behavioral revolution, and that, in fact, it can be regarded as an almost integral element of the behavioral paradigm. This is undoubtedly a minority viewpoint. In most of the analyses that have been written about the traditionalist–behaviorist controversy, the different substantive images of anarchy v. world society are not mentioned at all. For instance, Michael Haas discusses four traditionalist critiques of behavioral research in international relations, all of which concern questions of method and approach.[28] Richard B. Finnegan mentions six, and Robert L. Pfaltzgraff lists eight, characteristics of behaviorally oriented scholarship, and again all of these are methodological and epistemological in nature.[29] In their introduction to the multi-authored volume on contending approaches to international relations theory, Klaus Knorr and James N. Rosenau do raise the question of whether the traditional–behavioral debate involves any substantive issues, but they conclude that it is a purely methodological debate: 'the controversy is not over the substance of international politics. It is the mode of analysis, not its subject matter, that is the central issue'.[30]

Richard Smith Beal goes one step farther, and specifically considers the extent to which behaviorists have rejected the paradigm of international anarchy. Exaggerating the instances of non-coincidence of the behavioral and Grotian paradigms, he argues that the behaviorist approaches 'have unquestionably redirected the traditional focus of international relations, but they have not forced students of the discipline to make uncompromising choices. [They have] brought procedures of systematic inquiry to the traditional perspective and not destruction to its very premises'.[31] A similar conclusion is implied by Geoffrey Goodwin's assertion that 'international relations postulates the existence of an international society whose special characteristics derive principally from the fact that it is a society in which there is no overarching system of government with a monopoly of force'. *Within* the discipline, defined in this purely traditionalist way, he discerns a number of controversies such as the debate about the appropriateness of the scientific method.[32]

On the other hand, the strong challenge to the traditional notion of international anarchy has been clearly recognized by some of the most prominent traditionally oriented theorists. Hans J. Morgenthau, for example, objects to the behaviorists' tendency to treat international conflict as a special case of social conflict in general, because it overlooks 'the paramount distinctive factor that parties to international conflict are sovereign nations with a monopoly of organized force'.[33] Raymond Aron criticizes 'statisticians such as Lewis Richardson who count acts of violence or homicide without differentiating between murderers and soldiers', and he reaffirms his faith in the traditional paradigm, which seems to him to be 'closer to reality, more in keeping with experience, more instructive, and more productive'. He adds: 'Perhaps some modernists will condemn me for this. On this matter, I am a traditionalist'.[34] And Stanley Hoffmann has recently noted that 'the paradigm which prevails in the history of political thought ... – the "realist" image of the state of war, or troubled peace, among sovereign units in a state of nature – is now under sharp attack'.[35]

The link between the behavioral approach and the new theoretical paradigm that Deutsch's work has helped to establish is shown in the most explicit and unequivocal manner in Marcel Merle's important survey of international relations theory. Merle distinguishes between the classical conception of international relations, identical with the traditional paradigm, and the 'Anglo-Saxon' conception. The label 'Anglo-Saxon' is a somewhat misleading one because, as Merle admits himself, its adherents are primarily American rather than English, and not even all American theorists can be placed in this category; scholars like Morgenthau, Hoffmann, and Claude belong to the classical conception. What is important, however, is that Merle characterizes the 'Anglo-Saxon' conception in terms of *two* general tendencies: (1) the concern with methodological rigor, and (2) the denial that international relations has any specific and characteristic attribute, particularly the attribute of international anarchy.[36]

The new methodological and theoretical paradigms do not coincide perfectly, but if the major theorists of the post-Second World War era should be classified as either Hobbesians or Grotians and as either traditionalists or behaviorists with regard to methods, there is no doubt that a strong empirical relationship would appear. To a certain extent, the paradigms are also logically related. As Alger points out in the statement cited earlier, the rejection of the unique anarchical image of international relations logically clears the way for the use of methods developed in other fields and disciplines.[37] Merle argues that this pattern of influence is mutual: the application of methods borrowed from the social sciences also naturally encourages scholars to treat international relations exactly like these other sciences.[38] An extreme but revealing example of the view that the traditional Hobbesian paradigm logically necessitates a non-scientific methodological stance is that of Martin Wight. After noting 'a kind of recalcitrance of international politics to being theorized about', he explains that theorizing about domestic politics is possible because it falls 'within the realm of normal relationships and calculable results'. But, with the typical traditionalist emphasis on the notion of international anarchy, he continues: 'What for [domestic] political theory is the extreme case (as revolution, or civil war) is for international theory the regular case.'[39] This is tantamount to saying that the fact of international anarchy necessarily entails theoretical anarchy and logically precludes methodological rigor.

Moreover, it seems to me that it is significant that in the 'new science of politics' movement of the interwar years, which was the precursor to the behavioral movement that began in the 1950s, a concern with scientific method was also combined with a repudiation of key elements of the traditional paradigm of international anarchy. As William T. R. Fox writes in his essay about the significance of the so-called Chicago school for the academic study of international relations, nation-states were, for Merriam and his colleagues, 'only one class of associations to be related to each other and to various sub-, trans-, and supranational associations'. This meant that 'the idea of keeping separate the study of domestic and international politics was no longer a valid one', and that 'any difference in the treatment of state and non-state actors in world politics' was rendered unnecessary. The rejection of the state-as-the-only-actor and the state-as-unique-actor approaches is exemplified by Merriam's conclusion that, in his own words, 'many of the common distinctions between states and other societies distinguish little on close analysis'.[40]

Obstacles to the Recognition of the New Paradigm

There are a number of reasons that can explain why the emergence of the new theoretical paradigm and its relationship with the behavioral revolution have not been recognized more widely. First, the new paradigm has a negative quality that makes it less striking than the traditional paradigm. It rejects the image of international anarchy but does not offer a very clear positive image to replace it. There are no generally accepted terms to describe the new paradigm's special characteristics. In this chapter I have used the terms 'world society' and 'world politics' but these are not sufficiently distinctive and are unable to highlight the essence of the new paradigm. Behaviorist scholars who support the new paradigm tend to do so quite inconspicuously. One example is J. David Singer's famous discussion of the level-of-analysis problem in international relations. The two levels that Singer distinguishes, the level of the national state and that of the international system, correspond to Waltz's second and third images respectively. But whereas Waltz's third image is the image of international anarchy, Singer contrasts the descriptive, explanatory, and predictive capabilities of the two levels of analysis without mentioning the sovereignty–anarchy contrast – but also without explicitly and emphatically rejecting this contrast.[41] In a later article, he describes the international scene as a global system with various subsystems; the subsystems are both state and non-state actors. There are no qualitative differences between the global system and the various subsystems, he argues, and the only sense in which the global system is unique is not that it is anarchic but that there is only one such system 'on and around the planet Earth'.[42] This is indeed the image of the new paradigm, but it is not stated emphatically.

The second reason is that too much attention has been given to the relatively few exceptional instances where adherence to the new paradigm does not coincide with the behavioral stand on methodology. In particular, it has probably caused considerable confusion that the two major protagonists in the traditional–behavioral great debate that was originally conducted in the journal *World Politics*, Hedley Bull and Morton A. Kaplan, are deviant cases as far as their views of the rival theoretical paradigms are concerned.[43] Five of Kaplan's well-known six international systems correspond with traditional models: three are different forms of balance-of-power systems, the 'hierarchical system' is a system of world government, and the 'unit veto system' is equivalent to a Hobbesian state of nature. In describing these systems, Kaplan explicitly relies on the sovereignty–anarchy contrast.[44] Bull, on the other hand, adopts the Grotian point of view and follows Deutsch's arguments when he states: 'Formidable though the classic dangers are of a plurality of sovereign states, these have to be reckoned against those inherent in the attempt to contain disparate communities within the framework of a single government'.⁴⁵

A third source of confusion has been that behaviorist scholars have continued to study the characteristics and behavior of nation-states, because states remain important actors on the international scene and also because it is easier to acquire the necessary empirical data on states than on the various non-state actors. This pragmatic choice of subject-matter does not imply an exclusively state-centric approach and even less the endorsement of the paradigm of international anarchy. Consequently, when George Modelski argues that the traditional Hobbesian image of anarchy is still 'the ruling paradigm for methodologically innovative contemporary research', he is in error – but it is an error that is understandable.⁴⁶

Fourthly, the new paradigm contains the promise of the development of theories that are applicable to both the international and national levels, because it denies that there are qualitative differences between these levels. There are some examples of such theories – Deutsch's own theory of integration provides the most striking example – but, on the whole, this promise has not yet been fulfilled.⁴⁷ Harry Eckstein is undoubtedly right when he notes 'the paucity of theories, or even mere theoretical approaches or frameworks, that apply both to polities and to their relations . . . except at very general and uninformative levels'. But it is not necessarily correct and, in any case, it is premature to regard this as a demonstration of the fact that there are 'manifest taxonomic differences between polities and international systems'.⁴⁸

The fifth and final source of confusion is that, although the logic of the new paradigm casts grave doubts on the desirability of world government or regional amalgamated communities, the emotional appeal of the ideal of world and regional amalgamations has remained strong, even among those who are clearly not traditionalists. Peace research scholars generally adhere to the new paradigm; they tend to believe that international conflict can be understood better in terms of intergroup conflict in general than in terms of the traditional emphasis on the uniqueness of conflict among sovereign states. It is therefore interesting to note that one of the leading peace researchers, Johan Galtung, has nevertheless retained a clear preference for amalgamated instead of pluralistic approaches. In a recent review of Galtung's extensive writings, Kenneth E. Boulding credits Galtung with the following important contribution to conflict theory: 'the distinction . . . between associative solutions to conflict situations and dissociative solutions'. This distinction is similar to the difference between amalgamated and pluralistic security communities: 'Associative solutions involve some kind of agreement, some merging of identity of the conflicting parties, perhaps some superordinate structure or organization. . . . Dissociative solutions are those which involve property or boundaries, good fences making good neighbors, keeping people away from each other, and so on'. Boulding points out that although Galtung is not opposed to dissociation in principle, 'he clearly has a very strong prejudice in favor of the associative solutions'. This stance is particularly remarkable because, as Boulding notes, it is inconsistent with Galtung's other biases as well: 'associative solutions to conflict tend to involve hierarchy, dominance, inequality, and a great many other things which he does not like'.[49]

Deutsch's Role in the Paradigm Shift: Alternative Interpretations

In the previous section, I have tried to give explanations for the fact that neither the new paradigm itself nor its place in the behavioral movement has been adequately recognized. There are two further questions that must be answered. Why has Deutsch's contribution to the emergence of the new paradigm not been given the same kind of recognition that he has fully and deservedly received for his role as a methodological innovator? And how can it be explained that Deutsch has been portrayed as a traditionalist, instead of as a theoretical innovator, by some analysts?

Of course, Deutsch's intellectual leadership has not escaped notice altogether. One scholar who has forcefully called attention to the paradigmatic novelty of Deutsch's writings on integration and to the contrast between this work and the traditional emphasis on power and the balancing of power is Hedley Bull. As expected, Bull is no admirer of what he calls Deutsch's 'fetish for measurement [and for the] indiscriminate collection of data about international politics', but he argues that

> his studies have raised vital questions which previously were left unasked [as to] what accounts for the fact that in some international relationships the expectation of war has disappeared on both sides, whereas in other international relationships it has not.... The view that in the case of international groups such as the English-speaking nations or the Scandinavian nations, within which there appears to be no expectation that conflicts will be resolved by war (the groupings which Deutsch speaks of as 'pluralistic security communities'), the cohesion and persistence of the grouping are to be explained in terms of 'political community' rather than in terms of the workings of the system of powers, is one pregnant with implications of a general theory of international relations.[50]

Similarly, Keohane and Nye contrast the traditional description of world politics as a 'Hobbesian situation in which independent units called nation-states are locked into patterns of fundamental conflict' with 'the pioneering work of Karl W. Deutsch and his associates', especially their 1957 book on integration in the North Atlantic area: the thinking initiated by Deutsch 'led scholars quite far from the Realists' assumptions.... The analysis of integration processes tended also to undermine another basic tenet of conventional analysis: that students of world politics should limit their focus to nation-states and their interactions. The "cybernetic" approach pioneered by Deutsch focused largely on transactions among societies and on changes in public attitudes within societies'.[51]

The first reason why – notwithstanding the above clear statements by Bull, Keohane, and Nye, as well as the analysis by Puchala in his contribution to this volume – Deutsch's role in the paradigm change has found scant acknowledgement is that in one respect the new paradigm closely resembles the traditional paradigm. Deutsch gives the highest priority to questions of peace and security, and these also constitute the dependent variable in the traditional outlook. Although Deutsch's explanatory variables are completely different from the traditional explanations in terms of sovereignty and anarchy, the common concern with the attainment of peace gives the rival paradigms a superficial resemblance.

Secondly, much of the research that has been done on political integration since the 1950s has focused on the patterns of co-operation and unification in Western Europe. The subject of principal interest to scholars of European integration has been amalgamation rather than 'integration' in the Deutschian sense: the development of joint capabilities for providing a variety of governmental services instead of the attainment of regional peace. Because Deutsch's concept of integration has lacked direct relevance in this limited geographical context, it has frequently been neglected. As Robert J. Lieber writes, if in the research on European integration 'the focus of attention is merely upon the pluralistic security community, this approach may be of limited use, for Western Europe has constituted such an arrangement since soon after the Second World War, and concentration upon this relationship does not tell us very much'.[52]

The third explanation for the relative neglect of Deutsch's crucial role in the establishment of the new paradigm is that the notion of security community has turned out to be resistant to precise operationalization, whereas Deutsch has been quite successful in formulating operational definitions and indicators for a host of other concepts. Consequently, the latter contributions have received the greatest scholarly acclaim and attention. It is ironic – and, it should be added, in accordance with the traditionalists' doubts about the value of methodological rigor – that the concept of security community is, in Nye's words 'not only one of the ... most intriguing from a value point of view but also one of the most difficult to make operational'.[53] Deutsch states optimistically: 'The test for ... dependable expectations of peace is simple. It is that there are no major fortifications, bases, or deployment of troops, ships, planes, or missiles in any ... country [belonging to a security community] directed against the others'.[54] But he does not specify how 'major' fortifications and so on should be measured. And the biggest problem is how to identify the country or countries against which war preparations may be directed.

Two Canadian political scientists, Naomi Black and Charles Pentland, have explicitly argued against the proposition that Deutsch has been the leading opponent of the traditional paradigm of international anarchy. In their eyes, he is more of a Hobbesian than a Grotian thinker.

Pentland asserts that Deutsch's pluralist approach to integration has close affinities with the realist school of thought. They share 'the belief that the nation-state is both the central fact of modern political life and the central focus of all political analysis'. Moreover, he writes, both Deutsch and the realists reject 'dramatic therapeutic approaches to peace' and, instead, place 'a great premium on the traditional virtues of diplomacy'.[55]

As far as the former statement is concerned, it is true that Deutsch is not a foe of the nation-state, but he cannot be said to be preoccupied with it; on the contrary, as was pointed out earlier, his new paradigmatic perspective logically entails the outright rejection of the state-centric model. The latter statement has a degree of validity but it should be pointed out that Deutsch and the realists diverge sharply in their conceptions about what the 'traditional virtues of diplomacy' consist of. For the realists, the skillful balancing of power in order to deter or counter aggressive behavior is the main concern, whereas Deutsch maintains that 'dependable co-ordination cannot be built by deterrence and bargaining alone. A world of deterrent powers, a world of bargaining powers will, as a total system, be ungovernable'.[56] The North Atlantic area study also found that 'contrary to the "balance of power" theory, security communities seem to develop most frequently around cores of strength' – in other words, in situations of imbalance rather than equilibrium.[57] Moreover, it is interesting to note that in the well-known article on bipolar and multipolar balances of power, co-authored by Deutsch and Singer, the analysis is entirely in terms of interaction opportunities and attention patterns – in sharp contrast with the usual emphasis on combinations and recombinations of power in the traditional balance-of-power literature.[58]

Finally, Naomi Black presents an unusual reinterpretation of both the traditional and the Deutschian paradigms. She argues that the traditional approach to international politics is to view it as 'defective domestic politics' – a difference of degree rather than a qualitative distinction. The novelty of Deutsch's work is his emphasis on the domestic–international contrast, exemplified by his finding that 'integration does not operate in the same way within and between national communities'.[59] This interpretation is so utterly at variance with the views that I have presented in this chapter that it is difficult to present new arguments against it. One additional strong counter-argument, however, is that Deutsch's concept of sovereignty, instead of entailing a sharp boundary between domestic and international politics, is a relative and fluid concept. In his book on nationalism he distinguishes between the 'legal form' and the more important 'political substance' of sovereignty and he emphasizes that 'there are shades and gradations of sovereignty ... on both sides of the legal borderline'.[60] The strict classical notion of sovereignty thus gives way, as Ghita Ionescu suggests, to the concept of 'interpenetration of different degrees of autonomy'.[61]

Moreover, it seems to me that Naomi Black is mistaken when she claims that there are fundamental differences between Deutsch's theory of national integration and his theory of international integration. Of course, a number of differences can be identified, but these should not be exaggerated. The consensus among international relations scholars, with which I find myself in agreement, is that, as James E. Dougherty and Robert L. Pfaltzgraff conclude, there is a clear isomorphism in Deutsch's theory 'between the process of community building both at the national level and beyond the nation-state', and that, in Johan K. De Vree's words, a conspicuous characteristic of Deutsch's integration theory is its 'extremely wide scope and generality'.[62]

In fact, as I have argued above, one of the reasons why Deutsch's theory of integration is so important is that it is the major example of a *general* theory in political science that is applicable not only at the international level but also at the national and subnational levels. This aspect of the theory is, of course, closely related to the principal thesis of this chapter: the main theoretical significance of Deutsch's work on integration is that it must be regarded as the single most important contribution to the paradigmatic reorientation that emerged from the theoretical revolution in international relations.

Notes: Chapter 10

I should like to express my gratitude for the many helpful comments and suggestions that I received from my former colleagues at the University of Leiden, Leo M. van der Mey and Alfred van Staden, and from the editors of this volume, Richard L. Merritt and Bruce M. Russett.

1 See Arend Lijphart, 'The structure of the theoretical revolution in international relations', *International Studies Quarterly*, vol. 18, no. 1 (March 1974), pp. 41–74; and *idem*, 'International relations theory: great debates and lesser debates', *International Social Science Journal*, vol. 26, no. 1 (1974), pp. 11–21.
2 Robert L. Pfaltzgraff, Jr, 'Karl Deutsch and the study of political science', *Political Science Reviewer*, vol. 2 (Fall 1972), pp. 90–111, esp. p. 90.
3 This section is largely drawn from my two articles cited in note 1.
4 Two excellent discussions of Martin Wight's ideas are Hedley Bull, 'Martin Wight and the theory of international relations: The Second Martin Wight Memorial Lecture', *British Journal of International Studies*, vol. 2, no. 2 (July 1976), pp. 101–16; and Brian Porter, 'Patterns of thought and practice: Martin Wight's "International Theory"', in *The Reason of States: A Study in International Political Theory*, ed. Michael Donelan (London: Allen & Unwin, 1978), pp. 64–74.
5 Thomas Hobbes, 'The state of nature', in *World Politics: The Writings of Theorists and Practitioners, Classical and Modern*, ed. Arend Lijphart, 2nd edn (Boston, Mass.: Allyn & Bacon, 1971), p. 53.
6 Jean-Jacques Rousseau, 'The state of war', in *The Theory of International Relations*, ed. M. G. Forsyth, H. M. A. Keens-Soper, and P. Savigear (London: Allen & Unwin, 1970), p. 170.
7 Inis L. Claude, Jr, *Power and International Relations* (New York: Random House, 1962), p. 9.
8 Kenneth N. Waltz, *Man, the State and War: A Theoretical Analysis* (New York: Columbia University Press, 1959), pp. 137–56. Wight classifies the Marxists in the third of his basic categories, the Kantian paradigm; see Porter, 'Patterns of thought and practice', pp. 66–8.
9 See Hedley Bull, 'The Grotian conception of international society', in *Diplomatic Investigations: Essays in the Theory of International Politics* ed. Herbert Butterfield and Martin Wight (London: Allen & Unwin, 1966), pp. 51–73

10 Karl W. Deutsch *et al.*, *Political Community and the North Atlantic Area: International Organization in the Light of Historical Experience* (Princeton, NJ: Princeton University Press, 1957).
11 ibid., pp. 5–6.
12 ibid., p. 7.
13 ibid., pp. 29, 58, 66.
14 ibid., pp. 30–1, 105.
15 Karl W. Deutsch, *The Analysis of International Relations* (Englewood Cliffs, NJ: Prentice-Hall, 1968), pp. 193–4.
16 Karl W. Deutsch, *Political Community at the International Level: Problems of Definition and Measurement* (Garden City, NY: Doubleday, 1954), pp. 39–40; emphasis added.
17 Karl W. Deutsch, *Nationalism and Its Alternatives* (New York: Knopf, 1969), p. 190. One problem that this approach does not solve is what the relations are, or should be, *between* the different regional pluralistic security communities. The prospects for peace in an increasingly interdependent world remain uncertain unless there is a global security community, but a further problem is whether Deutsch's conclusions concerning the regional level can be transferred intact to the global level.
18 Karl W. Deutsch, 'The impact of communications upon international relations theory', in *Theory of International Relations: The Crisis of Relevance*, ed. Abdul A. Said (Englewood Cliffs, NJ: Prentice-Hall, 1968), p. 92.
19 Karl W. Deutsch, 'National integration: some concepts and research approaches', *Jerusalem Journal of International Relations*, vol. 2, no. 4 (Summer 1977), p. 18.
20 R. Harrison Wagner, 'Dissolving the state: three recent perspectives on international relations', *International Organization*, vol. 28, no. 3 (Summer 1974), pp. 436–8. He argues, however, that these assumptions are not 'strictly implied' by the notion of international anarchy (p. 438).
21 Arnold Wolfers, 'The actors in international politics', in *Theoretical Aspects of International Relations*, ed. William T. R. Fox (Notre Dame, Ind.: University of Notre Dame Press, 1959), pp. 100–1; emphasis added.
22 P. Dale Dean, Jr, and John A. Vasquez derive this assumption as well as the state-centric assumption from the 'power politics or Realist paradigm', and hence indirectly from the paradigm of international anarchy; see their 'From power politics to issue politics: bipolarity and multipolarity in light of a new paradigm', *Western Political Quarterly*, vol. 29, no. 1 (March 1976), pp. 16–17. See also John W. Burton *et al.*, *The Study of World Society: A London Perspective* (Pittsburgh, Pa: International Studies Association, International Studies Occasional Paper No. 1, 1974), pp. 30–1.
23 Karl W. Deutsch, *Nationalism and Social Communication: An Inquiry into the Foundations of Nationality* (Cambridge, Mass.: MIT: and New York: Wiley, 1953).
24 Chadwick F. Alger, 'Trends in international relations research', in *A Design for International Relations Research: Scope, Theory, Methods, and Relevance*, ed. Norman D. Palmer, American Academy of Political and Social Science Monograph No. 10, Philadelphia, Pa, October 1970, p. 25.
25 Joseph S. Nye, Jr, and Robert O. Keohane, 'Transnational relations and world politics: an introduction', *International Organization*, vol. 25, no. 3 (Summer 1971), pp. 331, 344–5.
26 Graham Allison, *The Essence of Decision: Explaining the Cuban Missile Crisis* (Boston, Mass.: Little, Brown, 1971).
27 James N. Rosenau, 'Pre-theories and theories of foreign policy', in *Approaches to Comparative and International Politics*, ed. R. Barry Farrell (Evanston, Ill.: Northwestern University Press, 1966), pp. 27–92; and *idem* (ed.), *Domestic Sources of Foreign Policy* (New York: The Free Press, 1967).
28 Michael Haas, 'Bridge-building in international relations: a neotraditional plea', *International Studies Quarterly*, vol. 11, no. 4 (December 1967), pp. 320–38.
29 Richard B. Finnegan, 'International relations: the disputed search for method', *Review of Politics*, vol. 34, no. 1 (January 1972), pp. 40–66; and Robert L. Pfaltzgraff, Jr, 'International studies in the 1970s', *International Studies Quarterly*, vol. 15, no. 1 (March 1971), pp. 104–28. See also Andrew Mack, 'World Politics and the behavioral revolution', *Politics*, vol. 12, no. 1 (May 1977), pp. 167–74.

30 Klaus Knorr and James N. Rosenau, 'Tradition and science in the study of international politics', in *Contending Approaches to International Politics*, ed. Klaus Knorr and James N. Rosenau (Princeton, NJ: Princeton University Press, 1969), pp. 13–14.
31 Richard Smith Beal, 'A contra-Kuhnian view of the discipline's growth', in *In Search of Global Patterns*, ed. James N. Rosenau (New York: The Free Press, 1976), p. 160.
32 Geoffrey Goodwin, 'International relations and international studies', in *The Year Book of World Affairs 1973*, ed. George W. Keeton and Georg Schwarzenberger (London: Stevens, 1973), Vol. 27, pp. 383–4.
33 Hans J. Morgenthau, 'Common sense and theories of international relations', in *Theory and Reality in International Relations*, ed. John C. Farrell and Asa P. Smith (New York: Columbia University Press, 1967), p. 26.
34 Raymond Aron, 'What is a theory of international relations?', in *Theory and Reality*, ed. Farrell and Smith, pp. 12–13.
35 Stanley Hoffmann, review of Fred I. Greenstein and Nelson W. Polsby (eds), *Handbook of Political Science* (Reading, Mass.: Addison-Wesley, 1975), Vol. 8, *International Politics*, in *American Political Science Review*, vol. 71, no. 4 (December 1977), p. 1635.
36 Marcel Merle, *Sociologie des Rélations Internationales* (Paris: Dalloz, 1974), pp. 89–91, 125. The third basic trend in international relations theory outlined by Merle is the Marxist conception.
37 See note 24.
38 Merle, *Sociologie des Rélations Internationales*, p. 125.
39 Martin Wight, 'Why is there no international theory?', in *Diplomatic Investigations*, ed. Butterfield and Wight, p. 33.
40 William T. R. Fox, 'Pluralism, the science of politics, and the world system', *World Politics*, vol. 27, no. 4 (July 1975), pp. 598–9. See also Albert Somit and Joseph Tanenhaus, *The Development of American Political Science: From Burgess to Behavioralism* (Boston, Mass.: Allyn & Bacon, 1967), pp. 109–17.
41 J. David Singer, 'The level-of-analysis problem in international relations', in *The International System: Theoretical Essays*, ed. Klaus Knorr and Sidney Verba (Princeton, NJ: Princeton University Press, 1961), pp. 77–92.
42 J. David Singer, 'The global system and its subsystems: a developmental view', in *Linkage Politics: Essays on the Convergence of National and International Systems*, ed. James N. Rosenau (New York: The Free Press, 1969), p. 30.
43 See Hedley Bull, 'International theory: the case for a classical approach', and Morton A. Kaplan, 'The new great debate: traditionalism *v.* science in international relations', in *Contending Approaches*, ed. Knorr and Rosenau, pp. 20–38, 39–61.
44 Morton A. Kaplan, *System and Process in International Politics* (New York: Wiley, 1957), p. 49.
45 Hedley Bull, 'Society and anarchy in international relations', in *Diplomatic Investigations*, ed. Butterfield and Wight, p. 50.
46 George Modelski, 'The promise of geocentric politics', *World Politics*, vol. 22, no. 4 (July 1970), p. 617.
47 A few promising possibilities are suggested by Bruce M. Russett, *Trends in World Politics* (New York: Macmillan, 1965), pp. 55–66.
48 Harry Eckstein, 'Authority patterns: a structural basis for political inquiry', *American Political Science Review*, vol. 67, no. 4 (December 1973), p. 1158.
49 Kenneth E. Boulding, 'Twelve friendly quarrels with Johan Galtung', *Journal of Peace Research*, vol. 14, no. 1 (1977), pp. 82–3.
50 Hedley Bull, 'The theory of international politics, 1919–1969', in *The Aberystwyth Papers: International Politics 1919–1969*, ed. Brian Porter (London: Oxford University Press, 1972), pp. 42–3. See also Hedley Bull, *The Anarchical Society: A Study of Order in World Politics* (London: Macmillan, 1977), pp. 283–5.
51 Robert O. Keohane and Joseph S. Nye, Jr, 'International interdependence and integration', in *Handbook of Political Science*, ed. Greenstein and Polsby, Vol. 8, pp. 363–5.
52 Robert J. Lieber, *Theory and World Politics*, St Antony's Publications No. 6 (London: Allen & Unwin, 1973), p. 58. On the confusion in the integration literature about what should be the dependent variable, see Bruce M. Russett, 'Transactions,

community, and international political integration', *Journal of Common Market Studies*, vol. 9, no. 3 (March 1971), pp. 224–45.
53 Joseph S. Nye, 'Comparative regional integration: concept and measurement', *International Organization*, vol. 22, no. 4 (Autumn 1968), p. 873.
54 Deutsch, 'The impact of communications upon international relations theory', in *Theory of International Relations*, ed. Said, p. 92. See also *idem*, *Political Community at the International Level*, pp. 33–4.
55 Charles Pentland, *International Theory and European Integration* (London: Faber, 1973), pp. 35–6.
56 Karl W. Deutsch, 'Between sovereignty and integration: conclusion', *Government and Opposition*, vol. 9, no. 1 (Winter 1974), p. 115.
57 Deutsch *et al.*, *Political Community and the North Atlantic Area*, p. 28.
58 Karl W. Deutsch and J. David Singer, 'Multipolar power systems and international stability', *World Politics*, vol. 16, no. 3 (April 1964), pp. 390–406.
59 Naomi Black, 'Inside the elephant: intellectual leadership in the study of international relations', *International Journal*, vol. 31, no. 4 (Autumn 1976), pp. 605, 608.
60 Deutsch, *Nationalism and Social Communication*, p. 53.
61 Ghita Ionescu, 'Between sovereignty and integration: introduction', *Government and Opposition*, vol. 9, no. 1 (Winter 1974), p. 5.
62 James E. Doughetry and Robert L. Pfaltzgraff, Jr, *Contending Theories of International Relations* (Philadelphia, Pa: Lippincott, 1971), p. 286; and Johan K. De Vree, *Political Integration: The Formation of Theory and Its Problems* (The Hague: Mouton, 1972), p. 187.

11

Domestic Structures and Political Strategies: Austria in an Interdependent World

PETER J. KATZENSTEIN

A preference for political autonomy in an interdependent and peaceful world has preoccupied Karl Deutsch in his research and teaching during the last forty years. Because they were inimical to his vision, Deutsch disliked xenophobic nationalism and political isolation as much as unworldly internationalism and premature political unification. From the perspective of contemporary Austria, the successor to the Habsburg Empire which was Deutsch's country of birth, this chapter discusses the possibilities which continue to exist for maintaining political autonomy in an increasingly interdependent world.[1]

In his contribution to this volume Donald Puchala has pointed out that the particular strength of Deutsch's approach to questions of integration was its focus on mass attitudes and mass behavior. What Puchala calls the motivational and political dynamics of the integration process, in contrast, have received much less attention. In a number of pathbreaking and controversial articles on changing trends in international interdependence, Deutsch and his associates established a putative relation between the size of the international sector of a country and the distribution of power among groups in domestic politics. They argued that 'each political interest group has a power base, or a power potential, somewhat proportional to the share of the national income which the members of its constituency command',[2] and they concluded that the size of the international sector was probably declining in the twentieth century. 'Clearly, if true, this "law of the declining importance of foreign trade" would have a direct bearing on the relative weight of economic interest groups directly engaged in international trade, as against other interest groups whose main and most immediate concerns are concentrated within the domestic economy.'[3] Although Deutsch took into account other variables affecting a group's power potential, these variables remained largely unexplored perhaps because the underlying assumptions informing Deutsch's view of domestic politics were drawn from the theory of pluralist democracy.[4]

Within Deutsch's framework Austria offers an interesting case study for two reasons. First, in the light of Deutsch and Eckstein's finding of a declining international sector the positive association between trade dependence and per capita income among the world's small states is surprising. According to Peter Lloyd this anomaly 'is no doubt based on the higher level of trade in manufactures among higher industrial countries'.[5] Secondly, Austria shares with most other small European states a distinct form of domestic politics which deviates from the precepts of American pluralism. In short, inspired by recent research on questions of international interdependence and political economy, this chapter focuses on the motivational and political dynamics of one small facet of current world politics.

In its focus on the intimate relations between domestic and international structures this chapter resembles Rokkan's contribution to this volume. Its emphasis on the political autonomy of a small European state does not neglect the political and economic constraints which are central to the analysis of political realism and dependency theory. In their analysis of the international political economy Gilpin and Krasner, among others, have singled out the international distribution of power as an essential precondition affecting national strategies of foreign economic policy.[6] Dependency theorists discussed elsewhere in this volume by Duvall et al. have, on the other hand, focused on the shackles which world capitalism imposes on national strategies.[7] But these contrasting perspectives downgrade a puzzling fact which provides the starting point for this paper. Austria's political strategies in international and domestic markets offer areas of choice and potential for change which can be explained neither by the enduring features of the international state system nor by the encompassing logic of world capitalism.

In an era of declining American influence, differences in domestic structures are of increasing importance in explaining the divergent foreign economic policies of advanced industrial states.[8] This chapter focuses therefore on Austria's domestic structure as a critically important determinant of her political strategies in international markets. This emphasis contradicts the conventional wisdom. A recent review article of the literature on small states, for example, concludes that 'a common feature of the studies on economic problems of small states presented here is that they concentrate on the external conditions, apparently regarded as the dominating determinants for the policy of small states in their foreign economic relations. Small states have, however, reacted in different ways to similar external conditions and one reason for this could be the internal structure of the small states themselves, a factor wholly neglected in the studies'.[9] In terms of their political strategies and structures, Austria and the other small European states hold a distinct place among the weak or small in world politics.[10] In her political strategies Austria, like the other small European states, offers a centrist solution (a modified liberalism) and eschews political strategies both of the left (Leninism, self-reliance or selective dissociation) and of the right (mercantilism and imperialism).

Austria's strategy is conditioned not by democratic 'pluralism' but by the 'consociationalism' of her political parties and the 'neo-corporatism' of her interest groups which according to Lijphart and others characterize the small European states more generally.[11] During the last two decades this strategy has avoided sole reliance on either the political intervention of the state bureaucracy or the unrestricted play of market forces. Instead Austria's strategy is geared to the principle of social compensation. To the working class the strategy has assured low rates of unemployment; to Austria's business community low rates of inflation; and to the general public political stability as well as economic prosperity. Today Austria's well-tested political formula and successful economic performance is challenged by an economic crisis in international and domestic markets which a growing number of policy-makers no longer regard as cyclical. Possible changes in Austria's political strategy may have only a minor impact on the current international regime governing the economic relations between states; but they would have a lasting effect on Austria's domestic structure of power.

International interdependence, domestic structures, and political strategies are influenced strongly by a country's historical evolution. Although he is interested in a different aspect of politics, Rokkan's explanation of Austrian fascism in this volume is in basic agreement with the analysis of Alexander Gerschenkron. Austria's weak development of capitalist instincts and market structures in a process of late industrialization in the nineteenth century was compensated for by a concentration of economic and political power in the hands of banks and government bureaucracies at the national level.[12] And the modernization of the Austrian state bureaucracy in the late eighteenth century as well as the organization of Austria's mass parties and ancillary interest groups in the late nineteenth century have also shaped the country's domestic structures until the present. By way of contrast, a still later process of industrialization in Latin America in the twentieth century assured foreign firms a much greater influence in domestic politics. The strategy of social compensation which is characteristic of the Austrian experience requires a concentration of political power at the national level. It is not feasible in Latin America where that concentration of power is centered on an international coalition of multinational firms, state bureaucracies and segments of the national bourgeoisie.

Only for the purposes of this chapter is Austria characterized as a typical representative of the small European states. Within the European context Austria's domestic structure of power reveals its own distinct mixture of political features. Its dominant social coalition integrates organized labor and constrains the business community in numerous ways. Austria's policy networks are centralized and the differentiation between the public and the private sector is small. In Switzerland, by way of contrast, organized labor is largely excluded from the dominant coalition, the business community enjoys an unchallenged position, policy networks are decentralized, and the differentiation between the public and the private sector is large.[13] Among Europe's small states social democracy and *laissez-faire* capitalism are just two political formulas which elucidate Deutsch's notion of the compatibility of political autonomy with international interdependence and lend some support to his hope for the possible emergence of a peaceful community of states without world government.

Political Strategies at Home and Abroad

In the postwar era Austria's strategy for managing the mechanisms by which the Austrian economy is linked to international markets has consisted of a slow and cautious opening of domestic markets to foreign competition, a half-hearted effort at strengthening Austria's export drive on international markets, and dilatory efforts at improving the structure of Austrian industry. Under the impact of the energy crisis and the prolonged economic recession after 1973, the Austrian state bureaucracy is beginning to assert itself in fashioning an Austrian export strategy. But these recent political initiatives have been constrained by Austria's domestic structure of power.

Austria's strategy in international markets has been based on full employment and a stable currency as the two overriding objectives. In the climate of economic growth which prevailed in the 1950s and 1960s both objectives could be met. Austria's labor market became sufficiently tight in the early 1960s that foreign workers were, for the first time in 1962, admitted in greater numbers. Until 1976 when the Austrian government, like most other West European countries, began to apply tighter restrictions on the influx of immigrant labor, the proportion of foreign workers increased steadily.[14] This was considered an effective weapon to alleviate inflationary pressures.

Fear of inflation was also an important stimulus for liberalizing imports. For example, when the German mark was revalued in 1969, the Austrian government countered the inflationary effect on the Austrian schilling with a number of specific policy measures, among them the liberalization of imports in about seventy product categories.[15] The liberalization of trade with Eastern Europe in the middle 1970s was similarly motivated at least in part by a fear of inflation.[16] Although priorities may be changing in the coming years, until recently in Austria, as in West Germany, fear of inflation rather than creation of new export markets or the rejuvenation of Austria's industrial structure was the major stimulant to the liberalization of imports. The objectives of maintaining full employment and a low inflation rate thus set the parameters for the intersection of commercial, investment, and industrial policy from which the Austrian strategy of managing international interdependence has been fashioned.

Compared to its traditional protectionism dating back to the beginning of the nineteenth century, Austria's strategy of gradually liberalizing its import trade during the last two decades constitutes an important break with past policies. But compared to Western Europe (and in particular its smaller states), which moved to limited forms of economic integration in the 1950s and 1960s, Austria's liberalization strategy is distinguished by hesitation and delay. Numerous studies conducted over the last twenty-five years show Austrian tariffs, on the whole, to be comparable to those of the larger West European states, but considerably above those of the Benelux countries, Switzerland, and the Scandinavian states. Among the small states of Western Europe, Austrian protectionism is an anomaly.[17] Liberalization forced itself upon the Austrians by the institutionalization of a liberal international economy in the form of GATT and regional economic integration in the EEC and EFTA. But the Austrian government succeeded in delaying for a long time the full impact of foreign competition, especially on its consumer goods industry. Thus early efforts at import liberalization in 1953 were carefully designed to leave domestic producers unaffected by growing imports. The calculation of Austrian tariffs based on the value, rather than weight, of imported goods resulted in 1958 in an increase in the average value of tariffs.[18] That Austria had a very detailed list of products in her tariff code facilitated pressure for high protection by groups or industries potentially affected by import competition.[19] In the 1960s and 1970s Austria's liberalization strategy was accelerated greatly under the impetus of joining first EFTA and then, on a qualified basis, the EC. Furthermore, because it wished to strengthen the process of détente and hoped to secure new export markets, Austria became the first OECD country which voluntarily extended GATT regulations to its trade with Eastern Europe in 1975.[20] And like other advanced industrial states, Austria has granted less developed countries preferential access to Austrian markets. For the first time since the 1860s, this slow evolution of policy has led Austria to adopt the liberal stance in international markets which has been a distinctive feature of other small states such as Switzerland and Sweden.

A traditional scarcity of capital and the urgent need to reconstruct Austrian industry with Marshall Plan aid after 1945 encouraged a much earlier Austrian participation in the liberalization of capital markets.[21] A stable political climate, low wages, and a strategic location close to Eastern European markets have ensured Austria of a steady stream of direct foreign investment over the past two decades, especially from the Federal Republic, the United States, and Switzerland. Political unease about the extent of direct foreign investment has been more than offset by economic advantages. Due to direct foreign investment, some traditional industrial sectors, such as the garment industry, have rapidly expanded in the 1960s. And a policy of limiting the foreign indebtedness of the Austrian state was reversed when mounting budget deficits in the middle 1970s led to a fivefold increase in gross capital imports from 6 billion schillings in 1972 to 30 billion schillings in 1975.[22]

The instruments through which Austria's strategy of import liberalization has been implemented do not, however, relinquish political control over imports once and for all. Despite the elimination of virtually all quotas in the 1960s, the legal foundations for centralized state intervention in the control of foreign trade continue to exist in the 1974 amendment to the Trade Act of 1968.[23] And, as is true of others, the Austrian government has at its disposal legislation which protects Austrian producers against foreign dumping (*Anti-Dumping Gesetz*) and also ensures orderly market arrangements (*Antimarktstörungsgesetz*). But since the typical mode of Austrian politics operates not by administrative decree but by political consensus, neither of these two laws has ever been used. Austria's stocking industry, for example, in 1977 was threatened by imports from Israel, France, and Italy which sold at only a fraction of Austrian production costs. Five thousand jobs in this industry were in danger. Faced by mounting political pressures from both business and unions, the Minister of Trade and Industry responded not by imposing a quota or price guidelines; instead he worked out a gentleman's agreement with Austria's importers which entitled them to the import of one inexpensive pair of stockings for every five domestically produced pairs. Such flexibility in its political arrangements at home made the Austrian government an easy convert to the incremental advances of politically organized trade in international markets in the middle 1970s. By early 1977 the Austrian government had negotiated eleven voluntary export trade agreements, mostly with textile producers in the Third World; and the Austrian government was a strong proponent of the renewal of the International Textile Agreement which was renegotiated at the end of 1977.[24] Furthermore, in its recently liberalized trade relations with Eastern Europe, Austria has insisted on what amounts to an escape clause should bilateral negotiations fail on particularly sensitive import items. In its gradual import liberalization the Austrian state has thus retained an informal political supervision of trading arrangements both at home and abroad, which may be as effective in protecting particularly exposed industrial sectors or products as any of the formal legal controls which the government so far has refrained from using.

The expansion of Austrian exports in growing world markets has been a corollary to the strategy of import liberalization. After 1945 Austria quickly re-established commercial relations with an increasing number of its traditional trading partners in Western Europe. Between 1945 and 1953, it concluded twenty-seven bilateral trade treaties with countries covering about three-quarters of its total trade; and the Austrian government joined the GATT in 1950. But the underlying orientation and overall economic consequence was one of securing rather than enlarging traditional export markets.[25] This orientation was also very evident in the Austrian debate over European integration.[26] Under the mounting pressures of a prolonged economic downturn and increasing international competition since 1973, there are, however, several signs which suggest that Austria is now beginning to gear up to a more concerted and sustained drive on export markets.

This shift is illustrated by recent changes in Austria's export credit and insurance programs. Although the establishment of these programs dates back to the early 1950s, and although they have been continuously enlarged and modified, particularly between 1964 and 1967, recent changes in both complexity and scale have been dramatic.[27] There exist now twenty different guarantee or insurance programs which are supervised by four different institutions, which tightly link the exporter, his bank ('Hausbank'), the Austrian Control Bank (Österreichische

Kontrollbank), the Austrian National Bank, the Federal Economic Chamber, and the Finance Ministry.[28] Between 1974 and 1975 export guarantees underwritten by the government doubled and covered roughly one-third of Austria's total exports and two-thirds of exports to Austria's non-European partners. In 1967, by way of contrast, only 9 per cent of Austria's total export trade had been so covered.[29] Government credit facilities for exports also increased sharply in 1974–5. And with the rapid deterioration of Austria's trade balance in 1976–7, the government has increased further its financial guarantees (from 60 to 80 billion schillings) and export credits (from 30 to 40 billion schillings). In January 1977 further government support measures for Austrian exports were announced.[30]

These measures have been supplemented by an export drive on Eastern European markets by which the Austrian government has tried to compensate for the erosion of Austria's position in the markets of Western Europe.[31] In consultation with Austria's business community, the federal government has assisted Austrian companies and trade associations in concluding numerous contracts with state trading corporations in Eastern Europe. The Federal Economic Chamber has organized special export promotion drives in Austria to increase Eastern trade.[32] Most important, the Austrian government greatly extended the credit facilities (*Kreditrahmenverträge*) open to its trading partners in the East. Poland, in particular, has been favored with total credits amounting to more than 15·5 billion Austrian schillings in 1975 and 1976. Although normal international practice reserves such credits for the trade in investment goods only, Austria extended long-term credit for the purchase of Austrian consumer goods as well.[33]

Since the late 1960s, furthermore, Austria has begun, on a small scale, to export capital. The protectionism of the Habsburg Empire in the nineteenth century and the expropriation of Austrian subsidiaries in the successor states in the twentieth century have left the Second Republic with virtually no firms engaged in international production. And as late as the middle 1960s, Austria's traditional capital shortage prompted occasional criticism of export support measures as ill-advised attempts of draining the country of capital badly needed in the modernization of its economy.[34] But increases in Austria's currency reserves in the late 1960s, and early 1970s made capital exports a choice which the Austrian government preferred to imported inflation or revaluation of the schilling.[35] Joint ventures with Eastern European countries have been registered with the Federal Economic Chamber since 1970 and number now more than 140.[36] Austria's nationalized industry has been at the forefront of moves to build up production facilities in countries such as South Africa or Greece under the colonels. Like many other banks throughout Western Europe, Austria's financial community and, in particular, the largest public sector banks have also moved rapidly into international markets.[37]

But it would be a mistake to interpret Austria's recent political initiatives in the area of export policy as indications of a longstanding strategy of export-led growth. When Austria experienced high economic growth, full employment, and a balance-of-payments equilibrium before 1974, the government turned a deaf ear to the demands of the export sector for stronger support. In 1973, for example, the sales tax rebate on exports was eliminated without compensation because exports were viewed as an undesirable stimulant of inflation. And both the government and the private sector had deep-seated reservations concerning the involvement of state agencies in the organization of export trade. These reservations are still visible in the new strategy which has been adopted to compensate for the economic downturn in international markets since 1973. In questions of export finance, for example, strictly commercial considerations continue to determine the policies of the Austrian Control Bank. In its two-tier system of interest rates, the variable portion fluctuates widely in response to changes in international money markets.[38] Indeed, the financial foundation of Austria's export support system follows market trends rather than compensating for them. This system is financed jointly by both government and the representative of the business community, the Federal Economic Chamber, which is entitled to collect a foreign trade fee of 0·003 per cent of the value of all goods crossing Austrian borders. In 1975, for example, the 825 million schillings of revenue thus generated was the Federal Chamber's contribution to Austria's system of export subsidies. But with the drop in Austrian exports in 1976, the Federal Chamber received less revenue and was thus forced to reduce its financial contribution.[39] And, although the government's relative share in the funding of export credit facilities increased from 2:1 in 1975 to 3·5:1 in 1976, mounting budget deficits set stringent limits to the various forms of export aid which different state agencies could grant.[40] Furthermore, export support programs could not be targeted on particular, critical industrial sectors or products but were applied generally. As the financial contributor as well as the benefactor of these programs, Austria's business community was simply unable to agree on a list of priorities for funding.[41] The veto which Austria's National Bank imposed on the extension of export credits for the financing of production periods of less than a year (as is typical in consumer goods industries) is perhaps the best illustration of the limitations which are imposed on recent government efforts to spur exports. Under the guise of export promotion, such credits, the bank argued, amounted to a politically motivated improvement of the capital base of particular firms or industrial sectors. And this, it thought, was antithetical to the tenets of Austria's market economy.[42] In short, recent political initiatives of the Austrian state bureaucracy to aid Austrian exports are attempts to compensate for the downturn in the international economy and the balance-of-payments and employment problems it has created for Austria. But numerous limitations are imposed on Austria's budding neo-mercantilism. It seems improbable that current efforts will yield a long-run strategy of export-led growth masterminded by the Austrian state.

This impression is reinforced by the way in which Austria modernizes its industrial structure. Although the Austrian state bureaucracy commands, at least in title, a nationalized sector which is larger than that of any other OECD state, throughout the postwar period it has eschewed a statist strategy and favored an indirect, global rather than a direct, sectoral approach to Austria's industrial problems. Typical of this indirect approach was Austria's pursuit of a stable currency throughout the postwar period, which, it was thought, would strengthen the structure of Austrian industry across the board.[43] The imperative governing Austria's industrial policy has been geared to ensuring full employment through a rationalization and modernization of Austria's industrial structure. 'For Social Democrats the first objective of economic policy . . . is to secure and create jobs.'[44] Fluctuations in the business cycle rather than sectoral characteristics of the Austrian economy have thus informed Austria's strategy of dealing with its industrial structure.

In the early postwar years, these later developments could hardly have been predicted. The distribution of the economic aid which Austria received from the Marshall Plan required a full-blown planning effort which left responsibility for the reconstruction and rejuvenation of Austria's industrial structure with state agencies. But by the end of the aid program, striking economic gains provided the political climate in which the Austrian adoption of the West German social market economy in the Raab-Kamitz era could flourish in the 1950s.[45] Fear of European integration and Austria's diminishing economic growth rates in the middle 1960s renewed public debate and resulted in the programmatic commitment of both major parties in 1968 to modernize the structure of Austria's economy through political efforts. Legislation passed in 1969 gave financial incentives to the merger of firms.[46] The Ministry of Industry and Trade was reorganized so as to include sections dealing with particular branches of industry and some of its civil servants received additional training. New sectoral data were collected and published regularly from 1973 on.[47] But whatever their intent, these measures had, by all accounts, no more than a cosmetic impact. Between 1954 and 1974, Austria's deficit in fees paid out for patents and licenses rose continuously from 41 to 976 million schillings. Its share in the total number of Austria's industrial licenses dropped from 27 per cent in 1960 to 19 per cent in 1970. While concerted efforts to increase Austria's research and development budget have almost doubled its share in GNP from 0·6 per cent in 1970 to 1·17 per cent in 1977, these efforts have fallen far short of planned increases and leave Austria among the advanced industrial states with the lowest research and development budget.[48]

Recent changes in Austrian policy in two areas suggest, however, that the Austrian state bureaucracy is becoming more directly involved in sectoral policy. One area of change is the deliberate attempt of the Austrian government, still in its early stages, to rejuvenate Austria's industrial structure by concentrating its efforts on six or seven major projects in industries such as paper and pulp, automobiles, chemicals, textiles, and magnesium. Motivated by diverse objectives – imbalance of trade in automobiles, unemployment in textiles, rationalization and modernization in paper and chemicals – these state-initiated efforts are a deliberate attempt to introduce major changes in Austria's industrial structure at the very time at which similar efforts in France and Italy, for example, have not fared well. These policies show the present SPÖ government, like social democracy throughout central and northern Europe, to be well disposed toward industry, especially large-scale industry, even though it often does not trust Austria's business community; the ÖVP opposition, on the other hand, typically favors business, especially the interests of small and medium-sized firms, over industry.

An instrument critical to the government's new industrial strategy is its control over several public investment funds which provide it with direct access to capital markets, and give it some control over investment decisions in the private and public sector. In the words of Chancellor Kreisky, 'in Austria [unlike Germany] we do not have to talk about investment controls; for that task we have the public funds'.[49] The Development Fund, for example, between 1969 and 1975 played the role of a lender of last resort and generated with its 1·3 billion schilling guarantees investments totalling more than 3 billion. In 1975, for example, of a total budget of 274 million schillings it invested 134 millions in a reorganization of Austria's textile industry.[50] The counterpart funds of the European Recovery Program have, since 1962, served a similar function as the Development Fund. The retraining of Austrian coal-miners in Fohnsdorf, for example, has so far required the creation of two thousand new jobs at the cost of about a billion schillings, of which the ERP Fund has carried about a third. At times the Austrian government can rely on its large nationalized sector to help it in achieving its industrial policy. The Zeltweg investment project, for example, is aided greatly by the involvement of the nationalized VOEST steel combine and its investment of 270 million in the construction of coal-mining equipment.[51] The diversity of public investment funds notwithstanding, the government evidently feels that it has to centralize credit instruments if it is to change the defensively oriented, employment-guaranteeing programs which past policies have preferred.[52] This explains why the Development Fund was changed in 1976 to a Finance Guarantee Corporation which not only permits investment in the modernization of Austrian industry but grants the government an opportunity to become a shareholder in individual firms.[53] Funded in 1977 at a level of 6 billion schillings, this fund is intended to strengthen the capital base not of ailing firms in stagnant sectors but of dynamic firms with growth potential which is not fully realized due to the limitation of Austria's capital market.

But this new Finance Guarantee Corporation illustrates the limitations of Austria's changing industrial policy as much as its potentialities. Although it presents another source of potential weakness of Austria's private sector, government participation in private firms is planned for a limited time-period (seven to fifteen years) only.[54] Furthermore, the Finance Guarantee Corporation represents the kind of government support for Austria's medium-sized firm which the business community has long asked for. The corporation is a source of venture capital which Austria's underdeveloped capital markets have so far denied to small or medium-sized firms with high growth potential. In view of the fact that Austria's two business peak associations are jointly minority partners with an ownership of 10 per cent of the stock of the new corporation, it is reasonable to interpret the corporation's establishment as an attempt of the government to allay widespread fears in Austria's business community that its policy of pushing ahead with large industrial projects will undermine further private initiative in Austria's market economy.

But the limitations which impinge upon Austria's 'new' industrial policy are evident in other instances as well. The new Commission on Industry set up in 1976 and chaired by the Chancellor evolved not into a centralized planning body which eventually might become a political alternative should Austria's praised system of social partnership crack under existing economic strains; instead, it became still another body of consultation in charge of preparing detailed position papers on critical industrial sectors. And the commission did not push for a policy of concentration, as business had feared, but encouraged instead, in its early sessions, an enlargement of co-operative relations between Austria's medium-sized and small firms.[55] Furthermore, important political questions, such as the employment problems of Austria's coal industry, were settled in the informal, personalistic, and secret bargaining between Chancellor Kreisky and the head of the Austrian Trade Union Federation, Benya. Austrian industrial policy is also hampered by its inability to influence the investment strategy of nationalized industry, which controls a quarter of Austria's total industrial investment funds. And some of the government aid which is expended on industry goes to foreign-owned corporations over which the government has little control.[56] In short, although the Austrian bureaucracy in recent years has moved toward greater direct involvement in the restructuring of its industrial base, that movement has been slow and has encountered numerous obstacles.[57]

The present economic crisis has led to contradictory tensions operating on Austria's strategy of managing international interdependence. In its import policy, Austria's traditional protectionism has given way to a policy of trade liberalization. In its export and industrial policy, on the other hand, one can detect limited moves toward a more direct intervention of state agencies in economic affairs. These tensions in Austria's strategy are shaped by a distinct, slowly changing domestic structure.

Austria's Domestic Structures

Austria manages its terms of interdependence with a domestic structure which is particularly adept at compensating for the disturbances which changes in international markets create in the traditional arrangements of domestic industry. That structure is not, however, well suited for the pursuit of a coherent strategy based on a particular set of premises, be they statist or capitalist. In theory and practice, Austria's domestic structures favor a system of social partnership (*Sozialpartnerschaft*) between organized business and organized labor which leaves little room to deliberate policy responses of the state bureaucracy or to the spontaneity of a vigorous capitalist system. In response to international interdependence, Austria's domestic structures embody the principle of political compensation rather than capitalist innovation or bureaucratic intervention.

The politics of the Second Republic cannot be understood without referring at the outset to the Great Coalition which united the Christian Democratic, Austrian People's Party (ÖVP) as the spokesman of the business community with the Socialist Party of Austria (SPÖ) as the representative of the working class. Although that coalition was formally dissolved in 1966 – when Austria moved to a system of one-party government dominated first by the ÖVP and, since 1970, by the SPÖ – in different spheres of Austrian politics it has continued informally ever since. One reason is the large number of ancillary interest groups, locked into a 'para-coalition', which reflect the distinct interests and mentalities which still separate 'Blacks' from 'Reds' in Austria.[58] This para-coalition assures members of both major parties easy access, mutual consultation, and ample opportunity for political bargaining. The concept of 'social partnership' is an apt description of the consensual politics which result.

The great coalition, it is important to remember, functioned in a society still marked by notable class and status divisions, regional disparities, and intermittent ideological conflict. The legacy of the instabilities of the interwar period and, in particular, of the civil war of 1934 have resulted in a defensive consensus in which both major parties agree on the virtue of political demobilization and strict limitations on unilateral political initiatives through carefully worked out political compromises. These compromises are facilitated by the character of organized business and labor in Austria. A meek business community, traditionally oriented towards domestic markets, found it easy after 1945 to strike pragmatic bargains with Austria's powerful, that is 'responsible', Trade Union Congress (ÖGB). Austria's para-coalition neutralized the large concentration of power which rests in its hands and legitimates incremental political compensations of economic sectors or social groups.[59]

The task of political compensation channels the energies of Austria's political leaders into the details of political bargaining with which they protect or marginally enlarge the benefits accruing to their respective constituencies. Through various political devices – mutually agreed upon political patronage (*Proporz*), log-rolling (*Junktim*), and sectoral opposition (*Bereichsopposition*) – the tightly linked party and interest group elites have specialized in delaying rather than accelerating economic change and in cushioning the impact of competition in domestic and international markets.[60]

Austria's policy network which links different political actors (both groups and individuals) managing international interdependence is highly centralized in both the public and the private sector, and the distinction between public and private is all but lacking.⁶¹ Distinctive of Austria's 'chamber state' is the prominent role of its publicly licensed economic chambers with compulsory membership. The Federal Economic Chamber (*Bundeswirtschaftskammer*) represents the crafts, commerce, industry, and business interests more generally; Austria's Federal Chamber of Labor *Arbeiterkammertag* speaks for wage and salary earners, as well as for consumer interests. Austria's private interest groups, the Federation of Austrian Industrialists (*Industriellenverband*) and the ÖGB, co-operate closely with 'their' chamber.⁶² There exists, of course, ample room for conflict between the interests of natural partners and for 'perverse' temporary alliances. For example, the interest which the Federal Chamber of Labor as spokesman of consumer interests has had in trade liberalization has dovetailed neatly with the demands of the Union of Industrialists for a more internationally oriented, outward-looking export policy. Since the Federal Economic Chamber represents the myriads of Austria's small firms most likely to be affected adversely by import competition, it has been a less enthusiastic proponent of a liberalization strategy. Law, tradition, and expertise assure these groups a central role in the development of major pieces of legislation and in the implementation of policy. The continuity in their leadership and their osmotic relations with political parties make organized capital and labor powerful spokesmen in Austrian society.

Membership of Austria's Federal Economic Chamber was made compulsory soon after 1945. Its six sections – commerce, industry, trade, banking and insurance, transportation, and tourism – cover virtually all Austrian enterprises, both private and public. It speaks for about 400,000 members who overwhelmingly support the ÖVP.⁶³ Sheer size and the heterogeneity of its clientele mean that on controversial issues the Federal Chamber is spending a good deal of time hammering out a business stance which somehow accommodates the divergent interests of its different sections. Once such a consensus, however tenuous, has been created within the Chamber, it becomes authoritative for all its members. The Union of Austrian Industrialists, by way of contrast, has a much smaller, voluntary, and homogeneous membership of about 15,000. Since it faces fewer internal restraints, the Union is more flexible, maneuverable and outspoken on controversial issues than is normal practice of the Federal Chamber. Even so, the Union maintains intimate contacts with the Federal Chamber, in particular its industry section. Because the Union represents big firms and can raise big money for political campaigns, its views are well heeded. Conflicts of interest between the two organizations are rare but seem to occur on some critical issues of international interdependence. The government's effort to create national champions and encourage the concentration of firms within industrial sectors has met with the approval of the Union of Industrialists but has been viewed critically by the Chamber. More generally speaking, conflicts between the two organizations are likely to exist on issues which pit big corporations against small firms and which set internationally oriented growth sectors of industry apart from domestically oriented mature or stagnant sectors. Even when they remain concealed, such conflicts can mute the powerful voice with which the Austrian business community speaks out on questions of international interdependence.

The organization of Austrian labor mirrors that of Austrian business. At the behest of the trade unions, the Chamber of Labor was created as a body of public law in 1920. Since 1945, this organization has assured the unions of formal representation in all major legislation. Although membership in the ÖGB is voluntary, it includes about two-thirds of all employees in Austria.[64] Organized on an industry-wide basis, the sixteen industrial unions are strictly controlled from the top. The power to engage with business in collective bargaining rests with the leaders of the ÖGB, not with the Chamber of Labor or the industrial unions. In practice, though, the ÖGB delegates the negotiations of agreements to industrial unions or their subdivisions. But no agreement stands without the ÖGB's consent.[65] And the ÖGB, not the industrial unions, controls the union finances and strike funds.

At first glance the unique centralization of political power in Austria's private sector is duplicated in the organizational structure of the government and state bureaucracy. Austria's federal system is weak, and Vienna remains the undisputed center of the country's political life.[66] And the Second Republic can look back on an administrative tradition of a strong bureaucratic state dating back to the mercantilist unification of the German core of the Habsburg Empire under Maria Theresa and her son, Joseph II, in the eighteenth century.

But the realities of Austrian political life are more complex and undercut the cohesiveness and *esprit de corps* of the state bureaucracy. Before 1966 political power was centralized in institutions which bypassed the state bureaucracy. The coalition committee (*Koalitionsausschuss*) provided the leaders of the ÖVP and SPÖ with a forum for settling virtually all important political issues in secrecy outside of the cabinet and parliament and unimpeded by the state bureaucracy. And the semblance of consensus politics portrayed by the Great Coalition rested on the *Proporz* system by which different ministries, as well as high-ranking administrative positions within ministries, were alloted to either ÖVP or SPÖ. This has reinforced the decentralization inherent in all large-scale bureaucracies. Since the break-up of the Great Coalition in 1966, the disappearance of the coalition has shifted the forum for high-level decision-making not to the state bureaucracy but to the top echelons of political parties and 'their' ancillary interest groups. While developments since the consolidation of the SPÖ hold on government power in 1971 are gradually moving in another direction, it still continues to be true that politicization at the top thus voided much of the administrative tradition of the Austrian state bureaucracy and prevents it from seizing independent political initiatives backed by its relationships with particular firms, economic sectors or trade unions. The initiatives of the state bureaucracy are carefully screened by channeling them through an elaborate policy network of committees on which Austria's 'social partners' are both represented. Within that network, the authority of the state bureaucracy, though important, is not overwhelming; outside of it, political initiatives by particular agencies or ministries would often lack the legal basis and always the legitimacy which are needed in order to translate political blueprints into practice. Virtually all political strategies affecting the terms of interdependence must be discussed with, ratified, and sometimes implemented by Austria's powerful interest groups. United in their dislike of vigorous state intervention or market competition, these groups typically prefer striking intricate bargains on questions of social compensation such as prices, wages, and questions of employment.

Austria's system of trade missions offers a good illustration of the relations between the state bureaucracy and private groups. In this area, as in many others, the government relies heavily on the instruments provided by the Federal Economic Chamber.[67] Although the Chamber plays, like all other economic interest groups, a minor role in Austria's foreign affairs generally, it holds a critically important place in the implementation of Austria's commercial policy. With a staff of more than 400, the eighty foreign trade missions which Austria maintains abroad stand under the supervision not of a ministry but of the Federal Economic Chamber which employs more than a hundred people in its foreign trade section in Vienna. A computerized system stores information on 4,500 firms and 17,000 products, thus covering more than 90 per cent of all export firms. Seventy of Austria's eighty trade missions have direct access to this data bank which is consulted sixty times a day. Within a year or two the trade missions will be able to reach directly virtually every export firm in Austria. For Austria's numerous medium-sized and small firms in particular, the traditional weakness in the marketing area is at least partly offset by this system of trade missions which the Federal Chamber has organized.[68]

The essence of Austria's policy network which fashions political strategies in international markets is the fusion of public and private power in the hands of a very small number of political leaders which control Austria's partisan camps. As bodies of public law, some of Austria's major interest groups exercise, in addition to their normal, autonomous operations, administrative powers delegated by the state. This makes these groups subject to the supervision of the government which cannot function adequately without the expertise which only the interest groups command. Equally ambiguous is the relation between party elites, parliament, and cabinet ministers who are normally members of particular interest groups, often their spokesmen but rarely their tools. The informality engendered by these interlocking corridors of power is revealed in what might be called 'government by commission'[69] and is best illustrated by the Joint Commission (*Paritätische Kommission*) as the lynchpin of Austria's celebrated incomes policy.[70] The Commission is the institutional response of the late 1950s to the challenge of inflation which in the late 1940s had been countered by a series of five wage–price agreements concluded by the big four interest groups without government participation. Composed of representatives of industry, labor, and government, the Commission lacks legal standing, and its decisions command no formal sanctions. And although it brings the representatives of organized business and organized labor to one table with the power-brokers in charge of the 'commanding heights' of the Austrian state, the Commission operates by the unanimity principle. With government officials, including the Chancellor, present but not voting in the literally hundreds of meetings which the Commission has held since its inception, it illustrates the traditionally subordinate role which the government and state bureaucracy have played in Austria's system of 'bilateral corporatism.'[71] Rather than initiating political strategies, the Austrian government is expected to ratify decisions reached in bilateral negotiations between Austrian interest groups.[72] The Commission's control over wage and price increases, as well as an active subcommittee which investigates the prices of imports, have the effect of harnessing Austrian business and unions to a policy of low inflation and of restraining competition.[73] In short, the Commission blunts the force of both market competition and state initiatives and provides instead a forum for making marginal economic adjustments and political compensations.

Austria's nationalized industries illustrate the same point, although here the emphasis naturally lies on the neutralization of state power. The nationalization of 'German property' after the Second World War and the enlargement of the public sector with the hundreds of enterprises which the Soviet Union relinquished when it signed the Austrian State Treaty in 1955 have left Austria with a public sector which is larger than that of any other advanced industrialized state. Yet since the ÖVP and SPÖ have persistently disagreed on the role of the public sector in the economy, the potential for economic management offered by the sheer size of Austria's public sector has remained unfulfilled. The ÖVP has traditionally been interested in limiting the scope of the public sector and in having management conform to strictly 'economic' considerations. SPÖ leaders, on the other hand, have always believed that since a planned and market economy were mutually complementary, the nationalized sector should consider the effects of its economic strategy on the whole economy (and in particular on labor markets), rather than on company profits alone. These conflicting conceptions of the purpose of economic power which Austria's two major parties have adhered to have blunted both the potential for state intervention in the economy and the potential for invigorating competition in Austrian markets. Instead, the nationalized sector seems to play, at least to some extent, the role of a buffer which protects Austria's domestic labor markets from higher rates of unemployment.[74] The compromise on the principle of compensation is assured by the fact that management in the public sector is appointed through Austria's *Proporz* system. Different positions within firms or, more typically, different firms in the same economic sector tend to be either 'Black' or 'Red',[75] Eschewing the harsh dictates of both market and state, Austria's public sector has shown a remarkable degree of internal conflict. Even under the reorganization effort which has taken place since the late 1960s, the organizational simplification which has been brought about by a systematic concentration policy within different industrial sectors has left the central holding company of all nationalized industries with little control over individual firms.[76]

Austria's management of interdependence is conditioned by domestic structures which avoid the logic of unmitigated market competition and of decisive state intervention. The particular competence of these domestic structures does not lie in the making of rules (*Ordnungspolitik*) (be it in the interest of either market competition or sectoral reconstruction), but in an incomes policy aimed at compensating groups adversely affected by economic change.[77] Austria's domestic structure links organized business and organized labor in an elaborate institutional network which yields easily marginal compensations for affected interests but resists strongly a vigorous development of entrepreneurial initiative or bureaucratic leadership. For the government typically affirms the political bargains struck between the 'social partners' and is involved in these bargains primarily through the fusion of public and private power and through the close alliance between political parties and interest groups. In sum, Austria's domestic structures are neither capitalist nor statist but corporatist.

Austria in an Interdependent World

The small European states are deeply entangled in the international economy. In the 1960s and 1970s, for example, this group of states exceeded all others in its dependence on foreign trade. Varying between a high of 94 per cent for the Netherlands and a low of 44 per cent for Finland, the foreign trade/GNP ratio of nine small European states averaged 66 per cent.[78] In 1975, for example, thirty-one economic ministers from other countries visited Vienna, and fourteen bilateral trade negotiations were conducted.[79] But the terms of interdependence of the small European states differ from both the less developed countries and the larger states. Unlike many less developed countries, the small European states do not suffer greatly from instabilities in exports, imports, and income; from low rates of economic growth; or from an enormous concentration of their foreign trade on a few trading partners.[80] And unlike their larger neighbors, they are not only more dependent on foreign trade but also experience qualitative imbalances in their trade. These imbalances in exports and imports are due to the dominance of 'traditional' over 'modern' industries in total output and exports. In the 1950s and 1960s the small European states lagged the larger states by 10 per cent in the proportion of modern industries in total manufacturing output and by 18 per cent in the proportion of modern industries in total exports.[81] In 1969 two-thirds of Austria's 1 billion schilling investment in its textile industry was paid out for the import of machinery. And Austria's dynamic machine tool industry relies on the imports of all electronic components and equipment even though it claims to have the technological capacity to produce virtually all of that equipment domestically.[82] In short, the small European states face a 'trade gap' of their own which results from their particular industrial structure and their dependence on imports in basic metals and in the investment goods sector.[83]

The absence of an indigenous automobile industry illustrates well the imbalance in Austria's industrial structure and foreign trade. Due to American influence, Austria refrained after 1945 from building up an indigenous automobile industry and signed instead a licensing agreement with Italy's largest car manufacturer, Fiat.[84] As a result, of the 1·1 million cars registered in Austria in 1969, less than 6 per cent were domestically produced. Economic dependence was costly. West German, French, and Italian cars were sold in Austrian markets at mark-ups varying between 2 and 27 per cent.[85] The dependence on car imports has enormous effects on Austria's balance of payments. The value of the 200,000 cars imported in 1971, for example, exceeded 12 billion schillings. This is twice the production value of Austria's greatest truck and bus manufacturer (Steyr) with its 18,000 employees.[86] When, in 1976, Austria's balance-of-payments deficit began to take on serious proportions, the Austrian government tried unsuccessfully to encourage foreign car producers servicing the Austrian market to purchase more of Austria's semi-manufactured goods. The fiscal retraints with which the Austrian government sought to master its financial crisis in late 1977 thus affected directly the imports of automobiles.[87] Perhaps most important in the coming years are the consequences of economic dependence for domestic labor markets. In order to maintain full employment, Austria will need to create 3,500 new jobs annually by 1985. The uncertain prospects of the automobile industry notwithstanding, the political interests of the SPÖ government and the economic interests of Austria's under-utilized steel industry thus both point in the direction of developing an indigenous car industry or of convincing foreign producers to open a plant in Austria.[88]

Yet despite their economically exposed position, the small European states have avoided economic impoverishment and political instability. They have been well served by their pursuit of a liberal trade strategy in international markets. As is true of the less developed countries, increases in the international division of labor have not alleviated and may, in fact, have intensified the trade dependence of the small European states during the last three decades. But, in contrast to the less developed countries, increases in the international division of labor have mitigated the imbalance in industrial structure and trade which characterize the small advanced industrial states. The predictions of neo-classical trade theory about the absolute and relative gains of small states in a liberal international trade regime have been borne out by the facts. Here is a case in which liberals can rejoice. Economic growth has occurred together with economic development.

The central argument of this chapter points to the importance of domestic structures. In contrast to the less developed countries, the domestic structures of the small advanced industrial states are more autonomous from the international political economy. And, unlike the larger advanced industrial states, these structures facilitate at least in the case of Austria a strategy which focuses on the social compensation of both the unions and the business community rather than fostering economic competition of the market or political intervention of the state bureaucracy. Austrian economic prosperity and political stability is due, at least in part, to the special competence which it has developed in adjusting to changes in the international economy rather than accepting these changes passively or trying to alter the rules of the game in international arenas.

Wolfgang Biermann, a popular writer in Germany, has characterized Austria unkindly as an 'economic appendix' of the Federal Republic. ('Österreich ist der wirtschaftliche Wurmfortsatz Deutschlands.') But compared to most other small advanced industrial states, Austria's economic dependence on West Germany is not unusual. In fact, Austria is somewhat less involved in and exposed to international markets than are most of its small European neighbors. In 1964 Austria's foreign trade accounted for only 52 per cent of her GNP, a figure that was well below the average for the small European states as a whole.[89] The same is true of Austria's outlays for research and development, as well as the share of 'modern' industries in manufacturing output and exports.[90] This is a consequence of Austria's domestic structure and the political strategies it has adopted for managing international interdependence.

Like most other small advanced industrial states, the prolonged economic recession in international markets confronts Austria with new economic challenges in the years ahead. In hoping for a quick recovery in the capitalist world economy, Austrian policy-makers countered the early phases of the recession with expansionary fiscal and monetary policies in 1975 and 1976. But the continued sluggishness in the international economy has led to gaping holes in the national budget, large deficits in the balance of payments, and the danger of rising unemployment. The early stages of serious political debate reveal two premises shared by all protagonists. Austria's interdependence with regional and world markets is irreversible; a small country cannot dream of insularity or autarchy. Secondly, in the short run, neither devaluation (as in Sweden) nor job reduction (as in Switzerland) is an instrument acceptable in the reduction of aggregate purchasing power.[91]

These shared premises do not exist when one considers long-term strategies. A difference of opinion on which strategy to choose cuts right through the center of Austria's governing SPÖ and the central bureaucracy.[92] The majority views Austria's current economic problems as the result of a cyclical growth of consumer demand for foreign goods which can be paid for through a determined export offensive in international markets; the minority sees in the current crisis a secular shift toward import dependence in both the consumer goods and investment goods sectors which may require selective import controls. But short of the most serious economic and political crisis the instrument most likely to improve Austria's standing in competitive international markets – devaluation and a decline in real wages – is politically infeasible under a SPÖ government. And a concerted export drive which does not rely on such Draconian measures may simply fail in restoring Austria's foreign trade balance. On the other hand the special tax levied in 1977 on cars and imported luxury goods illustrates how the SPÖ could protect its political base at least in the short run by shifting the costs of a strategy of selective controls to its political opponents. In a country still very much aware of its civil war of 1934, the obvious disadvantage of this political strategy consists in shifting the guiding principle from social compensation to social retribution. Because the logic informing either strategy has obvious political flaws, the veneer of political compromise within the SPÖ is not yet wearing as thin as might otherwise be expected.

But even if they were adopted in a moderated form, the two strategies have important consequences for Austria's domestic political structure. The liberal strategy requires a new state capitalism based on the selective intervention of the state bureaucracy in specific industrial sectors; the neo-mercantilist strategy demands a rejuvenation of Austria's old and waning system of social corporatism and the improvement of the capital base and investment climate of small and medium-sized firms. The liberal strategy thus would move Austria's bureaucracy and government toward 'multilateral' bargaining with interest groups, industrial sectors, and firms; the neo-mercantilist strategy seeks to preserve the system of 'bilateral' bargaining between the major interest groups which is then ratified by government and bureaucracy. Although this debate has started within Austria's SPÖ, it is likely to affect the ÖVP and its ancillary interest groups as well. The attitude of the political representatives of big business appears more favorable toward the liberal strategy (and the support of big business which it entails) than that of the Federal Economic Chamber which, as the spokesman of small and medium-sized firms, favors a more aggressive use of non-tariff barriers as a retaliatory measure.

The mixture of liberalism and protectionism which will inform Austria's strategy in the years ahead has obvious implications for the structure of the international economy. An export offensive would strengthen directly a liberal international trade regime; selective imports controls would strengthen the force of neo-mercantilism. Conversely, the degree of liberalism or protectionism in international markets will affect the balance of costs and benefits of strategies or economic competition in international markets or of social compensation in domestic politics. Confronted with strategic choice in their domestic and foreign policies, Austrians are beginning to ask themselves whether their country is what the pope in 1974 called 'an island of the blessed' (*Insel der Seeligen*) or whether it is, as the New Left argues, a system of 'peripheral capitalism' (*Peripherer Kapitalismus*). The three answers which one hears most often in Austria – something must happen (*da muss was geschehen*), nothing can be done (*da kann man nichts machen*), we'll have to muddle thorough (*man wird sich durchwursteln*) – capture the contradiction the country experiences as well as its resolution. This chapter has argued that in the contemporary capitalist world economy no man, and no country, is an island; but Austria's experience shows that even peripheral countries can be blessed.

Notes: Chapter 11

Research for this chapter was supported by a Rockefeller Fellowship in Conflict in International Relations. For their comments on an earlier draft I should like to thank Jorge Domínguez, Robert Keohane, Stephen Krasner, David Laitin, Andrei Markovits, Hans Mayrzedt, and Michael Pollak.

1. I have developed a similar argument for Austrian domestic politics in 'Center-periphery relations in a consociational democracy: Austria and Kleinwalsertal', in *Territorial Politics in Industrial Nations*, ed. Sidney Tarrow, Peter J. Katzenstein, and Luigi Graziano (New York: Praeger, 1978), pp. 123–69.
2. Karl W. Deutsch and Alexander Eckstein, 'National industrialization and the declining share of the international economic sector, 1890–1959', *World Politics*, vol. 13, no. 2 (January 1961), p. 268.
3. ibid., p. 271. See also Karl W. Deutsch, 'International communication: the media and flows', *Public Opinion Quarterly*, vol. 20, no. 1 (Spring 1956), pp. 143–60; Karl W. Deutsch, Chester I. Bliss, and Alexander Eckstein, 'Population, sovereignty, and the share of foreign trade', *Economic Development and Cultural Change*, vol. 10, no. 4 (July 1962), pp. 353–66. Karl W. Deutsch and Bruce M. Russett, 'International trade and political independence', *The American Behavioral Scientist*, vol. 6, no. 7 (March 1963), pp. 18–20.
4. Deutsch and Eckstein, 'National industrialization', pp. 270–2. This is also evident in Karl W. Deutsch and Lewis Edinger, *Germany Rejoins the Powers: Mass Opinion, Interest Groups, and Elites in Contemporary German Foreign Policy* (Stanford, Calif.: Stanford University Press, 1959).
5. Peter J. Lloyd, *International Trade Problems of Small Nations* (Durham, NC: Duke University Press, 1968), p. 25. See also the criticisms, revisions, and extensions of Deutsch's interpretation in Simon Kuznets, *Modern Economic Growth: Rate, Structure and Spread* (New Haven, Conn.: Yale University Press, 1966), pp. 316–17; Robert E. Lipsey, *Price and Quantity Trends in the Foreign Trade of the United States* (Princeton, NJ: Princeton University Press, 1963), pp. 36–40; Richard Rosecrance *et al.*, 'Whither interdependence?', *International Organization*, vol. 31, no. 3 (Summer 1977), pp. 425–71; Peter J. Katzenstein, 'International Interdependence: some long term trends and recent changes', *International Organization*, vol. 29, no. 4 (Autumn 1975), pp. 1021–34.
6. Robert Gilpin, *American Hegemony and the Multinationals: The Political Economy of Foreign Investment* (New York: Basic Books, 1975); Stephen D. Krasner, 'State power and the structure of international trade', *World Politics*, vol. 28, no. 3 (April 1976), pp. 317–47. For a different formulation from a similar vantage point see also Kenneth N. Waltz, 'Theory of international relations', in *Handbook of Political Science*, ed. Fred I. Greenstein and Nelson W. Polsby (Reading, Mass.: Addison-Wesley, 1975), Vol. 8, pp. 1–85.
7. See also the recent special issue of *International Organization*, vol. 32, no. 1 (Winter 1978), pp. 1–300, which James A. Caporaso edited under the title 'Dependence and dependency in the global system'.
8. Peter J. Katzenstein (ed.), *Between Power and Plenty: Foreign Economic Policies of Advanced Industrial States* (Madison, Wis.: University of Wisconsin Press, 1978), previously issued as a special issue of *International Organization*, vol. 31, no. 4 (Autumn 1977), pp. 587–920.
9. Niels Amstrup, 'The perennial problem of small states: a survey of research efforts', *Cooperation and Conflict*, vol. 11, no. 3 (1976), pp. 163–82, esp. p. 176.
10. David Laitin, 'A classification of strategies designed to overcome dependency and economic backwardness', La Jolla, unpublished paper, 1978.
11. Kenneth McRae (ed.), *Consociational Democracy: Political Accommodation in Segmented Societies* (Toronto: McClelland & Stewart, 1974); Arend Lijphart, *Democracy in Plural Societies: A Comparative Exploration* (New Haven, Conn.: Yale University Press, 1977); Martin O. Heisler (ed.) *Politics in Europe: Structures and Processes in Some Postindustrial Democracies* (New York: McKay, 1974).
12. Alexander Gerschenkron, 'Economic backwardness in historical perspective', in *Economic Backwardness in Historical Perspective: A Book of Essays*, ed. Alexander

Gerschenkron (Cambridge, Mass.: Harvard University Press, 1962), pp. 5–30; *idem*, *An Economic Spurt That Failed: Four Lectures in Austrian History* (Princeton, NJ: Princeton University Press, 1977). For the twentieth century, see Gustav Otruba, *Österreichs Wirtschaft im 20. Jahrhundert* (Vienna: Österreichischer Bundesverlag, 1968).
13 These categories inform the comparative analysis of the foreign economic policies of the large advanced industrial states in Katzenstein (ed.), *Between Power and Plenty*.
14 Beirat für Wirtschafts- und Sozialfragen, *Möglichkeiten und Grenzen des Einsatzes Ausländischer Arbeitskräfte* (Vienna: Ueberreuter, 1976); Ernst Gehmacher, 'Foreign workers as a source of social change', in *The Dynamics of Public Policy: A Comparative Analysis*, ed. Richard Rose (Beverly Hills, Calif.: Sage, 1976), pp. 157–76; Österreichisches Institut für Wirtschaftsforschung, *Monatsberichte*, vol. 35, no. 5 (May 1962), pp. 232–6; vol. 36, no. 11 (November 1963), pp. 411–15; vol. 47, no. 4 (April 1974), pp. 214–24.
15 Karl Gutkas, Alois Brusatti, and Erika Weinzierl, *Österreich 1945—1970: Fünfundzwanzig Jahre Zweite Republik* (Vienna: Österreichischer Bundesverlag, 1970), p. 302; Österreichisches Institut für Wirtschaftsforschung, *Monatsberichte*, vol. 42, no. 11 (November 1969), pp. 450–7. For the crisis in 1973 see *Monatsberichte*, vol. 46, no. 2 (February 1973), pp. 45–8.
16 *Der Kleinstaat in der Europäischen Wirtschaftlichen Zusammenarbeit aus der Sicht Ungarns und Österreichs* (Vienna: Verlag für Geschichte und Politik, 1975), p. 77.
17 *Monatsberichte* vol. 26, no. 6 (June 1953), pp. 194–6; vol. 26, no. 9 (September 1953), pp. 276–90; vol. 27, no. 2 (February 1954, supplement 24); vol. 34, no. 10 (October 1961), pp. 431–6; vol. 35, no. 1 (January 1962), pp. 40–3; vol. 36, no. 11 (November 1963), pp. 416–22; Curtis E. Harvey, 'A case study of the adaptation of a small national economy's industry to international competition: Austria', PhD thesis, University of Southern California, 1963, pp. 106, 264–6; Fritz Breuss, *Komparative Vorteile im österreichischen Aussenhandel* (Vienna: Verlag der österreichischen Akademie der Wissenschaften, 1975), pp. 220–1.
18 Franz Nemschak, *Liberalisierung und Zollpolitik in Österreich* 'Vorträge und Aufsätze', Vol. 8 (Vienna: Österreichisches Institut für Wirtschaftsforschung, 1954); Jan Stankovsky, 'Austria's foreign trade: the legal regulations of trade with East and West', *Journal of World Trade Law*, vol. 3, no. 6 (November–December 1969), pp. 595–639, esp. pp. 611–12, covers preferential imports especially of investment goods; *Monatsberichte*, vol. 26, no. 6 (June 1953), p. 195; vol. 34, no. 10 (October 1961), p. 435; vol. 35, no. 1 (January 1962), p. 41; vol. 48, no. 7 (July 1975), p. 314.
19 This situation is not unlike the American case. See Theodore J. Lowi, 'American business, public policy, case studies and political theory', *World Politics*, vol. 16, no. 4 (July 1964), pp. 677–715.
20 Egon Matzner, *The Trade Between East and West: The Case of Austria* (Stockholm: Almqvist & Wiksell, 1970); Thomas A. Wolf, 'The effects of liberalization of Austrian quantitative restrictions on imports from CMEA countries', (Berlin: International Institute of Management, 1975); Gerhard Rosegger, 'East–West trade: the Austrian example', *Journal of Central European Affairs*, vol. 22, no. 1 (April 1962), pp. 79–95. There are also numerous articles and reports in the *Monatsberichte* of the Österreichische Institut für Wirtschaftsforschung.
21 This literature is growing very rapidly. See *Monatsberichte*, vol. 21, no. 6 (June 1948), pp. 222–7; vol. 26, no. 5 (May 1953), pp. 160–6; M. Dillinger, O. Höll, and H. Kramer, 'The state and international economic power: the case of Austria', discussion paper prepared for the ECPR workshop 'The State and International Economic Power', Louvain, 8–14 April 1976; Otmar Höll and Helmut Kramer, 'Österreich im Internationalen System 1955–1975: Datenzusammenstellung Teil I' (Vienna: Institut für Höhere Studien, November 1976); Oskar Grünwald and Ferdinand Lacina, *Auslandskapital in der österreichischen Wirtschaft* (Vienna: Europa Verlag, 1970); M. Koch, 'Contemporary Austrian foreign policy elite attitudes concerning consensus and decisionmaking', PhD thesis, Brandeis University, 1974, pp. 160–71; Eckard P. Imhof. 'Ausländische Investitionen in Österreich im Rahmen eines Internationalen Vergleichs unter besonderer Berücksichtigung der Direktinvestitionen', PhD thesis, University of Vienna, 1960; Wiener Arbeiterkammer, *Das Eigentum an den Österreichischen Kapitalgesellschaften* (Vienna: Vorwärts, 1962); 'Ausländische Direktinvestitionen in

Österreich', *Monatsberichte*, vol. 33, no. 7 (July 1960) pp. 310–15; 'Eigentumsübergang von Industriebetrieben an Ausländer', *Monatsberichte*, vol. 46, no. 8 (August 1973), pp. 382–92; Kurt Bayer *et al*., *Der Eigentumswechsel in industriellen Mittelbetrieben: Studie erstellt vom Österreichischen Institut für Wirtschaftsforschung* (Vienna: Bundesministerium für Handel, Gewerbe und Industrie, 1973); Josef Peischer, 'Ausländische Direktinvestitionen in Österreich: Aufteilung nach Wirtschaftsbereichen, Rechtsformen, Bundesländern und Herkunftsländern', Diplom, University of Linz, 1975; P. Schaposchnitschenko, 'Stille Invasion des westdeutschen Kapitals in Österreich', *Deutsche Aussenpolitik*, vol. 11, no. 12 (December 1966), pp. 1468–75; Fritz Diwok, *Die Bedeutung des Auslandskapitals für Österreichs Wirtschaft* (Vienna: Verlag für Geschichte und Politik, 1959); Johannes Hofer, 'Die Rolle des Auslandskapitals in der österreichischen Wirtschaft: Vorteile und Gefahren für die Volkswirtschaft', Diplom, Vienna, Hochschule für Welthandel, 1971; Franz Jurokowitsch, 'Die deutschen Direktinvestitionen in der österreichischen Industrie: Motivation, Ausmass, Auswirkungen', PhD thesis, University of Vienna, 1971. In addition, Austria's Federal Reserve (Nationalbank) has regularly monitored the role of foreign investment in Austria since the early 1970s.

22 See also *Monatsberichte*, vol. 38, no. 2 (February 1965), pp. 49–54; vol. 38, no. 5 (May 1965), pp. 163–71; *Die Presse*, 10 December 1975.

23 Stankovsky, 'Austria's foreign trade', *Internationale Wirtschaft*, no. 28, 12 July 1974.

24 *Neue Zürcher Zeitung*, 21 January 1977.

25 *Monatsberichte*, vol. 26, no. 9 (September 1953), p. 278.

26 Peter J. Katzenstein, 'Trends and oscillations in Austrian integration policy since 1955: alternative explanations', *Journal of Common Market Studies*, vol. 14, no. 2 (December 1975), pp. 171–97; Edward E. Platt, 'Political factors affecting the Austrian government's decision to join EFTA', PhD thesis, University of Connecticut, 1967; M. Dillinger *et al*., 'Die europäische Integration und Österreich', *Österreichische Zeitschrift für Politikwissenschaft*, vol. 1 (1976), pp. 65–87; Thomas O. Schlesinger, *Austrian Neutrality in Postwar Europe: The Domestic Roots of a Foreign Policy* (Vienna: Braumüller, 1972), pp. 92–111; Theo Öhlinger, Hans Mayrzedt, and Gustav Kucera, *Institutionelle Aspekte der österreichischen Integrationspolitik* (Vienna: Verlag der österreichischen Akademie der Wissenschaften, 1976).

27 *Monatsberichte*, vol. 24, no. 3 (March 1951), p. 138; vol. 25, no. 10 (October 1952), pp. 292–4; vol. 33, no. 2 (February 1960), pp. 62–8; vol. 34, no. 10 (October 1961, supplement 67), p. 15; vol. 41, no. 8 (August 1968), pp. 319–28; Michael Pronay, 'Exportförderung in Österreich unter besonderer Berücksichtigung des neuen Exportfinanzierungsverfahrens der österreichischen Kontrollbank AG', Diplom, Vienna, Hochschule für Welthandel, 1975; *Arbeiterzeitung*, 18 March 1976; Thomas Klestil, 'Einrichtungen der äusseren Volkswirtschaftspolitik, mit besonderer Berücksichtigung der Aussenhandelsförderung in Österreich in den Jahren 1945–1956', PhD thesis, University of Vienna, 1957; Sozialwissenschaftliche Arbeitsgemeinschaft, *Probleme der Exportfinanzierung in Österreich* (Vienna: Sozialwissenschaftliche Arbeitsgemeinschaft, 1958); Helmut Richter, 'Aktuelle Probleme der Exportfinanzierung in Österreich', PhD thesis, University of Vienna, 1965; Willy Kummerer, *Methoden der Exportfinanzierung* (Vienna: Sparkassenverlag, 1965); Helmut H. Haschek, *Haftungen der Republik Österreich zur Förderung des Exportes* (Vienna: Grenzverlag, 1965); Erich Staringer, 'Die Ausfuhrförderung in Österreich', *Quartalshefte der Girozentrale*, vol. 1 (March 1967), pp. 67–75; Bundeskammer der gewerblichen Wirtschaft (ed.), *Export, Import in der Praxis* (Vienna: Österreichischer Wirtschaftsverlag, 1974); Isolde Faulhaber, 'Exportfinanzierung in Österreich sowie Begünstigungen der Exportwirtschaft im österreichischen Abgaberecht', Diplom, Vienna, Hochschule für Welthandel, 1974; Helmut Haschek, *Exportförderung, Finanzierungen und Garantien: Internationaler Vergleich und österreichische Praxis* (Vienna: Molden, 1976).

28 *Wiener Zeitung*, 12 September 1976.

29 *Monatsberichte*, vol. 41, no. 8 (August 1968), p. 326.

30 *Die Presse*, 4 November 1975; ibid., 9 January 1976; *Oberösterreichische Nachrichten*, 22 January 1977.

31 On the traditional orientation of Austria to Western Europe see Peter J. Katzenstein,

Disjoined Partners: Austria and Germany Since 1815 (Berkeley, Calif.: University of California Press, 1976), pp. 199–218; Koch, 'Contemporary Austrian foreign policy', pp. 183–8. See also Meinhard Supper, *Struktur und Wettbewerbseffekte im österreichischen Aussenhandel 1961—1970* (Vienna: Bundeskammer der gewerblichen Wirtschaft, n.d.); Österreichisches Institut für Wirtschaftsforschung, *Der Export als Wachstumsmotor* (Vienna: Bundesministerium für Handel, Gewerbe und Industrie, 1972); Lutz Beinsen, *Die Wirkung der Ausfuhr auf das inländische Wirtschaftswachstum* (Vienna: Verlag der österreichischen Akademie der Wissenschaften, 1975).
32 *Die Presse*, 19 April 1975; *Neues Volksblatt*, 17 April 1976; *Wiener Zeitung*, 5 June 1976.
33 *Die Presse*, 4 November 1975; ibid., 9 January 1976; *Österreichische Textilmitteilungen*, no. 39, 3 October 1975.
34 *Monatsberichte*, vol. 33, no. 2 (February 1960), p. 69.
35 *Die Presse*, 17 March 1973.
36 *Wiener Zeitung*, 21 February 1976.
37 *Die Presse*, 9 March 1977. Capital export of Austrian industry has traditionally concentrated on building up foreign sales organizations rather than production facilities. The stock and annual flow of Austrian foreign investment amounted to less than one-quarter of the foreign investment in Austria and to less than 3 per cent of Austrian exports. See Dillinger, Höll, and Kramer, 'The state and international economic power', pp. 16–21, and Höll and Kramer, 'Österreich im internationalen System,' pp. 17–19. This explains why union opposition to capital exports has remained muted. See *Die Wirtschaft*, no. 35, 26 August 1975; *Volksstimme*, 7 December 1974; Ferdinand Lacina, 'Multinationale Konzerne und Gewerkschaften', *Wirtschaft und Gesellschaft*, vol. 1 (January 1975), pp. 41–2.
38 *Internationale Wirtschaft*, no. 28, 12 July 1974; *Die Presse* 25 October 1976.
39 ibid., 9 January 1976.
40 ibid., 12 February 1975.
41 *Wiener Zeitung*, 6 November 1974.
42 In 1975 that policy was changed to permit again the granting of short-term credits covering production periods; these credits were, however, granted at commercial rates and simply eased the liquidity problem of the firms without strengthening their capital base. See *Die Presse*, 12 February 1975; *Die Wirtschaft*, no. 26, 25 June 1975.
43 See the article of Deputy Chancellor and Finance Minister Hannes Androsch, 'Die Rolle der österreichischen Wirtschaft in der arbeitsteiligen Weltwirtschaft der achziger Jahre', *ÖIAG Journal*, vol. 1 (April 1977), pp. 3–5; Horst Knapp, 'Spätherbst oder neuer Frühling: Informationen und Impressionen zur Industriepolitik', *Finanznachrichten*, no. 4, 28 January 1977, pp. 1–8; *Die Presse*, 27 January 1977. See also the informative article by Helmut Kramer, 'Glanz und Elend der Strukturpolitik', *Die Industrie*, no. 28, 12 July 1974, pp. 5–7. On Austria's industrial policy in general see Organization for Economic Co-operation and Development, *The Industrial Policy of Austria* (Paris: OECD, 1971), and Beirat für Wirtschafts- und Sozialfragen, *Vorschläge zur Industriepolitik* (Vienna: Ueberreuter, 1970).
44 Deputy Chancellor Androsch as quoted in the *Arbeiterzeitung*, 9 January 1977.
45 Eduard März, 'Austrian investment policy in the post war period', *Zeitschrift für Nationalökonomie*, vol. 23, nos. 1–2 (1964), pp. 163–88; Franz Nemschak, 'Vorträge und Aufsätze', *Längerfristiges Wirtschafts wachstum und Wirtschaftsplanung in Österreich*, Vol. 23 (Vienna: Österreichisches Institut für Wirtschaftsforschung, 1965); Othmar Peham, 'Walter Eucken und seine Auswirkungen auf die Wirtschaftspolitik, insbesondere in der Ära Kamitz in Österreich', Diplom, Vienna, Hochschule für Welthandel, 1975; Herbert Reisenhofer et al., 'Kommentar zum Johnstone Bericht 1952', Vienna, unpublished manuscript, 1952.
46 Egon Matzner, *Modell Österreich: Skizzen für ein Wirtschafts- und Gesellschaftskonzept* (Vienna: Europa, 1967); Gutkas, Brusatti, and Weinzierl, *Österreich 1945–1970*, pp. 293–9; Friedrich Placek, 'Bankenkonzerne: Machtkonzentration oder Strukturpolitik?', *Wirtschaftspolitische Blätter*, vol. 2 (March–April 1976), pp. 102–13, contains data for the years 1969–76.
47 *Arbeiterzeitung*, 31 July 1975; *Branchenindikatoren: Studie erstellt vom*

Österreichischen Institut für Wirtschaftspolitik im Auftrag des Bundesministeriums für Handel, Gewerbe und Industrie (Vienna: Bundesministerium für Handel, Gewerbe und Industrie, 1973).
48 Breuss, *Komparative Vorteile*, p. 143; Wilhelm Ambichel, 'Strukturschwächen der industriellen Klein- und Mittelbetriebe Österreichs', PhD thesis, University of Vienna, 1971; Androsch, 'Die Rolle der österreichischen Wirtschaft'.
49 Quoted in *Kurier*, 23 May 1976. See also Oskar Grünwald, 'Industrieadministration in Österreich'. *IBE-Bulletin*, vols 21-2 (August 1976), pp. 11–15.
50 *Die Presse*, 3 March 1976.
51 ibid. 24 November 1976. In other related cases, such as Austria's pulp industry, the source of funds is not yet clear. See ibid. 30 September 1976.
52 ibid., 14 December 1976; *Wochenpresse*, 3 August 1977.
53 *Arbeiterzeitung*, 29 September 1976; *Salzburger Nachrichten* 1 July 1977.
54 *Die Presse*, 17 August 1977; *Arbeiterzeitung*, 29 September 1976. Placek's essay 'Bankenkonzerne' is a one-sided treatment of the whole question.
55 *Die Presse*, 8 June 1976.
56 *Neue Zeit* [Graz], 1 May 1977; *Kurier*, 30 March 1970; *Volksstimme*, 23 January 1977; Wolfgang Hobl, 'Die Reform der verstaatlichten Buntmetallindustrie in Österreich: In Erfüllung der Forderungen des ÖIG-Gesetzes', Diplom, Vienna, Wirtschaftsuniversität, 1975.
57 *Die Presse*, 4 June 1976.
58 Rodney P. Stiefbold, 'Segmented pluralism and consociational democracy in Austria: problems of political stability and change', in *Politics in Europe*, ed. Heisler, pp. 123, 173.
59 Incisive for their political analysis of the Second Republic are the books of a journalist, Alexander Vodopivec, which have appeared since the early 1960s. See also Rodney P. Stiefbold, 'Elites and elections in a fragmented political system', in *Sozialwissenschaftliches Jahrbuch für Politik*, ed. Rudolf Wildenmann (Munich: Günter Olzog, 1975), Vol. 4, pp. 119–227.
60 Reisenhofer *et al.*, 'Kommentar zum Johnstone Bericht', See also Dieter Bös, 'Machtproportionen in den paritätischen Organen', *Berichte und Informationen*, vol. 24, no. 1207 (10 October 1969), pp. 1–4.
61 References to the literature are included in Stiefbold, 'Elites and elections', and 'Segmented pluralism', and in McRae (ed.), *Consociational Democracy*. See also Rudolf Steininger, *Polarisierung und Integration: Eine vergleichende Untersuchung der strukturellen Versäulung der Gesellschaft in den Niederlanden und in Österreich* (Meisenheim am Glan: Anton Hain, 1975).
62 Theodor Pütz (ed.), *Verbände und Wirtschaftspolitik in Österreich* (Berlin: Duncker and Humblot, 1966); Herbert P. Secher, 'Representative democracy or "chamber state": the ambiguous role of interest groups in Austrian politics', *Western Political Quarterly*, vol. 13, no. 4 (December 1960), pp. 890–909; Alfred Stirnemann, *Interessengegensätze und Gruppenbildungen innerhalb der österreichischen Volkspartei* (Vienna: Institut für Höhere Studien und Wissenschaftliche Forschung, October, 1969).
63 Wolfgang Oberleitner, *Politisches Handbuch der Republik Österreich, 1945—1960* (Vienna: Österreichischer Bundesverlag, 1960), pp. 62-3. See also the articles on different interest groups in Heinz Fischer (ed.), *Das politische System Österreichs* (Vienna: Europa, 1974).
64 The organizational strength of its unions puts Austria at the very top among the advanced industrial states.
65 Kurt Steiner, *Politics in Austria* (Boston, Mass: Little, Brown, 1972), p. 298. See also Fritz Klenner, 'Der Österreichische Gewerkschaftsbund', in *Verbände und Wirtschaftspolitik*, ed. Pütz, pp. 437–501.
66 Günther Engelmayer (ed.), *Die Diener des Staates: Das bürokratische System Österreichs* (Vienna: Europaverlag, 1977); R. Kneucker, 'Austria: an administrative state. The role of Austrian bureaucracy', *Österreichische Zeitschrift für Politikwissenschaft*, vol. 2, no. 2 (1973), pp. 95-127; Alexander Vodopivec, *Die Balkanisierung Österreichs: Die Große Koalition und ihr Ende* (Vienna: Molden, 1966).
67 Koch, 'Contemporary Austrian Foreign Policy', pp. 206–7, 256–60; *Die Presse*, 19

April 1975; ibid., 25 October 1975; ibid., 16 April 1976; Josef G. Maier, 'Die Entwicklung der Exportförderung durch die Aussenhandelsstellen', Diplom, Vienna, Hochschule für Welthandel, 1976; Erich Staringer, 'Die Ausfuhrförderung in Österreich', *Quartalshefte der Gironzentrale*, vol. 1 (March 1967), pp. 67–75.
68 *Die Presse*, 18 March 1975. It should be noted though that the technological sophistication of this foreign trade system is to some extent misleading. Computer print-outs are only a partial remedy for the traditional weakness of Austrian firms in the area of marketing and aggressive salesmanship.
69 Dieter Bös, *Wirtschaftsgeschehen und Staatsgewalt: Wieviel Staat hat die Wirtschaft zu ertragen?* (Vienna: Herder, 1970).
70 Hannes Suppanz and Derek Robinson, *Prices and Incomes Policy: The Austrian Experience* (Paris: Organization for Economic Co-operation and Development, 1972); Alfred Klose, *Ein Weg zur Sozialpartnerschaft: Das österreichische Modell* (Munich: Oldenbourg, 1970); Eric Schiff, *Incomes Policies Abroad, Part II: France, West Germany, Austria, Denmark* (Washington, DC: American Enterprise Institute, 1972); 'Die Preiskontrolle der Paritätischen Preis-Lohn Kommission', *Monatsberichte*, vol. 37, no. 5 (May 1964), pp. 173–8; Institut für Angewandte Sozial- und Wirtschaftsforschung (ed.), *Zur Paritätischen Kommission für Preis- und Lohnfragen* (Vienna: Jupiter, 1966); Dieter Bichlauber and Anton Pelinka, *Wissenschaftliche Politikberatung am Beispiel der Paritätischen Kommission* (Vienna: Institut für Gesellschaftspolitik, n.d.); Wilhelm Braun, *Die Paritätische Kommission: Einkommenspolitik in Österreich* (Cologne: Deutscher Industrieverlag, 1970); Johann Farnleitner, *Die Paritätische Kommission: Institution und Verfahren* (Eisenstadt: Prugg, 1974).
71 Gerhard Lehmbruch, 'Liberal corporatism and party government', *Comparative Political Studies*, vol. 10, no. 1 (April 1977), pp. 91–126. See also Egon Matzner, 'Sozialpartnerschaft', in *Das politische System Österreichs*, ed. Fischer, p. 433; Heinz Fischer, 'Die Sozialpartnerschaft im politischen System Österreichs', *Europäische Rundschau*, vol. 2, no. 3 (1974), pp. 103–20.
72 The Raab–Boehm Agreement of 1957 and the Raab–Benya Agreement of 1961 which led first to the creation of the Commission and subsequently to the enlargement of its jurisdiction are clearer illustrations of this bilateralism than one would find today since the government and the state bureaucracy are now more directly involved in the preliminary negotiations between interest groups.
73 A third of all consumer prices are controlled by the Commission while an additional quarter of all consumer prices are set by the government. See Gerhard Lehmbruch, 'Consociational democracy, class conflict, and the new corporatism,' paper prepared for the IPSA Round Table, Jerusalem, 9–13 September 1974, p. 4. See also Manfred Majer, 'Der Beirat für Wirtschafts- und Sozialfragen: Problematik einer neuen Institution', PhD thesis, University of Innsbruck, 1965.
74 *New York Times*, 12 October 1975, p. 3. In the 1950s this policy required keeping down prices in Austria's nationalized industries in order to facilitate the reconstruction and renovation of Austrian industry.
75 This is true, for example, of Austria's nationalized steel industry and financial institutions. See the analysis of Alexander Vodopivec, *Wer Regiert in Österreich? Die Aera Gorbach-Pittermann* (Vienna: Verlag für Geschichte und Politik, 1962); idem *Wer regiert Österreich: Ein politisches Panorama* (Vienna: Verlag für Geschichte und Politik, 1960; idem, *Die dritte Republik: Machtstrukturen in Österreich* (Vienna: Molden, 1976). Chancellor Kreisky has recently reaffirmed that principle even though the SPÖ has made notable gains in the staffing of top positions throughout the public sector. *Arbeiterzeitung*, 11 May 1977; *Kurier*, 22 May 1976.
76 Hobl, 'Die Reform der verstaatlichten Buntmetallindustrien'; Gutkas, Brusatti, and Weinzierl, *Österreich 1945–1970*, pp. 210–14, 252–6, 289–303; Steiner, *Politics in Austria*, pp. 83–90. Although Austria's banks are less politicized than nationalized industry, their strong influence in particular industrial sectors is, typically, used to bail out weak firms rather than to assist in the task of rationalization as is true of West German banks. See Hobl, 'Die Reform der verstaatlichten Buntmetallindustrie', p. 81. For the situation in the industrial sector more generally see Edmond Langer, *Les Nationalisations en Autriche* (The Hague: Nijhoff, 1964); Stephan Koren, 'Sozialisierungsideologie und Verstaatlichungsrealität in Österreich', in *Die*

Verstaatlichung in Österreich, ed. Wilhelm Weber (Berlin: Duncker & Humbolt, 1964), p. 335; Christian Smekal, *Die verstaatlichte Industrie in der Marktwirtschaft: Das österreichische Beispiel* (Cologne: Heymann, 1963); Anton Tautscher, *Die österreichische Wirtschaftsordnung* (Salzburg: Pustet, 1971); Rupert Zimmermann, *Verstaatlichung in Österreich: Ihre Aufgabe und Ziele* (Vienna: Volksbuchhandlung, 1963); Herbert Slavik, 'Die Reform der österreichischen verstaalichten Eisen- und Stahlindustrie: Gemäss Bundesgesetz zur Zusammenfassung der Unternehmungen der verstaatlichten Eisen- und Stahlindustrie', Diplom, University of Vienna, 1973; Gerhard Handler, 'Die Verstaatlichung in Österreich nach 1945', PhD dissertation, Vienna, Hochschule für Welthandel 1966; Siegfried Hollerer, *Verstaatlichung und Wirtschaftsplanung in Österreich, 1946–1949* (Vienna: Verband der Wissenschaftlichen Gesellschaften Österreichs Verlag, 1974); Leopold Waller, 'Staatskapitalismus in Österreich', *Politische Studien*, vol. 14, no. 149 May–June 1963), pp. 299–313.
77 Lehmbruch, 'Liberal corporatism', pp. 5–6, 8–9, 41–55.
78 Lloyd, *International Trade Problems of Small Nations*, p. 33.
79 *Wiener Zeitung*, 16 December 1975.
80 Peter J. Katzenstein, 'International dependence and strategies of association: the small European states', paper prepared for the Institute for World Order NIEO Colloquium, Cascais, September 1977, pp. 7–18.
81 Simon Kuznets, *Economic Growth of Nations: Total Output and Production Structure* (Cambridge, Mass.: Harvard University Press, 1971), p. 124; M. Carmi, 'The economics of small developed states', Jerusalem, unpublished paper, 1975, p. 32.
82 *Mitteilungen der Handelskammer Niederösterreich*, 18 September 1970; *Oberösterreichische Nachrichten*, 12 April 1973.
83 Katzenstein, 'International dependence', pp. 15–16.
84 Herwig Kainz, 'Produktpolitik der österreichischen Kraftfahrzeugindustrie', Diplom, Vienna, Hochschule für Welthandel, 1972; Helmut Krackowizer, 'Die österreichische Kraftfahrzeug-Industrie, ihre volkswirtschaftliche Bedeutung und ihre wirtschaftlichen Probleme', PhD thesis, University of Innsbruck, 1952.
85 *Arbeiterzeitung*, 14 August 1977; ibid., 24 August 1971; *Kurier*, 17 June 1971.
86 *Volksstimme*, 24 March 1972. It should be noted in this context that Austria's technologically advanced and competitive truck industry is increasingly integrated into an international division of labor. See *Die Presse*, 1 December 1972; *Die Wirtschaft*, no. 11, 15 March 1977.
87 *Die Wirtschaft*, no. 15, 12 April 1977; *Der Spiegel*, vol. 31, no. 48 (21 November 1977); p. 159.
88 The initial investment is estimated at about 1 billion schillings. See *Der Spiegel*, vol. 31, no. 33 (8 August 1977), pp. 114–15.
89 Lloyd, *International Trade Problems of Small Nations*, p. 33. See also Kurt W. Rothschild, 'Size and viability: the lesson of Austria', in *Economic Consequences of the Size of Nations: Proceedings of a Conference held by the International Economics Association*, ed. E. A. G. Robinson (London: Macmillan, 1960), pp. 168–81.
90 M. Carmi, 'The economies of small developed states', (Hebrew University: The Jerusalem Group for National Planning, Small States Project, 1975), appendix.
91 *Oberösterreichische Nachrichten*, 26 March 1977; *Der Spiegel*, vol. 31, no. 37 (5 September 1977), pp. 116–26; vol. 31, no. 41 (3 October 1977), pp. 191–2; *Frankfurter Allgemeine Zeitung*, 4 October 1977, p. 13; *Süddeutsche Zeitung*, 5 October 1977, p. 21.
92 H. Androsch, 'Die Rolle der Österreichischen Wirtschaft', *Oberösterreichische Nachrichten*, 26 March 1977. The conflict pits Deputy Chancellor and Finance Minister Androsch against the Head of Austria's National Bank, Kienzl, with Chancellor Kreisky remaining so far silent on the issue. It is worth pointing out that the logic linking either of the two interpretations of the economic crisis to particular policy prescriptions is political, not causal.

12

Dissociation and Autocentric Development: An Alternative Development Policy for the Third World

DIETER SENGHAAS

> A narrowing of the North–South prosperity gap will be possible, in our opinion, only if the developing countries can be successfully integrated more closely into the world economy ... The decisive factor is support of an 'export-oriented' development strategy in the less developed countries.
>
> From an address by former Federal Minister for Economic Affairs Hans Friderichs at the University of Mainz, quoted from *Spiegel der Presse No. 3* (FRG: Federal Ministry for Economic Co-operation, 1976), p. 67.

> Manifestly this is not the science that teaches how *productive forces* are engendered and nurtured and how they are suppressed and destroyed.
>
> Friedrich List, *Das nationale System der politischen Ökonomie* (The National System of Political Economy) (Tübingen: Mohr Verlag, 1959; 1st edn 1841), p. 147.

> The school [meaning the still prevailing economic theory] cannot deny that the internal market of a nation is ten times more important than the external one, even where the latter is in full flower; but it has failed to draw from this the so-obvious conclusion that it is ten times more important to cultivate and safeguard the domestic market than to seek riches abroad, and that only in nations who have raised their domestic industry to a high level of development can foreign trade attain importance.
>
> Friedrich List, loc. cit., p. 138.

> Once a nation has succeeded in fully developing its factory system and also its agriculture, and in bringing both into equilibrium in such manner that the consumption of the one corresponds to the output of the other sector of the economy, such a nation has made certain for all the centuries to come of

> its progress in its productive forces and wealth, in its national power, prosperity and civilization; while a nation that is dependent on foreign countries with respect to manufacturing capacity is exposed to all the disturbances and perturbations to which we ... have drawn attention.
>
> Friedrich List, *Das natürliche System der politischen Ökonomie* (The Natural System of Political Economy) (Berlin: Akademie Verlag, 1961; 1st edn 1838), pp. 75–6.

This study has been conceived as a contribution to the current development theory and development policy debate.[1] That debate is concentrated at present on the Third World's demand for the replacement of the old world economic order by a New International Economic Order.[2] The dialogue, which is pursued primarily in international forums and which vacillates between confrontation and co-operation, has so far brought no results capable of changing the traditional world economic order. As numerous diagnoses have shown in the meantime, it is threatening to end in a blind alley. At the same time – regardless of all development policy debates – new structures of an international division of labour are looming up, though they are hardly calculated to bring a solution to development problems.[3]

In the light of this situation, which has been examined thoroughly elsewhere, this chapter analyses some of the factors which – in the light of historical experience up to now – have formed the basis for relatively successful development. From this analysis, there are several programmatic, development theory, and development policy conclusions to be drawn.

In this connection, it is not a vital issue at present to reflect on details of the practical changes of a dissociative and autocentric development policy. That must be left to a diversity of region-, country-, and sector-specific studies, whose object should be to scrutinize the hitherto distorted or completely untapped development potential in the light of the following deliberations. Nor is it the purpose of the following study to justify dissociative development policy as a problem-free development policy passepartout. In a political and scientific setting in which, almost without exception, people expect the solution to the familiar development problems to be found in more widespread integration and closer association of the Third World into the present world market, the following arguments may be regarded – as has mostly been done so far in the debate on 'integration or dissociation' – as theoretically and historically quite valid, but illusionary in practical respects. Is it, none the less, permissible to continue to inquire into the illusions of the presently prevailing practical policy?

Economic Foundations of Viable Economies

Comparative historical studies show that a precondition for successful economic and social development is the shaping of a specific structure and dynamic process of capital formation (capital accumulation) in a society and economy. From a purely economic standpoint, the combination of the following factors is of fundamental importance:

(1) a positive increase in agricultural productivity, by which the basic food supply for the domestic population and supplies of agricultural raw materials for industry are ensured;
(2) industrial production of consumer goods that are within the reach of the mass of the population (mass consumer goods as opposed to luxury consumer goods);
(3) industrial production of means of production:
equipment for agriculture; means of producing consumer goods (e.g. light mechanical engineering); means of producing intermediate products (e.g. heavy mechanical engineering); means of producing other means of production (machine tools, computers, telecommunication, control technology);
(4) production of intermediate products: intermediates for consumer goods (iron and steel industry, chemicals, energy); intermediates for producer's goods (iron and steel industry, energy, non-ferrous metals);
(5) creation of an infrastructure and goods for collective consumption (transport and communications systems, training facilities, public health system, etc.)

The history of viable economies builds upon differentiated development and gradual mutual interlinking of the above-mentioned sectors and subsectors. The high degree of differentiation of the production structure and the growing extent of interrelationships and intermeshing tend to lead in such an economy to structural cohesiveness and to interlinkages which enable such economies to become economic and social entities of high coherence. In principle, different degrees of such coherence are measurable by analyses of intrasectoral and intersectoral intermeshing (input-output analyses). Such economies have the following basic capabilities.

(1) The mass of the people in them are integrated productively into the economy; people find work, receive incomes, and become consumers, in consequence of which needs can be satisfied to varying degrees, depending on the level of development.
(2) In these economies there is an inherent interrelationship (congruence) among the production facilities, level of employment, income distribution, and structure of consumption (consumption profiles).
(3) Such congruence results – in the long run – in an organic development process from the simple to the complex, in which at the development level reached at any given time the complexity of the consumption profiles matches the organically evolved complexity of the production facilities and technology. There tends to be feedback between the rise in the level of productive capacity and the level of real wages.
(4) Such economies are distinguished by high innovative capacity;

technical progress determines the dynamics of development to a considerable extent.
(5) Structural change is a persistent concomitant of such economies (high transformability), different degrees of active and passive transformability (also combined with differing degrees of innovativeness) being observable.
(6) Successful development processes are hallmarked by the growing homogenization of the production level of the various sectors, though perfect homogenization is unattainable on account of technical and social change. The acid test is whether a society and economy become more fragmented (heterogeneous) or more homogeneous in consequence of the development of productive forces. The tendency towards homogeneity is apparent in the never complete, but nevertheless far-reaching correspondence of the costs of factors such as land, capital, labour, etc., *within* the various sectors and in the never closable, but also never crass, gap of such factor costs between the various sectors. The pertinent, absolute, and relative differences can be determined empirically by a study of real wage levels, interest rates, profit rates, productivity levels, etc.

Up to now, every successful development process has been marked by specific successions of stages and accentuations, which were dependent in each case on the initial situation within the stage of development reached by the international economy. In this connection, recent systematic, historical development theory has drawn attention to the constraints imposed by the structure of the modern world system on the nature and form of internal development; but it has also pointed out the compass-bearing influence of internal political and socioeconomic constellations on the nature and form of individual development processes.[4] The historical variability of development processes attributable to the two factors named is impressive;[5] for the current development policy debate, however, it is more remarkable that both the development of metropolitan capitalism in the present OECD countries and the development of socialist economies in the Soviet Union and in Eastern European societies, although enacted by capitalistic methods in the one case and staged by socialistic methods in the other, have led to the same configuration of burgeoning productive forces that has been outlined above. Furthermore, it is remarkable that those developing countries which now – in contrast to a few decades ago – no longer number among the acute problem cases of the Third World (such as China, North Korea, Albania, Cuba) are aspiring to a systematic development of their productive forces in all the cited subsectors of a viable economy with the predictable attainment of a comparable depth structure: by the encouragement of agricultural productivity, by the building-up of industrial sectors for the manufacture of producer's goods and the creation of technologies for making intermediate products and mass consumption goods, and by the systematic expansion of their infrastructure.

All three of the above-mentioned cases – metropolitan capitalism, metropolitan socialism, socialist developing countries – are characterized by an identical coherent structure of capital formation, although the social conditions present exhibit most striking differences, not only as between capitalistic and socialistic development processes, but also within capitalistic and socialistic systems. None of these processes is free from crises; each of them develops specific symptoms; some symptoms are all-embracing (e.g. the ecological problems); but in all cases there is the capability – at completely different development levels – of attaining the above-mentioned basic economic accomplishments, which in their turn constitute the essential basis for social accomplishments.[6] (And carried by the tide of such a dynamic interlacement process, those social accomplishments, in their turn, dynamify the basic economic performance.)

Structural Characteristics of Peripheral Economies

The societies and economies of the Third World (peripheral economies) are characterized by exactly the opposite of what has been outlined above as a viable economy and its basic accomplishments.

(1) Only the export-oriented segment of agriculture is marked by some degree of dynamic impetus; for the most part, no substantial increase in agricultural productivity occurs on a broad basis. Hence, an essential precondition for a successful development process is unfulfilled. The same applies to the raw materials sector. True, in many places this sector is highly productive, but no more than an exclave of metropolitan economies and therefore not integrated into a coherent, intermeshed domestic economy.

(2) The industrial production of mass consumer goods is stagnant compared to the import of industrially produced, luxury consumer goods, or, in some instances, to local production of luxury consumer goods. This structural distortion reflects the crass, and in most cases still increasing, income differentials in peripheral capitalistic societies. This phenomenon, too, reflects the incapability of such economies of integrating the mass of the population productively into the capital-forming process.

(3) As a rule, a sector for domestic production of means of production is completely lacking and its development has been prevented by asymmetrical division of labour between metropolitan and peripheral economies. Hence, peripheral economies are systematically deprived of vital development impulses. In the few cases in which such production facilities are built up they are typically oriented to the dominant growth poles (and thus, for example, to the production of equipment for manufacturing luxury consumer goods and the related infrastructure).

(4) The production of intermediate goods is but little developed, and this, together with the lack of production of equipment and technologies, is the cause of the far-reaching technological dependence of peripheral capitalistic economies on the industrial

societies, which is resolving to an increasing extent into hopeless financial dependency.
(5) The collective consumer goods (education, health, etc.) and the development of the infrastructure have not, as a rule, contributed toward homogenizing the society of the Third World, but toward accentuating the disparities between growth poles and the hinterland.

Peripheral economies lack the vital production sectors (productive agriculture, mass consumer goods industry, equipment industry, broad infrastructure) that are essential for a viable society and they lack interlacement of those sectors. They may therefore be described as structurally crippled.[7] Their basic problems do not lie in the fact that no productive forces develop in them; in the period from 1950 to 1975, for instance, the economic growth of the developing countries attained orders of magnitude never achieved by the industrial societies in any comparable period prior to 1950.[8] As a general rule, the peripheral economies are decidedly high-growth economies, or to be more accurate, growth-pole economies. Their problem lies in the fact that their growth is concentrated on a few, mostly export-oriented, sectors, and that even where domestic industrialization processes have made good headway, the growth processes oriented to the home market are strictly limited sectorally and in terms of stratification. The result is structure-conditioned fragility of such economies. Their lack of coherence is attributable to:

(1) a lack of intermeshing of agriculture and industry (no forward or backward linkages);
(2) lacking depth of production, i.e. the lack of complete economic cycles: part of the capital-forming process, especially the production of technologies and equipment and to a substantial extent the production of intermediate products and consumer goods, takes place in the industrial societies; the economic spin-off effects of such reproduction are continually lost to the peripheral economies and find expression in the structural crippling already mentioned;
(3) the inherent, sociologically conditioned tendency of industrialization stages up to the present to satisfy the demand of high-income strata (landowning oligarchy, import-export oligarchy, the urban middle class, members of the services sectors, the public administration, the military, segments of the better-paid workers in urban centres), while the production of mass consumer goods remains relatively stagnant on account of the only less-than-average or even negative growth of the purchasing power of the masses (farmers, informal sector, workers);
(4) the consequent, by no means natural, narrowness of the domestic market, which has been brought about by historical and sociological processes and which is the logical outcome of incomplete economic cycles and of a non-coherent reproduction dynamic.

On the Genesis of Peripheral Economies

Underdevelopment has nothing to do with traditional backwardness and it is not the outcome of inadequate development of productive forces (for then the economies in question would be *un*developed); underdevelopment is rather a manifestation of misguided development of productive forces. The problem of the economies of the Third World lies not in their incapacity to form capital, but in a wrongly structured accumulation, which has detrimental effects for the majority of the people. The capital formation is not designed to open up a country's domestic market. It is oriented to the metropolitan economies, whether through the high-pressure production of goods for the world market or through taking over metropolitan consumer goods, consumption patterns, and technologies, all of which reflect a far higher and more complex (and hence more capital-intensive, more energy-intensive, and also more costly) development level, the products of which must necessarily act as structure-deforming foreign bodies in economies with less advanced and distorted development of productive forces.

This conventional structure of misdirected capital formation is the result of integrating the societies of Latin America, Africa, and Asia into a system of unequal international division of labour during the phase of colonialism and imperialism. It is remarkable that right up to the present day, the current debate on development theory still knows no concept of unequal division of labour. As a rule, it adheres to the classical, free-trade dogmas of foreign trade theory. According to that theory's prevailing doctrine of comparative advantages, all participants in international trade benefit, provided they specialize in the production of those goods for which they can make the best use of locally available factors (land, natural resources, capital, labour, technological know-how, etc.). In this context, in the theory the question has never been consequentially raised of what specific effects specialization conforming to the postulates of the doctrine of comparative advantages will exert on production structure, income distribution, consumption profiles, labour market, and infrastructure in the case of trading partners on unequal initial levels. If this question had been raised, the fundamental difference between trading structures of a symmetrical and an asymmetrical nature would have become evident. The above-diagnosed effects on a peripheral economy are manifestly the consequence of integrating the economies of Latin America, Africa, and Asia into an asymmetrically structured international economy which is permeated and dominated by metropolitan capitalism. That metropolitan capitalism is hallmarked by relatively productive, viable economies; its dynamic vigour stems from a gradual, systematic opening up of countries' own domestic markets. However, the viability of these economies was facilitated by the relations with the overseas economies: by the plundering of large areas of the Third World in the phase of primitive accumulation; by the possibility of importing cheap agricultural and mineral products, cheap energy, and cheap labour from the colonies or of using cheap labour there for the local production of mineral and agricultural raw materials and, later on, of finished goods requiring little processing – factors which have all contributed and still do contribute to the reduction of production costs in metropolitan economies.

In the course of this process, not only was locally accumulated capital drawn off from the southern continents; a much more radical result was the transformation of fairly viable subsistence economies into defective and crippled peripheral economies, the dynamic reproduction process of which brings specific effects.

(1) There is incapability of integrating the mass of the population productively into the economic production process.
(2) There is growing incapability of feeding the mass of the population with locally produced agricultural goods.
(3) There is incapability of inventing and manufacturing their own means of production, equipment, hand tools, and technologies and of adapting existing goods of these types to local needs.
(4) There is incapability of originating technical progress geared to local problem situations (innovative incapacity) and of changing traditional structures (transformative incapacity). These latter disabilities reflect the lack of structural differentiation, which in extreme cases takes the form of a monocultural economy.
(5) The structural crippling is evidenced by a striking and growing heterogeneity of peripheral societies and peripheral economies. If homogeneity or heterogeneity is measured operationally with indicators such as labour productivity, wage levels, qualification of labour, degree of organization of capital and labour, capital intensity and labour intensity of production, etc., it can hardly be denied that in the peripheries the fissures between 'modern' growth poles and the rest of the economy have widened during the past decades. This is equally true of the primary, secondary, and tertiary sectors. The relevant differences, e.g. between the by-no-means-disappearing minifundium and the capital-intensive agro-business groups which produce as a rule for the world market, but in the meantime also for the domestic, urban, luxuries and semi-luxuries market, are undoubtedly more marked than the traditional differences between minifundium and latifundium. In other spheres, comparable hierarchization can be observed, e.g. between groups with multinational operations, local undertakings, local crafts and trades, and the informal sector.
(6) This heterogeneity and hierarchization matches up with a very unequal distribution of political organization: the mass of the population remains or is placed under political tutelage, notwithstanding intermediate phases of a different stamp (e.g. populism). This phenomenon is in contrast to the growing political structuring of all levels of metropolitan societies, and particularly to the increasing degree of political organization of labour – a result of a long drawn-out and wearisome struggle of the union labour movement.
(7) The dialectics of misguided growth and mass penury generate a

substantial amount of conflict potential which is the background for the growing internal militarization of societies of the Third World. The danger of such internal militarization forming the foundation for building up classical international and intersociety conflict fronts is becoming ever more manifest.

Many years ago Karl Schiller described the development path of the countries of the Third World under the present system of division of labour as follows:

> In the raw material countries overseas, on their coming into touch with the capitalist world, the process began, so to speak, with the second act (some proponents of the theory of comparative costs often forget that in Ricardo's example, of course, before the inception of foreign trade, both countries, Portugal and Britain, can produce both products, wine and cloth, and after its inception specialize in wine or cloth, each country maintaining its respective national employment volume. So in that case a stage is attained where productive forces are developed even before specialization is presupposed). Modern production processes were transferred to the various countries, which, according to the 'law', were appropriate there for participation in world trade. The first act of step-by-step 'education' of the whole economy toward a modern mode of operation was omitted. Thus an overseas economy came into being, which has very modern production facilities, but on the whole only in those lines in which it is a specialized exporter. The overseas economy was developed in its modern segment, that is to say, not across the full breadth of its structure as, say, in the principal European-American countries, but at 'focal points' that were complementary 'counter-structures' to these latter countries. The 'tendency of production to spread' did not even start to take effect across the full breadth of overseas economies. ... So up to now, in the case of many overseas countries we have only lopsided or top-heavy integration into the modern economy, so to speak, which is geared solely to 'worldwide division of labour'.[9]

The question of what would have happened to the countries of the Third World without any integration into the international division of labour dominated by the metropolitan economies can hardly be of any interest today; all that remains for us is to record the lack of total development across the board which was diagnosed by Schiller, that is, the lack of 'full-breadth development' or the lack of development of a 'full-breadth structure'. The task of development theory and development policy is to consider the preconditions and measures which make development in breadth possible – an economy with internal, mutually fructifying, complementary effects.

A clear conception of the structural make-up of a peripheral economy is essential in order to arrive at meaningful development policy guidelines. If, as conventionally assumed, the economies of the Third World are regarded as traditionally backward in contrast to metropolitan modern economies, if they are conceived as embyronic, miniature editions of early phases of metropolitan economies to which it is only necessary to impart dynamic impetus, the failure of development policy strategies based on such conceptions is already built into the initial interpretations, as has meanwhile been demonstrated incontestably by abortive development policy in the past decades. For this reason it is necessary for every development policy measure, regardless of its point of departure, to pose the crucial question of how the traditional structure of the peripheral economy will be affected by it. That traditional structure is an 'in-depth structure', the essential characteristics of which can be observed everywhere in the societies and economies of the southern continents with greatly varying development of productive forces (in Haiti or Senegal just as much as in Indonesia or Brazil).[10] This is the objective reason why it is possible to draw, as a first step, general conclusions from the foregoing argument.

Capitalism and Cryptocapitalism in the Peripheries

To get an adequate grasp of the current development problems in the Third World it is necessary to classify the modes of production that are predominant there. In the above, the thesis has been advanced that metropolitan capitalism undergoes a process of homogenization, in the course of which, at least on a national scale, integrated market structures tend to come into being, within which specific adjustment and compensation processes take place, though homogeneity is never actually achieved or even achievable. The thesis concerning the tendency toward homogenization implies two things: on the one hand, it means the tendency toward thorough going capitalization of all essential spheres of life; on the other, it affirms the observation that in metropolitan capitalism intra- and intersectoral differences repeatedly become clearly apparent, for example, in the productivity of labour (in consequence of technical progress and social change), but ultimately undergo an equalization process and within integrated market structures remain as a rule inside certain limits. However, it must not be forgotten that metropolitan capitalism includes spheres which obstinately resist thoroughgoing capitalization. Of these the most striking example is non-capitalization of the work of housewives and mothers, that is, housework in general, which is of essential importance for the reproduction of society as a whole.[11] Notwithstanding this significant sphere, it is admissible to advance the thesis that in metropolitan capitalism the capitalistic mode of production tends to assume an exclusive function – and hence pre-capitalistic and non-capitalistic modes of production are dying out.

In peripheral economies, however, the capitalistic mode of production predominates only in the dynamic salient sectors, while in the subordinate sectors, though oriented to the dominant, capitalistic growth poles, widely differing forms of production can be observed. Peripheral social structures are marked by the combination of hierarchically mutually associated forms of production. This fact gives rise to the serious theoretical difficulty of defining clearly those forms of production which are subordinate to capitalist production. Are they pre-capitalistic, feudal, mixed modes of production, or modes of production of a singular type?

It is a peculiarity of the capitalistic mode of production that it tends to revamp modes of production of preceding stages to suit its own requirements. Whereas in metropolitan capitalism the capitalistic mode of production assumes in this process an exclusive function that is determinative in all spheres of the economy and society (this being *inter alia* the reason for the vitality of metropolitan capitalism), in peripheral capitalistic social structures it can be observed that all spheres tend to be affected and permeated by capitalistic growth poles, but without the capitalistic mode of production becoming exclusive in the metropolitan sense. In the light of the empirically demonstrable high degree of permeation and revamping of subordinate forms of production to gear them to the dominant poles, also precisely where the illusion of traditionalism and non-capitalism is preserved, it is wise to designate such subordinate forms of production, not as feudal residues, as supposedly pre-capitalistic, traditional forms of production, but as cryptocapitalistic.

Cryptocapitalistic modes of production do not exist autonomously and separately; they are conceivable only together with a higher-order capitalistic mode of production. While cryptocapitalistic modes of production outwardly exhibit non-capitalistic attributes (consider, for instance, the small commodity-farming producer in West Africa, who has land and means of production with the help of which he produces enough for his subsistence and a small surplus) such forms of production have no identity of their own, even though they preserve the illusion of being different, that is, non-capitalistic.[12] The term 'cryptocapitalistic mode of production' is used here in an attempt to define semantically the so-ambiguous character of the forms of production subordinate to capitalistic production. The capitalistic mode of production attempts to make the entire economy serve its purposes without becoming exclusive in the peripheries. The result of this historical process is a social configuration hallmarked by structural heterogeneity.

The great diversity of empirical observations summarized above are important, because they turn our attention to the traditional theory of dualism. It will be recalled that according to this theory the peripheral economies can be subdivided into a modern and traditional sector which, strictly speaking, coexist more or less without any symbiotic relationships. Recent debate has also drawn attention to the dubiousness of such a notion, and the development policy pursued in the developing countries in the past thirty years has demonstrated that this theory is wrong. For according to the theory, it should be possible, for instance, to 'develop' dualistic structures in their entirety by dynamifying growth poles by massive capital input, transfer of technology and of scientific and management personnel, inducing irradiation of the rest of the economy with their dynamic forces with such positive effects that an initially dualistic configuration gradually becomes an integrated structure, a metropolitan economy in miniature. It is now hardly contested that this idea of development was deceptive, although the reasons are perceived only vaguely on account of the lack of a clear-cut definition of the peripheral economy.

Peripheral capitalism, though a product of metropolitan penetration, is not comparable fundamentally to the structure of metropolitan capitalism. This is true not only in the economic domain but also in the social structure and in the form of political organization. The essential 'service' performed by peripheral capitalism consists in the constant supply of a mass of cheap labour, which is continually reproduced within its own framework.[13] In metropolitan capitalism, too, labour was freed and proletarianized, but then absorbed by the dynamic reproduction system oriented to the domestic market which has been outlined above. No comparable opening up of the domestic market takes place in peripheral capitalistic countries today. No building-up of a comparably differentiated production structure or a consequent macroeconomically relevant dynamic intermeshing process can be observed; nor is that political precondition for the increasing opening-up of countries' domestic markets observable, that is, the political organization of labour, without which particularly metropolitan development would have been inconceivable, quite apart from other factors such as the spreading of standardized discipline of labour, and so on.[14]

As mentioned above, the peripheral economies were extremely useful for the building-up of metropolitan capitalism in the sense that the goods they supplied (raw materials, food, human labour, etc.) enabled production costs in metropolitan capitalism to be kept lower than would ever have been possible without such inputs from the Third World. As union organization of labour spread, the settlement of political issues between capital and labour was thus facilitated. In this sense, the traditional pattern of relations between metropolitan economies and the peripheries proved positively helpful and expedient for the development of metropolitan capitalism although the real accomplishments of metropolitan capitalism were achieved by its own virility, that is they resulted from the forced growth of productive forces in the respective domestic markets.[15]

The economically crippled structures which do not make the opening-up of domestic markets on a broad basis possible in the peripheral economies are the outcome of a profound, long drawn-out historical process which integrated the societies and economies of the Third World into an unequal international division-of-labour system, with disastrous results. Although, as has just been said, that integration was highly efficacious for the development of metropolitan capitalism, it now proves that the distortion and narrowness of local domestic markets resulting from that integration is a barrier to thoroughgoing capitalization on capitalistic lines. What development-minded critics of the classical liberal theory of international trade and development like Friedrich List farsightedly predicted with respect to the development chances of the centres of metropolitan capitalism[16] is now really coming true with a vengeance on a worldwide scale with respect to the relationship between industrial society and the Third World.

Three Imperatives of Development Policy

Which are the implications resulting from the preceding analysis? Three imperatives for a sound development policy will be spelled out: the imperative of dissociation, the imperative of internal restructuring, and the imperative of a new division of labour among economies of the Third World.

The Imperative of Dissociation

In the long run, the Third World has a chance of building up self-reliant and viable economies and societies only if it dissociates itself temporarily from the prevailing international economy, namely, the metropolitan economies. As Karl Schiller correctly analysed, the developing countries lack 'the first act of in-breadth development' necessary for a successful development process. Historical experience of capitalistic and socialistic development processes that resulted in more or less viable structures shows that without a period of self-centredness, the duration of which may vary from case to case, that is without protection motivated by development policy, an intensive (as opposed to an extensive) development of productive forces is hardly possible. Mercantilism, phases of purposive protective policy, enforced or voluntarily self-imposed autarchy, constitute, in the light of these systematic aspects, merely variations of one and the same requirement.[17] And is it just coincidence or of more fundamental significance that in that area of Western and central Europe in which the development processes of our modern age began development was determined by 'temporary severance from the main arteries of previously prevailing trade'?

> In the Carolingian age, an important area did, in fact, centre itself for the first time around a focal point lying very far inland. Society was confronted with the task of developing inland communications more intensively. As it succeeded in doing so in the course of the centuries, in this respect, too, the heritage of antiquity had new conditions imposed upon it. The foundation was laid for configurations unknown to antiquity. It is from this standpoint that certain differences between the integrated units of antiquity and the others which slowly evolved in the occident must be considered: states, nations, or whatever those units may be called, comprised for the most part ethnic groups clustered around inland centres or capital cities and linked with each other by inland arteries.[18]

Is it not precisely the growth of inland interlacement as the nucleus for political control capacities, development of economic productive forces, and cultural identification, which peripheral societies typically lack and which they cannot attain as long as they remain integrated in the traditional world market structures as they have been in the past decades and centuries?

Self-centredness of this sort, with the goal of intensive development of productive forces in a country's own area, need not necessarily be identical with autarchy, although in the light of history it would seem scarcely to be a coincidence that, in view of the ever greater differences between the average productivity level of economies within the international economy, protection is being built up more comprehensively on all fronts, that is, autarchy is gaining importance as an instrument of development policy. Since, as mentioned above, peripheral economies are characterized by a lack of innovative and transformative capacity, such a course of development – quite apart from the political circumstances – is considered to bring heavy losses in terms of short-run cost-benefit assessments. However, such an assessment changes nothing in the sound development policy thesis that development can be brought to fruition only by one or the other form of dissociation.

Even assuming dissociation, trade with the more productive, dominant metropolitan economies is possible, but that trade is a consequence of an inward-oriented dynamic accumulation process in the sense that it is merely expedient and does not determine the dynamic impetus of the entire reproduction process. Trade must be pursued selectively, and only that form of selective co-operation should be practiced which benefits the building-up of a viable internal structure in the countries of the southern continents. Hence what is involved, as shown in a study of such widely differing cases as the development of Japan and that of the Soviet Union, is calculated isolation coupled with selective utilization of the world market, in which connection the authors point out that present-day China, more than any other country, seems to be repeating this scenario 'of calculated isolation, insistence on the vitality and superiority of strategies internally developed, and selective borrowing'.[19]

For the majority of countries of the Third World, dissociation nowadays means, in particular, a break with the traditional, export-oriented economy and instead mobilization of their own resources with the goal of making such resources utilizable for their *own* purposes. This would mean, specifically, a break with the production of raw materials, which are processed mainly in the metropolitan economies; a break with export-oriented industrialization, which will very soon prove to be very costly and a new cul-de-sac in the traditional development process; but also a break with misguided industrialization geared to import substitution, which, where it was pursued, patently satisfied chiefly the demand of high-income strata and was not oriented to the potential demand of the impoverished masses.

The Imperative of Restructuring

The second imperative relates to the building-up of coherent accumulation structures in the countries of the Third World themselves. This sort of autocentric development is hardly conceivable without organic linking of the following activities:

- renewed prospecting of locally available resources;
- local utilization of local resources;

- building-up of a domestic industrial sector for the production of means of production and intermediate goods;
- invention and reinvention of suitable technologies, and further development and adaptation of existing technologies to local needs;
- in-breadth productivity improvement in agriculture;
- industrial production of mass consumer goods designed to satisfy the basic needs of the masses;
- building-up of a broadly effective infrastructure.

Only the convergence of these activities permits step-by-step opening-up of the domestic market, by which the mass of the population is integrated into productive activities, purchasing power can be achieved, and dynamic impetus imparted to the demand for agricultural and industrial equipment and mass consumer goods, and for private and public services on the spot, all oriented to the satisfaction of local needs.[20]

Though the individual requirements of such a guideline may meanwhile have gained acceptance also in traditional development programmes, there can be no doubt that a development programme that would further the realization of all named factors in combination is opposed. The reason is that such a development programme is not conceivable without far-reaching repudiation of the traditional doctrine of comparative costs and advantages. What does this mean?

In an international economy in which national economies of differing development levels and average degrees of productivity coexist, goods of every type (consumer goods, machinery, technology, etc.) can be purchased by less productive economies in economies with higher productivity at less than the cost of producing them themselves. If trade is carried on within an asymmetrical structure, for example, between a metropolitan economy and a peripheral economy, comparative cost calculations result in peripheralization of the less productive economy: The less productive economy buys on the world market in more productive economies at lower cost – and in return, if it does not follow first and foremost an autocentric development path, it suffers fundamental structural defects. It saves itself the learning costs that are indispensable for building up a viable economy, only to be divested in the end of its capacity to invent, develop, adapt, and produce its own or foreign tools, equipment, and technology.[21] This is the reason why, in specific phases of the history of their development, most developing countries not only experienced predatory competition from industrial goods from the metropolitan economies to the detriment of handcrafted products (which in metropolitan development was an important phase in opening up the domestic market), but also phases of industrial regression, that is, elimination of already achieved industrial development levels.[22]

The consequence is that foreign machines and foreign technologies and the more complex consumer goods of an economy with higher average productivity are transferred as finished products to a less, and moreover defectively, developed economy and there necessarily act as economic foreign bodies with distorting socioeconomic effects.

If the countries of the Third World are really to develop, it is essential to break away from an unequally structured international division of labour and the doctrine of comparative costs; the costs necessary for building up a coherent economic structure must be classified – as in the case of every viable economy – as inevitable learning costs. They are a burden; but unwillingness to bear them would only mean carrying over the present structural defects and their social consequences into the future (unemployment, marginality, uncontrollable population growth, crass inequality of incomes, etc.).

> Industrialization means . . . step-by-step development of production capability by a steady, slow and patient process of learning by doing. It means much more than just setting up certain production capacities, which if need be, of course, can be imported from abroad. If the broad mass of the population is given a part to play in production and is to receive income via that production, suitable conditions must be created for the integration of the broad masses into the ever more differentiated process of division of labour. To this end it is essential that basic knowledge of alphabetization, technology and organization be imparted and furthered systematically. Similarly, the organizational prerequisites for industrial production must be created and all involved familiarized with appropriate organizational know-how. It is precisely these things which no country can import, but must accomplish itself. It is possible to import ideas, certain finished solutions to problems, which can then be adapted in every country concerned. But the adaptive capacity itself must exist or be systematically built up and developed.[23]

It is not against the doctrine of comparative costs *per se* that criticism is levelled. That doctrine appears to be fairly meaningful in development planning and assessment of trade processes when the economies concerned are in fairly similar situations (e.g. France and the Federal Republic of Germany at the present time), because in such a case the comparable initial situations permit expectation of a fair benefit for all involved. If peripheral economies follow the doctrine of comparative benefit and hence allocation calculi of the international economy, optimal allocation of a given stock of factors from a cosmopolitan standpoint can be expected (e.g. input of cheap labour for export-oriented production of finished goods in free production zones), but not the building-up of domestic development potential, the gaining of depth of production and coherence.[24] Friedrich List emphatically drew attention to this fact in the debate with the proponents of classical English economics (theory of value); he enumerated his arguments relating to the building-up of domestic development potential in a theory of the production of productive forces.

In dealing with the demands of the Third World, the Western capitalistic societies now resort, in the final analysis, to the doctrine of free trade. As demonstrated by Friedrich List more than a hundred years ago, that is a doctrine which caters for the interests of highly productive economies. In such pleas it is forgotten that in the history of every single capitalistic metropolitan economy, regardless of whether they were densely or more sparsely populated societies, there were phases in which only by disregarding free trade economic and development policy, that is, by disregarding the price mechanism as a means of controlling development processes, could an untapped development potential be opened up with the object of opening up an economy's domestic market, expanding it, and making it into an integrative structure.[25]

By the tapping of cheap labour sources by industries transferred from the metropolitan countries to the peripheries, superficially a development potential would seem to be created. In reality, grafted-on industrialization is extremely dubious from the standpoint of development policy, because it amounts to mere treatment of symptoms: cheap labour – according to the doctrine of comparative advantages the input factor *par excellence* of the Third World – is placed in the service of production oriented to the world market without eliminating in the process the structural causes of ever-renewed engendering of cheap labour. Like earlier economic activities of the industrial societies in the age of colonialism in the Third World (raw material production, plantation cultivation, etc.), grafted-on industrialization is also characterized by fragmentariness and enclave-type organization of production. This is clearly evident where transplantation is limited to the production of labour-intensive components of a complicated final product which is ultimately manufactured in the industrial societies. The enclave character becomes manifest when the grafting-on of industrialization occurs in so-called free production zones. Because they are grafted on from outside and oriented to the world market, such industries do not as a rule generate any enduring, dynamic intermeshing impetus. The sole result of grafted-on industrialization – which mostly serves to produce goods for the world market with the same productivity as in the industrial societies but for crassly unequal remuneration – is the exploitation of cheap labour – all other development policy objectives, though well meant, remain wishful thinking. 'For this reason', to quote Ludwig Erhard, 'nothing is so unwise and wrong for enduring development as the often asserted view that in development policy top priority should be given primarily to promoting the exports of the developing countries'.[26] A liberal theory which is oriented to and furthers the interests of metropolitan economies regards such procedure as development-promoting (however dubious the details of the justification may be). From the viewpoint of List's theory of the production of productive forces, such a procedure is highly reprehensible, because it does not help to enhance and further a given development potential with the goal of establishing a viable economy.

It is remarkable that the development policy debate on – academically speaking – the theory of value and the theory of the production of productive forces not only played an important role in the development process of the capitalistic, metropolitan economies (as evidenced by the theory and agitation of Friedrich List, to cite just one example); the same problems played a comparable role also in the debate on international division of labour and foreign trade co-operation among socialist societies with differing development levels.

The Sino-Soviet altercation on the appropriate development path for China in the second half of the 1950s and early 1960s related *inter alia* to this controversy.[27] And the dispute between the Soviet Union and North Korea, a case made interesting by the differences in size and development level, revolved in the second half of the 1950s around the issue of whether a developing country like North Korea could afford to pursue a development path intended to build up a heavy industry designed to stimulate light industry and agriculture – or whether it would not be more expedient to arrange far-reaching division of labour between the Soviet Union, which is productive in every respect, and a North Korean economy in which only subsectors should be built up and become specialized on the division-of-labour principle.[28] In 1965, in a lecture given in Indonesia, Kim il Sung described the controversy in retrospect as follows:

> The anti-Party elements lurking within the Party, and the revisionists and dogmatists both at home and abroad loudly protested against the line of ensuring the priority growth of heavy industry while simultaneously developing light industry and agriculture. According to their arguments, everything should have been directed to the daily need of consumption, leaving the future out of account. *Their purpose*, in the final analysis, *was to prevent our country from building its economic foundations*.[29]

In autumn 1963 the official party organ of North Korea wrote:

> Today some people ... have unilaterally repealed their agreements with fraternal countries and have virtually cut off the relations of economic and technical co-operation. They brand the construction of an independent national economy a 'nationalistic tendency' ... Those who oppose the building of an independent economy advocate, instead, the establishment of an 'integrated economy' of the socialist countries ... Under the signboard of 'integrated economy' they want to stamp out the economic independence of fraternal countries ... and make them subordinate to others ... It goes without saying that the loss of independence in economy will make it impossible for any country to maintain its genuine independence and sovereignty ... 'Aid' with strings attached or 'aid' given as a precondition for interference in others' internal affairs, as practiced among capitalist countries, cannot exist and must not exist among socialist countries.[30]

Elsewhere, Kim il Sung depicts the same facts systematically as follows:

> We do not intend by any means to oppose the economic co-operation of countries and to build up socialism in isolation. What we do oppose is the trends pursued by the great powers which, under the excuse of 'economic co-operation' and 'international division of labour', amount to no less than impeding the independent and complex development of the economy of a country and subjugating that economy. We are of the opinion that every country must co-operate with others on the basis of developing its own national economy, and that only then can economic co-operation among countries be unremittingly expanded and further developed according to the principle of completely equal rights amd mutual benefit. Today, our country is building up its economy with its own technology, with its own resources, with the strength of its own cadres and its own nation, and covers domestic demand for the products of heavy and light industry and for agricultural products largely from domestic production.[31]

The debate on international division of labour and economic co-operation within Comecon is likewise an indication of the problems raised here, which are of importance also in relations among socialist countries.[32] Faced with the alternative of far-reaching international socialist division of labour on the one hand or relatively costly building up of a broad-based agricultural and industrial structure on the other, the countries of Eastern Europe have evidently decided in favour of List's solution, which is evidenced by, among other things, the relatively small degree of integration in Comecon. Particularly the south-eastern European states, which were hallmarked up to the Second World War by all the attributes of peripheral-capitalistic social formations, regard international specialization of production as a process which, though important, does not have to be given priority under all circumstances and in all spheres of production. Hence the concentration on mobilization and utilization of domestic resources and efforts serves also within the framework of international division of labour among socialist societies a protective function similar to that which List provided for in his strategy of temporary dissociation.

The empirical examples cited here from the domain of development of capitalist and socialist metropolitan economies and of socialist developing countries underline an observation recently formulated by Paul Streeten. In a paper on self-reliance, he writes that the new argument is tantamount to protection (if not to autarchy) – at least in principle – of all economic activities:

> By opening up a society indiscriminately and too widely, we reduce the incentives and opportunities to develop indigenous processes and products appropriate for the low-income groups in developing countries, for their small and low-income markets, for their scarcity

of physical and human capital and for their desire for the wide spread of the benefits of development. The education, psychological and institutional arguments against a move toward world free trade, for capital flows and general openness point to the need to protect all activities from the eroding influences of the advanced world economy and, more important, they point to the need for constructive indigenous efforts, which, of course, do not result automatically from looking toward like-minded countries, but which may be hampered by an excessively outward-looking strategy and by emulation of the style of the rich.

Something like this also underlies the distinction between self-reliance and dependence, between autonomy and domination. Countries and groups of countries that generate their own technological capability, their own social institutions and organizations (not only in technology and industry but also in land tenure and rural institutions) will be able to mobilize their efforts more effectively than those that always look at how they order these things in the metropolis.[33]

The Imperative of a New Division of Labour

Another, third imperative of development policy relates to evolving *new forms of division of labour among the economies of the Third World itself*. Nowadays the term 'collective self-reliance' is used to describe this imperative. But an international division of labour in the subregional, regional, and continental domains – and also among the three southern continents – will have little success without dissociation of the peripheries from the dominant industrial societies. If they remain integrated in the world market as it is today, the idea of collective self-reliance is interesting, but without any real significance for development policy, as new market arrangements (e.g. free trade zones and the like) extending beyond individual economies would very easily prove to be nothing more than enlarged areas providing enhanced possibilities for penetration by the metropolitan economies.

Dissociated from the world market, the peripheries would have the chance of developing their economies in relation to each other, that is by mutually complementary processes. In this connection, importance would attach not merely to division of labour in the pure economic sense, but also to the building-up of subregional, regional, and continental infrastructures with provision for common transport and communication systems, means of transport, insurance companies, news agencies, and so on. This would contribute toward to dehierarchization of the present grossly hierarchized international society[34] and hence to the formation of effective counterweights to the so-called metropolitan economies.

If we proceed from the primary requirements of development policy, that is, satisfaction of the basic needs of the masses, the translation of this third imperative into practice in a first stage of meaningful development policy is less dramatic than it seems at first.

This building 'from the ground up' involves a basic fabric of economic activities which are needed by all mankind and can be pursued nearly everywhere. It involves the production of and demand for 'local goods'. Determination of the necessary assortment – for instance, according to the balanced growth principle – is not an unsolvable problem, especially in the early development stages, and above all: production of and demand for such goods are relatively independent of the world economy. The problem of co-ordination is not really acute. There is good reason to believe that in this apparently unpretentious sphere, which, however, would embrace the great mass of the non-integrated population, lie the best development chances for nearly all developing countries.[35]

The imperative of collective self-reliance involves two specific lines of attack.

(1) It is necessary to build up structures of reciprocal relations among societies and economies with similar development problems, which can never be achieved by the traditional type of asymmetrical integration of such economies into the world economy. This sort of horizontalization of the relations among the societies of the Third World would lead to repression or elimination of the metropolitan economies as mediation agencies.[36] New institutions through which mutual aid could be given would have to supplement such more close-meshed structures of relations.

(2) Strengthening the basis for Third World solidarity, above and beyond rhetorical proclamations, could bring a significant increase in the political weight of the Third World *vis-à-vis* the metropolitan economies and enable a change in the international division of labour to be achieved, both of which would lead to a new, essentially multicentrically structured international economy (a really new international economic order). The crassly biassed, traditional hierarchy of the international economy based on division of labour between the metropolitan economies and the peripheries would give way to a structure in which there were more independent, if not self-sufficient, viable economic areas with their own autonomous communication and decision-making systems. Whether such economic areas would be possible only where especially dense populations are to be found,[37] as suggested by spatial economic theories, is a question which would have to be examined thoroughly. Collective self-reliance among the countries of the Third World would undoubtedly have repercussions affecting the metropolitan economies, which in the latter would result in structural adjustments that ought also to raise the degree of self-reliance in these economies, too. It is the function of a theory of a multicentric world economy prompted by considerations of development policy and spatial economic analysis[38] to reflect on

these relationships, our view of which has hitherto been obstructed by one-sided concentration on liberal free trade theory and its underlying, generally accepted allocation calculi.

The well-known economist W. Arthur Lewis expressed the practical philosophy underlying this imperative in 1969, when he wrote:

It is true that the prosperity of underdeveloped countries has in the past depended on what they could sell to the industrial countries, but there is no reason why this should continue. The underdeveloped countries have all the resources needed for their own development. Taken together they have a surplus of fuel, fibres, iron ore, copper, bauxite, and practically every other raw material. In agriculture they are perfectly capable of feeding themselves, through exchange with each other, and do not have to beg the United States to buy more tea and coffee so that they can pay for American grain, when they could produce more grain for themselves. The underdeveloped countries are short of skills, but these can be learnt, so they could do all their own manufacturing. Apart from skills the development of Asia, Africa and Latin America could continue even if all the rest of the world were to sink under the sea. If this is so, it must mean that these countries have the solutions of their problems in their own hands, and should stop thinking all the time only in terms of what they can sell to or buy from the industrial countries.[39]

Conclusions for a Program of Autocentric Development

From the foregoing arguments we can draw several general conclusions for a development programme that would lead in the short run to considerable structural changes, but in the long run – if pursued energetically – would offer the chance of a solution to the development problems currently under discussion. Three of them should be given special emphasis:

(1) a well-balanced accumulation structure,
(2) the intermeshing of resource mobilization and resource utilization in the domestic sphere,
(3) the organic development of structures ranging from the simple to the complex.

(1) According to currently received development theory, it is necessary for the developing countries to specialize in their foreign and domestic trading behaviour within the international economy in line with their 'natural factor endowment'. Autocentric development, however, presupposes differentiated development of productive forces and balanced capital formation. If, as in many countries of the Third World, sufficient natural resources are available, this sort of strategy would assign priority to the building-up of a domestic heavy industry in so far

as it would contribute *simultaneously* to the dynamification of agriculture, light industry, and mining.

> ... it is erroneous to neglect the rehabilitation of heavy industry and the re-enforcement of the country's economic base; but it is no less erroneous not to establish a light industry which is called for to ameliorate the people's living standard, by only putting emphasis on heavy industry. To improve the people's livelihood it is necessary to increase rapidly the production in its totality, increase production of necessity goods and systematically lower the prices.⁴⁰

What appears to be nonsensical from the profitability standpoint, because it is uneconomical, that is, the building up of production facilities which, in the initial phase, are only capable of producing goods at greater cost than if they were bought on the world market, gains strategic significance in a process of autocentric development. The problem is illustrated graphically by the observations of two North Korean economists:

> When the Party had set out this line [of building heavy industry simultaneously with light industry and agriculture] factionalists within the Party were against it. Some foreign friends also interfered into the policies of our Party. The factionalists said we were putting too much emphasis on heavy industry: 'How can machines produce rice?' they asked. In other words, they wanted us to 'eat' all resources and foreign aid, living well for a short period and then have nothing. Our Party rejected this line because without giving priority to heavy industry, we would have been unable to stabilize the people's livelihood, our defense power would have suffered, and we would have been unable to lay the foundation of an independent national economy. As a matter of fact, machines can also produce rice! Heavy industry is the foundation for agricultural and light industrial development. When we make more agricultural machines, we produce more rice; when we make building equipment, we produce many more houses; and with vessels we catch more fish.⁴¹

This example is cited in this context because at that time, in the second half of the 1950s and the early 1960s, the North Korean administration was advised to import more consumer goods instead of machinery and equipment, and on the other hand to concentrate on the production of raw materials. The rejection of this recommendation and the will to oppose received allocation calculi were the basis for pursuance of a course of independent development borne by confidence in one's own strength. This is also one of the few cases in which the development slogan 'confidence in one's own strength' (self-reliance or, as the North Koreans say, *juche*) really assumed operative significance.

The principle of balanced development extends also to a balance between the requirements of massive capital formation on the one hand

and the requirements of steady improvement of the material and cultural living conditions of the mass of the population. The setting of wrong, that is, one-sided, priorities in this respect may have disastrous consequences for the entire dynamic development process.

The principle of balanced development applies also to the technology mix (within the spectrum range from labour intensity to capital intensity), in which connection 'balanced' does not mean uniform in all sectors. Especially in industries producing preliminary products for further processing in subsequent production stages, it is possible, even in an economy with a low average productivity level, for a more capital-intensive production to impart substantial dynamic impetus, if only because it enables such products to be turned out at lower cost, if appropriate allowance is made for economies of scale. Such products can then be further processed by less capital-intensive methods so that the labour-saving effects of the first stage can be offset by work-creating effects in the second and subsequent stages. A prerequisite for this, however, is growing coherence of the local economy, which, in its turn, is enduringly strengthened by such an association of heavy industry, light industry, and agriculture. The relevant, more recent planning debates in China and North Korea since 1955 have formulated the practical problems encountered. In particular, they demonstrated the dubiousness of the distinction drawn in the traditional development debate between a development programme with balanced growth and one with unbalanced growth. Although, in an unbalanced, crippled economic structure a strategy of unbalanced growth leads to further dynamification of already existing growth poles – and thus to the further disruption of already disrupted structures – elements of that strategy nevertheless have a positive and constructive role in a balanced development process in which new 'disproportional' emphasis is placed temporarily on further dynamification of what is in essence a balanced economic structure.

(2) Such a development path is marked by the convergence of resource mobilization and resource utilization geared to priorities in a country's *own* economy.[42] This is exactly the opposite of what can be observed in present-day peripheral economies, whose outward orientation continually cuts the ground from under any such development design. Linked with this is the fact that equilibration of needs and demand occurs. This form of intermeshing is likewise lacking at present in the peripheral economies, as the effective demand is extremely top heavy and on account of the lack of a broad-based economic structure the satisfaction of the needs of the masses does not provide a sound basis for the economy. As a result, not only is the development of productive forces distorted and misdirected; in addition, considerable latent, that is, mobilizable, development potentials remain untapped in such crippled development processes.

(3) Successful development processes proceed essentially and in line with priorities from the simple to the complex. An organic process of this sort lays the foundation for sound growth and broad-based effectiveness. The fact that in the course of such processes it is possible,

as mentioned above, for disproportional development impulses (e.g. by the selective input of a technology that is more complex than the average achieved level of technological development) to have a substantial impact on the remainder of the economy and exert a dynamifying effect on it, makes it clear that this development principle is not a plea for linear, unbroken development. An organic process complying with a definition of that sort presupposes an income distribution which stimulates demand for standardized, mass consumer goods. The top-heaviness of the demand profiles in the existing peripheral economies with their bias toward complex, capital-intensive, and energy-consuming consumer durables for the respective upper stratum and urban middle class are in contradiction to this development principle.

The operational test of whether there is autocentric development in a specific case depends on the answers to the following questions:

- Does the coherence of an entire economy improve in the course of the development process?
- Can such an economy provide certain, basic services as defined above for the mass of the population as a result of development?
- Is there an improvement in the capability for selective co-operation which can be made to benefit a country's own development?

The learning costs of political, administrative, economic, and technological experimentation cannot be set at a low level even in a process of autocentric development, but in the long run those costs bring a pay-off in the shape of increased independence, a fairly coherent economic structure, and satisfaction of the basic needs of the mass of the population.

The Third World must now start out from the empirical fact that in the past three hundred years there has not been a single case of successful development in which central determinants of autocentric development did not take combined effect:

(1) the differentiated development of productive forces in all important spheres: agriculture, capital goods industry, production of intermediate goods, invention and production of technology, mass consumer goods industry, private and public services – with the goal of attaining depth of production and interlinking effects;
(2) the growing capacity for independent self-control and self-steering of politics, society, the economy, and culture, i.e. the attainment of autonomy;
(3) the achievement of individual and collective, specific identities – and thus also of a specific identity of the political culture;[43]
(4) exchange with social units beyond a country's own frontiers, initially on a strictly selective basis and in later development phases on a more widespread basis.

As can easily be seen from this enumeration, the current development scene is topsy-turvy:

(1) Exchange processes under unequal international division of labour result in
(2) deformed development of productive forces, which
(3) keeps the potential for independent self-control and self-steering limited, and
(4) does not permit a country to find its own identity.

Consequently, autonomy, self-control, skills, and learning capacities are structurally distorted and remain limited.

A threefold revolution – in the sense of a complete *volte-face* – is needed to arrive at a solution to the fundamental problems of the Third World: revolution of the production structure and its social preconditions, revolution of ideology and culture, including mobilization of the mass of the population, and lastly, the revolutionizing of consumption styles and regaining of self-reliant technological skills. Is there any chance of this?

On the Feasibility of Autocentric Development

The question as to the possibility of translating the development programme elements outlined above into practice is less dramatic than it might seem at first sight. For is not this question equally applicable to all other development programmes, and precisely to those which are now actually being pursued with political authority? Are the alternatives to autocentric development really feasible? Or are they regarded as feasible only because they are pursued with political authority? We must earnestly query whether traditional development theory and development policy can claim to have a recipe for solving the problems of the Third World and the international economy, when practical development policy does not even succeed in solving the development problems close to home, for example, within the framework of the European Community, despite greater possibilities of control and greater resources and funds. On leaving the development policy problem areas of a structure like the European Community behind us and approaching its peripheral zones, for example, the southern European developing countries, here again the question must be raised of how a policy is to be successful worldwide if it cannot even solve the development problems in neighbouring areas. Can a breakthrough in solving development problems really be expected of export-oriented industrialization, the small farming projects of the World Bank, the projects under the world employment programme of the International Labour Organization, and so on, whether individually or cumulatively and in combination? Why, therefore, can such programmes, however well meaning or Machiavellian their intentions may be, be declared to be the quintessence of actual practice-oriented and practicable development policy, if they are so obviously incapable of attaining even their self-set development objectives? And why, on the other hand, should lines of argument which endeavour to work out an alternative development programme be considered unfeasible simply because in the majority of cases they admittedly lack the backing of political authority? After all, historical experience in the development of Western, capitalistic, metropolitan economies, of socialist metropolitan economies, and, in particular, also of a few developing countries which have overcome the worst maladies of underdevelopment in the space of a few decades speaks for the rationality and practical effectiveness of an autocentric development path.

Nor is the objection that history is not reproducible exactly plausible. Not a single case of autocentric development among the cited temporally and structurally widely differing cases is comparable with any other in all its facets and peculiarities. This is just as true of the Western metropolitan economies relative to each other as it is of the profound differences between Western capitalistic development and the cases of socialist development since 1917. Comparative historical research has demonstrated the differing initial situations, basic conditions, and so on. Nevertheless, as emphasized at the beginning, in the final analysis all these cases have in common a basic economic configuration which constitutes the manifest, indispensable foundation for viable societies and economies. Britain's development path could not be followed in Japan any more than that of the Soviet Union could be copied in North Korea. And for all that, despite all the differences, Britain, Japan, the Soviet Union, and North Korea all exhibit an astoundingly similar basic configuration. Cannot such experience be turned to account in development theory and development policy?

The question of feasibility becomes interesting and fruitful only when the big doubts have been left behind and we venture into more detailed issues, for example, the following:

- Are there any countries in the Third World which, on reorienting their economic policy to opening up their own domestic markets (and thus also reorienting their agricultural production to satisfaction of local needs) would be unable to mobilize sufficient resources to feed the mass of the population with their own output? Where, on the basis of such reorientation, could agricultural surplus areas be developed, which could help satisfy the food requirements that such countries cannot cover themselves?
- What countries have the potential to build up without any great difficulty a sectorally complete economy such as the theory of autocentric development indicates, and what countries will be unable to build up parts of an essentially desirable, complete economic structure because they lack the necessary natural resources (e.g. raw materials)?
- What sectoral components are non-essential, because within the framework of collective self-reliance expedient, complementary developments extending beyond the relative national frontiers take place (self-elected incompleteness where complementarity is agreed upon)?

- Are political controls capable of offsetting internal deficits by way of foreign relations in such manner that even in exchange processes with more productive economies structural gaps can be closed without endangering the further progress of autocentric development? The development of the European metropolitan economies, of Japan, and, more recently, particularly of China provides a wealth of illustrative material in this respect.
- What parts of the capital goods industry should initially be built up with high priority in a process of autocentric development? For what equipment for agriculture and the mass consumer goods industry can potential mass demand be assumed, for which reason the argument of narrow domestic markets is invalid from the start?
- What type of equipment production has the greatest intermeshing effects in the production sector itself and is capable of triggering self-accelerating growth in that sector? What combination of subsectors that are to be built up has the greatest effect with respect to extension and dissemination of technological knowledge, disregarding the implied learning costs? How can a country or group of countries which find themselves constrained, in spite of all their own efforts, to import foreign technologies succeed in escaping from the typical cycle of economic dependence, which was recently described as follows:

    > A country which produces no equipment sterilizes its technological research capacities and becomes progressively less capable of producing its own equipment and technology. Therefore it must import more, therefore earn foreign exchange, therefore seek new sources of finance, which are tied up with the renewed import of equipment and new direct investments, and so forth.[44]

- With what temporal priority should autocentric economic structures be built up in a given case? And what is the time horizon, if any, up to which a more or less sound, balanced economic foundation can be achieved?
- How can political motivation for this sort of development path be mobilized, assuming that political leaders are prepared to follow such a path? By what forms of political organization can the different demands with respect to massive capital accumulation on the one hand and satisfaction of basic needs on the other be met constructively in practice? What structure of political organization is capable, and by means of what blend of central leadership and decentralization, of resolving the accumulation–consumption dilemma in such a manner that the 'development motivation' of the broad masses which is essential for a process of autocentric development does not peter out? What role can the educational system play in all this? What importance attaches to a new political culture and a new cultural identity? What starting points can be found for this in a country's own past? And what experience out of the abundance of

cultural accomplishments of other nations can be turned to account eclectically?

Concluding Remarks

For the foregoing questions there are no prefabricated answers which might prove satisfactory in individual cases. An abundance of studies is necessary in order to formulate concrete, empirically tested recommendations. It is worthy of note, however, that in recent utterances of development theorists who have supported traditional development theory and development policy in prominent positions in the past fifteen to twenty years the programmatics of autocentric development have been formulated and discussed. Very recently, for instance, Paul Streeten, at present a special consultant to the World Bank, attempted in an article a comparison of the pragmatic implications of the traditional and the new development theory. His deliberations conclude with a reconciliation of integrative and dissociative programs.

> The interesting question is not 'do the developing countries gain or lose from coexistence with developed countries?', but 'how can the developing countries pursue selective policies which allow them to extract benefit from the positive forces without simultaneously exposing themselves to harm from detrimental forces?' These countries should therefore take a close look at the details of the whole balance sheet, at the entries on the debit and credit side, and not just the net balance. If the problem is looked at in this way, the question arises of what selective policies must be drawn up for aid, trade, foreign investments, transnational business groups, technology, education abroad, population emigration, etc. The correct answer will be neither complete self-isolation nor wide open integration, but a policy of enlightened differentiation and discrimination.[45]

However, the compromise between integrative and dissociative strategies, which seems agreeable at first sight, will not hold water; the recommended golden mean is illusory. For also within the traditional structure of relationships between the metropolitan economies and the peripheries, peripheries select from what is offered by the metropolitan economies that which they consider expedient for progress along the traditional development path. In this sense, even in the past decades the developing countries have always pursued a strategy that is a mixture of inward and outward orientation. Streeten's recommendation of a middle course is bootless because it was not preceded by analysis of the structural and reproductive dynamics of peripheral economies. In his approach, the problem is reduced to the question of different development styles and development highlights within the traditional framework. But considering the experience gained with studied development policy in the past three decades, this is taking too short a grip on things both analytically and practically. There is no way to avoid a macrosociological and macroeconomic analysis of peripheral societies and economies, if a fruitful new beginning is to be found in development policy.

Dissociation promises no easy and simple development path.[46] Accumulation has never been conceivable without sacrifices and hardships. But it seems to me that dissociative development programmes are more likely to show us a way out of the clearly discernible cul-de-sac of traditional development policy for the benefit of mankind than the present development strategies backed by political authority. So far, the traditional international economic order and the traditional social and economic orders in the Third World can still be stabilized tolerably well. But conflict sources are growing and the progressing militarization of the Third World is a clear sign that the traditional orders can no longer stabilize themselves without increased repression. At the present time, it can certainly be assumed that the geopolitical and economic map of the international economy in the year 2000 will be substantially different from what it is today. It would be irresponsible to take it for granted that dissociation will become the predominant development programme of the Third World in the course of time without raising any problems. But that the number of 'dissociative cases' will grow is something that can be predicted in the light of the failure of traditional development policy and of the abortive North–South dialogues at international conferences and of the ever more aggravated social conflicts in the Third World. In view of such prospective radical changes, it would seem important for the metropolitan economies to learn in good time to distinguish clearly between short-term setbacks to their interests and long-term potential gains. This includes first and foremost being able to sense why a dissociative development strategy is an indispensable foundation for a sound development path in a long, first phase of broad-based development of productive forces.

Notes: Chapter 12

1 This chapter picks up the thread of development theory and development policy studies outlined in my *Weltwirtschaftsordnung und Entwicklungspolitik: Plädoyer für Dissoziation* (Frankfurt: Suhrkamp Verlag 1977). Since I attempted there to evaluate the present position in the scientific debate thoroughly, in the following I shall refrain from detailed annotation. The debate on autocentric development, although started in the past century, is still in its beginnings.
2 On the debate concerning a New International Economic Order, see the interesting book by Mahbub ul Haq, *The Poverty Curtain: Choices for the Third World* (New York: Columbia University Press, 1976).
3 Regarding the emerging structure of a new international division of labor, see Folker Fröbel, Jürgen Heinrichs, and Otto Kreye, *Die neue internationale Arbeitsteilung: strukturelle Arbeitslosigkeit in den Industrieländern und die Industrialisierung der Entwicklungsländer* (Reinbek bei Hamburg: Rowohlt, 1977).
4 On this see especially Immanuel Wallerstein, *The Modern World-System* (New York: Academic Press, 1974); *idem*, 'Alternative development strategies', *Economic Review* [Sri Lanka] (February 1976), pp. 29–31; André Gunder Frank, *L'accumulation*

mondiale, 1500–1800 (Paris: Calmann-Lévy, 1977); Hartmut Elsenhans *Geschichte und Ökonomie der europäischen Welteroberung* (Frankfurt: publication forthcoming).

5 On this see the essay by Stein Rokkan, 'Dimensions of state formation and nation-building: a possible paradigm for research on variations within Europe', in *The Formation of National States in Western Europe*, ed. Charles Tilly (Princeton, NJ: Princeton University Press, 1975); and S. N. Eisenstadt and Stein Rokkan (eds), *Building States and Nations*, 2 vols (Beverly Hills, Calif., and London: Sage, 1973–4).

6 It is self-evident that the development processes in the three types of society named were not linear. Considerable structural disruptions are just as characteristic of them as the difficult attainment of economic coherence and corresponding political constellations. In particular, in no case was there a development plan intended to be implemented by a dynamic political leadership and an economic elite.

7 The term 'crippled', taken from Friedrich List, corresponds to the current concept of 'structural heterogeneity'. For a recent discussion of this concept, see Armando di Filippo and Santiago Jadue, 'La heterogeneidad estructural: concepto y dimensiones', in *El Trimestre Económico*, vol. 43, no. 1 (169) (January–March 1976), pp. 167–214.

8 A recent analysis in this field can be found in David Morawetz, 'Twenty-five years of economic development', *Finance and Development*, vol. 14, no. 3 (September 1977), pp. 10–13.

9 Karl Schiller, 'Zur Wachstumsproblematik der Entwicklungsländer', in *Kieler Vorträge*, n.s., no. 15 (Kiel, 1960), pp. 1–24, esp. pp. 8–9.

10 Regarding the analysis of this identical in-depth structure, see my *Weltwirtschaftsordnung und Entwicklungspolitik*, esp. pp. 65ff.

11 See Eva Senghaas-Knobloch, 'Weibliche Arbeitskraft und gesellschaftliche Reproduktion: Eine Problemskizze', *Leviathan*, vol. 4, no. 4 (1976), pp. 543–8.

12 In the cited example of the small commodity-farming producer in West Africa, this is the case if only because his production is completely tied in with the national and international price structure, which reflects higher productivity rates. In reality, though he still possesses means of production, his existence is proletarianized – regardless of all apparent traditionality.

13 See Samir Amin, *Die ungleiche Entwicklung: Essay über die Gesellschaftsformationen des peripheren Kapitalismus* (Hamburg: Hoffmann & Campe, 1975).

14 In his 'Dimensions of state formation', Stein Rokkan uses European examples in diagnosing four typical phases of development: the penetration and consolidation of territories; the standardization of experience, language, culture, etc.; achieving participation; and redistribution. With respect to all four phases and their material content, development in the peripheries is fundamentally different.

15 On this point, see the preface by Samir Amin to Michel Beaud, Bertrand Bellon, and Patrick François, *Lire le capitalisme: Sur le capitalisme mondial et sa crise* (Paris: Anthropos, 1976).

16 Friedrich List, *Das nationale System der politischen Ökonomie* (1841; new edn, Tübingen: Mohr [Siebeck] Verlag, 1959).

17 On this see also Harald Jürgensen, 'Autarkie und welwirtschaftliche Arbeitsteilung', in *Seewirtschaft: Beiträge zur ökonomischen Entwicklung in Seehäfen und Seeschiffahrt* ed. Central Association of German Seaport Administrations (Hamburg: Verlag Okis, 1966), pp. 83–93.

18 Norbert Elias, *Über den Prozess der Zivilisation*, 2 vols (Frankfurt: Suhrkamp Verlag, 1976), Vol. 2, p. 74.

19 Cyril Black *et al.*, *The Modernization of Japan and Russia: A Comparative Study* (New York: The Free Press, 1975), esp. pp. 233ff.; quotation from p. 235.

20 See Rolf Steppacher, *Surplus, Kapitalbildung und wirtschaftliche Entwicklung: Zur Relevanz der Physiokratie und der institutionellen Ökonomie für das Problem der Kapitalbildung in unterentwickelten Ländern* (Liebefeld/Berne: Verlag Peter Lang 1976).

21 This is one of the most important and enduring findings formulated by Friedrich List in his discussion of classical English economics.

22 For one of many examples, the dismantling of sugar production in Cuba, see Horst Fabian, *Strategien zur Überwindung peripherer Gesellschaftsformationen: Das Beispiel Kuba* (Frankfurt: in preparation).

23 Alfons Lemper, 'Collective self-reliance – eine erfolgsversprechende

Entwicklungsstrategie?' in *Mitteilungen des Verbunds Stiftung Deutsches Überseeinstitut*, no. 4 (Hamburg: Institut für Überseeforschuung, 1976), pp. 61–88; quotation from pp. 75–6.
24 On this see Hans-Gerhard Voigt, *Probleme der weltwirtschaftlichen Kooperation* (Hamburg: Hoffmann & Campe, 1969), pp. 7ff, and 121ff.; and Samir Amin, *L'impérialisme et le développement inégal* (Paris: Editions de Minuit, 1976), pp. 25–44.
25 André Gunder Frank, 'Über die Begrenzung des Binnenmarktes durch die internationale Arbeitsteilung und die Produktionsverhältnisse', in *Herrschaft und Befreiung in der Weltgesellschaft*, ed. Klaus Jürgen Gantzel (Frankfurt: Campus-Verlag, 1975), pp. 161–211.
26 *Frankfurter Allgemeine Zeitung*, 10 November 1976, p. 11.
27 On this see Ulrich Menzel, *Theorie und Praxis des chinesischen Entwicklungsmodells: Ein Beitrag zum Konzept autozentrierter Entwicklung* (Opladen: Westdeutscher Verlag, 1978), pp. 293ff.
28 On this see Ellen Brun and Jacques Hersh, *Socialist Korea: A Case Study in the Strategy of Economic Development* (New York: Monthly Review Press, 1976), pp. 180ff.
29 ibid., p. 181.
30 ibid., p. 184.
31 Kim Il Sung, *Reden und Aufsätze* (Frankfurt: Verlag Roter Stern, 1971), Vol. 1, p. 289.
32 See Uwe Stehr, *Sozioökonomische Bedingungen des Aussenverhaltens der RGW-Staaten* (Frankfurt: Hessische Stiftung für Friedens- und Konfliktforschung, No. 17, 1977).
33 Paul Streeten, 'Self-reliant industrialization', paper presented at the 18th Annual Convention of the International Studies Association, St Louis, Mo., 1977, p. 22.
34 In what respects spatial economic considerations may be a potential help in this connection was indicated several years ago by Hans-Jürgen Harborth in an essay 'Zur Rolle der Entwicklungsländer in einer multizentrischen Weltwirtschaft', *Jahrbuch für Sozialwissenschaften*, vol. 22, no. 2 (1971), pp. 244–56. At the present time, Harborth's arguments should be developed further from the standpoint of the theory of autocentric development.
35 Hans-Jürgen Harborth, 'Anforderungen an eine revidierte Integrationstheorie für Entwicklungsländer', in *Integration der Entwicklungsländer in eine instabile Weltwirtschaft: Probleme, Chancen, Gefahren*, ed. Winfried von Urff (Berlin: Duncker & Humblot, 1976), pp. 65–88; quotation from pp. 84–5.
36 See Samir Amin, 'Self-reliance and the New International Economic Order', *Monthly Review*, vol. 29, no. 3 (July–August 1977), pp. 1–21, especially pp. 18ff.
37 Hans-Jürgen Harborth, 'Dissoziation – mit welchem Ziel?' *Entwicklung und Zusammenarbeit*, nos 7–8 (1977), pp. 17–18.
38 On this see Alfons Lemper, *Handel in einer dynamischen Weltwirtschaft: Ansatzpunkte für eine Neuorientierung der Aussenhandelstheorie* (Munich: Weltforum-Verlag, 1974), ch. 4; Hans-Jürgen Harborth, *Neue Industriezentren an der weltwirtschaftlichen Peripherie* (Hamburg: Hoffmann & Campe, 1967): Voigt, *Probleme der weltwirtschaftlichen Kooperation*; Harborth, 'Zur Rolle der Entwicklungsländer' and, more recently, also Friedrich Buttler, Knut Gerlach, and Peter Liepmann, *et al.*, *Grundlagen der Regionalökonomie* (Reinbek bei Hamburg: Rowohlt, 1977).
39 W. Arthur Lewis, *Some Aspects of Economic Development* (Accra: Ghana Publishing Corporation, 1969), p. 15.
40 Kim Il Sung, as quoted in Brun and Hersh, *Socialist Korea*, p. 154.
41 ibid., p. 168–9.
42 See especially Clive Thomas, *Dependence and Transformation: The Economics of the Transition to Socialism* (New York: Monthly Review Press, 1974).
43 On these problems, see the early study by Karl W. Deutsch, *Nationalism and Social Communication: An Inquiry into the Foundations of Nationality*, 2d edn (Cambridge, Mass.: MIT Press, 1966).
44 *Le Monde Diplomatique* (September 1977), p. 19.
45 Paul Streeten, 'Changing perceptions of development', in *Finance and Development*, vol. 14, no. 3 (September 1977), pp. 14–16; quotation from p. 16.
46 See Galal A. Amin (professor of economics and economic adviser to the Kuwait Fund for Arab Economic Development), 'Dependent development', *Alternatives*, vol. 2, no.

4 (1976), pp. 379–403, which coincides entirely with my own view. In this article, the author refers back, as I do, to List as a starting point for working out a dissociative development program. Amin criticizes the fact that the countries of the Third World are taught the value of internationalism before they have achieved national socioeconomic integration. He advises them to pursue a policy of isolation similar to that adopted in Japan, Russia, and present-day China. He also considers the earlier examples of Britain and Germany to be instructive. He, too, does not aim at permanent isolation, but at a temporary, though quite prolonged, period of isolation lasting until the country can compete economically and culturally with integrated societies. The infant-industry argument should not only cover the entire economy, but should also be extended to cultural and economic life. He concludes (p. 402):

> The real difference between the Old International Economic Order and the New can therefore be seen as little more than the difference between selling cheap and selling dear. To those who reject the whole transaction of buying and selling, not merely as unjust but as dehabilitating, it matters little what price is being offered. An alternative analogy is that of the difference between a race in which two competing but unequal parties are unjustly required to start from the same point, and another race in which the weaker party is given the advantage of starting a few steps ahead. We are inclined to reject the whole race as wasting the energies of the weaker party in an unworthy pursuit.

13

A Formal Model of 'Dependencia Theory': Structure and Measurement

RAYMOND DUVALL, STEVEN JACKSON, BRUCE M. RUSSETT, DUNCAN SNIDAL, and DAVID SYLVAN

Introduction

'Traditional' theories of development have recently been subjected to strong and pointed criticism accompanied by alternative theoretical arguments about the causes of underdevelopment in the modern world. Latin American social scientists have been especially critical. Not long after the Second World War, the 'nationalists' and 'structuralists' associated with the Economic Commission for Latin America ECLA pointed to several weaknesses in traditional theories. More recently, new perspectives have come from those responsible for the formulation of so-called 'dependencia theory', a set of arguments offered as much in critical reaction to the ECLA structuralist positions as to the 'traditional' theories.

But the acceptance and continued development of 'dependencia theory' is not now limited to Latin Americans; nor is 'dependencia theory' now an altogether easily isolated and distinguishable set of arguments. Rather, the label signifies a broad set of contemporary discussions about imperialism, global inequality, and underdevelopment that focus on the economic, social, and political 'distortions' of 'peripheral' societies which result from their incorporation into the global capitalist system. Certainly that is the primary concern of those Latin American scholars generally identified as 'dependencia theorists', such as Dos Santos, Cardoso, and Quijano.[1] In the same vein, several Europeans and Africans have made substantial contributions to the literature on 'peripheral capitalism' with exactly the same concerns as those of the Latin Americans,[2] and hence they too can be viewed as dependencia theorists. And the diversity of theorists is associated with a diversity of particular theoretical arguments. Indeed, the Latin American theorists are currently engaged in heated controversy with one another over the precise transformations that occur under different conditions of incorporation into the global capitalist system[3] 'Dependencia theory', then, is not a single, unified argument; rather, it is a broadly based critical perspective on development and underdevelopment in the capitalist world.

The diversity of scholars and of particular analyses provides a breadth of perspective that can only imperfectly be captured in a single, precise theoretical structure. Within the diversity, however, there is reasonably clear convergence on a set of analytical concepts and fairly substantial agreement on some very basic arguments. Our attempt to model 'dependencia theory' in this chapter is focused on this convergence of conceptual set and of basic arguments. Thus we refer to arguments about the financial and technological penetration of peripheral societies by the developed capitalist centers, the creation of an unbalanced economic structure both within the peripheral society and between the periphery and the center, structural constraints on self-sustained economic growth in the periphery, the emergence of distinctive peripheral capitalist class relationships, and transformation of the role of the peripheral capitalist state.

The basic arguments about these phenomena are more complex and plausible than North American scholarship has always recognized. To date, there has been, in Cardoso's terms, a poor 'consumption of "dependency theory" in North America',[4] On the one hand, this has meant an apparently pervasive misunderstanding of the complexity and sophistication of the basic arguments, and a concomitant equating of 'dependencia theory' with common-sense interpretations of the term dependence. On the other hand, it has led to premature and uncritical rejection, partly from general misunderstanding and partly because dependence theory is too facilely equated with Marxist-Leninist theories of imperialism.

We hope for a better 'consumption' in North American scholarship of 'dependencia theory' as a sophisticated, complex, often plausible set of arguments. By this, we do *not* intend for ourselves the role of advocates, promoting a wholesale, uncritical adoption. Rather, we hope for a careful assessment, probing the extent and conditions of the validity of the basic arguments. This chapter is intended as a step in that direction. In it we present our understanding of the structure of the basic arguments of 'dependencia theory' in a more precise verbal form than is common; from that we develop a formal, structural-equation model, and discuss measurement of the separate conceptual elements of the model as a step toward a comprehensive test of hypotheses from the theory.

In terms of the foci of this volume – and of Karl Deutsch's basic perspectives – we are delineating a theory of how international, transnational, and 'domestic' variables interact; of how economy and society constrain the polity. In these concerns, and in our emphasis on the need for mathematical formulation and quantitative measurement, we are of course squarely within the tradition established by Deutsch – for example, as described in the contributions by Foltz, Lijphart, and Puchala in this volume. Nevertheless, the attention to international and transnational constraints on development shares more in common with Deutsch's work on international political integration than with his research on national development. The latter, as noted by Hudson's contribution, shares with 'traditional' development theorists like Almond and Huntington a narrowly intranational focus.

The magnitude of the total effort to understand dependence is beyond what any single group of researchers can, or should, attempt by themselves. But we believe progress in understanding can be based on three convictions. (1) Dependencia theory addresses a set of problems sufficiently central to world politics and economics to deserve the most serious attention. (2) Dependence is a phenomenon of a complexity that demands rigorous specification of a variety of variables and complex relations among them. (3) Despite the complexity, the fundamental processes are sufficiently similar, and amenable to scientific measurement, to permit a general investigation.

A brief preview of the ultimate concerns of our research may be seen by looking at the countries whose development we believe dependencia theory is attempting to explain. We begin by considering *all non-OECD market or mixed economies of nation-states independent in 1965*. To this we add the less developed countries of the 'European fringe' even if they were OECD members (i.e. Greece, Cyprus, Malta, Portugal, Spain, and Turkey). (The socialist countries may be added to our sample in the future for comparative purposes.) Our initial focus will be on cross-sectional assessments of the model to be presented below but later uses will attempt to obtain diachronic assessments for a limited subset.

The total time period at issue in our project (roughly 1955–75) is short, but has the advantage of encompassing a period of moderate industrialization for many Third World countries. It is post-colonial for Africa, but precedes the period of major industrialization for a few countries (especially in Latin America, notably Brazil and Mexico). The decision to include all Third World states is supported by arguments from much of the dependencia literature.[5] At the same time, we recognize the importance of distinctions among the mechanisms of dependence and certain social formations within this large group of countries.[6] In part this is acknowledged by our use of several different aspects of dependence in the model we develop (e.g. financial, technological, political, cultural, and trade dependence) and in the way the relationships are specified in the equations. But it also will be possible to remove some regions or groups of countries from the analysis to see if important changes in the model result (for example, whether the processes are markedly different for the 'European fringe' than for non-European countries and, on the whole, former colonial countries).

An Overview of the Model of 'Dependencia Theory'

The proposed model entails eighteen separate conceptual components, or variables, fourteen of which are endogenous (i.e. are affected by other variables in the model). The model consists of twelve structural equations and two definitional identities, each of which is presented here with a verbal interpretation and elaboration.[7]

We will begin to discuss our model in the context of the recent and contemporary international system. That is, we shall discuss each variable not only in terms of a concept derived from verbal theory of the 'dependencia' school, but also in terms of an appropriate measurement strategy for use of the concept in the context of empirical testing. The verbal theory is often imprecise, and most theorists have given little attention to problems of indicator construction and large-scale empirical testing. Especially for an analysis that is intended to apply to many countries, limited data availability will require us to accept some indicators that are not as valid or reliable as we would wish. Nevertheless, careful specification of measurement strategies, and a thorough search for information that includes some innovations in the use of familiar data for new purposes, can reduce these problems to manageable proportions. Somewhat different measurement decisions would be made for single-country longitudinal studies than for the large-sample cross-national application we discuss in this article. But the spirit of this inquiry – that we want to specify *and test rigorously* a set of hypotheses – requires an integral discussion of theory and measurement together. Report of data analytic results, however, will have to await later publications.

Before entering upon a detailed discussion of the model, a summary overview should be helpful. We begin with a set of processes whereby less developed countries are in important ways penetrated by, and transformed into a dependence upon, the world economy and especially the capitalist/industrial world. While these processes have developed over a long historical period, we shall concentrate on the later stages, which have been characterized by various writers as 'the new dependence' beginning roughly in the 1950s. In some respects the crucial factor is the extent to which the capitalist/industrial world system as a whole has penetrated the society. In other respects the patterns of concentration of penetration and dependence are significant (that is, the degree to which such ties are concentrated upon a single industrial country or diversified among several such countries). Penetration includes financial and technological aspects (foreign modes of production as manifested in the importation of liquid capital and capital goods, and the use of foreign patents, licences, and copyrights), as well as cultural and political ones. As a result, the dependent society incorporates major elements of the value system of advanced industrial societies. By adopting such values regarding consumption and productive activity, it becomes more dependent on the developed capitalist center. These various aspects of long-term continuing penetration and dependence are grouped together in the first box in Figure 13.1.

The historical and continuing fact of penetration and dependence, it is alleged, has led to a pattern of economic activity characterized by the predominance of trade and the development of export enclaves, the now common syndrome of 'export economies' (box ii in Figure 13.1). Foreign trade became of progressively greater importance to the less developed country's economy, and that trade often became highly concentrated upon one or a few industrial countries and, in exports, upon a few products – generally, but not exclusively, products from the extractive and agricultural sectors. These processes and the resulting syndrome are largely taken as historical background by most

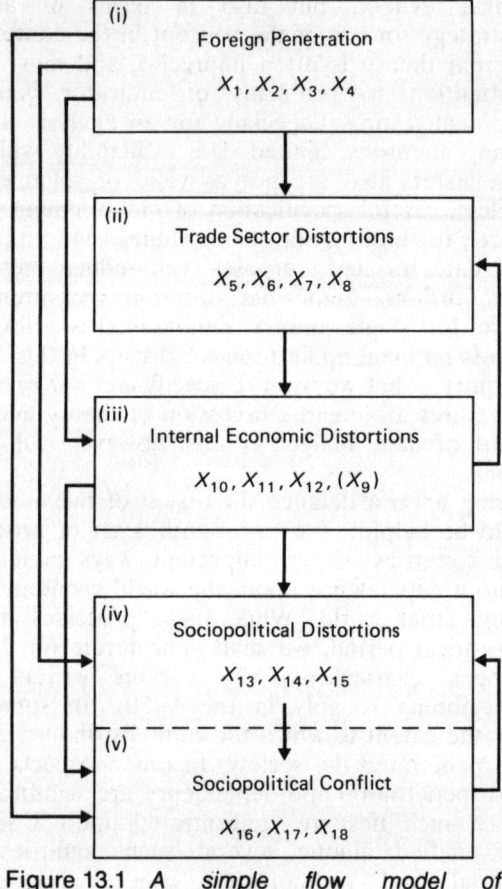

Figure 13.1 *A simple flow model of dependencia.*

dependencia theorists,[8] one of whose interests is in explaining any contemporary changes in aspects of this export syndrome. Although early identified in dependencia theory, trade sector distortions are no longer considered central to the theory.

The patterns of penetration, dependence, and export orientation nevertheless promote and are promoted by a kind of economic growth which is marked by severe internal structural 'distortions' (box iii in Figure 13.1). First, development is uneven, being much greater in some sectors (those most subject to foreign penetration, generally the export enclave) than in others. Secondly, the economy is poorly integrated; that is, the various sectors tend to be poorly connected or articulated. For example, even though a substantial manufacturing sector may develop, it will be little oriented to producing capital goods for the agricultural sector. Thirdly, the economy is marked by severe sectoral heterogeneity; that is, the returns to factors of production, especially labor, will be much greater in some sectors (e.g. manufacturing) than in others (agriculture).

Many aspects of this pattern of 'distorted' development have been recognized by a wide variety of theorists, including Raoul Prebisch and his school, by other predecessors to the dependencia school, and indeed by many neo-classical economists. Nevertheless, the dependencia school is notable in the way it compares this pattern of development with different (often vague and imprecise) norms of development, and by the emphasis on this pattern of development as a virtually necessary consequence of penetration and dependence. Moreover, dependencia theorists emphasize the *linkages* between financial, technological, and cultural penetration and further 'distortions' in the social and political systems. Finally, the reciprocal formulation between trade sector distortions and internal economic distortions in Figure 13.1 explicitly takes account of the view of recent dependencia theorists that changes in export enclave development are constrained by other structural changes in patterns of productivity. Thus amelioration of the export syndrome is not a simple policy matter as the Prebisch school seems to imply, nor is it a short-term historical aberration as neo-classicists argue.

The main distinguishing feature of contemporary dependencia theory, however, is the argument that particular social and political 'distortions' result from, or develop out of, capitalist penetration, trade dependence, and distorted economic development. These political and social 'distortions', which are represented by the final box in Figure 13.1, include increasing governmental involvement in the economy, creating a particular form of state capitalism. In addition, dependence and the distorted pattern of economic development lead to the suppression of interests of the laboring classes, and increasing inequality among social classes. In turn this leads to class conflict which promotes the imposition of coercive, authoritarian rule by the state. Some of the earlier dependencia theorists (e.g. Frank) treated these undesirable political and social consequences as the direct result of characteristics of dependence. However, contemporary dependencia theory is considerably more sophisticated in recognizing the intervening role of 'distortions' in the domestic economy, and in attempting to articulate the complex processes through which the social-political structure of peripheral societies is transformed by these economic 'distortions'.

Finally, the theory anticipates some 'feedback' from social and political 'distortion' to the forms and extent of penetration. For the most part this is seen as a continually reinforcing process, though there is some speculation about ways in which penetration and the dependence situation might be reversed or altered by political action in the periphery. These last linkages, however, are very poorly specified in the dependencia literature, and do not at present enter into our model. Penetration and the dependence situation remain, here, exogenous factors.

The Ties between Center and Periphery

Our model begins with a set of variables representing the principal linkages between a given less developed country and the 'core' of the global economic system. These are the variables of the first two blocks in Figure 13.1. The stronger these connections are, the more a country is said to be integrated into the international capitalist system, and, in turn, in a situation of dependence. There are at least three major channels through which the power of the industrial capitalist countries at the 'center' may come to bear on dependent countries in the 'periphery'. The first, and in many ways most important, is that of financial and technological penetration. The first two variables discussed below (X_1 and X_2) are concerned with this. The second channel linking the periphery to the center is that of cultural penetration. By culture we mean the principal shared attitudes and predispositions of the elite with respect to economic, political, and social means and ends; in this usage we borrow from Quijano's notion of 'la cultura dominante'. Both X_3 and X_4 tap this dimension. The final connection is through trade, asymmetric incorporation in the international system here being a reflection of the weakness which the dependent country presents when it comes as a buyer or seller to the international market in goods and services. Variables X_5 through X_8 are of this type. Variables X_1 through X_4 are aspects of the first block in Figure 13.1 while variables X_5 through X_8 are located in the second block in Figure 13.1. In this section we discuss the conceptualization and measurement of these eight variables; in the next section we will model processes.

Systemic financial and technological penetration (labelled X_1) may be defined as the extent to which the effective capital stock of a given national economy has been supplied by foreigners.[9] As penetration is viewed principally as the means by which a peripheral economy is integrated into the world capitalist economy, we shall focus upon that capital supplied from the 'core' of the global economy, that is, roughly speaking the OECD countries.[10] The capital stock includes financial, fixed, and disembodied forms of capital. Effectiveness of a unit of capital is a function of both its type and its age. As capital is normally supplied in anticipation of future needs, its full utility may not be realized until some time after it is introduced into the stock. On the other hand, capital depreciates with time, as a result of physical wear and obsolescence.

Note that the notion of control (or influence) does not appear in our definition of penetration *per se*. But in dependence theory it is influence over the economy that is the important aspect of penetration. In a world of two countries, X and Y, a high degree of penetration of country X is consistent with either a high degree or a low degree of penetration in country Y. We might call the situation in which the level of penetration in both countries is high symmetric penetration, or interdependence. We might likewise call the situation in which the level of penetration is high in one country and low in the other asymmetric penetration, or dependence. Stable and pervasive influence is more likely to be the result of asymmetric penetration.[11] Thus, our model is brought forward with respect to countries whose penetration of the core economies is negligible. This basic idea of examining a country's reliance on external sources of capital as a determinant of a nation's domestic policy, that is, as an influence relationship, is not new to neo-classical economics or to dependencia theorists,[12] of course.

Two major simplifying assumptions are necessary, however, to obtain a reasonably practical measure of penetration. The first is that the weight or effect of all of the different types of capital, whether supplied by foreigners or nationals, is the same. This is not implausible. The second assumption is that the three categories of capitalist penetration may reasonably be treated as equal in their impact. Therefore, in aggregating the types of capital, we standardize the amounts of each type cross-sectionally, and then sum the standardized units. With the aid of these two assumptions, we can express our measure of penetration as the sum of foreign-supplied financial, fixed, and disembodied capital, over the sum of all such capital in the economy.

As indicators of financial penetration, we have compiled data on accumulated foreign debt, and foreign investment. Ideally we would like to look at the percentage of the stock of financial resources which are provided (and in some sense controlled) from abroad. For debt, we have taken figures for the stock of external public debt from the World Bank *World Debt Tables*. We do not have a value for the total financial stock of a country at a given time, so we have chosen to approximate this level (that is control for it) by using gross domestic product (GDP). For investment, we found insufficient information on the stock of foreign investment for any large number of countries. Therefore, we have relied on an approximation using annual figures for net long-term private capital flows from the IMF's *International Financial Statistics*, divided by total of gross capital formation.

For fixed capital, we are concerned with the import of capital goods as a proportion of gross domestic investment. The importation of capital goods represents an introduction of the physical tools of technology into a society, and hence of the penetration of the products of outsiders into the plants and factories of a country. The importation of such goods thus may result in strong and inappropriate imitation of productive methods (e.g. toward greater technical sophistication, and higher capital intensity) and may be associated with greater emphasis on the production of luxury consumer goods.[13] Data are in the *UN Yearbook of International Trade Statistics*.

The role of 'disembodied' capital in penetration has been stressed by several dependencia theorists, notably Osvaldo Sunkel.[14] Particularly as modern technology tends to come in large packages of products and processes, acceptance of foreign *patents* for substantial parts of such packages is likely to entail continuing dependence for other parts. Our basic measure, therefore, is the percentage of patents registered to foreign nations. Unfortunately, data on total stocks – patents in force, by foreign or domestic origin – are not available. But we have data on flows from *Industrial Property*, the journal of the World Intellectual

Property Organization (annex to December issue for each year). An alternative indicator for disembodied capital is trademarks. Although largely neglected in the dependencia literature, the names, brands, and titles so important to modern marketing practice, which are restricted in use by trademark protection, are another part of the 'technological package'. Data on foreign and domestically held trademark registrations are available in the same source as that for patents. Each indicator (patents, trademarks, and capital goods) measures related but still distinct aspects of technological penetration.

Concentration of external financial and technological penetration (X_2) is a special aspect of the more general systemic penetration. As we shall specify more carefully below, some theorists are concerned especially with the penetration of a peripheral society or state by a single capitalist nation. Important here are the binding ties that constrain the programmatic alternatives of peripheral states and that allegedly stem from an excessive concentration of relations upon a single center country. In the Latin American 'dependencia' tradition the concern, of course, is usually with penetration specifically by the United States. But a more general application requires us to treat concentration of penetration by any metropole (e.g. Britain, France) as equivalent (though at some point in our empirical analysis we shall investigate whether important differences in effect can be attributed to penetration by *particular* metropolitan countries). There is some tradition in empirical studies of using variants of a concentration index first devised by Albert Hirschman for trade, whereby dispersion (of sources of penetration in this case) over several of the most prominent external actors is measured. Such indices take into account the relative size of the second, third, etc., most prominent actors as well as simply the largest one. For purposes of dependencia theory, however, it is probably appropriate to take into account only the largest, with a simple measure of the percentage of total penetration of any form (e.g. investment capital) that comes from any one metropolitan state.[15] The country-to-country data equivalent to the various dimensions of systemic penetration we used above for X_1 are generally available for this concentration measure (X_2).

Underdeveloped countries are of course penetrated by more than just foreign capital, even when capital is defined quite broadly. Local culture is also permeated with foreign elements, and we shall now explore this concept of systemic cultural penetration (X_3). Voluminous literature exists on this subject. On the one hand, numerous writers, beginning with Durkheim and continuing through Parsons and his successors, have viewed indigenous cultures as backward. To them, the transmission of Western ideas and values is all for the good, leading to 'modernizing', 'rational' societies.[16] On the other hand, there are those in the Marxist tradition who see culture as an instrument of class domination. To them, 'cultural imperialism' falsely represents certain values as universal, leading to a 'mystification' of 'objective' social relations.[17]

Rather than discuss the causes and consequences of cultural

penetration, we shall confine ourselves here to explicating the concept and its measurement. We define culture, following Geertz,[18] as a set of symbols which convey meaning about the beliefs, values, and aspirations of a group of people. Our job, therefore, is to assess the extent to which domestic symbols are permeated by foreign ones.[19] The simplest way to do this is to derive some way of counting symbols; for each type of symbol, we then need only determine the proportion of foreign ones to the total. These proportions can then be added together, and the resulting figure used as an index of cultural penetration.

Symbols, of course, cannot simply be counted up. In any society there are innumerable symbols representing all manner of subjects, and it is clearly impossible to assess their number. Thus, in order to arrive at a workable strategy for measuring cultural penetration, we must use indirect indicators of foreign and domestic symbols. We shall focus on two such groups of indicators. The first may be viewed as *carriers* of foreign symbols; the second, as *correlates* of cultural penetration.

Ideas do not arise by themselves; art, music, and the myriad other symbols comprising a society's culture come from people. This suggests that one way to discover how many foreign symbols currently exist in a given society is to find out how many people have supplied them in the past. Accordingly, we gathered data on several types of people who can reasonably be considered carriers of foreign culture.[20] The first, from Unesco *Statistical Yearbooks*, is students studying abroad, which we divided by total national university enrollment. The second, from the IUOTO *International Travel Statistics*, is foreign tourists, which we divided by the national population of the host country. It has long been known, of course, that foreign study is a means by which foreign culture is transmitted to a segment of a country's future elite. Tourists, too, bring their cultures along with their cameras; while not true in every case, their tastes and attitudes have a tendency to diffuse into the general population. Both students and tourists are leading indicators; the full cultural impact of current study and tourism will not be felt until some time in the future. Accordingly, we weight these indicators to reflect this rising (and, after a certain time, declining) influence.

Just as symbols do not come from some ethereal universe, neither do they remain divorced from everyday life. People's behavior tends to reflect their beliefs, values, and aspirations, as do their symbols. In particular, we would expect that just as a positive view of foreign things should result in a large number of favorable symbols relating to those things, so too it should induce people to seek out foreign ties. The word 'seek' should be emphasized. While nations are bound to each other by all sorts of ties, it is those ties that are actively *sought* which best reflect attitudes toward foreign things. Thus we have looked for non-routine ties requiring both planning and pleading. One such tie is foreign aid; another is arms transfers. We therefore gathered data (1) from the OECD Development Assistance Directorate on net flows of economic assistance and (2) from SIPRI on the dollar value of major weapons imports.[21] Both indicators were then divided by government spending (data gathered from the UN *Yearbook of National Accounts Statistics*). Since deliveries of both economic aid and major weapons tend to be 'lumpy', we computed five-year moving averages for those indicators.

To measure the concentration of cultural penetration (X_4), we use the same indicators as for systemic cultural penetration. The only difference is that here we compute orientations toward specific countries rather than toward the international system as a whole. We gathered penetration data (for each peripheral country) on every other nation which was the main partner on at least one indicator. This in principle restricted our efforts to at most four partners per periphery country – and, in practice, to fewer than that. We then summed the measures of dyadic penetration to construct a measure of the concentration of cultural penetration. Because different nations may be 'largest partners' for different indicators, it is necessary to add the four (each weighted equally) for a combined measure.

The four variables above enter into our model as predetermined, or exogenous, variables affecting a variety of economic, social, and political conditions in less developed or peripheral countries. The first group of the latter concerns aspects of the development of an 'export economy syndrome'. One aspect of this syndrome is trade partner concentration (X_5), or the concentration of international economic trade relations on a particular central economy. This is a concept familiar in the literature on dependence, so discussion of its measurement can be kept brief. As with the measurement of concentration in sources of penetration, X_2 and X_4, we prefer the simple 'percentage of trade going to the largest partner' to the somewhat more complex concentration measure devised by Hirschman. Data on country-to-country trade are available in the *IMF Direction of Trade Annual*.

A related concept, also by now familiar, is trade product concentration (X_6), or the concentration on a small number of products in the export profile of the peripheral economy. A major background theme of dependencia theory is the historical transformation of colonies and other peripheral societies into export-oriented, undiversified economic units, especially during the periods of formal colonial domination but extending at least to the early twentieth century. The agricultural and extractive export enclaves that were created tended to be the only 'dynamic' sectors, so that the peripheral economy became totally oriented to their maintenance and growth. In large part, this pattern has continued to be characteristic even today, but an important distinction for dependencia theories is between those peripheral countries which have remained basically export enclave economies, and those like Mexico, Brazil, Taiwan, and South Korea which have diversified their export profiles and now even export a large variety of industrial goods.

Attention to the concentration of export profiles is common in empirical research, and the data are available in the UN *Yearbook of International Trade Statistics*, with classifications of commodities into fifty-two divisions. Here both our understanding of the dependence literature and the existing tradition of empirical analysis[22] lead us to favor the Hirschman measure of dispersion or concentration, attending to concentration among several major commodities rather than only the percentage of the largest. We have computed our product concentration indices based on exports of the top five commodities relative to total exports. Inclusion of additional commodities makes relatively little difference in the index; indeed, in many peripheral countries of the 1960s, the largest commodity accounted for over 60 per cent of total exports.

The relative economic importance of foreign trade (X_7) has been used often by trade theorists. Historically, peripheral economies were transformed not only to economies exporting a few products to a few markets, but also into economies overwhelmingly oriented just to those sectors which produced for export, and in turn met many of the needs of their cash economies (for consumption as well as capital goods) by importation. Since we are here concerned with the impact of imports as well as exports, we simply take an average value of exports and imports as the size of the foreign trade sector and divide it by GDP.

A final variable in this group is trade vulnerability (X_8), which is simply a composite of the preceding three. Frequently in the verbal arguments below we shall refer to X_8 as the extent of export enclave development. It is a measure of the vulnerability of the economy to external manipulation through rates of exchange of products, and is defined as the economic importance of trade weighted by the extent of product and partner concentration of trade patterns. Thus it is expressed as the identity:

[I1] $$X_8 \equiv X_5 \cdot X_6 \cdot X_7$$

Sources of the Export Enclave Syndrome

The point of departure for dependencia theory in its divergence from the previously prevalent assessment of the problems of development was a decrease in the emphasis on the importance of the trade connection. Prebisch and his ECLA colleagues, as well as Myrdal and the European structuralists, had fastened on the trade concentration and terms of trade problems as sources of bargaining weakness in international markets, and the critical barrier to economic growth in Latin America and elsewhere in the so-called Third World. Dependencia theorists moved away from this position in two ways. First, they denied the appropriateness of the inordinate emphasis on trade to the exclusion of financial and cultural-political considerations. Secondly, they denied the fundamental causative nature of trade, seeing it rather as the derived effect of the other, more basic forms of penetration, financial, technological, and political-cultural. It is this latter aspect, that is, the extent of export enclave development as effect rather than root cause, which is the subject of the first three equations in our model.

Our first equation attempts to capture the simple proposition that 'trade follows the flag', in the sense that foreign trade will be concentrated upon a particular metropolitan partner as some function of the degree to which cultural, financial, and technological penetration are concentrated. That is, concentration of a peripheral nation's value structure upon a metropolitan partner will produce concentration of trade. Political, cultural values will shape consumption preferences and production habits so as to increase demand for goods from the dominant metropolitan country; similarly the means of production obtained from that country will shape economic development so as to require further inputs from that source of capital.[23] Here we capture the early arguments of dependencia theory attempting to trace the roots of post-Second World War trade patterns to a history of connections to particular countries in the capitalist center. Generally, then, X_5 at any time is a function of current and past values of X_2 and X_4.

The dynamic process is not appropriately represented by any short-term change formulation. Rather, we need a formulation that reflects slow, historically extended processes. In this instance, the current concentration of trade partners is said to be affected by current and past levels of economic and cultural penetration, with the past variables having a diminishing but non-negligible impact over long periods of time. This kind of argument is represented as:

$$Y_t = \alpha + \beta_t X_t + \beta_{t-1} X_{t-1} + \ldots + \beta_{t-\infty} X_{t-\infty} \qquad (I)$$

where $|\beta_t| > |\beta_{t-1}| > \ldots > |\beta_{t-\infty}|$ reflecting the decreasing impact of past history. Now we cannot estimate equation I directly because we do not have information on any X-variable back through all history. However, if we make the assumption that there is a smooth and steady decline in the impact of more distant history on the present which can be approximated by a geometric distributed lag, i.e. where $\beta_{t-i-1} = \lambda \beta_{t-i}$, and $0 < \lambda < 1$, then the model takes the form:

$$Y_t = \alpha + \beta_t X_t + \lambda \beta_t X_{t-1} + \lambda^2 \beta_t X_{t-2} + \ldots + \lambda^\infty \beta_t X_{t-\infty}. \qquad (II)$$

While this form also appears intractable, in fact it can be readily converted to a convenient estimating form. By taking the expression in II for the previous time period (Y_{t-1}), multiplying both sides by λ and then subtracting the result from II we obtain

$$Y_t = (1 - \lambda)\alpha + \lambda Y_{t-1} + \beta_t X_t \qquad (III)$$

which is an estimable form.[24] We shall apply this form to most of our following equations. In the particular application here we model the argument that the longer and stronger the continuous history of penetration by agents of a capitalist metropole (X_2), and the historically greater the orientation of dominant values to a metropole (X_4), the more concentrated on the metropole will be trade relations (X_5). The basic equation is therefore:[25]

[1] $$X_{5t} = B_0 + A_0 \sum_{i=0}^{\infty} L^i X_{2_{t-i}} + A_1 \sum_{i=0}^{\infty} L^i X_{4_{t-i}}$$

where L^i is the geometric lag coefficient appropriate for each independent causal process.

The next equation captures the basic argument that changes in the concentration of export product profiles (X_6) are reflections of changes in the evenness or unevenness of development of economic sectors, and that the degree to which changes in the latter produce changes in the former depends upon the degree of structural integration, or connectedness, of the economy. To discuss this, however, we must first explicate these two new variables. We will also introduce here another economic variable that will be important below, namely, the level of economic activity.

The level of economic activity (X_9) is perhaps the most imprecise and controversial concept in all of dependencia theory. Much of the confusion arises because the term connotes something of both neo-classical economists' use of aggregate per capita production as an indicator of 'well-being' and the Marxist notion of the transformation of the relations of production as an economy moves into the phase of industrial capitalism. Other labels such as modernization, industrialization, or level of capitalist development fall into the same genre of ambiguous terminology. Because of the confusion surrounding the concept and because it does not have quite as central a role in more recent works in the dependencia tradition, the exact definition of 'level of economic activity' is often obscured in the literature. Nevertheless it remains an important concept in the theory.

The level of economic activity – often referred to as development – has two distinct analytical traditions. In one context it is used to refer to the totality of economic productive activity *and* to the consequences thereof. Frank and his associates generally use the term in this way. They view a high level of economic activity as a condition for an economy to be self-sufficient, wealthy, and egalitarian. Other theorists, such as Cardoso, argue that this conception is overly broad, and they use the term to refer to a much more limited phenomenon. They derive their conceptualization from conventional Marxist theory and so emphasize the process of capital accumulation. For Marx, a crucial feature distinguishing the capitalist mode of production from pre-capitalist modes is that, in capitalism, the processes of reproduction of the means of production lead to ever greater accumulation of capital. Thus Cardoso is able to characterize the level of economic activity by the extent of capital accumulation.

We agree that the conception offered by Frank is overly general and would in fact embrace virtually the entirety of the last three blocks in Figure 13.1. We also are not aware of any available measure of the extent of capital accumulation. Thus we use an imperfect surrogate measure which reflects the extent of accumulation of capital but is somewhat broader in indicating the level of economic productive activity actually carried out. Our measure is the aggregate market valuation of production standardized by the size of the population (i.e. GDP per capita). The problem, of course, is that GDP is affected by things other than the extent of capital accumulation. Factors such as land fertility, climate, and natural resource endowments are also crucial determinants of GDP. In particular, some oil-producing countries (e.g. United Arab

Emirates, which is in fact not included in our 'sample') provide an extreme example of the dangers inherent in this surrogate measure. In these cases, it clearly reflects aggregate wealth more than simple capital accumulation. Although per capita GDP may be extremely high for such countries, certainly they have not achieved a comparable capacity for economic production. Thus, it is essential to pay special attention to locating instances where high GDP per capita reflects the direct sale of natural endowments (both renewable and non-renewable portions) instead of using natural endowments as a basis for producing further value.

We analyze the level of processing to ascertain the extent to which income is a function of higher production rather than a fortuitous happenstance of natural endowment.[26] The whole of the measurement strategy outlined above is consistent with a neo-classical economics approach of examining how successfully aggregate production is carried out given the available endowments of land, labour, and natural resources. Data on GDP per capita are available from the UN *Yearbook of National Accounts Statistics*.

Uneven development (X_{10}) refers to the extent to which different sectors of the economy are at different levels of economic activity and capital accumulation.[27] The underlying theoretical notion is that the transformation of the peripheral economy toward a capitalist mode of production occurs at very different rates for different sectors of the economy. Because this pattern of differential growth tends to be unbalancing – capital accumulation is greatest where productive capacity is already largest – the result, over some range, is ever-increasing levels of uneven development. In keeping with a general historical perspective in modeling dependencia theory, we cast our presentation of the argument in terms of this end-state variable rather than in terms of the process (i.e. unbalancing growth) by which it arises. Unbalancing growth may, of course, be ascertained by looking at changes in the level of uneven development.

Consistent with our definition and measurement of the level of economic activity, we measure uneven development by looking at output per worker for each sector. Our measure then is an indicator of variation among levels of output per worker across sectors. This measure is the weighted sum of deviations of the sectors from the weighted mean. Each sector is weighted by its relative size since large sectors have more impact on the level of uneven development than do small sectors. Data are based on material from the UN Statistical Office and its *Yearbook of National Accounts Statistics*, and labor breakdowns are available for many countries from the International Labour Office and its *Yearbook of Labour Statistics*. The logic for the use of sectors is outlined in the discussion in integration below; here we use data for three aggregated sectors: (1) agriculture and mining, (2) industry, and (3) services.

Use of large-scale aggregates implies the strong assumption of homogeneity within sectors. While this assumption is not strictly correct, differential growth rates in small subsectors frequently cancel out in near-random fashion. Moreover, our basic theoretical perspective specifies foreign penetration as usually having occurred within the industrial or extractive sectors of the economy. As a result, these sectors increasingly become separated from the rest of the domestic economy and experience a different growth pattern, depending largely upon external links with the capitalist metropole. In this context an assumption of basic homogeneity within sectors, and of large between-sector variation, usually seems reasonable.

Economic disintegration (X_{11}) (or 'disarticulation', as in Amin) is a second aspect of the structure of development, related conceptually to uneven development. It is concerned with the phenomenon whereby goods and services produced for domestic consumption are used only in limited sectors of the economy. By integration we mean the degree of well-connectedness of an economy. Our notion of connectedness contains three components: existence and balance of sectoral linkages relative to the overall level of activity in the system. The first says simply that an economy with a flow of production between the i_{th} and j_{th} sectors is better connected, *ceteris paribus*, than is an economy lacking such a flow, and the larger the flow, the better connected. By an extension of this reasoning, the second criterion, balance, implies that an economy with equal resource flows among sectors is better integrated than is one where the flows are very high between some sectors and very low between others. Regarding this latter case, imbalanced economies are 'hierarchical' ones with many vertical but few horizontal connections.[28] Finally, if the sum of all flows in one economy is greater than in another, then *ceteris paribus* the first economy is better connected and hence more integrated. Of course the theoretical maxima are unlikely to be found empirically. We simply do not expect agriculture to feed directly into steel production.

It is somewhat problematic as to what 'parts' of the national economy dependence theorists are referring. The common distinctions of traditional, transitional, and modern sectors often used by the development school are inadequate in that they are defined to be non-overlapping, and hence the lack of integration follows by definition. A similar deficiency is relevant with respect to Marxist class or functionalist divisions. However, Pinto[29] has used a sectoral division very similar to that employed in neo-classical economics (i.e. agriculture, mining, manufacturing, etc.) and this is the approach which we follow. It has the advantage of dividing the economy into homogeneous groupings which are relatively well defined in terms of their productive activity and are comparable across nations.

The connectedness or integration of an economy can best be measured by analyzing the flows among sectors of the economy. An input-output table is a matrix representation of flows of goods and services between sectors of the economy wherein each entry reflects the outputs from one sector which enter as inputs into another sector. Such an input-output representation would constitute our preferred measure, as can be seen in a full exposition of the status of the concept and our measurement strategy which has been presented elsewhere; readers are referred to that statement.[30] Unfortunately, however, input-output tables are not generally available and appear only sporadically for various countries. We decided, therefore, to use the available input-output tables only as the basis by which to check the validity of other indicators of integration which are more readily available.

In devising other indicators we relied on the obvious point that if goods are exchanged they must be transported. We assume that most firms in the same industry are located relatively close together, while different industries are relatively farther apart. Thus most inter-industry trade will cover long distances relative to the size of the country. By gathering information on the volume of domestic train, plane, and truck traffic from the UN *Statistical Yearbook*, controlling of course for the size of the country's geographic area and economy (GDP), we have been able to produce indirect estimates of the level of integration.[31] These indirect estimates correlate highly with the measure we derived from input-output tables where the latter are available.

The second equation in our model captures the basic argument that changes in the concentration of export product profiles (X_6) are reflections of changes in the evenness or unevenness of development of economic sectors (X_{10}), and that the degree to which changes in the latter produce changes in the former depends upon the degree of structural disintegration of the economy (X_{11}). At an early state of development, the rapid growth of a few export-oriented sectors (uneven development) results in overwhelming emphasis on a few exports only (the classic mono-sectoral export economy). According to some 'pre-dependencia' theorists (e.g. Prebisch), this trade product concentration can (and should) be reduced by developing additional 'dynamic' sectors (generally engaged in the production of consumer goods to substitute for imports). From such a perspective, trade patterns are seen as relatively volatile; if more productive sectors are developed, their products will probably be exported and thereby decrease trade product concentration. Dependencia theorists generally seem to accept this line of argument, but modify it substantially by arguing that the extent of volatility of trade profiles in response to more or less even development depends on the domestic economic repercussions of the latter changes, and this, in turn, is determined by the structural integration of the economy. In particular, if the peripheral economy becomes less dis-integrated, greater opportunity arises for traditional exports in the concentrated export profile to be diverted into domestically growing industries. The products are apt to be processed both for domestic use and for export as a more diversified line. Hence with more even development and greater integration, Brazil and Mexico have been able substantially to reduce the product concentration of their exports, whereas Zambia, with only a single important sector in which growth has been promoted, has experienced an increased concentration on exports from that sector. We capture this short-term sensitivity not in the distributed lag formulation used above, but in the simpler, first differences, form which reads

[2] $$X_{6_t} = B_0 + X_{6_{t-1}} + B_1(X_{10_t} - X_{10_{t-1}})X_{11_{t-1}}.$$

In the same way that peripheral economies today differ in the extent to which their export product profiles remain undiversified, so, too, they differ in the extent to which the products produced for export dominate productive activity in the economy. Some peripheral economies export a very high proportion of the value produced, and in complementary fashion, import a great deal of what is consumed, while others today have geared a substantial amount of production to the provision of domestic needs.

The ability of a peripheral economy to make this transition and the consequences for it in doing so or in failing to do so have been major theoretical issues for some time. The import-substitution industrialization recommendations of ECLA 'nationalists' were aimed precisely at overcoming this problem. The critiques by dependencia theorists of these recommendations, in turn, have pointed to a replacement of the export economy syndrome by a 'new' dependence on financial and technological penetration in response to policies of import-substitution industrialization. Since this shift to the 'new dependence' is by far the major concern of dependencia theory, a crucial argument is that offered to account for changes, especially decreases, in the relative economic importance of foreign trade.

The argument entails two distinct parts. First, because formal political and cultural penetration (i.e. X_3, especially in the form of colonialism) served historically to create export enclaves oriented overwhelmingly to foreign trade (X_7), the weakening of that dependence serves to weaken the basis for the maintenance of that orientation. Thus, the decline of 'state imperialist hegemony' and the emergence of relative state autonomy in the periphery contributes to a partial reorientation of the peripheral economy toward greater domestic production and consumption. Conversely, contemporary resurgences or a strengthening of political-cultural ties of dependence serve the same purposes as they did historically, namely, to promote a greater external orientation of the economy. Secondly, and most important, the economic importance of foreign trade is affected by changes in the financial and technological penetration of the economy (X_1), given a certain level of development of the economy (X_9). In particular, for less developed economies, increasing capitalist penetration increases the importance of trade, whereas for more developed economies, increasing capitalist penetration decreases trade importance. This is because at low levels of development, penetration serves to create or expand export sectors (especially of extractive and agricultural production), whereas at higher levels of development, penetration is aimed much more at production for domestic consumption (i.e. there is a switch to a new type of dependence, on that penetration itself). As these too are long-term historical processes, we return to the distributed lag formulation employed for equation (1), and express the preceding argument as derived:

$$[3] \quad X_{7_t} = B_0 + A_0 \sum_{i=0}^{\infty} L^i X_{3_{t-i}} + A_1 \sum_{i=0}^{\infty} L^i X_{1_{t-i}}(c - X_{9_{t-i}}).$$

The three aspects of the export enclave syndrome (X_5 through X_7) combine as indicated above in the identity to form a new variable, X_8, which plays a role in contributing to 'distorted' patterns of economic development within dependent countries. In addition simply to a constrained level of economic activity (X_9) there exist three relevant distortions: uneven development (X_{10}), sectoral disintegration (X_{11}), and sectoral heterogeneity in the returns to labor (X_{12}, to be discussed below). These three structural distortions are related but conceptually distinct components of the process of marginalization which occupies such a central place in the dependencia literature. We use these three variables plus the level of development (X_9) in a bloc of equations, with the central argument being that as penetration, dependence, and/or the export economy syndrome increase, the extent to which the economy becomes constrained and/or distorted in one way or another also increases. That the equations in this bloc are highly interrelated reflects our understanding of the sense in which the different characteristics of marginalization feed upon one another. It also reflects our attempt to model the holistic view of the dependent economy in opposition to the neo-classical view of the 'dual economy'.[32]

Modeling Structural Transformations in the Peripheral Economy

Arguments about the determinants of development (as capital accumulation and the level of productivity) generally focus on two phenomena. On the one hand, there is the issue of self-sustaining growth, and on that there is general agreement, even among dependencia theorists, that development (as here defined) is a somewhat self-reinforcing phenomenon. This is *not* to say that there is an acceptance of a 'take-off stage' argument – clearly there is not. However, it is to say that there is a recognition that through processes of circulation, accumulated capital (in use) generates new capital, and production stimulates new productivity. Thus, if all other things are equal, less developed economies grow less rapidly than do more developed economies. The extent to which the process is domestically self-reinforcing, however, depends heavily on the extent to which foreign control of the means of production serves to channel the process of circulation externally (e.g. through repatriated profits, repayment of loans, etc.). Where circulation of capital is largely external, self-reinforcement is largely eliminated, and this occurs where financial and technological penetration is high.

A second, independent, line of argument turns the above around some, and focuses on the external stimulation of development through the importation of capital, that is, through increased penetration. The argument is that more capital is accumulated and productivity is increased with increases in capitalist penetration, but changes in development stimulated by penetration are greater in economies where the export syndrome is low than in economies of high trade dependence. Said differently, greater penetration of an economy that is highly vulnerable to external manipulation of returns on its production generates less new capital and raises productivity less than does the same increase in penetration of an economy that is more internally oriented. Conversely, disinvestment (declining penetration) reduces development, and most severely in low trade dependent economies. These arguments mean that

$$[4] \quad \frac{X_{9_t} - X_{9_{t-i}}}{X_{9_{t-i}}} = B_0 + B_1 \sum_{i=0}^{\infty} L^i X_{9_{t-1}} X_{1_{t-1}}^{-1} + B_2 \sum_{i=0}^{\infty} L^i X_{9_{t-i}} X_{8_{t-1}} + B_3 \sum_{i=0}^{\infty} L^i X_{9_{t-1}}.$$

The first and foremost concern of dependencia theorists in the economic sphere, however, is not with the level of development so much as with distortions in the pattern of development. Conventionally, the structure of the peripheral economy is marked by highly uneven development, low integration, and high heterogeneity, as one or a few sectors are 'dynamic' in accumulating capital and increasing productivity, while others stagnate or even die out entirely. As mentioned above, the 'dynamic' sectors are most generally oriented to foreign trade, and hence have few economic linkages to other sectors in the economy – neither their material nor their capital inputs are produced domestically, nor are their products consumed domestically. Moreover, the 'dynamic' enclave tends to be characterized by wage levels far above those prevailing in the economy at large. This is partly because the foreign ownership of the dynamic sector serves to raise wages in that sector, and partly because the aforementioned structural distortions depress wages in general through processes of 'marginalization' of large labor pools – the creation of underemployment so marked in contemporary peripheral economies. But while this distorted pattern is pervasive it is not universal, for some peripheral economies (Brazil, Mexico, Taiwan, and South Korea are probably most notable) have developed several dynamic sectors, oriented domestically in part. Thus theorists have faced the need to account for changes in the patterns of distorted development generally inherited from colonialism.

In explaining uneven development, dependencia theorists have emphasized two aspects of the foreign economic relations of the peripheral economy: its export syndrome and its penetration by foreign capitalists. For the first, the argument is straightforward – increasing export enclave development (X_8) promotes uneven development (X_{10}) by strengthening the dominance of export sectors, whereas lessening enclave development, in de-emphasizing the central importance of export sectors, facilitates balancing growth across sectors. Moreover, in the long run enclave development contributes indirectly, in delayed fashion, to the stagnation of other sectors.[33]

For the second, dependence theorists argue that increasing capitalist penetration of a peripheral economy (X_1) operates over the long run to stimulate uneven development. This occurs primarily because penetration promotes growth chiefly in the penetrated sector, *and* because penetration is very generally directed to sectors that have already proven to be 'dynamic'. Thus, foreign capital works to change the structure of peripheral economies by making dynamic sectors even stronger. The extent to which this is consequential for uneven development, however, depends heavily on the number of 'dynamic' sectors in the economy and the relative dynamism of each. In particular, capitalist penetration of an economy already marked by highly uneven development will generally greatly exacerbate that unevenness because a few, clearly dominant sectors are apt to be strengthened. On the other hand, if penetration of a more evenly developed economy increases, it will often have a much less noticeable impact on the balance of development because of the relative equality of several dynamic sectors, each remaining strong in the presence or absence of greater penetration, *and* each likely attracting some of the increased penetration. Disinvestment, or declining penetration, *may* stimulate more even development but it will do so only by contributing to the relative stagnation of dominant sectors, and thus is likely to do so only in economies already marked by highly uneven development. These arguments are represented formally as:

$$[5] \quad X_{10_t} = B_0 + A_0 \sum_{i=0}^{\infty} L^i X_{8_{t-i}} + A_1 \sum_{i=0}^{\infty} L^i X_{1_{t-i}} (X_{1_{t-i}} + c X_{10_{t-i-1}}).$$

Arguments in dependencia theory about the determinants of structural integration or disintegration (X_{11}) are quite simple and straightforward, Economic sectors become more integrated with one another as either or both the importance of foreign trade (X_7) or the degree of uneven development (X_{10}) declines. Conversely, increasing trade importance or increasingly uneven development contributes to economic structural disintegration or disarticulation. While the argument is simple, it would give the distinct impression of being tautological if a common-sensical meaning were given to structural integration. That is, if integration involved merely greater domestic production and consumption (i.e. greater self-sufficiency), then changes in the importance of trade would provide no explanation of changes in structural integration for the relationship would be definitional. But tautology is not involved because, as indicated above, integration is concerned with the connectedness of the domestic economy rather than anything about the extent to which the conomy is externally oriented. Since the concern is the degree to which domestically oriented production flows throughout, or is utilized throughout, the economy, changes in trade importance (and uneven development) are conceptually unrelated to changes in structural integration. However, as we stated above, they are not *causally* unrelated. On the contrary, disintegration responds, slowly over time, to these changes because greater foreign orientation promotes a less widespread and balanced domestic orientation and because a less even development pattern across sectors promotes a less articulated set of relationships among sectors. These are not relationships by definition.[34] They are represented as:

[6] $$X_{11_t} = B_0 + A_0 \sum_{i=0}^{\infty} L^i X_{7_{t-i}} + A_1 \sum_{i=0}^{\infty} L^i X_{10_{t-i}}.$$

The third aspect of distorted development characteristic of peripheral economies is economic structural heterogeneity (X_{12}), which refers to activities occurring within various sectors rather than with linkages between sectors. Highly homogeneous economies contain sectors whose internal characteristics are very similar; strongly heterogeneous economies contain sectors which vary widely. All economic sectors, in varying degrees, utilize different factors of production: land, labor, and capital. But we cannot expect that all economic sectors have open to them the same range of production functions. Hence to measure the divergence of economic sectors we are more interested in the rates of return to factors of production than in the amounts of the factors themselves.

At first sight, a multiple indicator of heterogeneity would compare sectors according to their rates of return on all three factors. In point of fact, however, such a comparison is neither necessary nor possible. Impossible, because data on profit rates by economic sector simply are unavailable. Unnecessary, because any variation in rent among non-agricultural sectors is likely to be miniscule. More important, dependencia theorists in fact are concerned primarily with the degree to which wages in different economic sectors systematically diverge. Some have emphasized the rise of local bourgeoisies in producing this phenomenon; others have stressed the marginalization of peasants and small tradesmen; still others have resurrected the Leninist idea of a 'labor aristocracy'.[35] Whatever the proximate causes - and the ones cited by no means preclude each other - disparities in wage rates possess far greater potential for exploitation and class conflict than do disparities in either rent or profits.

We have collected data (principally from the ILO *Yearbook of Labour Statistics* on total compensation of employees in each economic sector (using the same sectors as for uneven development, and roughly the same number of sectors for each country). We divide those figures by the population employed in that sector. This quotient represents the wages paid over a year's time to an average worker in each sector. (We cannot measure variations within sectors.) Then, following the same procedure as with uneven development, we compute the standard deviation of these average wages across sectors, weighting each sectoral component by the size of the population employed in that sector.[36]

The extent of structural heterogeneity (X_{12}) is due, like so many other phenomena as described in dependencia theory, to the capitalist penetration of the economy (X_1). It changes in response to changes in penetration. But again, the extent of change depends on other aspects of the penetrated economy. An increasing penetration of economies of low development (X_9) and low integration (X_{11}) serves, over time, to reduce homogeneity by buttressing wages in the 'dynamic' sector with little or no multiplier or spillover consequences for other sectors. Alternatively, an increase in penetration of an economy that is more highly developed and more integrated can promote greater homogeneity by reducing the pool of marginally unemployed labor (through multipliers to other sectors, etc.) more rapidly than increasing the wage levels of those sectors directly affected. Penetration of moderately developed, moderately integrated economies reduces homogeneity, but not as severely as does the same penetration of a less developed, less integrated economy. Disinvestment, or declining penetration, has just the converse effects. All this is given as a lagged process, and in fairly complex form, as:

$$[7] \quad X_{12_t} = B_0 + A_0 \sum_{i=0}^{\infty} L^i X_{1_{t-i}} (X_{9_{t-i}}^{-1} X_{11_{t-i}} - c).$$

Modeling Structural Transformations in the Peripheral Capitalist Polity

To this point we have modeled dependencia theory as an almost entirely economistic set of arguments – changes in the economic structure of peripheral societies are explained largely by economic relations. Furthermore, many of these economistic arguments can be found (with different emphases and evaluations, to be sure) in the writings of neo-classical economists. But to stop here would be grossly to distort dependencia theory and to neglect many of its unique features, which deal with the nature of the state, the activities and policies of government, and the forms of social relationships. Indeed, the economistic arguments presented above are only the common, *basic* themes in dependencia theory, and as such do not capture all of the intricacies of the original verbal materials. A substantial part of the verbal intricacy is given over to analyses of *particular* governmental characteristics or actions and *concrete* social relationships, and how those constrain, modify, or determine the economistic arguments presented above. We have not attempted here to capture the verbal intricacy; rather, we have opted only for the economistic core because the intricacies are so generally developed in very particularistic form. In a word, the 'theory' component of dependencia theory often ends at the economistic level.

But while the non-economic determinants of economic structural transformation are difficult, if not impossible, to model, it is quite feasible to represent formally the basic arguments in dependencia theory about some key social and political processes. We attempt to do so here by distinguishing six non-economic concepts central to dependencia theory. For each, we develop an equation which represents our understanding of the basic verbal arguments about transformation processes.

The first of these concepts, X_{13}, is the extent of governmental involvement in the peripheral economy which, conceptually, includes both the relative size, or importance, of state-owned or -controlled economic sectors, and the degree, or pervasiveness, of governmental regulation of economic activity. A particular fascination of dependencia theorists has been with the emergence and expansion of state involvement, which is said now to be creating the truly modern distinguishing characteristic of peripheral capitalism, namely, a state-dominated capitalism.

Governments intervene on behalf of a stable economic order in a number of ways. They provide social services in order to increase the attractiveness of the modern sectors as opposed to the traditional sector. In this way they seek to ensure a stable workforce in the modern economy. Governments also provide educational and health services which might be viewed as enhancing the value of the working force. In this way they improve the functioning of the modern sector which is so dependent upon trained personnel. They enter into the economy directly through the creation of public enterprises, and the regulation of private industries, giving direction and stability to the national economy. Finally, they provide police and military services in order, among other things, to provide a stable environment for investment.

With these activities in mind, we have used figures on government consumption basically from the *Yearbook of National Accounts Statistics* of the UN. These figures include spending on community services, social services, and economic services, and include the activities described above.[37] However, we omit public investment from our measure for two reasons. First, it would probably be confounded with certain other measures in our model, in particular financial penetration. Secondly, it is not nearly so readily available as is government consumption as a percentage of GDP, which certainly reflects the extent to which the state enters into the capitalist economy for purposes of providing stability. The government consumption measure correlates closely with a measure of government employment as a proportion of the labor force, where reliable data are less generally available. Our concept here requires attention to economic activity by all levels of government, though for the final variable in our model, coercive authoritarianism of the state, it is appropriate to focus primarily on the role of the central government.

The next concept, X_{14}, is economic marginalization; that is, the extent to which groups are incapable of maintaining their economic position in society.[38] 'Economic position' can be interpreted in two ways, each of which has considerable historical cachet. The first meaning, discussed as far back as Ricardo, refers to the living standards of those actually working, the degree to which workers approach or remain at an economic 'margin'. The second meaning refers to the importance of labor in the productive process: while there may be a 'labor aristocracy', many members of the laboring class become 'marginal' to the economy and hence unemployed or underemployed. Marx was among the first to study this phenomenon; his term, 'reserve army of the unemployed', remains with us today. Writers in the dependencia tradition consider both phenomena to be present in peripheral societies.[39]

The measurement of marginalization is relatively straightforward. Our measure of stagnating living standards can be derived from the change in real wages over time. To compute this, we gathered data on average non-agricultural wages principally from the ILO *Yearbook of Labour Statistics* controlled by the rate of consumer price inflation as reported in the same source. The second meaning of marginalization – the economic importance of the workforce – can be measured by the proportion of economic activity accounted for by wages. These data are from the *Yearbook of National Accounts Statistics* on total wages paid, divided by GDP.

Economic inequality, X_{15}, is in part the consequence of marginalization. Here we refer to inequality in access to valued goods and services, substantially a function of inequality of income. Perhaps the most common focus is on comparing the incomes of different social groups. For the dependencia literature, these groups are social classes, defined according to conventional Marxist criteria. With data on the incomes of the various social classes, we could compute an index of inequality like that suggested by Kuznets. But very few countries in fact report incomes even by occupational groups, and the measurement of social class as a distinct phenomenon is in any case a matter of considerable difficulty.[40]

While class inequality may be the primary concern of dependencia theorists, they also discuss regional or geographic inequality, and such intra-class inequalities as implied by the creation of a labor aristocracy. A more general type of economic inequality for which data do exist is size distribution of income, which reports which percentages of the total population receive what percentages of total income.[41] Nevertheless the completeness and comparability of income distribution data have long been subject to some skepticism, and recently have come under sharp attack from Kuznets.[42] While Jain's data remain the best and most complete set available, it is necessary to have some other information for countries and years not covered there and to develop an index not quite so subject to reliability problems.

We do so by beginning with the simple notion that the impact of additional income on individual behavior is different at different income levels. One way this can occur is through a declining marginal impact of expenditures in meeting a particular goal. Whenever we have instances of non-linear impact of income on individual decisions then the results of those decisions also tell us about the relative incomes of individuals.

Access to health services – and thus in large measure to health – is related non-linearly to ability to pay for those services. For example, a variety of investigations have established that the gains in various indicators of health, whether using individual or cross-national data, are sharpest for increments to income at low income levels, and tail off considerably in the upper income ranges.[43] In addition, access is related to an individual's geographical distance from health care services. In rural areas one must often bear the time and money cost of long-distance travel to reach health care facilities. Moreover, in most countries the provision of health service is strongly concentrated in urban centers and away from rural areas. Together, these considerations argue that an individual's level of health should be a function (non-linear) of income, population density, and urbanization. Recognizing that an individual's income is a function both of the average level of income in the country and of the distribution of income within the country, we can aggregate these factors over all individuals in the country to produce an equation to predict health. Then, by appropriate algebraic manipulation we can rearrange terms so that we have an equation predicting income inequality from income level, urbanization, population density, and health.

By similar reasoning, which will only be very briefly summarized here, we produced an equation to predict acquisition of another basic kind of 'good': children. The 'new home economics' of demography treats the child as both a product (investment) and a consumer good. By this reasoning fertility is the result of rational economic choice within the household, and can be predicted by a non-linear function of the household's income (again a function of average level of income and the distribution of income and the probability of children dying – infant mortality rate). While we do not find this rationale wholly convincing, reasonably accurate descriptive statements suffice to allow us to use the empirical relations to generate an equation predicting the average level of fertility within a society. Again we can rearrange terms to make this an equation for predicting income inequality.

Finally, we take the estimates of income inequality produced by each of the equations, and combine them. These combined estimates correlate with an r^2 of approximately 0·75 with the Gini estimates published by Jain for a sample of thirty-seven less developed countries. Since data for the predictor variables are available for nearly all underdeveloped countries, the result is a basis for producing estimates of access to basic goods varying over time and space, where the standard household income distribution data are unavailable or unreliable.

Latent conflict, X_{16}, is the potential for civil strife. Class conflict is of course a key variable in any understanding of the social and political consequences of dependence. Latent conflict, however, is not measurable by any instrument presently available for use in large-scale cross-sectional analysis. For example, a strong manifestation of class conflict would seem to be in strikes or other overt labor–management disputes. Some cross-sectional data on strikes in capitalist countries are available. But the validity of such an indicator when used to tap latent conflict is hopelessly compromised by different patterns of political intervention by national governments. In some states labor organization is relatively unconstrained and strikes or other organized work-stoppages are rather freely permitted. In others, labor organization is sharply restricted, or illegal, and strikes are forbidden. To assume that latent class conflict is low simply because such manifestations are infrequent in such states would be ridiculous. Much the same would be true of other possible manifestations of conflict, such as riots or demonstrations, in states possessed of highly coercive regimes. Possibly, detailed interviews could begin to tap such a dimension, but on a cross-national basis that implies an enormous project and, even so, would face insuperable obstacles at the hand of repressive regimes. At the moment, therefore, we have no direct empirical referent for this variable. But since it is theoretically central, we retain it in our model and will show below how it can be estimated as a function of the level of economic activity and economic inequality.

Manifest conflict, X_{17}, however, is a measurable variable. The problems of inter-class, intra-class, and regional inequality that are associated with the structural transformation of the peripheral economy often give rise to manifest expressions of conflict over the societal distribution of economic goods. These may occur either in the labor–management arena, or in more directly politically relevant forms as general strikes, riots, demonstrations, and terrorism. As the state becomes more deeply and pervasively involved in the economy, conflict is frequently stimulated over access to state power. All told, the picture of the underdeveloped society is often a picture of society in turmoil, with a major consequence of the several processes of structural transformation which are experienced through incorporation in the international capitalist system being conflict, often intense conflict, over the nature and direction of those transformations. Nevertheless, underdeveloped societies differ tremendously in the form, extent, and severity of conflict that is manifested within them.

For the measurement of manifest conflict, Ted Gurr, in particular, has compiled data on the social extent (person-days) and severity (deaths) of conflict.[44] We use Gurr's composite person-day and death scores, but delete the contribution of conflict events that do not concern the distribution of economic goods and/or access to state power. We supplement Gurr's data with information compiled by Charles L. Taylor for the projected third edition of the *World Handbook of Political and Social Indicators*.

The final concept in our model is the *coercive authoritarianism of the regime*, X_{18}. This is certainly a related notion to the concept of governmental involvement in the economy, but it is also quite distinct. The concern of theorists here is with the apparent growth in a number of peripheral societies of a statist class interest that grows out of the bourgeois control of the state, but develops beyond that to a point where new class interests come to the fore and express themselves in coercive authoritarian policy. These class interests remain closely tied to those of the bourgeoisie but have their own basis in the apparatus of the state – in the control of the means of coercion. Dependencia theorists have recently been very concerned with an understanding and explanation of the emergence, and in some societies, the dominance of these statist class interests which are centered largely in the new military establishments. As the military emerges as a politically dominant force and loses its class ties to the aristocracy and the bourgeoisie, it creates this new coercive 'state bourgeoisie'. Coercive authoritarianism may not be a new phenomenon for many Third World countries, but its development and socially pervasive centralization, rather than being decentralized to village or latifundia, is often notable.

In measuring this concept we are concerned with three phenomena: the relative size of the coercive apparatus of the state; the political-governmental role played by coercive agencies; and their social-political activities. In a word, we are concerned with the development of a large, politically dominant, and socially regulatory coercive apparatus. So, X_{18} = size × governmental role × social control, of the coercive forces of the state. As the last element is perhaps most central to the theory, and certainly varies more sharply over relatively short time-periods than does the first element (which is subject to delays in expansion and to bureaucratic inertia in shrinkage), we weight the last element most heavily in our analyses.

We measure the size of coercive forces by estimating manpower actively employed in military armed forces and in paramilitary (and gendarmerie) agencies. Thus we exclude reserve forces and civil police (although attempts are being made to include the latter). Our estimates of the size of military and paramilitary forces are based on convergence, as much as possible, of at least two independent sources, including, but not limited to, the US Arms Control and Disarmament Agency, the International Institute for Strategic Studies, *The Statesman's Yearbook*, military almanacs, and country studies. The degree of convergence among sources has been less than anticipated or desired, although for approximately 80 per cent of our sample reliability is quite high.

The political-governmental role of coercive agencies is assessed by measuring the extent to which governmental positions (at or above central cabinet levels) are held by persons who also (continue to) hold roles in hierarchies of the armed forces. For the data we rely primarily (but not solely) on a variety of cross-national and country-specific compilations. Our indicator is the percentage of time central cabinet positions are held by military personnel. We find this superior to the various judgemental scales of military involvement which have appeared.[45]

For the extent of coercive social control by armed forces, we use the frequency and severity of coercive negative sanctions targeted at social collectivities, based on estimates reported in standard compendia.[46]

We now can present the final bloc of equations. The central verbal arguments offered to account for increasing government involvement in the economy (X_{13}), or the rise of state dominated capitalism in peripheral economies, are fairly straightforward. First, the extent of governmental involvement is treated in the literature as a growth phenomenon – to our knowledge, no theorist implies that it declines in contemporary peripheral capitalist countries in situations of the 'new' dependency. Rather, this 'state capitalism' feeds on itself, so that a 'state bourgeoisie' gradually becomes institutionalized as a major class in its own right. Hence the first term in our equation reflects a slow, self-promoting, auto-regressive growth process. Overlaid on this, governments respond, in the short term, to substantial changes in financial and technological penetration (X_1) and to increases in latent conflict (X_{16}). The latter are short-term change phenomena, the consequence of conscious regulative action in an adjustment/reaction process.

Governments are said to respond to changes (either positive or negative) in foreign capitalist penetration by increasing their level of involvement and regulatory activity. Hence we use the absolute value of such changes in the following equation. However, the extent of change in government involvement is conditioned by the level of economic activity of the economy (X_9). The more 'developed' the peripheral economy, and thus the more likely the peripheral state is to be controlled by capitalist class interests, the more the government involves itself in response to changes in penetration. For the final term, government involvement is determined by increases in latent conflict in the society. But again, the extent of involvement is variable, depending on the coercive, authoritarian character of the state (X_{18}). In particular, highly coercive states become involved quickly and extensively in economic affairs in the face of increased conflict, and the larger the increase in conflict, the larger still the governmental response. Coercive authoritarian states do not, however, much reduce the level of their involvement in response to any reduction in the level of latent conflict. Thus in the last term of the following equation we introduce a dummy variable (γ) that would be zero if conflict declined. We model these arguments as:

$$[8] \quad X_{13_t} = B_0 + B_1 X_{13_{t-1}} + B_2 |X_{1_t} - X_{1_{t-1}}| X_{9_t} + \gamma B_3 (X_{16_t} - X_{16_{t-1}}) X_{18_{t-1}}.$$

Two arguments are usually given in the literature to account for the degree of economic marginalization (X_{14}). The first is economic, the second, political. The economic argument focuses on capital-intensive growth. Writers since Marx have viewed an increase in capital intensity as contributing to increases in unemployment; dependencia theorists see financial and technological penetration (X_1), mostly by multinational corporations, as leading to capital intensification.[47] By increasing the size of the 'reserve army', downward pressure is exerted on the wages of those still working.[48] These effects can be exacerbated by the level of structural heterogeneity in the economy (X_{12}). If there are large disparities between economic sectors, an increase in the capitalization of high-wage sectors will attract workers from outside the market economy. Given that capital-intensive investment reduces the need for labor, for any given level of productivity, the newly arrived workers will not find employment in the high-wage sectors, and will end up as part of the 'reserve army' in the shanty-towns of urban areas.

A second argument – a political one – is more direct. It sees coercive authoritarian regimes (X_{18}) as capable of lowering wages through repressive means. This capability will be utilized depending on the extent to which the government is involved in the economy (X_{13}).

Typically, it is argued, the peripheral capitalist government becomes economically involved (both because of its class origins and because of its technocratic orientation) to assure stable and increasing productivity, which generally means the suppression of labor's demands for higher real wages.[49] In this situation, with productivity outstripping wages, the economic importance of workers (as a class) falls relative to that of capital.

These arguments can be represented as follows:

[9] $$X_{14_t} = B_0 + A_0 \sum_{i=0}^{\infty} L^i X_{1_{t-i}} X_{12_{t-i}} + A_1 \sum_{i=0}^{\infty} L^i X_{18_{t-i}} X_{13_{t-i}}.$$

The degree of marginalization in the economy (X_{14}) is important in its own right, but also because it affects the degree of economic inequality (X_{15}) more generally. Dependencia theorists pay considerable attention to economic inequality as a result of the degree of marginalization, conditioned by the relative size of the labor class. If labor has low economic importance (as measured by a relatively small total wage bill), even though the number in the laboring class may be relatively large, its ability to obtain substantial increases is low and the average wage will continue to stagnate. After a series of small, negligible, or even negative increases in wages, a high level of economic inequality *between* classes will prevail. The higher the level of economic activity (X_9), the more industrialization will proceed, and the more people there will be in the laboring class – that is, outside the traditional, subsistence sectors – and hence subject to this stagnation. In addition, uneven development (X_{10}) contributes to increased inequality *within* the laboring class. Uneven development means that both capitalists and workers (the labor aristocracy) within the most highly developed sectors are more highly rewarded, with stagnation for both workers and bourgeoisie elsewhere. Moreover, uneven development almost always promotes regional inequality because dynamic regions are generally geographically concentrated. Thus we have the equation:

[10] $$X_{15_t} = B_0 + A_0 \sum_{i=0}^{\infty} L^i X_{14_{t-i}} X_{9_{t-i}} + A_1 \sum_{i=0}^{\infty} L^i X_{10_{t-1}}.$$

A standard argument in social conflict theories, and one adopted in dependencia theory, is that economic inequality (X_{15}) fosters conflict, especially latent conflict (X_{16}). Indeed, dependencia theory sees the origins of conflict as primarily economic.[50] Unequal distributions of the 'national pie' tend to be conflict-inducing. Moreover, this potential for conflict is affected by the nature of changes in the over-all national income. In particular, in societies marked by high inequality, any appreciable change (either positive or negative) in the level of economic activity (X_9) will stimulate greater conflict over how the expanded or contracted 'pie' should be divided. Reductions in the level of economic activity stimulate more conflict than do expansions of equivalent magnitude. Societies marked by low inequality respond rather differently to changes in the level of economic activity. In such societies, economic growth does *not* promote greater conflict but reductions do, albeit less dramatically than from an equivalent reduction in development for a highly unequal society. This may be represented as an identity:

[11] $$X_{16_t} \equiv X_{15_t} + \Phi(X_{9_t} - X_{9_{t-1}})[(X_{9_t} - X_{9_{t-1}}) - X_{15_{t-1}}^\theta]$$

In the above equation, the coefficient ϕ represents our uncertainty about how to scale the two components in the second term. This cannot be estimated in the present formulation, because latent conflict is an unmeasured variable. However, subsequent equations provide an opportunity indirectly to estimate ϕ, and the flexibility of this parameter is appropriate to simulation efforts. The status of latent conflict is thus left as that of an unobservable construct of key importance in modeling manifest conflict (X_{17}) and the coercive authoritarian character of the state (X_{18}).[51] The coefficient, θ, would be set to +1 for declines in economic activity, and to −1 for increases in economic activity.

Manifest conflict (X_{17}) is of course in part a function of the level of latent conflict (X_{16}) in a society; a substantial level of latent conflict, built up over fairly long historical periods, is likely to become manifest in various acts against the authorities. Similarly, low and/or declining levels of latent conflict are likely to be reflected in low levels of manifest conflict. Yet the first part of this relationship is incomplete, since the manifestation of latent conflict is also a consequence of political authorities' actions. Over substantial ranges of government coercion (X_{18}), especially that typically employed by democratic or liberal bourgeois regimes, conflict feeds on government coercion. Scattered arrests or other moderately severe restrictions on civil liberties merely stimulate further manifestations of conflict from segments of the populace. Government coercion produces further protest; force induces counterforce.

At some point in the escalation of violence, however, the nature of the government's response changes markedly. Severe censorship may be imposed; large-scale arrests may occur; the security forces may be given much greater freedom of action in dealing with dissidents; the constitution and its guarantees may be suspended or a new 'constitution' imposed. Sometimes these may occur within an already moderately authoritarian context, but during the past decade sharp regime shifts from liberal to military governments in Chile, Uruguay, the Philippines, and elsewhere illustrate how discontinuous the change may be. The result of such a government crackdown is likely to be a sharp, discontinuous reduction in the manifestation of conflict. Protesters are either incarcerated or intimidated, terrorists may be eliminated by establishment terrorism, the dissemination of dissidents' ideas is inhibited by censorship and restrictions on free assembly. The regime's opponents must retreat from open conflict to conspiracy. The harsher the measures employed against dissidence, the more rare will be overt manifestations of dissidence.[52] If we use γ as a dummy variable to represent the point of discontinuity where government coercion exceeds some identifiable threshold, these arguments can be represented as:

[12] $$X_{17} = B_0 + A_0 \sum_{i=0}^{\infty} L^i X_{16_{t-i}} - \gamma B_1(X_{18_{t-1}} \cdot X_{16_{t-1}})$$
$$- (1 - \gamma) B_2(X_{18_{t-1}} \cdot X_{16_{t-1}}) + \gamma B_3.$$

These same discontinuities show up in modeling the other side of what is in large part an interactive process, the determinants of the coercive authoritarian character of the state (X_{18}). But other influences operate as well. No single source in the dependencia literature provides a complete and explicit explanation of the extent of coercive authoritarianism in peripheral states, so the development of our equation is based on a creative interpretation and synthesis of diverse arguments.[53]

For the first element, where manifest conflict (X_{17}) is intense, pervasive, and historically long-lived, the coercive apparatus of the state is expanded and its political importance strengthened. Recent high levels of conflict are especially relevant. This is particularly true where the government is actively and deeply involved in economic affairs, for in such circumstances statist interests are especially concerned with the control of de-stabilizing economic conflict. On the other hand, short-term reductions in manifest conflict are likely to have little effect in reducing coercion. The development of coercive authoritarianism can only with difficulty be reversed, due to the bureaucratic inertia built up by the security forces and the memories of past conflict held by the elite.

The second influence is cultural and political penetration both upon the capitalist world center in general (X_3) and as focused upon a particular capitalist metropole (X_4). Here we give special attention to the political-military aid process, the extent to which the regime in the peripheral country is and has been externally supported. To the degree external support is extensive, has been carried on for a long period of time, and is concentrated on a particular source, the coercive apparatus of the peripheral state is appreciably strengthened. Furthermore, the regime's traditional domestic class ties are weakened, and its political interests are made more homogeneous and similar to those of its dominant external source of support, increasing its need to exercise coercion. Alternatively, lower levels and long-term reductions in political dependence encourage the development of autonomous state interests.

Finally, levels of state coercion respond to long-term historical processes in the development or amelioration of latent conflict (X_{16}). Again using γ to signify a dummy variable, this time for a sharp discontinuity in the expression of manifest conflict, we express the preceding arguments as:

[13] $$X_{18_t} = B_0 + A_0 X_{13_{t-1}} \sum_{i=0}^{\infty} L^i X_{17_{t-i}} + A_1 \sum_{i=0}^{\infty} L^i X_{3_{t-i}} X_{4_{t-i}}$$
$$+ A_2 \sum_{i=0}^{\infty} L^i X_{16_{t-i}} + \gamma A_3.$$

The foregoing provides a statement of our model of dependencia theory, and a cursory justification and elaboration of the model in terms of our understanding of relevant theoretical arguments. It attempts to capture the basic set of propositions by which external penetration and dependence is alleged to lead to the coercive force of authoritarian states in the Third World. One further link, however, is discussed only in cursory fashion in the dependencia literature, and that is the loop back from the coercive state, increasingly bound up with external interests, which digs itself into further penetration and dependence. In substantial part, the whole process is seen as continually self-reinforcing. Most dependencia theorists of course abhor such actions, and may exhort their readers to work toward the elimination of the feedback loops – dramatic political action to break free of dependence and its consequences. But since such recommendations are rarely fully articulated, and the mechanisms for their achievement only imperfectly specified, we do not attempt to model them here.[54] Our further work will nevertheless address questions of how the feedback loop may be reinforcing or, alternatively, be broken.

Notes: Chapter 13

We wish to thank Arne Disch and Andrew Willard for assisting in the research, and Albert Fishlow and Tord Høivik for comments, and to acknowledge, with gratitude, financial assistance from the National Science Foundation, German Marshall Fund, and Concilium on International Studies and Council on International Relations, Yale University. Of course all responsibility is ours. This chapter represents one of several from a large and continuing project devoted to specifying and testing theories of dependence and imperialism. For others, see Raymond A. Duvall and Bruce M. Russett, 'Some proposals to guide research on contemporary imperialism', *Jerusalem Journal of International Relations*, vol. 2, no. 1 (Fall 1976), pp. 1–27; Raymond A. Duvall, 'Dependence and "Dependencia" theory: notes toward precision of concept and argument', *International Organization*, vol. 32, no. 1 (Winter 1978), pp. 51–78; Bruce M. Russett, 'Data priorities for modeling global dependence', in *Problems of World Modeling: Political and Social Implications*, ed. Karl W. Deutsch, Bruno Fritsch, Hélio Jaguaribe, and Andrei S. Markovits (Cambridge, Mass.: Ballinger, 1977), pp. 153–9; Steven I. Jackson and Duncan Snidal, 'Integration in "Dependencia" theory: its meaning and measurement', paper presented at the 18th Annual Convention of the International Studies Association, St Louis, Mo., March 1977; Steven I. Jackson, 'Capitalist penetration: concept and measurement', *Journal of Peace Research*, vol. 16, no. 1 (1979), pp. 41–55; David Sylvan, 'Arms transfers and the logic of political efficacy', *Military Issues Research Memorandum* (Carlisle Barracks, Pa: US Army War College, Strategic Studies Institute, 10 July 1978), to appear in *Military Policy Evaluation: Quantitative Applications*, ed. James A. Kuhlman (Leiden: Sijthoff, 1980); Bruce M. Russett, 'The marginal utility of income transfers to the Third World', *International Organization*, vol. 32, no. 4 (Autumn 1978), pp. 913–28; and Steven I. Jackson, Bruce M. Russett, Duncan Snidal, and David Sylvan, 'An assessment of empirical research on *dependencia*', *Latin American Research Review*, vol. 14, no. 3 (1979), pp. 7–28. Many of the measurement decisions reported here are tentative and preliminary; others have merely been presented in bare outline. The above papers, and other working papers of the project, will discuss the decisions in appropriate detail. This chapter is an extensively revised version of a paper presented at the 10th World Congress of the International Political Science Association, Edinburgh, August, 1976.

1 Theotonio Dos Santos, 'The Structure of Dependence', *American Economic Review*, vol. 60, no. 2 (May 1970), pp. 231–6; Fernando Henrique Cardoso and Enzo Faletto, *Dependencia y Desarrollo en América Latina* (Mexico City: Siglo Veintiuno Editores, 1969), published in 1979 by University of California Press as *Dependency and*

Development in Latin America; see especially the preface to this edition; and Aníbal Quijano, 'Cultura y dominación', *Revista Latinoamericana de Ciencias Sociales*, nos 1–2 (June–December 1971), pp. 39–56.

2 For example, see Johan Galtung, 'A structural theory of imperialism', *Journal of Peace Research*, vol. 8, no. 2 (1971), pp. 81–117; Dieter Senghaas, 'Introduction' to special issue on Overcoming Underdevelopment, *Journal of Peace Research*, vol. 12, no. 4 (Autumn 1975), pp. 249–56, and Senghaas's contribution to this volume; and Samir Amin, *Accumulation on a World Scale: A Critique of the Theory of Underdevelopment* (New York: Monthly Review Press, 1973).

3 Several of the most important theoretical controversies are addressed explicitly by Fernando Henrique Cardoso in 'Some new mistaken theses on Latin American development and dependency', unpublished manuscript, n.d. Perhaps the most basic such controversy, and the primary one addressed by Cardoso, is whether peripheral capitalist development is viable.

4 See the preface to Cardoso and Faletto, *Dependency and Development*. See also Duvall, 'Dependence'.

5 For example Amin, *Accumulation on a World Scale*, p. 378: 'Despite their different origins, the peripheral formations tend to converge toward a pattern that is essentially the same'. On the same page he makes it clear that he considers the periphery to include at least all the former colonies outside of North America, Australia, New Zealand, and, in some dimensions, South Africa, Zimbabwe, and Israel.

6 For example, see the preface to Cardoso and Faletto, *Dependency and Development*.

7 For the technically minded, the system of equations is bloc-recursive in form. Equation 1 is structurally independent of, and causally prior to, equations 2–6, which stand as a reciprocal bloc that precedes equation 7, which is an independent equation. Finally, equations 8–12 constitute a reciprocal bloc for which all others are considered causally prior.

8 Discussions of the literature of dependence theory, and of its relation to other theories of economic and political development (both within less developed countries, and in the global system), may be found in the papers of the project cited above, especially in the article by Duvall, 'Dependence'.

9 Hélio Jaguaribe, Aldo Ferrer, Miguel Wionczek, and Theotonio Dos Santos (eds), *La Dependencia Político-Económica de América Latina* (Mexico City: Siglo Veintiuno Editores, 1970), ch. by Jaguaribe, 'Dependencia y autonomía en América Latina', p. 14. For a more extended discussion of this variable see Jackson, 'Capitalist penetration'.

10 Osvaldo Sunkel, 'Capitalismo transnacional y disintegración nacional en la América Latina', *El Trimestre Económico*, vol. 38, no. 2 (1971), p. 606. There is some ambiguity as to whether the USSR and the more developed states of Eastern Europe should be considered part of the core. Most dependency theorists seem to include only capitalist countries; see for example Immanuel Wallerstein, *The Modern World-System* (New York: Academic Press, 1974).

11 Amin, *Accumulation on a World Scale*, pp. 169–70, and Francisco C. Sercovich, 'Dependencia tecnológica en la industria Argentina', *Desarrollo Económico*, vol. 14, no. 53 (1974), pp. 36, 39. On influence under conditions of symmetric penetration, see Robert O. Keohane and Joseph S. Nye, Jr, *Power and Interdependence* (Boston, Mass.: Little, Brown, 1977).

12 For the former see, for example, Charles P. Kindleberger, *The Formation of Financial Centers: A Study in Comparative Economic History* (Princeton, NJ: Princeton University, International Finance Section, Department of Economics, 1974); and John Kenneth Galbraith, *Money: Whence It Came, Where It Went* (New York: Houghton Mifflin, 1975). For the latter see especially the lucid essay by Miguel S. Wionczek, 'El endeudamiento público externo y los cambios sectoriales en la inversión privada extranjera de América Latina', in *La Dependencia Político-Económica de América Latina*, ed. Jaguaribe *et al.*; and Pedro Paz, 'Dependencia finaciera y denacionalización de la industria interna', *El Trimestre Económico*, vol. 37, no. 2 (1970), pp. 299–301. See also the uses made in empirical studies by Christopher Chase-Dunn, 'The effects of international economic dependence on development and inequality: a cross-national study', *American Sociological Review*, vol. 40, no. 6 (December 1975), pp. 720–38; Robert R. Kaufman. Daniel S. Geller, and Harry T. Chernotsky, 'A preliminary test of

the theory of dependency', *Comparative Politics*, vol. 7 no. 3 (April 1975), pp. 303–30; and Richard Rubinson, 'The world economy and the distribution of income within states: a cross-national study', *American Sociological Review*, vol. 41, no. 4 (August 1976), pp. 638–59.

13 Norberto García, 'Dependencia tecnológica', in *Dos Temas para el Estudio de las Teorías del Subdesarrollo*, ed. Aníbal Quijano and Norberto García (Caracas: Editorial la Enseñanza Viva, 1973), p. 61; Denis Goulet, *The Uncertain Promise: Value Conflicts in Technology Transfer* (Washington, DC: Overseas Development Corporation, 1978); and United Nations, *The Acquisition of Technology from Multinational Corporations by Developing Countries* (New York: UN Department of Economic and Social Affairs, 1974).

14 See Sunkel, 'Capitalismo transnacional', p. 580. On the use of foreign-owned patents, see such North American and European writers as Richard Barnet and Ronald Mueller, *Global Reach: The Power of the Multinational Corporations* (New York: Simon & Schuster, 1974); and Helge Hveem, 'The "technocapital" structure and the global dominance system', paper presented at the Workshop on Multinational Corporations as Political Actors, European Consortium on Political Research, Strasbourg, 28 March–3 April 1974.

15 Albert O. Hirschman, *National Power and the Structure of Foreign Trade* (Berkeley and Los Angeles: University of California Press, 1945). For a discussion of this and some related alternatives see Charles Lewis Taylor and Michael C. Hudson, *World Handbook of Political and Social Indicators*, 2nd edn (New Haven, Conn.: Yale University Press, 1972), pp. 347–8. Empirical investigation can, of course, substitute one or another measure as seems more appropriate, but in fact they all are very highly correlated and hence empirically virtually equivalent. For example, on a sample of eighty-nine peripheral countries for 1965 a correlation coefficient of 0·96 was found between proportion of trade going to the top trading partner and a Hirschman concentration index for trade with the top eight partners. For all the dyadic measures, all East European socialist countries other than Yugoslavia were aggregated as a single 'metropole', because of the high unity in extra-European foreign policy evidenced by those countries during the period in question.

16 Emile Durkheim, *De la Division du Travail Social* (Paris: Ancienne Librairie Germer Baillière, 1893); Talcott Parsons, *Structure and Process in Modern Societies* (Glencoe, Ill.: The Free Press, 1960); Edward Shils, 'Primordial, personal, sacred and civil ties', *British Journal of Sociology*, vol. 8, no. 2 (June 1957), pp. 130–45.

17 Karl Marx, *The German Ideology* (New York: International Publishers, 1947); Quintin Hoare and Geoffrey Nowell Smith (eds), *Selections from the Prison Notebooks of Antonio Gramsci* (New York: International Publishers, 1971); Ariel Dorfman and Armand Mattelart, *How to Read Donald Duck: Imperialist Ideology in the Disney Comic*, tr. David Kunzle (New York: International Publishers, 1975); Quijano, 'Dependencia tecnológica'.

18 Clifford Geertz, *The Interpretation of Cultures* (New York: Basic Books, 1973).

19 Conceptually, it is somewhat difficult to distinguish 'foreign' from 'domestic' symbols. For a discussion of this problem, as well as a more detailed treatment of cultural penetration, see David Sylvan, 'Of colonies and Coca Cola: the concept and measurement of cultural penetration', Yale University, mimeo., 1978.

20 Karl Deutsch long ago called attention to these carriers of culture, and the measurement of their activity, in his work on international political integration. For a review of theory and an empirical application see Bruce M. Russett, *Community and Contention: Britain and America in the Twentieth Century* (Cambridge, Mass.: MIT Press, 1963), esp. chs 6–8.

21 We would like to thank Signe Ländgren-Backström for making the arms transfer data available to us. Although they co-vary strongly with data on total arms transfers, data on major weapons are more appropriate for our purpose, given that their purchase is not routine (as small arms imports often are). For a discussion of this issue, see Sylvan, 'Arms transfers'.

22 For a fairly early example see Benton F. Massell, 'Export concentration in export earnings: a cross-section analysis', *American Economic Review*, vol. 54, no. 2, pt I (March 1964), pp. 47–63.

23 Most frequently those dependencia theorists who are at all concerned with trade

partner concentration deal more with contemporary processes of de-concentration rather than the converse. The 'trade follows the flag' thinking entailed in their arguments, then, tends to involve declining political dependence and reduced concentration of national trading partners. On these notions of declining 'state imperialism' and one particular and early form of economic domination, see the chapters by Octavio Ianni and Aníbal Pinto in *Latin America and the United States: The Changing Political Realities*, ed. Julio Cotler and Richard R. Fagen (Stanford, Calif.: Stanford University Press, 1974).

24 There are some difficulties in estimating this equation, as becomes apparent when we move from the above exact form into a form where error terms are included. This error term $(e_t - e_{t-1})$ contains an auto-regressive process which, in general, leads to inconsistent ordinary least squares estimates when there is a lagged endogenous variable (Y_{t-1}) in the equation. This problem can be overcome by generalized least squares estimation but even here great care is warranted. Minor additional complications arising in equations containing more than one such historical process can also be readily resolved.

This form is simply a variant of the Koyck form for the distributed lag and the relevant estimating problems and procedures apply. Although for simplicity we have left out explicit consideration of error terms in this and subsequent discussions, the technically minded reader will note that in the present case there will be a first-order auto-regressive process in the error term. In combination with the presence of a lagged dependent variable as an explanatory variable in the estimating equation this will mean that using ordinary least squares is both a biased and inconsistent procedure. Further, the Durbin-Watson statistic is an inappropriate check for autocorrelation in these cases, as it is also biased. One solution is to combine generalized least squares estimation with a grid or iterative search procedure for the coefficient of autocorrelation. In addition to the standard econometric texts see P. J. Dhrymes, *Distributed Lags: Problems of Estimation and Formulation* (San Francisco: Holden Day, 1971); Zvi Griliches, 'Distributed lags: a survey', *Econometrica*, vol. 35, no. 1 (January 1967), pp. 16–49; Douglas A. Hibbs, 'Problems of statistical estimation and causal inference in time-series regression models', in *Sociological Methodology, 1973-74*, ed. H. L. Costner, Jr (San Francisco: Jossey-Bass, 1974). Finally the form of the estimating equation becomes more complicated and estimation correspondingly more complex when there is more than one historical process represented in an equation through this lag formulation. A simplifying assumption which can be used in such circumstances is that the coefficients decline in the same geometric manner.

25 Simple B_i notation will be used for each equation in this chapter; the Bs are not related across equations. Intercept terms (B_0) are included in all equations. Generally these pick up the level of the dependent variable which is determined by other variables not included in the equation. These intercepts are not always of theoretical interest, but are necessary for proper estimation.

26 A simple measure of this would be the proportion of GDP accruing to the non-primary sectors. This could be used simply as a check on residuals in any analysis where level of economic activity was present or might possibly by incorporated directly into the measure by redefining X_9 as

$$\frac{\text{GDP}}{\text{Pop.}} \times \frac{\text{Non-Primary Production}}{\text{GDP}} = \frac{\text{Non-Primary GDP}}{\text{Pop.}}.$$

27 Paul Streeten, 'Crecimento equilibrado versus crecimento desequilibrado', *Desarrollo Económico*, vol. 3, no. 3 (October–December 1963), pp. 361–74.

28 See Ernst Helmstadter, 'The hierarchical structure of inter-industrialized transactions', UN Industrial Development Organization, Vienna, *International Comparisons of Interindustry Data, Industrial Planning and Programming Series No. 2* (New York: United Nations, 1969), and Galtung, 'Structural theory'; Helmstadter's procedure originated with Wassily Leontief, *Input-Output Economics* (Fair Lawn, NJ: Oxford University Press, 1966).

29 Aníbal Pinto, 'Naturaleza e implicaciones de la "heterogeneidad estructural" de la América Latina', *El Trimestre Económico*, vol. 37, no. 1 (1970), pp. 83–100.

30 Jackson and Snidal, 'Integration'. Note that the concept of integration employed here

is very different from Deutsch's. The use of input-output tables to measure the integration of an economy has been suggested by writers in the dependencia tradition (e.g. Amin, *Accumulation on a World Scale*, and A. Ghosh and H. Sarkar, 'An input-output matrix as a spatial configuration', *Economics of Planning*, vol. 10, nos 1–2 (1970), pp. 133–42), but has been performed empirically only by economists working in the neo-classical mode of analysis (e.g. Tibor Barna, ed., *Structural Interdependence and Economic Development*, London: Macmillan, 1963).

31 On the importance of railroads in Marxist analyses of the integration of underdeveloped economies, see Karl Marx, 'The future results of the British rule in India', *New York Daily Tribune*, no. 3840, 8 August 1853; and 'Preface to the French and German editions', of V. I. Lenin, *Imperialism: The Highest Stage of Capitalism* (New York: International Publishers, 1939). For an early use of transportation network data for this purpose, see Norton S. Ginsburg (ed.), *Essays on Geography and Economic Development* (Chicago: University of Chicago Press, 1960).

32 For the former, see Cardoso and Faletto, *Dependency and Development*. The 'dual economy' view is exemplified by John Fei and Gustav Ranis, *The Development of the Labor Surplus Economy: Theory and Policy* (Homewood, Ill.: Irwin, 1964).

33 Recall that in equation 2 we had changes in export concentration (one of the dimensions of the export enclave syndrome) responding to changes in uneven development, so there is a degree of reciprocality in these relationships. Nevertheless, these are importantly asymmetrical, occurring at quite different rates, and hence are very different processes. In equation 2 we modeled the changes in export profiles and in sectoral development as very nearly contemporaneous. That is, export profiles are *relatively* volatile, and hence adjust to changes in the structure of the economy relatively quickly. The opposite relation, from trade dependence to uneven development, as modeled below in equation 5, is much slower and hence is represented as a long-term lagged process.

34 See Galtung, 'Structural theory'.

35 See respectively, Amin, *Accumulation on a World Scale*; André Gunder Frank, *Capitalism and Underdevelopment in Latin America: Historical Studies of Chile and Brazil* (New York: Monthly Review Press, 1967); and Giovani Arrighi and John Saul, *Essays on the Political Economy of Africa* (New York: Monthly Review Press, 1973).

36 Note that a less inclusive variant of this measure – the ratio of rural to urban wages – has often been used both in theoretical treatments of the dual economy (e.g. Fei and Ranis, *Labor Surplus Economy*) and in aggregate empirical investigations (e.g. Taylor and Hudson, *World Handbook*, 2d edn).

37 For a more precise specification of the contents of these categories, and a suggestive breakdown of the proportions of each in twenty-four developing countries, see annex 1, table 6, in UN Economic and Social Council, *Mid-Term Review and Appraisal of Progress in Implementing the International Development Strategy* (New York: United Nations, 1975).

38 It should be noted that other usages of this term exist (e.g. by Jaguaribe, 'Dependencia y autonomia'). We have opted to retain this meaning of 'economic marginalization', in part because other writers in the dependencia tradition use it in the same way as we have (e.g. Aníbal Quijano, *Definición de la Dependencia y Marginalización en América Latina*, Caracas: CENDES, 1971, mimeo.; Fernando Henrique Cardoso, *Commentario sobre os Conceitos do Superpopulacão Relativa e Marginalidade*, São Paulo: CEBRAP, Estudios I, 1971; Osvaldo Sunkel, 'Transnational capitalism and national disintegration in Latin America', *Social and Economic Studies*, vol. 22, no. 1, March 1973, pp. 132–76) and in part because of a long history of similar terminology by writers outside the dependencia tradition (e.g. Karl Polanyi, *The Great Transformation*, New York: Rinehart, 1944; and Paul Baran, *The Political Economy of Growth*, New York: Monthly Review Press, 1957).

39 See, for example, Amin, *Accumulation on a World Scale*; and Cardoso and Faletto, *Dependency and Development*.

40 Simon Kuznets, 'Quantitative aspects of the economic growth of nations: II, industrial distribution of national product and labor force', *Economic Development and Cultural Change*, vol. 5, no. 4, supplement (July 1957), pp. 1–111, offers the basic index. Kuznets, 'Quantitative aspects of the economic growth of nations: VIII, distribution of income by size', *Economic Development and Cultural Change*, vol. 11, no. 2, pt 2

(January 1963), pp. 1–80, and Taylor and Hudson, *World Handbook*, 2d edn, have computed income inequality by economic sector, but these are not coequal with social classes, and since some classes, such as the working class, are likely to be spread across most non-agricultural sectors, an index based on sectoral data is likely to obscure more about class inequality than it reveals. Anthony Giddens, *The Class Structure of Advanced Societies* (New York: Harper, 1973) discusses the measurement of social class.

41 Shail Jain, *Size Distribution of Income: A Compilation of Data* (Washington, DC: World Bank, 1975); and Felix Paukert, 'Income distribution at different levels of development: a survey of the evidence', *International Labor Review*, vol. 108, nos 2–3 (August–September 1973), pp. 97–125. On summary measures, see Hayward R. Alker, Jr, and Bruce M. Russett, 'Indices for comparing inequality', in *Comparing Nations*, ed. Richard L. Merritt and Stein Rokkan (New Haven, Conn.: Yale University Press, 1966); and Raymond Duvall, 'International stratification: concept and theory', PhD dissertation, Northwestern University, 1974, pp. 81–8.

42 Simon Kuznets, 'Demographic aspects of the size distribution of income: an exploratory essay', *Economic Development and Cultural Change*, vol. 25, no. 1 (October 1976), pp. 1–94.

43 See Russett, 'Marginal utility'. For details on the reasoning and procedures outlined in this section see Bruce M. Russett, Steven I. Jackson. Duncan Snidal, and David Sylvan, 'Health and population patterns as indicators of income inequality', *Economic Development and Cultural Change*, no. 29 (1980), forthcoming.

44 A summary of this data set is reported in Ted Robert Gurr and Vaughn F. Bishop, 'Violent nations, and others', *Journal of Conflict Resolution*, vol. 20, no. 1 (March 1976), pp. 79–110. His data set has been deposited with the Inter-University Consortium for Political Research in Ann Arbor, Michigan. Given the emphasis in the dependencia literature on urban conflict, it may be useful to distinguish urban and rural conflicts. For measurement of the latter see Jeffrey Paige, *Agrarian Revolution: Social Movements and Export Agriculture in the Third World* (New York: The Free Press, 1975).

45 See, for example, from Irma Adelman and Cynthia Taft Morris, *Economic Development and Social Equity in Developing Countries* (Stanford, Calif.: Stanford University Press, 1973); S. E. Finer, *The Man on Horseback* (1962; repr. Harmondsworth, Mddx: Penguin, 1975); and Lee Sigelman, 'Military intervention: a methodological note', *Journal of Political and Military Sociology*, vol. 2, no. 2 (Fall 1974), pp. 275–82. For a full discussion of data sources and measurement procedures for this variable see Raymond A. Duvall and Michael Shamir, 'The coercive state: cross-national, time-series indicators', paper for the conference on Indicator Systems, International Institute for Comparative Social Research, Wissenschaftszentrum, Berlin, June 1978.

46 Taylor and Hudson, *World Handbook*, 2d edn, and new data prepared by Taylor for the third edition of the *World Handbook*, forthcoming.

47 See Ronald Mueller, 'The multinational corporation and the underdevelopment of the Third World', in *The Political Economy of Development and Underdevelopment*, ed. Charles K. Wilber (New York: Random House, 1973), and Malori J. Pompermayer, 'Dependency and unemployment: some issues', in *Structures of Dependency*, ed. Frank Bonilla and Robert Girling (Stanford, Calif.: Stanford University Press, 1973). It should be emphasized that domestic sources of capital intensification exist; there is, however, a general presumption in the dependencia literature that foreign investment is likely to be more capital-intensive than previous domestic investment (e.g. Celso Furtado, 'The concept of external dependence in the study of underdevelopment', in *The Political Economy of Development and Underdevelopment*, ed. Wilber). Even when new domestic investment is highly capital-intensive, it relies heavily on capital goods and technology imported from abroad, and thus is still dependent on financial and technological penetration. This is one of the reasons – in addition to its complexity – why we have omitted O'Donnell's import-substitution 'ceiling' argument about the determinants of marginalization: it implies foreign penetration. See Guillermo O'Donnell, *Modernization and Bureaucratic Authoritarianism: Studies in South American Politics* (Berkeley: University of California, Institute of International Studies, 1973).

48 Aníbal Quijano, *Nationalism and Capitalism in Peru* (New York: Monthly Review Press, 1971).
49 See, Jorge Graciarena, 'Types of income concentration and political styles', *CEPAL Review*, vol. 1, no. 2 (1976), pp. 203–36.
50 See O'Donnell, *Modernization and Bureaucratic Authoritarianism*; and G. Arrighi and J. S. Saul, *Essays on the Political Economy of Africa* (New York: Monthly Review Press, 1973).
51 See Steven I. Jackson, Bruce M. Russett, Duncan Snidal, and David Sylvan, 'Conflict and coercion in dependent states', *Journal of Conflict Resolution*, vol. 22, no. 4 (December 1978), pp. 627–57, for some reports on simulation efforts and further articulation of the considerations underlying this argument and that of the final two equations in this article.
52 For a perspective sharing much of what is discussed here, see Ted Robert Gurr, *Why Men Rebel* (Princeton, NJ: Princeton University Press, 1970), ch. 8.
53 A number of works provide important arguments to be modeled, however. In particular, see O'Donnell, *Modernization and Bureaucratic Authoritarianism*; Julio Cotler, 'The new mode of domination in Peru', in *The Peruvian Experiment*, ed. Abraham Lowenthal (Princeton, NJ: Princeton University Press, 1975); Aníbal Quijano, 'Imperialism and international relations in Latin America', in *Latin America and the United States*, ed. Cotler and Fagen; Fernando Henrique Cardoso, 'Associated-dependent development: theoretical and practical implications', in *Authoritarian Brazil: Origins, Policies, and Future*, ed. Alfred Stepan (New Haven, Conn.: Yale University Press, 1973); Arrighi and Saul, *Essays on the Political Economy of Africa*. O'Donnell presents an argument, which we do not model here, that the size of the laboring class is an important determinant – major coercion is necessary only when the laboring class is large.
54 And indeed to do so would introduce very severe complications into any attempt to carry out empirical estimation of the model. For some thoughts on this matter, see the contribution by Senghaas to this volume.

Part Four

Political Cybernetics and World Order

14
From Political Cybernetics to Global Modeling

HAYWARD R. ALKER, JR.

Too many people identify political/administrative cybernetics with Forrester-Meadows world modeling.[1] Slightly wiser, too many others think cybernetic systems modeling reduces to Systems Dynamics, econometric modeling with error feedbacks and optimal control, or Lange–Samuelson–Przeworski systems theories.[2] Many more political scientists are likely to perceive one of the above three modeling approaches as the only valid scientific residue from earlier linguistic, social, administrative, and political theorizing by cybernetic writers like Noam Chomsky and George Miller, Karl Deutsch, David Easton, Harold Guetzkow, Morton Kaplan, Talcott Parsons, and Herbert Simon.[3]

De-emphasizing the contributions of early information processing research to cognitive psychology and computational linguistics, but including within political cybernetics suggestive work by Chomsky and Miller on communicative competence and the organizational simulations of Carnegie–Mellon modelers,[4] I want first in this chapter to correct such false impressions. Relevant contributions include communications-oriented redefinitions of the essence of politics; the reintroduction into logico-empirical inquiry of teleological ontology and epistemology; emancipatory cybernetic hierarchies of knowledge, linguistic understanding and action; scientific modeling of systemic reproductive and self-productive processes, as well as pathological and healthy, even innovative and creative transformations therein; and a non-economic vocabulary for evaluating political successes and failures.

Secondly, in this chapter I shall try to link the concern of Deutsch and others with national cybernetic models to Deutsch's surely distinctive, but less obviously cybernetic concern with the development of pluralistic security communities at the regional and global level. To accomplish fully this transformative rewrite of the political cybernetics tradition will not be possible within the short second part of this chapter. But I shall none the less illustrate how such a reconciliation might take place in several related areas of Deutschean scholarship. And I shall suggest as a Deutschean problematique for future, politically oriented global modeling, the dialectics of state formation in center–periphery systems.

Some Central Themes of Early Political Cybernetics

Emphasizing for the sake of brevity, coherence, and appropriateness the work done at MIT by Norbert Wiener, Karl Deutsch, and others during the 1940s and 1950s, I now want to restate some central themes of the early social and political cybernetics literature.

Because it is the single most impressive early book on political cybernetics, I shall focus on Deutsch's *The Nerves of Government* and related early cybernetic work by Wiener and von Neumann most appropriate for understanding the strengths and some of the lacunae of that book.[5] Its subtitle, 'Models of Political Communication and Control', quite consciously paraphrases Wiener's titular definition: *Cybernetics, or Control and Communication in the Animal and the Machine*.[6]

The Shift from Muscles to Nerves

A very key point in Deutsch's political cybernetics is his redefinition of the 'essence' of politics away from force, power, and Hobbesian anarchy toward communication, organizational steering, and learning, and the dependable co-ordination of behavior (see especially pp. 75–8, 116–27, 122, 242–8). Just as gold is a damage-limiting element in international economics, so force is a damage-limiting feature of politics. It is a narrower currency than influence, favor trading, habit, or voluntary coordination, hence 'Power is . . . neither the center nor the essence of politics . . . [which is] the dependable co-ordination of human efforts and expectations for the attainment of the goals of society' (p. 124).

In his introductory statement of Wiener's views and their relation to social science, he argues:

> the viewpoint of cybernetics suggests that all organizations are alike in certain fundamental characteristics and that every organization is held together by communication. *Power* engineering transmits quantities of electric energy. *Communications* engineering . . . transmits neither tons of freight nor kilowatts of power. It transmits messages that contain quantities of information . . . communication, that is, the ability to transmit messages and to react to them . . . *makes* [i.e. constitutes] organizations . . . of living cells in the body . . . pieces of machinery in an electric calculator . . . [and] social groups. Finally, cybernetics suggests that steering [the etymological root of 'cybernetics'] or governing is one of the most . . . significant processes in the world . . . (p. 77, my emphasis).

Since the nervous system steers and co-ordinates human activity and neural information processing is the fundamental organic analogy in early cybernetics, it may be fair metaphorically to characterize Deutsch's emphasis on the *nerves* of government as a shift away from preoccupation with political *muscle*.

The reader familiar with Arend Lijphart's chapter in this volume cannot help but see a strong, scientific basis in cybernetics for Deutsch's promotion of a worldview much closer to the Grotian image of pluralistic international community than to the traditional Hobbesian–Machiavellian paradigm of power politics and international anarchy.[7] Using advances in computational engineering and mathematics, structurally similar, yet previously unobservable, non-manipulable, non-quantifiable communication and control processes are made scientifically accessible.

Information is neither unanalyzable and immeasurable nor idealistically immaterial (pp. 76–84). If entropy (unusable energy or disorganization) tends to *increase* in closed systems (Gibbs's thermodynamics law would have made Hobbes very happy), it may *decrease* in open, living systems. Unlike the constant sum of matter and energy required by the conservation laws, information increases or dissipates. Material limits on information storage in artificial and human memories need not be debilitating. Hence, sustained organization or order as well as structural novelty, creative thought, increased or decreased complexity, and emergent human communities are both possible and synthetically analyzable.

The Broadening of Ontological and Epistemological Concerns

Deutsch prefaces his introduction of the political cybernetics perspective by reviews of the inadequacies of what I would call alternate social ontologies, but which he calls 'classical models' of Mechanism Organism, and Historical process (ch. 2 and p. 75). Somehow the examples he gives in the quotes above, which are faithful to Wiener's texts, conflate organic, mechanistic, and even social images. His discussion of fruitful analogies – those based on valid structural correspondences (p. 78) – is an early statement of a general systems perspective with which much of what is valid in cybernetics has merged.[8]

A central theme in early (and much more recent) political cybernetics is precisely its ambivalent or paradoxical ontological quality. Consider for a moment the analogical problem of trying to 'square' a circle. If this Greek geometric dilemma of trying to find a square with the same area as a given circle is only resolvable by the 'absurd' invention or construction of $\sqrt{\pi}r$ as a measurable side of a square, so cybernetics' viability depends on the equally 'absurd' structural correspondence of communication and control processes – information processing systems – in the human organism, in the modern electronic computer and in the social organization of society.

Wiener considered Leibniz the 'patron saint' of cybernetics; Deutsch argues that genuine development comes from 'crucial simplifications' (p. 252). A true Leibnizian would state and try to resolve the cybernetic ambivalence about organisms, computers, and societies more ontologically and directly. By faith, intuition, or construction, Leibniz posited that the world really consists of, or is decomposable into, basic unities that are living machines. This vision is a synthesis or reconstitution of Aristotelian, Judeo-Christian, Galilean, idealist, and materialist conceptions:

entelechies	≅	souls	≅	automata	≅	monads	(1)
(self-sufficient Aristotelian essences)		(immortal Judeo-Christian spirits)		(generalized Galilean mechanisms)		(active principles of unity, internally perceiving the world from their own points of view)	

After a decent period of exploratory and synthetic work based on this postulate, one would want to see what conflicts and mysteries still remained unanalyzable. The Leibnizian program assumed these would eventually be small.[9]

Why argue that, three hundred years later, the key ontological vision underlying political and social cybernetics is the *existence* of *animated, interwoven, mutually aware, information processing automata*? First, because I believe it has substantial historical precedents. Secondly, because I think Deutsch's cautious writing lacks this claim, while Popperian falsificationists interested in 'bold, falsifiable conjectures' should relish it. Thirdly, I shall argue below that much more recent work in political cybernetics is heuristically driven and programmatically clarified by it. Fourthly, I think it suggests the historical, synthetic, emancipatory, conflict-resolution potential of Leibnizian social cybernetic thought. With origins in the foundational period of the modern age, this potential has almost been buried by the physicalistic, mechanistic, technocratic, equilbrium thinking about science, computers, and societies to which Deutsch rightly objects. Fifthly, too many social modelers who think a few feedback loops or non-linear optimal control algorithms are the main or sole worthwhile contributions of the cybernetic tradition to contemporary social science. Is not the living, reproductive quality, the mutable viability of social relationships, a much more challenging issue – directly or indirectly addressed by Deutsch, Forrester, Wiener, von Neumann, Ashby, Simon, Miller, and others – than their mechanical stability? Does not the constructed, artificial quality of poorly communicating, self-reprogramming organizations convey a much more profound yet still analyzable and potentially changeable conception of our world, and its global insecurities, than physicalist, naturalistic, mechanistic, and simplistic studies of the outbreak of war?[10] Should not peace science try to analyze such relationships into their primitive, logically constituent parts, so that more just, more humane, and more enduring reconstitutions might take the place of war? Finally, do not these (or similar) ontological respecifications help further re-engage the interests and concerns of humanistic scholars in social scientific work, surely an important and partly successful objective of *The Nerves of Government*?[11] Even if there are no easy answers to the questions of the logical/ontological status of *social* entities and the ways they are interwoven with, constitutive of, or composed out of individuals, one can argue to a humanist or skeptical social scientist that social cybernetic modeling suggests ways of specifying and testing for the existence of animus, identity, unity, agency, purpose or direction *possibly* inhering in collective activities.[12]

The above ontological equation also points toward a major epistemological polarity surrounding the cybernetic investigation of purposive, self-steering agencies. Man's efforts to understand nature teleologically and to explain it causally were named by Kurt Lewin, respectively, the Aristotelian and the Galilean scientific traditions. In his *Explanation and Understanding*, von Wright has traced these concerns from pre-Socratic philosophy through modern social analysis.[13] Neither the Aristotelian nor the Galilean emphasis, he argues, should be labeled as 'modern', with the pejorative implication that the other is 'out of date'. Moreover, both approaches are scientific in their search for deep structures that account for/explain manifest behavior. Leibnizian ontology, general systems theory, and the physical/philosophical view of the complementarity of perspectives all point toward synthetic resolutions of this polarity.

In this dual perspective, modern political theorists like Karl Deutsch, David Easton, Morton Kaplan, Herbert Simon, and Talcott Parsons can be interpreted as attempting to apply the quasi-teleological ideas of evolutionary biology and communications engineering to the scientific, explanatory understanding of political systems. Their heavy reliance on systems theory, in general, and revolutionary cybernetic models of communications and control in man and the machine in particular, is not a simple rejection of all mechanistic, lawful explanation and related equilibrium analyses. Rather, using richer, teleological metaphors often suggested by medicine, physiology and modern computers, it is an attempt to deepen the insights generated by earlier, often simplistic causal explanations. Feedback systems are not acausal; but neither are they entirely externally determined. Rather, they are systems whose actual performance (outputs), self-transformational capabilities, and structural properties are better understood in the often less obvious, more fallible terms of quasi-teleological or purposive epistemology.[14]

The Recognition of Emancipatory Cybernetic Hierarchies within Understanding, Knowledge, and Action Processes

Leibniz ranked monads in their degree of perceptual activity, historical consciousness, and self-awareness; his thought was a furtherance of speculation about the 'great chain of being' linking inert matter to the eternal God. He also emphasized mathematical notions of fullness (continuity) and infinitude.[15] Reformulated, this root ontological idea similarly informs Deutsch and Wiener's work. One can even argue that other social cyberneticians – in particular Donald T. Campbell, Noam Chomsky and George Miller, James G. Miller, Herbert Simon, and J. Patrick Crecine – soon presented superior reconceptualizations of such hierarchies to those conveyed by either Deutsch's, Easton's, or Forrester's previously mentioned work.

A behavioristic, purposive hierarchy. Rosenblueth, Wiener, and Bigelow start from a definition of the 'behavioristic study of natural events', which 'consists in the examination of the output [externally produced change] of the object and of the relations of this output to the input [object modifications due to external events]'.[16] It is a measure of the extent to which Deutsch, Miller, Campbell, Simon, and others have carried us past the epoch of the black box behaviorism that Rosenblueth's *et al.*, immediately subsequent clarification strikes many of us as epistemologically untenable: 'This omission [study of "the specific structure and the intrinsic organization of the object"] is fundamental because ... functional analysis, as opposed to a behavioristic approach, [speaks] to the intrinsic organization of the entity studied'.[17]

But then Wiener and his colleagues get very modern in describing the following cybernetic hierarchy. *Active* behavior is distinguished from passive behavior as occurring when the 'object is the source of the output energy involved in a specific reaction'. *Purposive* active behavior 'may be interpreted as directed to the attainment of a goal', that is, a final, spatial-temporal correlation with some other object or event; it is typically 'voluntary activity', to be distinguished from orderly but non-goal-directed phenomena as well as random behavior. Further subdivisions of purposive activity are proposed. Besides feedback-based 'teleological' purposeful behavior, there is non-teleologically purposive behavior in which no error signals from a goal 'modify the activity of the object in the course of the behavior', for example, a frog snapping at a fly. Feedback-governed purposive behavior may be predictive (based on extrapolations or not): 'higher order interpretive' extrapolations, both of input and output, might be uniquely characteristic of human capacities.[18]

Deutsch's ordering of purposes. Although he does not make much of the animal–human distinction, which Chomsky treats in a Cartesian fashion as fundamentally the difference between finite and infinite automata, Deutsch follows up these cybernetic ideas. Arguing that more complex learning takes place in nerve-like networks than in the pursuit of an unchanging Aristotelian *telos*, he too orders purposes. A 'first-order purpose in a feedback net' seeks immediate satisfaction, adjustments, or rewards. A second-order, 'self-modifying' or goal-changing feedback seeks the greatest mediation-based probability of the 'net's continued ability to seek first-order purposes', or 'self-preservation'. A third order of interwoven, specialized purposive nets would seek the preservation of a group, species, or society, while fourth-order purposes might be species-transcendant or spiritual purposes such as the growth or preservation of life, mind, or order in the universe.[19]

Some improvements on classical notions. When compared to earlier Aristotelian or idealist views, several favorable comments on this early, yet fundamental cybernetic theme are in order. Although Rosenblueth–Wiener–Deutsch 'purposes' may be purely external configurations or their corresponding internal 'informational representations', these 'purposes' are not mere ideals, but states or properties consciously or unconsciously embedded in active systems. And purposive, teleological activities have, by observation and definition, a self-energizing as well as a self-steering (error-feedback-governed) quality to them much more clearly defined in information-energy terms than it was possible for the Aristotelian student of self-sufficient entelechies to conceive. Clear, valid, operational definitions and measures of information, entropy, and conserved matter-energy amounts are now less than a century old.

Roughly simultaneous cybernetic work by George Miller, Noam Chomsky, Herbert Simon, and others on augmented and embedded TOTE hierarchies clearly transcends, in conceptual and mathematical power, the treatments of feedback loop systems in Wiener's early writing, Easton's *Political Life*, Deutsch's *The Nerves of Government*,

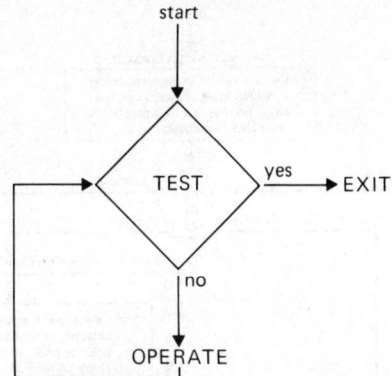

Figure 14.1 Basic structure of a TOTE.

and Forrester's *Industrial Dynamics*.[20] Since this is a strong claim, I shall at least try to illustrate my view in terms of a political cybernetics example from the work of a Simon student, J. Patrick Crecine.

The basic TOTE unit is nothing but a schematic, nicely formalizable feedback loop (Figure 14.1). A goal-matching TEST is made against the performance of some procedure or agency; a satisfactory match (indicated by 'Yes' in the figure) brings an immediate EXIT. An unsuccessful TEST result brings about a goal-seeking or gap-reducing OPERATE routine, and then a repeated TEST and, perhaps, EXIT.

TOTES can be generalized and embedded internally and hierarchically in one another, representing more complex forms of purposive activity. Figure 14.2 illustrates how this might be done.[21] The major boxes in the figure (Operations O_{-1}, O_1, O_2, O_3, etc.) are connected there with TEST polygon (T_0, T_{11}, T_{221}, etc.) and ellipsoid exit actions (E_0, E_{11}, E_{21}, E_{2231}, etc.). Ignoring the preliminary O_{-1} box, and collapsing O_1, O_2, and O_3 into a gigantic O_0 operation, one can see that the simplified mayor's budget recommendation program is nothing but a big, purposive, feedback-governed TOTE, specifically, T_0 O_0 T_0 E_0.

The articulated structure of the operations in the mayor's office, however, looks more like a sequence of budget initiation (O_{-1}), balance-testing (T_0), surplus (O_1), and/or deficit (O_2) elimination procedures, followed by 'final' budget preparations (O_3) and submission to the city council (E_0). Various series of operations might be expected to take place; for example, perhaps:

$$(O_{-1}\ T_0)\ (O_2\ O_3\ T_0\ O_1\ O_3)\ T_0\ E_0 \qquad (2)$$

This might correspond roughly to the following case:

> an initial deficit situation is removed (when up to *n* cuts in requests back down to the guidelines of a previous budget letter did not do

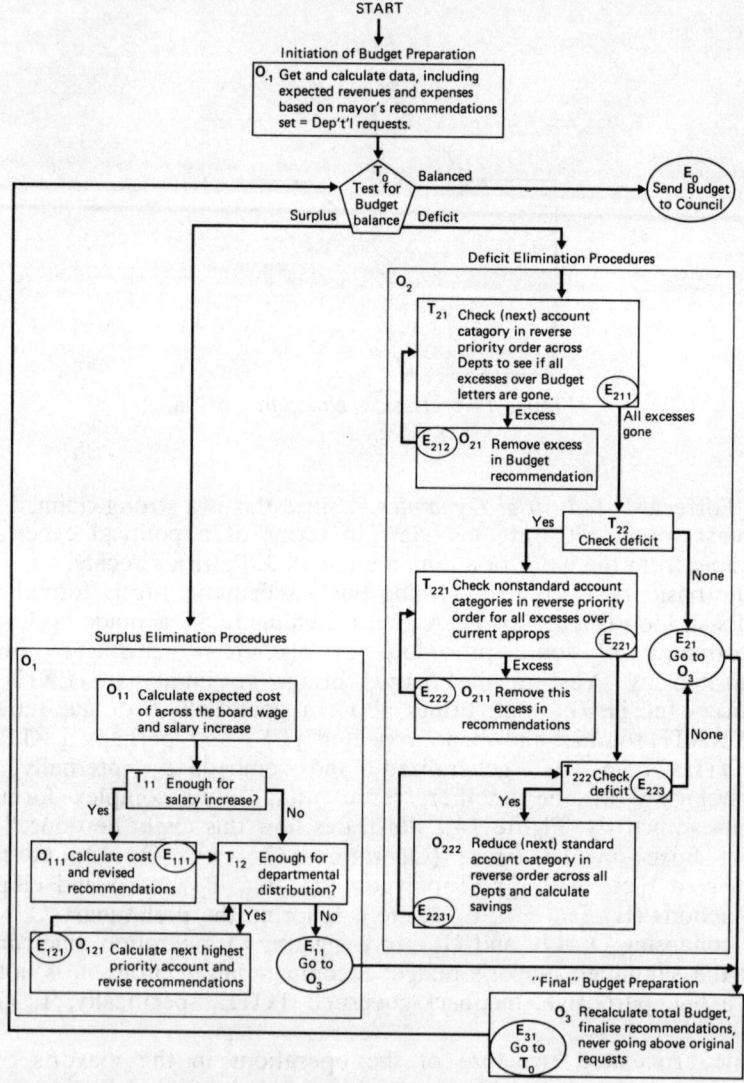

Figure 14.2 A mayor's budget recommendation routine in the form of a generalized TOTE hierarchy.
Source: Revised from J. Patrick Crecine, op. cit., Figure XI-2.

the trick) by recommendations to cut back maintenance and equipment requests in each Department back to current expenditure levels (say m cuts); this allows a small surplus, not enough for a salary increase, of course, but good for a few (say p) high priority, new Departmental programs to be funded.

Actually the list in (2) above must be rewritten several times to get down to the level of specificity of the above, purposive narrative. A

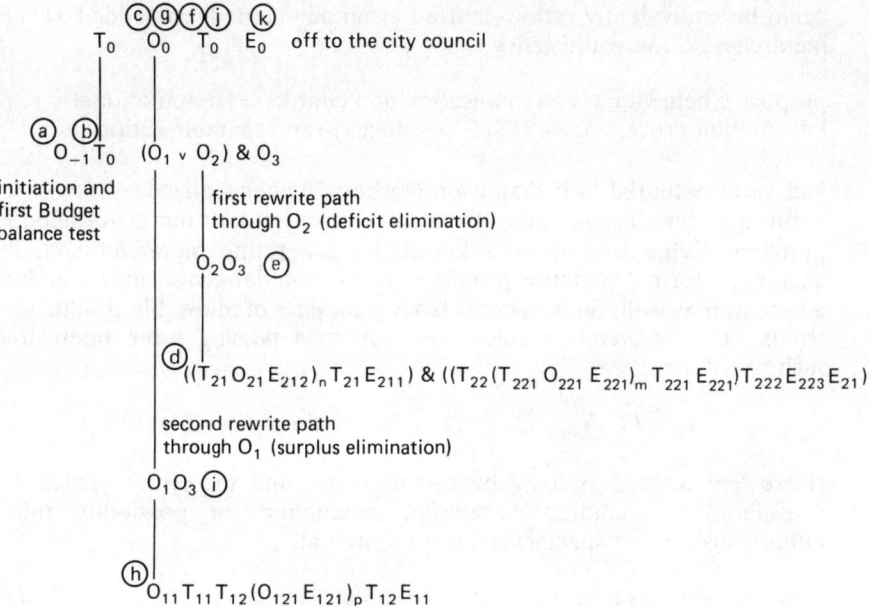

Figure 14.3 *TOTEs within TOTEs: the purposive deep structure within the budget-balancing simulation of Figure 14.2. Tracing through this structure from (a) to (k) gives a logically consistent budget preparation narrative.*

hierarchical graph suggestive of most of the basic rewrites involved is illustrated in Figure 14.3.

One can re-create the above purposive 'narrative' by a left-to-right (upside down) tree-climbing exercise, which should take the reader sequentially along the path in the tree from (a) to (b) ... to (k).

Now a few comments on the multiple cybernetic hierarchies invoked or implied in this little exercise.[22] First note that the pedestrian budget-balancing practice of Figure 14.2 and its roughly equivalent tree/list structures (2) and (3) instantiate a sublime ontological thesis that the author of *Monadology* might be proud of. If worldly practice can be decomposed into basic 'active principles of unity', TOTEs (mini-feedback loops) are a strong modern candidate for the multiple jobs of such unities. Tracking along the tree one finds (incompletely specified) TOTEs embedded within TOTEs embedded within TOTEs ... to a quite high degree. The subscript numbering system in Figures 14.2 and 14.3 attempts roughly to indicate the specifics of this vision, but the careful reader will notice that the lowest level of resolution in these structures is incomplete. Unindicated subparts, a plethora or paucity of Es and explicit or tacit preliminaries may also bother the rigorous at heart. One of the nicer mathematical results in early cybernetics, reported by Chomsky and Miller, was the *proof* that *any* well-formed program in ordinary (context-free) computer languages could be equivalently reflow-charted as an augmented, embedded TOTE hierarchy. So the equivalence:

$$\text{purposive behavior} \cong \text{communication and control} \cong \text{computational information processing} \cong \text{TOTE (feedback)-representable action} \quad (3)$$

had more potential to it than even Norbert Wiener realized.

But a second insight comes from the realization that our governmental problem-solving routine is a knowledge-generating hierarchy and, by analogy, a formal sentence producer or informal language understanding automaton as well. Such systems have *grammars* of allowable production, *rewrite*, or *interpretation* rules. We notice in passing some interesting such transforms:

$$T_0 + O_{-1}Y_0, \quad O_0 \rightarrow O_1 O_2 O_3 \quad \text{variously combined)} \quad (4)$$

(Here '$\rightarrow$' is read as 'may be rewritten as', and the entire expression considered a grammatical rewrite, production, or possibility rule.) Others, even more spectacular, were hinted at:

$$O_2 \rightarrow T'_2 O''_2 T'_2 E'_2; \quad T'_2 O'_2 \rightarrow T_{21} O_{21} E_{212})_n \quad (5)$$

Without going further into the formal language theory issues raised by these operational rewrites, it is perhaps enough to assert that Chomsky's most significant contributions to that theory are pregnant with implications of a rather different sort than the paradigmatic equivalence (3) might be taken to imply.

Chomsky and Miller have used their technical understanding of the computational capacities of different types of grammatical production rules to attack Skinnerian behaviorism and (inferentially) to criticize as subhuman the grammars of understanding and action implicit in typical feedback control models. Roughly, what makes such models inferior to the capacities inherent in the production rule grammars of the formal languages they are written in is the absence, within the model or program, of rewrite rules able to generate novel overt behavior from entirely unobservable, intermediate outputs. Simon and Crecine might put the point another way: with a little more clarity concerning negligible surplus/deficit stopping rules, Figure 14.2's program can generate only a finite set of budget-setting narratives. But recursive general problem solver programs (built up from TOTEs) that can indefinitely call or copy themselves in order to deal with their unsolved subproblems or purposes could *write* the specific program outlined in Figure 14.2; and they could also generate an *infinity* of comprehensible, *alternative* 'budget-setting' programs and narratives. Many of them would be richer in narrative complexity; some might be politically less pedestrian and more responsive to qualitative political ideals.

Let me conclude this section with a speculation on what such creativity might mean. In one of the most prophetic passages in *The Nerves of Government*, Deutsch intuits a very Chomskean restatement of the 'limits to growth' problematique. The 'politics of growth' crucially needs

> increases in *goal-changing* ability, in the range of different ends the society, culture or political system is able to choose or to pursue. Here we find learning capacity, not merely in terms of limited operational reserves but also in terms of the capacity for deep rearrangements of inner structure and thus for the development of radically new functions. Here we list ... growth in the possibility of producing genuine *novelty*, of applying some of the resulting new combinations of information to the guidance of behavior as *initiative*; and of producing eventually new patterns in the physical or social environment in processes of *creativity*.[23]

Have world reactions to pollution problems, energy 'shortages', population growth, or pervasive malnutrition ever displayed such qualities? Unfortunately, *none* of the world models to date adequately embodies such creative, emancipatory capabilities.

The Need to Go beyond Constrained Optimization and Conventional Economic Rationality to Heuristic Innovation and Linguistic Creativity

Almost all of the remaining themes in social and political cybernetics that we want to emphasize derive in some measure from an appreciation of the cybernetic hierarchies discussed above. An almost immediate one is the clear thrust of this literature beyond the decisional logic and mathematics of constrained optimization, which underlies so much of conventional 'rational' economic analysis in general and game theory in particular.

Karl Deutsch devotes his last chapter in *Nerves* prior to the introduction of a cybernetic model to von Neumann–Morgenstern's theories of games (ch. 4). He sees potential usefulness in the theory (p. 70), but reserves much of this chapter for a devastating list of its weaknesses, especially when applied to international deterrence relationships. Problems include the existence of fixed rules of play, narrow rationality assumptions, unchanging actors, and closed, static systems; and the unrealistic avoidance of information acquiring and processing costs which often drive human actors in well-defined situations to satisficing or trial and error problem-solving, and in more open and uncertain contexts, to adaptive and heuristic value-realization efforts.

In Figure 14.4 I have tried to synthesize Deutsch–Simon–Chomsky thinking on creative, goal-seeking problem-solving and value realization. In this synthesis, for example, one sees the typical structurally predefined (optimal) feedback control system less than halfway (at C) along the figure in the direction of fundamental creativity. The reader should recognize several features of Deutsch's cybernetic value ordering, his critique of game theory, and his non-revolutionary call for political learning and accelerated institutional innovation. (Politically, such reformists prefer changes more like those suggested at D and E in the

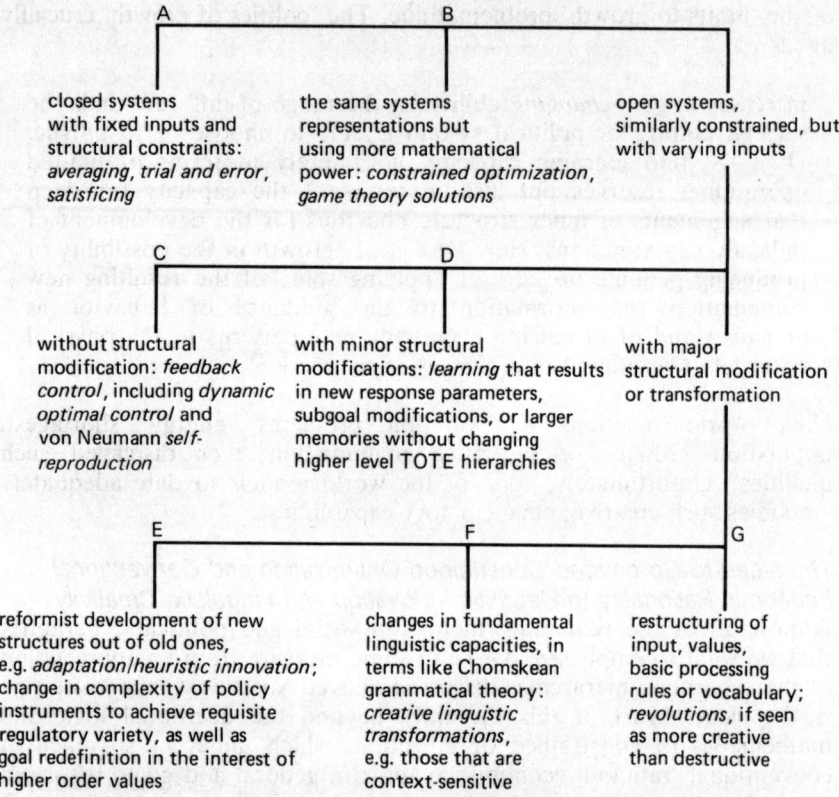

Figure 14.4 *Formal modes of sociopolitical value realization.**

*The idea of taxonomically organizing value realization procedures was suggested by the writings of Thomas Saaty. His preliminary concern was with the issue of what kind of mathematics the applied scientist should be exposed to. The lettered branches in the figure correspond to specific orientations mentioned at varying points in the text. The figure is neither exhaustively inclusive nor strictly exclusive of several points: there are hybrid types of value redefinition and realization. A general, but by no means strict rightward movement toward more fundamentally creative modes of realization is intended. An earlier version of this figure was discussed in my 'Cybernetic measures of political capabilities', op. cit.

figure; scientifically, the political cybernetic approach is more revolutionary, I believe, in emphasizing fundamental shifts in the basic vocabulary of power and control.)

Chomsky–Miller thinking about increasingly complex, purposive behavior is also very consonant with the figure and Deutschean creativity notions. Their five paradigmatic measures of purposive complexity start with (informational) *bit variance notions*, most applicable to the output of statistical and mathematical models (A, B, and C in the figure); then comes *degree of self-embedding*, clearly an important property of symbolically mediated communication, von Neumann reproduction models (discussed below), and higher-order Chomskean languages, at F and G; *depth of postponement* – this measure of memory load fits most naturally to existing TOTE intentions or plans, as at D, but has suggestive applications for rewrite capabilities farther to the right in the figure; structural complexity, the *ratio of total nodes* in a TOTE hierarchy *to* the number of *terminal ones* is a complexity measure not memory-oriented, but still applicable at C, D, E, F, or G. *Transformational complexity*, the number of important procedural changes necessary to handle a new situation, properly weighted to include cost considerations, might draw revolutionary creativity ideas at G into closer relation with inevitable complexities associated with cognitive, institutional, and linguistic readjustments at D, E, or F.

Political Cybernetics Goes beyond Equilibrium Analysis

Already in Wiener and Deutsch's early writings, and related to the hierarchies of section C above as well, another central theme of sociopolitical cybernetics attacks conventional economics. It is the cybernetic attempt to transcend equilibrium analysis.[24]

This dialectical accomplishment comes first from the reassertion of purposive analysis. As Deutsch correctly argues, 'from a historical point of view, the rise of [mechanistic] equilibrium analysis meant the neglect of problems of purpose' (p. 91). Introducing purposive, information-processing mechanisms, cybernetics subsumes equilibrium analysis by realistically generalizing it. Negative feedback can be equilibrating; positive feedback gives explosive growth or transformation. Whereas most formal equilibrium studies tend to ignore 'friction', cybernetic lag and gain (the *time* that error-induced corrections take up and the *extent* of the corrective action taken) provide measures of it (p. 90). Deutsch emphasizes also (p. 90) that Wienerian cybernetics handles probabilistic noise statistically.

A more powerful, and I believe more accurate statement might have been that cybernetic systems are open systems regularly exchanging information and matter-energy with their uncertain, but organization-containing environments. The organizing communicative network keeping such a system together – against Gibbsian rages of entropy increase – requires negative entropy to maintain its viability. This 'negentropy' is extracted from system inputs: 'what a [living] organism feeds upon is negative entropy'.[25]

But cybernetic transcendance of equilibrium thinking goes beyond statistical, dynamic, equilibrium analysis and active negentropy conservation. Recall that the higher-order goals of Deutschean cybernetics in particular emphasize autonomy, self-awareness, self-organization, even self-restructuring and self-transcending values. These are not the same as mechanistic or utilitarian equilibria and unreflective system stability in which symbolic identities or characteristic attributes remain uninvolved. Consciousness is defined by Deutsch in terms of second-order, self-referring symbols; historical self-awareness, a form of consciousness, is particularly important for achieving autonomy (pp. 206f.). Even Deutsch's preferred innovative adaptations point, as we have already seen, toward moderately smooth and non-violent redefinitions of identities and objectives. Such essential, inner relationships are not central to mathematical equilibrium analysis!

Other cybernetic thinkers also transcend, but sometimes less thoroughly, equilibrium perspectives: Ashby and Kaplan's interest in ultra-stability, Maruyama's concern with positive feedback growth and transformation, Sommerhoff's, Merton's, and Nagel's concern with directive behavior are all more than a decade old.[26]

A Shift to Reproductive, Self-Productive, and Transformative Concerns

Perhaps because of their preoccupation with neurological, computational, and social communication networks, neither Wiener nor Deutsch synthesizes many of the above cybernetic themes in terms of the precise idea of a self-reproducing system.[27] Von Neumann, however, did achieve, in the late 1940s and 1950s, the outlines of such a nearly miraculous synthesis, in which Aristotle and Leibniz again play a role.[28]

It is generally acknowledged that Leibniz's supreme metaphysical construction, the active, living, and perceiving monad, prefigures the modern idea of a self-sufficient and self-replicating biological cell. (For Leibniz, the recent revelation, through the first microscopes, that the world is teeming with invisible micro-organisms, lent realism to this view.) Neurons, of course, are also cells, highly reflective of each other's contents in that they are connected to hundreds of thousands of other neurons. Although they are self-repairing and originally self-reproducing, neurons have lost their independence and do not individually oversee human reproduction because in the 'modern', 'organic' division of labor within our bodies, at least, the reproductive function takes place elsewhere. None the less, very much as Leibniz foresaw, each cell of our body does contain a complete genetic 'blueprint' of an entire organism. This image is extended to political culture domains as well, if 'blueprints' may also be called 'little red books', 'constitutions', or 'charters'.

What von Neumann speculated about was that a 'cellular' automaton could be built that was a self-replicating system. He explicates the original idea in terms of the then ongoing discussion of 'complexity' in machines (to which Chomsky and Miller also contributed). Surely the intellectual world he was living in was fascinated with the 'living machines' idea: it must have sensed the proximity of a scientific theory of the origins and evolution of life at the level of genetic 'programs' for self-reproduction micro-organisms. (Parasitic or symbiotic, as well as mutative and destructive reproductive relationships – viruses, cancer, evolution, and so on – were soon fitted into this scientific worldview.) He presented a sustained lecture on this subject in 1948, introduced by the puzzle: could a generalized machine (i.e. an automaton) generate (evolve) products more complicated than itself? The test case would be to design and build (as was later done) a computer or computer program capable of building something as complex as itself, that is, copying itself. We have already seen the same visionary idea in a later version, *a world full of (re)generative TOTEs within TOTEs* ..., or one in which GPS routines race down life's evolving problem trees, copying themselves so as to leave little GPSs to solve subsidiary problems ... and then reintegrating their results later in to grand problem solutions!

Now, consider the following recent quote on von Neumann's self-reproducing cellular automata.

Von Neumann did not live long enough to bring his theory of automata [fully] into existence. He did live long enough to see his insight into the functioning of living organisms brilliantly confirmed by the biologists. The main theme of his 1948 lecture is an abstract analysis of the structure of an automaton which is of sufficient complexity to have the power of reproducing itself. He shows that a self-reproducing automaton must have four separate components with the following functions. Component A is an automatic factory, an automaton which collects raw materials and processes them into an output specified by a written instruction which must be supplied from the outside. Component B is a duplicator, an automaton which takes a written instruction and copies it. Component C is a controller, an automaton which is hooked up to both A and B, When C is given an instruction, it first passes the instruction to B for duplication, then passes it to A for action, and finally supplies the copied instruction to the output of A while keeping the original for itself. Component D is a written instruction containing the complete specifications which cause A to manufacture the combined system A plus B plus C. Von Neumann's analysis showed that a structure of this kind was logically necessary and sufficient for a self-reproducing automaton, and he conjectured that it must also exist in living cells. Five years later Crick and Watson discovered the structure of DNA, and now every child learns in high school the biological identification of von Neumann's four components. D is the genetic materials, RNA and DNA, A is ribosomes, B is the enzymes RNA and DNA polymerase, and C is the repressor and derepressor control molecules and other items whose functioning is still imperfectly understood. So far as we know, the basic design of every micro-organism larger than a virus is precisely as von Neumann said it should be.[29]

If Deutsch and Wiener's early cybernetic literature missed the profundity of this conception and its social implications, neither Leibniz nor Parsons did so, and both Wiener and Deutsch were quick to capitalize on their visionary syntheses. Unlike Galileo, whose mechanistic reductionism has so fascinated subsequent scientists, or Descartes, whose mind–matter dualism Leibniz rejected in terms of a theory of unified, active, self-productive agencies, Leibniz accepted the unity and the reality of all the Aristotelian categories of formal, final, material and efficient causes. But his clear logical mind probably saw the need for their more precise reformulation. As Table 14.1 suggests, there is a realistically good fit, then, between the Aristotelian–Leibnizian purposive-causal (!) categories and von Neumann and Burks's biologically prophetic formal realization of the self-reproducing monad-cell idea. What a new cast of characters for the vitalism–mechanism controversy of the last several centuries.

Table 14.1 *Corresponding theories of a self-reproducing system*

Aristotelean (Leibnizean) entelechy	Watson-Crick DNA model (von Neumann's letters)	von Neumann automaton	Parsons-Deutsch requisite function	Parsons's corresponding societal system
material cause	A. ribosomes	automatic factory: collection, processing, outputting (including copy of its instructions)	adaptive sector (A)	economy
formal cause	B. RNA/DNA polymerase enzymes	instruction duplicator	maintenance or reproduction of its own (latent) basic patterns (L)	household (with child-rearing, labor force restoring, kinship preserving functions)
efficient cause	C. repressor and derepressor control molecules, etc.	controller which copies in B and passes them to A, keeping original	attainment of whatever goals system has set for it (G)	polity
final cause	D. genetic RNA/DNA	written instructions causing A to manufacture A + B + C	integration and co-ordination of different functions and subsystems into a cohesive whole (I)	culture (education, religion, media)

It used to puzzle me why Karl Deutsch treats Parsons as a cybernetic theorist in *The Nerves of Government* (ch. 7, pp. 116–22), while von Neumann does not receive that honor. Later it puzzled me why there is no mention in the book of the self-reproducing automata theory. Of course Parsons in various places vaguely acknowledges his cybernetic perspective, and is very explicit on his intellectual indebtedness to other sociopolitical neurophysiologists than Rosenblueth and Wiener: Pareto, Henderson, and Karl Deutsch. But the final column of Table 14.1 shows an answer to all these puzzles and others as well. Parsons's famous 'AGIL' schema of (self-sufficient) societal organization fits von Neumann almost exactly. His puzzling claim that four centers of social interchange (Adaptation, Goal Attainment, Integration, and Latent Pattern Maintenance) are 'functional requisites' turns out to be *as strong a* logical argument as von Neumann's indisputably cybernetic 'Logical Theory' of self-reproducing automata.[30]

The precise, rigid, monotonous, conservative (and imperialistic?)

character of this version of the theory – von Neumann's automata clone themselves forever given sufficient computer time and spaces – is also put in mathematical perspectives. One could thus, perhaps, try to formalize dependency theories – where dependency is defined in terms of non-autonomous societal reproduction – in terms of variants of this kind of model, once the different ways in which cells and societies are dependent upon or interdependent with each other and their environments are better understood. Deutsch, Senghaas, Duvall, and Parsons all have a deep, unifying, cybernetic interest in this subject, but until now have not proceeded *formally* in this direction. Positive theories of self-productive (autopoietic) living systems are also needed, as modeled by Maturana and Varela.[31]

One should also take seriously Deutsch's important amendations to the von Neumann–Parsons theory in *The Nerves* (pp. 118–27) and elsewhere.[32] An evolutionary system theorist might suggest to von Neumann that one needs goal definition and adaptive goal redefinition 'routines' within this model, with much greater sensitivity to mutually transformative system-environment limits, as they affect autonomy, dependence, and interdependence relationships. Deutsch and Domínguez make exactly the right point in emphasizing the need for within-system goal definition and goal redefinition capacities, as well as the better understanding of self-transformative (autocentric) change.

The Enrichment of Normative Concepts for the Critique, Rationalization, and Reform of Political Practice

Surely the above discussion suggests the rich normative content of the political cybernetic approach. Nothing has been more inadequate in conventional economic optimization and equilibrium analysis than the paucity, weakness, and anti-egalitarian political bias of evaluative concepts like equilibrium, stability, GNP growth, and benefit-cost efficiency (as it is usually calculated). At roughly the same level of complexity are Deutsch's very Wienerian lead, lag, gain, and load pathologies in body co-ordinated, purposive systems. His treatment of modes of autonomy failure in chapter 13 is surely more inspired: they include loss of resource power, loss of intake, loss of co-ordinative steering capacity (which markets sometimes provide), loss of memory depth, loss of capacity for partial and/or fundamental rearrangement of inner structure. Perhaps even more provocative are Morton Kaplan's healthy and pathological cybernetic interpretations of *systemic* cathexis, learning, displacement, repression, sublimation, projection, introjection, isolation, and identification. Robert Abelson's insightful treatments of self-serving, defensive, rationalization are almost as rich. Both resonate with Deutsch and Senghaas's impressive, radical Freudian work on the fragile sanity of states.[33]

But does not political cybernetics have a more unifying vision than such a *tour de horizon*? Do not our ontological interpretation plus Figure 14.4 above and our discussions of self-restructuring, self-sufficient, and self-reproducing sociopolitical systems converge? *Dependency reversal or autonomy achievement and maintenance by self-renewing social communities* strikes me as this fundamental unifying concern, already apparent in the work done more than fifteen years ago. Political cybernetics' normative richness grows from these concerns. In attempting to understand better system performance, Deutsch focused in *Nerves* on positively valued communication capabilities such as problem-solving, creative learning, honesty, and ideological openness (as opposed to self-delusion). Conjoined with these were positively valued control-linked capabilities such as influence, shared goal-achievement, autonomy, power-sharing (democracy), conflict resolution, environmental adaptability, or negative self-closure and self-destruction.

A New Problematique for Global Modeling

Rather than review and assess fairly extensive world and global modeling literatures, and rather than summarize the extensive theoretical and methodological literatures in information-processing research or political cybernetics since the early 1960s,[34] I would like to conclude by outlining a new problematique for those global modelers who have come to that research concern out of the political cybernetic tradition. Some of the intellectual resources enabling productive scientific research on this problematique are already present in the tradition I have just reviewed; others need to be developed as revisions or rewrites of it. I believe this problematique also to be remarkably integrative of many of the concerns expressed in different chapters of the present volume. What I suggest is this: *the dialectics of state formation in center–periphery systems*.

Ways in which State Formation in Center–Periphery Systems Is a Dialectical Process

Perry Anderson, Jürgen Habermas, Barrington Moore, Stein Rokkan, Charles Tilly, and Immanuel Wallerstein have made major contributions to recent multidisciplinary literatures on European state formation in the sixteenth through twentieth centuries; Samir Amin, Enrique Cardoso, Johan Galtung, Hélio Jaguaribe, and Dieter Senghaas have energized a related literature on what is often called dependent development in Latin American, African and Asian peripheries of the European state system.[35] Not only is this literature a major, historically oriented, scholarly contribution to current debates about a new international order, it may also be the best source for substantive suggestions concerning the more politically sophisticated, structurally sensitive global modeling work that many critics of the world modeling tradition have called for. Put more negatively, most of the authors in this literature would agree with Wallerstein's observation about quantitative work on modern world development: 'Using the heavily narrative accounts of most historical research seems not to lend itself to ... quantification ... It is a major tragedy of twentieth-century social science that so large a proportion of social scientists, facing this dilemma, have thrown in the sponge'.[36]

In toto, this literature is heavily historical and not easily formalizable.

The principal reasons for such difficulties must surely be related to the dialectical qualities of its subject-matter. First of all, the work deals with *inner* (identity-involving or constitutive) relationships between centers and peripheries, and between national parts and systemic wholes. Thus writers like Amin, Cardoso, or Wallerstein will usually argue that exploitive and dependent peripheral development is necessarily related to, or constitutive of, the identity of central capitalist states in Europe, North America, and elsewhere. And Perry Anderson suggests that the rather Machiavellian modern state system has enjoyed mutually constitutive relationships with the militaristic, and until fairly recently absolutist, states directing the British, Austro-Hungarian, French, Spanish, Prussian, and Czarist Russian empires.

Secondly, this literature argues convincingly that the modern world is not made up (ontologically) of the same logically consistent, mutually aware, ageless, monotonously self-replicating agencies. Rather, it is at least partly a historical battlefield of mortal but evolving, contradictory, interpenetrating, self-organizing identities, agencies and principles. Their composite products include state forms, for example, absolutist states mediating contending class interests, national socialism, Maoist communism, Brazilian associated dependent development, frequently undergoing discontinuous development and decay. The relatively peaceful accommodation of such active collective agencies requires considerable hermeneutic capacities (those encouraging action-oriented, cross-culturally communicative consensus-building) plus dialectical sensitivity (especially concerning reproductive, self-productive, and transformative processes).

Thirdly, this literature contributes to a serious but difficult dialogue or debate about world order. If one recalls the origins of Western dialectics in the rules of Greek debate, one should not have too much difficulty intuiting many dialectical features in the rarely harmonious arguments among capitalists, socialists, feudalists, corporate authoritarians, and agrarian communists of the First, Second, Third, and Fourth Worlds.

How Deutschean Modeling May Be Reinterpreted in Dialectical Hermeneutic Terms

Both Karl Deutsch's earliest work on social communication processes in multigroup nation-building experiences and his subsequent scholarship on the creation of regional, pluralistic security communities, and the papers of many Deutschean modelers in the present volume can quite easily be assimilated to the specific problematique and its undergirding dialectical and hermeneutic research philosophy outlined above. Despite its conventional mathematical and statistical treatments, Deutsch's writings on the mobilization (toward a new center) of peripheral populations, often speaking different dialects or languages, never claimed that assimilation, integration, or 'national synthesis' into a communicating community was an easy, mechanical, continuous or automatically successful process. Stein Rokkan's marvellously integrative paper in this volume has shown more precisely how state formation in Western Europe was a very dialectical process, involving the often coercive resolution of major demographic-geographic, religious, economic, and political contradictions.

Deutsch's collaborative studies of multinational integration in the North Atlantic area and his current work on Switzerland can surely be reread to imply that the resulting amalgamated or pluralistic security communities have all gone through more or less fundamental, incorporative and integrative restructurings of somewhat contradictory national identities, practices, and organizing principles. (The especially American budget-balancing style of Figure 14.2 is a not wholly dissimilar constructed result of North American political history.) Internationally oriented studies by Deutscheans like Bruce Russett and Richard Merritt have also looked at the rise or decline in political community of those speaking dialects of the same Anglo-American language. The contradictory, dynamic unity of Berlin (Merritt's chapter in this volume) is also a very dialectical phenomenon.

Studies of dependency relationships and autocentric strategies for their reversal (Senghaas and Duvall *et al.* chapters) and my own dependency-inspired work on the transformation of power politics also point toward dialectical transformation possibilities in center–periphery relationships. Bruno Fritsch's concern with the increased capital formation requirements of modernizing nation-states exploitively interdependent with their environments adds an important ecological moment to state formation problematique as previously formulated.

What Political Cybernetics Needs in Order to Become Appropriately Dialectical

Had considerable, relevant progress not already been made, it would be foolish to suggest that political cybernetics can evolve into an appropriate modeling approach for the dialectical concerns reviewed above.[37] Surely the attentive reader will have seen certain hints of the appropriate development in the previous discussions of purposive political narratives, emancipatory cybernetic hierarchies, parasitic, symbiotic, and autonomous self-production and transformation processes.

But equally clearly, the attentive reader should realize the considerable ontological distance between the logically harmonious, mutually shared perceptions of eternally self-replicating monads and the interpenetrating, identity-changing interactions of often contradictory socioeconomic organizing principles or context-sensitive national identities. The inner relations of imperialistic powers and their self-reconstituting, power-balancing systems also seem a particularly recalcitrant problem for the would-be narratively oriented global modeler. And the dialectical hermeneutics research program briefly outlined above differs fundamentally from the logical positivism informing most political cybernetics work to date.

Without repeating arguments already made elsewhere,[38] it is worth noting that considerable progress has already been made on each of these issues. If nations, classes, or global systems can be identified in terms of their innermost, constitutive production modes or organizing principles, a fair approximation to such identities can be obtained using incompletely prespecified metaprograms, frames, demons, scripts, or production systems, as these procedural entities are currently conceived in artificial intelligence research. They represent considerable refinements of, but recognizable descendants from, the high-level TOTEs exhibited above. And they lead to much less monotonous, more reflective, dramatic and novel political narratives than the budget-balancing tale sketched above.

Similarly, extending the purposive-causal concepts above to include the category of systemic or structural determinations, and further revising power conceptions to include structural capabilities and class-biased systemic incapacities, one could approximately model the part–whole inner actions of states and their encompassing center–periphery systems.

Finally, the epistemological reconceptualization of political cybernetics in dialectical hermeneutic terms requires much more work on dialectical logics appropriate for the analysis of multiparty debates and contradictory organizing principles. Were such self-referential or self-modifying formalisms not already being discovered, political cybernetics would have little chance of becoming politically relevant global modeling.

Notes: Chapter 14

An earlier version of this chapter was presented at the 1978 Annual Meeting of the American Political Science Association in New York City. It contains reflections on nearly two decades of my acquaintanceship with *The Nerves of Government*, its author, Karl Deutsch, and the work following from the modeling tradition both represent. It has benefited as well from several years of co-teaching with Karl Deutsch a course on modeling complex social systems, and from the vigorous discussions with students and colleagues that this course has evoked. Its redrafting has been assisted by grant 7806707 from the National Science Foundation to the Center for International Studies, Massachusetts Institute of Technology.

1 Key works are: Jay Forrester, *World Dynamics* (Cambridge, Mass.: Wright-Allen Press, 1971); and Donnella Meadows, Dennis L. Meadows, Jorgen Randers, William K. Behrens III, *The Limits to Growth* (New York: Universe Books, 1972). Two important works transitional between the world modeling and the global modeling approaches are: Michael D. Mesarovic and Eduard Pestel, *Mankind at the Turning Point* (New York: Dutton, 1974); and A. O. Herrera, H. D. Scolnik, G. Chichilnisky, G. C. Gallopin, J. E. Hardy, D. Mosovich, E. Oteiza, G. R. Brest, C. E. Suares, and L. Talavera, *Catastrophe or New Society? A Latin American World Model* (Ottawa: International Development Research Centre, 1976). The more recent, more modest, and more inclusive approach of global modeling is described and ably defended in John Clark and Sam Cole, with Ray Curnow and Mike Hopkins, *Global Simulation Models* (London: Wiley–Interscience, 1975), which has influenced my own unpublished paper, 'Global modeling alternatives', at many points.

2 I take it as too obvious to require documentation that econometric or structural modeling is the leading data-oriented modeling tradition within contemporary political science (as in my earlier work, the Raymond A. Duvall *et al.* chapter in this volume, and the writings of John Ferejohn, Douglas Hibbs, John Jackson, or Gerald Kramer). Our most prominent political science optimal controllers are Dina Zinnes and the late John Gillespie; similar mathematics is used to advantage in the Latin American

(Bariloche) world model. The best texts on political interpretations of early feedback-oriented cybernetic work by Oscar Lange, Paul Samuelson, and others are Ronald D. Brunner and Gary Brewer, *Organized Complexity* (New York: The Free Press, 1973); and Fernando Cortes, Adam Przeworski, and John Sprague, *Systems Analysis for Social Scientists* (New York: Wiley, 1975). The former book is very Deutschean; the latter gives a number of examples of Althusserian structuralism using Forrester-like mathematics as well as some intriguing suggestions concerning modeling dependency relationships, about which more will be said below.

3 Consider that David Easton's 'An approach to the analysis of political systems' appeared in *World Politics* in 1957 (vol. 9, no. 3, April 1957, pp. 383–400); papers for Karl Deutsch's *The Nerves of Government: Models of Political Communication and Control* (New York: The Free Press, 1963) appeared in the 1950s; and Morton A. Kaplan's *System and Process in International Politics* (New York: Wiley, 1957) was also very early. All came before the defining work of Systems Dynamics. Jay Forrester, *Industrial Dynamics* (Cambridge, Mass.: MIT Press, 1961). Of course none of these efforts contained fully specified simulation models. The best single published source on international simulation models prior to *World Dynamics* also covers work from before 1961. It is Paul Smoker, 'International relations simulations', *Peace Research Reviews*, vol. 3, no. 6 (1970), pp. 1–84; a revision of this was published in *Mathematical Approaches to Politics*, ed. Hayward R. Alker, Jr, Karl W. Deutsch, and Antoine Stoetzel (New York: Elsevier, 1973), pp. 417–64. See also: Hayward R. Alker, Jr, and Ronald D. Brunner. 'Simulating international conflict: a comparison of three approaches', *International Studies Quarterly*, vol. 13, no. 1 (1969), pp. 70–110, and the review symposium on the Simulated International Processes Project in Frank Hoole and Dina Zinnes (eds), *Quantitative International Politics: An Appraisal* (New York: Praeger, 1976).

4 The best single source and most impressive bibliography of the Carnegie–Mellon school (emphasizing its cognitive psychological interests) is Allen Newell and Herbert A. Simon, *Human Problem Solving* (Englewood Cliffs, NJ: Prentice-Hall, 1972), which has numerous references to the later 1950s and early 1960s. Work by Guetzkow and Smoker has also constituted an important partial product of this modeling tradition.

5 Various pieces of the argument here have appeared in two earlier papers of mine: Hayward R. Alker, Jr, 'From information processing research to the sciences of human communication', Informatique et sciences humaines, vol. 11, nos 40–1 (1979), pp. 407–20; and Hayward R. Alker, Jr, 'Cybernetic measures of political capabilities', in *Mathematical Approaches to International Politics*, ed. Mario Bunge, Johan Galtung, and Mircea Malitza (Bucharest: Rumanian Academy of Social and Political Sciences, 1978), Vol. 1, pp. 50–68.

6 Although the original edition was available in 1948, I shall refer here to Norbert Wiener, *Cybernetics*, 2nd rev. and enl. edn (Cambridge and New York: MIT Press and Wiley, 1961); this is the edition cited in the 1966 paperback edition of Deutsch's book, to whose pages I henceforth shall also refer in my text. Wiener's most important additional contributions for our purposes are: Arthur Rosenblueth, Norbert Wiener, and Julian Bigelow, 'Behavior, purpose, and teleology', *Philosophy of Science*, vol. 10, no. 1 (January 1943), pp. 18–24; Norbert Wiener, *The Human Use of Human Beings* (Boston, Mass.: Houghton Mifflin, 1950); and Norbert Wiener, *God and Golem, Inc.: A Comment on Certain Points Where Cybernetics Impinges on Religion* (Cambridge, Mass.: MIT Press, 1964).

7 Arend Lijphart, 'Karl W. Deutsch and the new paradigm in international relations', in this volume.

8 The most extended and in some ways impressive recent statement of this view is James G. Miller, *Living Systems* (New York: McGraw-Hill, 1978), to be discussed below. All 1,051 pages are organized in terms of a seven-level correspondence of cells, organisms, groups, organizations, societies, and supranational systems.

9 I shall content myself in the text with a brief rationalization of this view. Its basic historical validity and contemporary heuristic utility is argued brilliantly in Jon Elster, *Leibniz et la Formation de l-Esprit Capitaliste* (Paris: Aubier, Montaigne, 1975); and Jon Elster, *Logic and Society: Contradiction and Possible Worlds* (New York: Wiley, 1978). My interpretations have been influenced as well by a considerable secondary

literature and by conversation with Jerome Lettvin at MIT, a co-worker with McCullough and Pitts (the authors of pioneering work on neural networks).
10 One may compare, for example, James Bennett and Hayward R. Alker, Jr, 'When national security policies bred collective insecurities', in *Problems of World Modeling*, ed. Karl W. Deutsch, Bruno Fritsch, Hélio Jaguaribe, and Andrei S. Markovits (Cambridge, Mass.: Ballinger, 1977), pp. 219–302, or Hayward R. Alker, Jr, 'Can the end of "power politics" be part of the concepts with which its story is told?', presented at the 1977 meetings of the American Political Science Association, with J. David Singer's or Manfred Kochen's contributions to the present volume.
11 Some modern philosophical discussions have translated metaphysical, including ontological, issues into pre-theoretical assumptions and queries (which form part of Lakatosian 'metaphysical cores', plus the negative and positive research 'heuristics' within scientific research programs). Deutsch follows the equally intriguing 'general systems' search for structurally valid analogies. Logical positivists since the early work of Whitehead and Russell have as well something to say about ontology. Typically they translate ontological issues into the choice of undefined logical or mathematical primitives, and then try to see if complex phenomena can be adequately formally represented using them.

An extremely provocative effort to respecify the basic unities of contemporary scientific thought, influenced by cybernetic thought, is Arthur Koestler's 'Beyond atomism and holism – the concept of the holon', *Perspectives in Biology and Medicine*, vol. 13, no. 2 (Winter 1970), pp. 131–53. It should also be noted at this point that James G. Miller's general systems-oriented *Living Systems* was inspired by Whitehead's later, rather Leibnizian (but more evolutionary) philosophy of organism; see *Living Systems*, p. xiii.
12 Miller, *Living Systems*, is very strong bibliographically on this point, citing Donald T. Campbell, Gerd Somerhoff, etc. See also my 'Le comportement directeur', *Revue Française de Sociologie*, vols. 11–12, special issue (1970–1), pp. 99–122.
13 George H. von Wright, *Explanation and Understanding* (London: Routledge & Kegan Paul, 1971).
14 That mechanistic or behavioristic teleology is not a contradiction in terms is a major argument of Wiener's most famous philosophical paper: '... purposefulness as defined here, is quite independent of causality, initial or final ... We have restricted the connotation of teleological behavior to purposeful reactions which are controlled by the error of the reaction – i.e. by the difference between the state of the behaving object at any time and the final state interpreted as the purpose [feedback] ... According to this limited definition, teleology is not opposed to determinism, but to nonteleology'. Rosenblueth, Wiener, and Bigelow, 'Behavior, purpose, and teleology', p. 225. A beautifully simple evolution of this view, based on the existence of uncontrollable state variables, is N. A. Coulter, Jr, 'The self-determinism of teleogenic systems', *Journal of Cybernetics*, vol. 5, no. 3 (July–September 1975), pp. 9–20. Such variables are shown to be necessary for a system to be capable of generating its own goals.
15 See Arthur Lovejoy's discussion of Leibniz, Descartes, and Newton excerpted in *Leibniz: A Collection of Critical Essays*, ed. Harry G. Frankfurt (Notre Dame, Ind.: University of Notre Dame Press, 1976).
16 ibid., p. 221.
17 loc. cit.
18 All quotes in this paragraph are from ibid., pp. 222ff., without original italics.
19 Karl W. Deutsch, *Nerves*, p. 92ff. Regular readers of *General Systems* and *Behavioral Science* will be aware of the considerable development and precision given to these ideas since the late 1940s by Ludwig von Bertalanffy, Donald T. Campbell, Kenneth Boulding, and James G. Miller. Having heard Deutsch exposit his marvellous functional diagram of information flow in foreign policy decisions (*Nerves*, appendix), I would say he comes quite close to the political application of Campbellian or Chomskian ideas about hierarchies of knowledge and understanding systems. This is clearest when Deutsch sequentially introduces and justifies the various complexities of attending, remembering, and responding processes.

Students familiar with Forrester's highly suggestive structural idea that interacting, higher order, non-linear feedback loops determine model performance will have already been exposed to another variant of the cybernetic hierarchy idea.
20 The relevant works were actually a bit earlier: Noam Chomsky, *Syntactic Structures*

('s-Gravenhage: Mouton, 1957), and George A. Miller, Eugene Galanter, and Karl H. Pribam, *Plans and the Structure of Behavior* (New York: Henry Holt, 1960), neither of which is cited in the 1966 edition of *The Nerves of Government* or in *Industrial Dynamics*. James G. Miller's review of Easton's systems models of political life in his chapter on societies is adequate and relevant here, but neither author appears to have grasped the deep structure of restructuring capacities inherent in human knowing, understanding, planning, or action systems. The several chapters by Noam Chomsky and George Miller in *Handbook of Mathematical Psychology*, ed. R. Duncan Luce et al. (New York: Wiley, 1963), Vol. 2, synthesize and update this view. See also Newall and Simon, *Human Problem Solving*. I am sure that a social and computer science citation search back to these and closely related items would produce thousands of citations. The uses made of these ideas, however, do not totally supersede Deutsch's or Forrester's somewhat different, if undeveloped, ideas.

21 My discussion follows J. Patrick Crecine, *Governmental Problem Solving* (Chicago: Rand McNally, 1969), pp. 208–15, at many points except that Crecine treats mayoral budgeting as an instantiated General Problem Solver (the famous artificially intelligent program of Ernst, Newall, Simon, and Shaw), while I choose here to emphasize the TOTE-like quality of such routines.

22 The reader may find certain similarities between what is said in the rest of this subsection and two of my earlier papers: 'Cybernetic measures of political capabilities' and 'cybernetic hierarchies within sociocultural change', paper prepared for the conference on Indicators of Social and Cultural Change within Computer Models of World Development, Moscow, 8–11 June 1976.

23 Karl Deutsch maintains he had never read Chomsky when he wrote this passage (*Nerves*, p. 253, his italics)! He certainly could not have read the Cocoyoc Declaration of the 1970s stressing the binding, but perhaps modifiable, nature of inner, sociopolitical limits to growth, prescribing the meeting of basic human needs.

The Chomskian critique of ordinary (context-free) formal languages is even stronger. He demonstrates that *natural human languages* are spoken and understood in an even more complex *context-sensitive* fashion (involving, for example, grammatical production rules like those in the second half of (6), which tell us that how O'_2 is to be rewritten depends on which test comes before it). Pronouns, tensed verbs, and expressions whose significance differs in different sociohistorical contexts all require context-sensitive generative/interpretive capacities. Ethnomethodologists and other critics of bureaucratic standardization can similarly claim, with varying degrees of validity, that political behavior itself cannot be adequately understood in simple quantitative terms for just this reason.

If the reader wonders how we possibly *can* understand such complexities, McCullough and Pitts showed that neural networks with circles in them have capacities even greater than those of context-sensitive grammars. Their relatively simple model, which inspired von Neumann's computer designs, in fact has the power of the top system in the Chomsky hierarchy, a Turing machine. See Warren S. McCullough, *Embodiments of Mind* (Cambridge, Mass.: MIT Press, 1965) for details.

The reader by now should have a somewhat fuller appreciation of the significance of Chomsky's cybernetic hierarchy of grammars, languages, and automata for social science and global modeling in particular.

24 János Kornai, *Anti-Equilibrium* (New York: Elsevier, 1971), carries this cybernetic theme to a paradigmatic conclusion, an adaptive planning orientation interpreted in Marxian terms as superior to market-oriented 'equilibrium' approaches. Political cybernetics does indeed have important affinities with socialist planning perspectives. But I cannot see that the connection is inevitable, or unique: otherwise Herbert Simon, John von Neumann, and Karl Deutsch would have converted to socialism twenty years ago.

25 E. Schrödinger, as quoted in Miller, *Living Systems*, p. 18. Concerning Wiener's recognition of the double translation: negentropy ⇆ information, O.C. de Beauregard makes a relevant comment:

> Let us note that the meaning of the word 'information' is not the same in the two senses: in the direction transition *negentropy* → *information*, 'information' signifies acquisition of knowledge; it is the current modern sense ... like the elementary process of *observation*. [Reciprocally] ... 'information' signifies *power of*

organization; it is the ancient Aristotelian sense, and the corresponding transition appears to be like the elementary process of *action*. To admit, as cybernetics does, reciprocity of the transition negentropy⇆information, is to admit ipso facto the equivalence of the two meanings, modern and Aristotelian, of the word 'information'.

Quoted and translated from Beauregard's 'Sur l'equivalence entre information et entropie', *Sciences* (1961), p. 54, by Miller, *Living Systems*, p. 42, n. 6 (italics in original).

26 A recent relevant paper by Talcott Parsons in his 'Some problems of general theory in sociology', in his *Social Systems and the Evolution of Action Theory* (New York: The Free Press, 1977), pp. 229–69. Many of the relevant references are given in my 'Le comportement directeur', and Miller, *Living Systems*, especially ch. 2 which uses non-symbiotic, non-parasitic independence as an organism-identifying criterion.

27 Wiener does, however, discuss von Neumann's astonishing preliminary results in the second, augmented edition of *Cybernetics* and in the last several chapters of *God and Golem, Inc*. It took some time for Arthur W. Burks to edit and complete posthumously John von Neumann's *Theory of Self-Reproducing Automata* (Urbana, Ill.: University of Illinois Press, 1966), from which has sprung much recent research.

28 Perhaps the revelatory quality of this synthesis accounts in part for von Neumann's reported conversion to Roman Catholicism late in his life. He was not the first to see certain compatibilities between Greek, Judeo-Christian, and modern thought. Neither is the Catholic Church a novice at self-reproductive behavior. As will become apparent, both von Neumann's and Parsons's models are highly conservative.

29 F. Dyson, as quoted in a superb article by the Michigan Logic of Computers Group: A. W. Burks, B. P. Ziegler, R. A. Laing, J. H. Holland, 'Biologically motivated automation theory and automation motivated biological research', *Proceedings of the Conference of Biologically Motivated Automata Theory* (McLean, Virginia, 1974). John von Neumann's lecture is conveniently available as 'The general and logical theory of automata', reprinted in *The World of Mathematics*, ed. James R. Newman (New York: Simon & Schuster, 1956), Vol. 4, pp. 2070–98.

30 And von Neumann's work is thus a much better 'formalization of functionalism' than Sommerhoff's, Lange's, or Forrester's. I use Nagel's phrase here from the debate among Merton, Gouldner, Parsons, Nagel, and Gunder Frank discussed in my 'Le comportement directeur', and N. J. Demerath and Richard Peterson (eds), *System, Change and Conflict* (New York: The Free Press, 1967).

31 The best summary volume on this subject to date, in a global modeling framework, is Deutsch *et al.* (eds), *Problems of World Modeling*. I have tried to synthesize these arguments in Hayward R. Alker, Jr, Karl W. Deutsch, and Andrei S. Markovits, 'Global opportunities and constraints for regional development', *Social Science Information*, vol 16, no. 1 (1977), pp. 83–102. An overview of autopoietic systems theory is given in Francisco Varela G., *Principles of Biological Autonomy* (New York: Elsevier-North Holland, 1979).

32 The clearest link Deutsch has made between his augmented Parsonian scheme, adding goal change and self-transformation functions, and the national development literature, is Karl W. Deutsch and Jorge I. Domínguez, 'Political development toward national self-determination: some recent concepts and models', *Comparative Political Studies*, vol. 4, no. 4 (January 1972), pp. 461–75. See also Domínguez's contribution to the present volume.

33 The relevant appendix 'On regulation' in Kaplan's *System and Process in International Politics* is rarely cited, but must be considered a classic piece. Robert P. Abelson's work in the 1958–1968 period is summarized in his 'psychological implication', in *Theories of Cognitive Consistency*, ed. Robert P. Abelson *et al*. (Chicago: Rand McNally, 1968), pp. 112–39. See also Karl W. Deutsch and Dieter Senghaas, 'The fragile sanity of states: a theoretical analysis', in *New States in the Modern World*, ed. Martin Kilson (Cambridge, Mass.: Harvard University Press, 1975), pp. 200–45.

34 These relevant tasks have been largely accomplished in many of the papers cited in the previous footnotes. At least half of the themes of my concluding section are previewed in Karl W. Deutsch's latest papers, especially his 'Toward an interdisciplinary model of world stability and change: some intellectual preconditions', *Journal of Peace Science*, vol. 2, no. 1 (Spring 1976), pp. 1–14.

35 The reader will find most of the relevant citations to this literature in Stein Rokkan's extremely integrative, empirical, and open-minded contribution to this volume, as well as the Duvall *et al*. and Senghaas chapters.
36 Immanuel Wallerstein, *The Modern World-System* (New York: Academic Press, 1974).
37 The best relevant technical work I know is incredibly expensive and difficult. It includes Robert Abelson, 'Concepts for representing mundane reality in plans', in *Representation and Understanding: Studies in Cognitive Science*, ed. Daniel G. Bobrow and Allan Collins (New York: Academic Press, 1975); Bertram Bruce and Denis Newman, 'Interacting plans' (University of Illinois at Urbana-Champaign and Bolt, Beranek, and Newman, Cambridge), mimeo., 1978; Hartmut Bossel and Michael Strobel, 'Experiments with an "intelligent" world model', *Futures*, vol. 10, no. 3 (June 1978), pp. 191–212; and Francisco Varela, *Principles of Biological Autonomy*.

Manfred Kochen's proposals for globalized computer communication systems, mentioned in this volume, unfortunately have almost none of the desired properties mentioned above. Who will use such systems? Who will have the resources and capabilities for doing so profitably? Without major changes in power, wealth, integration, and development levels, can we expect the national beneficiaries to be any other than those benefiting from them now?
38 In addition to my 'Can the end of power politics' ... paper, the most important epistomological writing on logical positivism and dialectical hermeneutics is critically summarized in my 'Learning how to do political and social science', mimeo., 1978.

15

Can the Global System Learn to Control Conflict?

MANFRED KOCHEN

Conflict of interest among parties in the global system arises when two or more intend to occupy or control the same space or exclusive position, to possess or control the use of the same objects, to reach incompatible goals or to use incompatible means to their ends.[1] Some writers have viewed conflict as a necessary concomitant of any viable innovative system, and that its elimination is both unfeasible and undesirable. Conflict is a systemic property of the international system. It depends to a greater extent on the relations and interactions among the states than on the attributes and behaviors of individual states.

The responses to conflicts of interest vary, including debates and mutually destructive fights.[2] Conflict *control* is a response of the system as a whole that maintains within tolerable limits the values of the total system of states. Conflict *management*, on the other hand, as a particular manager's responsibility, cannot be counted on as a response to a systemic condition that is tolerable according to the values of the system as a whole. A forest fire in an inaccessible region may be self-controlling even if it is unmanageable. None the less, individuals, institutions, states, transnational, and supranational entities can perhaps manage their part in a conflict so that it enhances the self-controlling dynamics of the global system.

Waltz[3] criticized international politics as lacking a hierarchic arrangement that would make a general-systems approach appropriate. Presumably the global system would be at the top level of such a hierarchy, as a new entity with a life and values of its own, even though such global values may have ultimately emerged from the values of individual parties and continue to be dwarfed by them. He is probably right in criticizing the systemic approaches he selected (which excluded seminal works of Boulding, Deutsch, Rapoport, and others[4] in this area) as being reductionist or reductionist in clever disguise. Alker, in his chapter of this book, proposes that elaborating theories of self-referential interpretive structures and developing data bases for script/frame/'dreme'-like analyses of belief structures might prove to be fruitful for a 'new' systems approach to international politics. Yet, work of the past two decades[5] on the dynamics of how belief systems are restructured may hold even more promise than the use of concepts such as scripts/frames/'dremes'. The bottom-up approach to systems that builds up a system from primitive components through frames, and so on, is more likely to become once again reductionism in disguise than a top-down approach combined with a bottom-up and a middle-to-top-and-bottom approach.

The key question addressed in this chapter is whether conflict control in the global system can be learned. I will first try to conceptualize with greater clarity some ideas of global conflict and its control as a systemic property. Then I will propose a conceptualization of adaptive learning, as it applies to global conflict control. In doing so, I will try to extend Deutsch's[6] view that the essence of a political system's capacity to *learn* is its ability to rapidly convert recommittable resources (tools, buildings, vehicles, subsystems) at all levels – from individuals to small and large communities – with a broad range of possible recommitments at low cost. I will also build on the system-theoretic approaches to conflict of Richardson, Boulding, Rapoport, and others[7] rather than more reductionist approaches,[8] by stressing the role of adaptive learning. Deutsch was among the first to introduce non-reductionist, system-theoretic learning concepts into political systems theory.

Conflicts of Interest

The concept of conflict has been applied to persons, as well as to groups. Some general systems theorists (e.g. Miller) believe that it can be conceptualized so as to make it usefully applicable to both, and independently of whether the conflict is inner, marital, economic, political, and so on. Applied to a person, it refers to a situation in which there is motivation to engage in mutually exclusive behaviors.[9] As a general notion, it refers to the situation of a system, A, that co-determines, together with A's behavior (output) and at least one other variable, a new situation which A evaluates for preference against its prior situation. What makes it a conflict situation A is that the other variables that co-determine how the situation changes may be the behavior of a second system, B, with a different basis for evaluating preferences among possible situations, so that A has only partial control over how the situation will change. A third system, G, viewed as a new entity emerging from the two interacting systems, A and B, may be interpreted to be 'motivated' to produce two different behaviors, one corresponding to A's preference and one to B's. If this general notion of conflict is applied to the third system, it specializes to the concept of conflict in an individual. We now specialize the general notion to apply to political conflict of interest in the global system of states, being careful not to de-emphasize that some of the parties are 'sovereign' and control strength to a greater extent than others.

To characterize a conflict situation, it is necessary to first specify the systems of interest, which are the parties in the conflict situation. The global system is a party and it is at the top level. At a level below that, supranational systems, such as NATO, are parties. At lower levels, transnational systems, countries and departments or ministries within states are other important parties. As Lijphart points out elsewhere in this book, the new paradigm in international relations pioneered by Deutsch liberated the field of inquiry from the limiting assumption that sovereign states are the *only* important actors in international politics and that states are unified, indivisible entities. Each of these parties may have different images and preferences of the situations (actual and possible) they all are (or can be) in. They may also perceive differently the behaviors (controlled or uncontrolled) that they and other parties generate, and how these change situations. Jervis,[8] for example, adopts the psychological hypothesis that decision-makers fit incoming information into their images.

Secondly, it is necessary to specify the field (ensemble, space) of situations, that both motivate, and result from, the behavior of the parties. Situations of political interest involve ownership and control of territory and material wealth, predominance of ideas and commitments of people. How a theorist specifies or represents the ensembles of situations (state-spaces) for each party should be sharply distinguished from (1) how each party represents its own field to itself and (2) how each party represents the other parties' fields, and possibly (3) how each party A represents certain other parties' representations of A. We know of no objective or canonical representation of the space of all possible situations that is independent of someone imagining and expressing it. Even a variable as seemingly 'hard' as who owns a particular geographic site at a specified time is subject to the interpretation of 'ownership'. It is somewhat easier to understand what representation means for an individual than for a ministry, a country, or the global system. When a person says that he wants to buy the land on which he stands, we are sure that he *imagines* owning that land, though we do not yet know how to ascertain this operationally. When the spokesperson of a country asserts the intention of acquiring a certain plot of land, we tend to ascribe the home of this idea to some collective imagination that may be represented by slogans or symbols. It is meaningless to speak of conflict in a system of two parties whose representation of the space of situations do not have at least some commonalities, or if the notions of 'representation' by a country and by a supranational agency are quite different.

Thirdly, each party's representation of its preferences over the ensemble of situations, as it perceives that, should be specified to characterize political conflict of interest. Again, it is also important to know how each party sees the preferences of other parties and even their perception of the original party's preferences. Fourthly, each party's representation of its own range of possible behaviors needs to be specified. These behaviors include proclamations by official representatives of the party about, for example, the ownership of land, actual troop movements ordered by a party to occupy land, and various other unit acts that can be implicated as co-determinants in situational changes. Fifthly, we need to know each party's representation of the 'laws' according to which it 'believes' situations change as a consequence of its own and other parties' behavior, of how each party 'thinks' other parties will respond to what they believe other parties' positions to be.

Finally, to characterize conflict we need to specify the options for management and for control of conflict. A party may 'believe' that certain of its possible behaviors can serve to manage conflict. It can 'imagine' itself fighting (as a deliberate move or as an automatic reaction to a situation), trading[10] (positively, where each party is and 'thinks' it is better off or negatively, where each party is and 'thinks' it is worse off), game-playing, talking (e.g. debating).

I have put quotes around such terms as 'thinks', 'imagines', 'believes' because it is even less clear what these terms mean when applied to a country or the global system than when applied to a person. The general concept of 'representation' as it has evolved since 1960 may help in clarifying not only what 'thinking' *by* a country means, but what it means in an individual. By a representation we mean a conjunction of weighted propositions denoting beliefs about the world. Some are of the form, 'If the situation is ____ and all the parties' behaviors are ____ , ..., ____ , then the situation will change to ____, which is preferred by parties____, ..., ____'. The weight reflects both how plausible and how valuable a party that stores such a hypothesis considers it.[11] We call those internal hypotheses to distinguish them from hypotheses of the form 'The situation is now ___' or 'The situation yesterday was ___' or 'Party A's current behavior is ____'. Yet another form of hypothesis is illustrated by 'war is politics by other means', a belief on which there may be consensus in the USSR.[12]

Inferring the beliefs held by a party such as a country may be easier than the corresponding task for individuals. All that we inquirers can ever hope to 'know' about another party's beliefs are hypotheses about them that are more or less confirmed by observed behavior. We ascribe a hypothesis to a ministry, country, or the global system if key spokespersons for such a party have expressed essentially the same belief without an assertion to the contrary from any key person of that party. For such consensus to occur, it is necessary that the statements from different spokespersons be in the same system of representation, generated from the same vocabulary and formation/transformation rules, inferred from the same axioms by the same rules of inference, based on a sufficiently overlapping corpus of prior knowledge (representation). Consensus is rare. Its existence, coupled with an ability to control strength or commit resources, may be used to define a party. In reality, therefore, fewer parties than one would expect need to be considered. The inquirer problem is to select them appropriately.

We cannot speak of conflict in a system G unless it is possible to ascertain what situations it is 'motivated' to attain and which behaviors such motivation is likely to generate. If G is steered according to a map or representation that makes ownership of a particular site (e.g. Jerusalem) a most preferred situation, then we assume that G is motivated to bring about that situation by behaviors believed to be instrumental. If G comprises two parties as subsystems, A and B, each of which seeks to own the site, then G is in a conflict situation if only A or B can own the site. Then G is motivated to produce two behaviors. One is to transfer ownership to A, the other to B. Only one of these can prevail. If, however, the word 'ownership' has a different meaning to A and B or if G stores two hypotheses using the same word but with different interpretations, then we cannot say whether there is or is not a conflict of interest.

By a system of representation we mean an applied predicate calculus (extended to accommodate self-reference)[13] with specified sets of variables, predicate names, and a specified system of interpretation – a mapping of the predicate symbols into a relational structure for a specified domain of discourse. For example, let the domain of discourse be the set of all integers, $Z = \{\ldots, -1,0,1,2,3, \ldots\}$, and select the subset of $Z \times Z$, $\{\ldots,(-1,0), (0,-1), (0,2), \ldots\}$ to illustrate a two-place relation. The assignment of this relation to the predicate symbol '>' or '___ is greater than ___' is an interpretation of that symbol.

Consider now the simplest illustration of this conceptualization of conflict. There are three parties, A, B, and G, the system of A and B in interaction. The field of situations is represented by five variables. The first three specify a region on the earth's surface by, say, latitude and longitude of the region's center and its radius. The fourth is the strength of A's claim to own the region and the fifth is the strength of B's claim. These two variables might be measured by the maximum magnitude of resources A is willing to commit to uphold the claim, to prevail. To depict various types of situations graphically, let us replace the first three variables by one, namely, distance d along a line at which a region consisting of a single point is contested. Assume for now that A and B have exactly the same representation and that the strengths of the claims indicate the preferences.

Figure 15.1 shows three types of situations, varying from no conflict to extreme conflict of interest. The solid curve in $15.1(b)$ or $15.1(c)$ shows A's strength of claim for ownership of various sites. It allows us to interpret point H, under the peak of the curve, as A's heartland or home base, the region of A's most essential, inviolable, non-negotiable national interests if A is a nation. It would include Texas, California, for the USA (in a dispute with Mexico) and Alaska (in a dispute with the USSR). The annular region R next to the heartland is also of great importance to A, but it can be negotiated at a high price. Next to that is a peripheral zone P, that can be negotiated more readily, and it is followed by regions that A does not contest much.

In addition to specifying the parties, the space of situations, the parties' preferences over it, we need to specify each party's representation of behaviors, the laws of change and options for conflict management. To complete the illustration started by Figure 15.1, we characterize A's behavior by a curve that indicates how much of A's resources A will in fact recommit and apply at point d in the line of Figure 15.1 in order to enforce its claim of owning that site. The difference between the strength of A's claim and A's strength to enforce that claim is the difference between intention and steps to attainment,

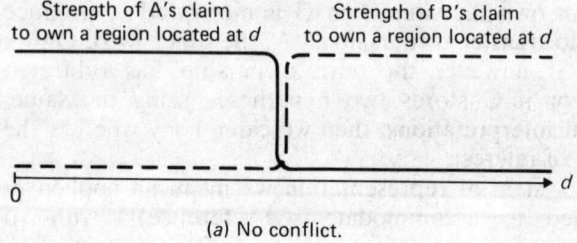
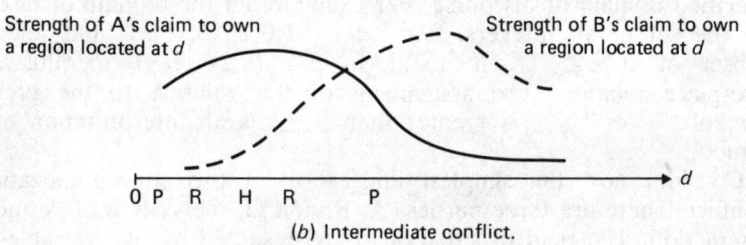
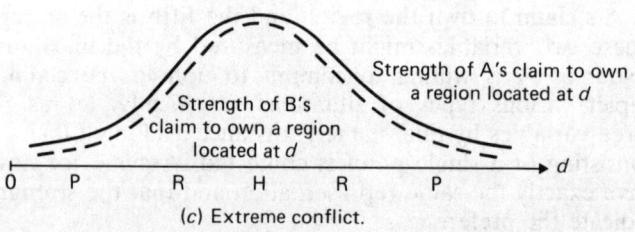

Figure 15.1 *Three cases of interest conflict.*

between desire and moves toward fulfillment, between interest and effective power. A's capacity for attainment is an intervening situational variable and it limits behavior. If A's strength curve does not essentially coincide with A's interest curve, with A and B both aware of this, we may have a pseudo-conflict of interest. This could generate stresses that are local and internal to A rather than to the system G. The situation becomes an interesting systemic phenomenon when B or A or both are unaware of the discrepancy between strength and interest curves, or when their representations are poor.

Representations of 'change laws' are most simply illustrated by imputing to A the hypothesis that if A applies its greatest strength where A's interest is strongest, and if B does the same, and the situation is one of extreme conflict (Figure 15.1(*c*)), then the party with greater strength at point H will own H. This is, of course, but one of many hypotheses that comprise A's knowledge of the world and of the specialities specific to the situation. Included are hypotheses held by A about A's own strength relative to B's.

The heart of the conflict concept is probably in the representation of the space of situations in which a preference ordering is assumed to exist for each party. That assumption is a myth. Figure 15.1 is not only an illustrative oversimplification, but a gross distortion. A situation space is hardly ever representable by one or five variables; indeed, individual decision-makers and countries even less may not represent situations in terms of variables, and relations among them, at all. When they do, they may devote top priority attention for a time to a variable such as d but without ever letting out of sight hundreds of variables such as 'mean life at birth', 'level of nutrition', and 'unemployment rate'. They may be aware of (hold hypotheses that they hold hypotheses about ...) constraints that make it impossible to act in their interest concerning every variable and that difficult trades must be made. Given limited resources, a party cannot provide as much as its interests in both a high standard of living and ownership of H require. In so far as a party can sort out separate variables that characterize situations and weight these differentially by importance, it is likely to be indifferent to choices among many pairs of situations; it is possible that a party does not even know with any certainty what really matters to it and whether or not it is indifferent except in the narrow sense in which attention is momentarily riveted on a contested region or resource. Confusion may predominate over both misperception and conflict, and local internal conflicts may predominate over the more systemic ones. (Jervis speaks of 'missing' concepts rather than confusion.)

Table 15.1 suggests an appropriateness relationship between types of situations and types of conflict management behavior. Of course parties can respond with any behavior that can escalate into a totally unconstrained fight or to a lightly constrained diplomatic game or a highly civilized debate.

Control of Conflict

I shall focus primarily on what it means for the (top-level) global system to remain in control. This involves a search for conditions under which self-regulating mechanisms in the total system maintain stable equilibria or smooth (non-catastrophic), non-equilibrium changes. If one subsystem A, of the global system G, can manage conflict so as to meet these conditions, it is because the self-regulating mechanisms of the global system are distributed or concentrated in local parties so that control by A is equivalent to self-control in G. The key question then is to characterize instability and catastrophe as instances of uncontrolled conflict.

The simplest balance-of-power[14] model leads to the notion of equilibrium. If each party tries to increase its total strength with the least effort and if it expends as little of its strength as is necessary to keep each other party from increasing its instantaneous strength, then every party's level of strength and its allocation will rise to a level where each just keeps the others in check. The equilibrium thus reached may be unstable if small changes from the equilibrium level by one party do

Table 15.1 Conflict management types

Situation types	Confusion, with underlying conflict	Misperception of conflicting interests	Local conflict internal to a party	Interest conflict among parties	Systemic conflicts of interest
Types of behavior	Automatic action and reaction	Misguided action and reaction	Deliberate indirect action	Trading and negotiation	Synthesis into higher levels of consciousness
Resulting dynamics	Escalation into a fight	Spiral into social trap	'Games parties play'	Bargaining, trading	Debates, dialectics

not bring all the levels back to their former value. If unstable, all the levels may still drift smoothly but in a predictable and desirable (with regard to G's 'preferences' or 'values') manner. As G drifts it may become locked into another stable equilibrium state or else it may be deliberately switched into one.

A stable equilibrium state of G may change its *nature* as a structural parameter changes continuously. The simplest example of this is a 2-party system with two behaviors (A_1 and A_2 for party A, B_1 and B_2 for party B) considered by each party and a preference function that can be represented by two pay-off matrices

$$\begin{array}{c} \\ A_1 \\ A_2 \end{array} \begin{array}{cc} B_1 & B_2 \\ \begin{pmatrix} 1 & X \\ -1 & 0 \end{pmatrix} \end{array} \quad \text{and} \quad \begin{pmatrix} -1 & -X \\ 1 & 0 \end{pmatrix}.$$

Here if party A does A_1 and party B does B_1 then A has a 'pay-off' of 1 and B has a 'pay-off' (penalty) of -1. The gradually varying structural parameter is X. As long as X exceeds 1, A should clearly choose A_1; B_1, realizing that A chooses A_1, will choose B_1. The pair of choices (A_1, B_1) is an equilibrium point. It is stable, because if A knows that B will choose B_1, A will not switch from A_1 to A_2.

As X decreases through 1 until it is less than 1, B will switch from B_1 to B_2. The new equilibrium point will be (A_1, B_2). As X decreases further through 0, until it is negative, A's realization that B chooses B_2 will motivate A to switch to A_2 (0 is preferred to a negative pay-off). But B, realizing that A would switch to A_2, will switch to B_1 (preferring 1 to 0). Therefore A would, in turn, revert back to A_1. B would revert to B_1, and so on.

To break this dynamic deadlock, A randomly spins a circular spinner that is divided into two sectors labeled A_1 and A_2, with A_1 occupying a fraction p of the circle. The value of p is chosen so as to maximize either the expected pay-off $p \cdot 1 + (1-p)(-1)$ (which is $2p - 1$, assuming B picks B_1) or $p \cdot X + (1-p) \cdot 0$ (which is $X \cdot p$, assuming B picks B_2), whichever is less. Figure 15.2 plots these two functions $v \cdot p$; for each value of p, the smaller expected pay-off to A is shown for $X = -\frac{1}{2}$ by the roof-like graph indicated by ___ · ___ · ___. Its peak or maximum occurs where the two lines ab and cd intersect, i.e. where $Xp = 2p - 1$. This occurs when $p = 1/(2 - X)$. Thus if $X = -\frac{1}{2}$, $p = \frac{2}{5}$.

Note that as X changes continuously from positive to negative through 0, the nature of the equilibrium changes from one where A and B choose one or the other behaviors according to a deterministic algorithm to one where they choose probabilistically, though with a deliberately chosen probability. It is another form of conflict control.

The mathematical theory of 'catastrophes' deals with changes in a function, such as the preference function of G over its space of situations, as a result of a continuous change in a parameter, where the number of extrema is changed. Suppose that A can behave by choosing the value of a continuously ranging variable s. The change in the

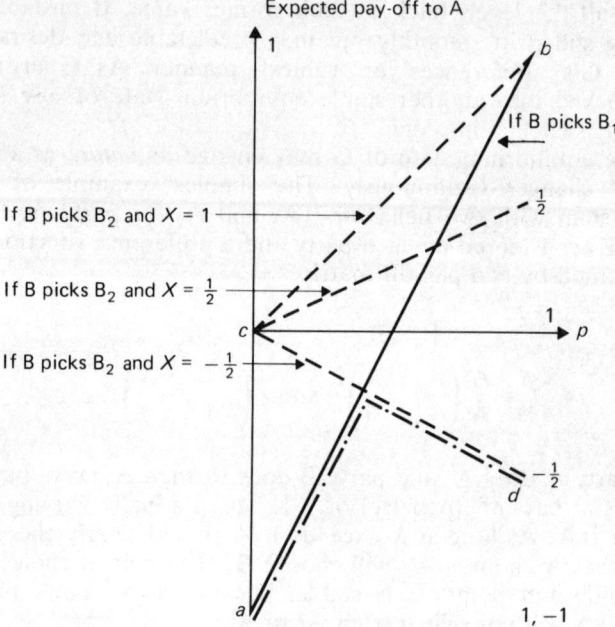

Figure 15.2 *Computation of a mixed strategy.*

situation is characterized by a real number k such that A represents the value of the new situation brought about by s as $ks^2 - s^4$. This is shown in Figure 15.3. If $k \leq 0$, the relation between A's utility and his behavior s is shown by the dashed curve; if $k > 0$, it is shown by the solid curve.

Note that as k varies smoothly through 0 from a negative to a positive value, the shape of the curve deforms continuously. But it changes its nature drastically, from where it had one peak as long as $k \leq 0$, to

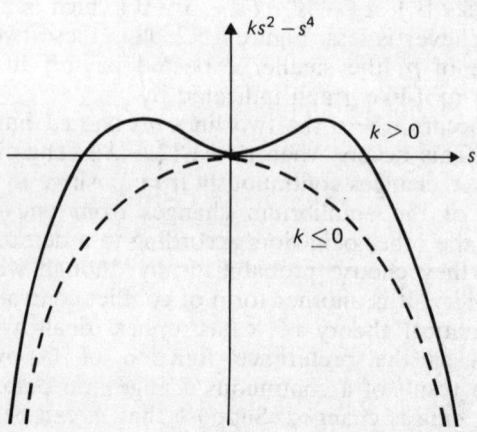

Figure 15.3 *Illustrating a 'catastrophe'.*

where it has two peaks when $k > 0$. The two peaks represent a conflict situation because A does not know whether to select

$$s = \left(\frac{k}{4}\right)^{1/3} \quad \text{or} \quad s = -\left(\frac{k}{4}\right)^{1/3}$$

(unless constraints prohibit one of these solutions). Keeping k from becoming positive is, therefore, a mechanism of preventing or controlling conflict in G.

Two analogies bring us a step closer toward adapting these concepts to control the conflict of political interest in the global system. The first is the 'Tragedy of the Commons', used by Garrett Hardin[15] to depict the situation of several herdsmen with a common grazing area for their cattle. If each herdsman acts in just his own best interest, the common will soon be overgrazed, to the detriment of all. If there is still enough grass, the rate of depletion increases with total number of cattle; when little enough grass is left, erosion may accelerate the further depletion of the remainder.

The analogue of common resources that are depleted as each party tries to increase its own strength while keeping all others from doing so should be introduced into balance of power models. That common resource may be the value derived from the cultivation and utilization of land that is owned. If two parties dispute a given region, they may divert some of their energies from cultivating and maintaining the region toward competition or combat with each other; moreover, combat in the region may devastate it, not merely allow it to wither from neglect. Its value for either party decreases even further. Processes similar to erosion may accelerate the deterioration of a disputed region as shown in Figure 15.4.

Conflict is controlled if each party behaves so that the long-term consequences are preferred by all parties, each according to its own basic values, even if it means forgoing short-term consequences that are preferable to each party. The value of controlling a region, less the cost of attaining such control, may in the long run detract rather than enhance the basic values of all parties in the dispute over control. The cost of losing control or the value of gaining it often seems greater during the heat of dispute than it does in retrospect.

The second analogy involves two archers. Each aims a bow loaded with an arrow at the other in order to gain control over a disputed object, the value of which may deteriorate or suddenly decrease if this situation continues. In addition to the two variables described previously to characterize conflict – strategic interest as depicted in Figure 15.1 and similarly distributed strength or capability – a third variable of great importance is dramatized here. It is the readiness to use strength. This may be interpreted as corresponding to tension in the bow. In the context of a system of parties in political conflict over territorially based strategic interests, readiness to use strength depends on such intervening variables as hostility, trust, resolve to use strength, volatility, and vigilance.

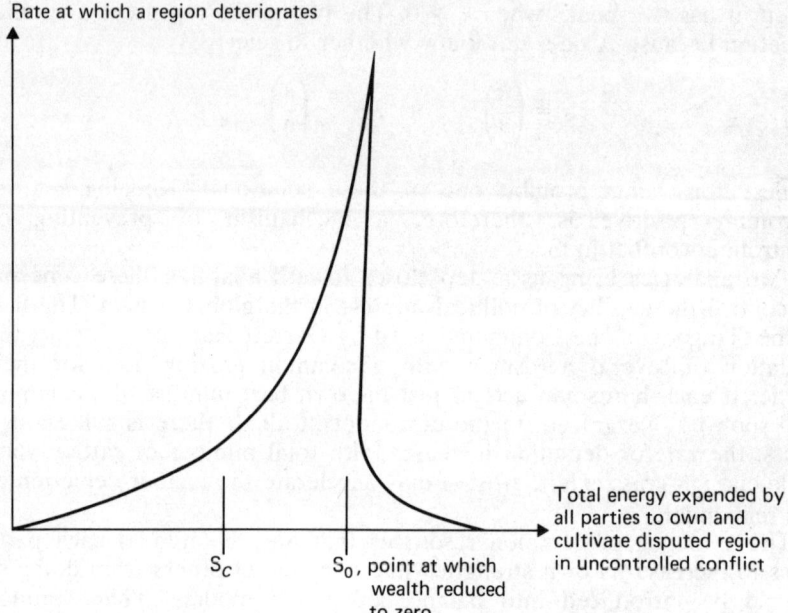

Figure 15.4 *Illustrating how the value of a disputed region may deteriorate with increasing applied strength.*

Consider a system G with two subsystems A and B, as before. Assume, with Boulding, that the readiness of A to use its strength against B increases by a multiplier, say m_A, for each unit of increase in B's readiness to use strength against A. Archer A responds to archer B's just noticeable increase in the tension of B's bow by increasing the tension of his own bow by a factor of m_A. Archer B responds similarly. The pair of response curves are shown in Figure 15.5. The dashed line specifies upper limits of readiness to use strength, where, in the case of the flexed bows, the tension is so great that it can no longer be restrained, and the arrows are released, damaging or destroying A and/or B and the object under dispute. At levels of tension below this critical threshold, system G's behavior is characterized by the zigzag path 1 – 2 – 3 – 4 ... – 0 in Figure 15.5. At 1, A has an unprovoked, initial readiness to use his strength against B as shown in Figure 15.5. When B realizes that, he increases his own readiness from his initial, unprovoked readiness to use his strength against A to the horizontal distance from 1 to 2. When A realizes the magnitude of that, he increases his readiness by the vertical distance from 2 to 3. B, in turn, responds by increasing his readiness by the horizontal distance from 3 to 4. This escalation continues, but in decreasing increments until the increments converge to 0 and a stable equilibrium situation occurs at 0. This is 'safe' or controlled by a 'balance-of-power' mechanism as long as the two response curves intersect and the intersection is in the safe region below the dashed line in Figure 15.5.

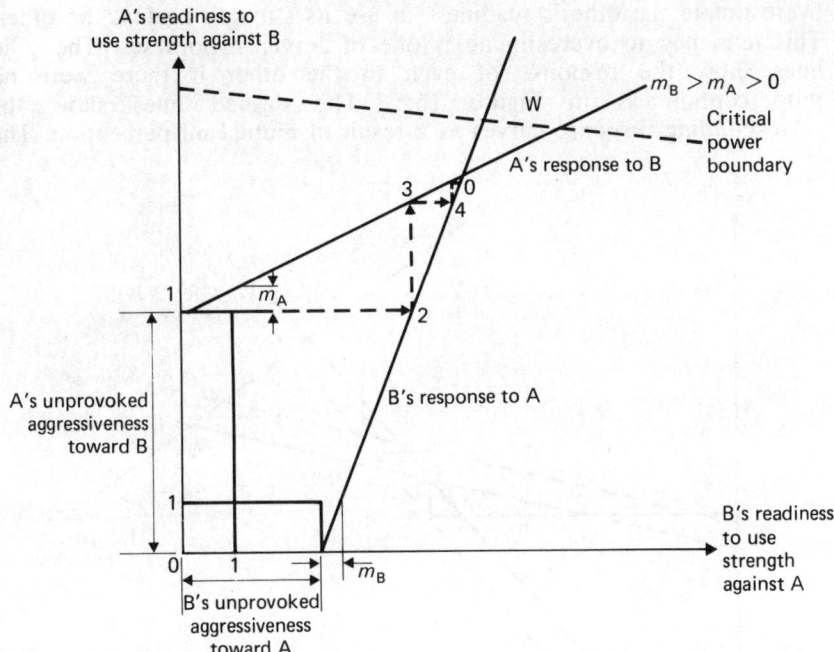

Figure 15.5 *Response of A's readiness to use strength to B's readiness to use strength and vice versa.*

What A and B realize about one another's readiness to use their strength against the other, however, depends on the perceptions and representations each has of the other. Thus, A does not respond to B's readiness to use force. Instead, A responds to A's judgement about B's readiness to use force. The increase in the tension of archer A's bow depends on how much he *thinks* B increased the tension on his bow. This perception may be accurate or biased, distorted or completely illusory. Jervis would have us believe that A's message to B about readiness to shoot would be perceived as clear by A, that A and B would tend to see one another more hostile than they are, that they see one another as more centrally controlled and co-ordinated than they are, that each finds it hard to believe that the other sees him as a threat.

The way A perceives the state of the world and the actions of others depends greatly on A's overall world-image and A's values. So does how A is likely to act. Values enter judgements of worth, and world-images give shape to dreams, hopes, ambitions as well as interpretations of self, others, and environment. Some modern Arab parties, for example, misperceive the intentions of Western countries and Israel partly because of a distorted or uncertain evaluation of their own worth and strength that may be the result of centuries of colonial subjugation. It takes part of A's strength to build, maintain, and enforce images and values, especially in A's heartland.

Figure 15.6(*a*) illustrates a situation for G in which A and B each

392 FROM NATIONAL DEVELOPMENT TO GLOBAL COMMUNITY

overestimate the other's readiness to use its strength against the other. This tendency to overestimate is one of Jervis' hypotheses. The solid lines show the response of each to the other if there were no misperception as in Figure 15.5. The dashed lines show the corresponding response curves as a result of mutual misperception. The

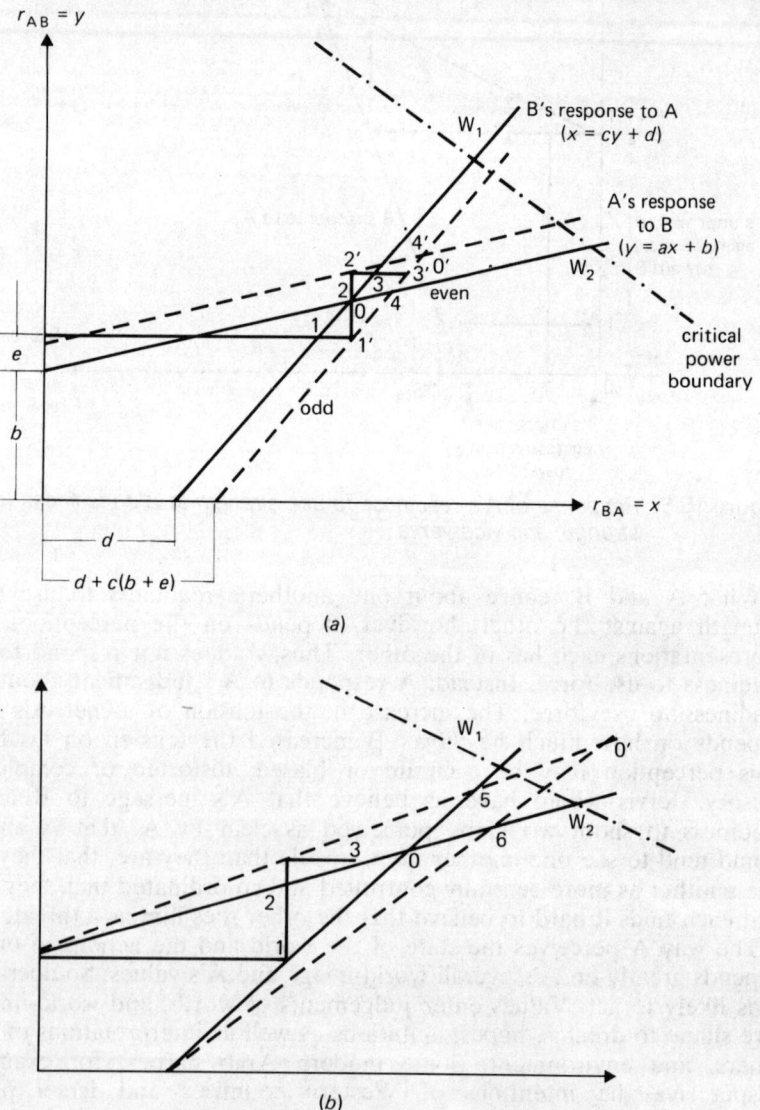

Figure 15.6 Illustrating the effect of misperception.
(a) Parties overestimate one another's readiness to use force.
(b) Case where overestimation to use force increases with level of readiness.

stable equilibrium point 0 is shifted to a new stable equilibrium 0', closer to the danger zone by an amount that depends not only on the extent of overestimation but on how close to parallel the two response curves are.

In Figure 15.6(b) the degree to which each party overestimates the other's readiness to use its strength increases with the level of readiness (tension in the archers' bows). This distorts the slopes of the response curves and results in a much larger shift of the equilibrium point toward or into the danger zone. Conflict control requires awareness about the possible consequences of such misperceptions. This does not imply that vigilance always improves the ability to control conflict, because vigilance does not guarantee the absence of misperception. Hypervigilance may well increase the chance of misperception. Lack of vigilance by one party can sometimes be to the system's advantage, as shown in the appendix to this chapter.

Adaptive Learning

A system is said to *learn adaptively* if it forms and uses a consensual representation of the world to recognize and control or master an increasing variety of challenging situations. By a challenging situation I mean in this chapter one characterized by conflict of political interest among subsystems of the global system. By a situation under control I mean system behavior that is consistent with the total system's long-term values. For sufficiently challenging situations, ability to control requires intelligence, that is, ability to quickly grasp the gist or essence of any situation. Learning extends the repertoire of situations that can be quickly grasped.

By 'representations of the world' we mean world images[16] that are composed of hypotheses (weighted 'if ... then' statements relating aspects of a situation and actions to their consequences) constructed from a changeable repertoire of concepts. For example, the concept of 'massive retaliation' based on overkill capabilities is new in history and had to be learned. Nearly all the concepts used to think about political global conflict – shortages and surpluses, dominance, ethnic bonds, national security – had to be learned at one time in the history of man. An adaptive learning process consists of: (1) changes of the weights in a fixed set of hypotheses (or in the procedures for generating them); (2) the change in such set of hypotheses; and (3) the change in the conceptual repertoire (and its structure) from which hypotheses are formed.

This proposed view of learning differs from existing ones. In a sense, it is narrower than Deutsch's[17] 'giving to the same class of inputs a new class of outputs' or 'increasing the probability of a response' in that it excludes from 'learning' the acquisition of counter-productive behaviors. To be sure, individuals learn to smoke, states learn to wage wars, and the system of states learns to waste resources through arms races. We are, however, concerned only with adaptive learning, not learning in general. Presumably the learners' values are such that the expected consequences of these behaviors are preferred to the expected consequences of abstaining from such behaviors, at least for the short run. A new class of outputs or mere changes in the probability of a response or just 'a behavioral change that results from experience',[18] could occur at random, and most unintended changes are likely to be undesirable both in the short and in the long run. Learning in practice often means that diplomats and militarists prepare to manage the conflicts that they had experienced in the past. That, too, is not learning in our intended sense. *The heart of the problem of learning is that we are uncertain and inconsistent about what we will consider desirable or valuable in the future.* Yet individuals do express and communicate their hopes and dreams. In aggregate, these help to shape shared images of a future world[19] and these images play an important role in how the world actually changes.[20]

One of the mechanisms of adaptive learning is that of making non-fatal errors and utilizing corrective feedback to improve future ability to prevent recurrence of similar errors and to rapidly and accurately detect those that do occur. Whether parties in the global system made 'errors' can be established by hindsight at best. Experiments have shown that hindsight is quite different from foresight.[21] Deeply rooted fears of an uncertain future may increase a party's resistance to changing its image as well as its behavior, and bring about interpretations of history consistent with an earlier image that does not admit or recognize 'error'.

Another of the mechanisms of adaptive learning is the concurrent correction of misperceptions. In a system of two states, each may correct its misperceptions of the other's values and outlook. In reacting to a move by B, A may increase the depth of moves to which A looks ahead. A takes account of how B is most likely to react. A may plan how it will react to that. A may anticipate B's likely response to that, and so on. Of course, look-ahead is of no value unless B's most likely responses can be accurately predicted. The system cannot respond appropriately unless both parties behave with a certain minimal level of intelligence.

Learning Is Possible

What mechanisms enable the system of states to control conflict? How do such mechanisms come into being? Once in operation, how do such control mechanisms adapt? These situations all have the property that the system can readily pass from trading moves to negative trading, analogous to the 'Tragedy of the Commons'. The shift from trading to negative trading, from involuntary mutual aid among conflicting parties to shared tragedy, from the invisible hand's patting to slapping, occurs sooner if each party's perception of the other is more uncertain, more distorted, more dissonant. As the set of options for action and image-formation by each party increases, the situations facing the parties increase in complexity. This increases the likelihood of misperception. This tends to shift the boundary at which trades become negative trades toward the earlier stages. It thus becomes increasingly important to control this kind of conflict.

An important mechanism for maintaining equilibrium within a safe region involves coping with complexity. Another is to detect and correct errors of perception, cognition, conation. Yet another is improved utilization and communication of information. There have been important advances in relevant aspects of system theory that have not been mentioned in Alker's chapter.[22] Some are current, but such basic 'principles' of cybernetics as are known persisted throughout his three stages.

If A receives feedback that it has misperceived a situation, it invokes hypotheses about what a more correct perception of the situation would be or about how it may have misperceived. Such hypotheses are chosen probabilistically. An example of such a hypothesis by A is that it overestimated the curves shown by a solid line in Figure 15.6 as shown by a dashed line. If A has no such hypothesis, it forms one. If the repertoire of building blocks for forming hypotheses is rich enough to represent all possible ways that A could misperceive or perceive situations, then appropriate hypotheses can, in principle, be formed. Once formed, there exist procedures for using them to select corrective actions.[23] Thus a corrective compensatory action for overestimation is to subtract. If the repertoire of building blocks is not rich enough, it can be extended, but this should be done slowly and in small steps.

We ask now how appropriate hypotheses and concepts come into being, particularly as new situations are generated. Man's ability to generate new actions and thus create new situations outstrips his ability to anticipate the outcome of that creativity.[24] But there is creativity of another kind, at another level: man can create images of situations that he has not experienced, that he perhaps cannot bring about or which could not exist. We cannot anticipate the outcome of our imaginative creativity either. It does not follow that we will be able to imagine all the situations we create nor all the ways that we can perceive or misperceive them. But we can take steps to ensure that the gap between what we imagine, wish, and what happens does not widen.

One of the forces tending to widen this gap is that which increases the complexity of the conflict situations faced by the global system. The increasing number of parties tends to increase complexity. For example, the situation over which Arabs and Israelis have conflicting views and interests is made more complex as more parties and spokespersons for each party become involved, and as no two perceive the situation quite the same way. Newer options for interaction and processing of information[25] may enable us to cope with this complexity and keep the gap from widening.

We are more unlikely to have a single or even a few uniformly held beliefs and visions than we need a diffuse scattering.[26] There is probably an optimal balance between diversity and coherence of values, images, perceptions. There are also natural social forces to establish and maintain that balance. Too much diversity begets excessive fragmentation into isolated pockets of belief-holders that soon lose their viability. Too little generates pressures for individual freedom of imagination that quickly expolodes and for consensual decision-making structure.

These same dynamics that bring about mechanisms for controlling conflict also bring about adaptations in these mechanisms to changing conditions. If we can design an organization capable of recommiting resources as needed in the first place, then we can redesign it to improve its recommitment procedures as the demand changes.

It is useful to distinguish between automatic or preplanned and voluntary or concurrently planned processes of controlling conflict. When two parties are in a high state of tension, perhaps in an unstable equilibrium state where any change in the readiness to use force by either party can trigger a series of escalations to disaster, there may not be enough time to detect and correct small errors along the lines we discussed. A pre-programmed automatic process must be triggered to thwart the spiral to disaster as quickly as that unwinds. It means defusing explosive situations after the fuse is lit or shifting the explosion after it has begun.

That requires anticipating explosive situations. Avoiding disastrous surprises is, of course, the responsibility of each party's defense and intelligence establishments. Their capabilities to do this are limited by the number and variety of leading indicators that they can think of and monitor to provide for early warning, and by the capability of adversaries to think of and create situations that cannot be anticipated with such leading indicators. The tendency of parties in conflict to try increasingly to outwit one another in this way could lead to negative trading, to conflict out of control. It could also lead to stable equilibria, analogous to the situation in Figure 15.5. Moreover, the behavior of parties in complex situations may unintentionally have the effect of 'outwitting' an adversary's intelligence.

In any case, increased communication or interaction through debates and use of newer information technologies among the parties may reduce this combat of wits. Each party may reveal more about its planned surprise moves as more of its behavior is available for sampling. It may also reveal more about its images and unplanned or unconsciously steered behavior patterns, as another party may be better able to analyze it.

It is not impossible that the Israelis can learn to change their own visions of what it is like to live with Arabs as genuine neighbors and colleagues, that Arabs can learn to accept and be attracted to the idea of a Jewish homeland, a Zionist state, in their midst. Until this happens, it is not impossible (and more likely) that both can learn to coexist, in full awareness of their conflicting interest in control of the same territory, but with a common interest in controlling conflict by communication rather then bloodshed. It is not impossible that the ruling whites and the majority of blacks in Africa can learn to see the situation from not only one another's perspectives but those of the rest of the world. There are few theoretical limits to human capacities to adapt and to learn, but there are severe practical constraints on the motivation, opportunities, and resources to do so.

Learning is quite possible. That does not imply that it is likely. If it is possible and unlikely, then perhaps there are steps countries can take to increase the likelihood. Could there be institutions that serve countries the way schools serve individuals? Who is to do the learning in the global community, how are they to do it, what is to motivate it, and what factors can make it efficient and effective? These are important questions that must be left for future study.

Is Adaptive Learning Likely and Can It Be Enhanced?

During the past century and a half, only one-tenth of the serious international disputes centered in Europe escalated to full-scale war.[27] I do not know the corresponding ratio for the century and a half preceding that and for comparable earlier periods. If we had such long-term data for the global system (disputes might have shifted from one region of the world to others), then we could check if the ratio has decreased during the course of history. Perhaps the ratio is decreasing right now and perhaps there are deliberate actions that parties or leaders of the global system can take to decrease it further. This would require learning in the sense of forming hypotheses about why some disputes erupted in war while others did not by creating new representations.

It is remarkable how often man did control conflict when he could so easily have lost control. Legislation to control pollution and to curb nuclear testing has been effective. Countries have spontaneously realized the dangers of, and refrained from the use of, nuclear, chemical, and biological weapons. Pricing mechanisms have functioned to some extent to curb energy over-use.

How a system responds to the trap of shifting from trades to negative trades depends greatly on the system's degree of integration. As Puchala points out in his chapter, the degree to which a population is integrated into at least a security community indicates the extent to which an international system is *pluralistic* rather than *amalgamated* to use Deutsch's terminology. In an integrated[28] neighborhood, community or society conflict may even be one of the activities that keeps the parties together, in creative tension, as it were. They need one another to spar, compete, dispute with. Constructive dialectic processes can result from such communities. Thus, New York during the 1965 brownout,[29] which presented a potential trap for passing from trades to negative trades, still responded as an integrated community.

A disintegrated or disintegrating community, however, falls into the trap. In 1977, New York responded to a power blackout with many parties looting stores that rapidly turned many shopping streets into disaster areas to the detriment of nearly all. It was similar to a 'Tragedy of the Commons', without effective controls. There was a shift from positive to negative trades. Similarly, Arab groups in Lebanon fell into the trap because of their weak state of integration. Integration is what enables a system to exist as a unit. According to Deutsch, it is a relationship among parties in which they jointly produce systemic properties which they would separately lack. Integration occurs as the result of adaptive learning through the formation of shared representations that are useful and their use in the control of internal conflict and interaction.

When parties are certain and consistent about what future they deem desirable, or what conditions they consider very undesirable, they learn to attain the desirable and avoid the undesirable. Both the USA and USSR have learned from Pearl Harbor and the Nazi 1941 invasion (Barbarossa) to guard at all costs against massive surprise attack.

In a number of conflicts since the Second World War the system of states faced the danger of a transition to negative trades that was controlled in the nick of time. During the 1948–9 Berlin blockade[30] and the Cuban missile crisis, remarkable control was exerted by all the parties involved. In the Korean War control was weaker, though it still remained remarkably limited. The United States had defined its defense perimeter. This led the North Koreans and the Chinese to believe that the USA would not come to the aid of South Korea. But it was a misperception. The USA erred in letting North Korea and China persist in their misperception. The USA then misperceived China's readiness to come to the aid of North Korea – which China regarded as in its sphere of influence – by crossing the Yalu River. It was a costly lesson for both sides. But there have been few uncontrolled conflicts with China since, possibly because of what was learned. Nor have there been serious uncontrolled conflicts with the USSR, also possibly because of what was learned in Berlin and Cuba. The conflict exists, to be sure, and Khrushchev's boast that the USSR will bury the USA may be made good, not through uncontrolled conflict, but through its development of the BAM,[31] for example. It is one example of shifting arenas of conflict from where strength was concentrated at a distance to where strength is close to the home base, where the pay-off is likely to be greatest. There are, of course, other examples of the USSR deploying strength far away from its home base and this contributes to the danger of uncontrolled conflict.

Many conflicts of political interest are likely to shift from disputes over ownership of material things and territory toward control over services. As Deutsch has pointed out, governments can and should be regarded as services to the governed. In a forthcoming research monograph,[32] Deutsch and I have argued that newer forms of organizing such human services are likely to be more decentralized in the sense that control is likely to be more distributed among service-providers and among clients. As Lijphart points out in his chapter, parties in conflict are more likely to be pluralistic, lacking a single center of authority, and should be perceived as such by other parties.

Deutsch and I have also argued that services should become more responsive and adaptive. We conceptualized decentralization in terms of pluralization, dispersion, functional specialization, feedback facilitation, flatness, delegation, participation in decision-making and in organizational redesign. We argued that organization structures ranking high on all eight dimensions would be more adaptive and responsive.

If we can learn to decentralize, we are likely to learn to develop resources that can be recomitted when and where needed. The use of US air power during the Berlin airlift and the success of the Marshall Plans are good examples. The persistent and clever use of guerilla warfare in the jungles of Vietnam was another example. Israel's ability to mobilize its reserves within forty-eight hours and deploy them to wherever they are needed is another instance.

Perhaps the strongest ground for believing that we will learn to control conflict more wisely is the awareness, concern, and creative thought about the wiser and more humane utilization of knowledge that is spreading throughout the world at all levels.[33] Community self-help groups and neighborhood as well as extended support groups are arising everywhere,[34] perhaps as an adaptive response to the dissolution of the extended family. Continuing and extended education enterprises are starting[35] to complement traditional schools. New social organs that do the thinking for countries much as the brain does the thinking for an individual, organs that would supplant human brains, are likely to evolve, partly because the idea has already taken root and the technology is likely to be available.[36] It is in this social organ, which serves as the nervous system to perform mental functions for the global community, where learning takes place and where control over conflict is exerted.

There has been a confluence of computer and communication technologies.[37] We are also becoming aware that human organizational factors, in managing the resulting information systems, are the paramount barriers to ensuring that these technologies enhance adaptive learning. That is the first step toward overcoming these barriers. These developments are likely to surprise even the most imaginative among us by the suddenness with which they will affect our lives. Procedures that effectively detect and expose lies, treachery, or deceit at high speed and with great reliability may soon be feasible. So are techniques for revealing to users of a system whether his inputs are inconsistent.[38] Newer methods of communication, such as computer conferencing,[39] are opening up new modes somewhere between speech and writing that may amplify the parties' abilities to debate in the sense of Anatol Rapoport, where each party understands the other. Systems to help people to realize that imprecise reasoning and communication is appropriate for some situations, and how to do it, are also new and promising possibilities.[40] All these offer new tools, new options for controlling conflict or at least its study.

If there is any validity to the exaggerated belief that in a complex computerized system anything that can go wrong will, then it is reasonable to postulate a counter-proposition for human systems: If anything can go right, it will. The problem is to give the global system a chance to go right. It would not be unreasonable to develop a pilot system of communication in which some opinion leaders in various countries learn to control conflict by acquiring new or modifying existing images and values in situations of conflict under controlled conditions. This could be done in the context of world models by bringing several groups of specialists into a multilogue.[41] A controlled experiment could be designed to test the hypothesis that learning occurs under those conditions.

Learning, especially as evidenced by the growth of science, seems to be man's greatest achievement and potential. There is no reason, in principle, why adaptive learning cannot apply to the control of conflict in the global system. Adaptive learning by any party requires great effort and will, and it may be costly and unpleasant. Yet it seems to be as much a property of any complex living system as conflict. This belief feeds my hope and conviction that parties in the global system are likely to learn conflict control and eventually 'neither shall they learn war anymore'.[42]

Appendix: Chapter 15

Imagine two parties, 1 and 2, on a collision course. Let V_i denote the event that party i, $i = 1,2$ pays attention (is vigilant, sees the course of the other party as salient and hence tracks it), and assume that it has perfect information. Let p_i denote the probability of V_i. If V_1 and V_2 are statistically independent, the probability of a collision is

$$p_c = (1 - p_1)(1 - p_2).$$

Suppose now that just one evasive action is available to each party and that it is chosen only if the party is on a collision course and knows it. If both choose it, then they are on a new collision course. If neither party pays attention, they collide, an event of probability p_c given above. If both pay attention, they also collide, an event of probability $p_1 p_2$. The probability of collision is

$$p_c' = (1 - p_1)(1 - p_2) + p_1 p_2,$$

which is greater than before, when no evasion was possible. If one pays attention and the other does not, no collision occurs, and this can happen with probability $p_1(1 - p_2) + p_2(1 - p_1) = 1 - p_c'$.

The option for evasive behavior does not always enhance control of a conflict situation. This simple model is readily extended to take into account situations with imperfect information, interdependence, misperception, and learning. It will be developed and reported elsewhere.

Notes: Chapter 15

1 Robert C. North, 'Conflict: political aspects', in *International Encyclopedia of the Social Sciences*, ed. David L. Sills, 2nd edn (New York: Macmillan and The Free Press, 1968, Vol. 3, p. 226.
2 Anatol Rapoport, *Fights, Games and Debates* (Ann Arbor, Mich.: University of

Michigan Press, 1960); and Karl W. Deutsch, *The Analysis of International Relations* (Englewood Cliffs, NJ: Prentice-Hall, 1968), ch. 11.
3 Kenneth N. Waltz, 'Theory of international relations', in *Handbook of Political Science*, ed. Fred I. Greenstein and Nelson W. Polsby (Reading, Mass.: Addison-Wesley, 1975), Vol. 8, pp. 1–85.
4 Major omissions by Waltz include: Kenneth E. Boulding, *Conflict and Defense* (New York: Harper, 1962); Karl W. Deutsch, *The Nerves of Government* (New York: The Free Press, 1963); Herbert C. Kelman (ed.), *International Behavior* (New York: Holt, Rinehart & Winston, 1965); Anatol Rapoport, *Strategy and Conscience* (New York: Harper & Row, 1964); T. C. Schelling, *The Strategy of Conflict* (Cambridge, Mass.: Harvard University Press, 1960); and T. C. Schelling, *Arms and Influence* (New Haven, Conn.: Yale University Press, 1966).
5 Manfred Kochen, 'Cognitive mechanisms', IBM Report, RAP 16, 1960; *idem*, 'Cognitive learning processes: an explication', in *Artificial Intelligence and Heuristic Programming*, ed. N. V. Findler and B. Meltzer (Edinburgh: Edinburgh University Press, 1971); *idem*, 'Representations and algorithms for cognitive learning', *Artificial Intelligence*, vol. 5, no. 3 (Fall 1974), pp. 199–216; *idem*, 'Cognitive science', in *Encyclopedia of Computer Science and Technology*, ed. Jack Belzer, Albert G. Holzman, and Allen Kent (New York: Marcel Dekker, 1976), Vol. 5, pp. 114–45; Manfred Kochen and John Stark, 'Representation and formation of hypotheses in learning programs', in *Proceedings of the International Conference on Cybernetics and Society*, IEEE (November 1978); and Robert P. Abelson and Milton Rosenberg, 'Symbolic psycho-logic: a model of attitudinal cognition', *Behavioral Science*, vol. 3, no. 1 (January 1958), pp. 1–13.
6 Karl W. Deutsch, 'On the learning capacity of large political systems', in *Information for Action*, ed. Manfred Kochen (New York: Academic Press, 1975), p. 76.
7 Lewis F. Richardson, *Arms and Insecurity: A Mathematical Study of the Causes and Origins of War*, ed. Nicolas Rashevsky and Ernesto Trucco (Pittsburgh, Pa: Boxwood Press; and Chicago: Quadrangle Books, 1960); Kenneth E. Boulding, 'Four concepts of conflict theory, in *Power and Conflict in Organizations*, ed. Robert L. Kahn and Elise Boulding (New York: Basic Books, 1964); Anatol Rapoport, 'Approaches to theories of large scale human conflicts', in *Progress in Mental Health*, ed. H. Freeman (London: Churchill, 1969), pp. 35–48; *idem*, 'Game theory and human conflict', in *The Nature of Human Conflict*, ed. E. B. McNeil (Englewood Cliffs, NJ: Prentice-Hall, 1965); *idem*, 'Game theory: strategies for resolving conflicts', in *1970 Britannica Yearbook of Science and the Future*, ed. R. J. Young (Chicago: Encyclopedia Britannica, 1969), pp. 54–63; Michael D. Intriligator and D. L. Brito, 'Formal models of arms races', *Journal of Peace Science*, vol. 2, no. 1 (Spring 1976), pp. 77–88; Nazli Choucri and Robert C. North, 'Dynamics of international conflict: some policy implications of population, resources and technology', *World Politics*, vol. 24, no. 1 (October 1972), pp. 80–122; Raymond Tanter, 'International system and foreign policy approaches: implications for conflict modelling and management', *World Politics*, vol. 24, no. 1 (October 1972), pp. 7–39; Charles A. McClelland, *Theory and the International System* (New York: Macmillan, 1966); and James G. Miller, *Living Systems* (New York: McGraw-Hill, 1978).
8 Robert Jervis, *Perception and Misperception in International Politics* (Princeton, NJ: Princeton University Press, 1976) (he focused on how individual decision-makers learn rather than learning in the global system); *idem*, 'Hypotheses on misperception', *World Politics*, vol. 20, no. 3 (April 1968), pp. 454–79; J. Lynn England, 'Linear learning models for two-party negotiations', *Journal of Conflict Resolution*, vol. 19, no. 4 (December 1975), pp. 682–707; and Raymond Tanter, 'International system and foreign policy approaches', also suggested, in passing, the introduction of reinforcement-type learning theories to explain how event–interaction patterns repeat or change.
9 Edward J. Murray, 'Conflict: psychological aspects', *International Encyclopedia of the Social Sciences*, ed. Sills, Vol. 3, p. 220.
10 Boulding, *Conflict and Defense*.
11 Manfred Kochen, 'Experimental study of hypothesis formation by computer', in *Information Theory*, ed. Colin Cherry (London: Butterworth, 1960); *idem*, 'Adaptive mechanisms in digital concept processing', in *The Growth of Knowledge*, ed. Manfred

Kochen (New York: Wiley, 1967); and Sidney L. Hantler and Manfred Kochen, 'ASP: a program using stored hypotheses to select actions', *Journal of Cybernetics*, vol. 3, no. 3 (July–September 1973), pp. 1–12.
12. Richard Pipes, 'Why the Soviet Union thinks it could fight and win a nuclear war', *Commentary*, vol. 64, no. 1 (July 1977), pp. 21–34. Pipes argues that the USA does not share with effective spokesmen of the USSR the belief that 'war is politics by other means', and that it does not recognize that leaders of the USSR hold this belief either. This kind of asymmetry can lead to dangerous misperceptions.
13. Francisco J. Varela, 'A calculus for self-reference', *International Journal of General Systems*, vol. 2, no. 1 (1975), pp. 5–24. Alker is right when he expresses hope elsewhere in this book that the 'new cybernetics' and general systems theory may show promise of developing in this direction. The notion of self-reference is probably essential for an explication of 'consciousness' as the ability to form hypotheses about a party's ability to form hypotheses. It is, in my view, increasingly important to place greater stress on the role of conscious deliberate and volitional behavior by parties in political conflict.
14. Morton A. Kaplan, *System and Process in International Politics* (New York: Wiley, 1964); Paul Seabury (ed.), *Balance of Power* (New York: Chandler, 1965).
15. Garrett Hardin, 'The Tragedy of the Commons', *Science*, vol. 162, no. 3859 (13 December 1968), pp. 1243–8. See also Garrett Hardin, *Exploring New Ethics for Survival* (New York: Viking Press, 1972).
16. Kenneth E. Boulding, *The Image: Knowledge in Life and Society* (Ann Arbor, Mich.: University of Michigan Press, 1956).
17. Karl W. Deutsch, 'On the learning capacity of large political systems', based on D. O. Hebb, *The Organization of Behavior* (New York: Wiley, 1949); and Ernest R. Hilgard, *Theories of Learning Instruction* (Chicago: University of Chicago Press, 1964).
18. W. H. Thorpe, *Learning and Instinct in Animals* (Cambridge, Mass.: Harvard University Press, 1956), p. 49.
19. Michael Marien, *Societal Directions and Alternatives: A Critical Guide to the Literature* (Lafayette, New York: Information for Policy Design, 1976).
20. Richard Jung, 'Systems of orientation: a revision', Papers in Progress 236A–77, Center for Advanced Study in Theoretical Psychology (Edmonton, Alberta: University of Alberta, 1977); John R. Platt, 'What's ahead for 1990', *The Center Magazine*, vol. 5, no. 4 (1972), pp. 21–8; John R. Platt, Social traps', *American Psychologist*, vol. 28, no. 8 (August 1973), pp. 641–51.
21. Bernard Fischoff, 'Hindsight ≠ foresight: the effect of outcome knowledge on judgment under uncertainty', *ORI Research Bulletin*, vol. 14, no. 13 (Portland: Oregon Research Institute, 1974).
22. G. T. Chaitin, 'Algorithmic information theory', *IBM Journal of Research and Development*, vol. 21, no. 4 (July 1977), pp. 350–9; and H. S. Linstone and M. Turoff (eds), *The Delphi Method: Techniques and Applications* (Reading, Mass.: Addison-Wesley, 1975).
23. Hantler and Kochen, 'ASP: a program using stored hypotheses to select actions'; see also note 5.
24. John Myhill, 'Some philosophical implications of mathematical logic', *Review of Metaphysics*, vol. 6, no. 2 (December 1952), pp. 165–98.
25. *Transnational Associations*, vol. 29, no. 10 (1977); Kochen (ed.), *Information for Action*; and William E. Colby, 'Modern intelligence and information', speech at Harvard University, Cambridge, Massachusetts, 31 October 1977.
26. Karl W. Deutsch, 'Nation and world', in *Contemporary Political Science*, ed. Ithiel de Sola Pool (New York: McGraw-Hill, 1967), ch. 8, p. 215.
27. J. David Singer, private communication, April 1978; it is a curious coincidence that at most 10 per cent of all scientific research publications are considered to contribute to the advancement of knowledge.
28. Rachelle and Donald Warren, *The Neighborhood Organizer's Handbook* (Notre Dame, Ind.: University of Notre Dame Press, 1977). They characterize neighborhoods in terms of their sense of identity or self-image, the extent of interaction within a neighborhood, and the degree to which a neighborhood is linked with outside parties. A neighborhood scoring high on all three dimensions is called integral, in contrast to

an 'anomic' neighborhood that scores low on all three aspects. Social psychiatrists have found the incidence of serious mental illness in a community to be lower in integrated communities. If the cultural artifacts located on the land of a region and the ideas and images that give it unity were taken into account, these concepts of neighborhood could perhaps be extended to apply to the parties – countries, ministries, transnational systems, etc. – that we are discussing.

29 Konrad Kalba, 'Sunglassed citizenry: New York during the blackout', *Planning Comment*, vol. 5, no. 1 (1967), pp. 30–43.
30 Raymond Tanter, *Modelling and Managing International Conflict: The Berlin Crises* (Beverly Hills, Calif.: Sage, 1974).
31 'Baikal-Amur Magistral', a new Russian railroad to replace the Trans-Siberian line; see Theodore Shabad and Victor L. Mote, *Gateway to Siberian Resources (The BAM)* (New York: Halsted Press, 1977).
32 Manfred Kochen and Karl W. Deutsch, *Decentralization: Sketches Toward a Rational Theory* (Cambridge, Mass.: Oelgeschlager, Gunn and Hain; Königstein/Ts.: Anton Hain, 1980).
33 Manfred Kochen, 'WISE: A world information synthesis and encyclopaedia', *Journal of Documentation*, vol. 28, no. 4 (December 1972), pp. 322–43.
34 Manfred Kochen and Joseph Donohue (eds), *Information for the Community* (Chicago: American Library Association, 1976).
35 Joe G. Eisley and Larry G. Coppard, *Extending Opportunities for Graduate Education in Michigan*, final report (Ann Arbor, Mich.: University of Michigan, 1977).
36 This idea is developed and debated more carefully in Kochen (ed.), *Information for Action*. Karl Deutsch and the author proposed the acronym WISE (World Information Synthesis and Encyclopedia) as the name for a movement and an emergent social organ – a realization of H. G. Wells's 'world brain' – that serves communities the way the brain serves an individual and that supplants brains; an improved acronym, WISDOM (Worldwide Intelligence Service for the Development of Omniscience in Mankind), due to Theodore C. Larson, has now replaced WISE.
37 This confluence was pointed out by the Program on Information Resources Policy, *Information Resources Policy*, vol. 1 (Cambridge, Mass.: Harvard University Annual Report, 1976–7), pp. 1–48. Oettinger coined the term 'compucnications' to denote the fusion between communication and computer technology that is now taking place. Its application to the study of international relations implies extending and bringing up on-line for real-world use, information systems such as CACIS. Hayward R. Alker, Jr, and Cheryl Christensen, 'From causal modelling to artificial intelligence: the evolution of a US peace-making simulation', in *Experimentation and Simulation in Political Science*, ed. Jean A. Laponce and Paul Smoker (Toronto: University of Toronto Press, 1972), pp. 177–224; and Harold Guetzkow, 'An incomplete history of fifteen short years in simulating international processes', in *Quantitative International Politics: An Appraisal*, ed. Francis W. Hoole and Dina A. Zinnes (New York: Praeger, 1976), pp. 247–58.
38 Manfred Kochen, 'Adaptive mechanisms in digital "concept" processing', *Proceedings of the Joint Automatic Control Conference*, American Institute for Electrical Engineers (1962).
39 Robin Crickman and Manfred Kochen, 'Citizen participation through consumer conferencing', to appear in *Technological Forecasting and Social Change*; and Robert H. Kupperman, Richard H. Wilcox, and Harvey A. Smith, 'Crisis management: some opportunities', *Science*, vol. 187, no. 4175 (7 February 1975); pp. 401–10.
40 Brian R. Gaines and L. F. Kohout, 'The fuzzy decade: a bibliography of fuzzy systems and closely related topics', *International Journal of Man-Machine Studies*, vol. 9, no. 1 (January 1977), pp. 1–68.
41 Manfred Kochen, 'Information systems for world models', in *Problems of World Modeling: Political and Social Implications*, ed. Karl W. Deutsch, Bruno Fritsch, Hélio Jaguaribe, and Andrei S. Markovits (Cambridge, Mass.: Ballinger, 1977), pp. 379–99.
42 Isaiah 2:4. From that same book (Isaiah 1:18) comes one of President Johnson's guiding quotes, 'Come now, and let us reason together', something he ironically left for the administration of President Nixon for controlling the Vietnam conflict.

16

Periodicity, Inexorability, and Steersmanship in International War

J. DAVID SINGER and THOMAS CUSACK

In reading, conversing, and collaborating with Karl Deutsch over the years, one finds certain themes to which he returns again and again. Despite the extraordinary breadth and depth of his conceptual repertoire, there seem to be a few basic concepts that are essential to his over-all paradigm. One of these is that of steersmanship. Borrowed from cybernetics and creatively developed by Deutsch in his frequent conversations with Wiener and others, the steersmanship concept emphasizes that we are not mere ships on the ocean of history. Rather, as our knowledge of the ocean, the vessel, and the self develop, we are increasingly able to estimate which course will bring us to our destination with the greatest facility.

Integral to this notion, of course – and implicit in the very metaphor – is awareness of the limits on our autonomy. The currents and waves of the oceans, not to mention the visibility and positioning of the stars that we steer by, are essentially beyond our control, and the craft in which we travel, be it fragile or sturdy, is largely inherited. But the more we know of geography, the more precisely we can set our objective; the better we comprehend the seas, the more likely we are to stay afloat; and the keener our mastery of navigation, the straighter will be our path.

The ways in which we comprehend and evaluate these limits will inevitably affect our orientation toward coping with them. We can set out on our voyage with an outlook that runs the gamut from the Ancient Mariner and the Flying Dutchman, through Beowulf, to the Owl and the Pussycat; each such orientation helps determine the effort we will make to comprehend and to control. Whether it be the seas, the heavens, the gods, or ourselves, humans have generally tried to make sense of it all. Confronted with what might otherwise be a mysterious conundrum or a vast, buzzing welter, we have devised all sorts of models and metaphors as a means of imposing coherence.[1] Our earlier metaphors – the wheel, the lever, the pyramid, the river – rested largely on observation and experience, but with increasing sophistication we turned to more complex and less directly experienced metaphors of an organic or a cybernetic sort.[2] Further, as our focus shifted from the 'natural' to the 'artificial world' – to use Simon's unfortunate distinction between physical and social phenomena[3] – these metaphors could be as stochastic as the capricious gods and as deterministic as predestination.

Cycles and their Implications

Whatever model or metaphor one chooses in order to cope with the complexities in our environment, certain assumptions are carried with it, and certain implications inhere. And among these assumptions, one of the most critical is that which reflects our views on the temporal unfolding of human experience. We may, for example, see social history as a long road to ultimate catastrophe, or as an inexorable path of continued progress, or as highly cyclical and perhaps even dialectic, or as a sequence of meaningless perturbations, to name the more obvious possibilities.

Further, each such assumed model carries with it certain notions of appropriate human response, particularly *vis-à-vis* the questions of predictability and controllability. If we lean toward secular trend models of human history (be they persistently toward *or* away from the specified conditions), we often accept notions of a teleological sort, assigning some cosmic purpose to it all. While such models may increase our belief in social *predictability*, the more extreme versions of them seldom encourage efforts to intervene in the process or to *control* our collective destiny. Similarly, assumptions of a more chaotic sort will probably not encourage efforts to understand or predict, but they need not – depending on the degree of fatalism that lies behind the stochastic model – discourage efforts at control. Again, if one's model of social reality is built around cycles and periodicities, prediction becomes a major preoccupation, but intervention seems less justified.

While most social scientists and some historians see the human experience as an elusive mix of these three – trends, cycles, and perturbations – we would suggest that discovering the nature of that mix is not only intellectually possible, but worth pursuing for pragmatic reasons. That is, the more fully we can ascertain how much of our fate is determined by Fate and how our chances are settled by Chance, the more accurately we can estimate how much control remains in our own hands. This is not, of course, to suggest that all of humanity can readily intervene in a highly co-ordinated fashion to head off one or another type of catastrophe. The plethora of conflicting interests that must be reconciled today is not dramatically different from those that, in years gone by, helped to shape the very state of affairs, be it menacing or benign, that confronts us in the present. But having a reasonable comprehension of the degree of conscious intervention that remains available, as well as which interventions are likely to produce which outcomes, could at least improve the odds. When neither of these is adequately understood, we are apt to become poker players operating in the dark, rather than aware and competent steersmen.

When it comes to war – a type of social event that is clearly the result of complex and interdependent processes – the tendency to fall back on one or another of these simple models is particularly acute. Whether we are practitioners of foreign affairs, scholars, or laymen, we suspect that the road to war is a murky and confusing one, and as a result we are all too prone to embrace one of the above models or metaphors. From among the inexorable trend (toward or away), the cyclical, and the stochastic models, modern man seems to prefer the cyclical. The trend model seems too teleological and the stochastic model seems too nihilistic, whereas the cyclical one has a certain aura of *a priori* plausibility in the twentieth century. After all, who amongst us is eager to embrace the implicit assumption of a largely beneficent, or essentially malevolent, or utterly capricious cosmos? Somehow, the notion that war comes and goes with some regularity seems to be the assumption that is least offensive to contemporary sensibilities.

Turning, then, from ontological speculation to empirical investigation, we will examine here the evidence and the reasoning that might support the assumption of cycles or periodicity in the incidence of international war. At the outset, we note that any such pattern may be sought or identified at several levels of social aggregation. The patterns could obtain at the systemic level, at the regional level, or at the national level, and the evidence found at one need not necessarily obtain at another. Thus, the intervals between the war experiences of the separate nations could be quite random, but when we look at the regional or global system level, there could emerge a clear regularity. That is, if we ignore the identity or location of the nations at war in a given year and ask only whether – somewhere in the system – war will occur at some fixed interval, the answer can be affirmative even though each nation's experiences occur in a highly irregular fashion. For the moment, then, we look only at the nation level, and will return to that of the international system later in the discussion.

Before examining the evidence, however, we might consider several of the possible reasons for expecting the war–peace–war cycle to be a strong and constant one for the nations. Leaving aside those who suspect that it is inherent in human nature or part of the cosmic plan, we find a few macrosocial models and a somewhat greater number of microsocial (and essential social-psychological) reasons for expecting such periodicity. At the macrosocial level, perhaps the most familar argument is that of the business cycle. Whether one proceeds from the perspective of a Ricardo, a Keynes, or a Marx, it is possible to posit the economic connection. That is, we may differ in our explanations of what 'causes' the business cycle, but nevertheless agree that it brings war ineluctably in its wake. One school of thought would have wars occurring near the peak,[4] another on the down side,[5] another at the trough,[6] and others on the rising side.[7] For each of these schools of thought, the link between one or another of the business cycles and war is somewhat different, but each tends to view fluctuations in national or global economic activity as a necessary and/or sufficient condition for the onset of war.

Another macro-level argument is the demographic one. Here, we note that wars are fought largely by young males, often in the train of decisions taken by older males. At the close of war, those who ordered it begin to retire or die, and those who fought in it move into positions of some influence. The former no longer *can* order it and the latter *will* not order it, given their experiences. But as memories of destruction are gradually replaced – by memories either of glory and victory, or of humiliation and defeat – and as a new generation of warriors comes of age, the nation once again is ready to resume the deadly cycle.

Then there are the more micro-level models, of which two are illustrative. First, there is David McClelland's 'Love and War' model,[8] which begins with the assumption of cycles in the cultural life of nations. These are the familiar need for affiliation, need for achievement, and need for power, whose existence has been demonstrated in several nations during certain periods, recent as well as remote.[9] Put simply, when the need for affiliation is on the rise in a nation, those who experience it most will soon recognize (and try to fulfill) the need for power as a means to domestic social reform. But given the incompatibility of these two norms, power soon dominates affiliative and altruistic concerns, leads to a more restrictive sense of in-group affiliation, and reinforces the concomitant tendency toward out-group hostility. Given the ubiquitousness of foreign provocation and opportunity, this hostility can readily lead to war, which leaves in its wake a new series of domestic inequities, thus generating yet another rise in the need for affiliation and thence for power at home, and so on to the next cycle.

Another social-psychological model pointing toward cyclical war involvement patterns is that of Frank Klingberg,[10] focusing on the shifts from isolationist to interventionist foreign policies on the part of the United States. After adducing some historical evidence for the existence of this periodicity, he goes on to suggest the psychological factors that might account for it. The introverted orientation that precedes and is associated with the isolationist period usually succumbs to the need for more action, new experiences and challenges, and a tendency toward national assertiveness. This shift to a more extroverted mood usually brings a more aggressive and interventionist policy in its wake, often culminating in war. But then there is 'the reaction to a long period of strain and tension – the need for a period of rest and relaxation'[11] and soon the nation has reverted to a more passive and less war-prone set of policies.

There is, as we might expect, other speculation and some mixed evidence as to why national war experiences should come and go in a cyclical pattern, from sun-spots[12] to grain and livestock cycles, to alternations between liberal and conservative regimes, to surges in technological innovation. But as is all too frequent in the social sciences, much of this speculation and model-building may be premature or worse. That is, should we invest in the effort to account for a particularly intriguing pattern of phenomena when it is not at all clear that such a pattern – however plausible – even obtains? Thus, let us shift now to the effort to ascertain whether or not there is indeed some periodicity in the war experience of the nations.

Examining the Evidence

Given the difficulties of comparing, combining, and integrating the results of macrosocial research – thanks to the limited and differing empirical domains from which we generalize, as well as the differing and often idiosyncratic ways in which we measure our variables – it might be appropriate to treat these two matters before examining the evidence adduced here.

The Empirical Domain and the Indicators

As to the temporal domain, we embrace in this study the same 150-year period from the Congress of Vienna up through 1965 that has characterized almost all investigations of the Correlates of War Project, with plans to extend that span up through the 1970s in future investigations. Regarding the nations under study here, we restrict ourselves to the major powers as defined by the consensus of diplomatic historians codified by the project.[13]

As Table 16.1 makes clear, industrial productivity or large population alone does not suffice for major power status. A variety of diplomatic, political, military, and economic attributes is essential, but the most obvious one is that which concerns us particularly in the study at hand: the ability to wage war frequently, and to win most of those wars. Thus we include in our population here the nations and years listed in the table. To this awesome array of relatively successful warriors, we add the Ottoman Empire/Turkey for the entire period 1816–1965, even though it was treated neither by the other powers of the time nor by most subsequent historians as a full-fledged member of the club. Although its power was on the wane during most of the period under study, Turkey fought seventeen international wars, of which eleven were interstate and six extrasystemic (colonial or imperial), making her the third most war-prone nation in post-Napoleonic history. This factor alone has led some scholars to classify Turkey as a major power up through the First World War, despite being on the losing side in six of the eleven interstate wars. In any event, all of our analyses have been run both with and without Turkey, and when her exclusion makes a difference in the generalizations we will so indicate.

Table 16.1 *The Major Powers and Their War Experience, 1816–1965*

	Years as major power	Number of wars	
		International	Interstate
United Kingdom	1816–1965	19	7
France	1816–1940; 1945–1965	19	12
Russia/USSR	1816–1965	15	10
Prussia/Germany	1816–1918; 1925–1945	6	6
Austria–Hungary	1816–1918	8	6
Italy	1860–1943	12	11
United States	1899–1965	5	4
Japan	1895–1945	7	7
China	1950–1965	3	2

Shifting from the years and the nations to the events, our population of cases begins with all international wars fought by the major powers when they were in the select class. But we also include the most recent war they experienced prior to moving into major power status, with the *ad hoc* exception of China, since it underwent a dramatic revolution between the close of the Second World War and its achievement of major power status in the crucible of the Korean War.

As to the two types of war, an interstate war is an episode of sustained combat engaging at least one sovereign state member of the system on each side, and leading to at least 1,000 battle-connected fatalities. By extrasystemic wars, we mean those in which the adversary of the major power was not a sovereign state, but a national political entity whose political and legal status was less than that of full sovereignty. The detailed coding rules, rationale, and resulting data are reported in *The Wages of War*.[14] We combine extrasystemic and interstate wars to arrive at the category of all international wars, and once again we will run our analyses both ways: for interstate wars only, as well as for all international wars combined. The results will always be reported for the combined category, but if they differ appreciably when interstate wars only are analyzed, those differences will be noted.

Turning next to the indicators that will be used in our search for periodicities in major power war participation, there are three important variables: (1) intervals; (2) outcomes; and (3) costs. As to intervals, our most frequently used indicator is that of years between the termination of one war experience and the onset of the following one. But as before, it is essential to assure that our findings are not an artifact of our measurement procedures, and we therefore also run our analyses using the longer interval: that which extends from the onset of the prior war to the onset of the subsequent one. If the longer of the two indicators produces appreciably different results, this will be duly reported.

By outcome, we mean simply whether the participant was on the victorious or defeated side; in only one case (the Korean War of 1950–3) was the outcome classified as a draw. While the coding criteria here are 'softer' than in most of our variables, the scholarly consensus was most impressive, reflecting a collective judgement as to which side enjoyed the dominant role in negotiating or imposing the terms of the armistice and the peace that allegedly followed.

By costs, we mean the damage sustained, and as one general indicator, we find battle-connected fatalities amongst combat personnel sufficiently valid; we label this the severity of the experience. But since some wars are short but bloody and others are longer but less severe, we also use an indicator of magnitude: the war months invested by the protagonist. Finally, just to be sure, we measure war costs in terms of two intensity ratios. One of these is battle-connected deaths per war month and the other is battle-connected deaths *per capita*, with the denominator reflecting the prewar population of the nation as a whole.

The Constant Probability Model of War Re-Entry

Having now summarized the empirical domain against which we hope to generalize, and the ways in which our variables are measured, let us return to the substantive questions that concern us here. The first question is that of the intervals between major power war experiences: are they the result of certain probabilities that rise or fall as time passes since the prior war? Or do they occur with more or less equal probabilities in *any* postwar year, regardless of the passage of time? To the extent that subsequent war experiences show a constant relative frequency in the ensuing years, we can infer that the passage of time has neither an enhancing nor a diminishing effect on the likelihood of another war entry. And to the extent that these relative frequencies increase and/or decrease across repetitive fixed intervals with the passage of time, we can infer that some cyclical process is at work.

Among the models that would reflect a constant probability of re-entry into war, regardless of the passage of time, is the exponential model,[15] and the better the fit between the historically observed distribution of interwar intervals and that predicted by the exponential model, the more readily we can reject the hypothesis that some periodicity inheres in the war-to-war histories of the major powers. This particular model is, of course, functionally equivalent to the better-known Poisson model in that the latter would predict (or in this case, post-dict) a random distribution of the interwar intervals, and to get such a distribution, the probability of a given nation entering into a new war would have to be independent of the length of the interval since its prior war. But since our concern is not with discrete phenomena, such as the frequency of each of a given class of events, but with the distribution of continuous temporal distances between those discretely measured phenomena of sequential war experience, the exponential model is most appropriate.

The first step in examining the fit between the predicted and observed number of war entries that occur during successive five-year periods is to calculate the number predicted by the exponential distribution model. The equation used for the calculation of the probability density is: $\int(X) = \theta e^{-\theta x}$, if $X \geq 0$, and where X is the time interval between war experiences, e is the base of the natural log, and θ is the estimated parameter of the distribution. But when, as occasionally occurs, X is less than 0 because of the nation's entry into a new war while still engaged in an earlier one, $\int X(X) = 0$. In any event, the value of θ is the inverse of the expected value – that is, the mean – of the *observed* distribution.

The probability that we will find an interval of a length that is greater than or equal to a, and less than or equal to b, is given by the following formula:

$$P_x\{a \leq X \leq b\} = e^{\theta a} - e^{\theta b}$$

Thus, if we wanted to know the probability that an interval between wars was between one and three years, and our estimate of θ was equal to 0.20, the following would hold:

$$P_x\{1 \leq X \leq 3\} = e^{-(0.20)1} - e^{-(0.20)3} = 0.27$$

So much, then, for the constant probability model, and why we might expect systematic deviations from it. Let us turn now to the empirical evidence and the extent to which such expectations are borne out by the historical patterns.

Passage of Time and the Probability of War Re-Entry

We turn, then, to the data summaries by which we can examine the validity of the null hypothesis, which states that the distribution of the observed interwar intervals for the major powers will be identical to that predicted by the exponential model, given the number of cases and the average length of these observed intervals. To cover the possibility that our patterns might differ if we look not only at *all* their international war experiences but at their interstate ones only, as well as not only the intervals from termination to onset but also from onset to onset, we need four different tabulations, as shown in Tables 16.2 and 16.3.

Looking first at the 101 cases in which a major power went from one interstate or extrasystemic war to another (i.e. all international wars), we find a rather close fit between the distribution of intervals predicted by the exponential model and the distribution that was actually observed. Whether the interval is measured from the *termination* of the first war to the onset of the second, or from one onset to the next, the significance of the chi-square values (0·20–0·10 and 0·50–0·30) indicates that there is little difference between the observed pattern and that predicted by the exponential model. In other words, the passage of time since the prior war experience seems to have little effect on the likelihood that the typical major power will soon find itself at war again; that historical likelihood remained constant, regardless of how long ago the previous war occurred.

Shifting now to the more restricted population of wars – those sixty-six fought against other sovereign states, be they major powers or not – we find a somewhat more ambiguous pattern. In the analysis of interstate war re-entries, when we measure from the *onset* of one war to the onset of the next (in the right hand column), the exponential model

Table 16.2 *Distribution of intervals between* all *international war experiences, compared to those predicted by exponential model (N = 101)*

Interval from termination to onset	No. of cases observed	No. of cases predicted	Interval from onset to onset	No. of cases observed	No. of cases predicted
<5	58	51	<5	50	44
6–10	13	25	6–10	17	25
11–15	14	13	11–15	13	14
16–20	7	6	16–20	10	8
21–25	4	3	21–25	4	4
26–30	3	2	26–30	4	2
>30	2	1	31–35	1	2
			>35	2	2

$\theta = 0·14$; $\chi^2 = 8·76$; $p = 0·20$–$0·10$ ‖ $\theta = 0·12$; $\chi^2 = 7·01$; $p = 0·50$–$0·30$

Table 16.3 *Distribution of intervals between interstate war experiences, compared to those predicted by exponential model (N = 66)*

Interval from termination to onset	No. of cases observed	No. of cases predicted	Interval from onset to onset	No. of cases observed	No. of cases predicted
5	31	23	5	25	21
6–10	9	15	6–10	9	14
11–15	5	10	11–15	8	10
16–20	3	6	16–20	5	7
21–25	10	4	21–25	6	5
26–30	4	3	26–30	8	3
31–35	0	2	31–35	1	2
36–40	0	1	36–40	0	2
40	4	2	41–45	1	1
			45	3	2

$\theta = 0.09$; $X^2 = 22.62$; $p = 0.01–0.00$ || $\theta = 0.08$; $X^2 = 14.00$; $p = 0.20–0.10$

Note: In this, as well as several other tables, the predicted number of cases appears to increase in the final half-decade, but this is merely a result of combining several such periods at the far end of the scale.

again does a fair job of predicting the re-entry rates that were actually observed. That is, the chi-square value of 14 is sufficiently insignificant (0·20–0·10) to justify rejecting the hypothesis that there is a strong difference between the predicted and observed distributions.

But when we return to the more intuitively reasonable cutting-point – from *termination* to onset (as on the left) – the significance level (0·01–0·00) is strong enough to suggest a distribution of observed interwar intervals different from those predicted by the model. Rather, we find a distinct bimodal distribution, with thirty-one re-entries within five years after the termination (compared to the twenty-three predicted by the model), then three periods with fewer re-entries than predicted, and then ten in the fifth half-decade, against the four predicted. While the unexpectedly high frequency of quick re-entries offers no support for

Table 16.4 *Distribution of intervals between termination and onset of interstate war experiences, with the eleven First and Second World War cases omitted (N = 55)*

	No. of cases observed	No. of cases predicted
5	27	20
6–10	8	10
11–15	4	6
16–20	3	5
21–25	5	4
26–30	4	3
31–35	0	2
36–40	0	2
40	4	3

$\theta = 0.09$; $X^2 = 8.49$; $p = 0.50–0.25$

the periodicity hypothesis, the high frequency during the twenty-one to twenty-five year span *would* seem to support that interpretation. However, a glance at the raw data reminds us that five of these ten re-entries are accounted for by the interval between the World Wars, and one suspects that this one case accounts for much of the belief that wars are cyclical. As a matter of fact, when the analysis is re-run without the eleven World War cases (Table 16.4), the chi-square value increases to 8·49, further supporting the equal interval hypothesis. In sum, any theoretical proposition that rests so heavily on a single set of outliers is not to be taken too literally.

Victory, Defeat, and the Probability of War Re-Entry

If the likelihood of getting into war in a given month or year is independent of *when* the last war was fought, is it possible that other attributes of the last war might be affecting this likelihood? If not the interval since the prior war, might it be, for example, its outcome in terms of victory or defeat, or its costs in battle fatalities? This certainly seems to be a reasonable question, and the answers are far from obvious. That is, victory in a prior war could certainly be a rewarding and reinforcing experience, making for more adventurous and war-accepting, if not war-seeking, policies in the aftermath of victory. Conversely, defeat could produce national resentment and 'revanchism', with early war re-entry again an all-too-likely event. Similarly, if the battle fatalities in the prior war were relatively few, this could reduce the inhibitions that usually follow very high casualty levels. But once more, the greater the losses in one war, the more eager some will be to avenge those losses. And, to complicate things further, a power can experience all possible combinations: victory with low or high fatalities, or defeat with low or high fatalities.

Turning first to the matter of outcome and its effect on the interval until the power's next war experience, we note in Table 16.5 that suffering military defeat seems to have no effect either way. The closeness of the distribution of war intervals actually observed to those predicted by the exponential, constant probability models tells us that

Table 16.5 *Distribution of intervals between military defeats and next experience in all international and in interstate wars, compared to those predicted by exponential model (N = 27 + 16)*

Interval from termination to onset, all wars	No. of cases observed	No. of cases predicted	Interval from termination to onset, interstate wars	No. of cases observed	No. of cases predicted
5	15	15	5	8	6
6–10	4	7	6–10	2	4
11–15	4	3	11–15	1	2
15	4	2	16–20	1	2
			20	4	3

$\theta = 0.17$; $X^2 = 3.18$; $p = 0.50$–0.40 || $\theta = 0.09$; $X^2 = 3.42$; $p = 0.50$–0.40

Table 16.6 *Distribution of intervals between military victories and next experience in all international and in interstate wars, compared to those predicted by exponential model (N = 71 + 47)*

Interval from termination to onset, all wars	No. of cases observed	No. of cases predicted	Interval from termination to onset, interstate wars	No. of cases observed	No. of cases predicted
5	40	34	5	21	16
6–10	9	18	6–10	6	10
11–15	10	9	11–15	4	7
16–20	4	5	16–20	2	5
21–25	3	3	21–25	7	3
26–30	3	1	26–30	4	2
30	2	2	31–35	0	1
			35	3	3

$\theta = 0.13$; $\chi^2 = 8.99$; $p = 0.20–0.10$ ∥ $\theta = 0.08$; $\chi^2 = 14.56$; $p = 0.05$

military defeat makes a major power neither more nor less likely to get into another war quickly. Neither the positive nor the negative reinforcement effect arises out of defeat, and the same holds true whether we look at all international war experiences or at interstate wars alone.

As to the effects of victory, the picture is a bit less clear, as Table 16.6 indicates. While the distribution of intervals between military victory and the next war is relatively close to that predicted by the model, there is – for all such war experiences and for interstate wars alone – a discernible propensity toward early re-entry into war. The model leads us to expect thirty-four and sixteen such entries respectively, but we actually observe forty and twenty-one cases in which the victorious nation is back at war within five years. Also deviating from the expected is the number of re-entries during the twenty-one to twenty-five year interval following victory in interstate war: seven as against the three that were predicted.

Another way to look at this is to compare (Table 16.7) the average intervals for the victorious war participants against those for powers that were defeated, and ascertain whether the differences are large enough to

Table 16.7 *Differences between interwar intervals of victorious and defeated powers*

		Victorious	Defeated	
Interwar intervals, all wars, termination to onset	mean: variation: N:	7·80 90·48 71	5·90 56·48 27	$t = 0.93$ $p = 0.35$
Interwar intervals, interstate, termination to onset	mean: variation: N:	12·44 177·39 47	10·79 172·91 16	$t = 0.43$ $p = 0.67$

have occurred by chance alone. Whether we compare these means for all war experiences or for interstate wars alone, the figures are quite close. As the significance levels show, differences between 7·8 and 5·9 and between 12·4 and 10·8 are sufficiently low to have occurred by chance alone.

Fatalities, Duration, and the Probability of War Re-Entry

An equally plausible factor, when it comes to predicting the war re-entry patterns of the major powers, is that of the *cost* of the prior war experience. Regardless of which side emerges victorious, each participant engages in combat for some number of months and loses some fraction of its population in the hostilities that ensue, and it is reasonable to expect the duration and casualty levels to affect its propensity to fight again in the near future. But as before, there is no obvious and compelling *a priori* expectation as to the most likely direction of the relationship. If the costs of the war were high, we *could* expect the memory of such devastation and the need to recuperate to have a fairly long delaying effect, but we could also expect the drive for revenge to stimulate rather rapid re-entry into war. And if the costs were low, with no inhibiting memory of devastation, war *could* become an acceptable option early on; but these low costs would also predict a low drive for revenge.

Before checking these equally plausible expectations against the historical evidence, let us recapitulate the indicators of cost that we will use. The most valid one would seem to be that of battle-connected fatalities measured in absolute terms, and the second might be that of war duration. A third and fourth might be the 'intensity' of that prior war experience, as measured first by fatalities per capita and secondly by fatalities per month.

What does the evidence suggest using these four indicators? Very simply, Table 16.8 contains not a single statistically significant correlation between any of these indicators and the interwar intervals of the powers. Whether we look at all 101 international war experiences, or the 66 interstate wars only, the product-moment coefficients range from 0·5 to 0·12 for the fatality indicators, and from 0·04 to 0·14 when the prior war's duration is used to reflect the war's cost. In other words, battle fatalities have a very slight prolonging effect and nation months had a very slight foreshortening effect on the interwar intervals.

Table 16.8 Product-moment correlations between indicators of costs of prior war and length of interval to next war

	Intervals for all wars (N = 101)	Intervals for interstate wars (N = 66)
Battle deaths	0·07	0·05
Battle deaths/capita	0·12	0·10
Nation-months	−0·14	−0·04
Battle deaths/nation-month	0·07	0·05

The Combined Effects of Outcome and Cost

If the separate effects of outcome and cost on interwar intervals are negligible, what about the *combined* effects? As Table 16.9 shows, the pattern continues to hold when we look at those war experiences that ended in military *victory*; this desirable outcome has little impact upon the effects of either fatalities or duration. But *defeat* in the prior war combines with the costs of that war in a relatively clear fashion. More specifically, we find that the greater the cost in nation-months, the *shorter* the interval until the next war, and the pattern is stronger for all types of war experience than for those associated with interstate wars alone.

Conversely, it turns out that the greater the battle fatalities sustained in defeat, the *longer* will be the interval before re-entry into war; again, this relationship is especially clear when we include the colonial and imperial war experiences as well as the interstate wars. Worth noting here is the fact that interwar intervals are especially lengthened by prior war experiences that were both severe and brief. One of the strongest associations in Table 16.9 is that with our intensity measure of battle deaths per nation-month (0·38), and if we exclude Turkey from the analysis, this coefficient rises to 0·53.

An interesting implication arises out of this finding. If high battle death levels in short wars clearly lengthen the interval until a defeated power again goes to war, it is reasonable to ask whether the length of that interval has – in turn – any effect on the severity, duration, or intensity of that next war when it finally occurs. As Table 16.10 shows clearly, the answer is affirmative, with the length of the interwar interval correlating 0·29 with the battle death level for the next war and 0·25 with the intensity measure of battle deaths per million population. And if we exclude Turkey, the coefficients again rise, to 0·39 and 0·36 respectively, significant at the 0·001 level.

We now have a rather suggestive chain of relationships, at least for those powers that suffer defeat in a given war. That is, Table 16.9

Table 16.9 *Product-moment correlations between indicators of costs of prior war ending in victory or defeat, and length of interval to next war*

	Victorious in Prior War		Defeated in Prior War	
	Interval for all wars (N = 71)	Interval for interstate wars (N = 47)	Intervals for all wars (N = 27)	Intervals for interstate wars (N = 16)
Battle deaths	0·04	0·03	0·40**	0·20
Battle deaths/capita	0·08	0·09	0·29	0·12
Nation-months	−0·02	0·02	−0·33*	−0·12
Battle deaths/nation-month	0·03	0·01	0·38**	0·31

*Significant at 0·10 level.
**Significant at 0·05 level.

Table 16.10 *Product-moment correlations between the interwar interval and the costs of the subsequent war*

	Interval since first war for all powers	Interval since first war, excluding Turkish cases
Battle deaths	0·29****	0·39****
Battle deaths/capita	0·25***	0·36****
Nation-months	0·19**	0·20**
Battle deaths/nation-month	0·21**	0·36****

**Significant at 0·05 level.
***Significant at 0·01 level.
****Significant at 0·001 level.

indicates that the more intense the costs of that war in battle deaths per nation-month, the greater the interval to the next war, and Table 16.10 indicates that the greater that interval, the greater the intensity of the *next* war experience.

Thus, one might discern the glimmerings of a slow and long-run secular trend in the war histories of the major powers. When they suffer military defeat, and pay a high price in battle deaths per month of war, they tend to avoid war for a longer time, and the longer they wait, the more intense the next war experience will be. It follows that if we wait long enough and there are more defeated than victorious powers in each successive war, the phenomenon might eventually disappear. While this would be a logical possibility if there are more powers on the losing side, the historical pattern – not surprisingly[16] – shows that the *victorious* side usually is more numerous. In any event, we can hardly pin our hopes on so slender a reed. To do so would be to repeat the naive error of Bloch[17] who – quite correctly – predicted the effects of weapons technology on the conduct of war and on the costs of preparing for war. But, like all too many social scientists from his epoch to ours, he assumed that awareness of these implications would lead us to seek other and more adaptive modes of conflict resolution. Knowledge may be *necessary* for rational human intervention, but the bloody pages of international history remind us that it is hardly *sufficient*.

Alternative Interpretations

Having found no discernible periodicity here in the intervals between major power war experiences, may we conclude more generally that there is no periodicity in international war since the Congress of Vienna? Not quite yet. First of all, there may be other and less obvious periodicities in the war experience of these nations, and secondly, it could be that the level at which to look is the systemic rather than the individual states.

Before attending to these possibilities, however, we digress long enough to treat the logical possibility that because our 'sample' is not representative, we might have overlooked such a periodicity in the war experience of other classes of nations. But a moment's consideration reminds us that if these particularly war-prone major powers, experiencing an average of 0·95 wars per decade, show no periodicity, there is little likelihood that the minor powers, with an average of fewer than 0·21 per decade, could show any periodicity in as brief a period as a century and a half.

Turning then to other possible periodicities in major power war, four considerations arise. One is that there exists a cyclical pattern, but without the constant length intervals; this could occur if national war experiences occurred in clusters of two or three in close sequence, followed by a much longer interval and then the next cluster. We find nothing in our data to support this surmise. Secondly, it could be that the periodicity being measured should not be the simple *occurrence* of war, but its magnitude or severity. That is, one could hypothesize that armed conflict, above as well as below the war threshold, is a relatively constant characteristic of the major powers' existence, but that peaks of particularly large amounts of war occur at regular intervals. Using spectral analysis and related techniques, we found no evidence for such, whether we looked at the battle death or the nation-month indicators.[18]

A third possibility in this context is that we have defined periodicity in too conventional a manner. Ordinarily, we mean approximately equal time-intervals between peaks and/or troughs of approximately equal magnitude, but one could extend the definition somewhat. And one possibility might be to define the intervals, not in fixed units of time alone, but these units weighted or multiplied by factors such as the outcome or cost of the prior war experience. But since our procedures are functionally equivalent to that sort of measurement, we can pretty clearly rule out such a possibility.

Turning to a fourth possibility, could it be that our search is at the wrong level of aggregation, and that the theoretically interesting question is whether there is a cyclical pattern of warfare when we move up to the systemic level? Somewhat like such physical phenomena as Brownian motion, one finds randomness in the behavior of each component, but a clearly discernible pattern at the aggregated level. In an earlier investigation we looked into this possibility from several perspectives, and found only the weakest suggestion of periodicity in system-level warfare.[19] That is, using spectral analysis and related techniques, we found no cyclical pattern between occurrences (measuring from onset to onset as well as from termination to onset), but a barely discernible one when measuring from peak to peak in terms of nation-months of war under way. Further, the periodicity was sufficiently ambiguous that we could only infer that it ranges between twenty and forty years.

We pursue this question farther than might seem necessary for two reasons. One is the well-understood danger of committing a type II error, in which a latent pattern goes undetected. Social scientists tend to be careful to avoid the type I error, and seldom are guilty of claiming the existence of a meaningful pattern when it could, for example, have occurred by chance alone. But it is equally important that we do not overlook some theoretically significant configuration merely because we used too few instruments of observation or too rigid a strategy of inference.

The second reason – returning to the matter of type I errors – is that a number of researchers claim to have discovered all sorts of periodicities in war, and there is thus a general tendency in our field to accept the proposition that war is indeed a cyclical phenomenon. Since we only presented the reasons for expecting this to be true in our introductory pages, and said little about the prior evidence one way or another, let us summarize that evidence here.

While we are merely the most recent in a long line of researchers to have examined the question, our predecessors have fared little better in their searches for periodicity, despite occasional claims to the contrary. Neither Sorokin[20] nor Richardson[21] – who had better data than the former, but worked in a much shorter time-span – was able to find any strong cyclical patterns at the regional or systemic level. But in a secondary analysis of the above data sets, as well as the data generated by Wright,[22] Denton and Phillips discerned an upswing in the incidence of war about every thirty years since 1680.[23] Similarly, in a secondary analysis of Wheeler's estimates,[24] Dewey claims to find a number of periodicities going back to 600 BC.[25] Another long-range study, but at the national and/or regional level, is Lee's analysis of Chinese internal wars from 221 BC to 1929, indicating a clear 800-year cycle, as well as less evident ones of a shorter duration.[26] And, as already noted, our own investigation – at the system level for the period 1816–1965 – also came up with ambiguous, but basically negative, results.[27]

Given the paucity of the evidence at the national level so far, as well as our skepticism regarding much of the methods and data used in the pro-cyclic literature, we find ourselves in agreement with Sorokin's dim view.[28] 'These considerations are sufficient', he said, 'until real evidence to the contrary is given, to ... conclude that ... no regular periodicity, no uniform rhythm, no universal uniformity of the curve of war movement in all of the countries studied are identifiable.'

Having addressed the proposition that national war experiences come at regular intervals in tune with some periodicity – foreordained or otherwise – all we have demonstrated is that the probability of the major powers getting into war is independent of when and with what effects they experienced their prior wars. Does this absence of periodicity permit us to infer that there is no underlying regularity, and that war experiences are randomly occurring responses to randomly occurring conditions? Clearly not, since it is quite possible that war requires the concatenation of several conditions, each of whose appearance is cyclical, but with different intervals. This *could* produce a periodicity in the war experiences of nations, but the concatenation of as few as three such cycles, even if they show (for example) three-, ten-, and fifty-year periodicities, would occur only once every 150 years. Thus the war cycle would be so long as to make its occurrence barely visible in the span under scrutiny here. Furthermore, since we know that the mean interwar experience interval is under ten years (depending on the class of nation) we can reject as impossible any fixed interval periodicity that is appreciably greater (or lesser) than that figure.

It follows, then, that whatever periodicities there *may* be in our unspecified predictor variables, these could not be exercising any cyclical effect on interwar experience intervals.

Conclusion

Is there anything in these findings that would strengthen our confidence in one or another of the orientations that we bring to the temporal incidence of war? Clearly the evidence does not support the cyclical view; the intervals are too irregular, and the occurrence of war entries has been virtually indifferent to the passage of time since the prior war. Moreover, when we control for the outcome of the prior war or its duration or its fatality level, we still find that the probability of the next war entry is basically unrelated to the passage of time.

And, of course, if there is no periodicity – as well as no upward or downward secular trend – we can more readily reject any suggestion of historical inexorability. As noted earlier, empirical confirmation of a cyclical pattern or clear secular trend would not demonstrate the existence of one or another of these inexorable historical laws, but the absence of such a pattern comes very close to refuting the proposition. To quote Sorokin[29] once more, 'History seems to be neither as monotonous and uninventive as the partisans of the strict periodicities and "iron laws" and "universal uniformities" think; nor so dull and mechanical as an engine, making the same number of revolutions in a unit of time. It repeats its "themes" but almost always with new variations. In this sense it is ever new, and ever old, so far as the ups and downs are repeated'.

We close, then, with the proposition that regularity and inexorability are far from identical. As suggested in the introduction, a fully determined and inexorable outcome need not be preceded by a discernible pattern of observed regularities. Just as chaos can mark the most teleologic of historical processes, pattern and regularity can characterize processes whose outcome remains very much in doubt. In sum, the purpose of systematic research into the correlates of war and the conditions of peace is to estimate as closely as we can how much variance in the outcome is explained by the deterministic processes of fate and the stochastic processes of chance, and how much is left for rational human steersmanship. The demonstrated absence of periodicity is no guarantee that we will either arrive at such an estimate or take advantage of the unexplained variance, but its presence would certainly have suggested an even more pessimistic conclusion.

Notes: Chapter 16

We are grateful to the volume's editors, to Michael Champion, Melvin Small, and Bradley Martin for their helpful comments, and to the National Science Foundation for research support under grant SOC71-03593 A05.

1 Jacob Bronowski, *Magic, Science, and Civilization* (New York: Columbia University Press, 1978); and Karl W. Deutsch, 'Some notes on research on the role of models in the natural and social sciences', *Synthèse*, vol. 7 (1948), pp. 506–33.
2 Norbert Wiener, *Cybernetics; or, Control and Communication in the Animal and the Machine* (Cambridge, Mass.: MIT Press, 1948); Walter Bradford Cannon, *The Way of an Investigator: A Scientist's Experiences in Medical Research* (New York: Norton, 1945); and Karl W. Deutsch, *The Nerves of Government: Models of Political Communication and Control* (New York: The Free Press, 1963).
3 Herbert A. Simon, *The Sciences of the Artificial* (Cambridge, Mass.: MIT Press, 1969).
4 Slavko Šećerov, *Economic Phenomena Before and After War: A Statistical Theory of Modern Wars* (London: Routledge; and New York: Dutton, 1919).
5 Miller Pontius, *A Study of the Recurring Economic Pattern Surrounding Major Wars* (New York, mimeo, 1958).
6 Niels Lindberg, 'The conflict theory and economic depressions, with some views on various political aspects of an anti-depression programme as supplementary to armament cuts' (Stockholm, Sweden: mimeo., 1967).
7 A. L. Macfie, 'The outbreak of war and the trade cycle', *Economic History* (supplement of *Economic Journal*), vol. 3, no. 13 (February 1938), pp. 89–97; and Ragnar Frisch, *Noen Trekk av Konjunkturlaeren: Med et Tillegg om Levestandard og Prisindeks* (Oslo, Norway: Aschehoug, 1947); summarized by Nils Petter Gleditsch, 'The causes of war: a research proposal' (Ann Arbor, Mich.: mimeo., 1966).
8 David C. McClelland, 'Love and power: the psychological signals of war', *Psychology Today*, vol. 8, no. 8 (January 1975), pp. 44–48.
9 David C. McClelland, *Power: The Inner Experience* (New York: Irvington, distr. Halstead Press, 1975).
10 Frank Klingberg, 'The historical alternation of moods in American foreign policy', *World Politics*, vol. 4, no. 2 (January 1952), pp. 239–73.
11 ibid., p. 262.
12 Norman Z. Alcock and Christopher Young, 'Evidence of an epochal cycle', *Peace Research*, vol. 5, no. 4 (April 1973), pp. 17–20.
13 J. David Singer and Melvin Small, 'Diplomatic importance of states, 1816–1970: an extension and refinement of the indicator', *World Politics*, vol. 25, no. 4 (July 1973), pp. 577–99; and Charles Gochman, 'Status, conflict, and war: the major powers, 1820–1970', PhD dissertation, University of Michigan, 1975.
14 J. David Singer and Melvin Small, *The Wages of War, 1816–1965: A Statistical Handbook* (New York: Wiley, 1972).
15 Cyrus Derman, Leon J. Gleser, and Ingram Olkin, *A Guide to Probability Theory and Application* (New York: Holt, Rinehart & Winston, 1973).
16 Bruce Bueno de Mesquita and J. David Singer, 'Alliances, capabilities, and war: a review and synthesis', in *Political Science Annual: An International Review*, ed. Cornelius P. Cotter (Indianapolis, Ind., and New York: Bobbs-Merrill, 1973), Vol. 4, pp. 237–80.
17 Ivan S. Bloch [Ivan Stanislavovich Bliokh], *The Future of War in Its Technical, Economic, and Political Relations: Is War Now Impossible?*, tr. R. C. Long (New York: Doubleday & McClure, 1899).
18 Singer and Small, *The Wages of War*.
19 ibid., ch. 9.
20 Pitirim A. Sorokin, *Social and Cultural Dynamics* (New York: American Book Company, 1937–41), Vol. 3, *Fluctuation of Social Relationships, War, and Revolution* (1937).
21 Lewis F. Richardson, *Statistics of Deadly Quarrels*, ed. Quincy Wright and C. C. Lineau (Pittsburgh, Pa: Boxwood Press; and Chicago: Quadrangle Books, 1960).
22 Quincy Wright, *A Study of War*, 2 vols (Chicago: University of Chicago Press, 1942).
23 Frank H. Denton and Warren Phillips, 'Some patterns in the history of violence', *Journal of Conflict Resolution*, vol. 12, no. 2 (June 1968); pp. 182–95.
24 Raymond H. Wheeler, *War, 599 BC–AD 1950: Indexes of International and Civil War Battles of the World* (Pittsburgh, Pa.: Foundation for the Study of Cycles, 1951).
25 Edward R. Dewey, *The 177-Year Cycle in War, 600 BC–AD 1957* (Pittsburgh, Pa: Foundation for the Study of Cycles, 1964).

26 J. S. Lee, 'The periodic recurrence of internecine wars in China', *China Journal*, vol. 14, no. 3 (March 1931), pp. 111–15; and vol. 14, no. 4 (April 1931), pp. 159–63.
27 Singer and Small, *The Wages of War*.
28 Sorokin, *Social and Cultural Dynamics*, Vol. 3, *Fluctuations of Social Relationships, War, and Revolution*, p. 359.
29 ibid., pp. 359–60.

17

Critical Factors of the North–South Relations Seen from a Long-Term Socioecological Perspective

BRUNO FRITSCH

After the UNCTAD IV Conference, held in 1976 in Nairobi, some of the major participants initiated a 'North–South' dialogue in Paris to discuss future relations between less developed countries (LDCs) and developed countries. It failed, however, to resolve such key problems as creating a stabilization fund for raw materials, reshaping the external debt structure of the LDCs, determining the status in the LDCs of multinational corporations, and appropriate means for transferring various levels of technology. The Paris dialogue, and with it the implementation of the New International Economic Order, ended in March 1977 in a stalemate.

Given the dimensions of these unresolved political and economic problems, the participating states deemed it imperative to create a new body which could assess them anew. Under the leadership of the former West German Chancellor, Willy Brandt, a group of independent, high-level representatives of LDCs and developing countries – people who had served in influential governmental positions in their careers and who were likely to play an important role in the future political development of North–South relations – met to consider the manifold ramifications of alternative development strategies.

This chapter, rather than re-examining the well-known details of development strategies or the political aspects of the North–South dialogue and the Brandt Committee, seeks to set the stage for a broader perspective: the socioecological trends that will determine the future of relations between the North and the South and hence the framework within which the political discussions must take place. It applies to this question new data on international economic relations, ecological constraints, and the 'reinforcement potential' of nations. Some alternative scenarios for future developments are explored to enable us to understand which of the various trends may turn out to be the most critical for these developments, those on which governmental and other experts must focus their attention if they would ensure long-term peaceful growth.

The starting point of any such analysis is a central fact: the interdependence of today's world. Economic development, demographic trends, and technological change do not proceed independently of one another, either within a single country or in the world as a whole. Growth in one sector or geographic region may upset an existing equilibrium in a way that works to the disadvantage of other sectors or regions. Similarly, the over-use of such natural resources as fossil fuels, besides incurring greater costs as substitutes are sought for the depleted resource, may have other secondary effects, in this case both unclean air in our cities and an accumulation of carbon dioxide and nitrogen oxide that can have an atmospheric greenhouse effect. As far as the production of degraded heat from energy consumption is concerned, of course, we are still far away from a significant disturbance of the biosphere (which might require energy consumption at 195 times the present level). The point is rather that, at least beyond a certain level of activity, equilibrium conditions for the steady growth of an economy may become inconsistent with the equilibrium conditions required to maintain the dynamic equilibrium of the ecosystem.

The fundamental relationship between economic growth and the overall ecological equilibrium within which the material and non-material needs of people can be accommodated rests upon the way in which societies organize matter and its transformation (including transport of matter as well as its transformation into consumption and investment goods), energy supply, and knowledge in both its pure and applied sense.

Following the practice of numerous international organizations and individual scholars, we might define people's material and non-material needs as follows:[1]

Basic Material Requirements	*Non-Material Needs*
Nutrition:	
3,000 kcal. per person, per day	'personal growth'
100 g protein per person, per day	diversity
Education:	equity
8 years min.	social justice
12 years max.	autonomy
	solidarity
Housing:	participation . . .
7 m^2 per person	

However, at our present social discount rate, which overestimates the immediate satisfaction of needs and underestimates future needs, it may be difficult to achieve this set of goals. The Bariloche model specifies the numerical values of an optimal solution for the achievement of the material goals. Under present socioeconomic conditions we observe, however, that an increase of growth is usually accompanied by a decrease of equity. Moreover, political decision processes usually do not follow an 'optimal path' as suggested in the calculations of the Bariloche model. The problem, therefore, is to minimize the required time for the attainment of the material goals without falling short in the fulfillment of the non-material needs. Although the non-material needs are difficult to measure, there exist indicators allowing for an indirect measurement.[2]

The Constraints

The political and economic constraints under which these two sets of goals can be attained are more restrictive than ecological factors. With a population of roughly 8 billion in 2020, at least 5 billion people will live in LDCs. Their situation in terms of income and wealth will then probably be improved (provided that we have managed to avoid a major nuclear war), compared with the misery of the 2 billion poor people living in the LDCs today. However, compared with the situation in the North, their income and wealth will still be considerably lower, their demands will be more pressing, but their capability to handle their own problems will have improved. If we assume the same IQ-distribution in the 'South' as in the 'North', 2·5 per cent will be highly gifted, that is, will have an IQ of greater than 130. In a stationary population of 5 billion people this implies 125 million highly gifted, intelligent people. Allowing for many retarding health and social opportunity factors which may still exist, the figure of 80–100 million probably reflects a fair proportion of the 'brain potential' of the LDCs, as compared with an absolute amount of something like 50 to 75 million highly intelligent people in the 'North'. Compared to the industrialized countries, the population of the LDCs then will still be 'younger', having a higher proportion of age-groups between 20 and 40 years than our populations.[3] In contrast to this situation, the 'North' will then be even more elderly ('overaged'), relatively affluent, still privileged, and hence conservative. Thus, we may arrive, by 2010 or 2020, at a globalization of what may be coined the 'Rhodesian syndrome'.

The 'South', however, will produce not only geniuses, but also desperate people, who will emerge from the continuous growth of the absolute number of marginalized individuals. Assuming that the ratio of these marginalized people who may turn to violence and even become desperate to total population may then correspond to what we observe currently in the industrialized nations, that is, one such person in a population of 2 million we will have in 2020, with a population of 5 billion people living in the southern hemisphere, a total number of 2,500 desperados, that is, persons who have to be counted as potential terrorists. Hence, along with the 'Rhodesianization', we will also get a 'Palestinization' of the world scene. Actually we do not know how many potential or actual terrorists there will be in 2020. But it seems likely that their number – subject to an operational definition of the notion 'terrorist' – will be higher in comparison to the present figure.

The dimensions of inequality, as shown in the table of indicators (see Appendix, Table A17.7), reflect the failure of our economic and political system to accommodate the material and non-material needs of all peoples. The inequalities, expressed in ratios, are not confined to per-capita income, energy consumption, or to the supply of food. They extend into many other areas of social life as can be seen below.

Although the inequalities tend to diminish, the speed of this improvement is probably too slow, compared with the speed of decreasing tolerance (or increase of intolerance) with which people assess such inequalities.

From these dimensions of inequality we may derive the tremendous absorption potential in areas of construction, water supply, and other infrastructure investments – to name just a few – which exists in the LDCs and which could be supplied by the industrial countries, provided the LDCs could either pay for it or acquire enough loans. Here, the complex problem of foreign aid and the future international division of labour enters the scene. If the LDCs are expected to pay for their imports, they must be given the chance of placing their exports in the industrial countries, which consequently would have to give up certain industries. We all know that any decision taken by governments to change the industrial structure is politically very sensitive. The envisaged combination of Western technological know-how with Arab money and low wages in the LDCs has not yet contributed to narrowing the existing inequalities.

On the other hand, one may argue that this sort of international division of labour is not a practicable way to solve the problems of the LDCs, and that the LDCs should focus more on self-reliance at some cost in material standard, once they have attained the minimal material needs. In view of the ever-increasing international proliferation of 'living standards', such a decoupling of the 'rest of the world' seems to be unlikely, though. The very fact that the most recent list of indicators, as presented by the UNRISD, reflects the present value system of the LDCs (since it was compiled with the approval and with the support of the LDCs governments) indicates that the self-reliance concepts proposed by *Western* scholars such as Dieter Senghaas or Johan Galtung are not shared by the majority of the LDC governments.

Energy Supply and Economic Development

Although there exists a nearly unlimited necessity for growth in order to satisfy the needs of the developing countries, there also exist some limiting factors which determine the speed, that is, the rate of growth attainable at a given technology, and hence the time needed until a certain number of needs can be accommodated. The relationship between growth, employment, distribution, use of resources, and inflation is determined by a complex set of economic interactions which cannot be easily loosened without a profound change of our existing economic and political system.

The Factors Limiting Our Growth Capacity:

- Renewable resources
- Non-renewable resources (fossil fuels)

Possible Extensions:

- Recycling
- Substitution by other energy sources (solar, nuclear, hydro, geotherm, wind, tides, etc.)

- Agricultural area

- Pollution

- Low levels of innovativeness
- Capacity to implement and diffuse innovations
- Managerial skills

- Land reclamation, increase of productivity by fertilizers, mechanization, high-yield varieties, water management, desalination of sea water, etc.
- Abatement technologies, environmental protection

All extensions listed above require *energy*. In addition, increased requirements for housing, transport and communication, increased industrialization, and so on, in conjunction with increased growth rates in the LDCs, require an overproportional extension of the energy system both in industrial countries and in the LDCs. This in turn implies an *increased investment ratio* from today's 20 per cent to at least 40 per cent of GDP,[4] that is, a higher capital accumulation. This follows from the fact that in any given technology, any energy-generating and transforming system, even in a stationary state, will itself use up energy in two ways. First, energy is directly absorbed in the transformation of one form of energy into another. Secondly, energy is indirectly absorbed by the system through the energy required to produce materials needed for reinvestment. In a growing economy with an increasing total consumption of primary energy, the long lead times of investment make the energy-generating and -transforming systems absorb even more energy. Thus, even with physically unlimited energy resources, the growth rates of the two systems, the energy-generating/transforming system and the non-energy production system of the economy, are mutually interdependent: one system cannot 'outgrow' the other.

The formal analysis of the problem shows that the strategic factors in the set of relations are the following:

- Investment rate and hence capital requirements
- The productivity of investments (capital/output ratio)
- Technical progress
- Proportion of investments going into energy systems
- The lead time of investments
- The efficiency of energy use (W/$): offsetting factors:
    increase of efficiency v. increasing share of industrial production in the LDCs
- Energy conservation
- The relation between attainable and expected increase of disposable income.[5]

Some Reference Scenarios

In order to solve their own economic problems, such as unemployment, inflation, resource availability, and so on, and in order to achieve an improvement in the intra- as well as in the international distribution of income, the industrial countries of the West (market economies) have to continue growing. However, whereas growth may ease some of the short-run problems, it causes, at the same time, in the long run, additional problems such as resource scarcities and hence price increases (which by no means are always offset by a corresponding increase of productivity), environmental disruptions, energy shortages, and so on.

The following five reference scenarios (Table 17.1) – not to be mistaken for forecasts – reflect some of the magnitudes involved in various assumptions about growth rates of population (POP) and gross national product (GNP) within the time horizon of 2020. These various scenarios have as their background the world's current situation (i.e. 1977), that is, a population of 4 billion people, gross national product of 5·3 trillion dollars, and energy production of 7·6 trillion watt (or 7·6 tera watt [TW]), as well as historically based growth rates of 2 per cent per annum for population and 4 to 5 per cent per annum for GNP in real terms.

Scenario A reflects UN estimates and targets proposed in various UN publications. The target growth rate for the GNP is a weighted average rate composed of the target rates of various world regions. The point we wish to make here refers to the implications of such target values: if population is assumed to stabilize somewhere between 9 and 10 billion in 2020 (which is the figure given most frequently), and if the GNP growth rate envisaged should really achieve 4 per cent per annum (the historical rate), we then would arrive in 2020 at a world GNP of 31 trillion dollars and – at the given efficiency of energy use of 1·43 watt per dollar of output – at an energy requirement of 44·3 trillion watt, i.e. 44·3 tera watt, which represents nearly six times the present energy consumption. There is no question that this required power cannot be provided by the classical fossil fuels any more. Rather, new energy sources must be made available. This in turn requires additional investment capital, which has to be generated within the developed industrial countries.[6]

Scenario B refers to the estimates resulting from the Bariloche model, a world model presented by a group of scientists from Latin America.[7] This model is based upon the above-mentioned definitions of basic needs. It is normative and redistribution oriented; however, it also requires growth. The implicit energy requirements of this scenario amount to 19·2 TW in 2020, i.e. more than 2·5 times the amount of present energy consumption.

Scenarios C and D simply show what the values for GNP and POP would be if a growth rate of 3 and 2 per cent p.a. were assumed for these two variables respectively, and what – at the historical efficiency rate – the corresponding energy requirements would be. Again, even at a GNP growth rate of only 2 per cent p.a. – which certainly is insufficient to absorb the growing numbers of people looking for jobs – we are faced with an increase of total energy requirements of 2·43 times the amount of our present energy consumption.

Scenario E finally represents the most unlikely case – it may be

Table 17.1 Reference Scenarios, 1975 Base Year and 2020

Year	World population (in billions)	World GNP (at 1975 prices) in trillions of US dollars)	World energy consumption (in TW = 10^{12} W at 1.43 W/$)	Per capita energy consumption (in kW)
1975	4.0	5.3	7.6	1.9
2020 Reference Scenarios:				
A Various UN estimates and targets, e.g. GNP growth rate of 4% p.a. and POP growth rate of less than 1.9% p.a.	9.0	31.0	44.3	4.92
B The Bariloche model	9.3	13.4	19.2	2.06
C With 3% growth rates p.a. for POP and GNP	15.1	20.0	28.6	1.9
D With 2% growth rates p.a. for POP and GNP	9.7	12.9	18.5	1.9
E With 3% growth rate for GNP 2% growth rate for ENCON 1.5% growth rate for POP	7.8	20.0	18.5	2.4

increase in efficiency* from 1·43 to 0·93 W/$

*The present W/$ ratio is : $\frac{7 \cdot 6}{5 \cdot 3} = 1 \cdot 43$.

Note: An improvement to 0·93 implies that energy is either conserved and/or the efficiency of energy conversion and energy use is improved through the technological progress by 54 per cent over a period of 45 years, i.e. on average, by 1·2 per cent per annum.

referred to as the 'dream scenario' – since it assumes an increase in the efficiency of energy use of more than 50 per cent and an increase of POP of only 1·5 per cent. Even here, however, we are confronted – at 3 per cent GNP growth rate – with the same increase of the total energy requirements.

The Problem-Solving Potential of the Industrialized Countries

One of the basic questions arising in this context concerns the individual capabilities of the industrialized countries to cope with these global problems. We have chosen for our analysis twenty-one countries, most of which are 'industrialized' in a broad sense (i.e. we have also included Ireland, Turkey, Greece, and Portugal in our comparison). The selection of countries and data was partly determined by the availability of comparable statistical data as offered by the Statistical Office of the European Communities. However, these twenty-one countries represent 73·6 per cent of world output and more than 85 per cent of the world energy consumption.

The concept which we have developed here is based on a comparison between the 'Reinforcement Potential' (REFOP) of each individual country and the 'Foreign Trade Dependency' (FODEP). The reinforcement potential is derived from a combined index reflecting the defense expenditures as a percentage of world defense expenditure and the degree of self-sufficiency in energy supply. This index is weighted with the 'Structuring Capacity Index' (STRCA), which is defined as a ratio of the 'Social Communication and Information Potential' (SOCIP) and the 'Material Energy Turnover' (MATE). The foreign trade dependency defines the imports as a percentage of the world exports. This index is weighted with the export value per capita.

The idea behind this concept relates to the correspondence of the basic notions 'energy' and 'information'. A bar of iron or aluminium, for example, represents a relatively high content of bound energy but has, at the same time, a low content of information. On the other hand, a microprocessor has little energy bound in its material content but represents much more 'information' in the sense that its occurrence, as a result of a random composition of the various parts it consists of, is highly improbable. The implicit assumption made here is that a combination of large quantities of formed matter with a dense package of information – for example, a space rocket or a nuclear submarine – indicates a high degree of reinforcement potential.

There is no satisfactory way in which one could empirically operationalize this concept. The way we chose here may be considered as a first approximation to an operationalization, subject to limitations set by the availability of comparable data. The degree of self-sufficiency in the energy supply, for example, combined with the defense expenditures, may be taken as the 'hardware' part of the social activity. If this 'hardware' part is mutliplied with the 'structuring capacity' – defined as the ratio of the communication–information potential and the index reflecting the use of material and energy – one may consider the product as a combined index of the reinforcement potential of a society. This potential is counterbalanced by any sort of dependency. We chose the foreign trade dependency: there are many other dependencies, of course. Basically, the relation between the reinforcement potential and the foreign trade dependency – as defined in the Appendix – was taken to determine the co-ordinates for the location of the twenty-one nation states included in our study.

Once the information content of products, combined with the hardware content of the total output of a nation is accepted as a concept relevant for the operationalization of 'power' – for which we use the term 'reinforcement potential' – then it is a matter of secondary importance whether the indexes are defined as roots of the product of the various components or as averages. Neither way is free of biases and hence both are subject to reservations. What is needed most, it seems, are proper and accurate data on the information content of products. The other components of our indexes, such as the energy consumption, the steel production, foreign trade, and so on, are less problematic.

The comparison between the reinforcement potential and the foreign trade dependency yields the following four groups of countries (see Figure 17.1).

(1) The USA and USSR represent the highest value of reinforcement potential combined with a relatively low foreign trade dependency. These two major powers, therefore, have the long-term potential to

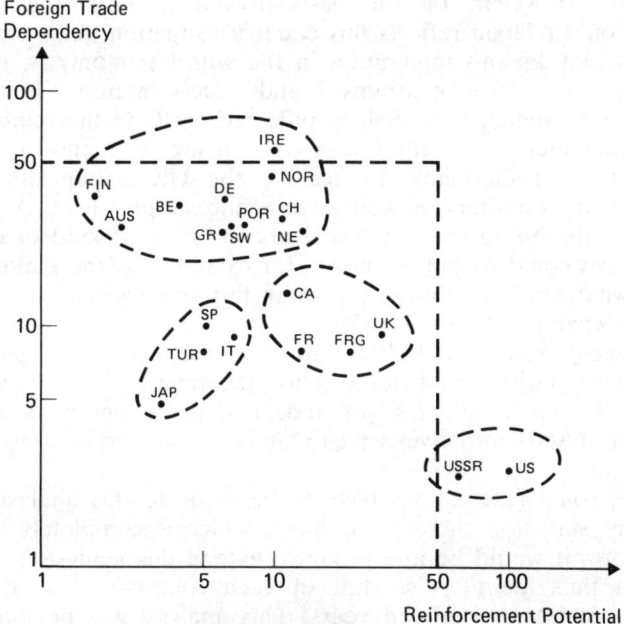

Figure 17.1 *Foreign trade dependency and reinforcement potential of selected countries.*

arrange between themselves, in a sort of 'duopolistic' manner, the conditions which occur to them as acceptable in pursuing their partly exclusive objectives. Taking into consideration the basic differences of the respective social and political system, any such duopolistic arrangement is highly unstable, however.

(2) Canada, France, the Federal Republic of Germany, and the United Kingdom in turn represent a group of countries with a lower reinforcement potential but with a somewhat higher value for foreign trade dependency (which does not necessarily mean more integration); these countries are in the position of serving as a mediator or as a bridge for activities leading to implementable concepts in the field of trade and energy policies. They are thus of great importance in the process of reshaping the international order.

(3) The third group, consisting of Austria, Belgium, Denmark, Finland, Greece, Ireland, the Netherlands, Norway, Portugal, Sweden, and Switzerland, seems to be involved in the international economic framework in the sense of somewhat greater dependence on the international system rather than being able to impose their own conditions upon this system. These countries are therefore the most likely candidates for political initiatives in the field of free trade, particularly opposing protectionist tendencies, and in the field of various activities related to peaceful settlements of conflicts (especially Norway, Netherlands, Switzerland, Sweden, Austria).

(4) The fourth group of countries comprises Japan, Turkey, Spain, and Italy. This seems, at the first glance, a surprising composition of a 'group'. However, on the basis of our analysis, the surprising 'location' of Japan reflects this country's situation quite correctly. It shows that Japan's integration in the world economy is, compared with the countries of groups 2 and 3, less intense. On the other hand, the military potential, as reflected partly in the reinforcement potential index, is – for reasons which are well known – smaller than that of Germany, France, or the UK. Japan thus can be subjected to military as well as to economic pressures. A glance at the events during the last few years shows what kind of economic pressures could be put on Japan, for example, by the United States, and what kind of military pressures this country may be subjected to, for example, by the USSR.

Turkey, Spain, and Italy are likewise not in a particularly favorable position and hence – for the time being – they are not likely to be candidates for independent autonomous economic and/or military initiatives which may be considered as constructive.

Of course, some reservations have to be made to this analysis. As we know from statistics, there is no index which is completely unbiased. Furthermore, it would be interesting to extend this analysis to previous years and thus identify the shift of each country's relative position during the last ten or fifteen years. This analysis will be made later; unfortunately the time available for this chapter did not permit such an extension. The indicators as presented by UNRISD (see Table A17.7) are given only for two years, namely, 1960 and 1970. We wanted, however, to include some more recent data and we therefore extended this analysis to a greater variety of available statistical material.

The Capital Formation and Redistribution Requirements

The world gross national product (GNP) is estimated at US$ 6,087 for 1975 at 1975 prices. Table 17.2 gives the distribution of this world GNP among ten regions or countries according to the figures given in the World Bank Atlas of 1977.

The gross domestic investment (GDI) is calculated on the basis of the data just released by the World Bank.[8]

The offical development assistance (ODA) from members of the OECD is 13·6 billion US$ (= 0·33 of the GNP); 5·5 billion are transferred by the OECD countries. The total amount of ODA for 1975 is 19·1 billion US$ which corresponds to 0·36 per cent of the donors' GNP, or 0·31 per cent of the world GNP.

This figure falls short of the net annual capital inflow of 65 billion US$ requested by the UNCTAD for the period 1976–80 in order to achieve the target of the International Development Strategy.[9]

While the ODA activities of the donor countries are usually expressed in terms of percentage of the GNP, we suggest linking them with the investment rate. If we, for example, propose to increase the non-industrial regions' (or countries') investment rate (GDI as per cent of GDP) by five percentage points for Oceania, two percentage points for South America and Central America respectively, and five percentage points each for Africa and Asia, then the total additional capital required for such an increase in the investment rate amounts to 57 billion US$ for 1975 at 1975 prices (see Table 17.2).

The burden sharing suggested here relates the 'donating capacity' of the industrialized regions and of the Middle East to the regions' respective investment rates and the relative shares in the total investment of the industrialized regions plus the Middle East, which amounts to 1,133 billion US$ (see Table 17.3).

It turns out that the additional increase of the 'donator regions'' investment rate would have to increase by maximally 1·4 percentage points (in the case of Japan), and 0·9 percentage point for the region (1), i.e. North America (see last column of Table 17.2). It thus appears that, from the economic point of view, an ODA of something in the neighborhood of 57 to 70 billion US$ (in 1975 prices) is perfectly feasible.

In comparison to the required additional investment for the new energy systems to be set up in the industrial regions, such an ODA amount is nearly negligible.

However, one could argue that precisely these additional capital requirements for energy systems will compete with the requirements for additional ODA by the less developed countries (LDCs). Basically, there are two major ways to reconcile these two seemingly opposing, or contradictory, objectives: *first*, new technologies are needed – and are

Table 17.2 Burden-sharing and Official Development Assistance (ODA), based on the investment rate

Regions or Country[a]	GNP in US$ 1975	GNP as % of world GNP	Gross domestic investment, 1975, in billion US$	GDI as % of GDP	Proposed increase of investment rate (GDI as % of GDP)	Corresponding amount in billion $	Proposed burden sharing (in US$)[d]	Investment rates after adjustment	Increase of GDI in percentage points
(1) North America	1,678	27.57	310	18.5			15.6	19.4	+0.9 (donor)
(2) Japan	496	8.15	163	33.0			8.2	34.5	+1.4 (donor)
(3) Oceania	94	1.54	14	15.0	+5	4.7		20.0	+5.0 (recipient)
(4) Europe, excl. USSR	1,971	32.38	473	24.0			23.8	25.2	+1.2 (donor)
(5) USSR[b]	649	10.66	162	25.0			8.1	26.2	+1.2 (donor)
(6) Middle East	153	2.52	25	16.0			1.3	17.2	+1.2 (donor)
(7) South America	224	3.68	45	20.0	+2	11.2		22.0	+2.0 (recipient)
(8) Central America[c]	103	1.69	20	20.0	+2	5.1		22.0	+2.0 (recipient)
(9) Africa	163	2.68	24	15.0	+5	8.2		20.0	+5.0 (recipient)
(10) Asia, excl. Japan	556	9.13	83	15.0	+5	27.8		20.0	+5.0 (recipient)
World	6,087	100.0	1,319	21.7		57.0	57.0		

Notes:
a Excludes Cambodia, Lebanon, and Vietnam in the aggregation.
b Estimates.
c Includes Mexico.
d The proposed burden sharing takes into account the total gross domestic investment of the industrialized regions or countries respectively, i.e. (1), (2), (4), (5), and (6) which corresponds to 1,133 million US$ and suggests a distribution of the 57 billion $ according to the regions' (or countries') relative shares of this amount, as shown in Table 17.3.

Sources: World Bank, *World Bank Atlas: Population, Per Capita Product, and Growth Rates* (Washington, DC: International Bank for Reconstruction and Development, 1977), p. 10; World Bank, *World Development Report, 1978* (Washington, DC: International Bank for Reconstruction and Development, 1978), *passim*.

Table 17.3 Burden-sharing and donating capacity of the industrial regions and the Middle East

	Gross domestic investment in billion US$ 1975	as % of the total	in billion US$
North America	310	27.4	15.6
Japan	163	14.4	8.2
Europe	473	41.7	23.8
USSR	162	14.3	8.1
Middle East	25	2.2	1.3
Total	1,133	100.0	57.0

being developed – by the industrial countries. They will undoubtedly increase the productivity of investments (i.e. decrease the capital output ratio, COR) and thus reduce the pressure of falling growth rates upon the absolute and relative amount of the ODA. As can be seen from the figures in Table 17.4, the historical patterns do not confirm the widely held belief that an inverse correlation exists between the slowdown of the growth rates in the industrial nations and the ODA in percentage of GNP spent by these countries.

Secondly, there is a positive correlation between per capita exports and the per capita ODA (Table 17.5).

Finally, I wish to point out that the redistribution of income does not necessarily exclude or prevent economic growth and industrialization.

Table 17.4 Growth rates of GDP, 1960–70 and 1970–6, compared with changes in the ODA/GDP ratio

Country	Growth rates of GDP 1960–70	ODA as % of GDP 1960–70	Growth rates of GDP 1970–6	ODA as % of GDP 1970–6
FRG	4.6	0.34	2.2	0.34
France	5.4	0.93	3.9	0.62
Italy	5.3	0.16	2.9	0.13
Netherlands	5.3	0.43	3.4	0.67
Belgium	4.7	0.65	4.0	0.53
UK	2.9	0.46	2.3	0.38
Denmark	4.7	0.20	2.2	0.51
Norway	4.9	0.20	4.5	0.52
Sweden	4.4	0.20	2.6	0.64
China	4.0	0.93	1.3	0.17
Austria	4.5	0.90	4.3	0.13
Finland	4.6	0.45	4.6	0.16
USA	4.3	0.44	2.5	0.27
Canada	5.6	0.26	4.8	0.47
Japan	10.5	0.25	5.6	0.23

Source: World Bank, *World Development Report, 1978* (Washington, DC: International Bank for Reconstruction and Development, 1978), Table 5, pp. 84–5, and Table 12, pp. 98–9.

Table 17.5 Correlation between per capita exports and per capita Official Development Assistance

Country	1975 per capita exports (index)	1975 per capita ODA (index)
FRG	52·06	39·2
France	34·47	57·3
Italy	22·08	4·7
Netherlands	90·21	64·3
Belgium	100·00	55·8
UK	27·64	22·2
Denmark	61·04	58·5
Norway	63·52	66·4
Sweden	75·30	100·0
China	71·32	23·2
Austria	35·41	12·2
Finland	41·44	14·7
USSR	4·63	2·9
USA	17·63	27·2
Canada	48·92	56·3
Japan	17·77	15·9

Note: The regression: $ODA/cap = 5(\pm 10) + 0.707(\pm 0.19) * EX/cap$
$r = 0.706 \quad R^2 = 0.5$.

The industrialized nations redistribute today between 4 and 15 per cent of their incomes (Table 17.6).

The domestic propensity of the industrialized countries to redistribute income is, on average, twenty-nine times greater ($9.49 \div 0.33$) than their propensity to redistribute income internationally. It is not the economic capacity but the political will which is lacking. The

Table 17.6 Redistribution of national income of industrial countries

1971 Country	Govt. expenditures as % of GNP	Share of social expenditures as % of govt. expenditures	Redistributed share of GNP (%)
FRG	27·8[a]	25·1	6·98
France	37·5	40·5	15·20
Canada	37·7	30·4	11·46
China	24·3	20·8	5·05
UK	37·0	37·6	13·91
USA	29·7	14·6	4·34
		Aver.	9·49

Note:
a 1970.
Source: W. W. Pommerehne, Quantitative Aspects of Federalism: A Study of Six Countries, in W. E. Oates (ed.), The Political Economy of Fiscal Federalism (Lexington, Mass.: D. C. Heath, 1977), pp. 275–355.

international community must seek *an optimal mix of technological advances, trade expansion, increased capital formation*, and an *accelerated international income distribution* in order to cope with the challenges of the future.

Conclusion

Coming back to our scenarios, it is evident that in the forthcoming years something must give way: either the growth rate of the GNP and/or the efficiency of energy use, expressed in the W/$ ratio, must drastically increase, and/or the private consumption expenditures must be curtailed while the investment rate has to increase.

It will be interesting to see what the outcome of the implied bargaining process will be, and whether the countries belonging to group 2, with the possible co-operation of other countries from other groups, such as Japan and the United States, will be in the position to extend their influence. In this context, the following concepts and notions must be borne in mind:

- Rising costs of missed, i.e. unutilized opportunities (threshold values, trajectories)
- The 'Quantum Jump' of the 'post-industrial societies', and
- The learning capacity of complex social systems
- The cost of failure to learn or to adapt to the ecological conditions relevant for the survival of the society.

The ultimate 'scarce goods', therefore, are:

- Time
- Options
- Values oriented to the future
- Capital formation

The fateful issue of our time is whether the industrialized countries will be able to facilitate the transition from an economy that is still increasingly destructive of resources (i.e. outside the limits set by the conditions of the thermodynamic equilibrium) into a situation of dynamic equilibrium with the impending stabilization – over the next forty to fifty years – of the world population at an estimated level of 8 to 10 billions. Physically and technically, such a *transition toward a global equilibrium* is perfectly possible. Energy production would need to be something like six to eight times greater than it is at present. The resulting waste heat would be unlikely to throw the thermal balance of the globe out, even though the problem of local instabilities might well become acute.

But the difficulties do not lie in the environmental constraints of such a 'final stage', but on the road toward it; they are of an economic and political nature. By the year 2010, nearly two-thirds of mankind will be living in urban agglomerations. For the first time in the history of Man, the farmers will be in a clear minority.[10] Social aims will be increasingly fulfilled, especially as regards literacy, and this in turn will lead to increased aspirations. These will be in conflict with the growing capital requirements. There will be decreasing tolerance of inequalities, and growing competition on world markets will lead to an increased propensity to form new cartels; this in turn, together with increasing demands on social services, combined with the decreased propensity to accept the burdens of labour, may result in a worldwide increase in stagflationary tendencies. As a further consequence of this, there is likely to be an intensification of social confrontations. These will be focused, more than they have been in the past, on demands for changing the basic principles of the present economic order, and less on a redistribution of wealth within the given order.

In the long run, the industrial countries will not be in the position to provide the urgently needed help to less developed countries unless they achieve the imminent 'quantum jump' in their own energy supply system. The absolute amount of *additional* ODA required for an accelerated development of the LDCs (corresponding to approximately 30 billion US$ at 1975 prices) does not pose any economic problems compared with the additional capital required for the establishment of future energy-generating systems such as new fast breeder reactors, reprocessing plants, fusion reactors, and hybrid solar systems. The total amount of capital needed for the latter purpose may well require an increase of the over-all investment rate in the industrialized countries from today's 20 per cent to something like 30 or even 35 per cent during the next two decades. The industrial countries must achieve this higher investment rate in conjunction with higher employment, less inflation, and smaller balance-of-payment disequilibria. If they fail, at the same time, to achieve an over-all economic growth consistent with *both* the social and the thermodynamic equilibrium conditions, then social unrest will follow. Then the political climate required for a constructive as well as effective support of the less developed countries will deteriorate.

Appendix: Chapter 17

REFOP   *Reinforcement Potential*

$$\sqrt{SESUE * DEFEX} * STRCA \text{ (Table A17.1, } a\text{--}d)$$

SESUE Self-Sufficiency in Energy Supply (Table A17.1, *a*)
DEFEX Defence Expenditures as % of World Arms Expenditures (Table A17.1, *b*)
STRCA *Structuring Capacity:* SOCIP/MATE (Table A17.5, *f*)
SOCIP Social Communication and Information Potential defined as:

$$\sqrt{COMO * IPRA} \text{ Table A17.4, } a\text{--}c)$$

COMO Communication-Mobility Index (Table A17.2, *a–f*)

IPRA   Information Processing and Retrieval Ability
        (Table A17.3, a–h)
MATE   Index of Material and Energy Use (Table A17.5, a–d)
FODEP   Foreign Trade Dependency: $\sqrt{ITRAR * EXCAP}$
        (Table A17.6, g)
ITRAR   International Trade Ratio: $\dfrac{IM/GDP}{EX/WEX} \cdot 100$
        (Table A17.6, a–d)

EXCAP   Export Value per Capita (Table A17.6, e, f)

Table A17.1 Reinforcement potential

1975	(a) Self-sufficiency in energy supply (%)[1] SESUE	(b) Defense expenditure as % of world defense expenditure[2] DEFEX	(c) $\sqrt{axb} \cdot$ STRCA structuring capacity	(d) Index: USA = 100
FRG	50·19	5·38	17·25	21·3
France	20·78	4·66	10·73	13·2
Italy	16·08	1·57	5·47	6·8
Netherlands	141·58	0·99	10·65	13·1
Belgium	15·41	0·66	3·19	3·9
UK	62·30	3·71	22·95	28·3
Ireland	24·07	0·04	8·43	10·4
Denmark	0·94	0·31	5·08	6·3
Greece	32·57	0·48	4·95	6·1
Turkey	50·32	0·73	4·24	5·2
Norway	127·63	0·31	7·74	9·6
Sweden	16·95	0·83	5·36	6·6
China	21·23	0·35	8·98	11·1
Austria	39·19	0·14	1·80	2·2
Portugal	11·73	0·36	6·00	7·4
Finland	6·78	0·13	1·38	1·7
Spain	26·74	0·57	4·21	5·2
USSR	116·99	41·33	49·37	61·0
USA	86·68	29·66	80·96	100.0
Canada	119·00	0·99	9·22	11·4
Japan	9·32	1·54	2·68	3·3

Sources:
[1] United Nations, Department of Economic and Social Affairs, Statistical Office, *Statistical Yearbook 1976* (New York: UN, 1977), Table 142, pp. 372–5.
[2] Ruth Leger Sivard, *World Military and Social Expenditures, 1976* (Leesburg, Va : WMSE Publications, 1976), pp. 21–3; world military expenditures are estimated to be $300 million (p. 10).

Table A17.2 Communication-mobility index

1975	(a) TVs per 1,000 pop.	(b) Cars per 1,000 pop.	(c) Telephones per 1,000 pop.	(d) Radio receivers per 1,000 pop.	(e) $\sum_{a}^{d} \div 4$ $a+b+c+d$	(f) Index USA = 100
FRG	305	280	302	337	306	33·6
France	235	288	236	324	271	29·8
Italy	213	257	246	228	236	26·0
Netherlands	259	257	344	284	286	31·1
Belgium	252	259	272	384	292	32·1
UK	315	251	366	750	420	46·2
Ireland	178	164	127	287	189	20·5
Denmark	308	248	428	336	330	36·3
Greece	106	39	204	279	157	17·3
Turkey	12	6	23	107	37	4·1
Norway	256	222	339	320	284	31·2
Sweden	348	323	633	378	420	46·2
China	264	265	594	314	359	39·5
Austria	247	217	262	288	253	27·8
Portugal	66	84	117	174	110	12·1
Finland	269	200	358	427	313	34·4
Spain	147	119	200	229	189	19·8
USSR	208	10	62	461	187	20·5
USA	571	495	677	1895	909·5	**100·0**
Canada	366	354	550	894	541	59·5
Japan	233	143	356	465	299	33·0

Sources: For (a), (b), and (c): Statistical Office of the European Communities, *Basic Statistics of the Community 1977* (Luxembourg: Centre Européen, Office for Official Publications of the European Communities, 1977), Table 130, p. 171, and Table 131, p. 172. For (d): Unesco, *Statistical Yearbook 1976* (Paris: United Nations Educational, Scientific and Cultural Organization, 1977), Table 15.2, pp. 1001–7.

Table A17.3 Information processing and retrieval ability

	(a) R & D expenditure as % of GNP		(b) Index US = 100	(c) Scientists and engineers per 1,000 pop.	(d) Index USSR = 100	(e) Book production 1974 per 1,000 pop.	(f) Index NOR = 100	(g) Average index	(h) Average NOR = 100
FRG	1.22	(1975)	53	2.9	60	0.36	47	53.3	67.5
France	1.15	(1975)	50	4.1	85	0.22	28	54.3	34.9
Italy	0.40	(1975)	17	1.1	23	0.06	7	15.7	19.7
Netherlands	0.96	(1975)	42	3.9	81	0.28	36	53.0	67.0
Belgium	0.72	(1975)	32	n.a.		0.25	32	32.0	40.5
UK	1.18	(1975)	52	2.8	58	0.25	32	47.3	59.9
Ireland	0.46	(1975)	20	1.08	22	0.09	12	18.0	22.8
Denmark	0.61	(1975)	27	2.4	50	0.62	80	52.3	66.2
Greece	n.a.		—	n.a.	—	0.11	14	14.0	17.7
Turkey	0.128	(1972)	5	n.a.	—	n.a.	—	5.0	6.3
Norway	1.56	(1974)	68	3.3	69	0.77	100	79.0	100
Sweden	0.88	(1974)	38	4.15	86	0.54	70	64.6	82.0
China	1.85	(1971)	81	2.85	59	0.69	90	76.6	96.9
Austria	0.30	(1972)	13	0.62	13	0.39	51	25.6	32.4
Portugal	0.25	(1972)	11	0.45	9	0.46	60	26.6	33.7
Finland	0.74	(1973)	32	0.39	8	0.40	52	30.6	38.7
Spain	0.31	(1974)	13	0.34	7	0.25	32	17.3	21.9
USSR	2.20	(1974)	96	4.80	100	0.23	30	75.3	95.3
USA	2.28	(1974)	100	2.48	52	0.09	12	54.6	69.1
Canada	2.16	(1973)	95	1.27	26	0.13	17	46.0	58.2
Japan	2.1	(1974)	92	4.45	93	0.17	22	69.0	87.3

Sources:
(a) For member countries of the European Community, Statistical Office of the European Community, *Basic Statistics of the Community 1977* (Luxembourg: Centre Européen, Office for Official Publications of the European Communities, 1977), Table 11, p. 21; for other countries, Unesco, *Statistical Yearbook 1977* (Paris: United Nations Educational, Scientific and Cultural Organization, 1978), Table 8.2, pp. 669–73.
(b) Calculated from Unesco, *Statistical Yearbook 1977*, Table 7.2, pp. 612–18; for listed countries, mostly 1973 or 1974 data.
(c) Books in social sciences, pure and applied sciences, calculated from Unesco, *Statistical Yearbook 1977*, Table 11.2, pp. 792–800; for listed countries, mostly 1974 or 1975 data.

Table A17.4 Social communication and information potential

	(a) Communication-mobility index (from Table A17.2, f)	(b) Information processing and retrieval ability (from Table A17.3, h)	(c) Social communication and information potential $\sqrt{a \cdot b}$
FRG	33.6	67.5	47.6
France	29.8	34.9	32.2
Italy	26.0	19.7	22.6
Netherlands	31.1	67.0	45.6
Belgium	32.1	40.5	36.1
UK	46.2	59.9	52.6
Ireland	20.5	22.8	21.6
Denmark	36.3	66.2	49.0
Greece	17.3	17.7	17.5
Turkey	4.1	6.3	5.1
Norway	31.2	**100.0**	55.8
Sweden	46.2	82.0	61.5
China	39.5	96.9	61.9
Austria	27.8	32.4	30.0
Portugal	12.1	33.7	20.2
Finland	34.4	38.7	36.5
Spain	19.8	21.9	20.8
USSR	20.5	95.3	44.5
USA	**100.0**	69.1	83.1
Canada	59.5	58.2	58.8
Japan	33.0	87.3	53.7

Table A17.5 Index of material and energy use structuring capacity

1975	(a) Production of crude iron, crude steel, and rolled steel in kg per capita		(b) Mining and construction as % of GDP, 1965–73		(c) Production of primary energy in tce per capita		(d) Index of material and energy use $\sqrt{a \cdot b \cdot c}$	(e) Social communication and information potential (from Table A17.4, c)	(f) Structuring capacity = (e) : (d)
	kg	Index		Index		Index			
FRG	1,606	54.9	10.2	78.5	2.75	21.3	45.1	47.6	1.05
France	1,053	36.0	11.0	84.6	1.10	8.5	29.6	32.2	1.09
Italy	885	30.3	7.9	60.8	0.62	4.8	20.7	22.6	1.09
Netherlands	868	29.7	9.6	73.8	7.57	58.7	50.6	45.6	0.90
Belgium	2,924	100.0	8.3	63.8	0.93	7.2	35.8	36.1	1.00
UK	819	28.0	8.1	62.3	3.13	24.3	34.9	52.6	1.51
Ireland	38	1.3	n.a.	—	0.61	4.7	2.5	21.6	8.60
Denmark	194	6.6	9.1	70.0	0.04	0.3	5.2	49.0	9.40
Greece	198	6.8	9.2	70.8	0.73	5.7	14.0	17.5	1.25
Turkey	85	2.9	6.8	52.3	0.33	2.6	7.3	5.1	0.70
Norway	510	17.4	9.3	71.5	9.77	15.8	45.5	55.8	1.23
Sweden	1,560	53.3	8.9	68.5	2.80	21.7	42.9	61.5	1.43
China	154	5.2	10.0*	76.9	2.14	16.6	18.8	61.9	3.30
Austria	1,327	45.4	10.7	82.3	2.05	15.9	39.0	30.0	0.77
Portugal	106	3.6	6.4	49.2	0.24	1.9	6.9	20.2	2.93
Finland	840	28.7	10.3	79.2	0.87	6.7	24.8	36.5	1.47
Spain	761	26.0	6.2	47.7	0.74	5.7	19.2	20.8	1.08
USSR	1,361	46.5	13.0*	100.0	6.74	52.3	62.4	44.5	0.71
USA	1,178	40.3	6.3	48.5	9.77	75.8	52.9	83.1	1.57
Canada	1,371	46.7	9.1	70.0	12.89	100.0	68.9	58.8	0.85
Japan	2,463	84.2	8.2	63.1	0.54	4.2	28.2	53.7	1.90

Note:
*Estimate.
Sources:
(a) Statistical Office of the European Communities, *Basic Statistics of the Community 1977* (Luxembourg: Centre Européen, Office for Official Publications of the European Communities, 1977), Table 67, p. 90.
(b) World Bank, *World Tables 1976* (Baltimore, Md. and London: Johns Hopkins University Press, 1976). Economic Data Sheet 1, National Accounts and Prices, pp. 250–83.
(c) Statistical Office of the European Communities, *Basic Statistics of the Community 1977*, Table 47, p. 69.

Table A17.6 Foreign trade dependency

	(a) Imports as % of GDP	(b) Exports as % of world exports	(c) $\frac{a}{b}$	(d) Index	(e) Per capita exports	(f) Index	(g) Foreign trade dependency $= \sqrt{d \cdot f}$
FRG	17·89	11·1	1·61	1·228	1,113	52·06	7·99
France	15·96	6·2	2·57	1·961	737	34·47	8·22
Italy	22·34	4·2	5·32	4·059	472	22·08	9·47
Netherlands	44·33	4·3	10·31	7·867	1,950	90·21	26·64
Belgium	50·14	3·5*	14·32	10·927	2,138	**100·00**	33·05
UK	23·33	5·3	4·40	3·357	591	27·64	9·63
Ireland	48·31	0·4	120·78	92·163	772	36·11	57·69
Denmark	29·18	1·1	26·53	20·244	1,305	61·04	35·15
Greece	27·50	0·3	91·67	69·950	207	9·68	26·02
Turkey	13·11	0·2	65·55	50·019	27	1·26	7·94
Norway	34·09	0·9	37·88	28·905	1,358	63·52	42·85
Sweden	26·10	2·1	12·43	9·485	1,610	75·30	26·72
China	24·54	1·6	15·34	11·705	1,525	71·32	28·89
Austria	25·05	0·9	27·83	21·236	757	35·41	27·42
Portugal	26·21	0·2	131·05	**100·00**	168	7·86	28·03
Finland	28·58	0·7	40·83	31·156	886	41·44	35·93
Spain	16·12	0·9	17·91	13·667	164	7·67	10·24
USSR	7·35	4·1	1·79	1·366	99	4·63	2·51
USA	6·33	12·9	0·49	0·374	377	17·63	2·57
Canada	21·24	3·8	5·59	4·265	1,046	48·92	14·44
Japan	11·76	6·8	1·72	1·312	380	17·77	4·83

Note:
*Including Luxembourg.
Sources:
(a) Statistical Office of the European Communities, *Basic Statistics of the Community 1977* (Luxembourg, Centre Européen, Office for Official Publications of the European Communities, 1977), Table 92, pp. 116–17.
(b) ibid., Table 93, pp. 118–19.
(c) ibid., Table 108, p. 135; value in EUR (1 EUR = $1·32; see Table 133, pp. 174–5).

Table A17.7 Dimensions of inequalities among nations

	Max.	Min.	Max/Min	Number of countries
Fertilizer consumption kg per ha arable land	886·8 (USA)	0·1 (Upper Volta)	1:8,868	81
Energy cons. per cap in kg coals equivalent	11,123 (USA)	8 (Burundi)	1:1,390	115
Telephones per 100,000 pop.	58,677 (USA)	53 (Nepal)	1:1,107	111
Higher educ. enrollment per 10,000 pop. 20–29	275 (USA)	0·3 (Central African Republic)	1:917	97
Cement consumption per cap in kg	2,328 (Hong Kong)	3 (Mali)	1:776	106
Steel consumption per cap in kg	734 (Sweden)	1 (Niger, Somalia)	1:734	108

Table A17.7 Continued

	Max.	Min.	Max/Min	Number of countries
Electricity consumption per capita in kWH	14,643 (USA)	3 (Yemen, A.R.)	1:488	116
Radio receivers per 1,000 pop.	1,415 (USA)	3 (Zaïre)	1:472	111
Dwellings with piped water as % of total dwellings	100 (many developed countries)	0·3 (Mongolia)	1:333	39
Foreign trade (EX + IMP) per cap in US$	2,297 (Belgium)	8 (India)	1:287	111
Death rate due to infectious and parasitical diseases per 100,000 persons	595,2 (Guatemala)	6 (Canada)	1:99	47
GDP per capita at current prices in US$	4,880 (USA)	55 (Mali)	1:88	109
Agricultural production per (male) worker at current prices in US$ (purchaser's value)	11,490 (USA)	150 (Niger)	1:76·6	70
Water supply : % of pop. with reasonable access	100 (many developed countries)	2 (Burundi)	1:50	84
Manufactured products per person active in manufacturing (in 1970 US$)	12,390 (USA)	430 (India) (no data for most of the African countries)	1:29	45
Infant mortality, rate per 1,000 live births	200 (Ethiopia)	11 (Sweden)	1:18	65
Dwellings with electricity as % of total dwellings	100 (many developed countries)	6·1 (Indonesia)	1:17	39
GDP derived from industry as % of total GDP	66 (Saudi Arabia)	4 (Burundi)	1:16·5	91
Savings as % of national income	34 (Libya)	3 (Vietnam)	1:11	51
Percentage of pop. 6–11 enrolled at school	100 (many European countries, Japan, Cuba, Australia, New Zealand, etc.)	10·0 (Ethiopia)	1:10	89
Literate as % of total pop. 15 and over	99·0 (USA)	12·1 (Mozambique)	1:8	65
Crude death rate per 1,000 pop.	26·8 (Ethiopia)	5·2 (Singapore)	1:5	78
Average number of persons per room	3·1 (El Salvador)	0·6 (Canada, USA)	1:5	44
Protein of non-animal origin, g per day per person	108·7 (Mongolia)	32·7 (Zaïre)	1:3·3	98
Expectation of life at birth	74·9 (Sweden)	38·1 (Ethiopia)	1:2	76
Calories per day per person	3,420 (Ireland)	1,700 (Tanzania)	1:2	98

Source: United Nations Research Institute for Social Development, *Research Data Bank of Development Indicators* (Geneva : UNRISD, 1976), Report No. 76.2, Vol. II, *passim.*

Notes: Chapter 17

I wish to thank Richard L. Merritt for his valuable comments and suggestions by which he decisively improved not only the English but, above all, the content of this article. Needless to say that the responsibility for all remaining shortcomings is entirely mine.

1 The material needs given in our example are those taken from the Bariloche model; see Amílcar O. Herrera, Hugo D. Scolnik *et al.*, *Catastrophe or New Society? A Latin American World Model* (Ottawa: International Development Research Centre, 1976). See also Unesco, Division for the Socioeconomic Analysis of Social Sciences and their Applications, *Handbook of the Latin American World Model* (Paris: Unesco, July 1977); and International Labour Office, *Employment, Growth and Basic Needs: A One-World Problem: The International 'Basic-Needs Strategy against Chronic Poverty'* (New York and London: Praeger, 1977).
2 Richard L. Merritt and Stein Rokkan (eds), *Comparing Nations: The Use of Quantitative Data in Cross-National Research* (New Haven, Conn., and London: Yale University Press, 1966); Bruce M. Russett and Hayward R. Alker, Jr, Karl W. Deutsch and Harold D. Lasswell, *et al.*, *World Handbook of Political and Social Indicators* (New Haven, Conn., and London: Yale University Press, 1964); and United Nations Research Institute for Social Development, *Research Data Bank of Development Indicators*, 3 vols (Geneva: UNRISD, Reports Nos 76·1–76·3m 1976).
3 This may be expected with a fair degree of probability, even if we allow for health improvements to take place in the forthcoming decades in the LDCs.
4 See Bruno Fritsch, 'Future capital requirements of alternative energy strategies: global perspectives', paper presented at the 5th World Congress of the International Economics Association, Tokyo, 29 August–3 September 1977.
5 For a more detailed analysis of the interrelations between economic growth and energy consumption, see Fritsch, 'Future capital requirements'.
6 For estimates about the future capital requirements of alternative energy stretegies, see ibid.
7 Herrera *et al.*, *Catastrophe or New Society?*
8 The World Bank, *World Development Report, 1978* (Washington, DC: International Bank for Reconstruction and Development, 1978), p. 84, table 5.
9 United Nations, Conference on Trade and Development, Secretariat, *Trade Prospects and Capital Needs of Developing Countries, 1976–1980* (New York: United Nations, UNCTAD, Document TD/B/C.3/134, April 1976), pp. 3ff.
10 See Karl W. Deutsch, 'Toward an interdisciplinary model of world stability and change: some intellectual preconditions', *Journal of Peace Science*, vol. 2, no 1 (Spring 1976), pp. 1–14.

Bibliography of Karl W. Deutsch, 1942–80

Editors' Note The bibliography was prepared on the basis of material provided by Professor Deutsch. It includes only original items, and hence neither excerpts and articles reprinted in other volumes nor most translations. It also does not include his many works in progress or in press.

1942
1 'Some economic aspects of the rise of nationalistic and racial pressure groups', *Canadian Journal of Economics and Political Science*, vol. 8, no. 1 (February 1942), pp. 109–15.
2 'The trend of European nationalism – the language aspect', *American Political Science Review*, vol. 36, no. 3 (June 1942), pp. 533–41.

1943
3 *Faith for Our Generation: A Study Unit on Youth and Religion* (Boston, Mass.: American Unitarian Youth, 1943).

1944
4 'Medieval unity and the economic conditions for an international civilization', *Canadian Journal of Economics and Political Science*, vol. 10, no. 1 (February 1944), pp. 18–35.

1945
5 'Anti-semitic ideas in the Middle Ages: international civilizations in expansion and conflict', *Journal of History of Ideas*, vol. 6, no. 2 (April 1945), pp. 239–51.
6 'The economic factor in intolerance', in *Approaches to National Unity*, Fifth Symposium of the Conference on Science, Philosophy, and Religion in Their Relation to the Democratic Way of Life, Inc. (hereinafter CSPR), ed. Lyman Bryson, Louis Finkelstein, and Robert M. MacIver (New York: Harper, 1945), pp. 368–86.

1947
7 'Problems of justice in international territorial disputes', in *Approaches to Group Understanding*, Sixth CSPR Symposium, ed. Lyman Bryson, Louis Finkelstein, and Robert M. MacIver (New York: Harper, 1947), pp. 237–70.
8 'The crisis of peace and power in the atom age', in *Conflicts of Power in Modern Culture*, Seventh CSPR Symposium, ed. Lyman Bryson, Louis Finkelstein, and Robert M. MacIver (New York: Harper, 1947), pp. 608–57.

1948
9 'The value of freedom: some long range implications for the social sciences', in *Learning and World Peace*, Eighth CSPR Symposium, ed. Lyman Bryson, Louis Finkelstein, and Robert M. MacIver (New York:

Harper, 1948), pp. 63–80; and *American Scholar*, vol. 17, no. 2 (Spring 1948), pp. 150–60, and vol. 17, no. 3 (Summer 1948), pp. 323–35.

1949

10 'Innovation, entrepreneurship, and the learning process', in *Change and the Entrepreneur: Postulates and Patterns for Entrepreneurial History*, ed. Research Center in Entrepreneurial History, Harvard University (Cambridge, Mass.: Harvard University Press, 1949), pp. 24–9.

11 'A note on the history of entrepreneurship, innovation, and decision-making', *Explorations in Entrepreneurial History*, 1st ser., vol. 1, no. 5 (May 1949), pp. 7–16.

1950

12 'Higher education and the unity of knowledge: an operational approach to the history of thought', in *Goals for American Education*, Ninth CSPR Symposium, ed. Lyman Bryson, Louis Finkelstein, and Robert M. MacIver (New York: Harper, 1950), pp. 55–139.

13 'The Middle Ages as a key to Western history', preface to *The Driving Power of Western Civilization: The Christian Revolution of the Middle Ages*, by Eugen Rosenstock-Huessy (Boston, Mass.: Beacon Press, 1950), pp. ix–xiv.

14 'Nationalism, communication, and community: an interim report', in *Perspectives on a Troubled Decade: Science, Philosophy, and Religion, 1939–1949*, Tenth CSPR Symposium, ed. Lyman Bryson, Louis Finkelstein, and Robert M. MacIver (New York: Harper, 1950), pp. 339–65.

1951

15 'Mechanism, organism, and society: some models in natural and social science', *Philosophy of Science*, vol. 18, no. 3 (July 1951), pp. 230–52.

16 'Mechanism, teleology, and mind: the theory of communications and some problems in philosophy and social science', *Philosophy and Phenomenological Research*, vol. 12, no. 2 (December 1951), pp. 185–223.

1952

17 'Communication theory and social science', *American Journal of Orthopsychiatry*, vol. 22, no. 3 (July 1952), pp. 469–83.

18 'Nationalism and the social scientists', in *Foundations of World Organization: A Political and Cultural Appraisal*, Eleventh CSPR Symposium, ed. Lyman Bryson, Louis Finkelstein, Harold D. Lasswell, and Robert M. MacIver (New York: Harper, 1952), pp. 9–20, 447–68.

19 'Nationalistic responses to study abroad', in *Report on the Conference on International Educational Exchanges* (New York: National Association for Foreign Student Affairs, 1952), pp. 9–20.

20 'On communication models in the social sciences', *Public Opinion Quarterly*, vol. 16, no. 3 (Fall 1952), pp. 356–80.

21 Review of *The Bias of Communication*, by Harold A. Innis, *Canadian Journal of Economics and Political Science*, vol. 18, no. 3 (August 1952), pp. 338–90.

1953

22 *Nationalism and Social Communication: An Inquiry into the Foundations of Nationality* (Cambridge, Mass.: MIT Press; and New York: Wiley, 1953;

2nd edn, 1966, with new chapter, 'Introduction: some changes in nationalism and its study, 1953–1965', pp. i–iv).
23 'Communication in self-governing organizations: notes on autonomy, freedom, and authority in the growth of social groups', in *Freedom and Authority in Our Time*, Twelfth CSPR Symposium, ed. Lyman Bryson, Louis Finkelstein, Robert M. MacIver, and Richard McKeon (New York: Harper, 1953), pp. 271–88.
24 'The growth of nations: some recurrent patterns of political and social integration', *World Politics*, vol. 5, no. 2 (January 1953), pp. 168–95.
25 'Tragedy and Karl Jaspers', preface to *Tragedy Is Not Enough*, by Karl Jaspers (Boston, Mass.: Beacon Press, 1953), pp. 7–20.
26 Review of *Modern Nationalities: A Sociological Study*, by Florian Znaniecki, *American Slavic and East European Review*, vol. 12, no. 3 (October 1953), pp. 401–3.
27 Review of *The Rise and Fall of Civilizations: An Inquiry into the Relationship between Economic Development and Civilization*, by Shepard B. Clough, *Journal of Economic History*, vol. 13, no. 1 (Winter 1953), pp. 109–10.

1954
28 *Political Community at the International Level: Problems of Definition and Measurement* (Garden City, NY: Doubleday, 1954; repr. Hamden, Conn.: Shoe String Press, 1970).
29 'Cracks in the monolith: possibilities and patterns of disintegration in totalitarian systems', in *Totalitarianism*, ed. Carl J. Friedrich (Cambridge, Mass.: Harvard University Press, 1954), pp. 308–33.
30 'Game theory and politics: some problems of application', *Canadian Journal of Economics and Political Science*, vol. 20, no. 1 (February 1954), pp. 76–83.
31 'On scientific and humanistic knowledge', *Confluence: An International Forum*, vol. 3, no. 1 (March 1954), pp. 29–40.
32 'Problems and prospects of federation', in *Challenge in Eastern Europe*, ed. Cyril E. Black (New Brunswick, NJ: Rutgers University Press, 1954), pp. 219–44; repr. Port Washington, NY: Kennikat Press, 1971).
33 'Self-referent symbols and self-referent communication patterns: a note on some pessimistic theories of politics', in *Symbols and Values: An Initial Study*, Thirteenth CSPR Symposium, ed. Lyman Bryson, Louis Finkelstein, Robert M. MacIver, and Richard McKeon (New York: Harper, 1954), pp. 619–46.
34 Review of *The Genius of American Politics*, by Daniel J. Boorstin, *American Historical Review*, vol. 59, no. 2 (January 1954), pp. 383–4.

1955
35 'Symbols of political community', in *Symbols and Society*, Fourteenth CSPR Symposium, ed. Lyman Bryson, Louis Finkelstein, Hudson Hoagland, and Robert M. MacIver (New York: Harper, 1955), pp. 23–42.
36 Review of *People of Plenty: Economic Abundance and the American Character*, by David M. Potter, *Yale Review*, vol. 44, no. 2 (Winter 1955), pp. 292–5.
37 Review of *Mathematical Thinking in the Social Sciences*, ed. Paul F. Lazarsfeld, *American Journal of Sociology*, vol. 60, no. 4 (January 1955), pp. 398–9.
38 Review of *Military Organization and Society*, by Stanislaw Andrzejewski,

American Journal of Sociology, vol. 61, no. 2 (September 1955), pp. 177–8.

1956
39 An Interdisciplinary Bibliography on Nationalism, 1935–1953 (Cambridge, Mass.: MIT Press, 1956).
40 'Autonomy and boundaries according to communications theory', in Toward a Unified Theory of Human Behavior, ed. Roy R. Grinker (New York: Basic Books, 1956; 2nd edn, 1967) pp. 278–97.
41 'Joseph Schumpeter as an analyst of sociology and economic history', Journal of Economic History, vol. 16, no. 1 (March 1956), pp 41–56.
42 'Shifts in the balance of communication flows: a problem of measurement in international relations', Public Opinion Quarterly, vol. 20, no. 1 (Spring 1956), pp. 143–60.

1957
43 (With Sidney A. Burrell, Robert A. Kann, Maurice Lee, Jr, Martin Lichterman, Raymond E. Lindgren, Francis L. Loewenheim, and Richard W. Van Wagenen), Political Community and the North Atlantic Area: International Organization in the Light of Historical Experience (Princeton, NJ: Princeton University Press, 1957; paperback edn, 1968; repr. New York: Greenwood Press, 1969).
44 'Mass communications and the loss of freedom in national decision-making', Journal of Conflict Resolution, vol. 1, no. 2 (June 1957), pp. 200–11.
45 'Language and nationalism since 1920' (bibliographies on selected areas), in 'The most dangerous decades: an introduction to the comparative study of language policy in multi-lingual areas', ed. Selig S. Harrison, Language and Communication Research Center, Columbia University, New York, 1957, mimeo., pp. 37–69.
46 Review of International Communication and Political Opinion: A Guide to the Literature, by Bruce Lannes Smith and Chitra M. Smith, Journal of Modern History, vol. 2, no. 4 (December 1957), p. 418.
47 Review of La querelle de la C.E.D., ed. Raymond Aron and Daniel Lerner, American Political Science Review, vol. 51, no. 4 (December 1957), pp. 1113–14.

1958
48 'Scientific and humanistic knowledge in the growth of science', in Science and the Creative Spirit: Essays on Humanistic Aspects of Science, by Karl W. Deutsch, F. E. L. Priestly, Harcourt Brown, and David Hawkins, ed. Harcourt Brown (Toronto: University of Toronto Press, 1958), pp. 1–51.
49 'The place of behavioral sciences in graduate training in international relations', Behavioral Science, vol. 3, no. 3 (July 1958), pp. 278–84.
50 (With Lewis J. Edinger), 'Foreign policy of the German Federal Republic', in Foreign Policy in World Politics, ed. Roy C. Macridis (Englewood Cliffs, NJ: Prentice-Hall, 1958, pp. 78–131; rev. edn, 1962, pp. 91–132; 3rd edn, 1967, pp. 102–55).

1959
51 (With Lewis J. Edinger), Germany Rejoins the Powers: Mass Opinion, Interest Groups, and Elites in Contemporary German Foreign Policy (Stanford, Calif.: Stanford University Press, 1959; repr. New York: Octagon Books, 1973).

52 'The limits of common sense', *Psychiatry: Journal for the Study of Interpersonal Processes*, vol. 22, no. 2 (May 1959), pp. 105–12.
53 'The impact of science and technology on international politics', *Daedalus*, vol. 88, no. 4 (Fall 1959), pp. 669–85.
54 'Jaspers' challenge to the universities', editor's note to *The Idea of the University*, by Karl Jaspers (Boston, Mass.: Beacon Press, 1959), pp. ix–xiii.
55 Comments on 'American intellectuals: their politics and status', by Seymour Martin Lipset, *Daedalus*, vol. 88, no. 3 (Summer 1959), pp. 488–91.

1960
56 'Toward an inventory of basic trends and patterns in comparative and international politics', *American Political Science Review*, vol. 54, no. 1 (March 1960), pp. 34–57.
57 (With I. Richard Savage), 'A statistical model of the gross analysis of transaction flows', *Econometrica*, vol. 28, no. 3 (July 1960), pp. 551–72.
58 'The propensity to international transactions', *Political Studies*, vol. 8, no. 2 (June 1960), pp. 147–55.

1961
59 'On social communication and the metropolis', *Daedalus*, vol. 90, no. 1 (Winter 1961), pp. 99–110.
60 (With Alexander Eckstein), 'National industrialization and the declining share of the international economic sector, 1890–1959', *World Politics*, vol. 13, no. 2 (January 1961), pp. 267–99.
61 (With William G. Madow), 'A note on the appearance of wisdom in large bureaucratic organizations', *Behavioral Science*, vol. 6, no. 1 (January 1961), pp. 72–8.
62 'Soziale Mobilisierung und politische Entwicklung', *Politische Vierteljahresschrift*, vol. 2, no. 2 (July 1961), pp. 104–24.
63 'Social mobilization and political development', *American Political Science Review*, vol. 55, no. 3 (September 1961), pp. 493–514 (expansion of item 62).
64 (With Walter Isard), 'A note on a generalized concept of effective distance', *Behavioral Science*, vol. 6, no. 4 (October 1961), pp. 308–11.
65 Review of *The Politics of Mass Society*, by William Kornhauser, *American Political Science Review*, vol. 55, no. 1 (March 1961), pp. 148–9.
66 Review of *Fights, Games, and Debates*, by Anatol Rapoport, *Yale Review*, vol. 50, no. 3 (Spring 1961), pp. 429–33.
67 Review of *The Strategy of Conflict*, by Thomas C. Schelling, in *Annals of the American Academy of Political and Social Science*, vol. 336 (July 1961), pp. 170–1.

1962
68 (With Chester I. Bliss and Alexander Eckstein), 'Population, sovereignty, and the share of foreign trade', *Economic Development and Cultural Change*, vol. 10, no. 4 (July 1962), pp. 353–66.
69 'Towards Western European integration: an interim assessment', *Journal of International Affairs*, vol. 16, no. 1 (1962), pp. 89–101.
70 'Communications, arms inspection, and national security', in *Preventing World War III: Some Proposals*, ed. Quincy Wright, William M. Evan, and Morton Deutsch (New York: Simon & Schuster, 1962), pp. 62–73.
71 'Strategies of freedom: the widening of choices and the change of goals', in *Nomos IV: Liberty*, ed. Carl J. Friedrich (New York: Atherton Press, 1962), pp. 301–7.

72 'Anarchism', in *Encyclopaedia Britannica* (Chicago: Encyclopaedia Britannica, 1962), vol. 1, pp. 867–9.
73 'Representative government', in *The Encyclopedia Americana* (New York: Americana Corporation, 1962), Vol. 23, pp. 387e–h.

1963
74 *The Nerves of Government: Models of Political Communication and Control* (New York: The Free Press, 1963; 2nd edn, 1966, with new introduction, 'The study of political communication and control, 1962–1966', pp. vii–xxiii).
75 (With Rupert Breitling), 'The German Federal Republic', in *Modern Political Systems: Europe*, ed. Roy C. Macridis and Robert E. Ward (Englewood Cliffs, NJ: Prentice-Hall, 1963), pp. 269–398; 2nd edn [with Eric A. Nordlinger], 1968, pp. 229–450; 3rd edn, 1972, pp. 308–473; 4th edn [with D. Brent Smith], 1978, pp. 175–291).
76 (With William J. Foltz), editor, *Nation-Building* (New York: Atherton Press, 1963; Atheling edn, 1966, with foreword, 'The study of nation-building, 1962–1966', pp. v–xi).
77 'Nation-building and national development: some issues for political research', in *Nation-Building*, ed. Karl W. Deutsch and William J. Foltz (New York: Atherton Press, 1963, pp. 1–16; Atheling edn, 1966).
78 'Outer space and international politics: a look to 1988', in *Outer Space in World Politics*, ed. Joseph M. Goldsen (New York: Praeger, 1963), pp. 139–74 (originally published in RAND Corporation Report R-362-RC, 5 May 1960).
79 (With Harold D. Lasswell, Richard L. Merritt, and Bruce M. Russett), *The Yale Political Data Program* (New Haven, Conn.: Yale University, Political Science Research Library, Yale Paper in Political Science No. 4, February 1963); appears in *Comparing Nations: The Use of Quantitative Data in Cross-National Research*, ed. Richard L. Merritt and Stein Rokkan (New Haven, Conn., and London: Yale University Press, 1966), pp. 81–94.
80 (With Bruce M. Russett), 'International trade and political independence', *American Behavioral Scientist*, vol. 6, no. 7 (March 1963), pp. 18–20.
81 (With Norbert Wiener), 'The lonely nationalism of Rudyard Kipling', *Yale Review*, vol. 52, no. 4 (Summer 1963), pp. 499–517.
82 'The commitment of national legitimacy symbols as a verification technique', *Journal of Conflict Resolution*, vol. 7, no. 3 (September 1963), pp. 360–9; and *Journal of Arms Control*. vol. 1, no. 4 (October 1963), pp. 454–63.
83 'Zur Theorie der Abschreckung', *Politische Vierteljahresschrift*, vol. 4, no. 3 (September 1963), pp. 222–32.
84 'Challenge to liberal education', *Journal of the American Association of University Women*, vol. 57, no. 1 (October 1963), pp. 20–3, 40.
85 (With Stein Rokkan and Richard L. Merritt), 'International conference on the use of quantitative political, social, and cultural data in cross-national comparisons, Yale University, 10–20 September, 1963: summary report', *Social Sciences Information*, vol. 2, no. 4 (December 1963), pp. 89–108.

1964
86 (With Bruce M. Russett, Hayward R. Alker, Jr, and Harold D. Lasswell), *World Handbook of Political and Social Indicators* (New Haven, Conn., and London: Yale University Press, 1964).
87 (With Philip E. Jacob, Henry Teune, James V. Toscano, and William L. C.

Wheaton), *The Integration of Political Communities*, ed. Philip E. Jacob and James V. Toscano (Philadelphia, Pa: Lippincott, 1964).

88 (With Morton A. Kaplan), 'The limits of international coalition', in *International Aspects of Civil Strife*, ed. James N. Rosenau (Princeton, NJ: Princeton University Press, 1964), pp. 170–84.

89 (With J. David Singer), 'Multipolar power systems and international stability', *World Politics*, vol. 16, no. 3 (April 1964), pp. 390–406.

90 'Introduction', in *Strategy and Conscience*, by Anatol Rapoport (New York: Harper & Row, 1964, pp. vii–xv; repr. New York: Schocken Books, 1969).

1965

91 (With Richard L. Merritt), 'Effects of events on national and international images', in *International Behavior: A Social-Psychological Analysis*, ed. Herbert C. Kelman (New York: Holt, Rinehart & Winston, 1965), pp. 132–87.

92 (With Leroy N. Rieselbach), 'Recent trends in political theory and political philosophy', *Annals of the American Academy of Political and Social Science*, vol. 360 (July 1965), pp. 139–62.

93 (With Hermann Weilenmann), 'The Swiss city canton: a political invention', *Comparative Studies in Society and History*, vol. 7, no. 4 (July 1965), pp. 393–408.

94 (With J. David Singer and Keith Smith), 'The organizing efficiency of theories: the N/V ratio as a crude rank order measure', *American Behavioral Scientist*, vol. 9, no. 2 (October 1965), pp. 30–3.

95 Discussion contribution on 'Max Weber und die Machtpolitik', by Raymond Aron, in *Max Weber und die Soziologie Heute: Verhandlungen des 15. Deutschen Soziologentages*, ed. Otto Stammer (Tübingen: Mohr [Paul Siebeck], 1965), pp. 138–45; and *Max Weber and Sociology Today*, ed. Otto Stammer (New York: Harper & Row, 1971), pp. 116–22.

96 'Quincy Wright's contribution to the study of war', preface to *A Study of War*, 2nd edn, by Quincy Wright (Chicago: University of Chicago Press, 1965), pp. xi–xix.

1966

97 'External influences on the internal behavior of states', in *Approaches to Comparative and International Politics*, ed. R. Barry Farrell (Evanston, Ill.: Northwestern University Press, 1966), pp. 5–26.

98 'The future of world politics', *Political Quarterly*, vol. 37, no. 1 (January–March 1966), pp. 9–32.

99 'Integration and arms control in the European political environment: a summary report', *American Political Science Review*, vol. 60, no. 2 (June 1966), pp. 354–65; and 'Rüstungskontrolle und Integrationsbestrebungen im Geflecht der europäischen Politik', *Politische Vierteljahresschrift*, vol. 7, no. 3 (November 1966), pp. 330–63.

100 'On theories, taxonomies, and models as communication codes for organizing information', *Behavioral Science*, vol. 11, no. 1 (January 1966), pp. 1–17.

101 'Power and communication in international society', in *Conflict in Society*, ed. Anthony de Reuck and Julie Knight, Ciba Foundation volume (Boston, Mass.: Mass. Little, Brown, 1966), pp. 300–16.

102 'Recent trends in research methods in political science', in *A Design for Political Science: Scope, Objectives, and Methods*, ed. James C. Charlesworth (Philadelphia, Pa: American Academy of Political and Social Science, Monograph No. 6, December 1966), pp. 149–78.

103 'Social resources for the growth of science: some issues for research and policy', *Public Policy*, Vol. 15, ed. John D. Montgomery and Arthur Smithies (Cambridge, Mass.: Harvard University Press, 1966), pp. 179–98.

104 (With Hermann Weilenmann), 'The social roots of Swiss national identity: the conflict of feudalism and cantonal self-government in the social order of medieval Europe', *Yale German Review*, vol. 2, no. 2 (Spring 1966), pp. 23–30.

105 'Some quantitative constraints on value allocation in society and politics', *Behavioral Science*, vol. 11, no. 4 (July 1966), pp. 245–52.

106 'The theoretical basis of data programs', in *Comparing Nations: The Use of Quantitative Data in Cross-National Research*, ed. Richard L. Merritt and Stein Rokkan (New Haven, Conn., and London: Yale University Press, 1966), pp. 27–55.

107 *Arms Control in the European Political Environment: Final Report* (New Haven, Conn.: Yale University, Political Science Research Library, January 1966).

108 (With Lewis J. Edinger, Roy C. Macridis, Richard L. Merritt, and Helga Voss-Eckermann), *French and German Elite Responses, 1964: Code Book and Data* (New Haven, Conn.: Yale University, Political Science Research Library, January 1966).

1967

109 *Arms Control and the Atlantic Alliance: Europe Faces Coming Policy Decisions* (New York: Wiley, 1967).

110 (With Lewis J. Edinger, Roy C. Macridis, and Richard L. Merritt), *France, Germany, and the Western Alliance: A Study of Elite Attitudes on European Integration and World Politics* (New York: Charles Scribner's Sons, 1967).

111 'Changing images of international conflict', *Journal of Social Issues*, vol. 23, no. 1 (January 1967), pp. 91–107.

112 'Nation and world', in *Contemporary Political Science: Toward Empirical Theory*, ed. Ithiel de Sola Pool (New York: McGraw-Hill, 1967), pp. 204–27.

113 'Nature de la légitimité et usage des symboles nationaux de légitimité comme technique auxiliaire du controle des armements', *L'Idée de légitimité* (Paris: Presses Universitaires de France, Annales de Philosophie Politique No. 7, 1967), pp. 129–46.

114 'On the concepts of politics and power', *Journal of International Affairs*, vol. 21, no. 2 (1967), pp. 232–41.

115 (With Hermann Weilenmann), 'The Valais: a case study in the development of a bilingual people', *Orbis*, vol. 10, no. 4 (Winter 1967), pp. 1269–97.

116 Review of *Human Behavior and International Politics: Contributions from the Social-Psychological Sciences*, ed. J. David Singer, *Behavioral Science*, vol. 12, no. 1 (January 1967), pp. 49–53.

1968

117 *The Analysis of International Relations* (Englewood Cliffs, NJ: Prentice-Hall, 1968; 2nd edn, 1978).

118 (With Stanley Hoffmann), editor, *The Relevance of International Law: A Festschrift for Professor Leo Gross* (Cambridge, Mass.: Schenkman, 1968; paperback edn, Garden City, NY: Doubleday Anchor, 1971).

119 'The probability of international law', in *The Relevance of International Law: A Festschrift for Professor Leo Gross*, ed. Karl W. Deutsch and

Stanley Hoffmann (Cambridge, Mass.: Schenkman, 1968, pp. 57–83; paperback edn, Garden City, NY: Doubleday Anchor, 1971, pp. 80–114).
120 'The coming crisis of cross-national and international research in the United States', *Newsletter of the American Council of Learned Societies*, vol. 19, no. 4 (April 1968), pp. 1–17.
121 (With Richard W. Chadwick), 'Doubling time and half life: two suggested conventions for describing rates of change in social science data', *American Behavioral Scientist*, vol. 11, no. 4 (March–April 1968), pp. 9–11.
122 'The impact of communications upon international relations theory', in *Theory of International Relations: The Crisis of Relevance*, ed. Abdul A. Said (Englewood Cliffs, NJ: Prentice-Hall, 1968), pp. 74–92.
123 'Knowledge in the growth of civilization: a cybernetic approach to the history of human thought', in *The Foundations of Access to Knowledge: A Symposium*, ed. Edward B. Montgomery (Syracuse, NY: Syracuse University, School of Library Science, 1968; distributed by Syracuse University Press), pp. 37–58.
124 (With Hermann Weilenmann), 'Die militärische Bewährung eines sozialen Systems: die Schweizer Eidgenossenschaft im 14. Jahrhundert', in *Beiträge zur Militärsoziologie*, ed. René König (Cologne and Opladen: Westdeutscher Verlag, Kölner Zeitschrift für Soziologie und Sozialpsychologie, Sonderheft 12, 1968), pp. 38–58.
125 'Problem solving: the behavioral approach', in *International Communication and the New Diplomacy*, ed. Arthur S. Hoffman (Bloomington, Ind.: Indiana University Press, 1968), pp. 64–88.

1969
126 *Nationalism and Its Alternatives* (New York: Knopf, 1969).
127 'On methodological problems of quantitative research', in *Quantitative Ecological Analysis in the Social Sciences*, ed. Mattei Dogan and Stein Rokkan (Cambridge, Mass.: MIT Press, 1969), pp. 19–39.
128 (With Manfred Kochen), 'Toward a rational theory of decentralization: some implications of a mathematical approach', *American Political Science Review*, vol. 63, no. 3 (September 1969), pp. 734–49.

1970
129 *Politics and Government: How People Decide Their Fate* (Boston, Mass.: Houghton Mifflin, 1970; 2nd edn, 1974; 3rd edn, 1980).
130 (With David V. J. Bell), *Instructor's Manual to Accompany Politics and Government* (Boston, Mass.: Houghton Mifflin, 1970).
131 (With David V. J. Bell and Seymour Martin Lipset), editor, *Issues in Politics and Government* (Boston, Mass.: Houghton Mifflin, 1970).
132 (With Richard L. Merritt), *Nationalism and National Development: An Interdisciplinary Bibliography* (Cambridge, Mass.: MIT Press, 1970).
133 'Efforts d'intégration dans le complexe de la politique européenne', in *Méthodes quantitatives et integration européenne* (Geneva: Institut Universitaire d'Études Européennes, 1970), pp. 34–64.
134 'The impact of complex data bases on the social sciences', in *Data Bases, Computers, and the Social Sciences*, ed. Ralph L. Bisco (New York: Wiley, 1970), pp. 19–41.
135 'Integration and autonomy: some concepts and data', *Ekistics*, vol. 30, no. 179 (October 1970), pp. 327–31.
136 'Kernwaffen und internationales Machtgleichgewicht', in *Zur Pathologie des Rüstungswettlaufs: Beiträge zür Friedens- und Konfliktforschung*, ed. Dieter Senghaas (Freiburg im Breisgau: Verlag Rombach, 1970), pp. 127–38.

137 (With Manfred Kochen), 'Decentralization and uneven service loads', *Journal of Regional Science*, vol. 10, no. 2 (August 1970), pp. 153–73.
138 'Research problems on race in intranational and international relations: social communication', in *Race among Nations: A Conceptual Approach*, ed. George W. Shepherd, Jr, and Tilden J. LeMelle (Lexington, Mass.: D. C. Heath, 1970), pp. 123–51.
139 (With Dieter Senghaas), 'Die Schritte zum Krieg: eine Übersicht der Systemebenen, Entscheidungsstadien und einige Forschungsergebnisse', *Aus Politik und Zeitgeschichte: Beilage zur Wochenzeitung Das Parlament* vol. 20, no. 47 (21 November 1970), pp. 3–40; and 'The steps to war: a survey of system levels, decision stages, and research findings', in *Sage International Yearbook of Foreign Policy Studies*, Vol. 1, ed. Patrick J. McGowan (Beverly Hills, Calif., and London: Sage, 1973). pp. 275–329.
140 (With Dieter Senghaas), 'Simulation in international politics: how to get your money's worth,' *Perspectives in Defense Management*, no. 10 (March 1970), pp. 37–40.
141 'Foreword', in *The German Democratic Republic from the Sixties to the Seventies: A Socio-Political Analysis*, by Peter Christian Ludz (Cambridge, Mass.: Harvard University, Center for International Affairs, Occasional Paper in International Affairs No. 26, 1970), pp. v–vi.

1971

142 'Abschreckungspolitik und gesellschaftliche Ordnung: zum Problem der sich wandelnden Gesellschaft', in *Jahrbuch für Friedens- und Konfliktforschung*, Vol. 1: *Bedrohungsvorstellungen als Faktor der internationalen Politik*, ed. Karl Kaiser (Dusseldorf: Bertelsmann Universitätsverlag, 1971), pp. 42–66.
143 (With Dieter Senghaas), 'Die brüchige Vernunft von Staaten', in *Kritische Friedensforschung*, ed. Dieter Senghaas (Frankfurt/Main: Edition Surhkamp, 1971), pp. 105–63; and 'The fragile sanity of states: a theoretical analysis', in *New States in the Modern World*, ed. Martin Kilson (Cambridge, Mass.: Harvard University Press, 1975), pp. 200–44.
144 (With John Platt and Dieter Senghaas), 'Conditions favoring major advances in social science', *Science*, vol. 171, no. 3970 (5 February 1971), pp. 450–9.
145 (With Richard L. Merritt), 'Data in international and comparative politics: the Yale Arms Control Project', in *Political Scientists at Work*, ed. Oliver Walter (Belmont, Calif.: Duxbury Pres, 1971), pp. 46–73.
146 'Development change: some political aspects', in *Behavioral Change in Agriculture: Concepts and Strategies for Influencing Transition*, ed. J. Paul Leagans and Charles P. Loomis (Ithaca, NY, and London: Cornell University Press, 1971), pp. 27–50.
147 (With Dieter Senghaas), 'A framework for a theory of war and peace', in *The Search for World Order*, ed. Albert Lepawsky, Edward H. Buehrig, and Harold D. Lasswell (New York: Appleton-Century-Crofts, 1971), pp. 23–46.
148 'On political theory and political action', *American Political Science Review*, vol. 65, no. 1 (March 1971), pp. 11–27.
149 (With Jorge I. Domínguez), 'Politische Entwicklung zur nationalen Selbstbestimmung: einige neuere Begriffe und Modelle', in *Theory and Politics, Theorie und Politik: Festschrift zum 70. Geburtstag für Carl Joachim Friedrich*, ed. Klaus von Beyme (The Hague: Nijhoff, 1971), pp. 417–55; and 'Political development toward national self-determination: some recent concepts and models', *Comparative Political Studies*, vol. 4, no. 4 (January 1972), pp. 461–75.

150 'Space and behavior', *Ekistics*, vol. 32, no. 191 (October 1971), pp. 299–300.
151 Discussion comments on 'Designing organizations for an information-rich world', by Herbert A. Simon, in *Computers, Communications, and the Public Interest*, ed. Martin Greenberger (Baltimore, Md, and London: Johns Hopkins University Press, 1971), pp. 52–9, 67–8.
152 'A community of ideas and an idea of community: the designs of Serge Chermayeff', review essay on *Shape of Community: Realization of Human Potential*, by Serge Chermayeff and Alexander Tzonis, *Yale Review*, vol. 61, no. 1 (Autumn 1971), pp. 101–10.
153 'Foreword', in *Political Science Enters the 1970s*, ed. Richard L. Merritt (Washington, DC: American Political Science Association, 1971), pp. v–vi.
154 'In memoriam: Quincy Wright', *PS*, vol. 4, no. 1 (Winter 1971), pp. 107–9.
155 'Serbelloni: where each day counted for Ted', in *Thoughts from the Lake of Time: A Group of Essays in Honor of the Villa Serbelloni and Especially John and Charlotte Marshall*, ed. John Burchard (New York: Josiah Macy, Jr, Foundation, 1971), pp. 265–7.
156 'Proposal: Institute for National Policy Research, issues which the proposed center should address', in *Collected Papers* (New York: Center for National Goals and Alternatives, 1971, multigraphed).

1972
157 *Peace Research: The Need, the Problems, and the Prospects*, The John Hamilton Fulton Memorial Lecture in the Liberal Arts (Middlebury, Vt: Middlebury College, April 1972); appears in *The International Yearbook of Foreign Policy Analysis*, Vol. 2, ed. Peter Jones (London: Croom Helm, 1975), pp. 245–66.
158 'The contribution of experiments within the framework of political theory', in *Experimentation and Simulation in Political Science*, ed. Jean A. Laponce and Paul Smoker (Toronto: University of Toronto Press, 1972), pp. 19–35.
159 'Friedensforschung – Grundsätze und Perspektiven', *Schweizer Monatshefte*, vol. 52, no. 6 (September 1972), pp. 392–402.
160 (With Thomas Edsall), 'The meritocracy scare', *Society*, vol. 9, no. 10 (September–October 1972), pp. 71–9.
161 'The nature of national power', *National War College Forum*, no. 16 (Fall 1972), pp. 1–13.
162 (With Manfred Kochen), 'Pluralization: a mathematical model', *Operations Research*, vol. 20, no. 2 (March–April 1972), pp. 276–92.
163 'Relating and responding: the adult', *Childhood Education*, vol. 48, no. 5 (February 1972), pp. 227–35.
164 'EWG-Integration: der Beitritt Englands wird noch mehr in die Richtung des Europas der Vaterländer wirken', interview in *Wirschaftswoche*, vol. 27, no. 3 (28 January 1972), pp. 25–7.
165 'Indikatoren der Fortentwicklung der Gesellschaftswissenschaften', in *Conference on Processes and Indicators* (Bonn: Universität Bonn, Institut für Politische Wissenschaft, and DATUM, August 1972).

1973
166 *Nationenbildung-Nationalstaat-Integration*, ed. Abraham Ashkenasi and Peter Schulze (Dusseldorf: Bertelsmann Universitätsverlag, 1973).
167 (With Hayward R. Alker, Jr, and Antoine H. Stoetzel), editor, *Mathematical Approaches to Politics* (San Francisco: Jossey-Bass, 1973).
168 'Quantitative approaches to political analysis: some past trends and future

prospects', in *Mathematical Approaches to Politics*, ed. Hayward R. Alker, Jr, Karl W. Deutsch, and Antoine H. Stoetzel (San Francisco: Jossey-Bass, 1973), pp. 1–60.

169 (With Manfred Kochen), 'Decentralization by function and location', *Management Science*, vol. 19, no. 8 (April 1973), pp. 841–56.

170 (With Richard W. Chadwick), 'International trade and economic integration: further developments in trade matrix analysis', *Comparative Political Studies*, vol. 6, no. 1 (April 1973), pp. 84–109.

171 'El poder internacional deberá ser compartido, no monopolizado', *Línea*, no. 6 (November–December 1973), pp. 3–8.

172 'Social and political convergence in industrializing countries – some concepts and the evidence', in *Social Science and the New Societies: Problems in Cross-Cultural Research and Theory Building*, ed. Nancy Hammond (East Lansing, Mich.: Michigan State University, Social Science Research Bureau, 1973), pp. 95–115.

173 'Der Stand der Kriegsursachenforschung', *Friedens- und Konfliktforschung*, no. 2 (September 1973), pp. 1–28.

174 (With Victor J. Marma), 'Survival in unfair conflict: odds, resources, and random walk models', *Behavioral Science*, vol. 18, no. 5 (September 1973), pp. 313–34.

175 'Zum Verständnis von Krisen und politischen Revolutionen: Bemerkungen aus kybernetischer Sicht', in *Herrschaft und Krise: Beiträge zur politikwissenschaftlichen Krisenforschung*, ed. Martin Jänicke (Opladen: Westdeutscher Verlag, 1973), pp. 90–100.

176 'Die Zukunft des internationalen Zusammenlebens', in *Die Zukunft der Politik* (Vienna: Vereinigung für Politische Bildung, Politische Akademie, 1973), pp. 20–7.

177 'Toward the study of political and social indicators across different social systems', in *Handbook of Soviet Social Science Data*, ed. Ellen Mickiewicz (New York: The Free Press, 1973), pp. xxi–xxvi.

1974

178 'Between sovereignty and integration: conclusion', *Government and Opposition*, vol. 9, no. 1 (Winter 1974), pp. 113–19.

179 'Imperialism and neocolonialism', in *Papers, Peace Science Society (International)*, vol. 23 (1974), pp. 1–25; and 'Imperialisme et néocolonialisme', *Bulletin de la Société Francaise de Sociologie*, vol. 1, no. 2 (June 1974), pp. 4–26.

180 'Impressions from Afghanistan', *International Educational and Cultural Exchange*, vol. 9, no. 4 (Spring 1974), pp. 4–7.

181 (With Manfred Kochen) 'A note on hierarchy and coordination: an aspect of decentralization', *Management Science*, vol. 21, no. 1 (September 1974), pp. 106–14.

182 'On the interaction of ecological and political systems: some potential contributions of the social sciences to the study of man and his environment', *Social Science Information*, vol. 13, no. 6 (December 1974), pp. 5–15; and in *Ecosocial Systems and Ecopolitics: A Reader on Human and Social Implications of Environmental Management in Developing Countries*, ed. Karl W. Deutsch (Paris: Unesco, 1977), pp. 23–31.

183 'Theories of imperialism and neo-colonialism', in *Testing Theories of Economic Imperialism*, ed. Steven J. Rosen and James R. Kurth (Lexington, Mass.: D. C. Heath, 1974), pp. 15–33.

184 'New national interests', *New York Times*, 22 November 1974, p. 39 [op. ed.].

1975
185 'Abhängigkeit, strukturelle Gewalt und Befreiungsprozesse', in *Herrschaft und Befreiung in der Weltgesellschaft*, ed. Klaus Jürgen Gantzel (Frankfurt/Main and New York: Campus Verlag, 1975), pp. 23-46.
186 'Über Abhängigkeits- und Emanzipationstendenzen in der Weltgesellschaft', in *Herrschaft und Befreiung in der Weltgesellschaft*, ed. Klaus Jürgen Gantzel (Frankfurt/Main and New York: Campus Verlag, 1975), pp. 47-67.
187 'The development of communication theory in political science', *History of Political Economy*, vol. 7, no. 4 (Winter 1975), pp. 482-98.
188 'On inequality and limited growth: some world political effects', *International Studies Quarterly*, vol. 19, no. 4 (December 1975), pp. 381-98.
189 'On the learning capacity of large political systems', in *Information for Action: From Knowledge to Wisdom*, ed. Manfred Kochen (New York: Academic Press, 1975), pp. 61-83; and 'Zur Handlungs- und Lernkapazität politischer Systeme', in *Handlungstheorien interdisziplinär IV*, ed. Hans Lenk (Munich: Wilh. Fink Verlag, 1977), pp. 307-28.
190 'The political significance of linguistic conflicts', in *Multilingual Political Systems: Problems and Solutions / Les Étas multilingues: problèmes et solutions*, ed. Jean-Guy Savard and Richard Vigneault (Quebec: Les Presses de l'Université Laval, 1975), pp. 7-28.
191 'Some common views', in *Man, Environment, and Resources in the Perspective of the Past and the Future*, 29th Nobel Symposium, ed. Torgny Segerstedt and Sam Nilsson (Stockholm: Nobel Foundation, 1975).
192 'Die Zukunft der Sozial- und Planungswissenschaften', *Transfer I: Gleiche Chancen im Sozialstaat?* (Opladen: Westdeutscher Verlag, 1975), pp. 129-37.
193 'Introduction', in *National Consciousness in Divided Germany*, by Gebhard Ludwig Schweigler (Beverly Hills, Calif., and London: Sage 1975), pp. 1-6.
194 'Koreferat: Atlantische Partnerschaft – Kooperation oder mehr?', in *Dokumente: Partnerschaft heute — unsere Politik nach aussen*, Aussenpolitische Bundeskonferenz der SPD, 17-19 January 1975 (Bonn: Sozialdemokratische Partei Deutschland, 1975), pp. 56-76.
195 'Some memories of Norbert Wiener: the man and his thoughts', *IEEE Transactions on Systems, Man, and Cybernetics*, vol. 5, no. 3 (May 1975), pp. 368-72.
196 'World order priorities', *Annals of the New York Academy of Sciences*, vol. 261: *Environment and Society in Transition: World Priorities*, ed. Boris Pregel, Harold D. Lasswell, and John McHale (New York: New York Academy of Sciences, 1975), pp. 261-2.
197 Review of *Main Trends of Research in the Social and Human Sciences*, ed. Unesco, *American Political Science Review*, vol. 69, no. 3 (September 1975), pp. 1010-12.
198 (With Manfred Kochen), review of *Means and Goals of Political Decentralization*, by Lennart Lundquist, *American Political Science Review*, vol. 69, no. 4 (December 1975), pp. 1429-30.

1976
199 *Die Schweiz als ein paradigmatischer Fall politischer Integration* (Berne: Verlag Paul Haupt, 1976).
200 (With Rudolf Wildenmann), editor, *Sozialwissenschaftliches Jahrbuch für Politik*, Vol. 5: *Mathematical Political Analysis: From Methods to Substance* (Munich and Vienna: Günter Olzog Verlag GmbH, 1976).

201 'America in its third century: nuclear target or world resource?', *Harvard Magazine*, vol. 78, no. 11 (July–August 1976), pp. 15–18.
202 'America's capacity to think,' *Nieman Reports*, vol. 30, no. 9/vol. 31, no. 1 (Winter 1976/Spring 1977), pp. 3–12.
203 'Toward an interdisciplinary model of world stability and change: some intellectual preconditions', *Journal of Peace Science*, vol. 2, no. 1 (Spring 1976), pp. 1–14.
204 Consultant, *University Divinity Schools: A Report on Ecclesiastically Independent Theological Education*, by George Lindbeck, in consultation with Karl W. Deutsch and Nathan Glazer (New York: Rockefeller Foundation, Working Papers, March 1976).

1977
205 (With Gerhard Schmidtchen), *Aussenpolitik und Öffentlichkeit in der direkten Demokratie*, ed. Daniel Frei (Berne and Stuttgart: Verlag Paul Haupt, 1977).
206 Editor, *Ecosocial Systems and Ecopolitics: A Reader on Human and Social Implications of Environmental Management in Developing Countries* (Paris: Unesco, 1977).
207 'Introduction', in *Ecosocial Systems and Ecopolitics: A Reader on Human and Social Implications of Environmental Management in Developing Countries*, ed. Karl W. Deutsch (Paris: Unesco, 1977), pp. 11–20.
208 'Epilogue: some problems and prospects of ecopolitical research', in *Ecosocial Systems and Ecopolitics: A Reader on Human and Social Implications of Environmental Management in Developing Countries*, ed. Karl W. Deutsch (Paris: Unesco, 1977), pp. 359–68.
209 (With Bruno Fritsch, Hélio Jaguaribe, and Andrei S. Markovits), editor, *Problems of World Modeling: Political and Social Implications* (Cambridge, Mass.: Ballinger, 1977).
210 'Toward drift models and steering models', in *Problems in World Modeling: Political and Social Implications*, ed. Karl W. Deutsch, Bruno Fritsch, Hélio Jaguaribe, and Andrei S. Markovits (Cambridge, Mass.: Ballinger, 1977), pp. 5–10.
211 (With Erwin Solomon and Hayward R. Alker, Jr), 'Relevance for policy: a brief exchange', in *Problems of World Modeling: Political and Social Implications*, ed. Karl W. Deutsch, Bruno Fritsch, Hélio Jaguaribe, and Andrei S. Markovits (Cambridge, Mass.: Ballinger, 1977), pp. 13–15.
212 (With Meinolf Dierkes), editor, *The Question of European Forward Studies: Public Scientific Symposium* (Berlin [West]: Institut für Zukunftsforschung, 1977).
213 'Der Einzelne und der Friede', in *Was der Mensch braucht: Anregungen für eine neue Kunst zu leben*, ed. Hans Jürgen Schultz (Stuttgart: Kreuz Verlag, 1977), pp. 94–107.
214 (With Hayward R. Alker, Jr, and Andrei S. Markovits), 'Global opportunities and constraints for regional development: a review of interdisciplinary simulation research toward a world model as a framework of studies of regional development', *Social Science Information*, vol. 16, no. 1 (1977), pp. 83–102.
215 'National integration: some concepts and research approaches', *Jerusalem Journal of International Relations*, vol. 2, no. 4 (Summer 1977), pp. 1–29.
216 'Prospects for the future', *Parameters, Journal of the US Army War College*, vol. 7, no. 2 (1977), pp. 77–86.

1978

217 *Gesellschaftspolitische Aspekte der Ökologie* (St Gallen: Aulavorträge der Universitat St Gallen, 1978).
218 'Schlüsselprobleme in der Sozialforschung', in *Zukunftsorientierte Planung und Forschung für die 80er Jahre: deutsche und amerikanische Erfahrungen im Bereich der Erziehungs-, Wohnungs-, Beschäftigungs-, Gesundheits-, Energie- und Umweltpolitik*, ed. Stephen J. Fitzsimmons, Rudolf Wildenmann, and Kenneth J. Arrow (Königstein/Ts.: Athenäum Verlag, 1978), pp. 225–48; and in *Applied Research for Social Policy: The United States and the Federal Republic of Germany Compared*, ed. Kenneth J. Arrow, Clark C. Abt, and Stephen J. Fitzsimmons (Cambridge, Mass.: Abt Books, 1979).
219 'Some prospects for world politics', *Law and State*, no. 18 (1978), pp. 7–20.

1979

220 *Tides among Nations* (New York: The Free Press, 1979).
221 'Die Aufgabe der Universität im Wandel der Zeit', in *450 Jahre Philipps-Universität-Marburg: das Gründungsjubiläum 1977*, ed. Wilfried Frhr. von Bredow (Marburg: N. G. Elwert Verlag, 1979), pp. 50–61.
222 'Economic and monetary policy', in *The European Alternatives: An Inquiry into the Policies of the European Community*, ed. Ghita Ionescu (Alphen aan den Rijn: Sijthoff & Noordhoff, 1979), pp. 493–8.
223 'Grundsatzentscheide in der Weltpolitik', in *Machtpolitik in der heutigen Welt*, ed. Daniel Frei (Zurich: Schulthess Polygraphischer Verlag, 1979), pp. 13–36.
224 'Major changes in the discipline', in *A Quarter Century of International Social Science: Papers and Reports on Developments, 1952–1977*, ed. Stein Rokkan (New Delhi: Concept Publishing Company, 1979), pp. 157–80.
225 'On world models and political science', *Government and Opposition*, vol. 14, no. 1 (Winter 1979), pp. 1–17.
226 (With Richard L. Merritt), 'Transnational Communications and the international system', *Annals of the American Academy of Political and Social Science*, vol. 442 (March 1979), pp. 84–97.
227 'Über Weltmodellarbeiten im Internationalen Institut für Vergleichende Gesellschaftsforschung', in *Jahrbuch der Berliner Wissenschaftlichen Gesellschaft 1978* (Berlin [West]: Duncker & Humblot, 1979), pp. 123–30.
228 'Zukunftschancen der Jugend unter politischen Aspekten', in *Die Jugend und ihre Zukunftschancen: ein Symposium mit Jugendlichen und Vertretern aus Wissenschaft, Wirtschaft, Politik und Verwaltung*, ed. Johannes C. Welbergen (Hamburg: Deutsche Shell AG, 1979), pp. 76–93.
229 'Foreword: how diplomats think and what can be found out about it', in *Patterns of Diplomatic Thinking: A Cross-national Study of Structural and Social-Psychological Determinants*, by Luc Reychler (New York: Praeger, 1979), pp. v–vii.
230 'Peter Christian Ludz zum Gedächtnis', *Kölner Zeitschrift für Soziologie und Sozialpsychologie*, vol. 31, no. 4 (1979), pp. 822–4.

1980

231 (With Javid H. Jodice and Charles Lewis Taylor), *Cumulation in Social Science Data Archiving: A Study of the Impact of the Two World Handbooks of Political and Social Indicators* (Königstein/Ts.: Verlag Anton Hain, 1980).

232 (With Manfred Kochen), *Decentralization: Sketches toward a Rational Theory* (Cambridge, Mass.: Oelgeschlager, Gunn & Hain; and Königstein/Ts.: Verlag Anton Hain, 1980).
233 *Política y Administración Pública* (Mexico City: Ediciones del Instituto Nacional de Administración Pública, 1980).
234 (With Bruno Fritsch), *Zur Theorie der Vereinfachung: Reduktion von Komplexität in der Datenverarbeitung für Weltmodelle* (Königstein/Ts.: Athenäum Verlag, 1980).
235 (With Andrei S. Markovits), editor, *Fear of Science — Trust in Science: Conditions for Change in the Climate of Opinion* (Cambridge, Mass.: Oelgeschlager, Gunn & Hain; and Königstein/Ts.: Verlag Anton Hain, 1980).
236 'Fear and trust: contrasting view of science in Western history', in *Fear of Science — Trust in Science: Conditions for Change in the Climate of Opinion*, ed. Andrei S. Markovits and Karl W. Deutsch (Cambridge, Mass.: Oelgeschlager, Gunn & Hain; and Königstein/Ts.: Verlag Anton Hain, 1980), pp. 3–6.
237 (With Andrei S. Markovits), 'On coping with science as a task of policy: a tentative summary', in *Fear of Science — Trust in Science: Conditions for Change in the Climate of Opinion*, ed. Andrei S. Markovits and Karl W. Deutsch (Cambridge, Mass.: Oelgeschlager, Gunn & Hain; and Königstein/Ts.: Verlag Anton Hain, 1980), pp. 223–35.
238 'Die Interdependenz zwischen Industrie- und Entwicklungsländern', in *Der neue Realismus: Außenpolitik nach Iran und Afghanistan*, ed. Helmut Kohl (Dusseldorf: Erb Verlag, 1980), pp. 140–68; and 'Sprengstoff im Süden: der Aufstand der Entwicklungsländer steht bevor', *Die Politische Meinung*, vol. 25, no. 190 (May–June 1980), pp. 58–70.
239 'An interim summary and evaluation', in *The Correlates of War II: Testing Some Realpolitik Models*, ed. J. David Singer (New York: The Free Press, 1980), pp. 287–95.
240 'On the utility of indicator systems', in *Indicator Systems for Political, Economic, and Social Analysis*, ed. Charles Lewis Taylor (Cambridge, Mass.: Oelgeschlager, Gunn & Hain; and Königstein/Ts.: Verlag Anton Hain, 1980, pp. 11–23.
241 'Political research in the changing world system', *International Political Science Review*, vol. 1, no. 1 (1980), pp. 23–33.
242 'Politische Steuerung auf dem Weg zur Kommunikationsgesellschaft', in *Sozialwissenschaften im sozialen Wandel: Wissenschaftliches Symposium aus Anlaß des 10jährigen Bestehens des Wissenschaftszentrum Berlin* (Berlin [West]: Wissenschaftszentrum Berlin, 1980, multigraphed), pp. 31–48.
243 'Technology and social change: fundamental changes in knowledge, technology, and society', *Human Systems Management*, vol. 1, no. 2 (September 1980), pp. 127–34.
244 'Eine veränderte Menschheit?', in *Technik und Gesellschaft: Fortschritt für den Menschen?*, selected contributions from *IBM-Nachrichten* (Stuttgart: IBM Deutschland GmbH, 1980), pp. 27–37 (appeared originally in February 1980 issue of *IBM-Nachrichten*).
245 'A voyage of the mind, 1930–1980', *Government and Opposition*, vol. 15, no. 3/4 (Summer/Autumn 1980), pp. 323–45.
246 'Der Westen – seine Merkmale und seine Strategien der Zukunft', in *Die Zukunft der westlichen Gesellschaft*, ed. Emil Bräuchlin, Theodor Leuenberger, and Erich Niederer (Berne and Stuttgart: Verlag Paul Haupt, 1980), pp. 43–62.

247 'Einleitung', in *Weltmodellstudien: Wachstumsprobleme und Lösungsmöglichkeiten*, ed. Stuart A. Bremer, Rolf Kappel, Peter Otto, Hannelore Weck, and Ulrich Widmaier (Königstein/Ts.: Athenäum Verlag, 1980), pp. 1-20.
248 'In memory of Stein Rokkan, 1921-1979', *International Political Science Review*, vol. 1, no. 1 (1980), pp. 9-11.

About the Contributors

HAYWARD, R. ALKER, JR, professor of political science at MIT, is the author, co-author, or co-editor of a number of studies in the areas of mathematical modeling, international relations, and philosophy of social science. Over the last two decades he has worked with Karl Deutsch in many ways, most recently in co-editing *Mathematical Approaches to Politics*, in leading an IPSA Research Committee on Mathematical and Quantitative Approaches to Politics, and in co-teaching a course on complex models of social systems.

THOMAS CUSACK, research scientist at the Science Center Berlin, received his PhD in political science from the University of Michigan in 1978. He is presently working with Karl Deutsch on the development of a new global model in Berlin.

JORGE I. DOMÍNGUEZ is a professor of government and a member of the Center for International Affairs, both at Harvard University. He is the author of *Cuba: Order and Revolution* and *Insurrection or Loyalty: The Breakdown of the Spanish American Empire*, senior author of *Enhancing Global Human Rights*, and author of articles on comparative and international politics. He studied with Karl Deutsch as an undergraduate at Yale, followed him as a graduate student to Harvard, and then joined him as a faculty colleague at Harvard, teaching jointly the introductory course on comparative politics for five years.

RAYMOND DUVALL is associate professor of political science at the University of Minnesota. His published research is on political processes in dependent societies, especially the role of the state and social conflict. He has not worked directly with Karl Deutsch, but through his association with Bruce Russett and the Yale dependence project can be regarded as a second-generation Deutsch student.

WILLIAM J. FOLTZ took his PhD at Yale University under Karl Deutsch's guidance, and later co-edited *Nation-Building* with him. He is now professor of political science and chairman of the Council on African Studies at Yale. His research and writing have concentrated on the domestic and international politics of Africa and on the study of political conflict and change in divided societies.

BRUNO FRITSCH is professor of economics at the Swiss Federal Institute of Technology, and was formerly professor at the University of Karlsruhe and the University of Heidelberg. He has frequently been a visiting professor at Harvard University, and in 1971 at the Australian National University and in 1960–5 the College of Europe. His publications on international political economy include *Growth Limitation and Political Power* and co-editorship of

Problems of World Modeling with Karl Deutsch, Helio Jaguaribe, and Andrei Markovits. He is acting president of the Swiss Association for Future Research.

MICHAEL C. HUDSON is professor in the School of Foreign Service at Georgetown University and director of Georgetown's Center for Contemporary Arab Studies. His most recent book is *Arab Politics: The Search for Legitimacy*. He was a student of Karl Deutsch at Yale and did his first book on Lebanon using Deutsch's social mobilization theory. Later he worked at the Yale World Data Analysis Program on the second edition of the *World Handbook of Political and Social Indicators*.

STEVEN I. JACKSON is an assistant professor of government at Cornell University; he received his PhD at Yale University. In addition to his work on dependency theory, his interests include the role of the state in dependent societies and applications of control theory to political phenomena. He has published articles in several journals, including the *Journal of Peace Research*.

PETER, J. KATZENSTEIN finished his dissertation under the direction of Karl Deutsch at Harvard in 1973, and is now associate professor of government at Cornell University. He is the author of *Disjoined Partners: Austria and Germany Since 1815*, editor of *Between Power and Plenty: Foreign Economic Policies of Advanced Industrial States*, co-editor of *Territorial Politics in Industrial Nations*, and co-editor of *Comparative Public Policy: A Cross-National Bibliography*.

MANFRED KOCHEN received his PhD in applied mathematics from Columbia University. While an undergraduate at MIT, as one of Karl Deutsch's students, he developed his interest in mathematical modeling of behavioral and social sciences. He worked in the von Neumann computer project at the Institute for Advanced Study from 1953 to 1955 where he was able to assist Karl Deutsch in his research on nationalism. He later joined the IBM Research Center for eight years, and has been at the University of Michigan since 1964, where he is professor of information science with a joint appointment as professor of urban regional planning and as research mathematician at the Mental Health Research Institute. He and Professor Deutsch are co-authors of *Decentralization: Sketches toward a Rational Theory*, and have co-authored about a dozen papers on this and related subjects.

AREND LIJPHART was appointed professor of political science at the University of California, San Diego, in 1978, after having held the chair in international relations at the University of Leiden in the Netherlands for ten years. He took his PhD in 1963 at Yale University, where he was a student of Karl Deutsch. His publications include *The Trauma of Decolonization, The Politics of Accommodation, Democracy in Plural Societies*, and other books and articles on comparative politics and international relations. He was editor of the *European Journal of Political Research* from 1971 to 1975.

ANDREI S. MARKOVITS is assistant professor of government at Wesleyan University and a research associate at the Center for European Studies, Harvard University. He has published numerous articles on comparative education, fascism, labor movements, and student politics. A collaborator of Karl Deutsch since 1975, he has co-authored an article with Professor

Deutsch on global modeling, co-edited *Problems of World Modeling: Political and Social Implications*, and continued collaboration on other projects funded by the Swiss National Foundation and the Science Center in Berlin.

RICHARD L. MERRITT is professor (and head of the department) of political science and research professor in communications, University of Illinois at Urbana-Champaign. His research has focused on issues of political communication, including the formation and change of public opinion in the Federal Republic of Germany. Among the books he has written or edited are *Symbols of American Community, 1735–1775, Comparing Nations, Systematic Approaches to Comparative Politics*, and, together with Anna J. Merritt, *Public Opinion in Occupied Germany* and *Public Opinion in Semisovereign Germany*. He is currently vice-president of both the International Political Science Association and the International Studies Association.

FRIEDER NASCHOLD was appointed professor of political science at the University of Constance in 1970 and rector of the University of Constance in 1974. Since 1976 he has been co-director of the International Institute for Comparative Social Research of the Science Center Berlin, together with Karl Deutsch.

WARREN OLIVER III is finishing a degree in philosophy, politics and economics at Magdalen College, Oxford University. As an undergraduate at Harvard University where he received his AB in 1977, he devoted much of his time to the study of social and political theory.

DONALD J. PUCHALA is professor of political science at Columbia University, and associate dean of the Columbia School of International Affairs. He took both his BA and PhD degrees at Yale, and later worked with Karl Deutsch on arms control and European integration. His publications include *International Politics Today, American Arms and a Changing Europe, The Global Political Economy of Food*, and numerous articles on problems of the European Communities and international integration.

STEIN ROKKAN (1921–79) was professor of sociology and comparative politics, University of Bergen, and director of research at the Chr. Michelsen Institute, Bergen. His own research, especially his many empirical articles and theoretic essays, placed him in the forefront of international political sociology. Many of these papers are included and elaborated upon in his *Citizens, Elections, Parties*. A very special talent that differentiated him from other leading scholars was his ability to work with others, including Karl Deutsch, to think together about and advance the state of knowledge on the interaction of empirical theory and quantitative indicators in crossnational, cross-temporal research. Among his important co-edited volumes in this vein are *Comparing Nations, Quantitative Ecology, Building States and Nations*, and *Party Systems and Voter Alignments*. His organizational efforts were instrumental in developing the structure of international social science, especially in the International Sociological Association, International Political Science Association, and International Social Science Council – all of which elected him as their president.

BRUCE M. RUSSETT is professor of political science at Yale University, editor of the *Journal of Conflict Resolution*, and chairman of the North American Advisory Council of the International Political Science Association. He is past president of the Peace Science Society (International), and has published fourteen books on international relations. He received his PhD from Yale University in 1961 as the first American student whose dissertation was supervised by Karl Deutsch, and taught at Yale and collaborated with Professor Deutsch in the World Data Analysis Program from 1962 to 1967.

DIETER SENGHAAS is professor of social science at the University of Bremen. He was formerly professor of political science at the University of Frankfurt, and from 1968 to 1970 was a research fellow at Harvard University and collaborator with Karl Deutsch. His publications include (English titles) *Deterrence and Peace, Aggression and Collective Violence, Armament Dynamics and Militarism, Arming by Arms Control, Violence, Conflict, and Peace*, and *World Economic Order and Development Policy*.

J. DAVID SINGER received his PhD from New York University (1956) and is a professor of political science at the University of Michigan; he has taught world politics at Vassar, Oslo, Geneva, and Mannheim, and has consulted for such agencies as the US Arms Control and Disarmament Agency, the Department of the Navy, and the Office of the Secretary of Defense. Among his earlier books are: *Financing International Organization*, 1961; *Deterrence, Arms Control, and Disarmament*, 1962; *Human Behavior and International Politics: Contributions from the Social-Psychological Sciences*, 1965; *Quantitative International Politics: Insights and Evidence*, 1968; *The Wages of War, 1816–1965: A Statistical Handbook* (with Melvin Small), 1972; *Beyond Conjecture in International Politics: Abstracts of Data-Based Research* (with Susan Jones), 1972, *The Study of International Politics: A Guide to Sources for the Student, Teacher and Researcher* (with Dorothy LaBarr), 1976.

DUNCAN SNIDAL is an assistant professor of political science at the University of Chicago; he received his PhD at Yale University. In addition to his work on dependency theory, he has done research on public goods and problems of international co-operation. He has published articles in several journals, including *International Studies Quarterly*.

DAVID J. SYLVAN is assistant professor of political science at Syracuse University; he received his PhD at Yale University. He has published in several journals and in the book *Military Policy Evaluation: Quantitative Applications*. His current research interests lie in the fields of dependence reduction and of influence processes in international relations.

CHARLES LEWIS TAYLOR, professor of political science at Virginia Polytechnic Institute and State University, is the author of *Aggregate Data Analysis World Handbook of Political and Social Indicators: Second Edition, Indicator Systems for Political, Economic and Social Analysis*, and other publications. He was a student of Karl Deutsch at Yale, was later his colleague in the Yale Political Data Program and is now working with him at the Science Center Berlin in the preparation of an updated *World Handbook* dataset.

Name Index
(Prepared by Anna J. Merritt)

Abel, Richard L. 43
Abelson, Robert P. 369, 377, 378, 401
Abu-Lughod, Janet 69
Adelman, Irma 349
Ahmed, Mesbahuddin 205
Alatas, S. H. 34, 43
Alcock, Norman Z. 421
Alford, Robert 140
Alger, Chadwick F. 240, 242, 249
Alker, Hayward R., Jr. 14–15, 16, 42, 163, 349, 374, 375, 377, 402, 403, 446
Allison, Graham 240, 249
Allport, Gordon W. 40, 45, 204
Almond, Gabriel A. 42, 67, 163, 164, 202, 313
Al-Salem, Faisal 68
Ambichel, Wilhelm 276
Amin, Galal A. 310–311
Amin, Samir 43, 69, 309, 310, 327, 345, 348, 370, 371
Amstrup, Niels 272
Anant, Santokh 205
Anderson, Perry 94, 370, 371
Androsch, Hannes 275, 276, 278
Apter, David E. 30, 42
Aron, Raymond 162, 241, 250
Arrighi, Giovanni 348, 350
Asad, Talal 44

Bahro, Rudolf 142
Bailey, F. G. 43
Baran, Paul 348
Barkan, Joel D. 43
Barna, Tibor 348
Barnet, Richard 346
Barrows, Walter L. 35, 43
Barth, Fredrik 43
Basso, Lelio 141
Baumgartner, Tom 44
Baumol, W. J. 113
Bayer, Kurt 274
Beal, Richard Smith 241, 250
Beaud, Michel 309
Behrens, William K. III 373
Beinsen, Lutz 275
Bell, Daniel 113
Bell, Wendell 43
Bellon, Bertrand 309
Belzer, Jack 401

Bendix, Reinhard 138, 141
Bennett, James 375
Berry, John W. 44
Bichlauber, Dieter 277
Biermann, Wolfgang 270
Bigelow, Julian 357, 374, 375
Bion, Wilfred R. 44
Birnbaum, Pierre 182
Bishop, Vaughn F. 349
Black, Cyril 309
Black, Naomi 246, 247, 251
Bliss, Chester I. 272
Bloch, Ivan S. 417, 421
Blohmke, Maria 138
Bobrow, Daniel G. 378
Bönisch, A. 139
Bös, Dieter 276, 277
Boettcher, Erik 139, 140
Bogardus, Emory 204
Bogs, Harald 138
Bonilla, Frank 349
Booth, John A. 43
Borcherding, Thomas E. 113
Bossel, Hartmut 378
Boudieu, Pierre 68
Boulding, Elise 401
Boulding, Kenneth E. 244–5, 250, 375, 379, 380, 401, 402
Bourguiba, Habib 52, 63
Brahimi, Addelhamid 68
Brandt, Gerhardt 138, 142
Brandt, Willy 208, 210, 423
Braun, Wilhelm 277
Bremer, Stuart A. 114
Brest, G. R. 373
Breuss, Fritz 273, 276
Brewer, Gary 374
Brinton, Crane 163
Brito, D. L. 401
Brittan, Samuel 139
Bronowski, Jacob 421
Bruce, Bertram 378
Bruce, Maurice 139, 140
Brun, Ellen 310
Brunner, Ronald D. 374
Brusatti, Alois 273, 275, 277
Brzezinski, Zbigniew K. 164
Buchanan, James M. 114, 139
Buckley, Walter 37, 44

NAME INDEX

Bueno de Mesquita, Bruce 421
Bull, Hedley 243, 245, 248, 250
Bundy, Colin 34, 43
Bunge, Mario 374
Burks, Arthur W. 377
Burns, Tom R. 44
Burrell, Sidney A. 163, 182, 229
Burton, John W. 249
Busch, Peter 164
Butterfield, Herbert 248, 250
Buttler, Friedrich 310

Cameron, David R. 27–8, 42, 141
Campbell, Donald T. 357, 375
Cancian, Frank 34, 43
Cannon, Walter Bradford 421
Cantril, Hadley 187, 188, 189, 203, 204
Caporaso, James A. 163, 272
Cardoso, Fernando Henrique 312, 313, 325, 344, 345, 348, 350, 370
Carmi, M. 278
Cauthen, Nelson R. 205
Chaitin, G. T. 402
Champion, Michael 420
Chase-Dunn, Christopher 345
Chenery, Hollis 103, 105, 113, 114
Chernotsky, Harry T. 345
Cherry, Colin 401
Chichilnisky, G. 373
Chomsky, Noam 353, 357–8, 361–2, 375, 376
Choucri, Nazli 401
Christensen, Cherly 403
Clark, John 373
Claude, Inis L. 163, 235, 242, 248
Cloward, Richard A. 140
Cochrane, A. L. 140
Cohen, Abner 43
Colby, William E. 402
Cole, Michael 44
Cole, Sam 373
Coleman, James S. 42, 67, 138, 164
Collins, Allen 378
Connor, Walker 28, 31, 42, 69
Converse, Jean M. 203
Coombes, David L. 164
Coombs, Clyde H. 203
Coombs, Lolagene 203
Cooper, Richard N. 164
Coppard, Larry G. 403
Cortes, Fernando 374
Coser, Lewis A. 138
Costner, H. L., Jr. 347
Cotler, Julio 347, 350
Cotter, Cornelius P. 421
Coulter, N. A., Jr. 375
Crecine, J. Patrick 357, 359, 376
Crespi, Leo P. 202
Crickman, Robin 403
Crow, Ralph 69

Crozier, Brian 114
Curnow, Ray 373
Curtin, Philip D. 43
Cusack, Thomas 17–18

Daho, Robert A. 41
Das, J. P. 204
Dasen, Pierre R. 44
Davison, W. Phillips 230
Dean, P. Dale, Jr. 249
de Beauregard, O. C. 376–7
de Bussy, Marie-Elisabeth 162
de la Serre, Françoise 162
Delorme, Hélène 162
Demerath, N. J. 377
Denton, Frank H. 419, 421
Derman, Cyrus, 421
Deutsch, Karl W. 1–19, 25–9, 37–41, 46–61, 64–7, 70, 96–8, 111–13, 116, 118, 145–6, 150–61, 165–79, 184–5, 191, 192, 206, 233–48, 252–3, 313, 353–73, 379–80, 381, 393, 397–9, 404
De Vree, Johan K. 248, 251
Dewey, Edward R. 419, 421
Dhrymes, P. J. 347
di Filippo, Armondo 309
Dillinger, M. 273, 274, 275
Disch, Arne 344
Diwork, Fritz 274
Domínguez, Jorge I. 9, 27, 42, 203, 204, 272, 377
Donelan, Michael 248
Donohue, Joseph 403
Doob, Leonard W. 45
Dorfman, Ariel 346
Dos Santos, Theotonio 312, 344, 345
Dougherty, James E. 248, 251
Durkheim, Emile 8, 26, 76, 117, 120, 137, 138, 139, 140, 165–79, 346
Duval, Raymond 13, 28–9, 42, 43, 64, 253, 344, 345, 349, 372, 373, 378
Dyson, F. 377

Easton, David 44, 164, 353, 358, 374, 376
Eberle, Friedrich 138, 142
Eckstein, Alexander 253, 272
Eckstein, Harry 244, 250
Edinger, Lewis J. 3, 155, 162, 272
Eisenstadt, S. N. 42, 94, 309
Eisley, Joe G. 403
Elias, Norbert 309
El Khatib, M. Fathalla 203
Elsenhans, Hartmut 309
Elster, Jon 374
England, J. Lynn 401
Erhard, Ludwig 295

Fabian, Horst 309
Fach, Wolfgang 137
Fagan, Stuart I. 162

NAME INDEX

Fagen, R. E. 44
Fagen, Richard R. 347
Faletto, Enzo 312, 344, 345, 348
Farah, Tawfic E. 68
Farnleitner, Johann 277
Farrell, John C. 250
Farrell, R. Barry 249
Faulhaber, Isolde 274
Fei, John 348
Feierman, Steven 43
Ferejohn, John 373
Ferrer, Aldo 345
Findler, N. V. 401
Finer, S. E. 95, 349
Finkle, Jason L. 202
Finnegan, Richard B. 181, 249
Fischer, Heinz 276, 277
Fischoff, Bernard 402
Fisher, William E. 162, 163
Fliess, Peter 192, 203
Flora, Peter 137, 138, 139, 141
Foltz, William J. 6, 15, 42, 43, 65, 96, 98, 137, 138, 140, 164, 313
Forrester, Jay 353, 359, 373, 374, 375
Forsyth, M. G. 248
Fox, Annette Baker 162
Fox, William T. R. 242, 249, 250
Francisco, Ronald A. 230
François, Patrick 309
Frank, André Gunder 43, 308, 310, 348, 377
Frankfurt, Harry G. 375
Free, Lloyd A. 204
Freeman, H. 401
Freeman, Walter E. 43
Frey, Frederick 204
Friderichs, Hans 279
Frisch, Ragnar 421
Fritsch, Bruno 18–19, 183, 344, 372, 375, 403, 446
Fröbel, Foler 308
Fromm, Erich 39, 44
Furet, François 95
Furtado, Celso 349

Gable, Richard W. 202
Gaines, Brian R. 403
Galanter, Eugene 376
Galbraith, John Kenneth 345
Gallopin, G. C. 373
Galtung, Johan 43, 164, 203, 244, 245, 345, 348, 370, 374, 426
Gantzel, Klaus Jürgen 310
García, Norberto 346
Geertz, Clifford 321, 346
Gehmacher, Ernst 273
Geller, Daniel S. 345
Gerlach, Knut 310
Gerschenkron, Alexander 254, 272, 273
Ghosh, A. 348

Giddens, Anthony 171, 179, 182, 183, 349
Giles, John J. 181
Gillespie, James M. 204
Gillespie, John 373
Gilpin, Robert 253, 272
Ginsburg, Norton S. 348
Girard, Alain 204
Girling, Robert 349
Gleditsch, Nils Petter, 421
Gleser, Leon J. 421
Gochman, Charles 421
Good, Robert, 186, 192, 202, 203
Goodrich, Leland M. 163
Goodwin, Geoffrey 241, 250
Gordon, Margaret S. 140
Gouldner, Alvin W. 182
Goulet, Denis 346
Graziano, Luigi 272
Graciarena, Jorge 350
Green, Reginald H. 34, 43
Greenstein, Fred I. 162, 250, 272, 401
Gregor, A. James 43
Griliches, Zvi 347
Grotius, Hugo 10, 234, 236, 354
Grünwald, Oskar 273, 276
Guetzkow, Harold 353, 403
Guldimann, Tim 139
Gurr, Ted Robert 338, 349, 350
Gutkas, Karl 273, 275, 277

Haas, Ernst 146, 160, 161, 162, 163, 164, 241, 249
Habermas, Jürgen 76, 94, 370
Hagtvet, Bernt 94
Hah, Chong-Do 138
Haim, Sylvia 68
Hall, A. D. 44
Halliday, Fred 68
Hamilton, Hamish 68
Handler, Gerhard 278
Hansen, Roger D. 162
Hantler, Sidney L. 402
Haq, Mahbub ul 308
Haque, Abdul 205
Harborth, Hans-Jürgen 310
Hardin, Garrett 389, 402
Hardy, J. E. 373
Harik, Iliya 69
Harvey, Curtis E. 273
Haschek, Helmut H. 274
Hayward, Fred M. 43
Hebb, D. O. 402
Heclo, Hugh 139, 140
Heimann, Eduard 120, 126, 139, 140, 141
Heinrichs, Jürgen 308
Heisler, Martin O. 272, 276
Helmstadter, Ernst 347
Herrera, Amílcar O. 373, 446
Hersh, Jacques 310
Hibbs, Douglas A. 347, 373

Hilgard, Ernest R. 402
Hill, Polly 34, 43
Hirabayashi, Gordon 203
Hirschman, Albert O. 44, 230, 320, 322, 323, 346
Hoare, Quintin 346
Hobbes, Thomas 234, 248
Hobl, Wolfgang 276, 277
Hodgkin, Thomas L. 164
Höll, Otmar 273, 275
Hofer, Johannes 274
Hoffmann, Stanley 162, 203, 241, 242, 250
Holland, J. H. 377
Hollerer, Siegfried 278
Holzman, Albert G. 401
Hoole, Francis W. 374, 403
Hopkins, A. G. 34, 43
Hopkins, Mike 373
Hopkins, Nicholas S. 44
Hourani, Albert 59, 69
Howard, Richard 162
Hudson, Michael C. 6, 17, 42, 67, 68, 69, 113, 313, 346, 348
Huntington, Samuel P. 26, 29, 42, 67, 114, 123, 141, 313
Hurwitz, Harold 230
Hussein, Saddam 58
Hveem, Helge 346
Hyman, Herbert 204
Hymer, Stephen H. 34, 43

Ianni, Octavio 347
Imhof, Eckard P. 273
Inglehart, Ronald A. 113, 162, 163
Inkeles, Alex 44, 191, 203
Intriligator, Michael D. 401
Ionescu, Ghita 247, 251

Jackson, John 373
Jackson, Steven I. 344, 345, 347, 349, 350
Jadue, Santiago 309
Jaguaribe, Hélio 183, 344, 345, 348, 370, 375, 403
Jahoda, Gustav 198, 204
Jain, Shail 349
Janowitz, Morris 139
Jervis, Robert 381, 391, 401
Jodice, David 17
Jürgensen, Harald 309
Juillard, E. 80–1, 95
Jung, Richard 402
Jurokowitsch, Franz 274

Kahn, Robert L. 401
Kainz, Herwig 278
Kaiser, Ronn D. 162
Kalba, Konrad 403
Kann, Robert A. 163, 164, 182, 229
Kaplan, Abraham 117, 138, 139
Kaplan, Morton A. 192, 203, 243, 353, 366, 369, 374, 377, 402

Karabel, Jerome 180
Karpat, Kemal 68
Kasfir, Nelson 26, 42, 138, 140, 141
Katzenstein, Peter J. 11–12, 163, 164, 272, 273, 274, 278
Kaufman, Robert R. 345
Keens-Soper, H. M. A. 248
Keeton, George W. 250
Keiderling, G. 230
Kelman, Herbert C. 203, 401
Kendall, Patricia 203
Kent, Allen 401
Keohane, Robert O. 162, 164, 240, 245, 249, 250, 272, 345
Kern, Horst 140
Khalidi, Walid 68
Kilson, Martin 377
Kim Il Sung 310
Kindleberger, Charles P. 345
Kirkpatrick, Jeane 203, 204
Klenner, Fritz 276
Klestil, Thomas 274
Klingberg, Frank 407, 421
Klose, Alfred 277
Knapp, Horst 275
Kneucker, R. 276
Knorr, Klaus, 241, 250
Koch, M. 273, 275, 276
Kochen, Manfred 15, 375, 378, 401, 402, 403
Koestler, Arthur 375
Kohour, L. F. 403
Kojima, Kazuto 203
Korbonski, Andrzej 161
Koren, Stephen 277
Kornia, János 376
Krackowizer, Helmut 278
Kramer, Gerald 373
Kramer, Helmut 273, 275
Krasner, Stephen D. 253, 272
Krauss, Herbert H. 205
Kreye, Otto 308
Kucera, Gustave 274
Kuhlman, James A. 344
Kuhn, Axel 95
Kuhn, Thomas 42, 117, 138, 139
Kummerer, Willy 274
Kunzle, David 346
Kupperman, Robert H. 403
Kuznets, Simon 272, 278, 336, 348, 349

Labisch, Alfons 138, 139
Lacina, Ferdinand 273, 275
Ladurie, Emmanuel Le Roy 43, 95
Ländgren-Backström, Signe 346
Laing, R. A. 377
Laitin, David 272
Lakatos, Imre 117, 136, 138, 139, 375
Landé, Carl H. 30, 42
Lane, Jonathan 203

NAME INDEX

Lange, Oscar 353, 374
Langer, Edmond 277
Lapidus, Ira 69
Laponce, Jean A. 403
Larsen, Otto N. 138
Larsen, S. U. 94
Larson, Theodore C. 403
Lasswell, Harold D. 16, 42, 164, 176, 446
Lebeaux, Charles N. 139, 140
LeDuc, Lawrence 203
Lee, J. S. 419, 422
Lee, Maurice, Jr. 163, 182, 229
Lehmbruch, Gerhard 141, 277, 278
Leibniz, G. W. 355–6, 366, 367
Lemper, Alfons, 309, 310
Lenin, V. I. 348
Leontief, Wassily 347
Lerner, Daniel 67, 185, 202
Lettvin, Jerome 375
Levy, Marion J., Jr. 140
Lévy-Bruhl, Lucien 44
Lewin, Kurt 356
Lewis, W. Arthur 300, 310
Lichterman, Martin 163, 182, 229
Lieber, Robert J. 246, 251
Liepmann, Peter 310
Lijphart, Arend 9–10, 181, 183, 229, 248, 254, 313, 354, 374, 381, 398
Lindberg, Leon N. 161, 162, 163, 164
Lindberg, Niels 421
Lindgren, Raymond E. 163, 164, 182, 229
Lineau, C. C. 421
Linstone, H. S. 402
Lipset, Seymour Martin 94, 138
Lipsey, Robert E. 272
Liska, George 186, 192, 202, 203
List, Friedrich 279, 280, 290, 294, 295, 296, 297, 309, 311
Lloyd, Peter J. 253, 272, 278
Loewenheim, Francis L. 163, 182, 229
Lovejoy, Arthur 375
Lowenthal, Abraham 350
Lowi, Theodore J. 273
Luce, R. Duncan 376
Ludz, Peter Christian 230
Lukes, Steven 180, 182

Macfie, A. L. 421
Macridis, Roy C. 155, 162, 179
März, Eduard 275
Magdoff, Harry 203
Magubane, Bernard 44
Maier, Charles S. 95
Maier, Josef G. 277
Majer, Manfred 277
Malitza, Mircea 374
Mapp, Roberta 198, 204
Marien, Michael 402
Markovits, Andrei S. 8, 183, 229, 272, 344, 375, 377, 403

Martin, Bradley 420
Martin, Lawrence W. 202
Marx, Karl 76, 92, 165, 177, 346, 348
Mason, Timothy W. 139, 141
Massell, Benton F. 346
Mattelart, Armand 346
Matzner, Egon 273, 275, 277
Mauss, Marcel 181, 182
Mayrzedt, Hans 272, 274
McClelland, Charles A. 401
McClelland, David C. 407, 421
McCullough, Warren S. 376
McNeil, E. B. 401
McRae, Kenneth 272, 276
Meadows, Dennis L. 353, 373
Meadows, Donnella 353, 373
Meltzer, B. 401
Mendel, Douglas H., Jr. 203
Menzel, Ulrich 310
Merle, Marcel 241–2, 250
Merriam, Charles E. 236, 242–3
Merritt, Anna J. 230
Merritt, Richard L. 9, 15, 16, 155, 162, 163, 164, 184, 192, 201, 203, 229, 230, 248, 349, 372, 446
Mesarovic, Michael D. 373
Miller, George 353, 357, 358, 361–2, 364, 376
Miller, James G. 357, 374, 375, 376, 377, 401
Mitchell, Robert C. 42
Mitrany, David A. 152, 163
Modelski, George 203, 245, 250
Montgomery, John D. 230
Moore, Barrington 93, 370
Moore, Clement Henry 52, 68
Moore, Sally Falk 44
Morawetz, David 309
Morgenthau, Hans J. 162, 241, 242, 250
Morris, Cynthia Taft 349
Morrison, Donald G. 42
Mosovich, D. 373
Mote, Victor L. 403
Müller, Gernot 141
Mueller, Ronald 346, 349
Murray, Alex 203
Murray, Edward J. 401
Musgrave, Richard A. 113
Myerhoff, Barbara G. 44
Myhill, John 402
Myklebust, J. P. 94
Myrdal, Gunnar 139

Naschold, Frieder 7, 138, 139, 140, 141
Nasser, Gamal Abdel 50, 55, 56
Navarro, Vincente 140
Nelson, Benjamin 181
Nemschak, Franz 273, 275
Nettl, John Peter 42, 140, 141
Newall, Allen 374

NAME INDEX 473

Newman, Denis 378
Newman, James R. 377
Nie, Norman H. 27, 42, 141
Nonn, H. 80–1, 95
North, Douglas 34, 43
North, Robert, C. 400, 401
Nye, Joseph S., Jr. 161, 162, 164, 204, 240, 245, 249, 250, 251, 345

Oberleitner, Wolfgang 276
O'Donnell, Guillermo 349, 350
Öhlinger, Theo 274
Offe, Claus 126, 140
Ogunlade, James O. 204
Oliver, Warren W. III 8, 229
Olkin, Ingram 421
Organski, A. F. K. 29, 42, 118
Oromaner, Mark Jay 180
Oteiza, E. 373
Otruba, Gustav 273
Owusu, Maxwell 44
Ozouf, Jacques 95

Packenham, Robert A. 138
Paden, John N. 42
Paige, Jeffrey 349
Palmer, Norman D. 181, 249
Parsons, Talcott 115, 353, 367–9, 377
Paukert, Felix 349
Payne, Stanley 95
Paz, Pedro 345
Peham, Othmar 275
Peischer, Josef 274
Pelinka, Anton 277
Pentland, Charles 162, 246, 247, 251
Perinbam, B. Marie 43
Pester, Eduard 373
Peterson, Richard 377
Pfaff, Richard H. 68
Pfaltzgraff, Robert L., Jr. 177, 183, 233, 241, 248, 249, 251
Phillips, Warren 419, 421
Pinto, Aníbal 327, 347
Pipes, Richard 402
Piven, Frances F. 140
Placek, Friedrich 275, 276
Platt, Edward E. 274
Platt, John R. 402
Polanyi, Karl 348
Pollak, Michael 272
Polsby, Nelson W. 162, 250, 272, 401
Pompermayer, Malori J. 349
Pontius, Miller 421
Pool, Ithiel de Sola 402
Porter, Brian 248, 250
Poulantzas, Nicos Ar. 139, 141
Powell, G. Bingham, Jr. 27, 42, 141
Pozzoli, Claudio 138
Prebisch, Raoul 317, 323, 328
Prewitt, Kenneth 27, 42, 141

Pribam, Karl H. 376
Pronay, Michael 274
Pryor, Frederic L. 100, 114
Przeworski, Adam 114, 353, 374
Puchala, Donald J. 8, 162, 163, 164, 169, 181, 182, 209, 229, 230, 233, 252, 313, 397
Pütz, Theodor 276
Pye, Lucian W. 30, 42, 140, 186, 202

Quijano, Aníbal 312, 345, 346, 348, 350

Randers, Jorgen 373
Ranis, Gustav 348
Ranney, Austin 94
Rapoport, Anatol 379, 380, 400, 401
Rashevsky, Nicholas 401
Rath, R. 204
Rein, Martin 123, 126, 139, 140
Reisenhofer, Herbert 275, 276
Renan, Ernst 210, 227
Richardson, Lewis F. 241, 380, 401, 419, 421
Richter, Helmut 274
Rimlinger, Gaston V. 139, 140
Rioch, Margaret J. 44
Robinson, Derek 277
Robinson, E. A. G. 278
Robinson, Ira E. 205
Rodenstein, Marianne 138, 139, 140, 141
Rokkan, Stein 6–7, 17, 42, 56, 94, 95, 98, 110, 141, 164, 253, 254, 309, 349, 370, 371, 378, 446
Rose, Richard 114, 273
Rosecrance, Richard 272
Rosegger, Gerhard 273
Rosenau, James N. 186, 202, 240, 241, 249, 250
Rosenberg, Milton 401
Rosenblueth, Arthur 357, 368, 374, 375
Rosenthal, Glenda G. 164
Rothschild, Kurt W. 278
Rousseau, Jean-Jacques 234, 248
Rubin, Milton D. 229
Rubinson, Richard 346
Runciman, W. G. 140
Russett, Bruce, M. 13, 16, 42, 113, 159, 162, 163, 164, 181, 182, 248, 250, 251, 272, 344, 346, 349, 350, 372, 446
Rustow, Dankwart A. 67

Sabel, Charles 141
Said, Abdul A. 249
Samuel, Raúl 204
Samuelson, Paul 353, 374
Sarkar, H. 348
Sathyamurthy, T. V. 44
Sattler, Charlotte 182
Saul, John 348, 350
Savigear, P. 248

Sayigh, Rosemary 68
Schaposchnitschenko, P. 274
Scheingold, Stuart A. 161, 162, 163, 164
Schelling, Thomas C. 401
Schiff, Eric 277
Schiller, Karl 287, 291, 309
Schlesinger, Thomas O. 274
Schmidt, Eberhard 141
Schmitter, Philippe C. 141, 161
Schneider, Harold K. 34, 43
Schneider, Jeanne 138
Schrödinger, E. 376
Schurman, Franz 141
Schuster, Peter 44
Schwarzenberger, Georg 250
Schweigler, Gebhart 230
Scolnik, Hugo D. 373, 446
Scribner, Sylvia 44
Seabury, Paul 402
Šećerov, Slavko 421
Seligson, Mitchell A. 43
Senghaas, Dieter 12, 15, 43, 64, 141, 345, 350, 370, 372, 377, 378, 426
Senghaas-Knobloch, Eva 309
Sercovich, Francisco 345
Shabad, Theodore 403
Shamir, Michael 349
Shils, Edward A. 30, 32, 42, 43, 346
Sicinski, Andrzej 203
Sigelman, Lee 349
Sills, David L. 400
Silva, Michelena, José A. 191, 203
Simon, Herbert A. 353, 357, 374, 376, 405, 421
Sinfield, Adrian 140
Singer, J. David 15, 17–18, 243, 250, 251, 375, 402, 421, 422
Sinha, A. K. P. 204, 205
Slavik, Herbert 278
Small, Melvin 420, 421, 422
Smekal, Christian 278
Smith, Anthony D. 43
Smith, Asa P. 250
Smith, David H. 44, 203
Smith, Geoffrey Nowell 346
Smith, M. Estellie 68
Smoker, Paul 374, 403
Snidal, Duncan 344, 347, 349, 350
Somerhoff, Gerd 375
Somit, Albert 250
Sorokin, Pitirim A. 419, 420, 421, 422
Sprague, John 374
Standfest, Erich 138, 139, 140
Stankovsky, Jan 273, 274
Staringer, Erich 274, 277
Stark, John 401
Starr, Paul D. 68
Stehr, Uwe 310
Steiner, Kurt 276, 277
Steininger, Rudolf 276

Stepan, Alfred 350
Steppacher, Rolf 309
Stevenson, Hugh M. 42
Stiefbold, Rodney P. 276
Stille, Frank 141
Stirnemann, Alfred 276
Stobel, Michael 378
Stoetzel, Antoine 374
Streeten, Paul 297, 307, 310, 347
Stulz, Percy 230
Suares, C. E. 373
Suleiman, Michael W. 69
Sunkel, Osvaldo 319, 345, 346, 348
Suppanz, Hannes 277
Supper, Meinhard 275
Swartz, David 180
Sylvan, David 344, 346, 349, 350
Syrquin, Moises 103, 105, 113, 114

Talavera, L. 373
Tanenhaus, Joseph 250
Tanter, Raymond 401, 403
Tarrow, Sidney 272
Tautscher, Anton 278
Taylor, Charles L. 7, 15, 17, 42, 68, 113, 346, 348
Tennstedt, Florian 138, 139, 141, 142
Teune, Henry 114
Thomas, Clive 310
Thomas, Robert Paul 34, 43
Thompson, Leonard M. 43
Thorpe, W. H. 402
Tilly, Charles 94, 309, 370
Tipps, Dean C. 137, 140
Titmuss, Richard 139, 140
Trevor-Roper, H. R. 43
Trucco, Ernesto 401
Turner, Henry A., Jr. 95
Turoff, M. 402

Upadhyaya, O. P. 204, 205

Váli, Ferenc A. 230
van der Mey, Leo M. 248
Vansina, Jan 43
van Staden, Alfred 248
Van Wagenen, Richard W. 163, 182, 229
Varela, Francisco J. 377, 378, 402
Vasquez, John A. 249
Verba, Sidney 250
Vincent, Joan 44
Vodopivec, Alexander 276, 277
Vogt, Winifred 141
Voigt, Hans-Gerhard 310
von Bertalanffy, Ludwig 375
von Ferber, Christian 138
von Neumann, John 354, 366–9, 376, 377
von Urff, Winfried 310
von Wright, George H. 356, 375

Wagner, R. Harrison 239, 249
Wagner, Richard E. 139
Wallace, Helen 162, 164
Wallace, William 162
Wallerstein, Immanuel 76, 89, 92, 93, 94, 137, 138, 139, 140, 141, 308, 345, 370, 371, 378
Wallner, Leopold 278
Waltz, Kenneth N. 235–6, 239, 243, 248, 272, 379, 401
Warren, Donald 402
Warren, Rachelle 402
Watanuki, Jōji 114
Webb, Carole 162
Weber, Eugen 95
Weber, Max 76, 165, 177
Weber, Wilhelm 278
Wehler, Hans-Ulrich 138, 142
Weinzierl, Erika 273, 275, 277
Welfling, Mary 28–9, 42
Wheeler, Raymond H. 419, 421
Whitaker, C. S., Jr. 43

Wiener, Norbert 14, 353–70, 374, 375, 421
Wight, Martin 234, 236, 242, 248, 250
Wilber, Charles K. 349
Wildenmann, Rudolf 276
Wilensky, Harold L. 139, 140
Willard, Andrew 344
Wionczek, Miguel 345
Witkin, H. A. 44
Wolf, Thomas A. 273
Wolfers, Arnold 239, 249
Wright, Quincy 419, 421

Young, Christopher 421
Young, Oran 203
Young, R. J. 401

Zaidi, S. M. Hafeez 205
Zapf, Wolfgang 137
Ziegler, B. P. 377
Zimmermann, Rupert 278
Zinnes, Dina 373, 374, 403

Subject Index
(Prepared by Anna J. Merritt)

Africa 33–5, 39, 42–3; attitudes toward alien minorities 194–5
Amalgamated security-community, *see* Security-community
Amalgamation: defined by Deutsch 152; difficulty of quantifying 154; relationship to integration 157; as distinct from integration 236–8, 246
The Analysis of International Relations 4, 179
Anarchy: and war 10; and pluralistic security-community 236–8; international, and behavioral revolution 240–3
Arab world: social mobilization theory and 6, 46–67; and Deutschian approach 47–67; general description 48–9; as single nation 54–6; viewed as separate states 56–9; as pluralistic security-community 56; and flaws in social mobilization model 64–7
Austria: and interdependence 11–12; fascism and model of Western Europe 87–93; relations between domestic and international structures 252–71; economy of and international markets 255–62; domestic structures and international economy 262–8; and world interdependence 268–71
Authoritarianism: coercive 338–43
Autocentric development, *see* Development, autocentric
Automata: von Neumann and 367–8

Balance of power 235
Berlin: political disintegration 9, 206–29; traffic patterns 212, 213, 214; visitors from East to West 213, 215–19; contacts between East and West 219–21; partisan activity 221–3; Eastern subscribers to Western newspapers 223, 224. *See also* West Berlin
Behavioralists: and international anarchy 241–3; and new international paradigm 243–5
Boundaries: importance to systems 39–40
Bureaucracy: in Austria 265–6

Catastrophe: mathematical theory of 387–8
Center: problem of defining 31; and periphery, in 'dependencia theory' model 318–23
Center-building: and suffrage 81
Center for Research on World Political Institutions 7
Change: and relationship between demands and capabilities 97
Chile: attitudes toward Argentina 194
Class conflict: and political-economic theory 130–2
Coercive authoritarianism 338–43
Collective conscience: in Durkheimian thought 166
Collective security 235. *See also* Security-community
Collective self-reliance 298–300
Colonies: transformation of dependency theory 322; and integrative learning 227–8
Communal consciousness: development of 59–60
Communication: and integration 157–8; in Deutschian thought 167–8, 175; between East and West Berlin 206–30
Communism: Durkheimian view of 170
Conflict: latent 337–8, 340, 341, 342, 343; manifest 338, 342, 343; origins 341; responses to 379; of interest among states 380–5; field of situations 381; control of 385–93, 399–400
Consciousness: Deutschian definition 365; communal 59–60
Correlates of War Project 408
Consociationalism: of Austrian political parties 253
Controllability: of human history 405
Creativity: and general problem solver programs 362–5
Cybernetic hierarchies 357–65
Cybernetics: Deutsch and 14, 37, 167–8, 178, 353–73; political 14–15

Data banks 16–17
Decentralization: and conflict control 398–9
Democracy: Deutsch and Durkheim on 170–1, 173, 179
Democratization: as strategy for national unification 81; variables needed for breakdown 89

SUBJECT INDEX 477

'Dependencia theory': and autocentric development 279–311; model 316, 344; and earlier development theories 323; trade and major concerns of 329; economics as source of conflict 341
Dependency 31; and penetration 315–16
Dependent development: literature on and global modeling, 370–1; as function of ratio of loads to capabilities 53
Development: Western European 77–80; autocentric 300–7; balanced 300–2; resource mobilization and utilization 302; organic growth 302–3; uneven 326–7, 328, 331, 332, 341; distortions in pattern of 331–4
Development assistance: and growth rates 433–7
Development policy: three imperatives for 291–300
Disintegration: Berlin as example of 206–29; economic 327–8, 330, 332, 334
Division of labor: in Durkheimian thought 166–7
DNA: von Neumann and 367

Ecological equilibrium: balance with growth 424
Economic activity: level of constrained 325–6, 329, 330, 334, 340, 341
Economic development: and energy supply, 426–7. See also 'Dependencia theory'; Development
Economic inequality, 336–7, 341
Economic marginalization, 335–6, 340, 341
Economy: of Austria, 255–62; viable, foundations, 280–3; peripheral, characteristics, 283–4; peripheral, genesis, 285–8; peripheral, modes of production, 288–90
Elites: transformation of, 51–2
Energy: supply of and economic development, 426–7; need for increased production, 437–8
Equilibrium: poltical cybernetics and, 365–6; and conflict control, 386, 387; global, possibility of 437
Ethnic identity 31, 43
Ethnicity: and Deutschian approach 64
Export enclave development 323, 331
Export enclave syndrome: sources, 323–30
Export profiles: concentration of, 322–3

Fascism: and model of Western Europe 86–93; development of in Austria 254
Foreign trade dependency, 444; compared to reinforcement potential, 430–3. See also Development, autocentric
France: compared to fascist victory countries 92–3

France, Germany and the Western Alliance 155

Gemeinschaft 33–4
German Democratic Republic 208, 211, 215, 219–20, 222–3, 226, 228, 229
Germany: social security system of 7: demands for reunification 211. See also Berlin
Germany, Federal Republic: national health care 117; Austrian dependence on 270. See also Legislative Health Insurance
Germany Rejoins the Powers 3
Global modeling: Deutsch and 18–9
Government: social mobilization and growth of 50–1, 96–7, 112–13; index of size 98–113; rate of growth 105, 112–13; functions of in Deutschian thought, 175–6
Gross domestic product: relation to government revenue 105–12
Gross national product: and relation between distribution of wealth and revenue 101–5; and North-South relations 428–30
Growth: governmental 96–113; politics of 363; relationship with ecological equilibrium 424; in GNP and population and North-South relations 428–30. See also Development; Modernization

Heterogeneity: and instability 58–9; structural 333–4, 340
Homogeneity: and stablity 58–9
Human rights: importance to Deutsch 170

India: opinions shaped by international events 199–201
Industrialized countries: problem-solving potential of 430–3
Inequality: dimensions of 425–6, 444–5
Instability: and heterogeneity/homogeneity 58–9
Integration: and unification 7–9; and communication 8, 157–8; and peace 9; and social mobilization 53; Deutsch and 145–7, 152–8, 167; difficulty of measuring 153–4; and amalgamation 157, 236–8, 246; and disintegration in postwar Berlin 206–30; European, Austria and 257, 260; of economy 325, 327–8; and conflict control 397–8. See also Amalgamation; Disintegration; Security-community
Integration studies: as opposed to integration theory 147
Integration theory: background 145–6; and Deutsch 152–8
International Institute for Comparative Social Research 18. See also Wissenschaftszentrum Berlin

International pluralism theory: lack of 160
International politics 9–13; Deutsch and new paradigm in 233–48; classical paradigm 234–6; significance of new paradigm 238–40; obstacles to recognition of new paradigm 243–5
Iraq: and threshold of integration 62–3
Italy: fascism and model of Western Europe 87–93

Labour: in Austria 264; division of in Third World 287; neeed for new division of in Third World 298–300; international division of 426
Latin America 27; attitudes toward one another 196–7; fascism and 254
Learning: integrative-disintegrative 227–8; adaptive 393–4, 397–400
Lebanon: as confirmation of Deutschian approach 61–4
Legislative Health Insurance 118, 120; and modernization theory 120–2; achievements 124–5; and social conflict 127; history of 132–3; and political theory of development 132–7
Less developed countries, 423–7, 433, 438. *See also* Development; Modernization; Third World
LGI: *see* Legislative Health Insurance
Limits: and autonomy 404

Marxists: and Deutschian approach 64
Mobilization:
  Political: 129, 132; and LHI 133–4
  Social: and nationalism 5–7; in Arab world 6; Deutsch and 25–6; reconsideration of model of 25–41; two-stage model of 26, 36; need for bigger government 50–1; and integration 53; flaws in theory 64–7; and growth of government 96–7, 112–13; secondary school enrollment as indicator of 99. *See also* Nationalism; Nation-building
Modernization: and Arab world 49; reversal 123, 125; effect on public opinion 185–7, 191. *See also* Development
Modernization theory 115–16, 137; revisionist and radical revisionist controversy 116, 136–7; national health care as test of 117; and German LHI 121–2, 132–7; and redistribution crisis 122; and reality 122, 126
Monads: Leibnizian 357, 366

National health care: and test of modernization theory 117. *See also* Legislative Health Insurance

Nationalism: and social mobilization 5–7; in Deutschian thought 168–9. *See also* Integration; Mobilization; National-building
Nationalism and Its Alternatives 179
Nationalism and Social Communication 3, 6, 37, 38, 53, 65, 70, 152
Nationalistic attitudes 197
Nation-building 6–7; and change 36–7
Nation-state: as unit of analysis 29–31; and new international relations paradigm 244
Neo-corporatism: of Austrian interest groups 253–4
Nerves of Government 3, 14, 37, 41, 167, 178, 179, 354, 356, 358, 362, 368, 369
New International Economic Order 280. *See also* Development; Less developed countries; Modernization; Third World
Newspapers: western, and East German readers, 223–4
North Korea: dispute with USSR on development policy 296–7, 301
North-South: prosperity gap, 279; relations, 423–6

Participation, political: government restrictions on 26; effect of economic change on 27
Partisan activity, in Berlin 221–3
Party systems: explanations of variations in 84–7
Patents: indicators for disembodied capital 319–20
Peace: integration and 9; importance in Deutsch's thought 150–1
Peace researchers: and new international relations paradigm 244
Penetration: systematic financial and technological 318–19, 329, 332, 334, 340; concentration of external financial and technological 320, 324; systemic cultural 320–2, 329, 343; cultural concentration of 322, 324, 343. *See also* 'Dependencia theory'
Peripheral capitalist polity: structural transformation 334–43
Peripheral economy: transformations in 330–4; governmental involvement 335, 339–43
Periphery 31; and center in 'Dependencia theory' model 318–23
Pluralism: defined by Deutsch 153
Pluralistic security-community, *see* Security-community
Political Community and the North Atlantic Area 3, 8, 151, 152, 153
Political Community at the International Level 152
Political cybernetics: themes 353–70; and global modeling 372–3

Political decay 26. *See also* Disintegration
Political-economic theory: concepts 128–30; and class conflict 130–2; usefulness in explaining German LHI 136–7
Politics: and Third World peasants 34–6; in Deutschian and Durkheimian thought 176; essence of in Deutschian cybernetics 354
Politics and Government 4, 179
Portugal: fascism and world of Western Europe 87–93
Power politics paradigm 145–6. *See also* International politics
Predictability: and human history 405
Public opinion: in less developed countries 184–202; and modernization 185–7, 191; volume of attention to international issues 185–92; attention focused on international subsystems 193–201; indicators of, in West Berlin 208
Purposes: Deutsch's ordering of 358
Purposive complexity 364–5

Redistribution crisis: origins 118–19; solution of according to modernization theory 122
Reinforcement potential: compared to foreign trade dependency 430–3
Representation: concept of 381–3
Reunification: German 211
Revenue: and government size 96–113; as percentage of GDP 100–5; relationship to GDP 105–12
Revolution: and social mobilization 27
RIAS: East German listeners 219–20

School enrollment: as indicator of social mobilization 99; relation to government growth rate 112
Science Center Berlin, *see* Wissenschaftszentrum Berlin
Scientification of social science 168
Security-community: defined by Deutsch 152–3; operationalization of 246 Amalgamated: focus of Deutsch's research 155–8 Pluralistic 158–60, 371–2; Arab world as 56; anarchy and 236–8
Self-replicating system 366–9
Social cybernetic modeling 356–7
Socialism; Durkheim on 170
Social mobilization, *see* Mobilization, social
Sociology: Durkheim and foundations of 165–7
Spain: fascism and Western European model 87–93
Stability: and homogeneity/heterogeneity 58–9
State: capacity to control 130–2; in development of LHI 134–5; Deutsch and Durkheim on 173–5; formation in center-periphery systems 370–1; formation of as dialectical process 371–2
Steersmanship 17–18; fundamental Deutschian concept 404. *See also* Cybernetics
Structural heterogeneity 333–4, 340
Subnational communities: and social mobilization theory 60
Suffrage: variations in sequence of steps toward 81–4
Sweden: systemic goal changes in 178
Systems: changes in, 38–9; and boundaries 39–40; center-periphery 370–1

Third World: autocentric development in 12, 300–7; politics in 34–6; scholars 36, 41; development policies for 279–308; division of labour 287. *See also* Development; Less developed countries; Modernization
TOTE hierarchies 358–63
Trade: foreign 323, 329, 330, 332
Trademarks: indicator for disembodied capital 320
Trade partner concentration 322, 324, 330
Trade product concentration 332, 325, 328, 330
Trade vulnerability 323, 330
Traditional society: views of 32–5
Traffic patterns: in Berlin 212–14
Transaction-integration balance 238
Transformation processes 334–43
Tunisia: and threshold of integration 63

Unification: and integration 7–9; model of political 155–6; shortcomings of model of political 156–8. *See also* Amalgamation; Integration
United Nations: attitudes in less developed countries toward 195–6
Unit of analysis problem 29–32
Urban networks: three types 80–1, *See also* Berlin

War: and anarchy 10; understanding causes of 17–18; effects of in Berlin 207–8; in traditional paradigm 237; typical model of road to 405–6; constant probability model 410–11; passage of time and probability of 411–13; victory, defeat, and probability of 413–15; cost and probability of 415–17
Welfare state: problem of conceptualizing 119–20; heterogeneous makeup 121–2; and redistribution crisis according to modernization theory 122; modernized nations and goals of 123–4; functions 126–7. *See also* Legislative Health Insurance
West Berlin, *see* Berlin; Wissenschaftszentrum Berlin

SUBJECT INDEX

Western Europe: model of 70–93; paradox of development of 77–80; conceptual map of 77–81
West Germany, *see* Germany, Federal Republic
Wissenschaftszentrum Berlin 18; world model being developed at 98
World Bank, Economic and Social Data Division 99–100

World government 235
World Handbook of Political and Social Indicators 16–17, 26, 50

Yale Arms Control Project 3, 10
Yale Political Data Program 3, 16–17, 26, 50
Yemen: and threshold of integration 62